Rufus

Paul F. Brown

RUFUS

James Agee in Tennessee

The University of Tennessee Press
Knoxville

Excerpts from LET US NOW PRAISE FAMOUS MEN. Copyright © 1939, 1940 by James
Agee. Copyright © 1941 by James Agee and Walker Evans. Copyright © renewed
1969 by Mia Fritsch Agee and Walker Evans. Reprinted by permission of Houghton
Mifflin Harcourt Publishing Company. All rights reserved.

Excerpt(s) from A DEATH IN FAMILY by James Agee. Copyright © 1938, 1956, 1957 by
The James Agee Trust. Used by permission of Penguin Books, an imprint of Penguin
Publishing Group, a division of Penguin Random House LLC. All rights reserved.

Excerpt(s) from A DEATH IN THE FAMILY, UK Edition, by James Agee. Copyright ©
1938, 1957 The James Agee Trust, Chapter 8 and Part of Chapter 13 copyright © 1957
by The New Yorker Magazine, Inc. Copyright © 1957 The James Agee Trust, copyright
renewed 1985 by Mia Agee, used by permission of The Wylie Agency LLC.

All other Agee materials, including poetry, letters, and excerpts not specified above,
used by permission of The Wylie Agency LLC.

LIBRARY OF CONGRESS CATALOGING-IN-PUBLICATION DATA
Names: Brown, Paul F., author.
Title: Rufus : James Agee in Tennessee / Paul F. Brown.
Description: First edition. | Knoxville : The University of Tennessee Press, [2018] |
Includes bibliographical references and index. |
Identifiers: LCCN 2018011934 (print) | LCCN 2018027498 (ebook) |
ISBN 9781621904250 (pdf) | ISBN 9781621904243 (hardcover)
Subjects: LCSH: Agee, James, 1909-1955—Childhood and youth. |
Agee, James, 1909-1955—Family. | Authors, American—20th century—
Biography. | Tennessee—Biography.
Classification: LCC PS3501.G35 (ebook) | LCC PS3501.G35 Z595 2018 (print) |
DDC 818/.5209 [B] —dc23
LC record available at https://lccn.loc.gov/2018011934

For Jessica

Contents

Illustrations

Preface

Identities change over time. Childhood nicknames often fall out of use with age. James Agee identified consistently with the name Rufus while he lived in Tennessee. In examining that period, his first fifteen years (covered in chapters 2–4), I refer to him only as Rufus from his birth up to the point in his life when he began answering to Jim, James, or Agee.

Of course, this tactic risks confusing the reader: Rufus was a real boy and adolescent, but he was also a fictional character in *A Death in the Family*. Rufus did not write that novel; James Agee did. Therefore, when referencing statements Agee made about his own childhood, this text occasionally employs phrases like "As an adult, Rufus" and "Rufus later" in an attempt to bridge the gap between the boy and the adult, avoiding jarring leaps between the two identities.

Justification for this approach is found in letters written both to and by Agee from the mid-twenties onward. While Agee's move to Exeter in fall 1925 roughly marked the inauguration of his adult name, he continued answering to Rufus among those people who had known him as a child. Hugh Tyler often referred to his nephew as Rufus, as in a 1948 letter to a friend. Laura Wright called her son Rufus his entire life, as evident in letters she wrote to him between 1946 and 1954, consistently addressing him as "Dearest, my Rufus."[1] Had Laura left us a memoir about her famous son, she almost certainly would have identified him as Rufus throughout the text, no matter his age in her reminiscences.[2]

In his own letters to Father James Harold Flye, James Agee invariably signed them as "Rufus" or "R" through June 14, 1943. By that time, Agee had been a professional writer for a decade. And while "Jim" became his preferred signature to Flye from October 30, 1943, onward, Agee continued to sign "Rufus" on occasion, even as late as his letter from March 2, 1948—significantly, the same letter in which he reported working on his "novel . . . about my first 6 years, ending the day of my father's burial." These letters provide continuity between the child and the writer, showing that even as Agee was becoming nationally known, close acquaintances still called him Rufus.[3]

A note should be made about the sources used in this text to document Agee's early life. Many of his writings are heavily autobiographical and therefore reveal clues about his past. *A Death in the Family,* for example, is closely based on Agee's childhood experiences leading up to and immediately following his father's death—as verified by the author himself in statements like the one above. However, that work is clearly a novel. Biographers have sometimes erred by lifting dialogue and situations from Agee's fiction and presenting them as facts without offering corroborative evidence from other sources. Agee never wrote a memoir; I have taken care here not to treat his work as such. At the same time, if his writings suggest autobiographical details, those clues are worth investigating.

Preference has been given to primary sources outside the novel—including interviews with family members, journals, letters, and notes Agee wrote while preparing his text. Agee revised constantly and left behind a paper trail of drafts that may help separate fact from fiction: some of his notes contain detailed, first-person recollections of his youth that read more like diary entries than fictional prose. Agee's actual words, and the written and spoken remembrances of those who knew him, are of primary importance to this book.[4]

The libraries at the University of Tennessee, Knoxville, and the University of Texas, Austin, hold a wealth of Agee's drafts, unpublished writings, and personal correspondence. Vanderbilt University's Heard Library contains the papers and audio recordings of Father Flye, many of which relate to Agee; a tape of Flye interviewing Laura Wright proved invaluable to this text. Knox County Library's McClung Historical Collection holds an album of Hugh Tyler's photographs, constituting the majority of available images of the family. The Agee Films website has made available audio interviews that Ross Spears recorded while preparing his documentary film about Agee.

James Agee wrote, "I feel that when historians get to work on anything, arteries begin to harden, in the subject and in the people interested."[5] While I do not consider myself a historian, only a person fascinated by history, I still hope to avoid hardening the arteries of readers interested in James Rufus Agee. May this book foster a growing interest in the writer's work and the region where he grew up, while contributing needed information to the body of Agee scholarship.

Acknowledgments

This project has been an obsession of mine for the past several years, ever since I read *A Death in the Family*. I lived near Knoxville from birth to age six, but grew up mainly in California. Not long after returning to the area as an adult, I happened to read one of Jack Neely's *Metro Pulse* columns, about a strange yearly commemoration held at a bar in Powell, Tennessee. Readers already know the story: on May 18, 1916, near the spot where the bar was later built, a man died in a car wreck; the man's son later wrote a novel about the tragedy. The date caught my eye, because I was born on May 18. Right away I became curious to read James Agee's account of the automobile accident that claimed his father's life, sixty years to the day of my birth. The novel captivated me and sent me investigating the people and events it depicted. Along the way, I realized that the hospital where I entered the world is located on West Clinch Avenue, only eight blocks west of the site of Agee's own birth and his father's funeral.

While I learned a great deal more about James Agee's life in Tennessee, I must acknowledge that my role has been much more compiler than discoverer, as many scholars prepared the way for this project through their earlier work (evidenced by the names that appear in my notes and bibliography). Thankfully, all the scholars and Agee aficionados I met expressed warm interest in my quest and at no time hinted that I was stepping on their toes; several indicated that at one time or another they also went through—borrowing author Larry McMurtry's wording—"an intense Agee phase."

In acknowledging the institutions and individuals that assisted me during five years of research, I am bound to leave off names by mistake. My apologies in advance.

I am grateful for the following libraries, archives, and their staff members: Kalamazoo Public Library (Alexander Merrill); Kentucky Department for Libraries and Archives (David Kirkpatrick); Knox County Archives (Eric Head, Phillip Smith, and others); Knox County Library, McClung Historical Collection (Steve Cotham, Sally Polhemus, and others), and Tennessee Archive of Moving Image and Sound (Eric Dawson and, formerly, Bradley Reeves); National Archives and Records Administration (Robert

Ellis); Phillips Exeter Academy Library (Tom Wharton); St. Andrew's–Sewanee School, Agee Library (Julie Jones); St. Clair County (Mich.) Library (Barb King); Tennessee State Library and Archives (Tom Kanon, Heather Adkins, Ronald Lee, Trent Hanner, Kayce Butler, and others); University of Tennessee, Knoxville, Special Collections Library (Bill Eigelsbach, Kyle Hovious, and others); University of Texas, Austin, Harry Ransom Humanities Research Center (Rick Watson and others); Vanderbilt University, Jean and Alexander Heard Library (Teresa Gray, Philip Nagy, and others); and Western Michigan University, Zhang Legacy Center (Sharon Carlson).

Thanks to the following organizations: Anderson County (Tennessee) Historical Society (Ron Evans and Stephanie Hill); Campbell County (Tennessee) Historical Society (Trulene Nash and the late Jerry Sharp); Campbell County Register of Deeds (Dormas Miller); Christ Church Episcopal, Chattanooga (Julia Cronin); City of Knoxville (Brently Johnson); *Clinton* (Tennessee) *Courier-News* (Brenda Foster); Columbia University (Claudia Wessberg); Corbin (Kentucky) Tourism and Convention Commission (Maggy Kriebel); Cowan (Tennessee) Railroad Museum (Maryann Knowles); Diller-Quaile School of Music (Kirsten Morgan); East Tennessee Historical Society (Michele MacDonald); Episcopal Diocese of South Carolina (Beth Snyder); Granville (Ohio) Historical Society (Theresa Overholser); Kalamazoo (Michigan) Historical Commission (Sharon Ferraro); Knox County Museum of Education; Knox Heritage (Kim Trent and Hollie Cook); *Knoxville News Sentinel* (Susan Alexander, Paul Efird, and Jack Lail); Knoxville Utilities Board (Bill Elmore and Pam Collins); Metropolitan Planning Commission (Terry Gilhula and Kaye Graybeal); Richland–West End Neighborhood Association (Mae Ambrose); Smoky Mountain Historical Society (Gwen Cody); St. Andrew's–Sewanee (Sherri Bergman, Sarah Core, and Faye Ricketts); St. John's Episcopal Cathedral, Knoxville (Melissa Dodson, Patty Dunlap, Debi McClure, and Douglas McKamey); Tennessee Department of Transportation Historic Preservation (Martha Carver and Tammy Sellers); the *Tennessean* (Ricky Rogers); TVA Maps (Peggy Cooper and Ron Jones); and the U.S. Postal Service (Stephen A. Kochersperger).

The following individuals, many of whom I met in person, deserve recognition for their assistance: Victor Ashe, Mary Barker, Vereen Bell, Carroll Bible, Albert Brenner, Ric Brooks, Sabra Brown, Perry Childress and Margaret Held, Bill Claiborne, Jay Clayton, Randall De Ford, Bill Dohm, Bill Edison, Ronnie Claire Edwards, Burki and Tom Gladstone, Lynne Glaus, Chris Hammond, Mark Heinz, David Herwaldt, Mark Hipshire, Jim

Hubbard, Roger Karlsson, Eileen Kearney, Michael Kreyling, Michael Lofaro, Dianne Luce, Molly MacMillan, Charles Mayo, Danielle Meyers, Randy Moats, Mary Dew Moody, Joseph Moon, Wes Morgan, R. B. Morris, Jack Rentfro, Lee Robbins, Alan Shayne, Donn Southern, Tom Southern, Ross Spears, Eddie Stair, Leigh Ann Theisen, Stanton Webster, Allison Wilson, and Diana Wolfram.

Thanks to the individuals whom I interviewed during my research: Michael Kearney, who was seven in 1962 when he came to Knoxville to play Rufus; Phil Hamlin, who once resided in the Agee home; Michael Hertzberg, an assistant director on *All the Way Home;* and Sam Tinsley, whose father arrived first on the scene of Jay Agee's accident.

I met or corresponded with several of Agee's relatives for the project. Annabel Agee, daughter of the late Dr. Oliver Agee, is a second cousin of the famous author; she met me on Market Square for coffee and kindly shared photos and memories of her family. By phone I conversed with Erik Van Valkenburgh and Addison Wardwell about their great-uncle Hugh Tyler. I was saddened to learn of the deaths in 2016 of two family members who had known Agee personally: his cousin (Hugh's daughter) Lydia Edison, and his daughter Deedee Agee. Although I never met them, both ladies blessed this project in their brief correspondences with me.

I am grateful to Paul Sprecher, trustee of the James Agee Trust, for allowing my use of the writer's words. (Thanks as well to Katie Cacouris at Wylie Agency for tracking down copyright holders.) Since Sprecher's tenure began, the trust has approved an impressive number of publications by and about Agee, and it continues to welcome new works. The University of Tennessee Press has attracted much of that scholarship due to its regional focus as well as the university's collection of Agee materials. Thanks to all at UTP who guided and shaped this book, particularly Thomas Wells, Jon Boggs, and Gene Adair.

Two individuals must be highlighted for the active role they played in improving this text. Paul Ashdown and Jack Neely each spent unpaid hours editing the manuscript and then going over their suggestions with me. Their expertise and advice were invaluable.

While writing about the lives of strangers, my thoughts often returned to my own past and the people and events that shaped it. Special thanks to my family—my father, David, and relatives on the Brown side; my mother, Rita, and relatives on the Hamby side; my siblings, Andrew and Pamela; and my relatives by marriage, the Bolings and the Klickas—whose love, faith, traditions, stories, and creativity energized my work. This project's completion was greatly hastened by the birth of my son, Benjamin, who delights me.

Most of all, I want to thank my lovely wife, Jessica, who gave my somewhat aimless research direction by suggesting I turn it into a book. As a writer herself, she cheered and inspired me through the entire process, and edited the earliest drafts. After four years of enduring the name Agee, trips to various libraries, and stacks of books around the house, she is as excited as I am to see this project finished. It would not have happened without her love, patience, and support.

Introduction

It happened one spring night more than a century ago. A Ford Model T traveling along a dark country road veered into an embankment and overturned, claiming the life of its sole occupant—a husband and father of two. His six-year-old son, asleep at home, learned of the accident the next morning and realized that the father he idolized, and from whom he sought approval in everything, was never coming home again. The loss devastated the boy, Rufus, who as a teenager began putting his thoughts—including poetic variations on his father's death—to paper. For him writing became not just a career, but a means of preserving his past and understanding how it had shaped him. He dedicated much of his life's work to reconstructing, through art, the lost moments of his early years.

James Rufus Agee's reputation as a writer has grown significantly since his death in 1955 at age forty-five. Although Agee completed only a handful of major works during his lifetime, he distinguished himself in a surprising number of genres. Agee won the Younger Poets Competition at Yale University, resulting in the publication of his early poems. His subsequent articles and reviews for magazines like *Fortune, Time,* and the *Nation* earned him the admiration of his journalistic contemporaries. One editor called him the greatest writer that *Time* ever had, and Agee is considered by many to be the father of modern film criticism. *Let Us Now Praise Famous Men,* his exposé of hardship and corruption in Alabama's cotton industry, is required reading for those studying Depression-era journalism. His screenplay for *The African Queen* received an Academy Award nomination. His Pulitzer Prize–winning posthumous novel, *A Death in the Family,* has been adapted as a play—which also won a Pulitzer—an opera, and two motion pictures, the first of which was filmed in Knoxville. The novel's stand-alone prologue, written decades earlier as a kind of prose poem, had a life of its own even before Samuel Barber set it to music; Agee's text, "Knoxville: Summer of 1915," is the most widely known piece of literature about that Tennessee city. Library of America has published three collections of Agee's works. And at this writing, the University of Tennessee Press is publishing a series, *The Works of James Agee,* in twelve volumes, five of which are now available.

Map of Knoxville, hand-drawn by Hugh Tyler in 1925. Tyler's map, showing the artist's interest in both landscapes and decoration, depicts "the buildings most important in the history of the town from its founding by Gen. James White to approximately 1865." N-6763, Thompson Photograph Collection, McClung Historical Collection, Knox County Library.

Read any capsule biography of James Agee, and you will find about one sentence identifying Knoxville as the place where he was born in 1909, and where his father was killed in a 1916 car wreck. St. Andrew's School in Sewanee gets about as much space, noted as the place where Agee met his lifelong friend and mentor, Father James Harold Flye. Then Agee is quickly sent packing up to New England, far from Tennessee's hills, never to return. Because all his major achievements occurred elsewhere, perhaps it is not surprising that his hometown receives only shallow attention. But this versatile writer, whose hard drinking and living became legendary, who mingled with the artistic elite of New York and Los Angeles, often surprised his peers by his quiet sensitivity and his fixation on the South. James Agee spent about a third of his life in Tennessee, most of that in Knoxville. That fact alone justifies a closer look at his first fifteen years and the region in which he then lived.

KNOXVILLE

Knoxville might rightly be called the "Literary Capital of Tennessee." The state's first novel was published there in 1832. Influential authors such as George Washington Harris, Frances Hodgson Burnett, Anne W. Armstrong, Cormac McCarthy, Richard Marius, Nikki Giovanni, and David Madden all lived and wrote there. And like Agee, many of them produced autobiographical works of fiction that were heavily inspired by Knoxville and the surrounding region.[1]

When founded in 1791, Knoxville—named for Henry Knox, George Washington's secretary of war at the time—was just a frontier settlement on a bluff overlooking the Tennessee River. A newspaper, the first in the state, soon began printing in Rogersville, but by October the following year it was rolling off a Knoxville press. A college was established there in 1794 that later evolved into the University of Tennessee (UT). When the state was formed in 1796, Knoxville became its capital and retained the designation until 1817. Even though Knoxville was a crossroads town—where wagons meandered over ridges toward Nashville, Lexington, and Richmond, and keelboats hauled goods downriver toward Alabama—it was still economically isolated.[2]

Then on a summer day in 1855, on a ridge near where James Agee later was born and spent much of his childhood, all of Knoxville's citizens gathered to witness the arrival of the first train into the city.[3] Eight years later, during the Civil War, the same hill was carved into an earthen fortress and guarded by Union soldiers, and then bombarded with Confederate shells in what became known as the Battle of Fort Sanders, part of a wider military campaign in and around the city. Knoxville's National Cemetery was established months before Arlington's.

The city grew immensely from the 1870s through the end of the century, a prosperous period of civic improvement during which Knoxville built an opera house, public schools and libraries, and a streetcar system; it also annexed communities to the north and west.[4] Within two decades of the local Civil War battle, developers had subdivided the eastern half of the scarred ridge into residential lots, a neighborhood consisting of working- and middle-class homes but also mansions for some of the city's more affluent citizens.

The region's natural resources—particularly coal, iron, timber, and marble—attracted northern capitalists, like Agee's maternal grandfather Joel Tyler, who partnered into a marble-cutting business after being drawn by East Tennessee's climate and hardwood forests. Around the turn of the twentieth century, railroad tracks were laid for transporting cut lumber out of the southern Appalachians. Between 1910 and 1913, Knoxville hosted three major expositions to promote the conservation of those resources. James Agee was a toddler when those events brought esteemed guests—such as William Jennings Bryan, Booker T. Washington, Helen Keller, and presidents Theodore Roosevelt and William Taft—to Knoxville.[5]

But not all Knoxvillians prospered, and neighborhoods were sharply divided by class. Tracts of humble working-class dwellings sprouted up along Knoxville's borders to house the growing population of manual laborers needed in local mills and factories. Agee's "solidly lower middle class" neighborhood of 1915, only a couple of blocks from the largest homes in West Knoxville, was one that many Knoxvillians would have envied. Despite civic improvements made decades earlier, parts of the city still lacked electricity and water. Infrastructure lagged behind the city's growing population of roughly forty thousand, an increase of more than ten times its size during the Civil War. While James Agee lived in comfort, existence was considerably harsher for another boy, James Herman Robinson, who in 1915 lived across town and witnessed the devastation of a rising creek as it uprooted homes and privies. Writing about it later, Robinson remembered the flood's two positive effects: "It swept away for a brief moment the stench of the outhouses and the slaughter pens," and, "It made us conscious of our oneness, black and white alike."[6]

Situated on a ridge west of downtown, Agee's neighborhood was also geographically separated from the racially mixed areas of town. Young Agee was probably more struck by the city's class divide than by its racial divide: family members later recounted his childhood awareness of and generosity toward less fortunate children. But aside from a few references in his Knoxville-inspired stories—hearing his nickname Rufus teased as a "nigger name," realizing that his nurse Victoria's skin color was darker than his, and seeing a black man made the target in a carnival ball-toss game—he wrote little about the racial tension that existed in the city during his childhood. White workers from the nearby mountains and black workers from the Deep South sometimes found themselves contending for the same jobs. And as Knoxville's manufacturers realized they could not keep pace with the more efficient northern factories, they increasingly cut wages and jobs to offset higher production costs. Dwindling jobs meant even more societal friction. The end of World War I coincided with a decline in Knoxville's prosperity as well as in relations between its black and white citizens. Agee may have been on a train to Sewanee with his mother and sister in late August 1919 when a major race riot erupted in downtown Knoxville.[7]

While Agee was insulated from the roughest parts of Knoxville, things still occurred that disturbed his otherwise peaceful neighborhood. He was almost certainly too young to recall the few months in spring 1913 when West Knoxville residents, frightened by a reported "barefoot burglar," locked their doors and kept weapons handy; one Highland Avenue woman's shotgun blast barely missed the intruder. The same bandit reappeared three years later, striking homes on Laurel and West Clinch and leaving sock prints at the scene. In July 1915 a body was found near the ruins of Fort Sanders where Agee liked to play; the suicide victim was the son of UT president Brown Ayres.[8]

Noise and grime pervaded the city. Agee recalled the sounds of the streetcar screeching past his family's house and the frequent rumbling of freight and passenger trains along the outskirts of the neighborhood. Scores of factories dotted the valley and contributed to Knoxville's industrial thrum. Even if Agee's youth made him oblivious to the city's darker side, he surely experienced the omnipresent coating of coal dust, the settled exhaust from stoves and factory chimneys. When Agee revisited Knoxville in the mid-1930s as a writer for *Fortune*, he noted the downtown's "sooty" and "smudgy" appearance.[9]

But Knoxville also had an appealing side, with many attractions for a boy of Agee's age. Motion pictures had been shown there as early as the 1890s and were no less novel when the city's first dedicated movie theater opened in 1907. By the time Agee was old enough to visit them, there were several theaters along Gay Street to choose from. Although his writings about

Knoxville say nothing about it, vaudeville was still a popular entertainment during Agee's youth. The Bijou, for example, was still two years away from converting to motion pictures when the Marx Brothers appeared onstage there in 1913. Then there was the nearby river, bordering the south side of downtown, where his father and he may have fished on at least one occasion. And east of downtown, Chilhowee Park was enormously popular during summer months, open daily for swimming, amusement park rides, and band concerts. In those days, during UT football's infancy, the city was much more known for minor league baseball, with Chilhowee Park hosting the Knoxville Appalachians—forerunner of the Tennessee Smokies—until Caswell Park was built in 1917.[10] Agee also saw the beginning of tourism in the Great Smoky Mountains. The same railroad that carried lumber out of the Smokies began hauling sightseers, including the Agees, to places like Elkmont, which consisted of a club hotel and cottages originally built for families of lumber mill employees. The area was part of what would become America's most-visited national park.

JACKSBORO AND SEWANEE

While Agee grew up primarily in Knoxville, other parts of Tennessee influenced him as well. He knew Campbell County, roughly thirty miles northwest of Knoxville, as his father's ancestral home. Migrating from Virginia, the Agee family had settled there between Cumberland Mountain and Powell River, more than a century before the Tennessee Valley Authority's Norris Dam flooded the valley and forever altered the landscape. In 1796, the same year Tennessee received statehood, U.S. Representative Andrew Jackson purchased two thousand acres nearby. Part of this land became the village of Walnut Cove, founded in 1806 as the county seat and renamed Jacksonboro in 1819 after Jackson, who by that time was considered a military hero but still a decade away from his presidency. The name was shortened to Jacksboro in 1887, but the town remained largely agricultural, with farms like the ones owned there by Agee's father and grandfather.[11]

However, Cumberland Mountain, part of a chain of ridges running through the heart of the county, was known to be a rich source of coal. In the 1890s the LaFollette Coal, Iron and Railway Company was established a few miles northeast of Jacksboro as a way to connect this energy resource to the wider region. Incorporated in 1897, the town of LaFollette became the county's industrial and business center.[12]

Several Agees distinguished themselves locally in politics, medicine, and business. James's uncle Frank Agee, for example, owned a mortuary in downtown LaFollette. But aside from Frank's brief, earlier venture into the coal business and another uncle, John, becoming a geologist, none of the family apparently profited from coal.[13]

When his father was still living, Agee observed the mountains of Campbell County during frequent trips to see his grandparents. In his writings, Agee depicted the area as both primitive and serene, and associated his father's humble upbringing there to what young Abe Lincoln must have experienced in rural Kentucky. The family farm that Agee knew sat below what is today the Eagle Bluff section of the rugged Cumberland Trail.[14]

James Agee wrote much more about another remote landscape, one located more than 125 miles to the southwest. Despite the distance, the wooded cliffs above Jacksboro are geologically linked to those forests Agee later explored near Sewanee. The counties of Campbell and Franklin both lay along the sandstone ridge of the Cumberland Plateau, which begins up in middle Kentucky and slices down diagonally through Tennessee, staying just west of both Knoxville and Chattanooga and ending in middle Alabama.[15] Sewanee, a quiet community near Monteagle that sits on the plateau's lower edge, is known primarily as the home of Sewanee: The University of the South, an Episcopal college whose longtime presence there influenced the proximate creation in 1905 of St. Andrew's—a boarding school for mountain boys. As a student there from ages nine to fourteen, Agee encountered daily the type of rural, impoverished children he saw only occasionally in Knoxville. His first major academic and spiritual challenges took place at the school, and the setting later inspired a novella, *The Morning Watch*. During his adult years, St. Andrew's became his home base when traveling through Tennessee: his mother and stepfather and his friend Father Flye lived on the St. Andrew's campus long after Agee had lost touch with Knoxville acquaintances.

Knoxville, Jacksboro, and Sewanee (Monteagle)—the three towns representing Agee's childhood—were by the early 1920s all designated points along the Dixie Highway, the first chain of north-south roads between Miami, Florida, and Sault Ste. Marie, Michigan. The same highway system also connected those towns to Kalamazoo and Port Huron, Michigan—important cities in Agee's maternal line.

THIS BOOK

Certainly Agee was both a southern writer and an Appalachian writer. But while he traveled throughout the South and wrote about places outside this sphere, his identity was firmly grounded in Tennessee, as this book's subtitle indicates. Naming East Tennessee as the region encompassing Agee's youth is only partly accurate, as he spent five academic years at St. Andrew's, in Middle Tennessee. The label "eastern Tennessee" would more accurately represent the Tennessee region Agee knew best (the city of Knoxville, the Great Smoky Mountains to the southeast of it, Campbell County and the land of Agee's paternal lineage to the north of it, and Sewanee in Franklin County to the southwest of it); however, the designation proves too unorthodox for repeated use here. In considering the Tennessee roots of James Agee then, one must acknowledge the scarcity of evidence in his writings that he lingered near Nashville, Memphis, or any other part of the state west of Franklin County.[16]

Rufus is the first literary biography to explore Agee's life and work in the context of his Tennessee heritage. Because of its focus, the book details parts of his early life that scholars have covered only sparingly or not at all. Chapters address the migration of his ancestors to East Tennessee and the circumstances that led his parents to meet in Knoxville and marry, as well as the people, places, and events that constituted young Agee's experiences in that city. The death and funeral of his father affected him greatly, and one chapter sheds new light on the accident and its aftermath. A subsequent chapter examines the unstable years following the funeral, as Agee transitioned from boyhood to adolescence. Accompanying the text, a large number of photographs, some previously unpublished, document Agee's connections to the region.

But while this book indeed tells the story of the writer's youth in Tennessee, it is also about the place itself, specifically the smaller places within it that Agee knew, and how they inspired him. During his varied career, Agee returned both creatively and physically to the region of his childhood. Images from his past—log cabins and Tennessee mountain farms, streetscapes in a southern industrial city, Victorian houses and potted ferns, boyhood games and mischief, a brave Lincolnesque father, a grieving family—resurface throughout his work. He continually, some would say obsessively, drew upon these and other memories for creative material. Without Tennessee's influence, the story of James Agee would naturally be quite different.

Finally, this book shows how the writer influenced the region he knew. While Jacksboro and neighboring LaFollette generally ignored Agee because of his controversial depiction of a respected family member, St. Andrew's School dedicated a library in his name. The city of Knoxville was slow to embrace Agee and recognize itself as any sort of literary capital; instead, local and regional citizens—including Ross Spears, David Madden, Wilma Dykeman, and R. B. Morris—and notable outsiders—including Alan Hall of the BBC, Steve Earle, Michael Stipe, and Garrison Keillor—became largely responsible for bolstering Agee's reputation there. Visitors familiar with the text "Knoxville: Summer of 1915" come to Highland Avenue each year looking for signs of the city that Agee described. The same fascination drew a Hollywood crew to the neighborhood in 1962 to film Agee's story, including depictions of fathers watering lawns and a family reclining on a backyard quilt. The film *All the Way Home*, more than the stage adaptation and perhaps even the novel that preceded it, motivated Knoxville's—and Tennessee's—first celebration of James Agee and is therefore worth studying in detail as a major factor in the author's regional legacy. In the decades since the film premiered there, Knoxville has dedicated a recording studio, a street, and a park to James Agee, and hosted three major Agee conferences. As Tennessee shaped James Agee's life and work, so his life and work, in turn, shaped Tennessee.

1

"By Some Chance, Here They Are, All on This Earth"

Ancestors, 1818–1909

His three names are biblical. James was the name of a brother of Jesus and of two of the twelve apostles. Rufus was the son of Simon the Cyrene whom Roman soldiers compelled to carry the cross of Christ. And long forgotten, buried deep in the Old Testament, was a Hararite—or mountain dweller— named Agee. Yet James Rufus Agee easily traced his names to both sides of his family.[1]

His paternal ancestors, he wrote, "were a blend of back-country British Isles . . . stock, Hessian mercenary, and Huguenot (the name Agee is a simplification of a French name I don't know)." The noble Huguenots, whose Protestant beliefs were considered heretical by the Catholic monarchy, were driven from France and migrated in large numbers to the English colonies of North America. One of them, Mathieu Agee, settled in Virginia in 1690, married, and had four children—including two sons, James and Anthony, whose wives gave Mathieu a total of twenty-four grandchildren. "James Agee" had survived as a name in the family tree for more than 180 years by the time James Rufus Agee was born. He was given the middle name of his father, Hugh James Agee, who was named after *his* grandfather, James Harris Agee, who was named after *his* father, James Agee, and so on.[2]

The name Rufus came from his mother's side, from her grandfather Tyler. Agee wrote of his great-grandfather: "My mother's father's father, whom she revered and of whom she has told me; I think well of him, and was burdened by his name; but I never knew him; I doubt I shall ever have occasion to tell my children of him; with this generation he vanishes from the memory of the human race." The young Agee endured much teasing on account of that name. Much later, when the writer re-created such childhood scenes for his novel, *A Death in the Family,* he imagined his mother soothing the insults with reassuring words: "It's a very fine old name. Some colored people take it too but that's perfectly all right and nothing for them to be ashamed of or for white people to be ashamed of who take it. You were given that name because it was your great-grandfather Tyler's name, and it's a name to be proud of." By the summer before his sixteenth birthday, Agee was apparently self-conscious enough about that name—about being a southern kid named Rufus about to enter a New England prep school—that he dropped it.[3]

So even though James Rufus Agee never knew his great-grandfathers Agee and Tyler, their names drew him into the distant past. As a writer attempting to describe and make sense of his own life, he could not help but reach "backwards beyond remembrance" to his mother's ancestors who came from Michigan, and New England before that, and his father's ancestors who came out of Tennessee's hills, and Virginia before that—back to strangers from faraway villages and times, whose faces and lives he could only imagine, as expressed in this autobiographical fragment:

> O my ancestral land, my tired old friends, my veterans:
> How little light there is, in so much darkness.
>
> You lived, as hungrily as I live now, and grew tired, or sorrowful, or Darkness suddenly grew tired of seeing you in the light; and where are you now.
>
> There are records of most, traditions and legends of many, genealogies for some; where are you now....
>
> It is possible to imagine those of you who were contemporaries of Charlemagne and of Shakespeare, to imagine you in the hovels and the strange ways of dressing which are hardly more than archaeology, than theatrical property, to me, but were your homes, the clothes you put on when you got up in the morning. One of yours is said to have been Wat Tyler. One of you was Archbishop of Canterbury under Elizabeth....
>
> Some of you were among the Huguenots who took refuge in Virginia and in the mountains below Virginia. It is possible to imagine you, it is possible to realize that every one of you existed, as fully as I exist, as fully as all those of whom I will try to write; but that is all that is possible, and where are you now?[4]

THE TYLERS: OHIO AND NEW YORK

Rufus A. Tyler, one of the great-grandfathers, came from New England. He was born in Essex, Vermont, on April 18, 1818. When he was fifteen, his family moved to Granville, Ohio, one of the larger townships of Licking County. He finished his education there.[5]

His mother, Prudence, transferred her church membership from Vermont to the local Congregational body, one of several houses of worship in Granville. His father, Judson, did not join the church, unwittingly setting a precedent that would repeat often through the Tyler line. When it came to spiritual matters, the women of the family would lead. Prudence was reportedly "a most excellent and Christian lady," and Rufus—like his twentieth-century namesake—was influenced by his mother's convictions. Rufus Tyler joined the church himself through baptism at age nineteen.[6] But his mother was not well. Some type of madness had eroded her mind, and in July 1838, at age forty-five, Prudence drowned herself. She was subsequently branded a "deranged" woman in the church records, which over the next few years also noted Rufus's absences from communion and his eventual suspension for "neglect of gospel ordinances." He had taught school in Granville during that interval, but by 1842 had moved several miles west to Alexandria.[7]

Shortly after relocating, Rufus helped get a bill passed in the state legislature to establish the Alexandria Literary Society. His motivation must have been more than civic, as his future descendants were endowed with an interest in literature: his daughter, son, and grandchildren would all share a love of books and learning; and his great-grandson would emerge from a classical education to become a gifted writer.[8]

In the early 1850s, New England was calling Rufus Tyler back, and he took off for unknown reasons to Clinton County, New York. There he met a woman, Sarah Potter, a native of the county and daughter of a cabinetmaker. Rufus and Sarah married in 1852 at Keeseville. Three years later, Sarah gave birth to a daughter, Jessie Potter Tyler, on March 8, 1855, at the nearby town of Black Brook. Another child came along the following year, but did not survive birth. On August 26, 1857, the Tylers were living in Au Sable Forks, a small village along the river, when the last-born member was added to the family—a son, Joel Claverly Tyler.[9]

The circumstances that drove Rufus and family back and forth across the Northeast are not known. By 1870 he had moved at least five or six times, about once a decade, from one northern hamlet to another. That July, the federal census found the family in Wilmington, Illinois, where fifty-two-year-old Rufus worked as a hardware machinist. But by the end of the year, he would make one last move, finally settling in a town where he would leave a legacy.[10]

THE TYLERS: MICHIGAN

When the Tylers arrived in Kalamazoo, Michigan, the place must have looked like a metropolis to them, as the town was about five times more populated than Wilmington. With all the industrial opportunities it offered, Rufus quickly partnered into one of three local lumber dealers, the one on the corner of Park and Water streets that was rebranded Tyler & Turner. While keeping busy in civic affairs, as an honorary member of the Kalamazoo Light Guard and later a trustee of Mountain Home Cemetery, Rufus also built the family a large house in 1872 that still stands at 1030 West Main Street, near Kalamazoo College. The two-and-a-half-story home, which was recommended for the National Register, is notable for Italianate details that include paired cornice brackets and tall, arched windows.[11]

Jessie and Joel attended Central High School, and in 1875 both received diplomas as the only graduates of their class. In September of the following year, they enrolled at Kalamazoo College and both traveled to Philadelphia to attend the Centennial Exposition—the first "world's fair" in the United States. After two years at the college, Jessie taught in St. Paul, Minnesota, in 1881. Meanwhile, Joel attended the University of Michigan in Ann Arbor

The Rufus Tyler home at 1030 West Main Street, Kalamazoo, Michigan.
Photo by and courtesy of Leigh Ann Theisen.

from 1877 to 1880, graduating with a master of arts degree. After college, he began teaching in St. Clair, Michigan. There he met an ambitious woman named Mary Emma Farrand.[12]

∞∞∞∞∞∞∞∞∞∞

The Farrands had lived in Port Huron, Michigan, on ten acres of what used to be the grounds of Fort Gratiot Military Reserve, near the mouth of the St. Clair River. The family's two-story, three-thousand-square-foot house, built facing north to offer a grand view of Lake Huron, was one of the largest in the area. Bethuel Farrand, a prominent attorney, and wife Laura Whitman Farrand had owned the house since 1847. Mary Emma Farrand, their second daughter, was born at the house on June 29, 1849. She would be called by her middle name.[13]

Emma was two when her mother died in 1852. Two years later, her father remarried and sold the property to Samuel Edison, whose son, Thomas, was seven years old at the time. During the family's decade in the house Thomas Edison's scientific experiments in the cellar laid the foundation for his famous, inventive life.[14]

From age four, Emma was raised by her stepmother, Helen Wheaton. Port Huron did not yet have a primary school, so Emma completed her early education at home before entering the public high school. Her love of literature was nurtured by Helen, who helped found the Ladies' Library Association of Port Huron in January 1866 and was appointed its first president. Emma served as financial secretary and librarian, and was part of the large audience that heard Frederick Douglass speak in February 1868 as the association's guest lecturer.[15]

In 1872, Emma taught music while living with her parents on the northwest corner of Eighth and Union. Later, Emma graduated from the University of Michigan with a bachelor of philosophy in 1877 and a master of philosophy in 1878. The next year, she taught English at the State Normal School in Whitewater, Wisconsin. Her sister, Laura Caroline Farrand Balentine, had founded and was president of the Somerville School in St. Clair and in 1880 brought Emma on as principal of the literary department, English literature and history. Emma met Joel Tyler, the man recently hired to head ancient languages and mathematics.[16]

At thirty-one, Emma was eight years older than Joel, but they were both single and intellectually compatible—and each with a parent who had helped establish a literary association. A relationship gradually developed. Joel "was reading medicine and going abroad to do some more of it," intending to become a doctor, as his daughter Laura recalled: "My father, you see, was getting ready to be a doctor, and he would've made a good one. And he met my mother and wanted very much to marry her right away. And grandfather Tyler was very generous about that. He said, 'If that's what you want, I'll take you into the business right now . . . and you will have your share of my estate now instead of at my death,' which was a lot for him to do. And so Papa went into that."[17]

In 1882, after two years in St. Clair, Joel abandoned his plans to practice medicine, and went to Kalamazoo, where he temporarily moved in with his parents on West Main and accepted a job in his father's lumber business. Paula Tyler, Laura's sister, later believed that their father sold himself short: "He was extremely intellectual, [had] a very fine mind, wonderful sense of humor. Unfortunately, he had a factory. He wanted to be a doctor until he got engaged . . . and then he had to get work. But he wasn't terribly interested in business."[18]

Emma stayed in Port Huron, teaching another year at Somerville, but remained in contact with Joel. They married on the afternoon of August 30, 1883, at the home of Emma's parents. Shortly after the new couple settled in Kalamazoo, Emma conceived; and on May 22, 1884, she gave birth to twins. She named the girl Laura Whitman, after the birth mother she barely knew. The boy, Hugh Claverly, shared his father's middle name.[19]

Rufus Tyler turned sixty-eight in April 1886. His former partner, Frank Turner, had retired in February, and Joel was now helping run the business, which had been renamed R. & J. C. Tyler & Company. Rufus was about a month away from seeing his only grandchildren turn two years old. But even though Laura would later tell her son about her grandfather, in truth she had no firsthand memories of the man who, in a family picture, "had gray whiskers along the edges of his cheeks and little corners on his collar" and "did not look very happy." On May 6 Rufus felt poorly all afternoon and by 9:00 p.m. complained of pain in his left side and arm. His visiting brother-in-law, Dr. Ira Fisk, told him there was no cause for alarm. When Fisk returned an hour later, Rufus Tyler was dead of "paralysis of the heart." A private funeral was held three nights later at Mr. Tyler's home, which he had built the previous year on the corner of Cedar and Park, former site of the Plymouth Congregational Church—the same denomination that had "suspended" him in 1847 for "neglect of gospel ordinances."[20]

Joel Tyler continued to run the lumber business with help from his uncle Ira. But Joel was increasingly plagued by illness during Michigan's harsh winters; and with his father no longer living, he began considering a move south to a milder climate, likely at Ira's suggestion. "And that was because the climate in Michigan was just killing our father," said Laura, who called his condition "grippe" and claimed he got it "every winter, very badly, and couldn't stand the snow and the damp." Although the archaic term usually referred to influenza, Laura may have been describing a recurring cold or other respiratory ailment.[21]

THE TYLERS: TENNESSEE

Around that time, Joel "and two or three other men up there heard about the wonderful uncut timber in the mountains of East Tennessee, and how cheap it could be bought," according to Laura. Except for small, local logging operations, Smoky Mountain timber had been largely untapped, partly due to the absence of any efficient method of transporting logs. "And they made them a party and went down into the mountains below Sevierville, and bought quite a number of thousands of acres down there, somewhere near Townsend, and all that part of the country," said Laura.[22]

Between July 1888 and June 1889, Joel invested in 2,200 acres of Smoky Mountain timberland in Sevier County, Tennessee, not far from Gatlinburg. One corner of the tract, which was deeded to R. & J. C. Tyler & Company, was located near the summit of Round Top mountain, roughly two and a half miles due north from Mount Le Conte. Another corner touched Roaring Fork Creek. "Wonderful timber," said Laura. "And Papa was the judge of timber. He'd learned to go through the woods and estimate it, and all that." Joel had heard of a new train line that was to be cut through the area, which was necessary for hauling timber. "So they bought with the assurance that there was going to be a railroad put through there, just right away, which would've made it very profitable." Joel held onto the acreage, expecting to hear updates about the railroad project. "And years went by, and years went by. No railroad," Laura said.[23]

As it turned out, the railroad did not go through as expected, and Joel held on to the land in vain for a decade before selling it ("for about what they'd paid for it," according to Laura) in 1899—just a year before a Pennsylvania man established the Little River Logging Company several miles to the east, starting his own railroad a few years later.[24]

Although Laura was only four years old at the time of her father's timber expedition, she later recalled the stories he told after returning home—tales that painted East Tennessee and its people as strange and "wild":

I remember when Papa came back to Kalamazoo from that trip. We were little things and didn't understand where he'd been . . . But he came in. I think Mama was dressing us in the morning. He was telling different things about it, how different it was down there. And they'd been invited to sleep in a cabin with a family who were being hospitable to them, but it was perfectly impossible, these three men and the whole family all in one room, and no air to breathe. So they went out and slept in their tent. And Papa drew a thing out of his satchel, a lump of something brown. And he said, "What do you think that is?" I said, "It's a rock." He said, "No, it is corn pone. They eat it down there." And then he told about some girl . . . she was eating green apple parings. And her mother said, "Don't eat no more of them apple parings, they'll make you sick." That struck me as a very peculiar thing. I got some funny impressions of the place. It was very wild, of course, in those days.[25]

With his sights already on the region, Joel somehow learned of a machine company, Knoxville Mill Supply, owned by William Savage, which would soon be in need of a new partner. "He'd met this Mr. Savage, W. J. Savage, an Englishman," Laura remembered. "And he was already in it in a small way, this flourmill machinery. And they went in together and built it up." William Savage, like Joel Tyler, was the son of a lumber dealer. Savage had left England for Canada and worked his way down to Knoxville in 1884, where he installed mill machinery at J. Allen Smith's White Lily Flour plant—the building of which still stands on East Depot Avenue. Younger brother Arthur Savage, though not as civically outgoing as William, was a talented millwright himself and later built a well-known rock garden in Fountain City.[26]

In early November 1891, the Tylers moved to Knoxville. Eleven years earlier, the city had trailed Kalamazoo's population by about 2,200. However, the 1890 census revealed that Knoxville's citizenry had increased by 132 percent in a decade—from roughly 9,700 to about 22,500—while Kalamazoo gained only about 6,000 persons during the same period. The Tylers' home at 2309 Magnolia Avenue was located a couple miles east of downtown, in a suburb whose street was "one hundred feet wide and well graded its whole length" and judged to be "one of the handsomest thorough-fares in the city." The streetcar track ran down the center of the avenue, "leaving a wide road on either side for carriage drives, and both sides . . . set out in shade trees." However, road maintenance in the city center had not kept up with the traffic increase. More than a year after the Tylers arrived, Knoxville leaders were still deciding between brick and asphalt paving to replace downtown's macadam, or crushed rock, roads, which "during a wet spell" looked less like "credible city street[s]" and more like "fields recently plowed for spring corn planting."[27]

During the first week of 1892, newspapers announced that the partnership behind the Knoxville Mill Supply and Machine Company was dissolved. The business would continue under the name Savage & Tyler, with Joel as the new partner.[28]

Laura and Hugh were already nine years old when a new little sister, and the family's first Tennessee native, was born on August 27, 1893. She was named Paula Farrand Tyler, and would be the last child for Emma, forty-four, and Joel, who had turned thirty-six the previous day. The crying infant immediately proved too much for one member of the household: "Tigee Tyler," the family's beloved cat—whom Joel had reluctantly left in Michigan in 1891 but retrieved a year or so later when "he went back for something" at the Kalamazoo house. "The day I was born," said Paula, "and [the cat] heard me cry, it left the house and never came back. And my father said, 'What an exchange!'"[29]

Within a year of the birth, the Tylers moved five blocks directly north from the house on Magnolia, to 2309 Coleman Avenue, the only house on that block at the time. Hugh Tyler described the property as "way out on a hill [in] back of Washington Avenue":

> The hill was blessed with a few giant chestnuts, now long since gone with the blight. We named them the King, Queen, Prince and Princess, and a prim cedar was the servant. But in the spring I can still smell, or fancy that I can smell, the dusty fragrance of their tassels. . . .
>
> Out there we had a grand view of Chilhowee and the towering Smokies beyond. One in particular we loved and used to call Big Top, because its three peaks with the sagging line between looked like an immense and distant circus tent. We didn't know it then, but it has since been identified as Le Conte, a mountain in which many Knoxville people take a fierce and almost personal pride.
>
> The hill next [to] ours was covered with a pine wood, full of wild canaries in the spring and cut by deep gullies with curious rocks which exposed to the hot Tennessee sun a net work of fossils scattered over their sides—
>
> We played Robin Hood and Maid Marian all over those hills and woods.

The twins mostly enjoyed free rein in exploring the neighborhood, though Joel and Emma had instructed them to stay away from a particular lot. Hugh's daughter, Lydia, told a story that likely took place on Coleman Avenue: "Hugh and Laura . . . were forbidden to climb on a house that was being built in their neighborhood. Of course they did, and were caught, and were given the choice of a spanking or no dinner. Laura's reaction was, 'What's for dinner?'"[30]

Despite the age difference, Paula remained close to her older siblings. "My sister seemed very grown up to me," she recalled. "She was going out to parties. I used to go and watch her get dressed in the evenings to go out somewhere. And she was very pretty. Hugh was like a companion to me. I used to go up to his room when I woke up early in the morning, and go in and get up on the bed with him and fix his hair."[31]

Sarah Tyler, mother of Jessie and Joel, was in poor health and moved with her daughter to Knoxville to be near Joel and family. Sarah's sister, Martha Fisk, also lived in Knoxville, having left Kalamazoo following the death of her husband, Ira.[32]

Sometime near the end of 1894, the Tylers' previous residence, the one on Magnolia, had burned. Another family occupied it at the time. About two decades later, during a streetcar ride to Chilhowee Park, Laura pointed out to her young son, Rufus, where the house once sat, among the "bushes and trees and lumps of clay."[33]

Not long after that house burned, disaster struck the Coleman Avenue home. On Sunday morning, January 13, 1895, the Tylers' upstairs water pipes were frozen. Sometime between eight and nine o'clock, Joel used an oil lamp to thaw them, concentrating the heat with a rolled piece of carpet. He went downstairs, leaving the lamp unattended for a few minutes. By the time he returned, the roof was on fire. The "magnificent residence," reportedly "one of the finest" in the neighborhood, was uninsured, and the Tylers lost most of the contents—including their caged canary, which "was set outside to save its life" but promptly "froze to death." The total loss was estimated at $6,000 to $7,000. Picking through the charred remains, Hugh found that liquid metal had dripped onto the cellar floor; he concluded that the extreme heat had melted a stack of coins. Word of the fire reached Kalamazoo, but details were altered—apparently to absolve Joel. The local paper made no mention of him wrapping carpet around an oil lamp: he was simply testing a smoke consumer stove.[34]

The accident forced the family to move again, this time to Cumberland Avenue, closer to downtown. The year had not begun well for the Tylers, and their sorrow was not over. On April 14, 1895, Easter Sunday, family matriarch Sarah Tyler died at age sixty-five of a "stricture of bowels." The funeral was held at the Tyler home the next afternoon, after which Sarah's body was sent back to Kalamazoo and buried next to her husband's. The death hit forty-year-old Jessie Tyler particularly hard, as she had lived with and taken "care of her mother until she died," recalled niece Paula Tyler. Jessie's great-nephew, James Rufus Agee, later wrote of her grief, "during which the

The interior of the Tylers' home in Knoxville, circa 1896. Twins Hugh and Laura Tyler are seated at left, and sister Paula at center. The woman at the far right is likely their aunt Jessie Tyler. According to Paula Tyler, this photo was taken one Sunday morning before Aunt Jessie took the children to St. John's Episcopal Church. Note the framed print, "Lions of Persepolis," hanging above the twins. Tyler Album 013, Hugh Tyler Collection, McClung Historical Collection, Knox County Library.

cross of living had first nakedly borne in upon her being, and she had made the first beginnings of learning how to endure and accept it."[35]

Jessie had been active in the Episcopal Church ever since moving to Knoxville, and her devotion may have increased in response to her mother's death. The marble edifice of St. John's Episcopal, on the corner of Cumberland

and Walnut, was only a year old in 1893 when Jessie was made an officer in the local chapter of the Girls' Friendly Society. Although its meetings were "mostly social," the group's "daily care for a hundred working girls" appealed to Jessie, who in the coming decades sacrificed more and more of herself to Christian service. She also joined the Altar Guild and helped prepare the church sanctuary for services by "polishing brass and silver, arranging flowers, sewing and laundering the linens and vestments." Jessie Tyler was confirmed at St. John's on December 29, 1895.[36]

Knoxville attorney Charles Seymour, writing about the congregation's history, stated that "Mr. Hugh Tyler . . . grew from infancy to manhood in St. John's." While church registers document Laura's involvement at St. John's, there are no such records for Hugh Tyler. However, he was briefly associated with the on-campus Episcopal Club while he attended the University of Tennessee.[37]

It is clear that Paula was connected with St. John's, at least during her childhood. One of her favorite family photographs shows her at roughly three years old, "sitting in a chair, waiting for Aunt Jessie to take me to church." Paula had "never been to church until that day," but had met the rector, Dr. Samuel Ringgold, when he visited the Tyler home. As she sat "with Aunt Jessie" on the pew during her first service, young Paula was confused when she saw the rector enter the sanctuary. "The procession came in, and I said, 'Why, Aunt Jessie, there's Dr. Ringgold in his nightgown!'" As she grew older, she became more involved at St. John's. "That's where I sang in the choir." Her small stature was somewhat of a handicap at the time, as she had trouble walking in the "long skirt" she had to wear: "I was so young, when I wanted to sing in the choir they made me come in the back door. I couldn't march with them." Paula "went to Sunday School" and saw herself as much "like the little church kids." And she might have gone further at St. John's, as Jessie and Laura did, had it not been for her mother. "I think when I was about twelve or thirteen, I wanted to join the church. And my mother said, 'I want you to wait until you're really old enough to understand what you're doing.' So I did." Paula never joined.[38]

It is not known whether Joel and Jessie were raised in any kind of religious environment, or if Rufus Tyler retained ties to the Congregational Church, out of which Unitarianism partly sprang. Father Flye spoke of the Tylers' religious views, specifically those of Joel Tyler. "In religion he'd be what they used to call a 'free-thinker,' or, we'd say, an agnostic. You would hardly say anti-religious, or certainly not a dogmatic atheist," said Flye, "but he felt, 'Well, I don't know. If you see something there, I'm glad you do; but I can't see it.' His wife belonged to the Unitarians once, and that isn't anything very dogmatic, I must say."[39]

Paula agreed with Flye's appraisal. "We're all agnostics except Laura," she said. "Well, I don't think my mother was. They went to the Unitarian Church in Knoxville for a while."[40]

The Unitarians' focus on social justice united seamlessly with Emma Tyler's civic and political associations. She was an active member of organizations concerned with child labor laws and women's rights, including the Consumers' League, Equal Suffrage Club, Southern Association of College Women, and Ossoli Circle—which was formed by fellow Unitarian and suffragist Lizzie Crozier French. Emma was known for her benevolence, even opening up her home to "wayward girls." Back in Kalamazoo, she had been on the board of Bethesda Home, created in 1890 to provide "relief, protection, care and reformation of such erring women and girls as shall voluntarily place themselves under its care, or may be so placed by their parents or guardians or by any municipal or other corporation." In 1896 the Florence Crittenden Rescue Home, a similar mission "for unfortunate women," opened on Knoxville's Central Avenue—known at the time as part of "the Bowery," a dangerous part of town rife with prostitution. Emma served as the organization's board president until early February 1898. Reportedly, her charitable care for women with venereal diseases exposed Emma to syphilis, an infection that contributed to her premature loss of hearing and eyesight. Those afflictions testified to her years of selfless service.[41]

Unitarians attempted to establish a church in Knoxville in 1895. As congregants dwindled in number, they often met in the Tyler home until the church folded in 1897. Although the religious body later reformed, Knoxville at the time was apparently "not ready for Unitarian doctrines."[42]

The Tylers' house at 703 West Cumberland Avenue sat on the northwest corner of Cumberland and Henley. It was a notable intersection. Samuel G. Heiskell, serving his first of four terms as Knoxville's mayor at the time, lived across the street on the northeast corner. And perhaps the Tylers learned of their house's connection to literature: it had briefly served as the home of Frances Hodgson Burnett, who left town about two decades earlier and by the 1890s was well known for her novel *Little Lord Fauntleroy*, among other works. Hugh Tyler remembered roasting "potatoes in an oven dug out of a backyard bank" behind the house. Roughly thirty years later, Tinsley Tire Company built a large store on that corner, "spilling over into what were 2 adjoining houses," observed Hugh, who had possibly met owner Stanley Tinsley at the scene of a fatal 1916 automobile accident—a tragedy that nevertheless contributed to the Tylers' own literary legacy, through the writings of Laura's famous son.[43]

The family moved to another corner house, diagonal from the last one, at 620 West Cumberland. During their brief occupancy there, Hugh "kept pigeons and white rabbits." This property, subsequently known as the Lizzie Crozier French house, was also lost to commerce a couple of decades later, when "an enormous filling station" replaced it.[44]

In May 1898 Joel and Emma purchased a large house and lot at 1115 West Clinch Avenue, in White's Addition, which along with Ramsey's Addition had been incorporated as West Knoxville a decade earlier. But the year the Tylers moved in, West Knoxville, also known as West End, was annexed by the city of Knoxville. The Tylers remained in the house almost thirty years. "We loved that place," said Laura. For Paula, who "was there through all my youth," Knoxville was an "awfully nice" place for a child to grow up. Perhaps

This 1930s aerial photograph shows the intersection of West Clinch Avenue (slanting up from the bottom toward the right side of the photo) and Twelfth (previously Fourth) Street (slanting left from the lower right corner). For almost three decades beginning in 1898, the Tylers owned the large, white-trimmed house on the corner. The one-story cottage that became Hugh Tyler's art studio is visible behind the main house. N-6702, Thompson Photograph Collection, McClung Historical Collection, Knox County Library.

comparing the city of her youth to Manhattan, where she spent much of her adult life, Paula said of Knoxville: "It was a small town. And the way we were situated, people's yards ran into each other, so that the kids at night—a bunch of them—would get together and play I Spy, or something like that, without anybody telling them what to do. [Our parents] never had to plan amusements for us. And of course, there were no [buses] for the schools; we just walked to school."[45]

The odors of coal smoke and honeysuckle always reminded Hugh of those early years in Knoxville. He recalled walking home to Clinch Avenue from a friend's house on Broadway: "I used to stroll home through the autumn twilight, with the smoke of the town gathering overhead, augmented by the tracks of the Southern crossing Broadway, and again, a few blocks further on, by the engines of the Louisville & Nashville, whose smoke drifted through the just lighted and sputtering arc lights. The hill of the university rose above a sea of river mist and smoke beyond the arches of the Clinch Avenue Viaduct, the Highland Avenue car would be grinding and squealing around the curve onto Clinch, and there would be the lights of home and the stone steps between the soot stained, ivy-covered wall, with probably a few crisp magnolia leaves to crunch underfoot."[46]

By September 1900 Jessie Tyler had moved to 1502 Laurel Avenue to live with her mother's widowed sister, Martha Fisk, called Patty by family members. "[Jessie] took care of her mother as long as she lived in Knoxville," remembered Paula. "Then she took care of her aunt, Aunt Patty. And they had a separate house." Patty was a greatly bereaved woman. She and her husband, Dr. Ira Fisk, lost their nine-year-old daughter in 1879; ten years later their son died at age twenty-four. Then in December 1891, a month after the Tylers moved to Knoxville, Dr. and Mrs. Fisk were summoned to Daytona, Florida, where Sarah Tyler had become "seriously ill" while vacationing. Shortly after he and his wife arrived at the hotel, Dr. Fisk died of "apoplexy." Laura Tyler was seven at the time. She might have retained memories of the heavy grief her great-aunt suffered—a grief that James Rufus Agee later fictionalized as he reflected on his own mother's bereavement. The writer imagined his grandfather Joel speaking to Laura about an episode that, if factual, would have occurred at the family's previous home on Magnolia Avenue: "Patty went to pieces you know, when she lost her husband, a lot later in life and a lot better warning than you got. Tore around like a chicken with its head off. 'Oh, why did it have to be *me*? What have *I* ever done that God picked on *me*?' . . . Butting her head against the wall, trying to stab herself with her scissors, yelling like a stuck pig; you could hear her in the next block." Now

From 1900 to 1910, Jessie Tyler lived with her aunt Patty Fisk in this house at 1502 Laurel Avenue, shown here in 2015. Photo by the author.

the Tylers lived a few blocks from Patty and Jessie. "My father always went up there in the evening to see her," recalled Paula. The house at 1502 Laurel Avenue still stands, directly across the street from James Agee Park, and is one of the rare Tyler homes remaining from the family's Knoxville years.[47]

Laura and Hugh entered the University of Tennessee as freshmen in fall 1901. Aside from his coursework, Hugh focused almost exclusively on his art lessons. That year, both joined the school's Episcopal Club and the off-campus Knoxville Art School led by Harriett Wiley—a native of Massachusetts who was unrelated to Catherine Wiley, the well known Knoxville artist who taught at UT around that time and later served as a president of Nicholson Art League, of which Hugh was a member. Laura, however, quickly integrated herself into the college community. She joined the Barbara Blount Club, as well as the Rouge and Powder Dramatic Club, becoming its secretary and treasurer.[48]

For Laura, life at the university revolved around the "Woman's Building," which opened in 1901 as Barbara Blount Hall. As UT's first female dorm, the hall also housed classrooms, a gymnasium, and the headquarters of Chi Omega, which was the only sorority on campus when the chapter formed in April 1900. Laura ambitiously applied to join the sorority, which required that she submit to an initiation ritual. One had to climb "four long flights of stairs" up to the attic of Barbara Blount Hall, where the door to the chapter rooms was emblazoned with "a ghastly skull and cross-bones." From there the candidate was led into a "secret room, where we keep the goat and other instruments of torture," wrote a Chi Omega officer in mock severity. It was up to this initiation room that Laura had to climb in the dark, as reported in the June 1902 edition of *The Eleusis*, Chi Omega's newsletter:

> At dusk one eerie, dismal Saturday afternoon, when the rain dripped with dreary monotony, and the gray winter twilight made weird shadows in the big, empty attic which is the ante-chamber to our rooms, Laura Whitman Tyler was conducted up the stairway that leads to Greekdom. . . . The ghostly drip, drip, of the rain, the attic full of eerie shadows . . . made it so fearsome an occasion that the more timid of our number felt a bit shivery and uncomfortable. . . . Laura, herself, came through bravely and is fulfilling all our expectations for her.[49]

Perhaps it was under the influence of this new clique of friends that Laura began attending a dancing class off campus. There she met a young, single man with a strong accent who had lived downtown since being hired as a post office clerk. His name was Hugh James Agee, but he went by James; those who knew him best called him Jim, or Jay. Laura came to know him as a "hearty, jovial, out-going man." Jay Agee has been called "rugged," presumptively comparing his rural background with the more refined culture of Laura's family. Two separate family lines converged in that dancing class.[50]

The Joel Tylers have been called "a substantial family of artists and musicians," and it is easy to accept such a statement when looking at their endeavors in the humanities and the fact that the family's strong appreciation for literature can be traced back, at least, to 1843, when Rufus Tyler helped establish the literary society in Alexandria, Ohio. But James Rufus Agee unpretentiously described the Tylers as a "middle-class" family "from Michigan out of New England," with "mainly business men with now and then a teacher or a doctor." His father's family is typically characterized as "quite different from the Tylers," hardworking but not as educated or artistically inclined. According to Father Flye, the Agees "were not illiterate, to be sure, but they weren't of [the Tylers'] kind of background." However, the way James Rufus described them, the Agees were no less substantial, made up of "mountaineers . . . a blend of country British Isles stock, Hessian Mercenary, and Huguenot. . . . They were farmers, with now and then a teacher or a doctor." And his list could have been more impressive by adding "with now and then" soldiers, county officials, and state legislators.[51]

THE AGEES

Jay's grandfather and namesake, James Harris Agee, was born in Campbell County on February 14, 1827, and named after *his* father, James Agee—a War of 1812 veteran and Tennessee legislator whose family migrated to Tennessee when he was young. James Harris was the first of his Agee line to be born in Tennessee.[52]

Jay Agee apparently inherited his grandfather's looks. James Harris, often referred to as J. H., was a striking figure standing six-foot-one and "dark-complexioned, with blue eyes and black hair." At age sixteen he farmed for a living while reading medical books. His father died in 1843. On November 22, 1848, J. H. married Mary Comer. Her parents were illiterate at the time, but her father—John, a farmer and ironworker—was in his sixties when he learned to read. Agee became a practicing physician about five years later. By 1860 James and Mary lived in the Campbell County town of Fincastle, five miles northeast of present-day LaFollette, with their five children. The eldest, born on August 24, 1850, was christened Henry Clay—a name chosen by many Whig families as a tribute to Kentucky senator Henry Clay, who greatly influenced Abraham Lincoln and was "almost worshiped" by the sixteenth president. Senator Clay was Lincoln's "beau ideal of a statesman" and had helped negotiate the end of the War of 1812, in which James Harris Agee's father served.[53]

J. H. was "an ardent republican" and did not keep his political beliefs private. He was "an aggressive Union man," who "took an active part in . . . various campaigns" as the country approached Civil War.[54]

Even though Campbell County voted to elect a pro-Union governor in 1861, the candidate lost, and Tennessee seceded that June. By the following year, many men had left the county to enlist in the Union army. J. H. moved his family to Pike, Indiana, where he taught school. On January 21, 1865, he enlisted as a First Sergeant in the Indiana Infantry, Company I, 143rd Regiment, which mustered in Indianapolis on February 21, just a week after he turned thirty-eight. A few days later, the regiment moved south to Nashville, and over a span of months continued down to Murfreesboro, Tullahoma,

James Harris Agee, Tennessee General Assembly, 1881. Reprinted by permission of Tennessee State Library and Archives.

and back up to Clarksville. He was discharged in Nashville on October 17. Late that year, the family returned to Campbell County, where Dr. Agee's medical services were greatly needed because of outbreaks of smallpox and other illnesses. After about four years of living under Confederate and Union occupations, the impoverished county residents had few provisions left.[55]

Dr. Agee entered politics a few years later and was elected to the state legislature, where "he was noted for his energy and activity. He had opinions on all vital questions, knew how to express them, and had the courage to stand by them." Between 1869 and 1883 he served three terms as a representative and one as a senator.[56]

In 1870 a bill was introduced in the House of Representatives to establish a new county in West Tennessee, to be named after Davy Crockett. Through Agee's efforts, the bill passed, and on January 20, 1871, he gave the following speech on the House floor:

Mr. Speaker: Upon returning to my seat, after an absence of some days, I found upon my desk a magnificent gold mounted walking cane bearing the inscription: "HON. J. H. AGEE, BY THE CITIZENS OF CROCKETT COUNTY."

I learn that this beautiful cane is presented to me by the good people of Crockett County as a token of their appreciation and endorsement of my action as a member of this house . . . [T]hat at least a portion of the citizens of our good and noble commonwealth indorse my legislative career is of more value to me than would be all the glittering diamonds that sparkle upon the plains of Alaska.

[I]t is but reasonable to suppose that the citizens living in that portion bordering upon the father of all waters would not entertain a very exalted opinion of me, hailing as I do, from the mountains of East Tennessee . . . ; but in this evidence of their kindness and partiality, I am convinced that they . . . do rise above all sectional prejudice. . . . I am proud to accept this token of their appreciation of my services of this honorable body . . . I hope the day is not far distant when . . . all the people of the state, irrespective of political parties or particular sections, will gather around the tree of our institutions like a band of brothers and fight only for God and our whole country.[57]

It was not the only time J. H. was honored by his constituents. The small town of Grantsboro, which sat at the forks of the Clinch and Powell Rivers in Campbell County, was renamed Agee when the post office reopened there on December 26, 1882. This was certainly an honor as well to J. H.'s family, including his son Henry, who later lived in the town.[58]

The post office at Agee, circa 1913. From *Campbell County Tennessee USA,* vol. 1. Reprinted courtesy of Campbell County Historical Society.

By that time, James Harris Agee was a self-educated lawyer as well as Campbell County court clerk and master, adding to his experiences as a physician, Civil War veteran, and state senator. A few years later, he was appointed as the county health officer, a position he held from about 1885 to 1890. He was a member of the Missionary Baptist Church, and many of his descendants were Baptists as well.[59]

On October 8, 1899, he died at age seventy-three in his LaFollette home, surrounded by his family. "He was a wide-awake, public-spirited man," eulogized Knoxville's *Journal and Tribune*. "Naturally aggressive, he sometimes made enemies; but he was sincere, hospitable and had a large number of warm friends, to whom he was always true and steadfast . . . . To his family he was . . . kind and lovingly devoted, and always took a profound pride in the welfare of his children." He had ten children in all and is one of several Agees buried in LaFollette's Dugtown Cemetery, including another James Harris Agee, a grandson who died in his mid-twenties. The cemetery is located within a block of where Dr. Agee lived, near the intersection of Seventeenth and West Beech Street.[60]

∞∞∞∞∞∞∞∞∞∞

Like his father, Henry Clay Agee farmed throughout his life starting at a young age, but he also taught school for forty-seven years in Campbell County, likely beginning at the small village of Craig's Ford. It sat on the Powell River, nine miles from the county seat in Jacksboro and eleven miles from Caryville, the nearest shipping point for packages brought in by the Knoxville & Ohio Railroad. The village site is now the area along Norris Lake known as Heatherly's Point. The settlement consisted of a post office, with semiweekly mail delivery, a Baptist church, two general stores, an iron smelting furnace and forge, and the district school. Henry Clay Agee and a cousin, William A. Agee, were the school's two teachers.[61]

William, a Civil War veteran, later met a tragic end. He was a nephew of James Harris Agee, but also became his son-in-law around 1875 by marrying Henry Clay Agee's sister Mary—a first cousin. After Mary died, William migrated to Indiana and remarried. In December 1904, William's body was unearthed in Oklahoma after a dog was found gnawing on the skull; the victim's horse and $15,000 were missing. Evidence pointed to James Bratcher, also a former LaFollette resident, and an accomplice who had been seen riding the horse out of town. Both men were arrested in Texas, confessed to the crime, and were sentenced to life in prison.[62]

Henry Clay Agee. MS.2730, box 6, folder
3, James Agee and Agee Trust Collection,
Special Collections, University of Tennessee
Library, Knoxville. Reprinted courtesy of
the James Agee Trust.

Moss Lamar Agee, circa 1925.
Knoxville Journal.

Henry was living in Craig's Ford when he met a young woman, ten years
his junior, from Anderson County. Serelda was her given name, but she went
by her middle name, Moss, or Mossie. The last born of six girls, Moss could
read but not write at age ten; however, later census records indicate that by
adulthood she could do both. Her father, Hugh B. Lamar, was a farmer de-
scended from the French Huguenots, as were the Agees. Her mother, whose
maiden name was Abigail Margraves, "had a Hessian ancestor who came
over for the Revolution." It is not known how Henry and Moss met. She
lived at Wallace's Crossroads (present-day Andersonville), located several
miles south of where Henry taught, so it is unlikely that she was a student
of his. Whatever the case, the two married in 1877, in a simple ceremony
officiated by Justice of the Peace H. L. Ridinour. Henry was twenty-seven
and Moss, seventeen. Exactly eleven months later, April 17, 1878, their first
child was born: a son, Hugh James Agee, named after both grandfathers.
From boyhood onward, he "was called Jim, James or Jay, but never Hugh."[63]

Between 1878 and 1896, Moss gave birth to eight children, but half of them died before reaching age four. Infant deaths were not uncommon in that place and time, but J. H. Agee, Campbell County's health officer, must have felt the acute irony in the high mortality rate of his own grandchildren. A possible cause for the deaths appeared in one his monthly health reports in 1885: "Cholera infantum prevails among the children from one to three years of age."[64]

Moss "was a very sweet, lovely person, a person of great strength of character, too," remembered her daughter-in-law, Laura. "And she was very pretty and very industrious, and extremely looked-up-to by the other women out there in the country. She'd always go if they were sick and help take care of them, [and] had a very broad charity in her toward everybody. She was a little thing . . . short, rather stocky woman." Laura's sister, Paula, remembered Moss as "an awfully nice old lady."[65]

In 1880 Henry and family still lived in Craig's Ford, where the June census recorded his occupation as "bootmaker," most likely a side job during his summer break from teaching. A couple of months later, another son, Alfred

Henry Clay Agee's three sons (from left): Frank, James (Jay), and John. MS.2730, box 6, folder 3, James Agee and Agee Trust Collection, Special Collections, University of Tennessee Library, Knoxville. Reprinted courtesy of the James Agee Trust.

Franklin (Frank), was born. The next two years saw the birth and death of two daughters. By the time the next son, John Henry, was born in 1887, the family had moved south roughly a mile and a half to Agee, the postal village formerly called Grantsboro, at the forks of two rivers. The final child, daughter Mossie Jane, was born in 1896. (By 1900 the Agee household had an additional member, Paralee Smith, an eleven-year-old "boarder" whom Henry and Moss would one day adopt.)[66]

Jay and Frank schooled their younger brother in the essential masculine skills of hunting, fishing, swimming, and baseball. Reportedly, John learned to pitch so well that after he was married "his mother-in-law, Sarah King, counted on him to 'catch' a chicken for Sunday dinner with a well-aimed rock."[67]

Jay Agee was largely self-educated, only finishing school to fourth grade. Although he was raised to work the family farm, he wished to become something more. For a few years around 1900, Jay taught school in Campbell County. His father had taught there for about three decades, was nowhere near retiring, and still had to scrape a living off of rented farmland. Henry Clay Agee had demonstrated that being "a country schoolteacher" was not a lucrative career choice. At least part of Jay's desire for a good city job was so he could give part of his earnings back to his family.[68]

In his spare time, Jay read law books, as his grandfather had. "My father," James Rufus Agee wrote, "was from the mountains forty miles upstate from town: had worked in his self-education and in the help of his family with a strength and courage that sickens me with shame of myself to think of." Rufus Agee's mother, Laura, described the lengths to which Jay pursued learning: "He never went further than the fourth grade himself, you know, and then he went to work. Kept on reading and reading and reading. He was avid for information and got it. . . . [The Agees] were poor; they had to work hard, and did. But he'd built a little room onto the house all by himself where he could be alone to read and not get into the family too much, so that when he was through working he could shut himself in and read. He bought books at auction whenever he could, and he had all of Blackstone's [*Commentaries on the Laws of England*]—read a great deal of that. He was interested in lots of different things."[69]

Jay's uncle Joseph was postmaster of Jacksboro and may have influenced Jay to consider a job with the post office. Newspapers carried announcements about civil service examinations, which were typically given twice a year. The clerk-carrier exam lasted up to four and a half hours and consisted of seven sections: spelling, arithmetic, letter writing, penmanship, copying text, geography of the United States, and reading addresses. Jay took and passed the exam sometime in 1900, but he was put on a waiting list for employment in Knoxville, as there were no clerk positions available there at the time. While waiting for an appointment, he continued living in Campbell County, perhaps teaching another year or working as a postal clerk in his hometown.[70]

At the end of June 1901, after several months of waiting, Jay received word that a vacancy had opened up in Knoxville's post office and that he would be hired as a "substitute clerk." If Jay was still teaching, the news conveniently arrived after the school year had ended. Presumably, he still lived with his parents and siblings near Jacksboro, as he had the previous June. As soon as he could, he packed his bags and boarded a train to Knoxville, where he rented a room downtown in preparation for his first day on the job on the first floor of the marble Custom House on West Clinch Avenue. James Rufus Agee wrote that his father "had at length, through civil service examinations,

The post office building, called the Custom House, on Clinch Avenue, Knoxville, 1900. LC-DIG-det-4a10874, Library of Congress Prints and Photographs Division.

The interior of Knoxville's post office, as it appeared circa 1894, roughly seven years before Jay Agee was hired as a clerk. McClung Historical Collection, Knox County Library.

got out of that country into town in the postal service. And here he was now, new, knowing no one much, [and] still reading late of nights."[71]

In some ways, as a transplant from the hills of East Tennessee, Jay found himself in good company in the prospering city. Between 1880, just after his birth, to 1900, Knoxville's population increased by almost 23,000. Many of those new residents were former farmers who had left "the hills and coves of Appalachia" to find factory jobs in Knoxville. Although Jay was somewhat different in that he now worked for the government, he lived in the same apartments and ate in the same restaurants and drank in the same saloons as did the other mountain folk. But mixed with the rural dialects he had heard since boyhood, Jay encountered unfamiliar accents and customs—not just from northerners but from people who had migrated from countries like Ireland, Germany, Switzerland, Italy, and Greece. Downtown Knoxville, and particularly the area where "dirt farmers from the hills" sold meat and produce, was perhaps unique in its heterogeneity. As one historian wrote, "Market Square could exhibit a cultural diversity unusual even in big cities," with its variations in "skin color and its Babel of accents both foreign and domestic." The new market house, a "brick leviathan" that "stretched from Union to Wall," was only three and a half years old when Jay arrived in town. On dedication day in December 1897, one distinguished orator characterized the market as truly egalitarian: "Today no Republican or Democrat, no gold-bug or silverite, no Methodist or Baptist, no Calvinist or Lutheran, no Catholic or Protestant, is here—but only Knoxvillians. Today none claim to be native or naturalized, Southern or Yankee, rich or poor, Irish or Swiss, white or black, or high or low, but everyone is proud to be a citizen of Knoxville and to share her renown." For the rest of his life, Jay struggled to reconcile this new urban existence with the rural one he had left behind.[72]

That summer, as Jay got to know his way around Knoxville, Laura and Hugh Tyler vacationed in Charlesvoix, Michigan, resting up before UT classes began in the fall. While attending the university, they lived at home on West Clinch, just a few blocks from campus, and several blocks down the street from the post office.[73]

DANCING SCHOOL

During her first year of college, Laura branched out beyond pure academics and made many friends. Besides her initiation and acceptance into the Chi Omega sorority, she participated in a few literary and artistic clubs. In April 1902 the Knoxville Art School exhibited student paintings, including selections by Laura and Hugh Tyler, at the Woman's Building on Main Avenue, directly across from the courthouse.[74]

The building also hosted a new dancing class, dubbed the 1902 Dancing Club, which had begun a month earlier. The class met each Monday night, with instruction from 7:30 to 8:30 and "an informal dance" afterwards. "A general invitation is extended to the young people of the city," the *Sentinel* had announced in March, "with whom dancing is a most popular form of entertainment." This may be the dancing class that Laura heard about and, perhaps with some of her Chi Omega friends, decided to attend.[75]

Laura "had from seven on lived in Knoxville," her son wrote. "Her girlhood had been on the outskirts of that city, her adolescence in its brick high schools and in a shingle house on middle-well-to-do West Clinch; in piano lessons and girlish poetry, amateur plays; picnics along the tall bluffs over the river; difficulty with mathematics on The Hill, the University of Tennessee; too much innocence, yet some strongmindedness; dancing school and dances. It was at a dancing school that she met my father." Jay, who was "new" to the city, "knowing no one much," came to the class to learn "a little how to dance and how to subdue his hands and feet." The tall country boy "had a rugged sweetness, a tenderness, a fine-chiseled handsomeness," and "a rollicking good humor" that perhaps distinguished him from the well-bred fraternity boys among whom Laura mingled. Paula Tyler remembered that Jay "was very good-looking. Laura met him at dancing school, night dancing school."[76]

Hugh and Laura continued as sophomores at UT, with Laura listed as a student in the education department. She rejoined the Rouge and Powder Club and sang with the Girls' Glee Club. And now Laura Tyler, newly elected as secretary of her sorority, was responsible for writing the chapter newsletter, which went out "to all the chapters of dear old Chi Omega, far and near," updating the sisters on local events of the past months. In November 1902 Laura and the other girls put in many hours, "nearly every spare minute," redecorating the chapter room in Chi Omega colors, as she later reported

Laura Tyler, center, stands among fellow members of the University of Tennessee's Chi Omega sorority, Pi chapter. 1904 UT yearbook, Special Collections, University of Tennessee Library, Knoxville.

in the newsletter. "You must try to imagine that our 'cuddy-hole' under the eaves is no longer upholstered throughout in irregularly patched expanses of burlap. . . . No, indeed, we have heroicly [sic] emptied our pockets and the room is all papered in deep red, the wood-work is painted deep cream, and as the matting which covers the floor is cardinal and straw, the room is all greatly improved." Laura was elected Chi Omega's treasurer by the end of that school year.[77]

Whereas Hugh graduated in spring 1905, Laura withdrew from the four-year track during her junior year and was relegated to a group of "special students" who took courses without pursuing a degree. She did not return to UT with Hugh that last fall. "Laura Tyler has deserted us," her Chi Omega sisters announced, "but as she lives in town we hope to see her often." Emma Tyler, an early female graduate from the University of Michigan and a leader in Knoxville's feminist circle, was likely disappointed by her daughter's decision, especially as Laura grew more deeply involved with the postal clerk from Campbell County.[78]

ENGAGEMENT

In November 1902, around the time Laura was refurbishing the sorority hall, Jay was likely working on the ground floor of the Custom House while outlaw Harvey Logan—"Kid Curry"—was being tried in the federal courtroom, two floors above, on charges of theft and forgery. At the time, Jay's annual salary was $800. It was raised by $200 in 1905. He had switched apartments about once a year since first arriving in Knoxville, but all of his listed downtown addresses—Oxford Place, the McCoy Building on Wall Avenue, South Gay Street near Staub's Opera House, the Vendome on West Clinch—were within a four-block radius of the Custom House.[79]

Now that Laura was no longer in school, Jay frequently called on her at her parents' home. "Sometimes I'd come home to our house, and we had high steps to the porch," remembered Paula Tyler, "and they'd be sitting on one of the porch steps talking." Jay's lack of formal education did not diminish his attractiveness to Laura. In fact, she believed there was "something like Lincoln" in the way he had advanced himself. "He had it all in his makeup, you know, the discipline of it and the knowledge," Laura recalled. Paula described Jay as "very intellectual. He liked reading very much, and he'd educated himself really by what he'd done after he'd left school."[80]

Joel and Emma were perhaps concerned initially about the relationship, especially when Laura chose not to finish college. However, after seeing

Jay's work ethic and common sense, Laura's father was finally won over. Joel "was an extremely independent person in his thought and opinions—the old American tradition of personal independence," remembered Father Flye. "This is where he stood and he wasn't modifying it for anybody. He wanted to stand on his own feet and pay his own way and not take any favors." Joel saw these qualities in Laura's suitor and confessed that Jay "needed college less than any man he had ever met."[81]

Jay proposed to Laura, and things appeared to fall into place for the couple to marry that autumn. He had a good job and was commended for his performance as a clerk. "Since he has been connected with the post office," wrote a local paper, "he has applied himself diligently, and has been painstaking, with the result that he has been given several promotions, and when the last increase budget for clerks and carriers . . . was put through, Mr. Agee came in for a nice increase in wages." With the extra income, Jay purchased one hundred acres near Jacksboro on October 31, 1905. Perhaps he imagined moving there with Laura after the marriage and farming in the foothills of Cumberland Mountain or at least holding on to the land until retirement, letting his parents live on it rent-free in the meantime.[82]

Then an opportunity arose that seemed too good to pass up—a transfer to Panama, where a historic canal project was underway, requiring many workers who would be well paid by the U.S. government. For doing essentially the same job he did in Knoxville, Jay could make about $800 more per year in Panama, more than twice the amount he made as a new postal clerk. Jay and Laura could marry as planned, reside in free Canal Zone housing for a couple of years, and return to Tennessee with enough money to buy a home. Jay applied for the transfer.[83]

But the appointment came on November 23, much sooner than expected. "James Agee, one of the best known of the clerks at the post office, has secured a good job at Colón in the Panama service looking after the mails for Uncle Sam," the newspaper announced, four days later. "He has received notice to report at Washington by December 1, for instructions, but does not think he will be able to do so by that time." The wedding would have to wait. Jay took his oath for duty on November 29 and moved out of his Clinch Avenue apartment.[84]

PANAMA

U.S. workers in Panama were generally more demanding and more susceptible to tropical diseases than their South American counterparts. Still, they were highly skilled, and the Isthmian Canal Commission (ICC) offered them generous salaries to be disbursed in gold coins and benefits like free housing for married workers, thirty paid sick days and forty-two paid vacation days annually, and access to social clubs and a growing number of amenities.

Along with the benefits, however, were some negative points to consider. Torrential rains soaked the isthmus from May to November, forcing workers to slosh through the muddy streets and cope with the pervasive dampness. Sanitary conditions always worsened during this time. Mosquito populations reproduced in swelling pools of fresh water, increasing the risk of diseases like yellow fever and, most prevalent, malaria in the region that became known as the "Fever Coast." After the turnover rate for U.S. workers rose to 75 percent by the summer of 1905, the ICC began working to retain their skilled employees, updating residences with plumbing, electricity, and screened porches. Recreational facilities, like bowling lanes, began to appear.[85]

Jay Agee departed from New York aboard a steamship on December 2, 1905. Seven days later, he moved into his single living quarters and reported for duty. On December 12, he was promoted from postal clerk to postmaster and assigned to run the post office at Corozal, a village named after the native corozo palm tree and located about three miles northwest from Panama City. The land was leased to the United States in 1904 and used primarily for housing Canal Zone workers. Compared to Knoxville's stately Custom House, the repurposed building that served as Corozal's post office was a major downgrade. But Jay could hardly complain about his starting salary of $1,500, paid in gold—more than he had ever earned in a year.[86]

Two regular events kept Jay particularly busy at the post office. One was payday. Workers were paid in gold but had nowhere to deposit it since the Canal Zone had no bank. Many took their coins to the post office and exchanged them for money orders, which could easily be mailed to their banks or relatives back home. The other big event was mail day. Mail was shipped in every five days to Colón, on the Atlantic end of the Canal Zone. Colón was connected to Ancon, on the Pacific end, by the Panama Railroad, which distributed mail to the twenty-six post offices along the forty-seven-mile track. Corozal was among the mail train's last stops before it reached Ancon. The mail could be delayed at any point, and recipients were eager to know the hour of its arrival. Even though Jay operated one of the smallest branches in the zone, on mail day he likely endured the same recurring question: "Heard any news of the mail train?" And even if that train did not reach Corozal until midnight, Jay was still expected to keep the office open "and distribute letters until the small hours."[87]

During Jay's first full month as postmaster, the U.S. Senate's Committee on Interoceanic Canals was investigating a scandalous rumor. In late October, before Jay arrived on the isthmus, a boat landed at Colón carrying a few hundred "colored" women from Martinique. A rumor quickly spread that the women were prostitutes and had been brought by the ICC to the Canal Zone for "immoral purposes." An official investigation began, and in January 1906 affidavits were collected from 167 of the women, including Miss Leonie St. Rose, who had been in Panama "a little more than two months and [was] now employed as a domestic in the house of the postmaster at Corosal [sic]." The inquiry put to rest rumors of debauchery, and concluded that the women, including Jay's domestic servant, "were wives, sisters or daughters of laborers" already working in the Canal Zone. However, allegations of unequal treatment and unsanitary working conditions were well founded, and it was clear that oversight was needed from higher up in the U.S. government.[88]

Back in Knoxville, marriage was heavy on Laura's mind. She had intended to become Mrs. Jay Agee the previous fall, but his transfer to Panama interrupted those plans. However, within a few months of separation, in letters sent to each other over land and sea, the couple decided that they could not wait for Jay's next extended leave. Laura would meet him in Panama as soon as Jay received approval for married housing. In preparation for the marriage, the Reverend Samuel Ringgold baptized Laura on April 8 at St. John's Episcopal Church, with Frances Nelson and Jessie P. Tyler as witnesses. Laura was listed as a communicant in the church register on May 27, 1906, only a few weeks before her arrival in Panama. When Jay contacted her about being assigned new living quarters, she made final arrangements for her trip. The *Journal and Tribune* carried the news on June 10: "Informal announcement has been made during the past week of the engagement and approaching marriage of Miss Laura Whitmann [sic] Tyler and Mr. James Agee.... As it is impossible for Mr. Agee to return home at this time, Miss Tyler and her brother Mr. Hugh Tyler will sail this week from New York. Upon arrival at Colón they will be met by a party of friends and the marriage will be solemnized at the Episcopal church in Cristobal."[89]

Hugh and Laura sailed from New York to Cristobal aboard the double-mast, single-funnel steamship *Finance*. On Wednesday, June 20, after six days at sea, they arrived at their destination. Jay and some friends were waiting there when the steamer arrived at port. "Laura spotted [Jay] from the ship, a long time before the ship docked," remembered Hugh. The party traveled

Jay Agee in Panama, sitting beside a native corozo palm tree. MS.2730, box 6, folder 3, James Agee and Agee Trust Collection, Special Collections, University of Tennessee Library, Knoxville. Reprinted courtesy of the James Agee Trust.

to Colón and from there to the Episcopal church, where the wedding was conducted. The groom was twenty-eight; the bride, twenty-two.[90]

According to one report, only Catholic marriages were recognized in Panama at the time Jay and Laura wed, and it was not until Theodore Roosevelt's March 1907 executive order that Protestant ceremonies were allowed. However, the newspaper announcement specified that the church was Episcopal; and according to the *Canal Record*, Protestant churches had been operating in Panama for over forty years at the time the Agees resided there. Perhaps non-Catholic marriages were not officially accepted by Panamanian government before Roosevelt's order but were still conducted and recognized by the American officials there.[91]

Jay and Laura would live near the post office in Corozal, a village "in the higher lands . . . three miles from the interesting old town of Panama." The day after the wedding, Hugh sent a telegram to Knoxville to report the wedding, and the Tylers relayed the information in cards to family and friends:

Mr. and Mrs. Joel Claverly Tyler
announce the marriage of their daughter
Laura Whitman,
and
Mr. Hugh James Agee,
on Wednesday, the twentieth of June,
one thousand nine hundred and six
Corozal, Canal Zone.[92]

After an eight-day honeymoon, Jay returned to work on June 29. On July 1 his annual salary was raised to $1,650. The new couple settled into their home, which aside from the bedrooms contained a kitchen, sitting room, piazza, and bathroom. Like the other wives, Laura shopped at the commissary. Jay now ate home-cooked meals regularly, rather than going to the government hotel with the other single men for thirty-cent dinners. But the hotel still had entertainment, becoming a clubhouse for American workers on Saturday nights, with singing and dancing and music from the corner piano. James Rufus Agee wrote of his parents attending "dances, in Panama," where his father would "stop except for dancing with her, [and] get sore if she danced more than a little with others." That Fourth of July, Jay and Laura likely joined in the American-style celebration.[93]

Hugh Tyler said goodbye to his sister and new brother-in-law and briefly visited Kingston, Jamaica, before returning home. This was his first of several trips to the Caribbean, the subject of many of his later painted landscapes, and he likely made sketches during his excursion. His 1914 watercolor "Tropical Scene, Panama" shows workers carrying clusters of bananas to the wharf and may be based on sketches or memories from his first trip to the isthmus. On July 12 Hugh was back on North American soil, arriving in New Orleans aboard the *Antillian*.[94]

Jay was out of work from September 23–29, 1906, due to an unnamed illness. A month and a half later, a ship, the U.S.S. *Louisiana*, anchored off the coast of Colón, carrying an important passenger on a history-making voyage. Theodore Roosevelt, in the first foreign trip by a sitting U.S. president, planned to inspect working and living conditions in and around the Canal Zone. His visit coincided with Panama's rainiest month, and he reported more than ten inches falling over a six-day period. "It would have been impossible," judged Roosevelt, "to see the work going on under more unfavorable weather conditions."[95]

During his three days ashore, November 15–17, the president made dozens of unannounced stops throughout the zone, conducting surprise examinations of work sites, hospitals, and housing to see firsthand what workers and their families had to endure. He visited Corozal, the village that a newspaperman had called a "hog wallow" because of its "marsh with a pond in the middle," where rainwater collected and harbored mosquito larvae. "Corozal," said Roosevelt, "was formerly one of the most unsanitary places on the Isthmus, probably the most unsanitary." While there, he saw that many improvements had been made, that "both the marsh and pond" had been "drained and the brush cleared off, so that now, when I went over the ground, it appeared like a smooth meadow intersected by drainage ditches. The breeding places and sheltering spots of the dangerous mosquitoes had been completely destroyed. The result is that Corozal for the last six months . . . shows one of the best sick rates in the Zone, having less than 1 per cent a week admitted to the hospital."[96]

Although the President's visit to Corozal was almost certainly unannounced, Jay and Laura would have likely noticed a large number of officials arriving at the small depot. Perhaps Roosevelt met the twenty-eight-year-old postmaster and asked whether conditions had improved in the village. But even if Jay missed seeing the president that day, he would have later opportunities in Knoxville.[97]

Roosevelt, having assessed the mosquito problem, noted another element affecting the quality of life in the Canal Zone: liquor. A directory of merchants from that time shows that in the cities of Colón and Panama the numbers of saloons were disproportionate to any other business, and the situation was obvious to Roosevelt after only a few days on the isthmus: "There seemed to me to be too many saloons in the Zone; but the new high-license law which goes into effect on January 1 next will probably close four-fifths of them. Resolute and successful efforts are being made to minimize and control the sale of liquor." Meanwhile, 1,900 miles to the north, another city was working to limit the availability of hard drink within its borders.[98]

Members of the Women's Christian Temperance Union had been advocating for a dry Knoxville since at least the 1880s. Many of the city's violent crimes were directly linked to alcohol, including the December 1901 shooting of two police officers by outlaw Harvey Logan at a saloon on Central Avenue. When the liquor ban issue was debated in Market Square's public hall in 1907, prohibitionists evoked Logan's name as a reminder of the violent stigma that saloons had attached to the city. In March 1907, Knoxville voted to close its bars, all 114 of them, leaving the town much drier than Jay had remembered.[99]

Around that time, Laura was welcoming a familiar bit of Knoxville to the isthmus. Her sorority sister Marcia Perkins came to Panama for an extended visit. It was Jay's and Laura's first contact with someone from home since Hugh left Cristobal following the wedding. Then on July 6, Laura finally got to travel to Knoxville after more than a year away, leaving Cristobal aboard the S.S. *Colón,* and arriving in New York on July 12. The next month, Jay was granted seventy-four days of paid leave and sailed from Cristobal on August 24 aboard the same steamer. He returned to duty in Corozal on November 7.[100]

By the end of spring, 1908, Laura had reached the limit of homesickness she could endure. Knoxville could be dirty and humid, but it could not rival the amounts of mud, moisture, and mosquitoes found in Corozal. Recent health reports claimed that the number of malaria cases in the Canal Zone had fallen by half since the previous April, but the threat of disease never abated. Every evening, Jay and Laura hid behind window screens and bed nets to avoid the night-feeding *Anopheles* mosquito, and may have taken regular oral doses of quinine as recommended by the ICC's chief sanitation officer. Quinine could prevent transmission of the virus but came with side effects and an unpleasant taste. Despite the best precautions, Laura contracted the virus and began suffering high fever and other flu-like symptoms. "I was shaking with malaria," she recalled. "I got it pretty frightfully down there." The nearest hospital at Ancon was most likely where doctors tested Laura's blood, placed her on a bed in a screened cubicle, and "injected" her "with large doses of quinine." In writing about the substance, "the only dependable preventive and cure for that ancient scourge of the tropics," James Rufus Agee described the symptoms experienced by a malaria patient: "First he has chills and his nails turn blue, then he has fever and his skin takes on a diseased rosiness, and finally he is drenched in sweat. This process recurs time after time over a period of years. . . . In due course of the malady, if nothing is done, he dies." By 1908, monthly deaths from malaria among the forty-five thousand canal workers had dropped to single digits; the disease was rarely fatal for patients with American privilege. Nevertheless, the ordeal sharpened Laura's resolve to return to Knoxville. Her appraisal of Panama was simple: "No place for white people."[101]

On June 21, 1908, the day after she and Jay celebrated two years of marriage and life together on the isthmus, Laura boarded the S.S. *Panama* at Cristobal and, for the last time, slowly withdrew from the port. By coincidence, she left the country just as 1,250 marines were heading toward it. In response to rising tensions as Panama's presidential election neared, the U.S. government sent troops to keep the peace. Even if Laura had not become ill, Jay might have insisted she leave because of the risk of riots spreading the few miles from Panama City to Corozal. At some point in the Atlantic, her steamer passed a ship carrying the first load of soldiers, who reached Panama just days before Laura arrived in New York. Activity at Jay's post office must have increased significantly after a marine battalion marched into Corozal and camped there until election day. However, voting was peaceful on July 12 after the opposing candidate withdrew his name from the ballot. On October 3, 1908, Jay was granted forty-two days of paid leave and sailed that day from Cristobal aboard the S.S. *Allianca*.[102]

During his first couple of weeks back in Knoxville, Jay and Laura stayed with her parents. By the end of October, the newspaper announced that "Mr. and Mrs. James Agee, of Corozal, Panama," were "visiting with relatives in LaFollette." On November 10, the paper reported that "Mrs. James Agee" was "visiting with relatives of her husband," but Jay's whereabouts were not mentioned, and the couple was no longer said to be "of Corozal, Panama." Three days later, near the end of his paid leave, Jay resigned his post.[103]

While Laura had likely recovered from malaria by that time, Jay "got it after he came back." He had probably been mosquito-bitten before leaving Panama. Depending on the strain, symptoms could start any time from a week to forty days after infection. Laura's sister, Paula, remembered that Jay "had malaria" after returning to the States and faced "difficulty" working because of the illness.[104]

"We were up on the farm quite a lot," Laura remembered. "Beyond La-Follette, up in the mountain there." Jay "had bought a farm . . . and built it up what he could. . . . And his father and mother moved out and lived on it. They were up there. And we were up there with them quite a lot of the time." But by spring, 1909, Jay had an urgent need for steady income, and Laura had a longing to be near her parents again. She was expecting.[105]

Contemplating his ancestors' movements from place to place, James Rufus Agee wrote that "few creatures are as capricious in their wanderings, or so dice-like in their destinies. . . . we meet and mate like apples swung together on a creek." Nine decades had passed since Rufus Tyler's birth and eight since James Harris Agee's. Those men, long dead, had been strangers to each other. Yet inside Laura grew their great-grandchild—the product of the choices and circumstances that led both families to East Tennessee.[106]

2

"In the Time That I Lived There"
Childhood, 1909–1916

Laura and Jay returned to Knoxville by summer 1909. Against his desire for independence, Jay agreed that they would stay with her parents on West Clinch Avenue, at least until after the child was born. The previous fall, Jay had resigned his position in Panama—a job he had thought would put him further ahead. Yet here he was, a year later, working again behind the post office counter in Knoxville.[1]

As Laura entered her final month of pregnancy, Knoxville began that November with a collective sigh after a wild night of Halloween pranks—like fire alarms being pulled in jest, milk bottles stolen from West Knoxville porches, road signs bent, and a gate stolen along with part of the rock wall to which it was anchored. The UT Volunteers also nursed wounds after their defeat by Georgia Tech 23–0, in a football game the *Sentinel* called "a contest of laughter and grief." The Vols were subsequently crushed by Vanderbilt, 51–0, and by Alabama, 10–0. Despite a Thanksgiving Day victory over Lexington's Transylvania University, Vols coach George Levene resigned at the end of an "unusually poor" season. Meanwhile, drought suspended boating operations on the Tennessee River, which had fallen to its lowest level in a decade.[2]

But Knoxville progressed in other areas that month, and in ways that would directly touch the Agees. At a local chapter meeting of the Southern Association of College Women, Emma Tyler reported the funds collected for purchasing school supplies and clothing for poor children. Her legacy of benevolence and social work would contribute to her grandson's early awareness of poverty. During his childhood, the boy would come to know the motion picture theaters of Gay Street, especially one that had recently

Knoxville postmen and clerks pose outside the Custom House in this detail from an undated photograph. The mustached man looking away on the top row, right, could be Jay Agee around the time his son, Rufus, was born. 200-071-006, Knox County Two Centuries Photograph Collection, McClung Historical Collection, Knox County Library.

reopened as the Majestic. He would attend the high school whose cornerstone was laid on November 10 in a Masonic ceremony attended by thousands of students from the city's schools. He would remember Chilhowee Park's "big fair buildings," whose designs were being planned on November 16 by officials of the forthcoming Appalachian Exposition—the *Sentinel* carried renderings of the buildings and grounds on the day he was born. And he would enjoy walking home with his father from the Majestic Theatre over the Asylum Avenue Viaduct, which was built beginning November 23.[3]

On November 27, 1909, Laura gave birth to him there at the Tyler home on West Clinch. It was a Saturday, Laura later wrote to her son, "the day you came into the world, at 7:15 in the morning, after a determined little journey of about seven hours—not so long, after all—from Infinity to here!!" He was "christened James Rufus," said Laura, "after his father and my paternal grandfather Tyler."[4]

This wicker bassinet, passed down through the Agee family, reportedly held James Rufus Agee when he was a baby. MS.2730, box 6, folder 3, James Agee and Agee Trust Collection, Special Collections, University of Tennessee Library, Knoxville. Reprinted courtesy of the James Agee Trust.

William Delpuech, the family doctor who delivered Rufus, lived directly across the street from the Tylers at 1114 West Clinch. He had graduated from Princeton University in 1879 with Woodrow Wilson and later helped found Knoxville General Hospital. Although Delpuech had a clinic in North Knoxville, he made house calls for births, as was common. Albert, his son, had suffered successive childhood bouts of pneumonia and meningitis that impaired his speech and mobility. Rufus came to know the man who "walked like a duck" as "Uncle Albert."[5]

Joel and Emma Tyler's house was full. Jay, Laura, Rufus, and Laura's sister, Paula, all lived there. Hugh Tyler might have been there part of the time, although his absence from the city directory probably coincided with the couple of years that he apprenticed in New York art and tapestry schools before studying in Paris and Rome in 1912. But even if Hugh was not there in early 1910, the Tyler house quickly seemed smaller with the addition of a crying newborn.[6]

The Reverend Walter Whitaker baptized the boy at St. John's Episcopal Church on March 20, Palm Sunday. Edward Slocum, Charles W. Turner, Frank

Nelson, and Jessie Tyler were recorded as witnesses. Among the congregants likely in attendance that day was an adolescent named Joseph Wood Krutch who, like Agee, would leave Knoxville as a teenager and become a respected critic and multi-genre writer—including magazine work for the *Nation*.[7]

A month later, the young family had moved to Jacksboro, where Jay still owned the hundred acres in Powell Valley at the base of Cumberland Mountain. He had purchased the land only a month before the unexpected job opportunity in Panama. His parents had lived on it until he could return to farm it himself. On the last day of April 1910, a census taker walked up to the Agee homestead to record the names, ages, and occupations of its residents. Jay, listed as James, was thirty-two and working on the "home farm." Laura was twenty-four and caring for their five-month-old son. Even though the land was Jay's, his father, Henry, was listed as the owner and employer of a "general farm."[8]

Curiously, though, when Knoxville's city directory was issued that July, Jay was again boarding with his in-laws on Clinch Avenue. No occupation was listed, and it is unclear how much time he spent in Knoxville and how much he spent in Campbell County. "Back and forth and back and forth" was how Laura characterized the moves between Knoxville and the Agee farm. Perhaps Jay farmed while waiting to hear back from potential employers in the city. Or perhaps he never fully retreated back to Jacksboro but was just on an extended visit, giving his parents time with their new grandson before returning to city life.[9]

CORBIN AND CIRCLE PARK

Sometime in early 1911, Jay heard that the Louisville & Nashville Railroad was growing fast in Kentucky and needing workers. Laura remembered Jay being hired "as an office man up with the L&N Railroad at Corbin, Kentucky. We went up there to live." The job in Corbin explains Jay's absence from Knoxville's city directory that year. A local paper reported in April that "Mrs. James Agee and infant son left for their home in Corbin."[10]

Corbin, located roughly seventy miles north of Knoxville, was the terminal for L&N's Cumberland Valley Division and the railroad's extension toward coal reserves to the east. The town was once notorious for its violence, bustling with railroaders and saloons. Laura recalled moving there when "Rufus was about a year and something old. We were there for about a year. And that was quite an experience. [Rufus] was very sick up there, cutting his teeth. Horribly sick." Toddlers commonly have slight fevers around the time a tooth appears. But if a child happens to pick up a germ at the same time that causes other symptoms like high fever, runny nose, diarrhea, or vomiting, a mother might misinterpret those as normal signs of teething, as Laura apparently did. But Rufus may also have suffered gastro-esophageal reflux disease, a condition suggested by statements he wrote much later about the frequent vomiting he experienced as a young child: "Semi starvation, first 2 years. Almost invariable regurgitation of whatever I ate, up to 7 or 8."[11]

Around June 1911, Laura visited a photography studio, possibly one in Corbin, and had a photo-postcard made of her holding Rufus. He stood on her lap in a one-piece outfit rolled up to his knees, and stared blankly at the camera while his mother looked lovingly at him. She sent the postcard to her mother, with a message on the back: "For dear 'Grabbie' with my love. I was feeling like a fight, but this is 'me.' Your grandson, Rufus, 19 mos." The card was likely sent from Corbin in time for Emma Tyler's birthday on June 29.[12]

Later in life, Rufus never mentioned Corbin in any of his writings or notes. He was too young when his father worked there to form any memories of the place. But he left a brief note that reveals a possible later trip to the area: "The night train, & tunnel. Only a few miles to Kentucky." He could have been thinking of a tunnel near Caryville, south of Jacksboro, or the series of tunnels approaching Jellico, the last Tennessee town en route to the Bluegrass State.[13]

All we know of Jay's time there is that after a short and unpromising stint with L&N, a "health problem" hastened the Agees' return to Knoxville. Details are elusive, as there are no employee records, city directories, or tax records to show where or how long they lived there. The 1908 L&N Station, still standing along Depot Street, was only a few years old when Jay came to town. Today, it is about all one can point to that marks his brief time in Corbin.[14]

Surely Jay felt pressure, as a husband and father and the eldest Agee son, to make a name for himself outside of a post office. His two younger brothers were stepping up in the world, though their schooling was possible largely because of his financial help. In 1911, after attending embalming school, Frank and his business partner opened Agee & Carden, a furniture store and mortuary in LaFollette, where Frank was also beginning his second term on the city council. And that spring John graduated from the University of Tennessee with a mining engineering degree and an impressive résumé of college service and associations. For Jay the L&N job was a major disappointment.[15]

Joel Tyler realized that the best way to solve his son-in-law's frustrations, while also keeping Laura and Rufus close, was to offer him a bookkeeping

As a toddler, Rufus lived in a small house that his parents rented on Seventh
Street, near Circle Park. The left foreground of this postcard image shows the rear,
southwest corner of the light-colored house, and the university on the hill beyond it.
Courtesy of Ronald Faulkner.

job at the machine company, which in 1904 had been renamed Ty-Sa-Man
after its three co-owners—Joel Tyler, Arthur Savage, and E. T. Manning.
"And then, in the course of that year, year and a half . . . my father wrote
and asked [Jay] if he'd come down and come into the office at Ty-Sa-Man
Company, which is what we did," said Laura. Jay gratefully accepted the job.
The large factory, which produced "flour and marble mill machinery," was
located at White Avenue's east end, just a couple of blocks from the Tyler
home. When he was older, Rufus visited the office where his father and
grandfather worked. Valuables were kept in a large safe, decorated with a
painted scene of "a white house on a green yard and a blue sky, and a wreath
of roses around it, every rose as big as the house." Joel had a paperweight
made of "glass on his desk to hold down papers, it had yellow flowers under
the glass." Nearby, his grandfather "had his picture of Oliver," the family's
"soft gray cat."[16]

Instead of moving in with her parents again, Laura recalled, "We moved down and had this little house off South Seventh Street. That's where Emma was born." Their modest, one-story rental home, number 955, was on the corner of South Seventh and Yale Avenue. From their east-facing front porch, Laura could easily point out Jefferson Hall, the Y.M.C.A. Building, Science Hall, Barbara Blount Hall, Estabrook Hall, South College, and the other edifices atop UT's Hill that she had seen as a student several years prior. When Laura needed groceries, W. T. Webb's store was only few doors down the other side of their street toward Cumberland. Jay could catch the Yale Avenue streetcar for a short ride to and from work. The house did not come with much of a yard where Rufus could play, but Laura took him to a grassy area up the street, one block west of their home. Rufus retained vague memories of "high rocks" at a "little park" called "Park Circle," though it was and still is called Circle Park. Now known for its Torchbearer statue and as a favorite tailgating spot before UT football games, the remodeled park is all that remains in that area from Agee's time, as the beautiful Victorian homes and circular drive around its perimeter and all of those university structures—except South College from 1872—are long gone. A decade or so after the Agees lived on Seventh Street, houses to the east were cleared and replaced by the Shields-Watkins Athletic Field. The spot near Circle Park where the Agees lived is a parking lot on the northwest corner of Phillip Fulmer Way and Peyton Manning Pass, directly across the street from Neyland Stadium's front gates.[17]

EMMA

Around the time Jay was hired at Ty-Sa-Man, Laura knew that Rufus would soon have a sibling. By his second birthday, she was about two months pregnant. Rufus later fictionalized the memory of his initial excitement when his mother promised him that a "surprise" was on its way: "Next day his mother told him that soon he was going to have a very wonderful surprise. . . . When he asked what he was going to be given she said that she did not mean it was a present, specially for him, or for him to have, but something for everybody, and especially for them." He also heard talk of things that he did not understand, like "bellybands."[18]

The surprise came on June 22, 1912, a Saturday, to the small house on Seventh Street, as Dr. Delpuech delivered the Agees' second child. Laura named the baby girl Emma Farrand, after her mother; as Rufus later imagined it, Laura settled on the name after rejecting as possibilities Moss, Lamar, and

Margraves—names associated with Jay's mother. She placed Emma in the same wicker bassinet Rufus had slept in as an infant. Years later she passed it along to her brother-in-law John, who used it for his children. The bassinet was last reported to be in the possession of Dr. Oliver Agee.[19]

The family rehired the "colored" nurse they had used when Rufus was born. Victoria Logan, a woman in her late forties, was "a well known nurse" and "much in demand" among the families of what was then West Knoxville. One local family had nine children, all delivered by Dr. Delpuech "at home," and one of the nine later remembered Victoria's influence. "She nursed seven of us—all excepting my two youngest brothers," said Arthur Seymour Sr. "When they were young and terrible brats, mother would attribute their behavior to the fact that Victoria had not nursed them and gotten them off to a better start in life." Rufus recalled Victoria's "gold spectacles" and the "Sweetcharryut" song she sang while giving him a bath when he was very young. "I do remember Victoria, a wonderful colored nurse," said Paula Tyler. "Everybody knew her, and she was quite well known, and the doctors all knew her. She was wonderful, and very, very kind." Paula described Victoria as "quite old" but "very handsome . . . and always wore a nice white apron, and nice uniform." Laura's good friend Hazel Lee Goff—who became the first graduate of Fort Sanders Hospital's nursing school before teaching there for four decades—also tended Emma on occasion, as Rufus remembered her "bathing the baby" with the "pale brown thin soap."[20]

In 1912 Laura Agee and her two children, Rufus and Emma, visited the Knaffl & Brakebill studio at 522½ South Gay Street to have this portrait made. Courtesy of St. Andrew's–Sewanee.

Dr. Whitaker baptized Emma on November 17, 1912, at St. John's Church. Mrs. Delpuech was chosen as Emma's godmother. Around this time, Laura and Jessie were the only members of the family listed as communicants of the church. They had their own seat assignment: left side along the main aisle, and fourth pew from the back.[21]

Just after Emma's baptism, her parents were preparing for another big change. Considering that Jay and Laura were now caring for both a toddler and an infant, it is not surprising that they desired a house with more space inside and out.

HIGHLAND AVENUE

On November 27, 1912, Rufus's third birthday, his parents signed the papers to purchase an eight-room house for $3,300. Located several blocks north of their Seventh Street rental home, the house at 1505 Highland Avenue sat on a fifty- by one-hundred-foot lot in the Ramsey addition of the West End neighborhood. This section of town was once outside the city limits and known as West Knoxville, with its own mayor and aldermen. The fire department's engine company number nine was located one block to the west, on the 1600 block, and Rufus's later memory of a "fire engine with white horses" could have been from one of the many times he saw and heard the engine clanging down the street.[22]

A block west beyond the fire station lay the remains of the old Federal fort that had been built into the ridge, which was stripped of trees during the Civil War. The ridge's south slope faced East Tennessee University (renamed the University of Tennessee in 1879) and the Tennessee River beyond it. The Battle of Fort Sanders was fought on November 29, 1863; Rufus was born two days shy of its forty-sixth anniversary. He later wrote: "I have had several clear mental images of that war, from almost as early as I can remember." He had just turned four years old in 1913 before the battle's fiftieth anniversary. And the day after his fifth birthday, the Daughters of the Confederacy dedicated a stone monument along Ninth (now Seventeenth) Street, north of Clinch. By the time Rufus was old enough to remember it, "the devastated Fort" was nothing more than a "waste of briers and of embanked clay." Veterans had reunited on the ridge for decades following the war, but despite a brief local movement to preserve the earthwork remnants as a memorial park, the site was eventually obliterated.[23]

Highland paralleled the top of the ridge and literally divided the larger upper-class lots and grand mansions of Laurel and Clinch avenues, down the south side of the ridge toward the university, from the humbler working-class dwellings of Forest and the misnamed Grand Avenue down the north side of the ridge toward the railroad tracks. Including the Agees', there were sixteen homes on the 1500 block, with the Epworth Methodist Episcopal Church at the western end of it. Rufus later poetically described this neighborhood in "Knoxville: Summer of 1915," one of his most famous works: "It was a little bit mixed sort of block, fairly solidly lower middle class, with one or two juts apiece on either side of that. The houses corresponded. Middle-sized gracefully fretted wood houses built in the late nineties and early nineteen hundreds, with small front and side and more spacious back yards, and trees in the yards, and porches. There were soft-wooded trees, poplars, tulip trees, cottonwoods. There were fences around one or two of the houses, but mainly the yards ran into each other with only now and then a low hedge that wasn't doing very well." As a boy, Rufus noticed the variety of fences in the neighborhood and the differences between "stick" and "iron & wood pickets." On the south side of the street, front yards were built up behind stone retaining walls.[24]

Occupations represented on Highland were not all as middle-of-the-road as the houses. When the family moved there, Jay Agee was thirty-four and working as a bookkeeper at his father-in-law's factory. His son remembered that other men on the block held similar "clerical" positions: "The men were mostly small businessmen, one or two very modestly executives, one or two worked with their hands, most of them clerical, and most of them between thirty and forty-five." However, the 1915 city directory shows that there were more executives than accountants living on the block. The Agees' neighbors included the owner of a stove company, a real estate broker, a superintendent at the cotton mill, a department store president, a clothing merchant, the manager of a dry goods store, and the owner of a sand company.[25]

Of his neighbors, Rufus was naturally most familiar with those immediately surrounding his house, as the playmates that he later named in his writings were from these families. His parents had "few good friends" on the block, just good acquaintances with whom they "nodded and spoke, and even might talk short times, trivially . . . and ordinarily next-door neighbors talked quite a bit when they happened to run into each other, and never paid calls."[26]

The King family lived next door on the corner, at 1501. Oliver King owned the Oliver King Sand & Lime Company and had named one of the firm's steamships after his eldest daughter, Annabel King, shortly after her birth. But the steamer sank in the Tennessee River on New Year's Eve in 1911 after hitting an old bridge pier. When the Agees moved to Highland, Annabel was twenty years old and in a relationship with Jay's youngest brother, John Agee—who had already graduated from UT but now had more than one reason to visit Highland Avenue. John had possibly met Annabel a couple of years earlier, when he roomed as a student at 1413, two houses down from the Kings. They certainly knew each other by the time John's sister Mossie— "Miss Agee of LaFollette"—came to Knoxville in June 1912 to be hosted and entertained by Annabel. Perhaps John was the one who told his brother of the house for sale next door to the Kings. As an adult, Rufus did not mention this uncle at all in his writings except for briefly noting a vague memory of one of John's visits: "John, Annabel & porch swing? Eavesdropping?" One can imagine the couple sitting close on the Kings' porch one evening, "rocking gently and talking gently and watching the street" while Rufus, the cute but sometimes annoying little nephew, crouched around the corner to spy

Rufus with Margaret King, left, and Josephine Stone in the King family's back yard, 1501 Highland Avenue. SPC 2017.005.002, McClung Historical Collection, Knox County Library.

The Agee house, 1505 Highland Avenue, as it appeared around 1962. Photograph by Robert Clay, 45033, box 45, folder 28, Robert Clay Papers, Library of Virginia.

on the embracing lovers or, from his upstairs bedroom window, strained to catch bits of their conversation. John and Annabel would marry a few years later, after the Kings moved to the Island Home neighborhood. Gladys King, one of Annabel's younger sisters, shared Rufus's birthday but was nine years his senior. Rufus had few friends his own age on the block, but did spend time with the Kings' youngest child, Margaret, who was six years older than him. The King house at 1501 appears to have been replaced in the 1920s.[27]

The Biddles, a young couple without children, lived at 1502, directly across from the Kings. Culan Biddle co-owned Biddle Brothers, a stove and range shop on Market Square. His wife, an amateur musician, would later be asked by Annabel King to provide music for her wedding. The house is still there and, though split into apartments, is one of the handsomest on the block. Standing at his front door, watching his grandparents and aunt and uncle walk home toward Clinch Avenue, Rufus would have lost sight of them as they passed "the corner of the Biddles' house."[28]

The Agee residence at 1505 Highland Avenue had been built in 1884. Like many in the neighborhood, it was of a gable-front-and-wing design. It had a front gable portion on the left—with a bay window downstairs and a sunburst fan decoration upstairs just below the attic vent—and a side-wing portion to the right, behind a front porch with decorative post brackets and gingerbread details between the posts. It was a typical folk Victorian, lacking the heavy ornamentation of the more "pretentious" homes at the top of the hill along Laurel.[29]

Passing through the front door beneath a transom window, one entered a central hallway. The first door on the left opened to the living room, or sitting room, which the Agees furnished with a sofa and Jay's favored "Morris chair," with "an ash tray on its weighted strap on the arm." Behind the living room, joined by a doorway, was the dining room, and behind that the kitchen and pantry. To the right, inside the front entrance, a door led to a parlor. Behind it, in the rear of the house, were a bedroom and small bathroom. Along the right side of the central hallway, a flight of stairs ran up to three bedrooms. A set of steep, narrow "back stairs" connected the second-story hall to the kitchen so that a servant, or children, could come and go without being seen by guests. The downstairs bedroom, in the rear of the house, had two doors, one that led to the kitchen, and the other that led to the parlor. The kitchen floor was covered with black and white checkered linoleum. A "rose-patterned carpet" may have covered the floor of his parents' bedroom. Passing long stretches of time as a boy with nowhere to go, Rufus often stared out through the windows and "screen doors," observing the "light & foliage through them, rain on screens, moiré patterns of screens," and the "bubbles & wavers in windowglass."[30]

Jay smoked, impressing Rufus by blowing "smoke rings," and often "rolled his own cigarets." His favorite tobacco brands were "Erin Go Bragh" and "Montenegro." Perhaps the metal container was empty when Rufus tried "blowing in [a] tobacco can" once and then "a second time." Jay sometimes brought home "little silk flags," or cigarette silks—squares of cloth printed with brightly colored pictures of flags, women, and other scenes: "He has little flags in the cigarette packs for us." They came rolled up inside the boxes of some brands of cigarettes and cigars; other brands of cigarette packs contained coupons that one saved up and redeemed for the silks by mail. Rufus remembered his father's "whiskers" and the way his face looked "with & without mustache." He recalled his father "fooling with garden hose" and his exclamations of frustration: "damn . . . & assorted grunts," all of which Rufus later "imitated."[31]

Having his father around the house made days special for Rufus, contrasting with the ordinary days of the workweek: "The days he was away all day were a good deal like each other but the days he was home were different." His family's daily routines included breakfast in the mornings, with Emma in the "high chair." Rufus followed Laura "around kitchen" as she did "housework & cooking." As they stood next to their mother, Emma and Rufus were roughly "knee and hip height" to her.[32]

When clothes needed to be made or mended, Laura operated the "sewing-machine, changing bobbins . . . working treadle." When shoe soles wore out, repairs began with "softening shoeleather for half-soling." New soles were fitted using shoe molds, or "lasts." Jay likely learned this process from his father, who made boots when Jay was very young. Other chores included canning mushrooms and "cutting & barreling" cabbage for sauerkraut, which the family stored in the basement. Fresh vegetables likely came from Joel Tyler's front-yard green house.[33]

Jay and Laura sang often around the house, as their son remembered "Mother singing" songs like "Aunt Rhoda." Laura's "voice was soft and shining gray like her dear gray eyes," he wrote. His father "always loved to sing. There were ever so many of the old songs that he knew, which he liked best, and . . . he also enjoyed the sound of his own voice." Rufus heard his parents singing "Swing Low, Sweet Chariot," which nurse Victoria had also sung to him when he was younger. "Stand Up, Stand Up for Jesus" was likely found in the hymnal at St. John's Episcopal, where Rufus "heard hymn-singing," and perhaps where he saw an "old woman in [a] brocaded linen bodice." In addition to the various songs and verses Rufus learned, Paula Tyler recalled a "nice little prayer" that he recited at bedtime, an English nursery rhyme of "rural" character that had been used in variation since at least the seventeenth century: "Four posts around my bed, / Four saints around my head. / Matthew, Mark, Luke and John, / Bless this bed that I sleep on."[34]

SEASONS AND STREETCARS

While the "routines of a day" typified much of the family's life on Highland Avenue, the seasons and certain "special days" distinguished themselves in Rufus's memory. Occasionally, one or both of his parents went "out to a party or a wedding." One such party was when Emma Tyler hosted a "thimble tea" for Laura in early 1913. Rufus vaguely remembered his parents leaving for another party one evening and his mother wearing "her rose-colored dress." And the latter half of 1914 saw two Agee family weddings. That July,

Jay's sister Mossie married Charles Hodges in Campbell County. And on New Year's Eve, his brother John married Annabel King at her parents' new residence near Island Home. Even though newspapers stated that the couple had no attendants during the ceremony, John chose Jay as his best man.[35]

"Then there were holidays," Rufus later wrote:

> Christmas, Easter, Fourth of July, Halloween, Thanksgiving, his birthday, Christmas again.
> And vacations.
> And different times of year, too, and different kinds of weather.
> Summer, Winter, Spring, Fall.[36]

In autumn the leaves of the cottonwoods and tulip poplars turned a golden yellow before blanketing the neighborhood lawns below. Rufus associated this time of year with "trips to Grandparents" in Campbell County—with "cider, ripe apples, hogs, [and] Sunday afternoons" at their farm—and with celebrating "Halloween, Thanksgiving, [and] his birthday." Thanksgiving coincided with his birthday only once while the family lived on Highland—on November 27, 1913, when Rufus turned four years old. That day, the family ate dinner together at the Tylers', and Rufus was given a little "celluloid swan" that floated in a dish of water and looked so tasty that his parents had to keep it out of his mouth.[37]

Christmas came less than a month later. Rufus and his family ate an early supper in the kitchen one Christmas Eve. Outside they heard a "train shuffling in snow, a snowy sound." On Christmas Day in 1915, dropping temperatures changed "a heavy downfall of rain" into snow. Rufus watched what the evening newspaper called "some of the largest flakes ever seen fall in this city." Seeing "snow outside [the] window," and "looking at fried egg on plate," Rufus felt "the just sense of, I will always remember this." He received a "Happy Hooligans doll" one Christmas, and his father lit a "fire in early morning."[38]

Rufus experienced winter in the house: "In Winter it got dark early. Hot dry air came up through the registers. If you put your finger into the squares of the registers you could even get burnt. Often Daddy built a fire in the fireplace besides. Outdoors sometimes it snowed. Then Mama would bundle him up." He remembered that "being bundled up" for winter weather included putting "copper caps on [his] shoes." Outside, the family built a snowman with "soft coal features." And Rufus and Emma sat in a box while being "pulled through [the] snow."[39]

Spring brought rain to Knoxville. For Rufus, that meant "poplar worms on damp spring pavement," "the full gutters" as water ran down the street, and "making dams" to divert the flow. When those "early spring" rains rutted the pike roads out toward LaFollette, making trips there by car impractical, the family searched "for wild flowers" closer to home.[40]

Another season passed, giving way to sweltering summer days in Knoxville, days hot enough to soften the asphalt beneath Rufus's feet: "In Summer, there were leaves all over and it was very hot. Some of the horses wore sponges and some wore hats just like people but with holes for their ears. On the hottest days you could make tracks in the street even if you were barefooted if you stomped hard enough, and you could rub pieces of the street together with your thumbs and pick it up and chew on it. It tasted tarry. When it began to get dark there were always locusts and they kept up as long as you stayed awake. It was hot all night."[41]

Of course, Rufus also experienced "summer evenings" outdoors, running free with his friends, playing "hide and seek" and watching the "bugs at the corners" circling around the carbon arc street lamps. He looked forward to "getting old carbons when the sticks are changed." It was also the time of day for singing with the family while "lying out all together on a quilt in the back yard."[42]

Martin Southern, an older boy on the street, shared memories of "nostalgic summer evenings" on Highland Avenue. "As for the street, I too felt the taste of it, the old-model automobiles (which we used to know as 'machines'), the electrics, and Stanley steamers, the numerous wagons, fewer buggies," Southern wrote. "I remember the hawkers of produce, especially in watermelon time. And the buttermilk and butter that we used to get at the curb. The street cars clanged by at half-hour intervals, although I rode them seldom."[43]

Two new viaducts, at Asylum and Clinch avenues, spanned the rail yards of Second Creek valley and connected West Knoxville to the city center. Streetcar tracks from Clinch turned north up the ridge at Third (now Eleventh) Street, ran west down Highland past the Agees' house and ended at Thirteenth (now Twenty-First) Street. The Agees could easily access downtown and the outlying areas of Knoxville via the Highland Avenue Line, which cousin Oliver Agee remembered was called Old Number Seven. "I can still feel that streetcar sway as I ride it," he said. The trolley was "an open car," Paula Tyler recalled, "with seats running straight across, and kind of a platform for the conductor to walk on and collect your fare." Martin Southern's "dream of maturity was to ride standing up on the narrow right-side platform, while the conductor stepped around me."[44]

With the light railway running up his street, just a few steps beyond the sidewalk, Rufus could not resist a little mischief: putting "toadfrogs and pennies . . . on the tracks" and waiting until "the streetcar ran over them." His notes even suggest a time he got separated from his parents while transferring between streetcars: "Sunday summer streetcars, I get lost, Saturday before Easter, transfers."[45]

The trolley passing Rufus's house every thirty minutes or so left him with vivid mental pictures and sounds that he later turned into poetry: "A street car raising its iron moan, stopping, belting and starting . . . and swimming its gold windows and straw seats on past and past and past, the bleak spark crackling and cursing above it like a small malignant spirit set to dog its tracks."[46]

After Knoxville discontinued its streetcar service in 1947, some sections of tracks were removed; many others were simply covered in layers of asphalt. Miles of worn, notched iron rails, still spiked onto their creosote-soaked crossties, lie buried beneath city streets to this day. Road crews digging up utility lines, or grinding away asphalt for repaving, sometimes unearth these century-old relics of the city's first electrified transit system.

CHILHOWEE PARK

"On Sunday afternoons we used to ride the open cars to Chilhowee Park . . . There were the Appalachian Expositions, fireworks, balloon ascensions, miniature trains," wrote Southern. His summertime experiences were remarkably similar to those of Rufus, who rode the same streetcar out to the park: "It was a long way out to Chilhowee Park but even the ride out there was fun because the streetcar was all open."[47]

The park was a popular recreation spot located a few miles east of downtown. In the weeks before its summer season opening, newspapers carried half-page advertisements with large block letters touting the daily attractions and entertainment. Typically, the season began the third Monday in May; but in 1913 it came early, May 4, as the National Conservation Exhibition needed the space that October. There had been two Appalachian Expositions before that, in 1910 and 1911. In a sense, these special events were precursors to the annual East Tennessee Division Fair that was inaugurated in 1916 and would continue a century later as the Tennessee Valley Fair. But Chilhowee Park was open every summer, not just during these expos. Dancing, baseball, concerts, boxing, vaudeville, swimming, and boating were among the daily summer offerings that attracted visitors to the park. For Knoxvillians who craved spectacle, Chilhowee was the place to be on Independence Day. Like most boys, Rufus was fascinated by the Fourth of July's festive explosions, rockets that popped and sparkled in the sky, whether shot off by adults or lit with his own fingers: "Firecrackers. Torpedoes. Niggerchasers [bottle rockets without the wooden sticks]. Roman candles. Sparklers. Balloons. Things blow up in his face. Strings of firecrackers under a tin pan."[48]

He had a vague memory about his parents arranging before one of the family trips to have someone babysit Emma: "We will go to Chilhowee Park & Paula will stay with the baby?" and "Argument re[garding] Emma? (Aged 1 year?)." Rufus would have been about three-and-a-half years old when Emma turned one in the summer of 1913. At that year's National Conservation Exposition—a two-month event attended by over a million people—his Uncle Hugh won the Cook medal for best collection of paintings in an art competition that had been organized by the Nicholson Art League. The family likely saw this exhibit at the Fine Arts building, and this could have been a first occasion at the park for Rufus. But his memories of Chilhowee were likely created during several visits between the ages of three and five.[49]

Among those memories was riding the Chilhowee Park and Burlington Line north on Gay Street, crossing the viaduct over the Southern Railroad tracks, and then turning east onto Park Avenue. Along Magnolia, the car passed the lot where Laura lived with her family the first year they came to Knoxville from Michigan, when she was not much older than Rufus. But she could not point to the house, only where it sat, because it had burned long ago. At the time, Magnolia Avenue ended at Lake Avenue (now Beaman Street), the southwestern edge of the park, but the streetcar tracks continued east to let passengers off at the main gate.[50]

As passengers got closer to the fairgrounds, the sights, sounds, and smells grew stronger and more tempting. Inside, the various attractions and exposition buildings were linked by walkways surrounding Lake Ottosee ("ought-to-see"), which stretched the length of the park and was divided into a "lower" section to the north and an "upper" section to the south. Guests entering the gate at the southern end of the upper lake were met with enticing views of park attractions, including what Rufus called the "rolly coaster," whose white wooden loops arched toward the treetops and could be seen from Magnolia Avenue. The tracks of the "narrow gauge" or "dwarf train" paralleled many of the walkways circling the lake before crossing the water over a wooden bridge. Even though riders were almost certain to get soot in their faces from the coal smoke, the miniature train was judged to be "the stellar attraction for the children." The merry-go-round sat at the edge of an upper

With the marble bandstand behind it, the miniature railroad steams past guests at Chilhowee Park during the National Conservation Exposition, 1913. GP-0645, Thompson Photograph Collection, McClung Historical Collection, Knox County Library.

lake peninsula, casting its rotating reflection in the water below, and there young Rufus may have pleaded with his parents to let him ride a carousel horse by himself. Nearby concession stands prepared popcorn and other snacks, while more substantial food was served at a small restaurant near the park entrance. Music "ranging from classical to popular" could be heard throughout the day at the marble bandstand, and at the dance pavilion.[51]

Guests promenaded in their best clothes down the main driveway, and carefree couples in canoes rowed across the upper lake. A boardwalk spanned the middle of the lower lake, and boys swam in the north end while women "sat on the banks and watched the fancy swimming and diving stunts." Fair promoters promised thrilling daily attractions like "Balloon Ascension and Double and Triple Parachute Drop Every Afternoon at 5." Rufus witnessed the "parachute jump from balloon" in the sky above the park.[52]

As daylight faded, all of the exposition buildings were illuminated, their edges strung with thousands of light bulbs. The Liberal Arts Building, easily the grandest expo structure on the grounds, created spectacular reflections in the nighttime lake. And on certain nights, crowds lined the banks of the lower lake to watch the fireworks display.[53]

Among the live entertainment offered, Rufus watched a circus at Chilhowee that was possibly related to an act from the 1910 exposition, "Big Otto's Trained Wild Animals." Another likely holdover from the same expo was Zach Mulhall's Wild West Show. For twenty-five cents' admission (fifteen cents for children), audiences were treated to a parade of rough riders and Indian braves, stagecoaches, and cowboy shoot-outs. The 1913 exposition hosted a similar show, performed in an area of the park called Joy Street. Laura likely insisted that the performance was too violent for her young son, as Rufus later remembered "leaving as Wild West Show starts (fire coming out of pistols)."[54]

Another time, the family left during "an outdoor movie." Chilhowee Park featured an open-air theater, which from the early 1900s was used for live performances during the hot summer months when downtown's Staub's Theatre temporarily closed its doors. In addition to plays and vaudeville acts, in 1906 Chilhowee Park Theatre began screening motion pictures, among the first ever shown in the city. Movies became a regular part of the park's summer activities, with newspapers advertising "FREE MOVING PICTURES Each Evening at 8:00 PM." Rufus likely saw his first motion picture there at the park, as his later note, "first movie, outdoors," seems to indicate.[55]

The lower lake is now a parking lot. At least two-thirds of the upper lake is still there. The only structure that survives intact from those early expositions is the refurbished 1910 marble bandstand. After the Liberal Arts Building burned in the late thirties, some of its wood and windows were saved, along with timbers from one of the incarnations of the wooden coaster, and rebuilt as the rabbit and poultry barn. Nowadays, during the Tennessee Valley Fair, there is no swimming or boating in the lake. But white swans still glide across its surface, a merry-go-round still turns, carnival barkers still invite guests to toss a ball and win prizes, and concession stands still lure the crowds with scents of cotton candy and popcorn.[56]

ooooooooooooooo

The five-mile trip out to Chilhowee was probably the farthest the Agees traveled by streetcar. Mostly, the light railway meant short rides to downtown shopping or, for Laura and the children, church on Sundays. Jay and Rufus might have taken the trolley partway during an "early Saturday" angling trip. "He takes me fishing," Rufus later wrote, without specifying a location; perhaps they carried rods and reels down to the bank of the Tennessee River or to Chilhowee's Lake Ottosee. While he did not indicate how the fish were biting that day, Rufus retained a hazy memory of hooking something else: "I catch a worm in my lip?" Apparently it did not ruin the trip, as he noted the incident was "not catastrophic."[57]

Whatever the mode of travel, the Agees largely remained within a thirty-five-mile radius from their Highland Avenue home. Before the family had a car, and perhaps when the roads were rough during rainy season, Jay and Laura took the children with them to visit relatives in Campbell County, making the "trip by train to LaFollette." But while his father was still living, the most memorable train trips Rufus took were to Elkmont.[58]

ELKMONT

Decades before there was a national park in the Smokies, Elkmont was a tourist destination, advertised as a place "for rest and recreation," especially "during the hot summer days." Back when Joel Tyler was a lumber dealer and purchased 2,200 acres of forest in the Smokies, perhaps he had envisioned a logging town where the railroad hauled out tons of cut timber every day. But another man, Col. Wilson Townsend, realized that dream and founded a logging company and railroad between 1900 and 1901. By the time Rufus was born, Townsend's Little River Railroad was carrying passengers back and forth from Knoxville to Elkmont. Daily service had begun in July 1909: "The Little River Railroad Co., known as the 'Scenic Route,' running through the beautiful canyon of east prong of Little river, will effective Monday, July 5, operate trains daily in connection with Knoxville & Augusta railroad, Knoxville to Elkmont and return, leaving Knoxville at 7:30 a.m., returning at 5:45 p.m. This makes an ideal trip right into heart of [the] Great Smoky Mountains." When demand for trips to Elkmont pushed the Little River Railroad train beyond its capacity, a Sunday-only train, the "Elkmont Special," was brought into service, with direct trips from Knoxville's Southern Station. The excursion from Knoxville to Elkmont—with in-between stops at Maryville, Walland, Sunshine, Townsend, Line Springs, and Wonderland Park—took two and a half hours.[59]

The Agees were there in Elkmont around October 2, 1914, when a train arrived carrying a team of women who planned a weeklong hike up to Siler's Bald and Clingmans Dome, with trail guides leading and pack mules hauling the bulk of supplies. Among the hikers, Laura recognized two of her fellow UT sorority sisters, Lucy Templeton and Laura Thornburgh. Years later, Templeton was known for her popular *News-Sentinel* columns and Thornburgh for her travel book, *The Great Smoky Mountains*.[60]

On a later occasion, the Agees traveled to Elkmont with Rufus's Uncle Ted and Aunt Kate, who were visiting Knoxville from Michigan. Rufus thought they were not really his aunt and uncle, just friends—that Aunt Kate was "a kind of cousin," because "she was Aunt Carrie's daughter and Aunt Carrie was Granma's half-sister." In truth, Emma Tyler and Aunt Carrie—Laura Caroline Farrand Balentine—were full sisters. Carrie's daughter, Katherine, married Theodore Heavenrich, a doctor from Port Huron. During the Elkmont trip, Ted teased Rufus, saying that if he wanted cheese, all he had to do was whistle, and the cheese would "jump off the table into his lap." Rufus was "just about six" at the time, according to Laura, who retold the incident and her reaction to it: "A cousin of ours came down with her husband at just about that time, and we all went up to Elkmont in the mountains for a couple of weeks to the cabin up there. And Ted Heavenrich, my cousin's husband, told Rufus, 'You see that piece of cheese on the table there?' Rufus said yes. He said, 'If you whistle for it, it'll come down to you.' Rufus whistled and whistled and whistled, and of course it didn't come down. And I blew up. I said, 'I don't know what you think you're doing, Ted, but Rufus has never been teased in his life that we can prevent. Never. Nor told false stories. We just don't do it.' And, well, he says, 'He'll have to learn to take things as they come.'"[61]

At the time, Elkmont was "an exclusive summer community," catering to members of the Appalachian and Wonderland clubs and their guests. Perhaps what Laura called "the cabin up there" was owned by a friend of the Agees, or by an associate of her father. Many Knoxville businessmen built cabins near the town as summer homes for their families. Typically, these cabins were simple structures with front porches and a few rooms, covered by metal roofs and board and batten siding; chimneys and fireplaces were often built of river stones. Jake's Creek flowed along the Society Hill and Daisy Town sections of the resort, up past the clubhouse, and joined into the Little River. Footbridges crossed the creek at various points, and a boardwalk led from the train station and clubhouse down to a cluster of cabins that lined the creek bank. Rufus remembered "snakes in [the] quick shallow branch" and "the fast stream," and being carried "across the fraying water" by his father. And "peeing."[62]

Elkmont's logging industry had been disbanded for almost a decade by the time the Great Smoky Mountains National Park was established in 1934. The town's cabins and other buildings became federal property, though many of the original owners were granted long-term leases that would not expire until the 1990s. Elkmont Historic District joined the National Register of Historic Places in 1994, and the National Park Service has since selected nineteen buildings for preservation, including the Appalachian Club (rebuilt in the 1930s following a fire) and a dozen or more cabins—some of which were standing when the Agees visited.[63]

THE CAR

Perhaps the family sensed, on the day Jay drove home from work in a 1915 Ford Model T, that life from then on—from vacations to everyday existence—would be different. Rufus, for one, was overcome with excitement and stared in awe at the shiny new auto: "It had round wide lights like eyes and they were edged with wide bands of yellow brass, and on a broad piece of brass at the top the name was stamped in writing. Ford. Up beyond that, the glass windshield was shining in the sun." Brass headlight rims were discontinued on Model T's in late 1915.[64]

Except for the front windshield, the car had no other windows, so passengers were not insulated from the outside temperature, fog, wind, or insects. Levers on the steering column controlled throttle and engine timing; three pedals on the wood floor controlled braking, reverse, and low gear. The driver's seat was three feet off the ground and directly above the gas tank. "The Model T was high-slung, narrow-wheeled and homely . . . it became the hero of 10[-cent] joke books," Rufus later wrote. Yet Henry Ford was "rather proud than ashamed of unmistakable usefulness and cheapness," and "shrewdly" turned jokes into good publicity: "Ford's own favorite joke was the one about the gravedigger who was asked why he was digging such an enormous hole. 'They're going to bury this fellow with his Ford,' the gravedigger explained. 'He said it had pulled him out of every other hole, it would pull him out of this one.'"[65]

Rufus's first trip in the car may have occurred as he later described, with the family piling in and riding west down Highland from their house, down to the "quirk" or "S" bend in the avenue at Ninth (now Seventeenth) Street.

As they approached the end of that block, a horse and buggy turned onto the street heading toward them, followed by a streetcar. Jay slowed the car and squeezed the horn a few times to alert the horse. This seems authentic, considering the law at the time. According to a 1905 Tennessee statute, when a motorized vehicle approached a horse being driven or ridden, and the horse looked frightened, the auto driver had to bring the vehicle to a stop until the horse passed. If approaching from behind, the auto had to slow and announce itself with a bell or horn; the car had to stop completely if the horse looked frightened, until the horse's owner could control it. As Rufus described the drive, his father made a loop back to the house, turning right at Ninth Street, "downhill towards the knitting mill," called Appalachian Mills, then "east on Forest Avenue," followed by two right turns, "onto Highland ... to their curb."[66]

Jay may have taken Rufus on a nighttime drive down Highland. At that time, the avenue's residential development ended at Eleventh (now Nineteenth) Street, with open land lying to the west—as represented in this excerpt from a story Rufus Agee composed at Harvard: "Highland Avenue projects various and diminishing qualities of paving through the suburbs of West Knoxville. It lies straight across a chaos of clay ravines, brambles, and tin cans. A few bungalows and signboards hang close on either side. The road lies straight across the field, and buries its head in a steep gravelly hill." He later remembered—or imagined—his father speeding west along the street. Accelerating faster and faster, the small houses on either side appearing as a blur, the headlights suddenly revealed the dead end ahead. Jay barely stopped the car before running head-on into the "high weedy bank." The episode is likely a fictional foreshadowing of Jay's ultimate fate, but it suggests that Rufus saw his father as adventurous and daring.[67]

Rufus guessed that Arthur Savage, one of Joel Tyler's two business partners, had taught his father how "to drive the Ford." This is very possible, as it turns out, because the Model T Jay drove home was actually owned by Ty-Sa-Man. It is not known whether all of its employees drove company cars, but the Model T, which cost roughly $500 at the time, was definitely an incentive for Joel's son-in-law.[68]

At the first of the year, beginning in 1915, Tennessee car owners had to pay an annual registration fee to the secretary of state—$7.50 for autos carrying more than four passengers; $5.00 for trucks and four-passenger cars; $2.50 for motorcycles—after which they received a certificate carrying the registration number, the owner's name, whether an individual or a business, the city of residence, and the type of automobile. Registered owners also received two plates—one for each end of the vehicle—displaying the five-digit registration number, the year, and the abbreviation "TENN" written vertically down the right side. Most likely, Jay's car would have been registered to "Ty-Sa-Man Machine Co.," with the factory's White Avenue address on the certificate.[69]

Perhaps reflecting on how the Model T had affected his family, particularly his father, during his childhood, the adult Rufus wrote of the automobile's advent in a 1934 article for *Fortune:* "God made the American restive. The American in turn and in due time got into the automobile and found it good. . . . It was good because continually it satisfied and at the same time greatly sharpened his hunger for movement: which is very probably the profoundest and most compelling of American racial hungers. The . . . automobile became a hypnosis . . . the opium of the American people."[70]

Whether or not the new Model T increased Jay's "hunger for movement," it meant more to him than just a quick jaunt to and from work. The car meant fewer streetcar fares, not having to plan his life around rail schedules. It offered the horse and buggy's mobility, but with fewer headaches and greater speed. By train, he had traveled at such speeds, but sitting in the car low to the ground while steering himself around curves and feeling every bump of the road was far beyond the experiences afforded by horse, tractor, or rail. The Model T would greatly alter his life's course.

THE AGEE FARM

Having a car also meant Jay could visit his parents and siblings in Campbell County more often. Before the car arrived, the Agees traveled to LaFollette by train, probably making the trip only a couple of times a month. By car the trip between Knoxville and Jacksboro could be made in about three hours via Clinton Pike, part of State Route 9 from Kentucky to North Carolina, which passed through the towns and communities of Powell's Station, Clinton, Coal Creek, and Caryville before arriving in Jacksboro. This route was the fastest, which is why in the summer of 1915 the Dixie Highway's organizers were considering it as a possible link in the north-south highway chain. The other route took drivers up Broadway out of Knoxville, through Fountain City, past Halls Crossroads and on to another crossroads at Loyston. Jay likely chose this route on occasion, because past Loyston one way to get across the Clinch River was by a ferry at the town of Agee, where he lived as a boy.[71]

Jay's parents lived about halfway between Jacksboro and LaFollette, north of the main highway. Approaching the house, his father drove up a "lane" beside a "small creek," as Rufus recalled; a "round hill" sat "forward to left of house," and the "spring, down hill to right." Today, the former Agee property lies at the end of Smith Oaks Lane. As the road winds around a barb-wired embankment, one sees a small, 1920s cottage on a low, flat hill, and a weathered garage down across the lane from it. Farther up the private lane is a larger, red-roofed barn, and above that at the end of a gravel drive-way is a more modern home, possibly built on the footprint of the Agees' old farmhouse. All of this is set against a forested hillside below a gently rolling ridge. Paula Tyler visited the Agee farm once and described the area as "really, truly rural." She remembered that the house sat "way up steep on a hill," which is how one might describe the placement of the newer home on the property. Rufus and his family made "trips to the country" during the spring and summer months, and picked "wild flowers, May apple, trillium," likely in fields near his grandparents' home. He remembered eating "Sunday dinner there" with his uncle Frank and aunt Mossie, with Grandma Agee "working" and Grandpa Agee "loafing" and playing "his violin." He recalled an "autumn trip," and associated the transition from summer to fall, and the leaves changing colors, with the "cider mill, apples, orchard, [and] pigs" that he saw on the farm in Campbell County. The orchard might have been on the hillside beyond his grandparents' home, as one of Rufus's later written fragments seems to indicate: "Late in the Sunday afternoon they strolled out behind the house and leaned on the fence and looked at the apple orchard. They leaned on the fence talking in deep rusty voices while they looked along an aisle of trees, and he stood with his toes on the lower rail of the fence and his chin on the upper rail. The fence was splintered silver. He ran his tongue along it; its taste was sour. . . . The orchard was one glow of golden light. The sun was down but from every yellow surface of fruit and leaf and leaf and turf and from the leafy ground and the red gold of the ground itself the light stood up in quietest splendor of gold, and in this gold, the crippled trunks smoldered their intense black like charcoal."[72]

On overnight stays at the Agee farmhouse, in bed, Rufus could smell the "wood smoke in quilts" from the "clayed or stone chimney." Rufus later expressed the primitive beauty of life on the Agee farm in his poetry:

> sweet tended field, now meditate your
> children , child , in your smokesweet quilt , joy in your dreams,
> and father , mother : whose rude hands rest you mutual of the
> flesh : rest in your kind flesh well.[73]

When he novelized his childhood memories decades later, Rufus described a trip in which the family crams into the Model T at the Agee farm and drives out to find the house of Jay's great-grandmother, whom they had not

Part of the former Agee farm property, off Smith Oaks Lane in Jacksboro.
Photo by the author.

seen in more than a decade. While struggling to remember the route through the hills of Campbell County, the novel's characters figure the old woman was born in 1811 or 1812 and was 103 or 104 years old at the time, which if factual would place the episode between 1915 and 1916, assuming Jay did not have the Model T until 1915. The ancient matriarch, called "Granmaw," is said to be Rufus's grandfather's grandmother. Laura confirmed that her son invented the episode for his novel: "That was a completely fictitious scene, and most people thought it was the realest thing." However, two brief notes, "Looking for a country place" and "hunting a house," appear among his other written memories of Campbell County trips. Could the imagined episode be based on a similar trip with the family? According to online genealogy sites, both of Henry Clay Agee's grandmothers had died by 1880. Although the boy Rufus had no great-great-grandparents living, he did have a single great-grandparent. "There was a grandmother for awhile—that is, it would've been Rufus's great-grandmother, of course," said Laura, "but she didn't live long after [Rufus and Emma] were born." Mary Comer Agee, Henry Clay's mother, was born in 1830 and died in 1918—outliving husband James

Harris Agee by almost two decades. She lived long enough that Rufus might have remembered her but was eighteen or nineteen years younger than the "Granmaw" character he later created.[74]

WEST CLINCH AVENUE

Not surprisingly, Rufus spent much less time with his Jacksboro grandparents than with his Knoxville grandparents, who lived at 1115 West Clinch, just a few blocks southeast of the Agee home on Highland. Paula Tyler remembered that the family got together often during the years when Rufus was a boy. Typically they had dinner together on Sundays. "Either they [came] up to us or we [went] down to them," Rufus later wrote, and "Sunday dinner [was] at 1115." It is not known whether the Tylers kept chickens or just brought them home live from the market, but one of Rufus's memories of

Clockwise from left, Joel, Emma, and Hugh Tyler, and Laura, Rufus, and Emma Agee stand in the Tyler yard in this circa 1917 photograph. Tyler Album 048, Hugh Tyler Collection, McClung Historical Collection, Knox County Library.

dinner with his Tyler grandparents involved "killing hens, wringing their necks." Ice cream was a favorite summertime dessert, freshly churned on the family's back porch. He recalled the "ice cream freezer. Licking the dasher. Too much salt."[75]

The Tylers' home stood on the northeast corner of Clinch Avenue and Fourth (now Twelfth) Street. Described as a "large frame residence perched on a high embankment," it lacked the gingerbread embellishments of neighboring homes. It was a two-story home when the Tylers purchased it, but they later flattened the roofline and built a third-floor cupola, or widow's walk, and surrounding porch. Approaching the house from the Clinch Avenue sidewalk, one would see "the dusty ivy on the wall" as one came up the "brick walk in the shade of the magnolia," and "the small glass house" sticking out from the front porch into the yard. This was not the only greenhouse in the neighborhood; someone had built a larger one a block west on White Avenue. In the back yard, the Tylers also built a small cottage that Hugh used as an art studio. Although Hugh kept it locked and its windows shaded, neighborhood boys peeking "through the north side windows" spied his "paintings and drawings of nudes."[76]

Hugh lived with his parents during Rufus's "early childhood," he recalled, "but went to New York when he was still a little boy." He is not listed in Knoxville's directories between 1905 and 1913, a period of travel and art apprenticeships. The winter before Rufus was born, Hugh was in the middle of a two-year design course "at Pratt Institute in Brooklyn." Immediately after that, he "worked for two years in the shops of the Herter Looms, N.Y.C. designing tapestry and rugs." He also learned "landscape painting at Woodstock, N.Y. with John Carlson." In 1912 he spent a year in Europe, "at Julian's in Paris and the French Academy in Rome." Two years later Hugh's name reappeared in the Knoxville directory under his parents' address, where he would remain until 1926.[77]

Like Hugh, Paula also studied in New York at various times. In 1915 she lived there at the Three Arts Club among dozens of female musicians, artists, and actors. The following year, after another New York trip, Paula opened a piano studio in the Tyler home. And a decade later, she would live in New York long term, teaching piano at the Diller-Quaile School of Music.[78]

For roughly a decade, Jessie Tyler had lived up on Laurel Avenue, faithfully caring for her aunt, Patty Fisk, who died about two weeks after Rufus was born. Jessie sold the house a couple of months later, possibly near the time Jay and Laura moved out, which would have opened up a spot for Jessie in her brother's house. She lived in Boston for part of 1912 but was back in Knoxville the next year. By mid-1916 she would live in Chattanooga, in preparation for a major step of faith.[79]

Rufus liked visiting his grandparents' house "because there were so many things there." Inside the front west room was "a big bay window with ferns and chairs and a table." A locked glass cabinet held "all kinds of rocks and shells and little eggs." The odd device his grandmother held up to her ear fascinated him; Rufus was curious about its waxy tip and recalled "tasting ear trumpet." He often saw his grandmother sitting at the "tall and dark brown" player piano. He got into mischief occasionally, including the times he was disciplined for "tearing page of book" and "matches burning piano keys." When Rufus was older, Aunt Paula gave him lessons at that piano, which his grandmother later bequeathed to him. Robert Fitzgerald remembered that Agee kept "the old upright" for two decades.[80]

Paula recalled a time when the three-year-old Rufus kept the family entertained by naming various objects and knickknacks in the house: "He was in the living room with me and my brother, and I guess some of the family. One wall was lined with bookcases. On top of the bookcases were ornamental things. And we would point to one of them and say, 'What's that?' and [Rufus would] say the name of it. We finally got to a lion [made of] plaster, and said, 'What's that?' And he looked at it and said, 'Something else.'" This might be the object Rufus later described as a "lion" that "was little and white. He lay on the mantle. He had a round thing on with a cross on it. He had [an arrow] sticking out of his side."[81]

The walls of the house were decorated with pieces of art, such as one depicting the "ruins of Athens." Rufus studied the framed print of "Lions of Persepolis," a work by Briton Riviere: "There was a picture with lions walking. It was dark and they padded along in the moonbeams. There were big stone stairs with weeds growing on them. There were big broken statues." Another painting, possibly one by Benjamin Champney, showed the rock formations of Ausable Chasm in New York, near where Joel and Jessie were born: "Great big rocks came up on both sides from the bottom to the top. There were trees on top of the rocks and a long thin ladder down and in between the rocks at the bottom there was a river." Another print, Luc-Olivier Merson's "Rest on the Flight into Egypt," depicted Joseph, Mary, and the baby Jesus, sleeping beneath a sphinx: "There was a big stone lion with a smooth face kind of like Uncle Hugh. Not a lion face but a man. He was lying down in the sand and in between his paws there were people sleeping. A man and a lady and a baby and a donkey. They had a little fire."[82]

Besides the Tylers' artistic influence, Rufus was also exposed to literature at a young age. He read a book written by a University of Michigan alumnus, Stanley Waterloo. *The Story of Ab* was a work for young readers about a caveman's adventures. An illustrated edition from 1904 featured several color prints by Simon Harmon Vedder. When Rufus remembered a "picture of wounded, killed man," he may have been thinking of one that showed the character Oak, killed with an ax by Ab, lying wide-eyed on the ground, a large red gash in his forehead. He read at least one of Joel Chandler Harris's books, possibly *Nights with Uncle Remus,* and recalled descriptions of "Miz Wolf in dark woods road, ax, whites of eyes." Other books he read were *Robinson Crusoe* and *King Arthur and His Knights,* Walter Scott's *Waverley Novels,* Booth Tarkington's *Penrod*—which Rufus later said was "like Tom Sawyer, yes, but more modern (I don't like the sound of that)"—and volumes of *Penny Encyclopedia.*[83]

Rufus was a "precocious child," according to his aunt, Annabel Agee. "At three years of age, he tired of nursery tales and liked to hear stories and myths of ancient Greece and Rome and their gods" and was "enchanted with stories like Ulysses and the one-eyed Cyclops." Margaret, Annabel's

Rufus with Margaret King, near the front porch of the King home, circa 1913. SPC 2017.005.001, McClung Historical Collection, Knox County Library.

sister, agreed: "Rufus, as we called him, was smart as he could be even at that early age and had advanced intelligence. He preferred stories of knights and dragons rather than the usual type of fairy tales cherished by children. He had a deep voice and was always asking questions."[84]

Rufus was about three years old when he asked, "Mama . . . who made God?" But often the boy's questions were more materialistic in nature, as in a story Oliver Agee, son of John and Annabel, shared about his cousin Rufus: "He used to go to my mother's parents' house—Mrs. Oliver King, who also lived on Highland. He'd go over and ask for cookies. But his mother said, 'Rufus, you must remember your manners; you must wait for Mrs. King to ask.' So he went back and said, 'Mrs. King, would you like to ask me if I would like any cookies?'" Annabel's sister, Margaret, remembered the story, too, but with Rufus expecting a different treat: "My grandmother, Mrs. David King, lived with us at the time and always kept fruit and candy in her room. She always gave Rufus fruit and candy. Rufus's mother chided him about asking for these little refreshments and told him not to mention them unless he were offered some. Well, Rufus came over to our home one day and stood looking up at grandmother. Finally, he asked, 'Grandmother King, why don't you ask me to have an orange?'" Although the two versions differ in some respects, the story shows how even as a boy, Rufus used words to his advantage.[85]

PLAYMATES

Ann Taylor, an older girl whose family lived down the street at 1642 Highland—now the site of Redeemer Church—recalled young Rufus's appearance: "He had hair that fell down in his eyes, cut in kind of a bang across the front, and wore Russian blouses. If you never heard of a Russian blouse, it was a long overblouse and generally had a belt. I remember when [my brother] David wore them."[86]

As many boys do, Rufus often preferred to play outdoors without shoes. However, his notes suggest that as a result of going "barefooted" he once broke out with "dew-poison," an infection causing sores on his feet and legs. As a four-year-old, Rufus "was run over by a bicycle, but later learned to love the irresponsible fellows," he later wrote.[87]

To Laura, her son "was a very normal, healthy, affectionate and happy little boy, with an endearing certainty that everyone surely loved him, as he loved everyone himself." To her friend Hazel, Rufus was a "beautiful and sensitive child." To Hugh Tyler, "He was the most generous, trusting, lovable little

Rufus stands in the front center of this group of children in the King front yard. Margaret King wears a large hat directly behind him. Although the other children cannot be positively identified, the two boys to the left of Rufus may be the Tripp brothers. The bell tower of Highland Avenue School is visible in the top right corner of the photograph. SPC 2017.005.003, McClung Historical Collection, Knox County Library.

fellow I ever knew." Laura remembered an example of Rufus's kindness, "an overflow of sympathy and generosity toward anyone whom he thought was hurt or wronged in any way." A friend of hers took Rufus out in a cart, hauled by a donkey, to visit "a settlement school . . . at the woolen mills." Laura retold the story: "The women brought their children, you know, and had to have people stay in the nursery all day while they worked in the mills. . . . Rufus said, 'Why do they have to stay in such a place? What are they there for?' And [my friend] explained that their mothers worked, and somebody had to take care of them, and that they were very, very poor—which they were. And she said, 'You know, some of them don't even have shoes and stockings to wear in the winter.' And Rufus's eyes commenced to fill up, and he was taking his shoes and stockings off right then and there to give her for whoever would need them. And that was like him, too. That continued to be like him."[88]

Another time, Paula Tyler recalled, "a little boy up the street" did not have a tricycle, "and Rufus gave him his. Of course when the family heard about it, they thought they'd better do something. So I think Laura, his mother, went up and talked to the family and got it back. He didn't mind that either. I don't think he thought anything about it."[89]

Laura felt that Rufus's sympathetic nature "remained one of his strongest traits all his life." But as her son mingled with the older boys of the neighborhood, she frequently witnessed them taking advantage of his sensitivity. "He was extremely trustful of the good will of everyone, and had some hard lessons to learn, that older boys were often teasing him and telling him tall stories just for fun," Laura said. Some of the oldest neighborhood children "never deceived [Rufus] or teased him . . . but just said, 'Hello, there,' and smiled as they went by, or maybe mussed up his hair or gave him a little punch, not to hurt or scare him, but only in play." Rufus distinguished between those boys and the ones closer to his age who "were mean to him, every time." After reading the fictionalized account of the boys teasing Rufus, Laura wrote in a letter that she could "easily identify the group of boys who gathered about my son."[90]

Martin Southern remembered Rufus "as a little kid with a perpetually running nose" and a "mop of black hair." In June 1914, the Southerns moved to 1413 Highland, a house where John Agee had roomed as a college student the year his nephew Rufus was born. Martin was four years older than Rufus; his brother, Charles, was four years younger. One of Charles's first words was "Chooten," a toddler's attempt to pronounce Rufus's name. Martin remembered "pudgy" Emma Agee and Charles sitting in a "coaster wagon" as Rufus pulled it along the sidewalk; but his overall impression of Rufus was that he was "a shy, studious youngster, who played a great deal by himself." The age difference between Martin and Rufus was somewhat of a barrier to friendship, and Martin regarded him with some disdain, as older children often dismiss younger children. However, Martin was especially interested in Rufus's copy of *The Boy Mechanic*, volume one—"a thick red book" containing "700 Things for Boys To Do." Rufus lent it to him, gaining some favor with the older boy; Martin "was inclined to keep" the book, and gave it back "with much reluctance."[91]

Rufus "was a lonely child because he was the wrong age to play with us," remembered Ann Taylor. Of Rufus's playmates, Alvin Tripp was closest to him in age. Around 1915 the Tripp family moved from Forest Avenue to 1509 Highland, next door to the Agees. Benjamin and Cornelia Tripp were members of St. John's Episcopal and sat way up on the front pew. They had two sons, both of whom were older than Rufus: Arthur by three years, and Alvin by almost three months. But to Rufus, "Alvin always seemed older because he was much less clumsy. . . . For Alvin was naturally skillful with his body and looked extremely dangerous when he got mad, and Arthur was soft-looking, with a rather girlish smile, and had curly hair."[92]

The Tripps kept rabbits in their back yard, and it was not long until Rufus wanted some, too. Jay and Laura apparently learned that the purpose of their neighbors' rabbits was "sex education," so as Rufus remembered, his parents brought home "white ones, same sex, as pets, for us." But while the rabbits did not help teach Rufus the birds and the bees, the experience ended with his first lesson in mortality. Details are scarce, but something, probably dogs, got into the hutch one day and killed the rabbits, leaving what Rufus described as "torn white bloody fur and red insides."[93]

Alleys ran east to west, parallel to the avenues, past the backsides of lots, separating backyards from those of houses on the street behind. It was common practice in Rufus's day for families to dump ash from their stoves and fireplaces in the alley behind their houses. He remembered walking back there and "listening to the cinders cracking under each step." Almost all the houses had barns in back of their lots along these alleys. Families with horses and buggies kept them in the barns, and when automobiles replaced the horses, the stables became garages. Mr. King's barn must have been the most inviting on the block, because Rufus and the Tripp boys chose it as their hideout when playing "Mexican spy," inspired by tales reported in the paper of General John J. Pershing and his "soldiers going to or coming from Mexico." Another activity Rufus remembered, though perhaps not as proudly, was "crapping in King's barn."[94]

During an interview much later in life, Dr. Alvin B. Tripp recalled that "Rufus was strange and lonely, a boy who had never learned to play baseball." One can almost hear young Alvin incredulously asking Rufus, "You don't know how to play baseball?" As many boys would, Alvin probably took every opportunity to flaunt his superior athletic abilities. But academically, Rufus had the upper hand.[95]

SCHOOL

On weekday mornings, "after his father had waved for the last time and disappeared," Rufus watched the students carry their books along the sidewalks past his house, which "was on the way to school for a considerable neighborhood." He could easily see the bell tower of Highland Avenue School one block to the east. The sound of the tolling tardy bell induced fear and quickened steps in students who had not yet reached their classroom seats. One girl lived across the street from the school but still "always had a horror of being late. I'd even dream about it. Some had to stay after school for being late, but I always managed to get there on time."[96]

Remembering his father, Rufus later wrote, "I'd be starting school that Fall before he died," which would have been the fall of 1915. However, school records show that Rufus began the previous year, despite being too young. Students entering in the fall had to be six years old by December, but Rufus was barely five years old in December 1914. Apparently, when Laura registered Rufus for kindergarten that June, she falsified his age as five years and six months, making him a year older than he actually was. She believed her son "was very quick" and could keep pace with the rest of his class.[97]

So on September 10, 1914, when the city schools opened, Rufus finally got to leave the house carrying his own lunch and books, and join the procession of students to the schoolhouse. On his first day of kindergarten (or "kindergartlen," as one of his grandmothers pronounced it), he was at least a year younger than all of his classmates, but he already knew most of the material. He recalled an early vowel exercise that his class practiced by rote: "tooby toob*ah* toob*iss* toob*eh* toob*ess*." Laura grew frustrated with the school's teachers, who criticized her for training Rufus at home: "[Rufus] already knew how to read, of course, before he got there. And they wished he didn't. It wasn't done according to Hoyle, you know. They said, 'Now, don't teach Emma anything before she gets to us. Please, don't teach her anything. Not to read or to count, or anything.' Insufferable. Just ridiculous. And Rufus was awfully smart, of course, and he was jumping ahead in everything all the time."[98]

Laura recalled that one of her neighbor's children was older than Rufus but had more trouble in school. She might have been thinking of Arthur Tripp, who was three years older than his brother, Alvin, but later graduated with him in the same class. "There was a boy on the other side of us up there on Highland . . . he was a little older than Rufus, but in the same grade," Laura said.

> And Rufus came home one day and said, "It was too bad about him. . . . You know, he just can't learn. He just can't learn." And I said, "Well that is too bad, but don't think any the less of him for that. If he can't, he can't. But you can. You have been given a good mind, I think, and you're supposed to do all you can with it. And not to look down on anybody who can't, but do the best you can."

Well, he got it, and he went and told the child, "Don't you feel bad because you can't learn. That's all right. I can, but you can't. But that's all right." And the little boy wouldn't play with him anymore for a long time. And [Rufus] said, "I don't know why he's mad at me." And I said, "Well, I do. It's not so mad as it's hurt his feelings." He said, "Well, I don't see why. I told him it was all right." And I said, "Well, it did hurt his feelings. It's too bad you did that. I never meant you to tell it to anybody."

While it could have been a different child, Arthur seems a likely match. Alvin later recalled Arthur not wanting Rufus to play baseball with them. The rejection could have been due to Rufus's admitted lack of physical co-ordination, but it could also be an example of Arthur harboring a grudge following Rufus's precocious insult. And since Arthur's mother, Cornelia Tripp—Highland Avenue School's PTA president that year—would surely have found out what Rufus told her son, such an episode agrees with the evident friction between the two families, which Rufus later wrote about. This minor school conflict also explains Jay's apparent rebuke—"Don't you brag"—that left Rufus "puzzled and rather stupid in school for several days, because of the stern tone in his voice."[99]

Rufus remembered the name of at least one kindergarten classmate: "Eliz Johnston dances, I try to imitate." Elizabeth's family lived at 1301 Laurel, a couple of blocks southeast from the Agees. Rufus mimicked her danc-ing one day in class, while his own movements were being watched and "burlesque[d]" by another student.[100]

By September 1916 Rufus's age discrepancy appears to have righted itself, although at six years, nine months, he was noticeably young to be entering his second semester of second grade. When school began the following fall, he was seven years, ten months, old, and a second-semester third grader. And in September 1918, after blowing through one and a half grade levels the previous year, he started fifth grade at age eight years, ten months.[101]

As an adult, Rufus wrote—tongue in cheek—about himself during these early school years: "After a brief sojourn in kindergarten, for which [Rufus] showed no more than average aptitude, he entered the public schools, and at these, and others, he spent no few years in ardent study of the back of the nearest head and of the nearest exit." However, it is clear that Rufus was not merely of "average aptitude" but rather quite gifted in grade school. And one wonders if bullies targeted him during this period because he not only was much younger and more sensitive than everyone in his class but also markedly smarter. Among his later story ideas based on Highland School experiences is one about a "teacher's pet"— a role his classmates surely accused him of playing often—and another, "Getting tough with Miss Murray," inspired by one of his teachers, Margaret Murray.[102]

The schoolhouse had been built in 1887, a year before the town of West Knoxville was incorporated. When Knoxville annexed West Knoxville in 1898, the high school grades were discontinued at Highland School, leaving only the elementary classes. Rose Staub—whose grandfather Jakob Staub was a first cousin to Knoxville mayor and businessman Peter Staub—had been one of the school's first teachers. Called "Miss Rose" by the students, she paddled infrequently, believing that corporal punishment was "a confession of weakness" and only to be used as a last resort. By the time Rufus started there, she had been principal for over a decade. The school was renamed Van Gilder in 1916. The following year, six rooms were added to the building's front to alleviate overcrowding. One student there in the 1950s later recalled "the huge old Victorian three-story brick building," which housed "the first- through fourth-grade classes . . . on the first floor, the fifth and sixth on upper floors." But throughout the school's life, the "small, gravely playground" remained about the same size. In 1957 a new school, Fort Sanders Elementary, opened and Van Gilder was permanently closed. It was demolished in 1960.[103]

THE CORNER

The northwest corner of Highland Avenue and Seventh (now James Agee) Street was, as Ann Taylor remembered, where Rufus and the other children gathered at "the most exciting time of the day . . . to see the fathers come home from work." But Rufus "began to anticipate going out to the corner with as much unhappiness as hope," as it was often the site of teasing, and even physical struggle, "sometimes with Tripps & Richard Williams & Johnny Breen," all boys whose families lived on Highland. "Everyone knew [Breen] was the best fighter his size in the block."[104]

Laura remembered a group of boys gathering on that corner: "It was on our side of the street that the boys congregated, three or four at once, generally. [They tried] to make Rufus sing to them. He had a sweet little voice, you know, and knew a lot of little songs and things. He was always obliging them. He was perfectly sure they meant it when he said they wanted to hear him, and so forth. 'Rufus Rastus Johnson Brown'—he knew that. And then they'd laugh because his name was Rufus, you see; that's where he got that horrible feeling about his name. And they would put ice down his neck, and hit him on his arm that had been vaccinated . . . I could have

Looking east down Highland Avenue in 1906. Almost a decade after this photo
was taken, older boys bullied Rufus Agee on the corner to the left, where the
picket fence and fireplug in front of 1501 Highland are visible. The row of houses
beyond it, on the 1400 block, remains largely intact more than a century later.
Note the streetcar tracks in the road. From *The City of Knoxville, Tennessee and
Vicinity and Their Resources,* Knoxville Board of Trade, 1906, Special Collections
Rare Books Oversize, University of Tennessee Library, Knoxville.

wrung their necks without any compulsion at all." Another song, "Whistlin'
Rufus," added to her son's "distaste for the name."[105]

While multiple boys bullied him to some degree, Alvin Tripp seemed
to be Rufus's primary antagonist. An early encounter with Alvin occurred
when Rufus and he "were both three," although considering that Alvin still
lived on Forest Avenue at that age, it might have been later. The doorbell
rang one day while Rufus sat at the table, eating. Still wearing his bib, he
got up to answer the door. When he opened it, there stood Alvin, who took
one look at Rufus and said, "If you wear a bib, you're a baby."[106]

Relations between the Agees and the Tripps became strained at one point. Rufus later wrote several pages of notes about an incident involving the Tripps but did not include it in his novel. On the surface, it seems like a typical boyhood spat. But he remembered it as a point of significant change in the family dynamic. When Rufus was a "small child," he was "much used for practical jokes and deceits; learned distrust slowly; no instinct to fight back about it." Concerning Alvin Tripp and the other boys who bullied him, he "[did] not understand why he should fight, and he [was] too trusting."[107]

Laura remembered the initial spark that ignited the feud with the Tripps. "That was a group on the corner, the Tripp boys and some others. . . . [T]hey wound this chewing gum right into his hair on the crown of his head, right down to the scalp," she said. "So I had to cut it all out, make a big round bare spot on his head. And they thought that was very funny." Alvin was apparently the main instigator, because Laura took Rufus next door to show the damage to Benjamin Tripp. "Mother cuts my hair and takes me over & shows [Mr.] Tripp," Rufus wrote. "I am taken along by her to Tripp but beyond being embarrassed & ashamed I understand little of it." Laura "complains" to Mr. Tripp about his son's behavior, "unaware that she shouldn't." Later, when Jay comes home from work, Laura "tells daddy about telling Tripp. He is appalled, and sore as hell. . . . When he learns from me that I didn't fight he whips me hard. Then he feels sorry and goes to town & comes back with an Indian suit." In the notes, Rufus even imagined part of his parents' conversation, with one lamenting that "he had such *nice* hair" and the other replying, "Personally, I'm glad it's cut."[108]

Rufus believed that his inability to fight made him a complete failure and a disappointment to his father. He was "several times whipped by my father in rage, then soon forgiven and apologized to or treated kindly. Bewilderment, fear of him, shame; I greatly respected him." The Indian costume was just one of the gifts Jay gave Rufus in short-lived apology. Soon after the first incident, Rufus was again confronted on the corner. "Next time I get the [Indian] suit ruined, feather pulled out, etc." Rufus recalled, or imagined, coming home after the fight: "Mother tries to fix the Indian suit? 'My nice suit!' Very deep crying." And again, Jay was furious at his son's refusal to fight. "Whipping again. Then ice cream." Rufus thought his father gave him a football another time as a consolation. Finally, he wrote, "He tries to teach me to fight." After much goading from his father—"*Hit me! Hit* me doggone it"—Rufus swung his fist. "I hit him hard enough in the eye to hurt & surprise him. I feel lousy about it."[109]

Rufus later imagined Mr. Tripp as his father's "main rival." Benjamin Tripp was a few years older than Jay, was "a city man," worked as a drafts-man at Weston Fulton's sylphon, or metal bellows, plant, and had "2 boys" to Jay's one. Perhaps Jay was "working to put himself ahead of" his next-door neighbor, and Rufus wondered whether this was what led his father to bring home the new, expensive machine one day after work: "He gets Ford in characterized competition with Tripp?" But it is difficult to know how much of this rivalry was real and how much was embellished. It cannot be known, for example, whether Rufus really heard his father say of Tripp in private, "Damn turkey neck *if he didn't wear glasses I'd bust him one.*" Or whether Rufus actually quoted that to the Tripps, which sent Mr. Tripp over to confront Jay, who responded, "Not that I wouldn't." Or whether Alvin said to Rufus, "My daddy can lick your daddy." Or even whether "Mother & Mrs. T" told each other a thing or two about "child raising," although Rufus did remember "Mrs. T" coming over for a "front porch talk."[110]

Alvin's bullying continued, but despite Jay's giving him fighting lessons, Rufus felt that "I am even more thoroughly a coward than before." To make matters worse, his three- or four-year-old sister was watching from the sidelines and saw Alvin humiliate him. "I begin to treat Emma badly."[111]

Margaret King remembered Emma "as a beautiful child with light curly hair." After the Tripp incident, Rufus believed that his father was beginning "to favor" Emma over him. As for teaching him how to fight, Jay "more or less gives it up" but teased Rufus and "over does his jestings" about the boy's inability to stick up for himself. In response, Laura "over-defends" her son and "tends to favor" him for being "misunderstood." Although Rufus was "quite unaware" of his father's roughness, he wanted "more than anything to have his approval." His sister, "hurt or jealous" that Rufus got all of their mother's attention, was "mistrustful of her." It seems that Rufus and Emma were each favored by one parent but wanted to be favored by the other: "Emma is 'his' and wants to be hers; I am 'hers' and want to be his." While children often complain of being treated unfairly compared to their siblings, Laura later confessed to seeing early signs that her daughter was dealing with something more than typical childhood insecurities.[112]

Rufus's parents "begin to take sides," he later wrote. "They divide even on my brightness." Laura argues that "smartness" is "superior to 'roughness.'" Her husband "has nothing against it to start with but he thus develops a prejudice against it. 'He's *your* boy.' She brings it up that Hugh could never fight . . . that Hugh & she never quarreled." Jay takes Laura's criticism "as a reflection on himself & his background."[113]

As a result of the dispute, Jay and Laura retreated into their own modes of comfort: "He begins to drink & fall more; she gets more religious. I am drawn more into that orbit, but more & more want to be in his." This was Rufus's first indication that his father may have had a problem with alcohol. Jay was "full of great energy and a fierce kind of fun, but also a feeling that things might go wrong." Rufus sometimes "overheard" his parents "arguing" about "whiskey." Elsewhere in his notes, he connected "drinking & moroseness" to his father "blaming me in regard to Emma," writing, "Mother is worried," apparently because of Jay's drinking.[114]

"Enter her plan to send me off to school." There are no other clues about this school, except that, concerning Rufus's father, his mother "wanted to send me to school to escape him." Perhaps Laura had in mind a place like the one Jessie Tyler told her about, the Episcopal boarding school near Sewanee, where Rufus would receive spiritual instruction while living among other boys his age. With regard to Laura's religious influence on the children, Jay "doesn't like what she is doing to [Rufus] either: but in general, feels it is none of his business." However, Jay was entirely against the idea of the school, and "he [put] his foot down."[115]

At some point, Laura apparently told her father, Joel, about her marital troubles, or he sensed something was wrong: "Grandpa warns her [about] the drinking. Maybe he spoke to [my father] about it?" Although there are no further details about the conversation, it resulted in an ultimatum, with Laura promising Jay: "If you do that again I'll leave you. (For *their* sake.)" And with that, the family quarrel—which began with a group of boys on the corner—apparently ended.[116]

THE MAJESTIC

Even before he was old enough to attend Highland Avenue School, Rufus was educated in the movie houses of Knoxville. He probably saw his first moving picture one summer night at Chilhowee Park. The flickering images strung together before his eyes developed in him an early aesthetic sensibility that his later writings display: in addition to his film criticism and screenplays, his descriptive powers reveal a cinematographer's sense of movement and detail.

Rufus and his family may have been part of the audience that sold out the Gay Theatre in December 1915 for the screening of a short film, "Aunt Sally Visits Knoxville," shot in the city by photographer Jim Thompson. Several locals appeared in the film, including Carrie Quincy, Marjorie Bailey, and

Dr. W. H. Richards. Another person, listed in advertisements as "Mr. Ochs," cannot be positively identified, as the film is now lost; he could have been Adolph Ochs, the owner of the *New York Times* who spent his boyhood in Knoxville. But if Rufus sat in the audience that night, he would have been most impressed by another onscreen local: his uncle Hugh Tyler.[117]

When he was older, it was not unusual for Rufus and his sister, Emma, to see "four films in four different theaters in a single Saturday." Movies were mile markers for Rufus, grounding his memories at particular points between childhood, adolescence, and adulthood. "Most of my time-identifying up to 20–21 is by movies. Or, rather, I identify the year of the movie by the memory of where I saw it when," he later wrote. He realized that movies, like "recorded music" but unlike memories, can be relived: "A movie was a more brilliant part of experience than much that surrounded it. It is the only part that can be exactly repeated."[118]

Some evenings after supper, Rufus and his father walked toward those downtown theaters instead of taking the streetcar or Model T—out Forest Avenue and across the viaduct, following Asylum Avenue until it ended at Walnut, then rounding the corner to Wall Avenue, and passing Market Square on the way to Gay Street. The trip was barely a mile one way.[119]

In 1916 seven of Knoxville's nine movie houses sat on Gay Street's west side, with four of those in the two blocks between Commerce and Union. Only a few of the theaters advertised daily in the newspapers, the others every few days or even less frequently, so the full spectrum of picture choices would only be known by walking the sidewalks past the movie posters and sandwich boards. Of the choices offered by the various theaters, Rufus and his father tended toward "westerns, and above all, Charlie Chaplin or his imitator Billy West." His mother disapproved of Chaplin, though it is unknown which element she found most unacceptable—the hobo dress and lifestyle, or the slapstick. "I remember my mother saying of Chaplin that 'he is so vulgar' and deploring our going, and my father's laughing that off. We both had a very good time watching him."[120]

Rufus visited a particular Knoxville theater, the Majestic, which despite its name was one of the smaller movie houses on the street—the Gay, Grand, and Bijou theaters were at least twice its size—and the large Haynes Block building next door made it appear even more diminutive. Compared to other small theaters, like the Crystal and Queen, the Majestic advertised infrequently in the papers. In June 1915, however, the ads showed more of a promotional effort than normal, touting giveaways ("Save the coupons given with each ticket to the Majestic—begin using Monday, and get a Statue of

The Majestic Theatre, right, as it appeared in 1921. *The Son of Tarzan* was showing at the time. N-1575, Thompson Photograph Collection, McClung Historical Collection, Knox County Library.

Chas. Chaplin. These miniatures are on display at the box office"), relief from the humidity ("Forget the heat of the day—there's a cool hour and a pleasant hour awaiting you at the Majestic Theatre Monday"), and live music ("Band Concerts & Moving Pictures EVERY NIGHT").[121]

Previously called the Lyceum, the theater began operating as the Majestic in late 1909, offering "moving pictures and vaudeville." Carl Haug managed it at the time of Rufus's early visits, and a young musician, Maynard Baird—known a decade later as leader of the Southland Serenaders, a successful touring jazz band—threaded the projector and occasionally performed onstage, possibly during some of those advertised nightly band concerts.[122]

On a typical night at the Majestic, moviegoers would have seen two or three short subjects in rotation—a mixture of dramatic action and comedy. In *A Death in the Family*, the Majestic's small auditorium is characterized by the odors of country bodies packed together in the heat of late spring and the feverish tones of a piano amid raucous laughter. The Chaplin movie is fiction, a synthesis of various cues from the comedian's films—the eggs-in-the-pants bit, for example, is found in the 1915 short, "The Tramp," but out of context from the rest of the described scene. Rufus greatly respected Chaplin and later stated, "The finest pantomime, the deepest emotion, the richest and most poignant poetry were in Chaplin's work."[123]

Rufus also recalled watching a William S. Hart western. Hart had first appeared in a Knoxville theater two decades earlier, though not on film: he was there in person, portraying a hunchback onstage at Staub's Theatre, five blocks south of the Majestic's location. The young Rufus, however, only knew him as a film actor, as the hard-featured cowboy with a billowing neckerchief. Later, as an adult writing for the *Nation*, Rufus Agee stated that Hart "at his best . . . was in his face and his way of handling himself almost as mythically and finely racial—or . . . national—as Lincoln." As he drew parallels between his father and the sixteenth president, perhaps Rufus also recognized something of his father in the cowboy actor. Many of Hart's early films are not readily available, and the brevity of Rufus's description makes it difficult to identify the film. It may be, as with the Chaplin film, an amalgam of images recalled from various Hart films.[124]

In *A Death in the Family*, the trip to the Majestic takes place the evening before Rufus's father is killed. Unfortunately, the local papers are no help in confirming this. The Majestic newspaper ads were usually sporadic, but that week there were none at all. Even checking all of Majestic's ads going back to the previous summer, as Ron Allen verified, "fails to turn up any record of a double bill that featured both Charlie Chaplin and William S. Hart films."[125]

The Majestic changed owners throughout the next decade. By 1931 the theater had closed and the building was consumed by the northward expansion of S. H. George's department store. In 1957, the sites of both businesses were cleared for the construction of W. T. Grant's new department store, which itself closed in the mid-1970s and became offices for Tennessee Valley Authority. The building was completely "gutted to the steel" before reopening in 1989 as TVA Credit Union's downtown branch. Today the northernmost fifth of the building's storefront marks the approximate site of the Majestic.[126]

DOWNTOWN

By late evening, when Jay and Rufus stepped onto the sidewalk outside the movie theater, Gay Street was ablaze with electricity, and "many of the store windows were still alight." Rufus "watched the absorbed faces pushing past each other and the great bright letters of the signs." The city had installed a new lighting system downtown the previous year, and one local paper reported "a cosmopolitan air about the streets" that you could sense if you "stand on one of the busy corners and watch the passing throng, listen to the honk of the automobiles, or catch the vari-colored twinkle of the electric signs." Rufus observed those electric "sign-letters" while "walking in dusk" with his father. One of the "lighted signs" he noticed along the way promoted "Cardui," a women's tonic that was probably sold at "Kresses & Woolworths," drug stores at 417 and 509 South Gay, respectively. "Sterchi's" sold appliances and furniture, and Rufus clearly saw its sign down the street at 412–414 South Gay. That building later became known for its long-term association with J. C. Penney. Another department store sign, "George's," was visible at the south end of the block from the theater.[127]

One block north from the theater was Morris Bart's clothing store for women. Bart, a Jewish merchant originally from Russia, kept a large "stuffed bear" on the sidewalk out front that reminded Rufus of a real animal he had seen in the mountains, maybe near Elkmont. The bear was so realistic that a farmer's hound dog once attacked it, pulling it by the snout onto Gay Street. Another Jewish businessman, Isadore Beiler, ran a corner newsstand and confectionery on Clinch Avenue, in the Plaza Block building across the street from the Custom House. Beiler, a Romanian immigrant, was known to stock "high class publications" and "reading matter that was elevating or at least something parents would permit their sons and daughters to read." Rufus bought "Jim Jam Jems, Whizbang, Argosy, Adventure," and other pulp magazines "at Beiler's." After visiting the store one day, possibly with his father, Rufus asked, "Why's he talk so funny?" The reply was blunt: "He's a Jew."[128]

Walking south on Gay Street, Rufus and his father passed S. H. George's store at the corner of Wall Avenue and likely turned west there toward Market Square. Another downtown sign that Rufus later remembered, "Economy Range," was almost certainly an advertisement for the "Economist Range" stove, sold by J. F. Walker at number 31 on the square's west side. Walker's store sat in the shadow of the 1897 market house, an imposing brick structure with a bell tower, whose bulk all but filled the square. The narrow lanes on either side of it remained cluttered with the horses and buggies of farmers

The 500 block of Gay Street, circa 1916, looking north past Union Avenue. Businesses along the west (left) side of the street include Aerial Billiard Parlor, Woolworth's 5 and 10 cent store, East Tennessee Savings Bank, Miller's department store, and, further down the block, Kress's 5 and 10 cent store. Businesses on the east (right) side of the street include Doll & Co. stationers, Clark & Jones pianos, Woodruff's hardware, and faintly visible beyond it, Cullen's china, and Sterchi's furniture. MS.0951, box 2, folder 8, Photographs of Tennessee Cities Collection, Special Collections, University of Tennessee Library, Knoxville.

camping out to sell their produce the next morning, a scene Rufus Agee later fictionalized: "They passed a wagon in which a lantern burned low orange; there lay a whole family, large and small, silent, asleep. In the tail of one wagon a woman sat, her face narrow beneath her flare of sunbonnet, her dark eyes in its shade, like smudges of soot." The lane on Market Square's west side was known as "Produce Row," and at the time, more fruits and

"Busy Spots in Knoxville." This 1921 drawing, looking north over downtown, shows the locations of businesses Rufus remembered from childhood: Bart's (A), the Majestic Theatre (B), George's (C), Sterchi's (D), Miller's (E), the market house (F), Harbison's (G), Beiler's (H), and the post office where Jay Agee had worked (I). *Knoxville Journal and Tribune*. October 15, 1921.

vegetables were sold there than at any other place in Knoxville. Even though the market house was demolished in 1960 following a fire, local independent farmers have continued to sell produce on the square, an unbroken tradition since the space was designated for that purpose in 1853.[129]

Jessie Tyler took Rufus shopping downtown once, riding the streetcar to Gay Street. Miller's, whose 1905 building still sits prominently on the corner of Gay and Union, was apparently "a profoundly matronly store in which Rufus's mother always bought the best clothes which were always, at best, his own second choice." He preferred the store on Market Square that only sold clothes for men and boys, and recalled Aunt Jessie buying him a coveted cap at Harbison's. Rufus thought it was "one of the nicest things . . . that had ever yet happened in my life":

> I had very particularly wanted a cap for a long time. Many boys of my age or size wore them; so did some boys who were smaller than me; all the big boys did: I wore little hats. These little hats I had recognized for quite some time as the badge of babyhood: worse. If I wore a hat at my age and size I was not only a baby, I was a sissy as well. Merely to wear a cap, I felt, would be more than enough to change all that. . . .
>
> And now that I was downtown with my Aunt Jessie, and she had done her shopping, she turned to me quite casually and said: "And now why don't I get you a cap. Would you like that?" And she even left me considerable liberty in picking out the cap I like best.
>
> I can't be sure I remember rightly, but I think I chose so recklessly, something loud with an enormous visor, that she felt she really had to set a limit, so that what I got was a compromise . . . [but] that made no difference to me. . . .
>
> For the moment I realized that I actually had a cap, the cap itself became secondary. The thing I wanted, above everything in the world, was to show it to my father, to have him see me in it, if possible, to surprise him with it.

While there was indeed a store called Harbison's, located at number 2 on the square's east side in 1916, newspaper ads reveal that it sold "Nothing But Shoes." As an adult, Rufus probably had it confused with Edington's, a clothing store for men and boys at number 12, which sometimes advertised as "Knoxville's Best Store for Boys."[130]

Most of the depiction of Market Square in *A Death in the Family* rings true with what is known about Knoxville at that time—that is, until Rufus visits the "market bar" with his father, walks "through the swinging doors," and immediately smells "beer, whiskey and country bodies." Since the "dry" law was passed in 1907, no place in Knoxville openly served liquor. And with the police headquartered on the market house's second floor, the square seems the least likely place in the city for a saloon. Was the bar just the novelist's fanciful invention? When asked in the late 1960s whether the scene was true, Hugh Tyler said he did not know, "but knowing Jay, it might well have been." Perhaps it was partly true. While the existence of an open saloon was unlikely at the time, there is an apparent reference in the novel to the city's dry status: Jay longs to stop at one of the all-night lunch rooms, where "you could get a shot or two of liquor" if you "looked like you could be trusted."[131]

If the Market Square saloon Rufus later described was actually based on a memory, perhaps what Jay visited that night was a speakeasy, where certain individuals could obtain a back-room drink and where certain police officers looked the other way. Billiard rooms were the most likely candidates for such an establishment on Market Square, and there were four nearby. Two sat just off the square: Central Billiards and Smoke Parlor on Wall Avenue and W. A. Allie's pool room on Union. Jay and Rufus would have passed one of those on the walk from the Majestic. And there were two billiard rooms on the square's west side along Produce Row: R. G. Mullins' place at 33 Market Square and W. M. McIntyre's at 21 Market Square, which had been a saloon, McIntyre & Cassady, back when Jay was single and still living downtown. When the law changed, McIntyre made it a billiard hall but perhaps still catered to his old bar patrons.[132]

THE WALK HOME

After passing through Market Square on their way home, Rufus and his father likely walked west on Wall, turned the corner onto Walnut, and proceeded a short way to Asylum Avenue, named after the Tennessee School for the Deaf and Dumb—once called the Deaf and Dumb Asylum—on the next block. In its early years, the institution was one of only ten schools for deaf students in the country. The Administration Building, constructed in Greek Revival style between 1848 and 1851, had been used as a hospital during the Civil War. As they passed by the building's columned front, Rufus observed that "its windows showed black in its pale brick, as the nursing woman's eyes, and it stood deep and silent among the light shadows of its trees." Farther up the road, "Asylum Avenue lay bleak beneath its lamps." No pawn or secondhand shops show up on this block in the city directory, so the objects "latticed in pawnshop iron" were probably the writer's invention. But he also described "a closed drug store" window, displaying "Venus de Milo, her golden body laced in elastic straps." Whether or not such a statue occupied his front window, Frank Johnson operated a drug store on

Looking east across the Asylum Avenue Viaduct towards the L&N Station and downtown Knoxville. Postcard from the author's collection.

the southeast corner of Asylum and Broadway. The businesses along this section of road were later obliterated with the widening of Henley Street and creation of Summit Hill Drive.[133]

Despite major changes to that intersection over several decades, the 1905 L&N Passenger Station still inhabits a prominent corner overlooking the Second Creek valley, which once echoed as "couplings clashed and conjoined" and "switch engine[s] breathed heavily." Even though the depot "smelled like chewing tobacco and pee, and like a barn," Rufus's parents preferred the L&N over "the Southern depot because there were so many country folks." Rail service was discontinued in 1968, and the rail yards became the site of the 1982 World's Fair. The building's ornate "stained glass" windows that "smoldered like an exhausted butterfly" were replaced by reproductions at some point. One of the original windows is displayed at the East Tennessee History Center. The former passenger station now houses the L&N STEM Academy. Although the site echoes only with the rumbling automobile traffic around it and not "the restive assemblage of the train" and "crumpling of freight cars," one lonely railroad track still traverses the valley behind the former freight depot.[134]

Passing the depot, Jay and Rufus crossed the Asylum Avenue Viaduct, over the rail yards on one side and the steel mill on the other, and leaned over the railing "to inhale the burst of smoke from a switch engine which passed under." Rufus was about the same age as the viaduct—its construction began five days before his birth. When completed the following August, the concrete bridge was hailed for its innovative continuous girder design, which became the standard for modern bridge building. Even though the street was renamed Western Avenue decades later, a bronze plaque implanted in the concrete railing preserved the viaduct's original name. "If you've never seen it by moonlight," wrote Knoxville journalist Jack Neely in July 1992, "you need to. It can give you a chill." His recommendation carried an urgent tone: "But look fast. It won't be there much longer." At the time, the city was planning to tear down the eighty-three-year-old viaduct as part of a reconfigured freeway on-ramp. "Knoxville will be distinctly less interesting," Neely lamented, "less worth visiting, for its loss."[135]

About half a block beyond where Forest Avenue branched off the end of the viaduct toward Rufus's home, there was "a vacant lot," described as "part rubbed bare clay, part over-grown with weeds, rising a little from the side-walk. A few feet in from the sidewalk there was a medium-sized tree and, near enough to be within its shade in daytime, an outcrop of limestone like a great bundle of dirty laundry. If you sat on a certain part of it the trunk of the tree shut off the weak street lamp a block away, and it seemed very dark." From where they sat at the corner, Rufus and his father looked "out over the steep face of the hill and at the lights of North Knoxville." At that time of night, spots of light would have shown from area houses, streetlamps, a few open businesses, and possibly churches with midweek services.[136]

When the viaduct was replaced, the east end of Forest Avenue was closed and made inaccessible from Eleventh Street and Western Avenue. North Knoxville's lights can no longer be seen from where the vacant lot was once located. Even if the view were not obscured by the raised Western Avenue overpass, Interstate 275 beyond it had already carved chunks out of North Knoxville as it followed Southern Railroad's tracks out of town.[137]

Rufus sat with his father at that lot and felt closer to him there than in any other place, because in those moments Rufus had his father all to himself. "It was a thing which brought us together, distinct from my mother, my sister, other relatives, etc." Years later, Rufus wrote a letter to his Jungian psychologist, Frances Wickes, detailing his recollections about those particular times

Detail of a 1919 aerial photograph showing locations along Asylum Avenue, including part of the School for the Deaf property (A), the drug store (B), the L&N Station (C), the viaduct (D), and the vacant lot (E) at the corner of Forest Avenue and Second (later Tenth) Street. N-1121, Thompson Photograph Collection, McClung Historical Collection, Knox County Library.

at the corner with his father: "When we stopped and sat at the corner, as we always did, he was always very quiet. Sometimes he would sing a little (but to sing was not unusual for him) but generally he was silent and so was I. I can't be sure but not impute to him that he felt a great deal of quiet homesickness for solitude and for country night, which I did not interrupt, and that he enjoyed stopping for 15 or 20 minutes, putting off getting home. My imputation is too, that women get in the way of this—at least change it. That few men have enough time alone. All we would do really was sit in the dark on the rock with the leaves around and more or less watch the stars."[138]

Later in life, thinking back to the times he had refused to fight, Rufus apparently struggled with thoughts that his father considered him a failure. But this was contradicted by reflections of his father's quiet tenderness during their outings together: "In the days I knew him I was not sharply aware of being a disappointment to him and I never had any doubt I was loved by him, or of my love for him; yet if I can remember correctly I had at this corner time a distinct and joyful sense of being fully accepted, and fully loved. . . . I remember his hands and his caressing of me as particularly gentle and feel that he was at these times not at all concerned that as a son I was discreditable to him, not at all aware of it."[139]

This trip downtown and back—walking together to see Chaplin and Hart, and then returning by way of Market Square, past the asylum and the L&N Station, over the viaduct, and sitting on a rock in a quiet lot—was one Rufus and his father made several times. And these memories were perhaps the clearest ones Rufus had of his father, because they were among the last impressions Jay ever made on his son. For as they sat "facing north through the night . . . towards the deeply folded small mountains and the Powell River Valley," neither of them knew the fate that waited in darkness somewhere out beyond the ridgeline.[140]

3

"The Hour of Their Taking Away"
Death, 1916

Up in Jacksboro that morning, Henry and Moss Agee likely showed each other a little more affection than normal. Henry was now sixty-five, exhausted from farming, and weakened further by spells of illness. Moss, fifty-six, faithfully managed the housework plus the tasks her husband was too weak to do. But that day may have begun with the happy thought of their marriage years ago, when she was seventeen and he was a twenty-five-year-old schoolteacher. This was May 17, 1916—their thirty-ninth anniversary.[1]

For their son Jay, it was just Wednesday, a normal workday. Coffee, breakfast, kisses for Laura, Emma, and Rufus—who was a month away from summer break—and then outside to crank his company car before puttering down the ridge to the plant on White Avenue. Joel had hired him four or five years ago as a bookkeeper but had not moved him up in the company. No records exist to show whether Jay's salary had been raised at all during that period. It is not known how satisfied Jay was with the job, or if he had considered other career options. But that Wednesday, he worked late, with Laura probably delaying dinner till he arrived home. Contrary to Rufus's later account, there was probably no trip to the movies that evening, and Jay likely went to bed shortly after supper.[2]

Sometime late in the night, he awoke to the telephone ringing downstairs. His brother Frank was calling from Campbell County with bad news. Their father had had a stroke that night and was not doing well. Sister Mossie Hodges had come all the way from Morristown to the Agee farm to be with him and was there now. Frank told Jay that he should come up as soon as

Taken in 1912, this is the only known photograph of Jay Agee with his children, Rufus and Emma. From *Agee: His Life Remembered.* Reprinted courtesy of Ross Spears, James Agee Film Project.

possible, that their father might not have long to live. "My father thought it likely that Frank was exaggerating—he sounded drunk, he told my mother," wrote Rufus, whose novelized version of the events portrayed Frank as a pathetic drunkard. But Annabel Agee, John's wife and Frank's sister-in-law, sought to set the record straight: "Mossie heard the conversation Frank had with Jim about the father's illness, and she told me there was nothing unusual about it—Frank was not drunk."[3]

Jay dreaded such a long drive at that hour but decided he should go since "it was just possible that his father was as sick as Frank said he was," Rufus later wrote. "My father dressed quietly in order not to wake me and my sister. I imagine that my mother got into a bathrobe and fixed him some coffee, and probably a breakfast." These may be details Laura later told her son. As an adult, Rufus guessed that Frank called "late that night, about two-thirty." Assuming that time was accurate, if Jay left the house within the hour, he would not arrive in Jacksboro until close to six o'clock that morning.[4]

Knoxville newspapers reported 4:28 as the time the sun rose that morning in 1916. Nowadays, the sun appears two hours later on May 18. Daylight
Savings, of course, had not yet been enacted in 1916, which accounts for one
hour. And Knoxville was not in the Eastern Time Zone but the Central,
whose eastern boundary at the time ran through Asheville, North Carolina.[5]

ROAD TO JACKSBORO

At sunrise, Jay was likely still on the road to Jacksboro. But how did he get
there? Obviously, he traveled alone that night on his last trip out of Knoxville, so unless he happened to mention the route to his family in Jacksboro,
no one knew for certain. There were at least a couple of ways he could have
taken. The adult Rufus, surely consulting his own memories of riding with
the family to Campbell County, imagined his father leaving the house the
same way they had walked to the movies and turning north on Broadway:
"He drove down Forest, across the viaduct, past the smoldering depot, and
cut sharply left beneath the Asylum and steeply downhill. The L&N yards
lay along his left. . . . Along his right were dark vacant lots, pale billboards,
the darker blocks of small sleeping buildings. . . . Before long the city thinned
out into . . . mean little homes, and others inexplicably new and substantial, set too close together . . . and alongside the road, between them, trash
and slash and broken sheds and rained-out billboards: he passed a late, late
streetcar . . . far out near the end of its run." On this route, Jay would have
crossed several Southern Railroad tracks downhill from the School for the
Deaf, as the Broadway Viaduct would not be built there for another decade.[6]

This was certainly one way Jay could have traveled. An 1895 map of Knox
County shows Broadway becoming Jacksboro Pike north of Knoxville; a remnant of this still remains in Fountain City. A piece of an Old Jacksboro Road
also lies along Old Andersonville Highway and Norris Freeway. One would
have driven through Fountain City and six miles past Halls Cross Roads
before turning left and traveling ten miles to the crossroads town of Loyston,
lying in a lush valley twenty-five miles from Knoxville. From there, one of
the roads led west seven miles to the convergence of the Clinch and Powell
Rivers. Two crossings—approached from the Anderson and the Campbell
sides of the Clinch—brought travelers over the waters into Agee, a speck of
a town, not much bigger than its post office. Even after a bridge was built at
one crossing in 1908, ferry traffic continued from the other crossing into the
1930s. Once across the river and through the town, one would either turn
left toward Jacksboro on the Kentucky Road or right toward LaFollette on

a newer lane, roughly what is now called Demory Road. Neither road was a straight shot, often meandering beside creek paths. Although not convenient, Jay likely chose this scenic route during family excursions as an excuse to visit the town of his boyhood. This was "the real, old, deep country," the family's "home country." Jay's brother John drove his own son through Agee in the early 1930s, telling him, "Oliver, I want you to see where I was born, for if you don't see it now, you'll never see it." That trip through Agee cannot be re-created today because of the changes Norris Dam brought to the landscape in 1936. When the dam's spillway was opened that year, Loyston, Agee, and other "ancient" valley towns were gradually submerged beneath Norris Lake, along with the connecting road to Jacksboro. One TVA worker noted that boats were now rowing above roads walked by oxen more than a century earlier. Some locals claimed that for decades afterward, whenever

Ferry across the Powell River at Agee, circa 1900. From *Campbell County Tennessee USA*, vol. 1. Reprinted courtesy of Campbell County Historical Society.

waters dropped below normal levels, the last Agee ferry could be seen on the lake bottom where it had been abandoned.[7]

As much nostalgia as Jay surely felt about the town named after his family, the urgency of that night's mission forbade any leisurely side trips. Fortunately, there was another, faster way to Jacksboro via Clinton Pike, which approximated an early-1800s stage route between Knoxville and Cumberland Gap. Leaving home, Jay could easily have taken this road by turning left instead of right onto Asylum Avenue; after only a mile or so, out past Knoxville College, Clinton Pike angled off to the north at New Gray Cemetery, and Asylum continued west as Ball Camp Pike. The Agees must have used that road at some point, because Rufus later remembered its name; however, the road he called Ball Camp Pike in his writings was actually Clinton Pike.[8]

More than likely, Jay drove north that night over this quicker route, because he certainly chose the same one for his return trip the following evening. Like all highways leaving Knoxville, Clinton Pike snaked over a series of parallel ridges that slashed the landscape from southwest to northeast. Jay traveled up McAnally Ridge and Black Oak Ridge, then crested Beaver Ridge before proceeding down into the valley near Powell's Station. Rumbling past an old house on his left that is known today as Lulu's Tea Room, he approached a grain mill on the bank of Beaver Creek. He crossed the creek noisily over the wood-plank floor of Bell's Bridge, a through-truss span built by the King Iron Company in 1888. Back from the road on the left sat the two-story, oak-log Fort Menifee, built in 1788 with portholes through which rifles could be fired at attacking Indians. Passing the 128-year-old fort, Jay ascended Copper Ridge into Anderson County and drove eight miles over narrower roads before making it to the Clinch River at the town of Clinton.[9]

Jay probably never stopped in Clinton longer than it took to ferry across the river. He may not have known that his grandfather, James Harris Agee, had finished school there, probably in the frame schoolhouse called Union Academy that later burned during the Civil War. On separate occasions during that war, Confederate and Union soldiers crossed the river at Clinton. General A. E. Burnside, remembering his passage in December 1863, called that ferry "an important one for the crossing of troops, trains and animals, and its maintenance absolutely necessary for the good of the service." Forty-five years later, the first automobile into Clinton rolled off the ferry onto the same riverbank. By 1916 the automobile had noticeably changed the way of life in Clinton. The ferry, wrote a local reporter, was "about the only reminder left of the good old days when walking was fashionable, and the ox team was the only vestibule service in the community."[10]

Had Jay crossed by ferry into Clinton or Agee, or any other Tennessee town, he would not have paid a toll. A February 1909 state bill mandated that each county was to pay the salaries of its ferry operators, making the service free to the public. But it turns out that early on May 18, 1916, on his last journey north to see his folks, Jay did not cross the Clinch by ferry.[11]

The previous fall, Anderson County began building four steel bridges. After several months of construction and weather-related delays, Clinton's bridge—525 feet between abutments—finally opened to traffic on May 5, roughly two weeks before Jay was summoned to his father's bedside. "The ferry boat has been anchored," reported the *Anderson County News,* "and the ferryman joined the tribe of lone fishermen who delight with rod and line to bask in the sunshine."[12]

As Jay came down the end of the bridge into town that Thursday morning, he may have noticed a smokestack off to his right that belonged to the town's biggest industry, the soon-to-be-expanded Magnet Knitting Mill. Coming in on Broad Street, he took a right onto dusty Jacksboro Street, past Clinton's imposing courthouse and its otherwise unexceptional homes, churches, and brick buildings, only a few of which still edge the old highway, now Main Street. Once through the town it was another eleven miles to the Campbell County line, through Coal Creek to Caryville. Jacksboro was only a few miles farther. This north-south highway is part of Tennessee State Route 9, and was chosen around 1920 to be part of U.S. Route 25-W, East Tennessee's link in the Dixie Highway chain.[13]

After Jay arrived at the farm in Jacksboro and entered the bedroom where his father lay, he quickly realized that Frank had greatly exaggerated the situation—at least, this is the scenario Rufus later imagined for his novel. In fact, Henry Clay Agee was "critically ill," "very low from a stroke of paralysis," and "not expected to survive long," according to a newspaper report. Henry's condition was so grim that, after spending the afternoon with him, Jay apparently decided to return home, pick up Laura and the children, and "take them back to his father's bedside." But he never made it home. Exactly what occurred in the moments before and after the tragedy is conjecture.[14]

THE CRASH

Jay likely called Laura to tell her the situation and say that he would be on his way soon but "not to wait supper." Jay's mother probably made him an early supper before he headed home. He was running on little sleep when he left the farm and had about a three-hour drive ahead of him. If he was

1915 Model T touring car. Photo Album of Dedication of Agee Library,
Special Collections, University of Tennessee Library, Knoxville.

indeed planning to bring his family back up to Jacksboro the next day, one
can imagine him pushing the maximum speed over the familiar gravel roads
so he could get home as soon as possible. Twenty miles per hour was the
fastest anyone could drive legally in town. Of course, speedometers were
optional on Tin Lizzies, so it did not matter much, especially at that time of
evening on an unpatrolled country highway. On a straight, flat section, Jay
could hit forty miles per hour. On a downhill stretch of good road, maybe
forty-five or fifty.[15]

However, Jay was losing daylight. If he left Jacksboro at 5:30 that evening,
the sun would have been as low as at 7:30 p.m. on May 18, 2016. Electric,
rather than kerosene, headlights were a new feature on the 1915 Model T.
Powered by the flywheel's magneto coil, the lamps' brightness varied with
the motor's rpms, and the beams projected only thirty to forty feet out in
front of the car. One Model T owner compared the car's dim headlamps to
"two jars of lightning bugs."[16]

On Highland Avenue, Jay's waiting wife and children ate "supper a little late." The whole evening, Rufus kept his new cap—the one Aunt Jessie had bought for him during their downtown shopping trip that afternoon—by his side, "ready as a cocked pistol," he remembered, "ready to put it on and rush out to him the instant I heard the car coming." He waited with "intensity and excitement and joy . . . for my father to come home." Emma and Rufus

A rare photograph of Bell's Bridge on Clinton Pike, looking northwestward toward Copper Ridge. The image shows the iron bridge structure and, past it on the left, the Samuel Bell house. The "NARROW BRIDGE" sign and white safety pylons lining the road were likely recent upgrades when the photo was taken around 1929. Note the low land surrounding the bridge approaches and how the sides of the road slope downward. Jay Agee's car could have easily dropped off the side of the road there; yet articles in the *Journal and Tribune* (May 19 and 20, 1916) stated only that the car ran "up a slight embankment at the side of the road" and "struck an embankment." The right foreground of the photo shows what may be part of the "slight embankment" that Jay hit. Courtesy of Vicki Barb and Diana Wolfram.

were even "allowed to stay up a little late, for mother thought it likely that he'd try to get home before we were asleep."[17]

Jay rounded the top of Copper Ridge sometime before 8:00 p.m. He was now back in Knox County, and despite the darkness, he may confidently have increased throttle as Clinton Pike began its gradual, mile-and-a-half descent toward Beaver Creek. Reportedly, Knox County highways were superior to those in Anderson, and Jay might have agreed with the judgment that sections of Clinton Pike south of Copper Ridge were "unusually good." Jay cut down the hill, passing farmland and the few spots of curtained light visible here and there among the lonely houses. His headlamps revealed a

Aerial photo of the area near Bell's Bridge, circa 1940. Structures visible in the photo include Charles McConnell house (A), William Dew's former blacksmith cottage (B), Samuel Bell's house (C), and Bell's Bridge (D) along Clinton Pike. The newer, wider Clinton Highway splits the image diagonally. McConnell owned the light-colored store wedged between the two roads. Other structures existing in 1916—Dew's blacksmith shop and grain mill, and Fort Menifee—had been torn down by the time this photo was taken. Courtesy of TVA Maps.

two-story house on the right near the primitive Fort Menifee, and as the car sloped down the grade, the iron girders of Bell's Bridge emerged from the dark, along with the grain mill on the opposite bank of the creek. If Jay were at all drowsy at this point in the journey, the car wheels bumping onto the bridge and loudly rumbling over its wooden deck likely would have roused him. Cars had a hard time crossing the creek quietly, as nearby residents knew too well. But on this night, an unfamiliar sound followed.[18]

Just seconds after passing the creek's south bank, Jay lost control of the car. Perhaps the wheels hit a rock or a rutted patch of road. But the car suddenly jerked toward the east side of the "over road," striking an embankment and sending Jay's chin hard into the steering wheel's dome-shaped bolt. The Model T's high center of gravity made it prone to tip-overs, and as the car rolled sideways off the bank, Jay was thrown facedown into the road and the Model T landed on top of him. Assuming the car was still in gear and the impact did not stall the motor, the raised rear wheel probably continued to spin until fuel flow to the tilted carburetor stopped and the motor died, extinguishing the headlights and blanketing the scene of the accident in darkness.[19]

William Dew, fifty-five, owned and operated the grain mill on the south bank of the creek, on the west side of the pike. He also had a blacksmith shop and a small L-shaped cottage where he had raised his family. According to his son Joe, Will did not work at the shop much but instead leased it out, providing the cottage nearby where the blacksmith could live; Dew would take a share of the blacksmith's income. The smith would also be responsible for sharpening the tools and saws and maintaining farm implements, and possibly straightening bent fenders of neighborhood autos. While census records that list Dew, his wife, and daughters do not show a blacksmith or any other hired hands on the property, there could have been such a person living there in 1916. According to that year's Knoxville directory, two blacksmiths resided somewhere on Clinton Pike from where it branched off of Asylum Avenue out to the county line. One lived in Lonsdale. The other, John R. Young, had a blacksmith shop on the west side of the pike and a house on the east side, in residential district eight. However, with Dew's cottage located on the west side of the pike, and because Dew himself is not listed in the directory, it is unlikely that Young was the smith who worked for him. Another possibility is Martin Roop, who in 1910 lived close to the Dews and worked as a blacksmith at a local tree nursery.[20]

The Charles McConnell family also lived nearby, immediately south of the Dews. In addition to their five children, Victoria McConnell was preg-

Looking north past the porch of Charles McConnell's house, a two-story building on Will Dew's property is visible in the background. The structure's function is not known, but it may have been part of Dew's grain mill, with the blacksmith shop attached or nearby. The new two-lane Clinton Highway, built in 1929, is barely visible to the right of the building. Courtesy of Vicki Barb and Diana Wolfram.

nant with a sixth and would deliver him ten days later. Living so near the site, Charles, a forty-year-old merchant, had almost certainly heard Jay's car turn over, as had Will Dew next door.[21]

Because there were at least a few occupied houses within a stone's throw of the crash site, it is surprising that the first person to find the wreck was not a neighbor but another motorist passing by on the pike. Stanley Tinsley had left Knoxville that evening, headed toward Clinton on a motorcycle. He was employed at the Motorcycle Store, a Harley-Davidson and Excelsior dealer on Gay Street, and was well known in the South for competitive racing. In September 1915 he broke records at Cal Johnson's racetrack near Chilhowee Park, where on his Excelsior he rode the half-mile in under thirty-three seconds. The same year, he completed a round trip from Knoxville to Chattanooga in seven hours, thirty-one minutes. "The way it worked, he sold motorcycles. And if you sold them and you raced them, and you won, then your sales went up," said Tinsey's son, Sam. "I think he was sort of an adventurer in his younger days. . . . I don't think he was a blowhard at all, but he was an adventurer. And the motorcycle thing attracted him."[22]

Not far from the bridge, Stanley Tinsley's single headlight caught a dark mass lying across the road, and, getting closer, he was shocked to discover it was a late-model Tin Lizzie on its side, with a man's body caught face down beneath it. Tracks leading up the roadside embankment showed where the car had flipped. Tinsley parked his motorcycle nearby and probably called out to the man and checked for signs of life, but got no response, movement, or pulse. He had no idea how much time had passed since the crash and needed to find a few men to lift the car off the victim.[23]

Dew and McConnell might have been outside their houses already by the time Tinsley arrived. Whatever the case, Tinsley and a few bystanders were able to lift the car. The Model T weighed about fifteen hundred pounds and could probably be righted by three strong men. Perhaps the car was lifted partway and the body pulled free before the car was settled back on its wheels. The victim was carried to the blacksmith shop. He was dead as far as bystanders could tell, but Tinsley telephoned for a doctor anyway from a nearby house—most likely Dew's or McConnell's. Who was the dead man? There had to be registration papers somewhere in the car, either in the stor-age area beneath the rear seat cushion or in a carrying pouch accessory that was strapped to the steering column. The car's papers were almost certainly found, because a call was made to the car's registered owner, Ty-Sa-Man Machine Company.[24]

Up the hill from Bell's Bridge, across the north bank of the creek, the lights were on at Samuel Bell's place, the last house Jay Agee had passed before reaching the bridge, about four hundred feet away. One can imagine Bell, a farmer in his late sixties, stepping off his porch and hastening down the road to help, while curious faces inside the house peered out the south windows. His daughter, Beulah, taught school in Powell's Station and lived with her parents. She did not see the crash and did not walk down to where it happened—which many women in those days would have considered improper. But she remembered people visiting the house that night and the next day, talking about the wreck and how sad it was that the man died so young: "He was a healthy, handsome man, and he had a pretty wife and two little children. What a pity!"[25]

Back in West Knoxville, Laura was worried, wondering why Jay had not arrived home yet. She already had told the children to "go on to bed and straight to sleep," Rufus later recalled, "and after a great deal of protesting, we knew we were beaten. . . . So we went to bed, determined to stay awake until he came, and restive with the promise that if he didn't come too late, we would see him. But try as we did to stay awake, we fell asleep—early enough that we did not hear the phone call which came at about eleven." Rufus might have speculated about the time and the method of communication. While the Agees' telephone undoubtedly rang that night, Hazel Lee Goff remembered how news of the accident first reached Laura: "When the husband of your very best friend dies, and under such tragic circumstances, it's not a thing you forget easily. . . . A man from Ty-Sa-Man Company where Jay worked came to the house in the middle of the night, all excited and shouting that Jay had been 'hurt bad' in a wreck. Laura called her twin brother, Hugh Tyler, and he went to the scene and returned to tell her Jay was dead." Arthur Savage was likely the Ty-Sa-Man employee who first notified Laura of the accident, as Rufus later wrote that Arthur drove Hugh out Clinton Pike to Bell's Bridge.[26]

Dr. William Delpuech, who delivered both Rufus and Emma, had just turned fifty-eight on May 17. As a friend and close neighbor of the Tylers, perhaps Delpuech came at the family's request; it is even plausible that he rode with Arthur and Hugh to the accident site. Or perhaps it was just by coincidence that Delpuech was summoned to Powell's Station that night, responding to Tinsley's call, and learned only on arrival that the victim was Jay Agee. But the presence that night of another city physician, William Cochrane, suggests that two separate calls were indeed made. After both doctors confirmed that Jay was dead, they conducted no autopsy but deduced from the circumstances that Jay "met death either by a broken neck from concussions received on the chin" or by suffocating under the Model T's weight. The car itself escaped the crash relatively unscathed, suffering only minor cosmetic damage.[27]

Several theories were offered to explain the accident's cause, but no one who investigated the site had a conclusive answer. Some pointed to the condition of the road. While Clinton Pike was overall well maintained through Knox County, the road at the accident site was "rather rough." Being a fairly low spot at the base of a ridge, the macadam or gravel pavement there probably washed away during heavy rains, when Beaver Creek could rise high enough to reach the front porch of Will Dew's cottage (the flooded, muddy creek would also shut down his grain mill, which needed clean water for its boiler). Rufus remembered when spring rains sometimes made the "roads not good enough to go to LaFollette." While the first half of May was relatively dry, more than four and a quarter inches had fallen in Knoxville during March and April; towns to the north, like Clinton, had received even greater amounts. On early Model T's, the "wishbone" suspension attached above the front axle, rather than below it, making the T particularly unstable over rough roads and causing its drive wheels to shimmy. Lacking any shock absorption, the wheels would "dance and hop, becoming intermittently airborne at anything above a relative crawl." And if the front wheel hit a rut or pothole, the wishbone flexed, shifting the wheel's caster angle rearward.[28]

Another explanation was that a "small stone" or some other object in the road caused the wheels "to turn quickly so as to run up the side of the embankment." In addition to poor suspension, the Model T's three-to-one steering gear ratio provided little leverage for a driver trying to control his vehicle. Even with the car parked and the driver anticipating it, someone pushing against one of the front tires could easily wrench the steering wheel out of his hands. Traveling at twenty miles an hour or more on a narrow road, Jay would not have had time to correct the steering if a stone suddenly knocked the wheels aside to full lock—especially if he failed to see the rock in the headlights' weak beams.[29]

A third explanation was simply that Jay was driving too fast. Both Knoxville newspapers opined that excessive speed was the primary cause. "It is thought that Mr. Agee was going at a very fast rate," the *Sentinel* reported, "as the pike just before coming to the scene of the accident is in excellent condition," allowing smooth acceleration. The *Journal* stated that "it is probable that Mr. Agee was going at a fast speed." According to one Model T owner, "Keeping the speed from increasing, downhill, is absolutely critical because beyond a certain value, the car will begin uncommanded acceleration and once that starts, all the driver can do is steer as best as possible and hope not to hit anything."[30]

A fourth theory is one Rufus might have heard from family members— that a cotter pin came loose from the steering mechanism. If not for one fact, this is certainly plausible. Model T owners can recount stories of accidents caused when a cotter pin was not in place, and a nut backed itself off a bolt, causing the linkage to disconnect and the steering to go wobbly as the car ran off the road. But those who inspected Jay's wrecked automobile reportedly "failed to disclose any defect in the steering apparatus." The car was deemed drivable.[31]

A fifth reason for the accident was told many years later and is probably the product of a faulty memory. Ann Taylor Brown, Rufus's childhood friend, remembered hearing about the death of his father: "He was driving his T-Model on Clinton Pike near what is now Emory Road. The motor of the car died, the lights went out, and the automobile ran off the road and overturned." As mentioned, the headlights were powered by the flywheel's magneto coils, so if the motor quit, the lights would indeed go out. But those who reported the accident probably did not consider this theory, since the car was drivable after the wreck.[32]

A sixth explanation, and seemingly the most popularly embraced, is that Jay was drunk. It is possible that back before sobriety checkpoints and Breathalyzer tests, drivers regularly got away with some level of inebriation behind the wheel and that accidents were discreetly blamed on bad roads and excessive speeds. Rufus's later writings reveal that his parents argued about his father's drinking and that after Jay's death the family seemed reluctant to consider that his drunkenness caused the wreck. If Jay had been drinking that night, the men who lifted his prostrate body off the road and the doctors who briefly examined it may have overlooked the odor of whiskey. But the evidence is silent on the matter. Years later, when Hazel Goff was questioned on this issue, she responded, "The Agees were not teetotalers; they served a social drink on special occasions. But I never saw Jay drinking in all the years I knew him."[33]

Goff explained what she thought caused the crash: "Laura always felt— and I do, too—that Jay fell asleep at the wheel. He had been working late the night before and had driven to the mountains to see his ailing father later that day. He never liked to stay away from his family all night, so he started home after midnight and ran off the road before he could get there." Despite Goff confusing the time of Jay's return trip to Knoxville, her assertion is reasonable. Driver fatigue must have contributed to the accident.[34]

The night of the crash, Stanley Tinsley, presumably, found out the car was registered to Ty-Sa-Man, and called the machine shop to report the accident and give directions to Will Dew's property. Arthur and Hugh made the roughly ten-mile journey, probably arrived while the doctors were still there (especially if Dr. Delpuech rode with them), and learned that Jay had indeed died. They might have taken the body to a Knoxville mortuary that night. Rufus later remembered a mortician named Roberts. Carl Roberts was a well-known undertaker at the time, whose funeral home was located on Union Avenue. Unfortunately, there are no records, not even a death certificate, to show which mortuary received Jay's body.[35]

Before leaving the crash site, Arthur Savage asked one of the bystanders to drive the wrecked company car back to Ty-Sa-Man's office. Among those men gathered near Bell's Bridge was Nicolai Knoph. Born in Copenhagen, Nick worked in the Smokies as a trainmaster for the Little River Lumber Company. On the job he somehow met a young woman, Neta Reagan, who lived with her parents in Powell's Station. He had arrived by train that evening and was presumably at the Reagan house when Jay Agee wrecked his Model T. How Nick ended up near Bell's Bridge is therefore somewhat of a mystery, since he would have been well out of earshot of the crash. The Reagans did not live near that part of Beaver Creek, but about two miles east of there, on Spring Street, near the Knoxville Brick Company plant where Neta's father was superintendent. But Ty-Sa-Man had done work for John Reagan, making him a likely acquaintance of Arthur's. Perhaps Arthur knew John was a local man of resource and called to explain the situation, and John responded by driving his future son-in-law to Bell's Bridge. That night, Nick Knoph was apparently one of the few in the area who knew how to operate an automobile. And however he happened on the scene, he agreed to drive the Model T to the machine shop in Knoxville. His girlfriend knew the way.[36]

As Nick and Neta drove out to White Avenue, possibly following Arthur's car there, it occurred to the young couple that the machine company now had a job opening and that if Nick could get a job there, he could live in Knoxville and be closer to Powell's Station. When they arrived at Ty-Sa-Man, they left the car with one of the owners, and Nicolai—or perhaps Neta, who was "much more aggressive," according to their son—asked him if the deceased man's job was still available. The couple also confessed their desire to marry but that Nick "wouldn't take a bride to the logging camp at Elkmont." After listening to their request, Joel Tyler asked Nick, "Young man, do you curse?" Knoph answered, "Mr. Tyler, I log with oxen." Joel, amused at the reply, hired him on the spot, and presumably lent him the Model T to drive back to Powell. Perhaps Joel, as a former lumberman, felt a kinship with the Dane. Joel kept him as a bookkeeper for several years before making him a partner around 1924. Knoph stayed with the company for more than thirty years, buying the company with his son in 1950.[37]

By the time Knoph delivered the Model T to Joel Tyler, Arthur and Hugh had probably made it back to the Agee home, where Hugh had the terrible task of reporting Jay's death to Laura. With the multiple visitors calling and other unusual activity at that time of night, the neighbors likely knew something was wrong. Possibly, in the stillness, they could sense the family's grief.

SPIRITS

While the Tylers were assembled in the Agee living room, something strange happened. As family members sat comforting one another, they suddenly felt an additional but unseen presence, which some of them interpreted as Jay's spirit returning to say goodbye. Hugh Tyler later verified the story, telling Father Flye that the family "did feel [Jay's] presence in the room" that night; Flye trusted his testimony, since Hugh was not a "credulous person." Considering the deep grief felt that night and the longing to at least say goodbye to Jay, the anecdote seems somewhat believable. What makes the occurrence incredible is that it was not the first unexplained phenomenon the family had experienced.[38]

In March 1892, Joel Tyler wrote two letters to parapsychologist Richard Hodgson, of the American Society for Psychical Research, to report what was probably "a case of auditory collective hallucination." The Tylers had then only been in Knoxville four months, and their household at 2309 Magnolia Avenue consisted of Joel, Emma, twins Laura and Hugh, Jessie, matriarch Sarah Tyler, and a hired servant. Around 3 p.m. on February 24, Joel and Emma were in their bedroom when they heard a woman speaking. He thought it was Emma's voice, while she had thought it was her mother-in-law's. "We immediately looked in the hall and in the adjoining room, and also on the verandah, through the glass door, and could see no one," Joel wrote. "We did this instantly, and so quickly that no one would have had time to get out of sight, and especially without making any noise. . . . The voice seemed to come or rather to be right in the room with us, and as you know it is hardly possible to confound the voice of persons in the same room with one coming from another room, and certainly impossible when that other room is on another floor, or separated from the room in which the hearer is, by other rooms." In his second letter, Joel confessed to Hodgson that he had dabbled in the occult practice of "automatic scrawling" both with and without the aid of a "planchette," a small triangular pencil holder on wheels that is held lightly in the hand to facilitate "automatic" writing. He also reported a separate occurrence that other family members experienced a few months prior:

> My sister [Jessie Tyler], who spent the winter in Fla. with my mother [Sarah Tyler], tells me she had two very disturbed nights there, following soon after the sudden death of my uncle [Dr. Ira Fisk], which occurred at the hotel where they stayed.
>
> The disturbance took the form of rappings which came from all parts of the room, being in the walls and ceiling, and continued for two successive nights. At this time they had just moved into a room above the one in which my uncle had died. She has had a similar experience once before. If you care to have it, I will try to prevail upon her to write the account, although she does not wish her name to appear in connection with it, and is quite reluctant to speak of it.
>
> She is very intelligent, and not at all superstitious.
>
> Very truly,
J. C. TYLER.[39]

A few things are noteworthy about Joel Tyler's testimony. First, these reports immediately relate to the later, nonaudible episode the night Jay died when the family sensed his spirit moving throughout the house. Second, Joel Tyler seems more open in these letters to the possibility of "psychic" activity, compared to the way Rufus portrays his grandfather's skeptical response to the "presence" felt by other family members, although even here Joel rationalizes his experience as a "hallucination." Third, with these letters plus Rufus's apparently factual novel account, we have a record of four such incidents experienced by the Tyler family—a presence felt after Jay's death in 1916, a voice heard by Joel and Emma in 1892, knocking heard by Jessie and her mother in 1891, and Jessie's earlier, "similar experience"—that could be interpreted as psychic activity. Apparently, it was not the family's last such experience. Years later, in his eighties, Hugh Tyler claimed that the ghost of his late wife, Mildred, resided with him in his Kent, Connecticut, home.[40]

NEWS

If the neighbors had wondered what was going on at the Agee house late Thursday night, May 18, many of them found out Friday morning. News of the accident had already begun to spread, as the morning *Journal and Tribune* carried this headline on page fourteen: "FOUND DEAD ON CLINTON PIKE—James Agee, of This City, Pinned Under Automobile, When Car Struck Embankment and Overturned." The article reported that Tinsley "was taking a party of men to Clinton in an automobile" when they "found the wreck lying across the road."[41]

While many Knoxvillians read the morning paper, Rufus and Emma woke as usual. Rufus later recalled that his main objective that morning was to find his father and show off what Aunt Jessie had bought him the previous afternoon: a new cap, of which Rufus thought his father would approve. But then Emma and he were told the sad and confusing news that their father would not be coming home again. After realizing that he was not going to school that day, Rufus wandered outside, where he talked to other neighborhood children on their way to school. Some of them had already read or been told about the article by the time Rufus saw them. Martin Southern, almost eleven years old at the time, lived three houses east from the Agees and later wrote of being "shocked" by Rufus's "blithe announcement" that his father had died. However, Martin's son Donn believed his father's reaction was less shock than indifference: "I wish I could recall exactly what Daddy told us he said to Rufus when they crossed paths a few days after

Rufus's father's funeral but my guess is that it was something like, 'I heard your Dad died,' and the answer was probably 'yeah.' I think our father was a little embarrassed in later years that he wasn't a little more sympathetic."[42]

Mrs. Tripp had heard disturbances coming from the Agee house Thursday night but apparently had not read the newspaper by the time Alvin and Arthur Tripp left the house the next morning. She warned her boys, "Well, don't go next door because from what I could hear last night that woman was having plenty [of] trouble with him, probably on a drinking spree." Alvin remembered walking with his brother to the playground that morning to play baseball. But since Friday was a school day, the ball game might have happened Saturday morning instead. "I saw Rufus when we were leaving the house," Alvin remembered. "He was on his walkway to his house. I think I nodded to him but didn't speak because it surprised me coming so soon after what my mother had said. Further down the street, I remember looking back at him and saying to my brother, 'Maybe we should have asked him to come along with us, he looked so lonely.' Arthur answered he didn't think that would do any good since Rufus was so strange and odd looking the way he moved; and we were going to play a game at the playground. . . . I told him that was because he had never learned to play ball and was awkward. Arthur answered that was just what he had meant and with a game coming up, it was no time to learn." The Tripps did not realize that Rufus looked especially lonely because he had just lost his father.

"It was a day or so later that we learned what had really happened next door," wrote Alvin. "I told Mother that I had heard that Rufus' father had died and that the commotion she had heard wasn't what she had thought it to be." According to Alvin, his mother felt the death did not affect Laura at all. Her response to the news seems to indicate a degree of animosity between the two families, as Rufus had remembered. "Much difference it had made," said Mrs. Tripp. "The funeral and all was over with in one day, [and] the woman was back at her sweeping and all."[43]

Frank Agee sent word to Alliance, Nebraska, where John worked as a civil engineer with the U.S. Department of the Interior and lived with Annabel and their infant daughter, Gladys. John and Annabel knew that his father was not doing well. When a telegram was delivered to the house that morning, Annabel opened it, expecting news that Henry Clay Agee had died. She recalled that it was "such a shock when I read, 'Jim killed last night Car turned over embankment Father no better Love Frank.'" She did not know what to say to her husband as she handed the telegram to him. "I'll never forget the grief on his face," she later wrote. Annabel and John were sorry to miss the funeral, but traveling by train all the way to Knoxville with a seven-month-old was not something they could presently endure. Annabel would visit in September.[44]

Another article appeared Friday evening. The Motorcycle Store, where Stanley Tinsley worked, sat adjacent to the *Sentinel* office on Gay Street. Presumably, a reporter from that paper had walked next door and interviewed Tinsley that morning. Whereas the *Journal* only briefly mentioned Tinsley, the *Sentinel* article relied heavily on him as an eyewitness, twice using the phrase "Mr. Tinsley states." The article, "Automobile Accident Fatal For James Agee—Body Is Found on Clinton Pike, Face Downward Pinned Under Machine," reports that Tinsley "was riding out the pike on a motorcycle," rather than in an automobile with other men—although "a party of men" might well have arrived at the scene by car not long after Tinsley—and also described Clinton Pike as "rather rough" at the spot where Jay's car lost control. The *Journal* article was published too early to include funeral arrangements, which were made by the time the evening *Sentinel* article appeared. The funeral would be conducted the following afternoon at the Tyler home, with burial to follow at Greenwood Cemetery.[45]

The story of the accident as fictionalized in *A Death in the Family* differed in several respects from the newspaper accounts. The paper reported that Jay was found facedown beneath the car; in the novel the body came to rest a foot away from the car, face up. The paper indicated there was nothing wrong with the car's steering; the novel suggested that the steering went wobbly when a cotter pin worked itself loose. If the novel's version was truly based on what Rufus's family told him about the accident, a possible explanation for the discrepancies is that Hugh Tyler attempted to soften the emotional blow to Laura by altering details—reporting that Jay's body was found uncrushed following an unpreventable crash. Rufus's later written account contains these conflicting details as well as some erroneous information, such as mistaking the site of the accident as "just on the north side of Bell's Bridge, on Ball Camp Pike." Although newspaper reports did not identify the exact location of the Clinton Pike wreck, it is now generally believed to have occurred south of the bridge. As remembered—or imagined—by Rufus, "The roadside, near the bridge, dips sharply down towards the creek" into a "sort of flat, wide ditch, about five feet down from the road" before rising "up an eight-foot embankment." Despite his apparent certainty about such details, Rufus later wrote, "I cannot even remember who it was who found my father."[46]

That forgotten man quit "the motorcycle selling and racing business" a few years after the accident and founded a successful Knoxville company, Tinsley

Stanley Tinsley on his motorcycle, 1914.
Knoxville Journal and Tribune, July 3, 1914.

Tires, which he later passed on to his sons. He never told them about the car wreck. By March 21, 1946, almost thirty years had elapsed since he had discovered the overturned Model T. That evening, Stanley Hale Tinsley was traveling home, probably along Cumberland Avenue, when he collapsed in his car. He died the same night. It is doubtful that Rufus ever met Tinsley or recalled his name. But when *A Death in the Family* came out more than a decade later, it contained veiled praise for the stranger who had called for help on Clinton Pike: "He was just as fine as a human being can be." Sam Tinsley, who was twenty-one when his father died, said that he had "always been sort of interested in this story, since it involved my dad."[47]

FUNERAL

Saturday, May 20, 1916. Two days before sharing a thirty-second birthday with Hugh and exactly one month before her ten-year wedding anniversary, Laura Agee had to bury her husband. That morning, the Reverend William C. Robertson arrived from Chattanooga, where since 1901 he had been rector of Christ Church—located on the corner of Douglas Street and McCallie Avenue, which today borders the University of Tennessee, Chattanooga. Jessie Tyler resided on Mabel Street, several blocks from the church, and likely had something to do with the clergyman's trip to Knoxville. But

Robertson was also well acquainted with the Reverend Walter Whitaker, rector of St. John's Episcopal, and on occasion had preached before the Knoxville congregation. As both churches were members of the Diocese of Tennessee, Robertson and Whitaker had also attended the organization's annual convention in Chattanooga on May 10 and 11. Now, less than a week and a half later, they were co-officiating Jay's funeral service.[48]

Rufus later wrote extensively about the day of the funeral. His notes reveal his uncertainty about many of the details, and contain as many questions about the events as memories. His recollections include seeing his father's body before the other guests arrived and then a second time when the room was full of people, the way the body looked in the coffin, being prayed over by Father Robertson, being shepherded through the Tyler house by family members, and staying at the Savages' house with Emma while the rest of his family attended the burial. "Morning of funeral, we were brought down to 1115," Rufus wrote.

> I think we walked. I remember Mother's face, through the veil. He was in the living-room (& Grandma would mention this room without consciousness of any irony: Grandpa overhearing her?). Over the colored-tiled hearth of the never-used fireplace. The coffin: was it open all the way down, or down to the waist? I remember the hand (right hand I think), laid over his stomach (the other along his side); the veins were strong in it and it looked as three-dimensional as if I had seen it through a stereoscope. The lower lip had a deep narrow bruise in it. There was another just under the point of the chin; but it looked strong and quiet, not swollen or in any way misshapen, but more conspicuous or focused because of the bruise. (Did someone, now or before or later, say, "Not another mark on him"? Did Hugh say something about their having wanted to powder and rouge him?) The black points of beard, shaven off close against the lifeless chin, made the jaw blue. The eyes were quietly shut. I think someone said, "He looks just as if he was asleep."
>
> As I remember it we were brought in first to see him alone, & unmolested. Then I think but am not sure, that I sneaked back in. Then if I remember rightly we were formally brought in once more, by Mother and perhaps Aunt Jessie, with Fr. Robertson, and I realized faintly that he was the boss of this occasion, and obscurely resented his bossiness and intrusion, his sureness of his right to be there. We were told we could look at our Daddy once more and that then we would not see him any more (?), then we were told to kneel down. We knelt down (I looking at the hand?) and each of us felt a hard hand, heavily clasping over the skull, and he said "The peace of God &c &c". Nothing more, I think. I had a faint sense that the water for a moment became enormously deep beneath me, that all direction was lost. When we came out was Hugh in the hall and was I startled and mystified by the rage that blazed through the grief in his eyes?[49]

The funeral began at one o'clock that afternoon, and Rufus was "pretty sure" he was taken to the Savages' home for lunch beforehand:

> I should find out what they fixed for Mother and what she ate. Or did we eat at the Savages (& did he come for us in his car?) By the time we left the house the chairs had arrived in a great load and were being arranged in rows, and I suppose we must by then have seen and smelled some of the flowers. During the morning (& the 2 days before) we must often have been told to sit quietly and be a good boy & girl. Did we talk, & if so, about him? But this time particularly, we must have been cleaned up early in the morning, and so, kept particularly still. Yes I am pretty sure we had dinner at the Savages. We were told to be good and we would be called for and we would see Daddy once more. I imagine what was done was, that we had lunch there and were then brought back up, then back again to the Savages. (Was Walter involved in any of this? I seem to remember his strongly hostile eyes in connection with it).[50]

It is unknown whether "Walter" was a reference to Dr. Walter Whitaker, the rector of St. John's Episcopal whom few if any would have ever described as "strongly hostile." If so, perhaps Dr. Whitaker disagreed with the decision that Rufus and Emma would not attend the funeral. Whitaker remained an influential figure in Rufus's life over the next few years as the boy became immersed in church ritual.

> When we got back to 1115 it was bright early afternoon. (Were the horses &c there yet?) As we came in through the screen door into the dark hall, we were drowned in the odor of flowers and in the near-silence of densely-crowded, uneasy people. A very different atmosphere from the coldly lighted East Room. Before I even knew they were there I knew it—deep from the country, much more wild and grim. How was all this done? I suspect we were brought back with a double purpose—that, more especially because we were not going to the funeral, it was felt that we simply had, for appearances' sake, to put in an appearance, if only a short one, and take the last look to satisfy the guests; also, to meet our father's relatives & to satisfy *their* sense of propriety. But also, they probably felt it was our right & their duty.
>
> I don't remember which-of-what happened first: meeting them, (& Frank, & hearing the wailings), or being brought into the living room and past the coffin (& did Mother take us past? I doubt it.) I do remember our going past, and seeing him, quite briefly, again. Very different in this context. I was most appalled by & interested in the strength of the odor of the flowers, & all their scarves and ribbons, and the feeling that everybody was looking at us. We went out (guided) through the Green Room.
>
> East-room: I think we were taken in to our Grandmother. Or was she brought out to us? I am not sure: I think she took us both and said "Bless your hearts". I think we were so maneuvered as not to meet most of them; hasty excuses about

our being so young; that John was very clean and rosily pale; that Frank made a stumbling, sobbing rush for us and bellowed, heavily drunk with whiskey strong & sour on his breath, how it was all his fault, he'd never forgive himself, never; and who? Hugh? Frank's mother? Both? Hurried to him saying *control yourself,* and the mother comforting him.[51]

The identity of "John" is unclear in these notes. Perhaps Rufus forgot that his uncle John Henry Agee was actually living in Nebraska at the time. Or perhaps he was thinking of his grandfather Henry, whom he renamed (or misnamed) John Henry in his novel. If Henry Clay was indeed "very gravely sick," it seems unlikely he would have attended the funeral. Because few embellishments are evident in these notes, with Rufus remaining quite tentative in his version of the story, the incident involving Frank's drunkenness seems credible. But when the novel was published, some family members took offense at the way Rufus portrayed Frank, and in some respects the writer's local legacy suffered as a result.[52]

Other funeral guests included friends of the family, like the Delpuechs from across the street, the Goffs, the Glenns, the Salmons, the Kings, and Laura's friend Marcia Perkins. According to Rufus, six men—his uncles Hugh Tyler, Frank Agee and Charles Hodges, plus Oliver King, Clifford Glenn, "and a man whom [he] had never seen before"—carried his father's "long, gray, shining" coffin "down the curved brick walk from the house to the street."[53]

The hearse was parked along the sidewalk in front of the Tylers' Clinch Avenue home. Rufus wrote, "When we come out the hearse" is "already drawn up with the black & chestnut horses." Laura's close friend, Hazel Goff, remembered that the large "hearse that took Jay to the cemetery was . . . beautifully decorated. The horses wore black ribbon rosettes on the sides of their heads and they stepped along the route with a measured tread—all very solemn." Herbert Hall, of Hall & Donahue Undertaking, said that mourners "would have been deeply offended if the driver had permitted the horses to go in any other gait than a walk. That was indeed dignified, but on a long trip it certainly was hard on the undertaker." While "motor hearses" were widely used by the mid-1920s, horses still pulled Knoxville hearses in the teens, as during the funeral procession that carried Tennessee senator Robert Love "Bob" Taylor's remains to Old Gray Cemetery in 1912.[54]

Rufus and Emma did not go to the cemetery but were taken again to the Savages' house at 707 Third (now Eleventh) Street, a couple of blocks southeast of the Tylers'. While Arthur Savage attended the burial, his wife, Hortense, babysat Rufus and Emma. To counteract the afternoon's heaviness, she played the children some upbeat and humorous phonograph records, a few of which Rufus remembered in his notes: "Too Much Mustard," a 1913 recording by the Victor Military Band; an unidentified record featuring the lyric "a pritt-ty lit-tle rabbit, and a *hunt*-ah"; a recording of Irish baritone Harry Lauder; and "Cohen at the Telephone," a 1915 comedic monologue by George L. Thompson.[55]

While at the house, Mrs. Savage also taught Rufus and Emma the best way to read "funny-books," as Rufus remembered: "Funnies: we are told how to read them. You lie down on your little stomachs. And you put your elbows down and your hands up under your chins. And you cross your feet, and bend them legs at the knee, and swing the feet *gently* back and forth, just like this. See? And then when you want to turn the page, you turn it like *this*, just reaching out with one hand. Does she say, just like a picture in a story-book or do I get that as an association? I am slightly embarrassed & bewildered but on the whole, rather pleased to have found out how to do it right, though it *does* seem a little bit sissy." Of the books Mrs. Savage showed him that day, Rufus wrote, "The only 2 I am sure I remember are Buster Brown & Foxy Grandpa. Maybe also Lady Bountiful, and Slim Jim & the Force, I'm not sure. I particularly remember Buster Brown's hard, round, terrible eyes & those of his dog." Mrs. Savage served refreshments, though what kind—"Candy? Iced tea? Fruit punch or grape juice?"—Rufus could not recall.[56]

That spring, the Savages may have added some much needed color to their "completely bare" yard. A neighbor, Karl Steinmetz, who lived behind on Fourth Street, planted "a long row of chrysanthemums" that caught Arthur's eye. Karl's flowers "bloomed so beautifully that . . . Savage went out and bought some to plant in his own very small backyard." He had a knack for gardening, and Karl said that Arthur "was either born with a natural talent for growing flowers or else he studied hard and learned it quickly. He was good at it." Rufus recalled that Arthur wore glasses with "large lenses" and "suits as brown and hairy as his mustache." In 1917, Arthur and Hortense moved to a larger property in Fountain City, where he opened his first rock garden—landscaped "with lily pool and bridge and effective Japanese pagoda with stone lanterns . . . and a profusion of flowers." Now known as Savage House and Garden, the private property is part of Garden Montessori School.[57]

GREENWOOD

The funeral party arrived at Greenwood Cemetery on Tazewell Pike in North Knoxville. It was a hot afternoon at eighty-three degrees, but still several degrees cooler than the previous Saturday. Upon seeing the decorated grounds some mourners may have noted that Jay could not have been buried on a more beautiful weekend. The whole cemetery was in bloom.[58]

On Thursday afternoon, before Jay left his parents' home in Jacksboro, Flower Day ceremonies had been held, during which all of the graves were "strewn with beautiful floral tributes" by the Greenwood Cemetery Flower Association and relatives of the deceased. Dr. Walter Whitaker had been the featured speaker that day, presenting a sermon titled "The Larger Life." As he spoke about what happens to the soul at death, he unwittingly addressed questions that Laura and other family members would ponder late that night as they sensed Jay's spirit enter the house. "God has set eternity in man's heart," said Whitaker.

> Human beings alone strive for what is beyond sense and experience. We are ever coming to ultimates and mysteries. Time and space are two of these, and we have to accept them and act in them. We cannot think of space as unbounded. Equally we cannot think of it as being limited. So of time. They are too vast for reason or for imagination to dogmatize about.
>
> Personality is a greater mystery than time and space. How is it possible for invisible personalities to communicate through material channels and for the physical to act on the spiritual as sound and motion stir the soul? The fact we know, and the fact we live by, but the law is a permanent mystery of life. . . .
>
> Individual destiny is shrouded at the grave, but it is not terminated. That the wires are down in a storm, and communication is suspended does not make us declare that the intelligent beings who were canvassing have been annihilated. No one can dogmatize negatively on the continual existence of the soul. The worst that any can say is, 'I don't know.' . . .
>
> Standing today amid the graves of our loved ones where all speaks of labors that are finished and of ties that are broken, our faith takes shape in a five-fold conviction as to those who are gone, whose memory is dear to us. . . .
>
> Personality continues unbroken, through the change of death, and the true self lives apart from the no longer needed instruments of earthly association. . . .
>
> It is true we cannot hear each other speak. But absence from those we really love is not forgetfulness of them. Often it happens that the dead are closer to us than when they lived. The little differences no longer arise, and we know them and are known by them, and soul can merge in soul as never before.[59]

The newspaper reports that Whitaker and Robertson conducted Jay's funeral jointly on May 20. Although Dr. Whitaker does not appear as a character in *A Death in the Family*, he is mentioned by name in its text, and comments about him indicate that Whitaker was well liked by Rufus and the family. However, Rufus wrote that he "obscurely resented" the visiting minister's "bossiness and intrusion, his sureness of his right to be there." It is true that some members of Christ Church were dissatisfied with the Reverend Robertson during his tenure. Some complained about his endorsing the High Church practice of kneeling during communion. Others found him irresponsible with church funds, as when he made a purchase without first consulting the finance committee, or when he planned additions to the sanctuary even though the church lacked the money to build them. But church records give no indication that Robertson was arrogant and insensitive, certainly not like the fictional priest that stubbornly refused to recite parts of Jay's funeral service. According to Hugh Tyler, the "man who came up from Chattanooga, Father Jackson in the book, was not as bad a fellow as Rufus made him appear." And although he had no firsthand knowledge

The Reverend William Robertson. Courtesy of Christ Church Episcopal, Chattanooga.

Jay Agee's grave, Greenwood Cemetery, 2016. Photo by the author.

of the man, Father Flye reported, "I asked James' mother about that detail and she said he was not that way at all."[60]

And Robertson had no reason to deny certain burial rites, because, in fact, Jay had been baptized at some point. Records from St. John's Episcopal Church show that while he was not a communicant, which would have required receiving communion at least three times during the preceding year, Jay was registered as a "baptized member only." It is assumed he was baptized before Laura and he were married, since there is no record of the baptism at St. John's.[61]

Jay was buried in a newer section of the cemetery. Within a twenty-foot radius, there was only one other grave near his: only a few feet away, a four-year-old girl had been laid to rest about ten days earlier. Jay's grave was marked with a simple chunk of marble, roughly one foot high and two and a half feet across, with name and dates in raised block letters. The stone—inscribed "In His Strength"—was a physical reminder of Jay Agee, something with weight and dimension that would not dissolve with the passage of time. There the family stood as the coffin was lowered into the pit. And there Rufus would stand years later as an adult, noting the epitaph, and perhaps pondering his own mortality.[62]

BUTTERFLY

When he returned home from the burial, Arthur Savage probably drove Rufus and Emma back to the Tyler house. Sometime before supper, late in the afternoon, Uncle Hugh took Rufus for a walk. "I assume the sign is tipped to get me along out of the house for a while, & Hugh does so," wrote Rufus. Although he recalled a few specifics from the walk, like passing the 1914 Confederate "monument" that still sits along Seventeenth Street, he was again tentative about the details. But he clearly remembered what Hugh told him about that afternoon's burial service:

> We walk west out either Clinch or Laurel (monument), a high, fair sunset.
> I feel odd & aware of my best clothes . . . as people move home from their ordi-
> nary business? Little or no talking. I doubt that we touch. Does he say, I expect your
> mother was right but now that I've seen it I wish that you could have been there?
> Does he say anything about or against Father Robertson? (Then [would he have]
> spoken also of the long ride as reason for not taking us? And might [he have] de-
> cided that I should stay home, rather than witness something Emma was deprived
> of?) I vaguely remember some bitter disparagement of the sort, very brief. But
> mainly I remember his needing to tell me about the butterfly. "If I ever believe in
> God, it will be because I remember what I saw today. The coffin, with your father in
> it, was just being lowered and was just level with the ground, when a perfectly *mag-
> nificent* butterfly alighted on it, and just stood there for several seconds while they
> kept on lowering the coffin, the fools, and then a short cloud came off the sun, and
> that had made everything dark, and just *drowned* everything in brightness, and it
> flew up straight at the sun." I don't know what magnificent means but through the
> word and the way he says it I am filled with a mysterious sense of glory. We walk
> to the edge of town (?) past the last blocks of [illegible] bungalows, (?) and a little
> beyond the crest of the hill, and look out over waning, open country. The sun is low,
> and setting. . . . He says abruptly (?) "Let's turn around, now," and we walk back.[63]

They had walked all the way to the ruined earthworks of Fort Sand-
ers. At the time, Clinch Avenue was virtually undeveloped west of modern Eighteenth Street, and Laurel had seen no development west of modern Seventeenth Street—which, by the time of the 1890 veterans' reunion, had been cut directly through the fort.[64]

As indicated by his frequent use of question marks, Rufus could only guess at certain details as he recalled that day's events. His notes include no clear memory of Hugh deriding Father Robertson, whereas in the novel's parallel scene, the uncle rants hatefully about the minister, leaving the impression of a great divide within the family. Laura wrote that Hugh was "hurt" over the portrayal, "that tho[ugh] we never see eye to eye on religion—yet there was not this bitterness" during or after the funeral, "& we were all *one*."[65]

Sometime that next week, Laura visited Jay's parents in Jacksboro. Henry Clay Agee, confined to bed, was clearly distraught and close to death. Besides the debilitating effects of the stroke, the guilt of his son's death was upon him, as he was the reason for Jay's long journey on May 18. Laura remembered her father-in-law lying there when she came in. When he saw her, Henry gestured with a finger towards his chest, and with much effort found enough voice to whisper: "My fault, my fault." He died on June 19, 1916, a month and a day after his son. He was buried in LaFollette at Woodlawn Cemetery. His headstone is inscribed: "Death is eternal life, why should we weep?"[66]

∞∞∞∞∞∞∞∞∞

Jessie Tyler returned to Chattanooga following Jay's funeral. On June 22, Corpus Christi Day, just after Rufus's grandfather Agee was laid to rest, Jessie and Father William Robertson founded St. Gabriel's Convent on McCallie Avenue, a block east from Christ Church.[67]

In September, Annabel Agee and her daughter, Gladys, came to Knoxville and "went to see Laura and the children first thing." Annabel wrote of the conversation she had with Laura about the accident: "I remember her saying, 'And just to think Jay (as she called him) was within 12 miles of home.'" During later visits to Knoxville, John and Annabel tried to spend more time with their nephew. "Rufus would go on rides with us after his father died," Annabel recalled. "I remember driving out in the country—a long time before there were bridges over every creek and we had to just go right through them. It fascinated him. He always wanted to go through another creek." But John and Annabel did not move back to Knoxville until the 1920s. Rufus wrote that, after the death of his father, "I got to see relatively little of his people."[68]

On April 25, 1917, roughly ten months after she buried her first husband, Rufus's grandmother Moss married Thomas Henry Oaks, who had probably worked as a hired hand on the Agee farm. The union was controversial, but not for its timing: Moss's new husband was twenty-seven years her junior—about the same age as John, her youngest son. Decades later, after his own remarriages had raised eyebrows in the family, Rufus stated his approval of Moss's choice: "Grandmother had the same humane understanding and good sense about the whole thing ... that people and their needs and their well-being mean a lot more than any principle."[69]

Barely a year after Rufus lost his father, a similar tragedy struck a family living next door to the Agees at 1501 Highland. Dr. C. E. Lones was about three years older than Jay would have been; his wife, Margaret, was about three years older than Laura; and their daughter was about three years older than Rufus. C. E. got in the car on a warm June evening and headed west out of the city. He had received a call about a sick person and was driving out for a visit. Probably wanting to get there and back before nightfall, C. E. was speeding down the pike, too fast for the sudden sharp curve. Out of control, the car slid onto an embankment at the side of the road and overturned. The impact broke several of Lones's ribs and punctured a lung, and he would die of his injuries about a week later. His body was brought back to 1501 Highland, where the funeral was held on a Wednesday afternoon. Laura Agee understood Margaret's grief and undoubtedly offered the new widow her help and comfort. Perhaps Rufus spoke to the daughter and told her that his daddy had died, too. Dr. Lones was buried at Greenwood Cemetery—about forty feet from Jay Agee.[70]

4

"Tell Me Who I Am"
Transitions, 1917–1925

The United States entered the Great War in early April 1917. In notes Rufus later wrote about this period, statements like "The War is Declared" suggest his early awareness of the overseas conflict that produced daily front-page headlines in Knoxville's papers—including stories of orphaned Belgians whose parents were "killed in the war." In the few years leading up to U.S. involvement, Rufus overheard his grandfather talking about "the Rooshuns" and "Brave-Little-Belgium, too proud to fight." Joel had contributed ten dollars in 1914 to *Life* magazine's charity drive to help Europeans "made homeless and destitute by the war." Bernadotte Schmitt, a University of Tennessee Rhodes scholar who lived a couple of blocks southwest of the Tylers, later wrote a book about the war and was awarded a Pulitzer Prize for the work in 1930. Eighty-five years later, Schmitt's former White Avenue home, facing imminent demolition, was moved to 1201 West Clinch Avenue, just one lot west of where the Tylers lived.[1]

By its fall semester, 1917, the University of Tennessee had formed a Student Army Training Corps for recruiting college men into military service. Richard Owen was a student cadet at the time. "Some of the old buildings on the Hill were turned into barracks," he recalled. "We were drilled and put on a semi-military basis." Owen and another UT student, Marshall Shoaf, found a room for rent in the home of a young widow and her children. "We got a room at 1505 Highland with Mrs. Agee whose husband had recently been killed in an auto accident," wrote Owen. "She had two children: Rufus (James) and a little girl. James, about seven, a very sensitive boy, cried a lot. It was a difficult adjustment, meeting his father's death."[2]

From left, Laura Agee, Paula Tyler, and Emma Tyler stand
with Emma and Rufus Agee in the Tyler front yard in
August 1917. Tyler Album 054, Hugh Tyler Collection,
McClung Historical Collection, Knox County Library.

More than a year after the tragedy, Rufus was still in emotional turmoil.
His life had been upset, and in some ways it never resettled. Since his father
died, his mother had opened the house to strangers, leasing out unused bedrooms. Earlier that year, Mrs. Marks, a teacher from Lonsdale, boarded with
the family; now two students—including cadet Owen—and a U.S. Marine
Corps recruiter lived there. And all around the city were constant reminders
that the country was at war. Stores raised prices as materials were needed
overseas, and automobile travel was restricted on certain days to conserve

gasoline. The fact that downtown had a Prince Street rankled some Knox-villians as akin to honoring German royalty, so the name was changed to Market Street. Anti-German sentiments were spreading to the point that some local families of German heritage changed their names.[3]

On May 18, exactly one year after Jay's death, Congress had passed the Selective Service Act, initiating the draft for males aged twenty-one to thirty-one. Draftees were selected by lot from the lists of registered men. John Agee was twenty-nine during the first registration on June 5, 1917. Frank, thirty-eight, registered on September 12, 1918, the day the draft opened to those aged eighteen to forty-five. Apparently, neither Agee brother was called to service.[4]

Hugh Tyler enlisted as a U.S. Merchant Marine, possibly in spring or summer 1918 after turning thirty-four. However, an accident aboard a cargo ship cut his tour of duty short—in fact, it only lasted one day. Family members later recounted the incident: on his first day, Hugh "followed his superior officer in the darkness between decks and fell thirty feet down an open hold and broke his wrist." He was out of commission, and the ship had not even left port yet. "They put him down on the dock and steamed off." His hospitalization coincided with the Influenza Epidemic of 1918, and Hugh returned home with "horrific tales of . . . a ward full of servicemen dying of the flu" and "the bodies of the flu victims being stacked like cordwood on deck." Much later, his daughter Lydia recalled "him telling about the terrible nonchalance with which someone came back from the toilet to tell of a dead man in there." According to another family member, Hugh reported these conditions to a congressman, which led to an official investigation; however, this claim has not been substantiated.[5]

Meanwhile, Knoxville continued to rally support for the war effort. Perhaps Laura and her children were among those who crowded downtown's sidewalks on April 6, 1918, to watch the Grand Liberty Parade, a forty-block procession reported to be one of Gay Street's largest ever. The event marked the one-year anniversary of the country joining the war. And that October, on behalf of the Southern Association of College Women, Emma Tyler headed a committee to collect and distribute magazines to American soldiers.[6]

By the second week of October, Knox County was reeling from the effects of Spanish flu, with reported cases numbering at least 850. And the news from overseas hit many local families hard. October 8 was a particularly tragic day, as twenty men from Knox County were lost in battle, more than on any other day of the war. However, on the same day, a Fentress County native singlehandedly conquered 150 German soldiers, and Alvin York became a household name.[7]

The war would not end before claiming the life of a former Ty-Sa-Man employee. Oscar Rider began working there as a machinist around 1915, and had therefore known both Joel Tyler and Jay Agee. Shipped overseas in July 1918, Rider endured months of fighting in France before November 11, the last day of the war. While engaged in the Argonne Forest that morning, one hour before the armistice, Rider was shot and killed—perhaps the last Knoxvillian to die in World War I combat.[8]

As he attempted to make sense of both the war and his father's absence, Rufus also suffered confusing physical maladies. Besides the frequent "re-gurgitation" that had plagued him since he was a toddler, he continued to wet his bed, a condition that likely worsened after Jay's death and happened "nearly every night, till 13 or so; frequently till 16." While 85 percent of children grow out of bedwetting by age five or six, some continue to suffer into their early teens. Rufus was shaken by another physical change around that time, one that was sudden and beyond his control. His mother insisted that he be circumcised—a procedure normally performed within the first few weeks of a male's birth. Rufus was seven at the time, and despite being under "total anesthesia" he remembered the pain the rest of his life. As an adult, he felt the act signified his mother's power over him: "Circumcised at 7: intense resentment as I came to realize that one aspect of my mother's motive was to reduce my erotic sensitiveness and hence my liability to 'temptation.'"[9]

Hidden in her brother's shadow, Emma Agee is often overlooked. Al-though relatively little is known about her childhood, evidence indicates that, emotionally, she struggled as much or more than Rufus did. If Emma grew up believing that her brother was the favored child, as suggested earlier, it might explain Laura's statement decades later that Emma "had a deep in-feriority complex about herself as related to or compared with [Rufus]." In fact, Emma "resented not being a boy" and suffered from mental illness as an adult. Laura realized, in hindsight, that "a great great many of the outward symptoms were there, even when [Emma] was still a child," she wrote to Rufus in 1946. "I do not believe (but am, of course, ignorant) that one can be *born* neurotic—but I fully believe one can be born with some mental kink that admits quickly of neuroses *after* birth, & this I believe of Emma."[10]

ST. ANDREW'S

Jessie Tyler had persevered through her own personal tragedies. She had cared for ailing loved ones—first her mother, then her aunt Patty—all the way through to their deaths, while continuing to minister within the Epis-

Jessie Tyler (Mother Mary Gabriel)
stands with her nephew Hugh Tyler
during a visit to her brother Joel's
residence in Knoxville, 1922. Tyler
Album 100, Hugh Tyler Collection,
McClung Historical Collection,
Knox County Library.

copal Church. "She didn't have a very free life," remarked her niece, Paula
Tyler, "but she'd always been a good churchwoman. Well, then she went with
real depth into it and became a nun." On May 30, 1918, Corpus Christi Day,
Jessie Tyler professed her vows at Christ Church, Chattanooga, and became
Mother Mary Gabriel. Along with the Reverend William Robertson, the
visiting minister who officiated at Jay's funeral, Jessie established Sisters of
the Tabernacle, a contemplative order of women, drawing up the rule based
on "The Fundamentals of the Religious State," by Father Hughson of the
Order of the Holy Cross.[11]

Episcopal monks from the same Order had founded a school thirteen years
earlier near Sewanee for the religious instruction of mountain boys. Jessie
knew of the school, called St. Andrew's, and likely suggested it to Laura as
a place where she could spend a restful couple of months with her children
away from Knoxville. The Cumberland Plateau's higher elevation offered a
more comfortable summer climate than East Tennessee's valleys did. But
Laura mainly wanted to inspect the campus and experience the school's

"country life and . . . religious atmosphere" as she considered alternatives to her son's public education. By that time Highland Avenue School had been renamed Van Gilder, and a six-classroom addition had been added on to the front of the building to help alleviate overcrowding. Not long after eight-year-old Rufus finished fourth grade there, he traveled with his sister Emma, six, and their mother to Sewanee.[12]

To get there from Knoxville in 1918, they left from the L&N Station to Chattanooga, and then boarded the train to Cowan on the Nashville, Chattanooga & St. Louis line. The small Cowan Depot still stands in the valley where Laura and her children arrived from Chattanooga and switched trains to Tracy City. Leaving the station, the train crossed a flat plain through wide, green tracts of farmland, with the Cumberland Plateau standing tall and gray beyond. It became clear why the train was nicknamed the Mountain Goat as it ascended—at the time that section of track was one of the country's steepest railway inclines—and the passengers, forced rigid against the seatbacks, were surely thankful when the chugging train reached the top.[13]

Visitors to St. Andrew's School had to request a stop at the Gipson Switch post office—the site of which is now marked by a state historical sign placed in honor of Franklin County pioneer Allan Gipson. A small dirt road led from the post office to the school, which was composed of a dozen or so buildings scattered amidst rolling farmland. "It was a rural setting," said Father Flye, "a property of perhaps 200 acres, some wooded, some under cultivation as a farm, a few dwelling houses, the school buildings, the small monastery or priory with chapel, refectory, library and guest rooms, where 4 or 5 members of the Order and 2 or 3 other men lived." The monastery was named after St. Michael. Other buildings were also named after saints. Dormitories were St. John's, St. George's, and St. Joseph's. St. Augustine, the main school building, contained classrooms, a woodworking shop, and a dormitory above. Even the "backhouse," which contained the outside toilets, was nicknamed "St. Maligog," as one student recalled: "Everything had to be called 'saint,' so we gave that one a name, too." There was also a gymnasium and a chapel, and several one-story dwellings for faculty members and their families. Laura, Rufus, and Emma stayed in a cottage that had been occupied by the Stroups, a well-known family at the school.[14]

The Agees were likely at the cottage in July when Laura received a message from LaFollette—perhaps arriving as a telegram or as a call to the one telephone on campus. The news was tragic. Frank and Vesta Agee's son, Wheeler, who was about nine months younger than Rufus, had contracted a bone infection, possibly staph. The boy died on July 10 and was buried at

Woodlawn Cemetery, just a few feet from his grandfather Henry Clay Agee. It is not known whether Laura and the children traveled back to Campbell County for the service.[15]

Near the end of Rufus's summer vacation, the Agees returned to Knoxville. Perhaps inspired by a couple of months at St. Andrew's, living simply in a manageable house, Laura decided to sell the family's large Highland Avenue home rather than continue to rent out rooms. On September 23, she signed the deed over to John D. Jett. Her living arrangement for the next several months is unknown, but she and the children likely boarded with her parents on Clinch Avenue.[16]

HUMANITIES

Rufus became immersed in the Tylers' cultural values. Around this time, he began earnestly studying art and music in his grandparents' home, contrasting his earliest attempts when he was perhaps more motivated by mischief—like setting piano keys aflame—than by artistic achievement. He had gazed at the framed prints on his grandparents' walls, maybe flipped through Uncle Hugh's copy of *The Grammar of Ornament*. Now an older and more complex boy whom Hugh was teaching to paint, Rufus was increasingly aware of the thriving arts scene in the industrial, mid-southern town he called home.[17]

At the time, Hugh was an active member of the Nicholson Art League. The group had formed in 1906 and until its dissolution in 1923 retained an impressive roster of local artists—including Lloyd Branson, Catherine Wiley, and Charles Krutch—whose works were widely known. If Rufus knew any of his uncle's colleagues, he must have known the family of Catherine Wiley, Knoxville's "one noted impressionist." The Wileys lived on White Avenue, a couple of blocks from the Tylers. And one of Rufus's later manuscripts includes a reference to "Nell Wylie," a family acquaintance; in fact, Nell (Eleanor) Wiley was a sister of Catherine and also a member of the Nicholson Art League. The league's greatest accomplishments were the art exhibitions it staged at Chilhowee Park's Fine Arts pavilion during the 1910–11 Appalachian Expositions and the 1913 National Conservation Exposition. Attended by thousands, the exhibitions introduced Knoxville artists to a national audience. Hugh himself was lauded during the latter expo when his collection of paintings won a top prize. And just as he had learned from his colleagues, so he influenced them. Hugh taught drawing to an artist about seventeen years his junior, Beauford Delaney, and with Branson paid for the artist's entry into a Boston art school in 1924. Delaney later became associated with the Harlem Renaissance and was regarded as "the best-known artist who ever lived in Knoxville."[18]

While he made his living as a muralist and decorator (sometimes in collaboration with a fellow Nicholson alumnus, architect Charles Barber), Hugh was drawn artistically to exotic landscapes, to places like Panama and French Polynesia. On a tour of Hiva Oa in 1921, he paid his respects to a French impressionist who had been buried there almost twenty years earlier. As the art lessons continued in the Clinch Avenue studio, Hugh must have told Rufus stories about his South Seas adventure—about painting "PAUL GAUGUIN" in white across the artist's headstone and placing decorative rocks on the previously unadorned, vine-covered grave. Although later in life Rufus spent relatively little time painting or drawing, without Hugh's influence he may never have written the 1953 screenplay *Noa Noa*, based on Gauguin's travelogue.[19]

Music remained a lifelong source of enjoyment for Rufus. According to his mother, he "showed great love for music" at a young age. Certainly the popular songs his parents sang at home contributed to this musical awareness and marked some of his earliest memories. But growing up in Knoxville afforded Rufus chances to hear a variety of music, performed live. In his many walks downtown, he must have occasionally encountered string players busking on Market Square or along the sidewalks near Vine Avenue, and perhaps he caught snippets of early country and blues music like the songs the Brunswick–Vocalion company recorded in 1929–30 at the St. James Hotel. Along Gay Street, pianists accompanied the images Rufus viewed in the movie houses; bands backed the musicals and minstrel shows that headlined on theater stages. Out at Chilhowee Park, a dance band performed every night during the summer season. Besides popular tunes, Rufus heard and sang sacred music as part of the regular Sunday services he attended at St. John's. Some downtown churches, including St. John's, also hosted recitals of music by classical composers. Although the Knoxville Symphony Orchestra was not formed until 1935, its founder and first conductor, Bertha Walburn Clark, led a small ensemble in the city while Rufus still lived there. Clark and Rufus's aunt Paula Tyler were roughly the same age, and likely knew each other.[20]

By the time Rufus started formal piano lessons, Paula had taught music for several years and was preparing for a permanent move to New York. In January 1920 the census found her teaching music in Manhattan while boarding with another music teacher, Mildred Haire (who became Mrs. Hugh Tyler in 1926). Paula joined the staff of the Diller-Quaile School of Music by 1922. And though she returned to Knoxville in 1924 long enough for her name to appear in the city directory, she remained in Manhattan for decades, serving as Diller-Quaile's co-director from 1941 until 1955. Rockefellers and other prominent families sent their children to the school; reputedly, Paula tutored young members of the Kennedy family during her tenure. But she always had more to say about her talented nephew. "I taught Rufus piano when he was little," Paula confirmed. "He was terrifically musical. When he was trying to make up his mind what he was going to do in his life—I guess when he was going to Harvard, or perhaps before he went—I said, 'Before you decide what you're going to do, don't forget that you could do wonders in music. You're very gifted.' And he said, 'Well, I think it's not hard enough for me. I want to do the writing.'"[21]

Besides learning from his aunt and uncle in the Tyler home, Rufus also witnessed his grandmother's continued activism in social causes. She was heavily involved in the Knoxville Equal Suffrage League and had been since her friend Lizzie Crozier French established the association in 1910. After repeated failed attempts to lobby Nashville lawmakers for almost a decade, and a war that diverted attention away from the voting issue, the group's efforts paid off in April 1919 when the state legislature passed a bill allowing women to vote in certain elections. For years Emma Tyler had edited a *Journal and Tribune* column, "In the Interest of Votes for Women," dedicated to Suffrage League activities. "At last the Tennessee legislature has followed the example of 26 other states, and conceded to women the right to vote in presidential and municipal elections," wrote Emma in response to the bill's passing. "The members from Knox county as usual were solidly for the measure. It would seem East Tennessee leads the states in the march of progress."[22]

That June, Congress approved the Nineteenth Amendment but needed the legislatures of three-fourths of the states to officially ratify it. Thirty-five states passed the amendment in quick succession over the next nine months before momentum stalled, one state's vote shy of ratification. On August 18, 1920, the nation took notice as Tennessee's House of Representatives convened to decide the issue. The poll was tied when Harry Burn's name was called. Feeling pressure from both sides, the McMinn County representative cast the deciding yes vote, admitting afterward that his mother's opinion had swayed him. Certainly Emma was proud of the parts her city and state had played in achieving equal suffrage. In one of her final *Journal and Tribune* columns, she reminded her sisters of the new obligations that accompanied their right to vote: "Knoxville women, as full fledged citizens, now have responsibilities that they do not wish to assume ignorantly and they are therefore taking steps to gain thorough information regarding questions of civic interest which will hereafter be incumbent upon them to help their brother-citizen in deciding, here in our own beautiful Knoxville. We were never more proud of its beauty and its promising future than today, and we desire with all the things we have in trust to serve our city well."[23]

Emma Tyler would have been pleased to see her city commemorate the cause through two works of public art. In 2006, a bronze sculpture by Alan LeQuire was unveiled on Market Square depicting three prominent Tennessee suffragists, including French. And in 2018, LeQuire completed a sculpture of Harry Burn and his mother, Febb, which now occupies a corner of Clinch Avenue just outside the old Custom House. In the twenty-first century, Knoxville has developed a reputation as one of the more progressive cities in the region. But in Rufus's time, despite his familiarity with the Tylers' political and artistic circles, he felt that the values of most Knoxvillians were quite different from his own and even believed his father would have "felt contempt" for his "interest in art." Years later, Rufus remarked to a friend that one's "fervent interest in the arts and in social justice must make East Tennessee a lonely place in which to live."[24]

CONFIRMATION

By his ninth birthday, Rufus had been almost solely under the influence of his mother and the Tylers for two and a half years. His early spiritual development can be attributed to his mother, "a devout Anglo-Catholic," and his great-aunt Jessie. Rufus regularly attended services at St. John's Episcopal—a church building constructed of Georgia marble in 1892 that still graces the corner of Walnut and Cumberland. Its interior, based on the Latin cross plan, was finished in red oak and featured, behind the altar, an Italian marble mosaic of the Ascension.[25]

Walter Claiborne Whitaker became rector of St. John's in 1907. His family had lived in Jackson, Tennessee, for a good part of his childhood. Walter remembered running out the back door and hiding in the woods when the local preacher visited the family's home. At the time, Walter's main interest in Sunday school was a church bookshelf that had been stocked with reading material of interest to boys like him. "I wasn't going to leave that Sunday school till I'd finished reading all of those books," Whitaker said. "I enjoyed reading them as all boys do. I even read Diamond Dick and all sorts of thrillers that came my way in paperback form. I have never had any

Dr. Walter Whitaker. Courtesy of St. John's Episcopal Cathedral, Knoxville.

patience with people who said those things were demoralizing. I never found an unclean line in them."[26]

Rufus was fond of Dr. Whitaker, perhaps relating to the minister's artistic and intellectual sensibilities. Whitaker, like Rufus, came from a musical family and considered becoming a concert pianist after graduating from the Alabama Polytechnic Institute (now Auburn University). According to one parishioner, Whitaker "loved the music of the Church and encouraged, during his ministry, the use of the best music in the Church Services." He wrote and published a book of poetry at age seventeen and later wrote several theological books and articles. Dorothy Whitaker Allen characterized her father as a Renaissance man of sorts: "He had so fine a mind, so keen a wit, so many talents and such a delightful personality that he was constantly being told by his friends that he should have been a lawyer, a professor, a musician, an actor, a writer, a lecturer or any number of other callings. So often did this happen that one day he ruefully remarked that, apparently, according to his friends, he should have chosen almost anything except the ministry."[27]

Whitaker was praised for his "intellectual ability and deep religious conviction" and regarded as "a man of quick sympathy and understanding, and real friendliness." As William Whaley recalled, "His services were beautifully conducted, reading clear and unaffected. His sermons were well prepared and sometimes 'over the heads of the congregation,' but were never lacking in erudition." Those sermons impressed Rufus, who later wrote that Whitaker "gave his words and phrases special emphasis and personal coloring, as though they were matters which required argument and persuasion." According to Whitaker's daughter, "Most people were agreed . . . that to few priests is given as beautiful and expressive a reading voice as was his, and the offices of the Church became ever more beloved as his voice read the various services."[28]

Under such leadership, Rufus's spiritual commitment grew. He was confirmed on January 26, 1919, a milestone that his mother remembered clearly: "He was confirmed by Bishop Gailor in Knoxville, and I think he was just nine that very fall when he was confirmed. And I can just see him. Most

The sanctuary of St. John's Episcopal in 1921, showing some of the intricate decorations that Hugh Tyler painted on the walls and archways. N-1578, Thompson Photograph Collection, McClung Historical Collection, Knox County Library.

everyone was a grown person that was being confirmed. And he went march-
ing up all by himself. He didn't kneel in the mob; he went off by himself a
couple of yards down the communion rail further, you know, and knelt all
by himself, and was confirmed."[29]

Following confirmation, Dr. Whitaker presented him before the congregation. On February 2, Rufus took his first communion. Around this time,
he became a member of St. John's youth choir. Rufus "grew up familiar with
the Book of Common Prayer and services of the Church."[30]

Near the end of the year, following morning services, a fire erupted in
the church basement and burned the floor, severely damaging the sanctuary. St. John's had only recently been remodeled, including the addition of
painted decorations by Hugh Tyler. After the damaged areas were rebuilt,
Hugh returned and, for the second time, painted new designs "as a gift to
his church."[31]

RELOCATION

In March 1919 Joel and Emma Tyler deeded property to Laura, a lot measuring one hundred by ninety-six and a half feet that contained two houses—1112
and 1116 Laurel Avenue. The property sat directly behind the Tylers' Clinch
Avenue lot. Rufus had memories of the move, of "Mother & her new house."
Laura and the children lived in one of the lot's two homes, "right behind
1115, up on Laurel Avenue—a pleasant little, smaller house up there." Curiously, Knoxville directories list other residents at those addresses, but not
Laura. Perhaps Laura, as a single mother without an income, rented out
part of the house, suspecting that a more permanent move to Sewanee was
forthcoming.[32]

Paula Tyler recalled an incident not long after Laura and the children
moved to the new house: "I remember once when she was living in the house
that my father let her have after her husband died, she was fasting through
Good Friday," which fell on April 18 in 1919, the last spring Laura spent in
the house. "And about half past five, Rufus and Emma came down to our
house and said they wanted some supper, that mama hadn't had anything
to eat all day. She was sick and couldn't do anything."[33]

When the school year ended, Laura and the children returned to St.
Andrew's to spend the summer of 1919 in the same cottage they had occupied
the previous year. It was during that visit that Rufus met James Harold Flye,
a thirty-three-year-old teacher who had only been at the school for a year.
He would become a lifelong spiritual advisor, mentor, and friend. "After my

first year of teaching at St. Andrew's," Flye wrote, "I stayed on through the vacation. Mrs. Agee, who had friends there, came from Knoxville with her two children for the summer, living in a cottage on the school grounds, and it was thus that James Agee and I first met. He was a bright, intelligent and interesting boy, and we formed a very happy friendship."[34]

The priest was struck by Rufus's "winsome manner, his mental and physical alertness, his zest for information . . . his clear voice and pleasant manner of speech—delightful mingling of elements childlike and mature . . . a very likeable and interesting boy." Rufus was not necessarily "a handsome boy," but Flye saw "in his face the expression of life and keen intelligence and real goodness. Clear . . . eyes, with often a look of things seen primarily with the mind, and a trace, too, of sadness, as of one whose sensitive soul was already knowing and would know much more whether in experience or in acute sympathy, of the pain . . . of the world."[35]

Father Flye had a heart for nurturing boys toward spiritual and intellectual maturity, and rejoiced with them as they progressed toward their full potential. "We look into the face of a boy," wrote Flye in 1921,

Father James Harold Flye, in a portrait by his wife, Grace Houghton Flye. Courtesy of Molly MacMillan.

it may be the child of common and ignorant folk, and notwithstanding faults whose traces may perhaps be there we are won by the infinite charm of youth, speaking to us of something purer and sweeter and higher than the hard, dry, practical, materialistic life which so many adults live. The child has his faults and failings, he is careless, his ethical standards may seem at times disappointing; and yet there is this delicate quality in his face which means innocence and faith, and love, and God, and the presence of the guardian angels—something which seems to say that the faults do not express his real self. . . . The appeals of the world make themselves heard, the broad way is inviting, the world's roughness has hurt and perhaps toughened him, low standards are constantly presented to him, and influences towards what is common and vulgar, and probably he has absorbed more or less of all this. But God's guidance has been about the souls so dear to Him. The boy can be touched by the appeal to what is high and pure.[36]

Laura sensed that Flye would be the strong male role model Rufus needed to guide him into adolescence. "At the end of the summer, with the cottage still available, Mrs. Agee decided to stay on through the winter and have the children attend the school," remembered Flye.[37]

The Agees likely returned to Knoxville to gather any belongings needed for their long-term move to campus. With school beginning on Tuesday, September 2, they may have departed Knoxville a few days earlier—just as the worst race riot in the city's history was erupting. It was supposed to be a time of celebration, a Labor Day weekend honoring "both workers and returning soldiers." Instead, on August 30, 1919, a mob of white citizens stormed the Hill Avenue jail where a mulatto man, accused of fatally shooting a white woman, had been locked up. Fearing such a reaction, police had transferred the prisoner to Chattanooga. But in its hunger for vengeance, the mob destroyed the jail anyway, raided several stores for firearms, and marched "toward the corner of Vine and Central avenues," where a group of "armed blacks" had supposedly gathered. Despite a military unit arriving to help keep the peace, the armed assault dragged on for several hours, with both black and white casualties and many injuries. Even though the actual body count was lower than expected, the violent episode revealed serious rifts in a city that during the Great War had seemed so unified. Shortly after the conflict, a local journalist lamented that Knoxville appeared to be headed on a "downward course to the valley of dissension, dissimulation, and ruin." Whether or not the Agees were there when it happened, news of the riot must have affirmed in Laura's mind her decision to leave town.[38]

ooooooooooooooo

"When I was eight," Rufus later wrote, thinking of his age during the family's first visit to Sewanee, "I was sent to St. Andrew's School, run by an order of monks, mainly at that time for mountain boys. I went to school there five years, spending vacations at my grandfather's home in Knoxville."[39]

Father Flye was pleased that Laura decided to enroll Rufus at the school, "glad indeed that our association was not to be broken off," he said. But Flye also "had some questionings and doubt." He wondered how "a boy like that" would "adjust" to the school's "regimen and surroundings." Flye did not know of "many boys (and certainly none of [Rufus's] age) with anything like his background, tastes and interests."[40]

The school was open to students whose parents were mountain folk. Some 15 to 20 percent of those enrolled were orphans, and tuition was kept at a minimum so poor families could afford it. "Most of us were people who had come from places where there was a plank shack and a log cabin and an old barn and a pigpen," said Oliver Hodge, who was a few years older than Rufus. "This was a school for poor mountain boys and most of us were just that."[41]

Rufus Agee and his aunt Paula Tyler hold kittens outside the former Stroup cottage, St. Andrew's School. Tyler Album 070, Hugh Tyler Collection, McClung Historical Collection, Knox County Library.

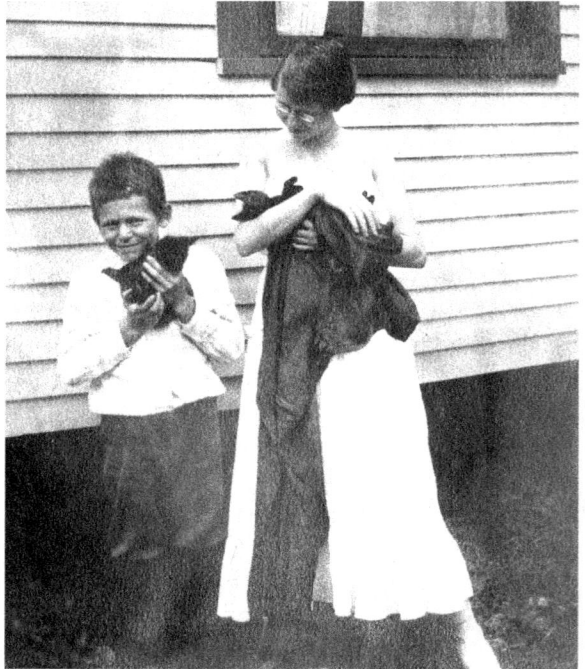

Although the Agees were from the Tennessee hills, Rufus was far less provincial and far better off than typical mountain children, who survived off what their parents farmed from the land. As an adult, Rufus stated, "I have hill-billy blood myself," but Father Flye argued against this: "Knowing these facts about Agee's progenitors I would write, 'he was not from hill-billy roots.'" Flye attempted to justify Rufus's claim to the contrary, writing, "Might it perhaps be that in that connection he was using broadly or even somewhat lightly the word 'hill-billy' to refer to people of the hill and mountain country of eastern Tennessee . . . or possibly thinking of those who might produce and enjoy what goes by the name of hill-billy music or ballads?" Ultimately, Flye did not know why Rufus identified himself as such: "But perhaps what I have written here may help to avoid some possible misconceptions."[42]

Despite not meeting the criteria, St. Andrew's admitted Rufus at a $100 yearly tuition, and the Agees officially moved into the former Stroup cottage. Mrs. Stroup "ran the pantry in the kitchen" on campus and had a son in New York who was a school alumnus. Seeing the cottage now occupied by strangers, students were naturally curious: "Who's in the cottage?" "It's the Agee family." "Who's that woman?" "She's a widow with two children, Rufus and Emma." Hodge recalled the sight of Laura and the children walking from their house to campus. "Along would come Mrs. Agee with that long, loping walk, with Rufus and Emma strung out behind her," Hodge said. "When they walked, they rose up from the heel. Every one of them walked that way, decidedly. The mother walked that way, and both children."[43]

When Rufus entered the school on September 2, he clearly stood out from the other students because of his middle-class upbringing. "Rufus didn't really belong there," remembered Hodge. "The fact that he came from a woman like his mother, this was already very, very unusual. We just didn't have people there of highly educated backgrounds. We hadn't had any contact with this kind of thing."[44]

Rufus knew he did not fit in and experienced "friendlessness" and a "profound mistrust of nearly everyone." Others around school considered him "somewhat of a loner" and "not too good a mixer." Because he read well in class and was spotted "always reading" outside of class, he quickly earned the nickname Socrates. "He knew a lot of the classics, and he read beyond the age of a boy like that," Hodge said. "It caused the students to think of him as a wise fellow, and they did it a little scornfully. The name wasn't altogether a compliment; it was a mixture of scorn and reluctant praise." For one thing, the other boys resented the fact that Rufus "could take off" to

The top image shows Laura Agee's cottage at St. Andrew's, circa 1920. The bottom image shows the remodeled residence as it appeared in 2016. Although Rufus only lived in it a short time, this cottage is notable as the last of his Tennessee homes left standing. Top photo: Tyler Album 064, Hugh Tyler Collection, McClung Historical Collection, Knox County Library. Bottom photo by the author.

his mother whenever he felt like it. "Having a mother there probably led somewhat to his reputation as a momma's boy because he had a momma to run to," recalled Hodge. "The rest of us would possibly have run to one, too, if we'd had one. But we didn't have anybody like that."[45]

The house Rufus ran to, built around 1910, still sits off the side of the road inside St. Andrew's stone-columned front entrance. The small red-shingled cottage with tan siding once consisted of little more than uninsu-

lated tongue-in-groove walls, beadboard ceiling, and one-inch wood flooring, its few small rooms heated by a coal stove. Although the cottage has
been altered over the decades, the front entrance remains the same, and the
central dining room retains much of its original wood.[46]

To help him develop friendships and a sense of independence, Laura
had made Rufus live in the dormitory with boys his age instead of staying
with Emma and her in the cabin. She limited her son's visits to one day per
week. Consequently, he suffered "intense homesickness first three years."
Later fictionalizing his St. Andrew's experiences for a novella, *The Morning
Watch*, he described

> watching his mother's cottage, the one place he was almost never allowed to go,
> sometimes by the hour; sometimes in ambush under dripping trees, relishing the
> fact that only he knew of the miserableness of that watch; sometimes openly, hang-
> ing against the fence, relishing the fact that she knew, and others could see, and
> that even though she knew, she would try to ignore him and stay out of his sight,
> and that when at last she could ignore him no longer, she would hurt him by trying
> to be stern with him as she told him to go away. . . . "Because dear, mother thinks
> it's best for you not to be too near her, all the more because you miss her so much."
> "Because your father—isn't with us." "Because mother thinks you need to be
> among other boys . . ."

He had lost his father and was now being separated from his mother, all
but banned from her cottage. As one scholar wrote, Rufus "was isolated by
death and distance from his parents."[47]

There were four dormitories—St. John's, St. George's, St. Joseph's and St.
Augustine's—the last two with classrooms on the ground floors. The name
of the dorm in which Rufus stayed is not known, although he may have lived
in more than one during his years as a student. But his writings suggest that
the chapel was "downhill" from his dorm, and St. Joseph's sat more uphill
than the others. He only briefly described his dorm's interior as a "long room"
with "alcove windows, and the aisled ends of the iron cots," which also suggests St. Joseph's, the three-story building with several gabled windows.[48]

Rufus found that even his dorm cot was a place of embarrassment, as
his bedwetting continued. The stress of being uprooted from Knoxville and
moved to this new school likely intensified his condition. He later fictionalized his morning ritual of checking his sheets for wetness: "By a habit of
their own . . . his hands searched and tested along the undersheet, and now
they told him that this time he had wet the bed so little that by morning
nobody would know."[49]

This work by Grace Houghton Flye is believed by her descendants to be a portrait of Rufus Agee. Grace gave the painting to her niece, Mary Houghton Boorman, who "seemed so certain" that it depicted Rufus, according to Mary's granddaughter. Courtesy of Lynne Glaus.

When feeling lonely and humiliated, teased by other boys but denied motherly comfort, Rufus sought the "shelter and friendship of a teacher." Former classmate Hodge said that Rufus "would run to Father Flye, so we all thought of him as a teacher's pet—which he was." Flye and his wife, Grace, lived on campus in a one-story frame house with a wide, columned front porch. Rufus enjoyed visits there, "for friendliness was certain," he wrote, "and often cookies and cocoa too." Grace was an artist who sometimes painted portraits of visiting students. The Flyes' 1915 bungalow sat across the road from the chapel but was relocated in 2006 to make room for a new performing arts building.[50]

Father Flye wrote that during this period Rufus was "*not* dwelling or brooding on [the] death of his father." The priest also insisted of himself that he was not Jay's replacement. "It has sometimes been suggested that James Agee found in me something of a surrogate for his dead father. I do not think so," Flye wrote. "I could have had the same dear and affectionate friendship with him, I feel sure, if his father had been living."[51]

Although Flye "did *not* see him constantly," Rufus and he managed to spend a lot of time together, walking along the "schoolyard [that] was skimmed with dusty gravel" and conversing about a wide range of subjects. "He was not a prodigy, but he had read lots of books—Booth Tarkington and Mark Twain, for instance," said Flye. "He was interested in fossils and shells, knowing many of these by their scientific names which he used fluently and naturally. Then there was the subject of possible pets, and we discussed monkeys, baboons, ponies, elephants, rabbits, pigeons and kangaroos, with citations from pet books and books of Natural History. Then foreign countries; and Indian life, and scout lore and woods craft. He wanted a bow and arrow, and we made a bow which he used some. Later he wanted a 22 rifle. It wasn't considered desirable to buy him one but we borrowed one and did some target shooting. He wouldn't have thought of shooting at birds or rabbits or other living things."[52]

Physically, Rufus was "large, soft, clumsy for my age, mild-timorous," compared to the "physically smaller, better-coordinated boys. Successful in fighting only when I was berserk." As a student, Rufus "was not especially prominent in the school life and activities," wrote Flye. "How he rated in academic records would vary with the subject and the teaching, and degree of his interest." Rufus believed that after age nine his academic skill was "split between precocity in chiefly English and near-imbecility in mathematics, manual training, sports (nearly all)." As a ninth grader, he scored 98 in history and 78.5 in math. The next year, his history grade was still high, 96, but the math score had sunk to 64.5. "He liked History," Flye remembered. This might be because Flye taught Rufus's freshman English history course, the first time the two had a class together. For the rest of his life, Flye saved a particular final exam, one taken on May 18, 1923, on which Rufus had penciled a note to his favorite teacher:

J. R. Agee
1115 W. Clinch
Knoxville, Tennessee.
Goodbye forever, till next fall!
(I'll see you at dinner)[53]

Unlike some of his classmates, Rufus was not rebellious, but his occasional lapses in judgment brought discipline. "He would undoubtedly be in trouble with rigidity of some school rules and requirements," Flye recalled. "Not intentionally, for he was not of defiant or non-cooperative spirit, but though of good intentions he was absent-minded, forgetful of details, absorbed in what he was doing, and with insufficient awareness as to time."[54]

Rufus was "far-out" and "dreamy," remembered Oliver Hodge, and "way off all the time" with his "head in the air." Hodge called Rufus "the sloppiest kid that ever lived, and full of sins of omission. He never did anything that was of a vicious nature, but he couldn't get to mass on time," said Hodge. Rufus was called before the student council for various other reasons—"for having shown up an hour late for school, or for going over to his mother's," Hodge recalled. "Probably the boys had beaten him up or something like that, and he'd take off for home. Of course, this was a dereliction; he had failed to go to school. And he'd come in front of the student council, and we would discuss the matter and vote on what the punishment would be." As student council president, Hodge was responsible for administering the punishment: "If it turned out to be a paddling . . . it was up to me to give it to him. It wasn't very hard; it was right on his butt, you know . . . and I laid it on, maybe four or five licks . . . with a paddle." Hodge said that Rufus didn't cry afterwards: "He'd take [the paddling]. He didn't like it, and I'm sure he remembered it years later, but there was nothing brutal about it."[55]

One activity that leaned closest to rebellion was walking to the Sand Cut, an area "about a mile" from the school "toward Monteagle" where silica had been excavated, leaving large, rain-filled pits. To get to the popular swimming spot, students traced a path east around the school's demonstration farm, through the woods and out toward the railroad tracks. The students' arrival there is described in *The Morning Watch:* "Along the far side of the track they saw the weathered oak tower and soon, walking more briskly along the ties, the relics of machinery and the dead cones of putty-colored sand and the wrinkled sandstone and, at length, the sullen water itself, untouched in all these cold months." Hodge remembered the site as "an overgrown mudhole where they had been digging out sand. It was deep enough to swim in and quite dangerous. There was an old mowing machine sunk in one end of it, and many a boy dived in there and knocked his head on it. But we all went swimming there. The railroad came by in those days carrying passengers: the 'Mountain Goat.' Of course the boys went swimming naked, and when the train would come everybody had to run and jump in the water—thirty or forty naked boys of all ages and sizes. It was very amusing."[56]

The former railroad track bed is now the Mountain Goat Walking Trail and still skirts the north edge of the Sand Cut property, currently owned by the Sequatchie Concrete Service, Inc. Satellite images of the property show a sandy area cleared with several small, manmade pools, tinted light blue compared to the dark lakes visible nearby and looking something like the holding ponds of a water treatment facility—but with machinery, conveyors, vehicles, and little buildings strewn about. A sandy smear of a driveway turns off the highway, crosses the walking trail where the train passed, and leads to the front gate, where the company sign—with its logo of a Native American man with multicolored headdress—directs visitors to check in at the office. Past the entrance one can see rusty conveyors and mounds of sand. "This is where he would sometimes go to think," wrote Father Flye of Rufus's swimming hole. "Of course the place isn't like it was then."[57]

FAITH

This dreamy boy from Knoxville, whose dearest friend was a priest, became immersed in what he later called "religiosity (Anglo-Catholic)." According to Flye, students were "required" to attend "daily chapel service and on Sundays and the Sung Mass and Evensong," and "encouraged to go to Confession and Holy Communion." While Rufus had been raised with the liturgy, the High Church rituals were foreign to many of the students. Nevertheless, "without any constraint many boys from other backgrounds became members of the Church," said Flye. Boys were recruited as "acolytes" and other assistants "in the Church services." Rufus later described his own service as an acolyte, in a sweeping sentence from *Let Us Now Praise Famous Men:*

> I used as a child in the innocence of faith to bring myself out of bed through the cold lucid water of the Cumberland morning and to serve at the altar at earliest lonely Mass, whose words were thrilling brooks of music and whose motions, a grave dance: and there between spread hands the body and the blood of Christ was created among words and lifted before God in a threshing of triplicate bells, and from the rear of the empty church stole forward a serene widow and a savage epileptic, softly blind, and knelt, and on the palms of their hands and at their mouths they took their strength and, blind, retired: and the morning was clangorous with the whole of a roused school when we were done, and out, and that was the peace of a day.

Regardless of whether Rufus actually saw "a savage epileptic" enter the chapel, services were indeed open to those from outside communities. Although "the religious tone was strong and pervasive," said Flye, services were conducted with "a friendly, natural and unaffected quality, far removed from anything of piousness or stuffiness."[58]

After the Agee cottage, the 1914 Spanish Mission–style chapel is the oldest structure on St. Andrew's campus and one of the few that remain from Rufus's time there. The vestibule, nave, transept, sanctuary, Lady Chapel, and vestry make up about 3,600 square feet of floor space, with a small balcony of about 360 square feet. The space feels smaller than one might imagine after reading Rufus's descriptions, most of which are incredibly accurate. Bronze "triplicate bells" hang from the bell tower. Visitors enter the rear of the chapel after walking up "the sandstone steps," just as Rufus did. The "big life-size" crucifix still hangs inside, though moved from the vestibule to the nave's north wall. Also moved from the vestibule is the "sandstone font," which now sits near the altar. The original altarpiece, an intricate reredos screen modeled after one by Italian Renaissance painter Carlo Crivelli, still backs the High Altar in the sanctuary near where the Moller pipe organ, with its "white stops and keys," is located. The Lady Chapel is tiny, but its Madonna statue stands in the corner just as Rufus described. Atop the Lady Chapel's wooden altar sit the tabernacle and the monstrance, with its "spangling sunlike gold and white center," although it is uncertain whether those are the same objects he saw. Just inside the north door is the vestry, where a row of hooks lines the "inward wall" that "was hung solid with cassocks," the clergymen's robes.[59]

St. Andrew's campus, circa 1920s. The Agees likely walked from their cottage to campus using the path shown in the photograph's left foreground. The buildings shown, from left to right, are St. Joseph dormitory, St. Michael monastery (farther back), St. Andrew's main building, and the chapel. Courtesy of St. Andrew's–Sewanee.

Since Rufus's time, the chapel interior has been altered, with some objects rearranged, others removed. Pews replaced the former rows of wooden, "cane-bottomed chairs." Plaques depicting the Stations of the Cross no longer line the walls of the nave. The balcony has been opened up. Carpet now covers "the waxed floor" that was once "brutal against" a kneeling boy's knees.[60]

"There was due observance of Lent, and other special seasons and days of the Christian year," Flye wrote. The most important of these "special seasons" is the forty-day period of fasting beginning at Lent, culminating in the Holy Week—including Maundy Thursday, Good Friday, and Holy Saturday—and ending on Easter Sunday, "the crown of the year." St. Andrew's observed the tradition called the Morning Watch, reenacting the Disciples' vigil while Jesus prayed in the Garden of Gethsemane. In preparation for the ritual, members of the school and community committed to keep watch through the night, as described in these notes from *The Morning Watch:* "Between the middle of the morning on Maundy Thursday and the Mass of the Pre-sanctified Good Friday morning the Blessed Sacrament was exposed in the Lady Chapel and the boys, teachers and priests of the School, and some of the people who lived nearby on the Mountain, signed the list on the bulletin board for half-hour periods in the continuous watch that was kept before it. Since there was no compulsion, even of an invisible kind, it is probable that most of those who signed and watched were sincerely devout (though some signed perhaps ostentatiously often)." As currently practiced by the school, the watch begins "at 10 p.m. after the Maundy Thursday service. Proctors wake boarders during the overnight hours and escort them to the chapel," where students serve "30-minute shifts of prayer and meditation." The watch ends with the "Eucharist service at 7 a.m."[61]

Rufus later wrote of his own struggle to remain focused in prayer during that watch. Though fictionalized, his account—set "in a deep country part of Middle Tennessee, in nineteen twenty-three"—accurately depicts the chapel's appearance on the night of Maundy Thursday. The chapel's interior never looked more solemn. According to custom, images of any kind—the altar settings, crosses, statues, and artwork—were covered. Neither the nave nor "the sanctuary lamps were lighted, but the night at the windows made just discernible the effigies and the paintings and the crucifix, no longer purple veiled but choked in black, and the naked ravagement of the High Altar." Along the walls of the nave, "he saw the spaced badges of blacker darkness where the Stations of the Cross hung veiled." The covered "Madonna stood, a blind black monolith," in the Lady Chapel, which "brimmed with shaken light" from "candles it seemed by thousands."[62]

Chapel interior, St. Andrew's–Sewanee, 2015. Photo by the author.

ooooooooooooo

Laura Agee possessed a "deep interest in church ritual," according to her brother Hugh. Campus neighbors and faculty remembered her devotion to the school and church and her strong convictions. Perhaps as payment for her rental cottage, she regularly cleaned the chapel, and dutifully "laundered the linens and kept the flowers fresh." A friend and neighbor, Mrs. Medford, recalled, "She took care of the chapel as long as I knew her." Sometimes Laura's "lively sense of humor" was seen; other times she lived in quiet reservation.[63]

Laura's manner impressed the students, some of whom she actually taught in a classroom. Oliver Hodge characterized Laura as "a bright woman. Beautiful, bright . . . tall and striking in every way . . . and just overwhelming with kindness and intelligence." On days when Father Flye had to miss his history class, Laura occasionally substitute taught for him. Whereas most of the boys "didn't have a very high opinion of women teachers," Hodge said, "we just sat gaga to hear this woman." Another former student remembered that Laura's "natural voice was just soft and soothing." The boys "recognized her as something out of this world. Anything this boy [Rufus] had, he got from mama," Hodge said. "His father might have been remarkable—well, he must have been to have married a woman like that."[64]

One wonders if Laura ever led the history class while Rufus was taking it. Years later, he considered teaching at St. Andrew's, imagining it might provide him both stable employment and "much and uninterrupted leisure." However, he quickly dismissed the notion as "a terrible idea."[65]

Inspired by her surroundings, Laura took to writing religious poetry, and in 1922 published a collection, *Songs of the Way*. One poem stands out as what seems a reflection on Jay's death:

> Man is a flower of the field,
> His summer-time shall pass,
> The winter wind shall blow.
> And down like grass
> Cut by the mower's blade
> He falls, and lieth prone,
> And giveth back to clay
> The elements that for a sweet, brief time
> Saw day.
>
> His joy and weariness are gone to rest,
> All pain of body ceases, -yea, forgotten, he,
> Save in the waning lights of memory,
> He lies,
> And in his utter sleep
> Sinks slowly down, into silent deep.[66]

Whereas Laura's devotion drew her toward creativity, Rufus struggled with "self-pity, desires for martyrdom or sainthood, [and] incessant ... guilt" during this time, symptoms of an immature spiritual life. Father Flye did not believe Jay's death was enough of "a wounding experience" to cause the boy dysfunction. But combined with the events that followed—the death of his grandfather Henry, circumcision, the death of his cousin Wheeler, leaving home, abandonment by his mother, humiliation by classmates—Rufus certainly took an emotional beating.[67]

If his later writings about this period are revealing, Rufus appears to have gone through a sort of crisis of faith after his first couple of years at St. Andrew's—a crisis in the sense that his faith could not surmount his adolescent angst. He wrote of being eleven years old when "the image and meaning of Jesus and the power and meaning of the Sacraments and of the teachings of the Church . . . established upon all his heart and mind their comfort, their nobility, their sad and soaring weight." But his devotion "had begun to fade away soon after Easter, with the good weather, and had vanished . . . completely during the free summer in Knoxville."[68]

The summer of 1921 was a particularly restless one for Rufus. As during other school holidays, he returned to Knoxville with his mother and Emma to stay with the Tylers on Clinch Avenue. He was in the throes of "hot early puberty," spending his "cavernous and gloomed" vacation at his grandparents' "large unsentineled home." He recalled lying on the "shaded boards" of the front porch, "while the air lay in the metal magnolia leaves asleep":

> and I, this eleven-year-old male, half-shaped child . . . thinking and imagining what I was able of the world and its people and my grief and hunger and boredom, lay shaded from the bird-stifling brilliance of the afternoon and was sullen and sick, nearly crying, striking over and over again the heel of my bruised hand against the sooty floor and sweating and shaking my head in a sexual and murderous anger and despair: and the thought of my grandfather, whose house this now was, and of his house itself, and of each member of his family, and of all I knew so keenly and could never say and of those I too did damage to, and of the brainless strength and mystery behind all that blaze of brightness, all at once had me so powerfully by the root of the throat that I wished I might never have been born.

Meandering "from vacant room to vacant room," Rufus felt imprisoned inside the stuffy house, in "the stench of ferns trapped in the hot sunlight of a bay window." He vainly sought to satisfy his boredom:

> trying to read; trying to play the piano; ravening upon volumes of soft-painted nudes; staring hungrily and hatefully into mirrors; rifling drawers, closets, boxes, for the mere touch at the lips and odor of fabrics, pelts, jewels, switches of hair; smoking cigars, sucking at hidden liquors; reading the piteous enthusiasms of ribboned letters stored in attic trunks: at length I took off all my clothes, lay along the cold counterpanes of every bed, planted my obscenities in the cold hearts of every mirror . . . I permitted nothing to escape the fingering of my senses nor the insulting of the cold reptilian fury of the terror of lone desire which was upon me.

Climbing up to the rooftop balcony, he stared "in anguish and contempt upon the fronded suffocations of the midsummer city." For Rufus, almost a teenager, Knoxville summers had changed: they were no longer characterized by evenings with families "lying out all together on a quilt in the backyard" but by stifling loneliness.[69]

In 1923, following another summer vacation in Knoxville, Laura, Rufus, and Emma returned to St. Andrew's. Rufus, now a sophomore and almost fourteen, began his final year at the Episcopal school with perhaps more of an aesthetic interest in church ritual than a deep religious faith. "I just think he saw the artistic side of it," said Oliver Hodge, who likened Rufus to "a lot of people at St. Andrew's who were . . . more artistic or given to the form and color" of Episcopal services "than they were actually pious." In a controversial event held on campus that winter, "form and color" indeed overshadowed any spiritual significance. Rufus was surely there on January 30, 1924, the day the school observed St. Charles Day without the Church's sanction at the insistence of Father Liston Orum, a great admirer of England's martyred king, Charles I. The chapel interior and vestments of the clergy were draped in red, the color of martyrs; white roses representing the "white king" decorated the altar; and a giant banner, created by Mrs. Flye for the occasion, depicted King Charles, axe in hand. One wonders if Rufus was among the group of acolytes who solemnly paraded down the aisle: "Thurifer, swinging censer and attended by two taper bearers, crucifer, four choir boys, thurifer, acolytes, sub-deacon in tunicle, deacon in dalmatic, celebrant in cloth of silver cope, hundreds of years old; banner of Our Lord, Bishop's chaplain, two attending deacons and the Bishop." But at the ceremony's high point, "a reliquary made at the Abbey of Caldey, off the west coast of Wales" was carried in on a velvet pillow and duly blessed. Inside was the venerated relic that all eyes strained to see—a whisker from King Charles's beard.[70]

∞∞∞∞∞∞∞∞∞∞∞

Meanwhile in Knoxville, Joel Tyler's health was declining. Perhaps "grippe," his old enemy, had returned from long ago, when it forced the Tylers' move south from Michigan. Although Joel had been ill the previous fall, he was "much improved" by Rufus's fourteenth birthday. But whatever now afflicted her father, Laura believed it was serious enough that she needed to be near him. She no longer owned a house in Knoxville, having sold the last parcel of her Laurel Avenue property in June 1922; so once again she moved into her parents' home on West Clinch. Some sources claim that Laura returned with the children to Knoxville in "late February 1924," with Rufus transferring into Knoxville High School partway through the spring semester. However, school records indicate that Rufus did not leave St. Andrew's until May, after he had finished the term. Apparently, Laura brought Emma back early but left Rufus in Sewanee to finish his sophomore year.[71]

She left someone else behind. Father Erskine Wright, a fifty-one-year-old teacher from Pennsylvania, had arrived at St. Andrew's the year after it was founded. His campus house was located a little east of the gymnasium. Laura and he had both lost spouses and were contemplating remarriage.[72]

CHATTANOOGA

There is evidence that in early 1924 Rufus traveled with his mother and sister to Knoxville, briefly visited his grandfather there, and then returned alone to St. Andrew's. He wrote in a later journal entry that he had once stopped in Chattanooga during a solo trip back to the school. Even though Rufus had not grown up in Chattanooga, he had personal connections there: "Friends of mine, and boys who beat me up, came from the slums of this town. The mothers of two were whores. My great-aunt established her convent here."[73]

He also recalled gorging himself on movies while in Chattanooga—something he could not do at St. Andrew's—turning what was supposed to be a brief layover into an entire afternoon, which resulted in school punishment (perhaps administered by Oliver Hodge) for returning late. In recounting that day in his journal, Rufus apparently confused his age, as he was actually fourteen years old when the film *West of the Water Tower* was released in January 1924. "Down the street when I was twelve, on my way back to school, I stopped in between trains to see West of the Water Tower. . . . I came in at ten minutes of one. I stayed through two showings, came out at five, ate a hot dog, saw The Flying Dutchman, by rushing, got back for the 7 o'clock showing, stayed through till eleven, spent the night on a bench in the Union Depot, and got to school late next morning. My mother was worried to death and I was seriously whipped at the school." Twelve and a half years later, he would travel through Chattanooga as a journalist, on his way to the cotton fields of Alabama.[74]

In late April 1924, Paula was hospitalized in New York, ailing to the point that her family traveled from Tennessee to be with her. Laura and, incredibly, both of her parents made the journey by train, indicating that by spring's arrival Joel had regained at least some of his strength.[75]

KNOXVILLE HIGH SCHOOL

By May 1924, after multiple illnesses and moves between Sewanee and Knoxville, the family was still struggling to regain the stability it lost eight years earlier. Rufus returned to Knoxville, joining his mother and Emma, now twelve, in the Tyler home. Whether Rufus knew it or not, a stepfather was on the horizon. And whatever friends he had made during his five years at

The front of Knoxville High School, as it appeared on
August 15, 1921, with the newly installed World War I
memorial. N-1504, Thompson Photograph Collection,
McClung Historical Collection, Knox County Library.

St. Andrew's, in the fall he would be starting from scratch at an unfamiliar
school.[76]

Just eight days before Rufus was born, the cornerstone for Knoxville's new
high school had been set, on November 19, 1909. A block-wide, three-story
building "of Colonial design" was constructed of "marble and red brick" at
North Central and East Fifth Avenue, and opened the following September. Its front entryway boasted "a porch forty-five feet long, supported by
solid marble columns twenty-one feet high and three feet in diameter and
approached by marble steps forty-one feet in length."[77]

The "Doughboy statue of heroic proportions," pedestaled near the school
entrance, was erected in 1921 to the alumni who were killed in World War I.
General John Pershing, whose Mexican exploits once inspired make-believe
battles between Rufus and his playmates, attended the dedication ceremony

in May 1922. Rufus noted that the sculpted soldier "struggled through one singularly unimposing strand of bronze-painted barbed wire."[78]

Rufus, aged fourteen years and nine months, walked up those steps and between those columns, entering the building as a junior on September 7. "School had begun." The population change from St. Andrew's to Knoxville High must have shocked Rufus, as he was suddenly lost among two thousand students. The mass of classmates apparently did little to cure his loneliness. "Year in a Tennessee City High School. No friends [my] own age," he later recalled. Alvin Tripp, his three-months-older rival from Highland Avenue days, was now a senior; Arthur Tripp, older by three years, curiously was also a senior.[79]

The school building was "endowed with . . . modern improvements," as Rufus later described: "The toilets had a five-foot wainscoating [sic] of white tile. . . . There was a library, branch of the Lawson McGhee Library. . . . In the basement was a large and glistening kitchen. . . . There was a salon for girls' gymnastics and for aesthetic dancing; there was an excellent basketball court; there were two laboratories splinterey [sic] with broken test-tubes; and there were, of course, a great number of most up-to-date classrooms— all this vast variety nestled under one great roof." As he walked the school hallways, Rufus observed sculptures and wall hangings depicting literary and historical figures: "In the corridors stood startling statues of Apollo (well dressed), Pocahontas, the Winged Victory and Abraham Lincoln. On the walls hung pictures of Aurora, General Grant, Whittier, Abraham Lincoln, Washington Crossing the Delaware, and General Knox. And everywhere in class-rooms were constant foot-prints on the sands. In Latin rooms Julius Caesar, an unrobed goddess, and a Latin crossword puzzle stared at each other impersonally. In the English classroom were pictures of good and great men, gentle men, whose works and, apparently, heads, were to be a perpetual inspiration for Youth."[80]

Academically, Rufus mostly repeated the pattern of his freshman and sophomore years, slumping through algebra and geometry while excelling in history. But unlike at St. Andrew's, where he kept much to himself outside of chapel service, he joined Knoxville High's Dramatic Club and was cast in the spring production in a sizeable role. *Turn to the Right*, a play by Winchell Smith and John Hazzard, had a Broadway run a decade earlier and in 1922 was adapted as a motion picture. Rufus's part was that of Gilly, the more serious half of a pair of comic ex-cons. The script describes the character as "hard faced but likeable," "rather seedy," and "dressed in a rather ill fitting suit of dark brown or gray, plain color."[81]

In one scene, Mrs. Bascom, a sympathetic matron who believes Gilly is a good person despite his past, nurses his bruised head while telling him that "the Lord himself" sent him there. Gilly replies, "I ain't used to havin' nobody take care of me much. . . . I ain't got no family." Learning that Gilly has no mother, Mrs. Bascom comforts him: "Well, she's watchin' and lovin' you just the same as if she was here." Considering how isolated he felt from his mother at St. Andrew's and how in her absence he found refuge in Father and Mrs. Flye, Rufus may have read his own loneliness into Gilly's dialogue with Mrs. Bascom.[82]

The play was presented on April 24 at 7:45 p.m. in the school auditorium, which, Rufus wrote, "boasted genuine theatre seats and a dubious capacity of 2500." During school hours, the space functioned "variously . . . as the Auditorium, Assembly Hall, Study Hall, or Chapel. . . . The walls were of pockmarked plaster, painted a dusty cream color, with a rash of white initials in guarded corners." Rufus also satirically detailed the theater decorations:

> There were two pictures, one (purely allegorical) depicting Education, a tall and lovely goddess surrounded by cypresses, quadrants, papyrus rolls and intense-browed bare youths; the other of Aurora, her chariot riding clouds wild as a ripped feather bed, as a belch on a winter morning. The stage was hung with green, shining cloths, presented by the Dramatic Club to conceal some interesting and ineradicable attempts at artistic self-expression which had been made once during a rehearsal. They were of use occasionally, irregularly twisted and irregularly hung, to represent "a woodland" in Shakespearean comedy or the tall timber surrounding "Jack Van Puyster's camp in the Rockies; late p.m." The green was in clever contrast to the lush velvet curtains of royal blue. Bold above the stage, in large brown letters, blared: "Ye Shall Know The Truth, And the Truth Shall Make Ye Free."[83]

A few of Rufus's earliest published writings were inspired by memories of Knoxville High. But his interest in writing would not be fully known until after he left the city and transferred to Phillips Exeter Academy. One of his Exeter short stories, "Knoxton High," about a provincial city school with delusions of grandeur, mixed satire with barely disguised details from his junior year. Besides describing the building itself, Rufus referenced several actual faculty members. The fictional "Principal [Elmans] from Toledo" was based on the real-life W. E. Evans from Ohio, who was principal of Knoxville High from 1917 until it closed in 1951. Knoxville City Schools superintendent Walter Ellsworth Miller bore no resemblance to the character "Superintendent Sherwood," who had been "imported from . . . Chicago," although near the end of Rufus's school year it was announced that a man named

Shepherd, born in Illinois, would replace Miller in the fall. "Mr. Hendricks" was based on J. L. Hendrickson, a science teacher and business advisor for the yearbook. "Evelyn Neibert," the "green" but idealistic young history teacher whose "body was tying itself into one great knot" anticipating the first day of school, was based on Jessie L. Neubert, who taught junior-level social studies and had just joined the faculty that year. Rufus was enrolled in her ancient history course.[84]

"Helene Mundy," the girl sitting at home "in scant glamorous pajamas" while practicing a Cicero oration through a mouthful of candy, was the real Helen Monday, the only student Rufus named in this 1927 story. Perhaps he gave her a prominent spot because he had seen her a couple months earlier as the lead in *Stark Love,* a movie shot in the Smoky Mountains using local talent and one that was widely acclaimed upon its opening in New York late that winter. Monday, billed as Helen Mundy, had been discovered in a Knoxville soda fountain. But there is doubt about whether Rufus and Helen actually attended Knoxville High at the same time. Although Helen was enrolled at KHS during the 1922–23 year and the fall semester of 1923, she received no grades the following spring; and by September 18, 1924—a week and a half after Rufus entered KHS—she had transferred to Central High School. It is unclear whether she just started late at Central, or began the school year at KHS before transferring out less than two weeks later. If the latter is true, Rufus and Helen may have lacked a chance to meet each other in that limited time and within such a large student population. Perhaps Rufus was simply smitten after seeing her in *Stark Love* and, reading in the papers that she was discovered as a high school student in Knoxville, he mistakenly assumed she had been at KHS with him.[85]

Still, it is odd that Helen would appear in "Knoxton High" if she had left the school before Rufus arrived, since so many of the story's details are based on his own observations. The likelihood is remote, but it is just possible that Helen was indeed enrolled in his ancient history class that first week before transferring, that Miss Neubert had indeed assigned a Cicero oration, and that Helen indeed butchered the recitation so badly—"Quo usque tandem . . . what's usque. whaddluh-dooooodledoodloodooo . . to what lenth . . . " —that the experience stuck with Rufus as an amusing memory. It is also possible that as Rufus watched Helen onscreen three years later, he remembered her classroom performance and was thankful her movie dialogue was not audible.[86]

Even if Rufus had missed meeting Helen at KHS, he still could have encountered her elsewhere in the city. She was locally well known as a solo "classical," "fancy and toe dancer" and performed at various banquets hosted by organizations like the Shriners and Les Amis Club. In May 1923 Helen danced onstage at the Riviera Theatre before a matinee screening of Harold Lloyd's comedy *Safety Last*. Two years later, she "drew several encores" while performing "the Hula Hula and other 'mean' dances" at North Knoxville's Whittle Springs Resort Hotel pavilion, as part of a state convention for furniture dealers.[87]

Aside from some inaccuracies and embellishments, the "Knoxton" satire is clearly based on Knoxville High School. Although Rufus's school transcript and a couple of references in the school newspaper confirm that he attended KHS, there appeared to be no photographic evidence. The 1925 yearbook provided little help; juniors, like sophomores and freshmen, were photographed in a massive group outside the front of the school, making it almost impossible to recognize individual faces on the printed page. However, a digitized version of that class photo reveals a familiar face along the top right side, although the student's brow is furrowed against the sunlight and his mouth slightly twisted, making him appear annoyed. He stands half a head taller than most of the young men nearby, with his hands in his

In this detail, a student resembling James Rufus Agee stands at the far right side of his junior class photo, taken in front of Knoxville High School, 1925. N-0845 A1, Thompson Photograph Collection, McClung Historical Collection, Knox County Library.

pockets, and his dark hair parted on the left—just as Rufus's hair is parted in later school portraits. If this is indeed Rufus, then the photograph may be the last one taken of him in Tennessee.

Knoxville High closed in 1951, and for several decades the large brick building housed the offices of the Knoxville Board of Education. In 1994 the building joined the National Register of Historic Places as part of the Emory Place Historic District. Renamed Knoxville High Independant Living, the former school now houses apartments for senior citizens.[88]

Twelve-year-old Emma may have attended Boyd Junior High School as a seventh grader while her brother was at KHS. The old Boyd School building on Union had recently burned, so classes were moved that year to the former Tennessee School for the Deaf property on Asylum Avenue. Hugh Tyler remembered Emma's "delicious sense of humor," and told a story of walking downtown with her, likely around this time. The identity of the "aunt" in Hugh's story is unknown: "One day in Knoxville Emma was on her way to see some relatives living in a section of the city called Summit Hill. After walking block after block, uphill in the hot sun, I said, 'Emma, where *does* this aunt of yours live anyway?' By this time Emma was quite breathless. 'O,' she gasped, 'it's the hair on the next Squase!' It was the most perfect 'Potterism' I ever encountered. We just sat down on the curb until we could speak again."[89]

Rufus remembered that his "year in Knoxville High School" ended "the year of the Scopes trial." Within a month and a half of him leaving Knoxville, controversy was brewing at a high school seventy miles to the southwest. John Scopes, a teacher in the small town of Dayton, was brought to trial for teaching the theory of evolution in his science classroom. Rufus may not have known that his Knoxville rector, Dr. Walter Whitaker, submitted testimony as one of "four religious experts" to Scopes's defense, which "sought to reconcile for the jury the theory of evolution with the biblical account of creation." One defense attorney, John R. Neal, was already a controversial figure in Knoxville, having been fired as a law professor by UT president Harcourt Morgan two years earlier for supporting evolutionary theory, Neal claimed. Former Knoxvillian Joseph Wood Krutch, covering the trial for the *Nation*, criticized Morgan and UT professors for lacking "the courage to stand up" for Scopes. William Jennings Bryan, the lead prosecutor and former secretary of state under Wilson, had spoken in Market Square's public hall in 1920. When he died in July 1925, five days after the trial, Bryan had been planning a trip to Elkmont. At the time, there was much interest in making the Great Smoky Mountains a national park, and promoter David C.

Chapman invited Scopes and his lead attorney Clarence Darrow to stay at Elkmont, where both learned of Bryan's death. The funeral train's route to Washington, D.C., included a brief stop in Knoxville, where "hundreds" of citizens gathered near the Southern Railway Station to pay their respects.[90]

oooooooooooooo

While Rufus observed and absorbed details of his high school during this transitional period, he also reoriented himself with the city of his younger years. Although several of the families he knew on Highland Avenue had moved on, the old neighborhood had not changed much physically. In another decade, his old home would be split into apartments. While Rufus was at St. Andrew's, John and Annabel Agee had returned to Knoxville from Nebraska and now lived about two blocks west from where John first called on her at the King residence. Rufus probably visited his uncle, aunt, and younger cousins, Gladys and Oliver, at 1710 Highland. (Property records indicate that the Craftsman bungalow at that address was built in 1925.) How often he visited them and his other Campbell County relatives is unknown; he admitted that he saw "relatively little" of them.[91]

Spending much time with the Tylers, Rufus developed a "profound attachment to [my] invalid grandfather to whom I read a great deal and talked." Rufus characterized Joel Tyler's somewhat incongruous personality as "bitterness and unhappiness" mixed with "calm, beauty and fortitude." One summer evening as the two sat together, something odd occurred which Rufus retold in a letter to the *Sentinel*, hoping to win tickets to the Riviera Theatre for the most "humorous, pathetic or unusual" story. "My grandfather has false teeth and they are not very comfortable for him," Rufus wrote. "The other evening he took them out and laid them on a table while he read. When he had finished he asked me to hand them to him. I picked them up and they were literally crawling with small red ants." Interestingly, Rufus signed his letter "James Agee," a name he would not use regularly until after moving away from Knoxville.[92]

He later outlined a story about this period, "with an invalid, failing grandfather, renewal and intensification of deep affection, filled on both sides with a sense that they are likely never to see each other again." Besides a love of literature and conversation, Rufus inherited from Joel "a lasting terror of marriage, earning a respectable living, having children: a virulent, defensive sense of being completely surrounded by traps, both malignant and merely well-meaning or conventional." Some of Rufus's marital insecurities might have formed the winter of his junior year when his mother announced her engagement to Father Erskine Wright, the school bursar.[93]

REMARRIAGE

She was listed in Knoxville's 1925 city directory, issued in March, as "wid Jas"—the widow of James—residing at 1115 West Clinch. That spring, less than a week after Rufus performed in the school play, Laura Agee traveled with Father Wright to the Polk County courthouse in Florida, where on April 30 they were issued a marriage license. Three days later, they wed at All Saints Episcopal Church in Lakeland, Florida, with the Reverend G. Irvine Hiller officiating. "My mother remarried when I was 15, a clergyman," wrote Rufus.[94]

Once school ended, Rufus, and apparently Emma, found places to go apart from the new Mr. and Mrs. Wright. In June the *Knoxville News* listed the names of forty girls—including one named Emma Agee—who spent two weeks in Townsend at a Girl Scout camp. And "early in the summer," Rufus left with Father Flye to tour England and France for several weeks. On their return to the Port of New York at the end of August, the customs agent recorded Rufus's summer address as Coronado Beach, Florida. The Wrights subsequently lived in Charleston, South Carolina.[95]

Laura's parents visited her in Charleston in early February 1926 before traveling to New York, where Joel was to undergo eye surgery. He was in Manhattan on February 28, about 260 miles south of his birthplace, when he suffered a fatal stroke. His body was cremated and the ashes taken to Kalamazoo. In a private ceremony at Mountain Home Cemetery, Joel's remains were buried near the graves of his parents, Rufus and Sarah Tyler.[96]

Later that year, the Wrights settled in Rockland, Maine. On August 26 Emma Tyler signed her last will and testament in Knoxville, naming Hugh as its executor and bequeathing "all of my property . . . to my three children, namely Laura Tyler Wright, Hugh C. Tyler, and Paula F. Tyler, equally, share and share alike." She spent the winter with Hugh in New York and returned to her Clinch Avenue home by summer 1927. It appears that Emma gave up the house within the next year or two, because Paula and she traveled from New York to spend Christmas 1929 with Hugh and his wife, Mildred, who had moved to Knoxville the previous month. At the time Hugh was working as a muralist for the local architectural firm Barber & McMurry. His intricate wall decorations can still be seen inside the Church Street United Methodist Church and in the James D. Hoskins Library on the UT campus. But other than the couple of years through about 1931 that Hugh and Mildred lived in Knoxville with their young daughter, Lydia, the Tylers spent most of their remaining lives in New England. Emma Tyler was living with the Wrights in Maine when she died on November 6, 1931. She was buried in Kalamazoo next to Joel. The obituary printed in Emma's hometown of Port Huron, Michigan, noted her lifelong interest in "education for women" and that she had been "the oldest living member of the local Ladies' Library Association."[97]

While Emma Tyler had primarily worked through secular and political organizations, her sister-in-law Jessie Tyler served within the Episcopal Church. Both women were zealous in their own spheres, devoted and persevering, putting others ahead of themselves to the detriment of their own health. The ministry exhausted Jessie, who once confessed to Laura that she "had no longing left" for an afterlife: "If I just was sure . . . when I get through with this life that I would never be conscious any more, how glad I should be—I'm so tired." But Jessie remained faithful, despite her weariness: "Unfortunately, I can't believe that. I have to go on, I think, myself." While caring for influenza patients in 1929, Jessie Tyler—Mother Mary Gabriel—contracted the virus herself and was "on the brink of death for five months." When she finally succumbed in Sewanee on August 11, Father Flye was present in the room, watching over her. She was buried at Park Cemetery in Bridgeport, Connecticut.[98]

<hr />

The 1924–25 academic year proved to be the last time that Rufus and his surviving family, perhaps excepting Paula Tyler, all resided in Tennessee. "After a year in Knoxville High School, the year of the Scopes Trial, I was sent to Exeter, where I spent three years; the vacations then, and thereafter, in Rockland, Maine," he wrote. "Then four years at Harvard, majoring in Latin and English." Of course, his editorial work for Harvard's *Advocate* magazine opened doors to a professional writing career.[99]

Laura Wright said of her son, "His life in Knoxville ended entirely with his entrance to Phillips Exeter." He only visited the city a handful of times as an adult, twice on assignment with *Fortune* magazine. By that time, everyone had stopped calling him Rufus, except his mother, Father Flye, and a few others. But he remained emotionally connected to the mountains he left behind, later stating that "Tennessee" was one of the few "places [where] I feel really at home," along with "more or less, anywhere in the South." Laura confirmed that Rufus "always had a deep love for the land, and for the South, which he very strongly felt his blood-tie to."[100]

In some ways, Rufus never left, as evidenced by his frequent use of childhood locales in his writings. As his friend Robert Fitzgerald wrote, "The native ground and landscape of his work, of his memory, was Knoxville and the Cumberland Plateau." Agee's recollections of Knoxville and the surrounding hill country became a source for his satire, plays, poetry, journalism, avant-garde experimentation, and his barely-disguised autobiographical fiction.[101]

5

"The Stars Are Wide and Alive"
Writings, 1925–1955

While Tennessee inspired so many of Rufus Agee's later writings, one wonders why there were few indications of his future vocation while he lived there. His old Knoxville neighbor, Martin Southern, had expected Rufus to enter some white-collar field such as business or medicine and was astonished to learn that he became a writer. The journal entries Rufus wrote while traveling with Father Flye in Europe were the first signs of creativity the priest had seen from the boy, who showed no such inclination at St. Andrew's. "I wasn't aware of his doing any writing that would be noticed until the summer that we went to Europe together, and he was to enter Phillips Exeter that fall," said Flye. "But I wasn't aware in his earlier days that he had any particular gift for writing or taste for it." Did his gift spontaneously emerge that summer after he left Knoxville?[1]

As it turns out, Rufus had been sketching story ideas for at least three years before that, as he stated in his Guggenheim application in 1932: "I began writing in Tennessee, at about twelve." He was that age the year his mother published her book of poetry at St. Andrew's, and perhaps one pursuit influenced the other. Unfortunately, there is no record of his early written experiments, though some likely survived as seedlings for his later fiction.[2]

But his first-ever published work, a book review, has come to light. It appeared in the May 8, 1925, edition of Knoxville High School's *Blue and White Weekly* newspaper—six months before the more prestigious *Phillips Exeter Monthly* printed his first story, and about fourteen years before he began reviewing books for *Time* magazine:

PETER AND WENDY
By J. M. Barrie
Reviewed by Rufus Agee

"Peter and Wendy" is a classic of gentle whimsy. Please read the book and then pass judgment upon it—and me. Most of you will laugh at it scornfully, call it a "baby book," and say that you enjoy real literature, and pick up "The Mine with the Iron Door" or some similar story of the big open where men wear their sleeves rolled and let the wind blow through their hair.

True, it is an ideal "fairy story," and one which children can enjoy immensely. But it is far, far more than that. It leaves the big, clean hills, and the big, red-blooded, double-chested Harold Bell Wright heroes who infest said hills, painfully behind, to be used by the unfortunate souls who care only for them.

For besides being a delightful fantasy, it is replete with the mellowest, most deftly written satire I have ever read.

The satire is not bitter, like that in "Alice in Wonderland," and it is never cutting. The book was probably not written with as definite an object in view as was Carrol's [sic] classic, but throughout the story one finds gentlemanly criticism in the form of travesty.

In fact, many of the sequences remind one of "Treasure Island," leaving that book in a ridiculous light, although all of Barrie's satire is so veiled and so gentle that one is not surprised to learn that he was an ardent admirer of Stevenson.

If you read it, do not go about it as you would peruse the Manufacturer's Record, or a report from the Presbyterian Missionaries in China, but try to enter into the spirit of the thing, and realize that it is a fantastic story of another world. I believe you will find it a delightful book. If you do not, return to the gripping stories of the big open spaces, and we'll all be happy, won't we, dears?

Although not a brilliant piece, Rufus's breezy voice comes through as intelligent and witty, making several outside references within a short review. Significantly, the byline bears his childhood name, showing continuity between the boy from Knoxville and the writer in New York. It is easy to imagine Rufus Agee as an outsider, withdrawn and sullen during the tumultuous decade following his father's death, never distinguishing himself in school. Yet here is evidence of his continued love of literature in his first published critique—indeed, his first published work of any kind—which foreshadows the future career he had not yet considered.[3]

POSSIBILITIES

As Rufus bicycled through European landscapes that summer, his mind conjured beautiful and evocative words, which he committed to paper. The trip might have been the first time Rufus imagined himself writing for a living, and his journal displays the same gift for imagery that characterizes his later work. In one of his first pieces published at Phillips Exeter Academy, Rufus described a war-ravaged cathedral he encountered at Amiens, France: "I retraced my steps and, at the western edge of the church, found the twisted ruin of the organ. The sun had set and the pale moon became brighter. By its light I saw wraithlike old images, bestowing upon the desolation a deathless, hopeless benediction." He entered Exeter in autumn 1925 with a clear interest in writing, through which he could express his longing and sadness and irony—and make the fleeting moments of his life more permanent.[4]

He also sought to make sense of his life, which still felt unsettled and haunted by his father's absence ten years after the fatal accident. He retained vivid impressions of the days between the death and funeral; now he had a creative means of expressing them. Not long after arriving at Exeter, Rufus stated in a letter to his mother that he wanted to write about his father's death and how it affected the family. According to David McDowell, "this was something that was in his mind all the time." Now at the New Hampshire prep school, awakened to his identity and calling, perhaps Rufus contemplated the series of events that led him there. After all, he was an Exeter student solely because his stepfather recommended it; and his mother would not have married Erskine Wright had she not been a widow. In all likelihood, the family would still be living comfortably in Knoxville had his father lived, with Rufus following some white-collared career path as his acquaintances expected. Jay Agee might have continued working securely for his father-in-law, eventually moving up from bookkeeper to partner, from partner to successor.[5]

But then, even with his father living, life might not have been as stable as one would imagine. As Robert Coles speculated, "Had [Jay] lived might he once again have started drinking heavily, pulling away even more from his family, frightening an older Rufus, depriving him of someone with whom he might identify?" Rufus might have come to resent his father's mountain heritage, instead of embracing it, and father and son might have divided over the son's artistic and political leanings. As an adult, Rufus himself pondered the scenario, writing, "If he had lived I am pretty sure that we would have fought for many years. He was much more simple, violent, direct in action, and courageous than I am and would, I am sure, have felt contempt for me on three main counts: 1) physical cowardice, 2) interest in art, 3) promiscuity." It is plausible that had his father not been killed, Rufus would have spent most of his life in Knoxville—eliminating the need for a transfer to

St. Andrew's and a mentor in Father Flye, who mused over such possibilities in a birthday letter to Rufus years later. "No doubt you think from time to time of events and decisions and often very small circumstances which have modified our lives," Flye wrote.

> Some slightly different circumstances in 1918 or before, and I would not have come to St. Andrew's; and so with you; and we would never have met. I am glad that in life it has not been a matter of my choice alone where I would go and whom I would meet, for if I could see all the elements, the alternatives, the future, I would not feel able to choose wisely and indeed would probably not dare to choose. However, it happily does not depend entirely on what we wish or plan or decide, and while some things may come out worse than we would have made them, others come out much better. At any rate, I am glad that in this way—the old name for it was Providence, which seems a very good term—you and I were brought to know each other.

"Providence," then, had worked within Jay's death to steer his son through channels of opportunity that would have otherwise been closed. In scholar Victor Kramer's assessment, "So many circumstances of his life developed as a result of his father's early death." This seems to be the paradox of Rufus Agee's life: without the tragedy he might have lived a longer, more secure life in Knoxville but possibly would not have become a writer—maybe music would have been his passion. But because of the tragedy, he departed the city in his youth and for the rest of his life could not shake the compulsion to recapture on paper what he had left behind.[6]

Rufus greatly respected his father and believed that, despite a few areas of conflict, they had much in common, including "veneration for 'nature' and for the simple, insulted & injured; & enduring kindness; hatred of snobbery; melancholy; ambition and a sense of defeated ambition; tendency to drink too much; essentially 'peasant' as against urban feelings; [and] a murderous temper." Wanting "to be identified with his father," Rufus now called himself James or Jim. And whether or not his father would have approved, James R. Agee was now a writer, and would eventually distinguish himself as a poet, journalist and critic, screenwriter, and author of fiction.[7]

EXETER

Agee entered Philips Exeter Academy in September 1925. While he would not write explicitly about the event for years to come, as a prep school student Agee meditated on his father's death and how he might express it poetically. By his second month on campus, Agee had already prepared several pieces of writing for publication, as he indicated in a letter to Father Flye: "I have written stuff for the *Monthly*, and I am to get a story and 2 or 3 poems in this month. This will get me into the Lantern Club, I hope." One of those poems, "Ebb Tide," is his first published work in any form that addresses his father's absence:

> He's gone, he's dead; he carried away my soul
> To empty space where stars sink sighing past.
>
> And now—my life to live, a gaunt, sad life . . .
> My life—it's like a little shallow pool
> Left in a hollowed rock by ebbing tide;
> A pool which slowly turns to bitter salt. . . .
>
> My life . . . a tepid slowly dwindling pool,
> To join—once more—the vastness of the sea.

Agee's phrase "empty space where stars sink" faintly echoes one from his mother's earlier poem: the "silent deep" into which Jay's body "sinks slowly down."[8]

The same November issue featured Agee's first use of a Knoxville setting in fiction, one of several Exeter pieces he would set in East Tennessee. "Minerva Farmer" is about a thirty-nine-year-old woman who graduates from the University of Tennessee before teaching at a local grade school. For the story, Agee likely drew not only from his mother's experience at the university and his own as a student at Van Gilder (Highland Avenue) School but also on his father's determined escape from an agricultural existence through self-education. After delaying college to help her blind father work the family farm, Minerva Farmer finally graduates from UT two decades later—her "gnarled, parboiled" hands and body mangled by years of "back-breaking labor." She is subsequently hired as a teacher at an unnamed "primary school," one evidently modeled after Van Gilder because Agee retains the name of his former principal from that school, Rosa (Rose) Staub. Like Jay Agee, Minerva gives up farming to "become a country school-teacher," which allows her "to save money for board and for books." And like Laura Tyler, she attends UT dances with "hair . . . puffed and knotted behind as was stylish at the time," and is "admired" by "young men" for "her determination and the soft gray eyes." However, the real Rose Staub, who felt that "one must love children . . . in order to be successful as a teacher," was probably not as intimidating as the fictional principal's "red-haired, red-faced, seamed pomposity."[9]

His first drama, "Catched," is set in "the simple interior of a log cabin in the Tennessee Mountains." Mag Felts, fifteen-year-old daughter of a moonshiner, is afraid that marrying a man from the hills will cause her to lose her beauty. When a traveling salesman from Knoxville, Sam Hayden, stops by the cabin, Mag sees him as her means of escaping to the "good-sized" city: "Oh, Lordy; they ain't no chanct fer me . . . unless I git to town." Mag's fears are realized when her plan to coerce Sam to marry her falls through. Although the characters and scenario are fictional, the play echoes with the hopelessness felt by many mountain people in the late nineteenth and early twentieth centuries, when large numbers of them found work in Knoxville factories. Of course, Agee remembered that among those transplants was his own father, whose postal employment brought him to the city. The name Felts later reappeared in *A Death in the Family*, as the name of the neighbors who lived "two doors away" from Uncle Frank in LaFollette. In "Catched," the Feltses have a neighbor named Gudger—another name Agee recycled years later as a pseudonym for one of the tenant families in *Let Us Now Praise Famous Men*.[10]

"The Circle" is Agee's first use of Campbell County, and specifically the town of LaFollette, as a story setting. LaFollette, of course, is the town near where his father's parents lived. His uncle Frank owned a furniture and mortuary business there, Agee & Carden, which was renamed Agee Furniture & Undertaking in 1936 and retained the name until after Frank Agee died in 1940. Like "Minerva Farmer" that preceded it, this short story centers on a main character's aspirations being crushed by unavoidable circumstances. After his father's death, Edgar Butler feels trapped in the position of caring for his aging aunt, and abandons his plan to study law: "My career has been warped by my father's decease, and college is for the present out of the question. I must stay with my aunt now, for I see nothing else I can do." Agee's setting is largely fictitious, as in the naming of "Kirby Street," "the LaFollette *Banner*" newspaper, "the Rex Movie Palace," and "the Broken Boat, a favorite trysting place for LaFollette couples." While census records show several Butlers living in Campbell County in the early 1900s, it is unlikely Agee was naming actual persons, as his firsthand knowledge of LaFollette was very limited compared to that of Knoxville. However, in describing the Butler Mansion as "LaFollette's pride" and "a conglomeration of every possible architectural monstrosity," Agee may well have had a house in mind called Glen Oaks, just a block or two east from downtown's main intersection. Erected around 1900 by the city's founder, the George Barber–designed, twenty-seven-room mansion on Indiana Avenue is indeed "the largest dwelling in town," as Agee stated of the Butler residence, and remains a striking example of Victorian design.[11]

May 1926 marked a decade since his father died. Agee composed a poem, "Widow," in which a woman buries her husband the afternoon of Christmas Eve but suppresses her grief in order to give her children a cheerful holiday. Agee fictionalized the event by setting the poem in winter, with the "coffin lowered in the sifting snow," but must have imagined his own mother's sorrow during the family's first Christmas without a father:

> The children are asleep, and now I sit
> Stringing flaky pop-corn, bit by bit;
> Polishing the apples till they shine—
> Hark! "Annie, won't you *ever* stop your whine?
> Yes, Santy Claus is comin'—go to bed,
> Dear"—(God, how memories pound through my head)!
> . . . .
> I've got to take things quietly, I can't
> Go raving crazy now, dear God, I shan't!
> More tinsel now, to decorate the tree—
> There, I step back a little bit to see
> The finished job. My, how they'll love all that!
> (They'll dance and squeal and howl and blab and blat
> And make my day a hell)—But they don't know;
> They can't see what I see now—*all* I see;
> The coffin lowered in the sifting snow
> Only this afternoon—and now to go
> Through Christmas, keeping up a silly sham
> Just to make those kids upstairs forget—
> Forget the thing they never understood! . . .
> That branch is thick—it spoils the symmetry.
> I'll get the hatchet now, and lop it off . . .
> How sharp and bright it is; how cold the blade!
> I draw my thumb along the edge; and think
> What it could do! Oh, God forgive me that!
> . . . .
> I cannot stand it more; with stifled shriek
> I creep to our old bedroom. I undress
> And lie . . . and wait a comforting caress . . .
> And your hard arms . . . and find but . . . emptiness.

Of course, it is presumptuous to assign all of these feelings—especially the improbable suicide-by-hatchet-blade fantasy—to the widowed Laura Agee.

However, it is not a stretch to imagine Laura feeling frustrated and over-whelmed while keeping up appearances for her two children. And regarding the widow lying in bed awaiting "a comforting caress" from her husband's "hard arms," it is worth noting that after Jay's death Laura confessed to her brother, Hugh, "how she missed her husband's body."[12]

There is no direct evidence that Agee's sketch "Revival" was based on a factual episode. But revivals were common events in Knoxville churches, as in late 1922 when such events were held at Central Baptist, First and Second Presbyterian, Lincoln Park Baptist, Washington Pike Methodist Episcopal, Hayes Chapel, and Centenary Methodist Episcopal—most of them headed by visiting ministers. St. John's and other Episcopal churches also hosted revivals, which they labeled "missions," a more subdued term. Agee's fictional church sanctuary, punctuated "with the penetrating odors of sweat, tobacco, bad whiskey, and perfume," appears much more informal than that of an Episcopal congregation and anticipated his later description of the Majestic Theatre auditorium. Although it is not known whether Agee had a real-life counterpart in mind for "Rev. Victor Moody," there was a Fountain City–based evangelist, Rev. George E. Moody, who led local revivals, like the one in South Knoxville just before Christmas 1924 that he wrapped up with a sermon provocatively titled "The Devil's Incubator." Moody apparently had a flair for the dramatic, as when he helped the sheriff's office destroy moonshine stills as part of its "Devastation Day." With Moody swinging the ax, the newspaper promised a "performance . . . filled with vigor and en-thusiasm." Even if Moody was not his model, Agee must have experienced firsthand the kind of charismatic preaching that he lampoons in "Revival." Robert Fitzgerald, whom Agee met when both attended Harvard, stated that on occasion Agee performed "a parody of a southern preacher in a hellfire sermon."[13]

Agee wrote a handful of satirical sketches at Exeter that reflect his teenaged impressions of Knoxville. The mocking tone of these stories suggests that there was no love lost when Agee departed his hometown, as though he considered Knoxville to be the graveyard of ambition. Of course, it is not uncommon for a teenager to disparage his hometown. Agee might have been using sarcasm at the time as a defense against his family's instability. But even as a student in Tennessee he had been familiar with satire, as evident in his *Peter and Wendy* review. "I was in the cheap-irony stage at about fifteen," he wrote to Father Flye. What appeared to be bitterness in his writings was likely the literary influence upon him of satirists like Sinclair Lewis. The previously mentioned "Knoxton High," published in April 1927, is a thinly-disguised story of Agee's year at Knoxville High School, where he perhaps felt that school administrators emphasized the building's amenities over the quality of education.[14]

Not as well known are a couple of earlier satires about a fictional town, "Jenkinsville, Tennessee." One could argue that in describing this Podunk locality Agee was really provincializing his former hometown. After all, Jenkinsville's "White Way"—a main street "carelessly splashed with asphalt, which lies along the street's center like a tattered and wrinkled ribbon"—connects the town's train station to its courthouse, just as Gay Street links Knoxville's courthouse to the Southern Depot. The shabbiness of the fictional town agrees with the 1925 account of a visitor who called Knoxville a "peculiar town" and noted Gay Street's "rickety appearance" and "whacked-up buildings." And with Jenkinsville's "General Supply Store" slogan, "The Best Is None too Good," Agee could have been satirizing the Knoxville grocer on North Central Avenue whose advertisements read, "If the BEST is good enough, buy your meats from A. J. Carroll." Furthermore, Agee writes that a section of Jenkinsville "has since the Dixie Highway's coming fallen into decay." By the 1920s, of course, Knoxville was a midpoint along that major highway, which entered town from the north via Central Avenue and left town via Kingston Pike and Asheville Highway.[15]

But other story elements suggest that any similarities are coincidental. For one, Jenkinsville's thoroughfare is only "a hundred yards long," about a tenth the distance Gay Street stretches between the courthouse and depot. Jenkinsville's courthouse, "a box-like" structure with "bilious monstrosities of slate and wrought-iron," does not resemble Knoxville's 1886 courthouse on the corner of Gay and Main; nor does the story's "scabrous and barnlike" depot remind readers of Knoxville's grand 1904 Southern Passenger Station on West Depot Avenue. While the fictional post office "blithely masquerades as a Greek temple," the vaguely neoclassical Custom House in Knoxville lacks the columned façade that such a caricature demands. Perhaps the strongest argument against the story being a Knoxville satire is found in Agee's companion sketch, "Jenkinsville II." Consisting of three character studies but fewer descriptions of the actual town, the text names Knoxville as a place separate from Jenkinsville. One resident, "Seigbert Pearson," owns a pool hall over which he and his wife live in a two-room flat. Annoyed by his wife's religious zeal ("she . . . shouted loudest, sang the shrillest, repented the most vehemently at every revival"), Sig often escapes Jenkinsville by train "for a lil' weekend" of carousing in Knoxville. If Agee had a real place in mind for his fictional setting, perhaps it was one of the smaller Dixie Highway towns he often passed when traveling in and out of Knoxville.[16]

Even if its setting is completely imaginary, as it may well be, "Jenkinsville II" employs a familiar Agee trope: a character, "Emerson Davis," is forced to trade ambition—in this case, writing "the Great American Novel"—for a mundane existence following the death of a loved one. Emerson's wife insists they leave New York and move back to Jenkinsville to live with her mother. There she dies, and Emerson's remarriage to her "aging, sad-eyed" sister cements his unhappiness. "Now he works in a Chain Shoe Store, of which Jenkinsville is inordinately proud."[17]

Besides "Knoxton High" and the "Jenkinsville" stories, there exists an even earlier satire that is rarely mentioned by Agee scholars, perhaps because of its being mistakenly categorized as a nonfiction article, rather than as fiction, in an often-cited Agee bibliography. "Largest Class in History of School Grads" appeared in the November 1926 issue of *Phillips Exeter Monthly*. What distinguishes this amusing piece, set in the town of Hydesboro, from the other satires is that specific Knoxville publications can be identified from which Agee borrowed details. For example, he seems to have relied heavily on the issue of Knoxville High School's *Blue and White Weekly* newspaper in which his review of *Peter and Wendy* appears—which suggests that he kept the newspaper with him at Exeter, or had possibly written part of the story before he left Knoxville. For the title of the satire, Agee pulled a line almost verbatim from the KHS newspaper: "This is the largest class in the history of K. H. S." While his real high school graduated 319 seniors in May 1925, Hydesboro High's largest class numbered seventy-nine. In satirizing his former school, then, he made it smaller and more provincial.[18]

Hydesboro's fictional commencement exercises were held at "First Baptist Church," with a "baccalaureate address" given "by Rev. Percy Knickerbocker, rector of the Baptist Church." While KHS held its baccalaureate and commencement services on separate nights, the former event was indeed held "at the First Baptist Church," though not officiated by Rev. Knickerbocker—a name Agee borrowed from an advertisement in the *Blue and White:*

Have You Heard
REV. J. P. KNICKERBOCKER
    Pastor of Church Street M. E. Church preach? It's the old gospel in a new setting. He'll hang golden lamps along your highways, open silver doors to your ambitions, and teach you the pathways to God. His religion is religion of addition and not subtraction. Come and laugh with the happy Savior.

Agee varied some of the details, such as Hydesboro's "school colors" of "yellow and blue" versus Knoxville High's blue and white. "The Hydesboro High

Orchestra, under the able direction of M. Arthur Garratt, instructor in violin, piano, piccolo and vocal," greatly resembles Knoxville High's orchestra,
which was "under the able direction of Prof. Garratt," as the *Blue and White*
stated; the paper also advertised that "Charles A. Garratt" taught "Voice,
Violin, Piano, and Harmony" at "The Garratt School of Music." Adding to
the list of similarities, the fictional school and its prototype also shared the
same sports rival, "Red Central," as well as the same principal, "William E.
Evans, B. S.," and the same Latin teacher, "Miss Sherwood."[19]

Laying aside the *Blue and White,* Agee flipped through another KHS
publication while composing Hydesboro's fictional senior class poem. His
line, "Four years of joy, and sorrows, too," almost exactly matches one, "Four
years of joy and sorrow," written by Knoxville's graduating class. But a more
remarkable likeness is found in one of Hydesboro's "two School Hymns,"
written by the fictional students "Adelaide Carver and Rebecca Cole":

> We, the class of '26, are leaving Hydesboro High,
> That we're the best that she's produced nobody can deny.
> We're sorry to leave Hydesboro High,
> We're sorry to leave Hydesboro High,
> But whatever we'll do we'll always be true
> To thy Name, dear Hydesboro High.
>
> —ADELAIDE CARVER

Compare that to Knoxville High's "Class Song 1925," the lyrics of which
were written by a real student named Rebecca Cole:

> We the class of Twenty Five are leaving Knoxville High.
> That we're the best that she's produced, no one will dare deny.
> We're sorry to leave Knoxville High
> To ever be worthy we'll try.
> But whatever we do we'll always be true,
> And we'll raise her standard to the sky.

The fact that Agee copied more than half of KHS's senior class song verbatim
indicates that he not only mined details from his high school newspaper but
also from the 1925 KHS yearbook, *The Voice.*[20]

Hydesboro appears again in Agee's "From the Life and Letters of an Exeter Man," an unpublished story told in a series of humorous correspondences
sent back and forth from Exeter student Alfred Rutledge to his parents and
friends in Hydesboro. These fictional letters are dated from September to
November 1926, the same semester Agee wrote his other Hydesboro-based

story, but the dates may be fictional as well. While Agee clearly pictured Hydesboro as a substitute for Knoxville in "Largest Class," here he identifies it as a town in Massachusetts. Perhaps Agee still had Knoxville in mind but simply set it in New England, as director Clarence Brown did for his 1935 film *Ah, Wilderness!*—modeling the story's Connecticut high school on his alma mater, Knoxville High. "Largest Class" and "Exeter Man" share something else in common: both contain a character named "May Belle Uldridge." Alfred Rutledge resembles Agee in several respects. For example, Alfred is disappointed in his Exeter entrance exam scores, "getting only Lower Middle ranking after being a Jr. at Hydesboro High, but I have had the Caesar before, so it ought not to be so bad." Likewise, Agee attended Knoxville High as a junior and later complained that "he fought Caesar's Gallic War for the third time" at Exeter. Another similarity is that Alfred does not get along well with his father, as his mother confirms in a letter: "Father has had a sick headache today, and is feeling cross. Alfred, you must write to him. It hurts him that you don't get along better with him, and while I can understand your various points of difference, you must try to narrow the gap, rather than letting Exeter widen it." At the same time, Agee had a somewhat strained relationship with his stepfather, Erskine Wright. Alfred also has an "advisor" who is "a sort of father by proxy." For Agee, of course, this was Father Flye. The name of Alfred's old Hydesboro girlfriend is Helene King, who calls Hydesboro "absolutely the *deadest* place I ever saw." Perhaps by coincidence her first name appears in another of Agee's stories around this time, attached to the "Knoxton High" student Helene Mundy.[21]

In another unpublished story, likely written around the same time, Agee again transplanted Knoxville details to a New England setting. Exeter student Ned Greene returns home and must quickly adapt to a new member of the household: the aged Aunt Etta Goodwin, in from Louisville. Meanwhile, he carries on a romance with girlfriend Martha, including drives out to a trysting spot. But since Ned plans to enter college next year, he's not sure how far to take the relationship. After a date one night, the conflicted Ned drives home along a "country road"—whose name Knoxvillians will recognize:

> Thursday night he left Martha early. Heedless of the glare-ice, he slithered along for miles over the humped back of Ball-Camp Pike. The windshield wiper wheezed unendingly, and through the beady crescent of clear glass an occasional parked car would loom toward him. As he swished by, the lights would flash on, and the motor would purr like a sleepy Bengal.
>
> He kept recognizing spots where—things had happened. But only once did he slacken speed; and then once more he abruptly jammed in his foot, and the motor sang in the bleak winter night.

Later, in *A Death in the Family*, Agee (mis)named Ball Camp Pike as the site of his own father's car accident, an event he might have alluded to here as one of the "things" that Ned remembered "had happened" along that road.[22]

A couple of months after "Knoxton High" was published, Agee submitted another drama to the *Monthly*, "Any Seventh Son," which he also set in "a little log cabin," presumably in Appalachia. The tone is ominous as, offstage, a midwife comforts a new mother, who just gave birth at midnight. Jed, the seventh boy in his family, has become the father of his own seventh son, Zeke. Hester Bright, the midwife, sees the birth as a bad omen and tells Jed that Zeke is "the seventh son un a seventh son," and though he will have mystical abilities, he was born badly deformed, with "little squinched-up lags." Jed rushes into the room, presumably to kill his baby boy, and the drama ends with a scream. The play is short and undeveloped, but it contains the type of unnerving superstitions that one encounters in mountain folklore, where a birth defect might be interpreted as a literal curse upon the family. Although the story's location is unspecified, one character looks out the door at the billowing storm clouds, which he says are "jist a bilin' up over Shake-Rag Rift." Agee must have based this name on Shake-Rag Hollow, an area west of St. Andrew's where he used to hike.[23]

He again employed a regional dialect in "Bound for the Promised Land," this time establishing his characters as lower-class southern blacks by having them speak lines reminiscent of Joel Chandler Harris. Agee probably drew from memories of his father's funeral in describing that of Leopold Rucker, as in this scene: "There was a long silence. Upward into the hot sweet dusk strained the lily flames. The shades were drawn, and eyes shone like bits of china. The men were lunged forward in their chairs, round heels hunched between shoulders. Between their knees dangled their hands, knotty fingers interlaced. Beneath puckered foreheads the white eyes stared, straight before them, hard and fearfully." Partway through the story, it is revealed that Leopold "had striven these seven years" to somehow achieve his own death so that his family could "sell da body" to Dr. Pinckney up at the local college, presumably for scientific research. Although Agee's reference to "Science hall," a building on UT's campus, suggests he set this story in Knoxville, his characters do not appear to be modeled on particular Knoxvillians. The name Pinckney does not show up in a search of university faculty members from that time period. There were a few Ruckers in Knoxville's 1925 directory, labeled (c) for "colored," including a pastor's family that lived on East Church Avenue, but there is no evidence that Agee knew them. The undertaker, "Mr. Johnson," also appears to be fictional. There were three black-owned mortuaries in Knoxville in 1925: two of them, Jarnigan & Son and Wheeler

& Son, were located on East Vine Avenue; the other, Lillison & Mills, was located on Cansler. "Reverend Sampson" also appears to be fictional, as a minister of that name does not appear in the city directory.[24]

In "A Sentimental Journey," Lula "ran off and married Alvin" Green years ago—not out of love but to spite her mother. Now, after a loveless marriage, Alvin is dead. Lula and her daughter, Ella, travel back home to Portersville, where they will live with Lula's mother and aunt Etta. During the train ride, Lula catches a glimpse of a man sitting behind her and fantasizes a relationship with him, even imagining his name is Quinn. Carried away with the delusion, she thrusts herself upon him and creates a scene. The setting is unclear, but descriptions suggest the South: as the train pulls into town "beneath Liberty Hill," it passes "the flickering windows of trackside tenements" and "a spatter of bungalows with garages of tin and front yards of red clay." (The fact that a railroad-traversed community named Liberty Hill exists in Grainger County, about thirty miles northeast of Knoxville, is probably coincidental.) While the characters do not resemble members of Agee's family, the relationships could. To Laura's parents, it might have seemed that she "ran off and married" Jay in Panama, although theirs was not a loveless marriage. After Jay died, Laura lived with her mother (and possibly her aunt) for a time, but there is no evidence of animosity between them.[25]

Agee graduated from Philips Exeter Academy in spring 1928. During his three years at the prep school, he published over thirty works, many of them set near Knoxville. While his writings were mostly undeveloped, as one would expect from a young author, they reveal Agee's emerging talent for capturing detail, his identification with characters stuck in mediocrity, and his fascination with his native South.

HARVARD

Even before entering Harvard in autumn 1928, Agee had a vision to "revive the Harvard *Monthly*, which died of wounds rec'd in the Great War. It was far, far ahead of the *Advocate*, in every way." He became editor of the *Advocate* and published more than thirty pieces during his four years, mostly poems—a large portion of which later appeared in *Permit Me Voyage*, the only poetry collection published in his lifetime.[26]

The bleak and undeveloped "A Walk Before Mass" was published in December 1929, while Agee was a student at Harvard. The main character, a man who feels stuck with an unfaithful wife because they have a son, bears

James Agee at Harvard. Courtesy
of St. Andrew's-Sewanee.

little resemblance to the writer except in his appreciation of A. E. Housman, whom Agee listed among other influential writers in "Dedication." One Sunday morning, the man rises early, and wakes his son, Jerome, who tries to dress himself but stands "puzzled, over a complication of buttons." In writing this, Agee might have recalled his own childhood struggle to button suspenders to his stockings and the way his father carefully showed him how to do it. Leaving the house, the fictional father walks the son "down the hill" on a road that "stretched downward like a hard cone" and out "to the end of the pavement." As a "country wind" blows rain at them, they walk "across the meadow and down to the river's edge." Just as one expects the man to confess his resentment and bitterness, he hurls his son into the cold rushing water. The story's location is not named, and there are few details that help place the action. Because Agee was a Harvard student and well acquainted with Housman's work at the time, one might assume that he set this story near the Charles River in Cambridge. However, descriptions of the landscape are also compatible with Knoxville's hilled Fort Sanders neighborhood and its proximity to the Tennessee River, where Agee and his father may have walked during an early morning fishing trip.[27]

No guesswork is needed, though, in determining the setting of his next short story, "Boys Will Be Brutes," the most autobiographical of Agee's

Harvard prose. In his first sentence, he reveals the location as the old neighborhood where he lived from ages three to eight: "Highland Avenue projects various and diminishing qualities of paving through the suburbs of West Knoxville." Two boys—Joe, "about eleven," and Richard, no "more than eight" but "nearly as tall"—are hunting sparrows with a BB gun in a field near the old Civil War fort. Agee turned eight in November 1917 and was that age when he first visited St. Andrew's during the summer of 1918. His mother, Laura, sold the Highland Avenue house that September after returning from Sewanee. So if "Brutes" is based on an actual incident, it may have occurred in the spring of 1918. Agee uses the name Richard here as an apparent pseudonym for himself, as he did later in *The Morning Watch* and in early drafts of scenes reworked for *A Death in the Family*. A possible candidate for Joe, the other boy, is Arthur Tripp, who was three years older and who probably would have seen Agee at "Sunday School," since the Tripps also attended St. John's Episcopal Church.[28]

"Death in the Desert" is Agee's story, narrated in first-person, of hitchhiking through the Southwest. Suffering from the heat and an infected ear, the narrator is picked up by a family. However, his own conscience is seared when the driver then leaves a black man stranded on the lonely desert highway, even though there is room for him in the car. It is possible that Agee based this story on an actual incident, as he had spent the summer of 1929 "harvesting wheat" as a migrant worker. While the setting is nowhere near the Southeast, Agee inserts details that relate to his Tennessee adolescence. Trying to make small talk, the young passenger "told of Maine a lie or two I had picked up in Tennessee." As the conversation ebbs, the young man lays his head on the seat cushion and begins to daydream, retracing "a path through the Tennessee woods; every turn of it, and every fork; and the place I used to leave it for a trickling ravine that ran down into Shake-Rag Hollow." This is the name of a wooded area about a mile west of St. Andrew's roughly equidistant from campus, in the opposite direction, as the forbidden swimming hole Agee visited. "There was a flat of sand half way down, printed with exciting tracks that I could never identify. Once, a little farther down, I had come suddenly upon a king snake and a rattler, fighting." The confrontation ended with the rattler being eaten by the king snake, "with rattles still purring between his jaws. I had walked home a little sick at my stomach." This episode evokes another snake that Agee may have encountered near St. Andrew's—the one his character Richard, in *The Morning Watch*, killed to make the other boys think he was brave. Continuing his daydream recollection: "There were abandoned coal mines in the hollow; shale and slate and coal were naked and flaky about the tumbled shafts. If you kicked a black stone it fell away in sheets like a broken book. The sheets were one great clear weave of black ferns, every vein and feather of them distinct. They were giants, but they could never have been larger than the ferns in the drop below, that sprang and drooped in the half-light, a sinister ferocious green. It was somehow too terrifying to know that they too would sink into the earth, that this blaring green would be flattened into blackness." But the narrator says he "was eleven" at the time and "had never seen and could not conceive such foliage stamped on stone." Like the story's narrator, Agee apparently daydreamed often of his earlier years in Tennessee, as glimpses of that prior life are revealed in his stories, sometimes overtly as in the above example from Sewanee, sometimes not.[29]

Some of Agee's Harvard story ideas exist only as sketches found in his old composition books. One sketch, another early variation on the loss of a parent, is about a young man, roughly Agee's own age, who visits his dying mother. "The last time the son . . . sees her, she is very weak." Following the visit, the mother "remembers that she'd meant to give him an apple" and wanted very much to place it in his hand herself in case she was "unconscious next time he comes. Very soon afterward she loses consciousness and shortly dies. The father solemnly passes on this last message and the apple." The story would follow the son "through the days of the funeral," focusing on "his conduct . . . and *centered about the apple*. At times he doesn't dare to touch it—it seems too sacred. He will sit & look at it by the hour—thinking—or musing—on his mother. . . . At other times he will pick up the apple . . . will rub it, cool, against his cheek & throat & breast—Then cup it in hands till it take[s] on a fleshlike heat. . . . The apple, of course, has become a symbol to him. . . . He begins to dream about his mother . . . of early childhood in which she gives him an apple—he wakes up realizing—for first time—that she wanted him to eat the apple." By that time, of course, "the apple will be rotten." While one wonders where Agee got the idea of the apple, the sketch foreshadows his later written reflections on his own father's death.[30]

For another story idea, Agee used the death of a family member—the aunt of a boy named Abbott Nolan—as the basis for a humorous scenario. "Abbott's mother had gone away, the night before, and she would not be back until tonight. She had gone to her sister's funeral, and in her absence, Mrs. Carson was taking care of Abbott." But unlike the serious nature of Agee's other death-related stories, this untitled fragment reads more like a situation comedy as two boys find mischief in an empty house. "Right after breakfast, George Carson and Abbott had hurried across the street to

Abbott's house," where they climbed in through an open basement window and "ransacked the house from top to bottom. . . . They stole from room to room, snickered before mirrors, flushed the toilets, danced stiff-kneed on every bed," and "gaudied their faces" with Mrs. Nolan's makeup. But as "George was struggling into one of Mrs. Nolan's dresses, and Abbott was simpering at himself in her mirror," Mrs. Carson called out from the front door, which immediately "galvanized" the boys "into silence." The rural setting is not described, except for the Nolan house being situated near a cornfield. But the untitled story is yet another example of Agee returning to the theme of death and its effect on a family, and further evidence that the writer was working out on paper the permutations of his own unresolved past.[31]

In the same composition book, Agee sketched a scenario based not on death but on a familiar scene from his Knoxville childhood. "A family is sitting in the back garden, on a summer evening," something he did often with his parents and his mother's family. "This is a habit and joy to them." For a real-life model, Agee noted that "nothing could be better than the Tyler family." But sadness enters the scenario, as the "daughter is late in pregnancy—very soon she goes to the hospital." Perhaps Agee imagined the daughter having to move away from the family after the birth, as "the girl's husband" has been offered a job elsewhere. Agee wrote, "They all know this is the last time she can sit out here with them—maybe the last time she ever will." As the family struggles to enjoy the last evening together, "their sense of sorrow and beauty and *living* is heightened, that evening." Agee specified, "The narrative should hover delicately over one of them after another." It is possible that Agee pictured his own parents on the eve of his birth, sitting in the backyard of the Tylers' Clinch Avenue home, faced with moving away for an undetermined length of time. But "in the end," the "husband . . . will *fail* to take his job," and "the whole business, so tenderly worked up, will break up like thawing ice"—apparently meaning that the family will stay together after all. Elements in this "summer evening" sketch prefigure ones Agee detailed several years later in "Knoxville: Summer of 1915."[32]

"A Short Story," one he hastily titled in February 1930 for his sophomore English class, depicts "a box-supper in the Tennessee hills" inside an old church building: "The loud thud of stamping feet beat out through the open windows, and the thready squeal of a single wild fiddle shivered through treetops and failed on the windy darkness." Joe Rickets, twenty, attempts to woo young Stella away from his rival, Buck. Meanwhile, country folk either "whirled in the dance" or watched from the side, with their "root-like hands between their knees, lean heads slung awry on their spines. The old men smoked or chewed, and talked and laughed, and jugs were oftener on their shoulders than on the floor." Seizing a moment when Buck is distracted by the passed-out fiddler, "Joe veered toward Stella's side" and, grabbing her, "hurried out, through the wagons and awakened horses and crying children, and onto the path towards her cabin." Joe and Stella take swigs from the jug and walk together, "drunk, glad and singing." Agee pictures a moonlit valley, the kind he must have viewed on trips to East Tennessee hills: "They stood just within the heavy ledge of woodland shadow, and looked across the valley. The tilled land lapped about the black-timbered prongs of the mountain, as if at high tide. Beyond the mountain's hold, the plain lifted toward the horizon in one fecund swell. The mountainside was scarred with dead streams, and landslides, and tilted farms. Deep in the cove below them treetops thrashed in a storm of moonlight." Enchanted by the scene, the lovers embrace; and Joe sees a place off to the side where they might lie together. "An ancient log lay there, bedded in moss, barkless and faintly silver ... the rich moss beyond it lusted for them." As Stella "gave him a long, blinding kiss," Joe "swung her about and drew her down upon the log." However, Joe misidentified the object he chose to bed on, and the writer describes the consequences with characteristic vividness: "The horse's carcass gave way with a crackle of splintering ribs: a swarm and whine of flies burst about them: and monstrous fluent putrefaction lapped their loving flesh around." As in many of Agee's stories, some unforeseen obstacle frustrates the main character's ambition. Agee's later fiction contains several names recycled from earlier works, and readers will recognize the name Rickets (Ricketts) as a pseudonym for one of the tenant families in *Let Us Now Praise Famous Men*.[33]

Most of the Tennessee-based stories Agee wrote at Harvard were more reflective and less mocking than those he wrote at Exeter, almost as if he was beginning to realize the value of what he had left behind. But his sense of satire was stronger than ever—and contributed to his start as a professional writer soon after graduation.

1930s

Agee had apparently been ambivalent about writing as a career until November 1930, just before his twenty-first birthday. By then he had ruled out "music and directing movies" as possibilities and wrote to Father Flye that "writing is my one even moderate talent," an "unhealthy obsession" that consumed "every waking minute, in one way or another." He was barely out of Harvard and had no experience writing business articles when *Fortune* hired him in 1932, based on a parody of *Time* magazine he had edited at the university. He quickly demonstrated a knack for manufacturing beautiful prose out of *Fortune*'s drab subject matter—economic issues that nevertheless reunited Agee with his homeland on multiple occasions.[34]

On May 18, 1933, exactly seventeen years after Agee's father died, President Franklin Roosevelt signed into existence the Tennessee Valley Authority (TVA), a federal corporation that promised to boost jobs and infrastructure in the Depression-crippled Southeast. Although the TVA Act specified that the agency would be based in Muscle Shoals, Alabama, the headquarters were instead moved to Knoxville. There, "in 106 offices," TVA could oversee its "most important present undertaking: the Norris Dam," to be built just north of the city. *Fortune* assigned Agee the story of TVA's first project, and his research took him to Knoxville in September 1933. It was likely the first time he had been back to the area since he left eight years earlier. He chose to open his article by charting the Tennessee River's journey from its birth at the Holston and French Broad rivers to where it "continuously dies into the Ohio": "The Tennessee River system begins on the worn magnificent crests of the southern Appalachians, among the earth's oldest mountains, and the Tennessee River shapes its valley into the form of a boomerang, bowing it to its sweep through seven states. Near Knoxville the streams still fresh from the mountains are linked and thence the master stream spreads the valley most richly southward, swims past Chattanooga and bends down into Alabama to roar like blown smoke through the floodgates of Wilson Dam, to slide becalmed along the crop-cleansed fields of Shiloh, to march due north across the high diminished plains of Tennessee."[35]

Knoxville, one of TVA's key cities, is notable for being "at the head of Tennessee, girdled with mines and quarries and timber, the first capital of the state of Tennessee, the seat of the University of Tennessee," Agee wrote, but also for being, in 1931, "the . . . twenty-eighth most murderous city, big or little, in the U.S." He added the latter statistic somewhat hypocritically, considering that in his previous sentence he suggested that writer Thomas Wolfe should have represented his native Asheville "more kindly."[36]

Agee noted Chattanooga as another important Tennessee city, a "self-styled Dynamo of Dixie" with "400 factories more or less" that was also a "great center for religious publications," with "more churches per capita than any other city in the U.S." Among those congregations was Christ Church, founded by the Reverend William Robertson, whom Agee met the day of his father's funeral.[37]

Some lesser Tennessee towns also made Agee's list: "Bristol and Kingsport and Johnson City and the villages down-at-heel like Dayton of blessed memory and Jacksboro and Tracy City." Besides his personal connection to Jacksboro, these places stood out to Agee from other small towns across the country because of "the fine soft slur of speech in the streets and the still goodly number of Model T Fords and the few deciduous southern mansions with their hitching posts and the 'nigger-towns' with their clay beaten down by bare heels and the whitewashed clapboard shacks." Throughout the state, you could still find the "Southern Gentleman of the old school, who ... nuzzles 'burbon' juleps and quotes Horace and talks 'hosses' and loves his country as the greatest battleground of all the war, next to Virginia." But the people most affected by TVA's plans were the simple farmers who worked Tennessee's valleys, and the particular breed of farmer who worked its hills: the "mountaineer." Agee called the mountaineer "the strong backbone of the Tennessee Valley," and surely grouped his own ancestors with "that incomparably pure American stock which produced such men as Lincoln." Despite the fact that Agee was praised for his reporting in this first TVA article, it mostly reads as if it could have been written from anywhere in the country using information gleaned from newspapers, correspondences, and official TVA publications—not by someone who was already intimately familiar with the region and had traveled there especially for the assignment.[38]

When *Fortune* dispatched him a year and a half later to follow up on the Norris Dam project, Agee's return to TVA headquarters yielded a longer and less detached appraisal. Joined by his wife, Via, and his mother, Laura, Agee arrived in Knoxville near the end of January 1935. Whereas he had remained a distant observer in his previous article, this time he offered a literal man-on-the-street perspective. Visiting TVA's offices in "smoky Knoxville," Agee walked "up sooty Gay Street" to "turn down smudgy Union"—a familiar route that took him past Market Square—and entered a six-story building "a block this side [east] of the Masonic Temple." Today, the Pembroke, containing forty upscale condominiums, quietly occupies the southwest corner of Union and Walnut. But in the mid-thirties, the New Sprankle Building, as it was known then, hummed with activity as TVA's hub of operations. Earle Draper, who planned the model town of Norris, J. W. Bradner Jr., creator of the innovative Norris Freeway, and Roland Wank, chief architect for Norris Dam and other agency projects, all worked from third-floor offices. The fourth floor contained the offices of TVA's three directors, whom Agee met during his tour. Chairman Arthur Morgan viewed TVA as a "benevolent" driver of utopian ideals, but he had also endorsed the practice of eugenics decades before its association with Nazi Germany. Harcourt Morgan, who would succeed Arthur as chairman, had of course been president of UT and, some felt, a particularly mute one during the controversial Scopes Trial. And

Looking north over the Tennessee River toward downtown Knoxville, circa 1930s. N-5620, Thompson Photograph Collection, McClung Historical Collection, Knox County Library.

David Lilienthal later served under President Truman as chairman of the new Atomic Energy Commission.[39]

Agee asked locals for their opinions of TVA, and in the process interviewed two people whom he may well have known from earlier days. Of course, then as now, using close acquaintances or family members as shortcut sources was considered unprofessional journalism. But it is possible that the "Knoxville marble man" who "is not so sure about the wisdom and efficiency of his government" was Arthur Savage—still one of the heads of Ty-Sa-Man Company, producer of marble-cutting machinery. Even though Joel Tyler was no longer living, the family still owned part of the company, and as a stockholder, Agee conceivably stopped by to see Arthur and ask about business.[40]

Roughly twenty-five miles to the north, where "the Norris Reservoir" would soon displace many rural cemeteries, Agee also spoke with a man hired to relocate "several hundreds of the coffins," who "holds that TVA is doing a fine work." The man, "a La Follette undertaker," is not named by Agee but could have been his own uncle Frank. For the young journalist, the river valley was sacred ground: his father had been born in one of the villages that in a year would be submerged beneath rising lake waters. Agee visited the Norris Dam construction site and reported statistics on how much hydroelectric power it would generate. He described the model town of Norris itself, its layout and available styles of worker housing, and the Norris Freeway, which ran east "from Coal Creek"—renamed Lake City the following year—"across the Norris Dam site around Norris Town and southward to join the Cincinnati-Knoxville highway," then known as Dixie Highway. In 1935 the two highways intersected in north Knoxville, at Central Street and Broadway.[41]

∞∞∞∞∞∞∞∞∞∞∞

With his entrance into professional journalism, the 1930s also saw the bulk of Agee's poetic output. Perhaps inspired by his trip to Knoxville the same year, his 1933 poem "Theme with Variations" highlights the cyclical agrarian life, laboring from dawn to dusk, and the mammals, birds, reptiles, and insects that would have been constant companions on the farm. In 1934 Yale University Press published *Permit Me Voyage,* a book of Agee's poems, most of which he had written at Harvard. It would be the only collection of his poems published in his lifetime.[42]

The collection's capstone is "Dedication," a benediction of sorts in which Agee acknowledged members of the human race—including his own father—who had most influenced his life: "To those who died in sorrow, and in kindness, and in bravery; to those who died in violence suddenly, and to all that saw not death upon them . . . to those who died in the time of the joy of their strength." Jay Agee would certainly belong to this group; he was buried under the epithet "In His Strength" and often characterized as "brave" by his son. The poetic memorial continued:

> [T]o all the dead in their generations:
>   And especially to Joel Tyler, and to James Agee my brave father, and to Jessie Tyler that became Mother Mary Gabriel, faithful maidservant of the most high God, and to Emma Farrand, the wife of Joel Tyler.
>   May they rest.

While Agee included both of his Tyler grandparents in the list of deceased relatives, his father's father, Henry Clay Agee, is notably absent.

> To those who, living, are soon to die: and especially to Via my wife, and to my
> mother, and to my sister Emma and to David Preston her husband, and to Gladys
> Lamar Agee my father's mother; and to Hugh Tyler, and to Paula Tyler, and to
> Erskine Wright, priest.

Among his list of living relatives, Agee mentions his mother, his stepfather, his sister, his brother-in-law, and his aunt and uncle Tyler. He leaves out all of his father's siblings. And while he allots space to his grandmother Moss Lamar Agee, he misnames her Gladys Lamar, after his first cousin. From this poem, it is clear that Agee did not retain close relationships with his Campbell County relatives. But he was much more careful to name the adults at St. Andrew's who helped nurture his adolescence: "And to James Harold Flye, priest, who befriended my boyhood with the wisdom of gentleness, and to Grace his wife; to Edwin Clark Whitall, priest, patient in all his life."[43]

In the same book of poems, Agee included a sequence of twenty-five sonnets, many of which contain autobiographical references. In the fourth sonnet, Agee reflects on his connection to all those who came before, from distant humankind up through his own family tree:

> I have been fashioned on a chain of flesh
> Whose ancient lengths are immolate in dust:
> Frail though that dust be as the dew's mesh
> The morning mars, it holds me to a trust:
> . . . .
> I have been given wings they never wore.
> I have been given hope they never knew.
> And they that were brave, who can be brave no more.
> And they that live are kind as they are few.

The line, "And they were brave, who can be brave no more," recalls his "brave father," listed in "Dedication." Those who died are no longer brave or strong, for "Strengthless they stand assembled in the shadow," as Agee writes in the fifth sonnet. He recalls the generations before him, his father's people whose plows "scored the April meadow" and whose "hands that gave their kind ungentle power / To summer's travail, autumn did not spare." Although the death in the eleventh sonnet is a metaphor for lost love, the idea of "strength" expiring appears again: "Woe though it was that wreck of strength to see / Thaw down and die, it was not by our will." The fourteenth sonnet contains more explicit references to his parents, and to his father, whose "strength" was cut short:

Not of good will my mother's flesh was wrought,
Whose parents sowed in joy, and garnered care:
The sullen harvest sudden winter brought
Upon their time, outlasting their despair.
Deep of a young girl's April strength his own
My father's drank, and draughted her to age:
Who in his strength met death and was outdone
Of pity and high purpose, grief, and rage.

At his death, all of Jay Agee's struggles and aspirations ended. But though he was robbed of "strength" and "high purpose," he also escaped a life of sorrow and lack of fulfillment. With the phrase "in his strength," the poet again references the engraved epithet on his father's tombstone. As in "Ebb Tide," Agee seems to be echoing his mother's poetic sentiment that Jay's "joy and weariness are gone to rest." Each in his time, Agee's forbearers loved and fought and aged, and saw their lives' inevitable decay from strength to weakness, from spring to winter, day into night. In the fifteenth sonnet, Agee affirms his own responsibility to continue where they left off:

But that all these, so hopeful of their day,
Highsouled in joy and hungry for the fight,
Loved all too well such loving to betray,
And linked in love declined into the night
Whose dusk is flesh, whose dark is family,
Whose midnight is despair full-wrought from love;
Despair of strength and the soul's entity;
Opposed to noon by this thick world's remove.

And since I burn so wrathfully with joy,
And love also, as kindly as did they,
And so would fight, and so would not destroy
Night-hearted love that shows so proud a day:
I'll choose the course my fathers chose before.
And, with their shadows, pray my son does more.[44]

The collection includes only one Exeter poem, "Ann Garner," written during Agee's last semester at the prep school. He later stated that the piece, which he reworked in 1929, "more or less gave me a chance to say everything I had to say or feel about nature and death." The folk ballad is Agee's first poem to include images of nature and agriculture that his paternal ancestors would have known intimately. Descriptions of the stark, unnamed hill country suggest the mountains of Appalachia, a rugged land cultivated by equally rugged people:

> Now the blue plowshare surged in the broad fields,
> The black earth, riven by the flame-like blade,
> In sinuous furrows flowed behind. Ann watched
> The plunging and inexorable plow,
> Watched her husband guiding it, and when
> The work was done, and over the quiet hills
> The sky glowed greenly, stealing out alone,
> Ann pressed her body to the raw, rich earth
> And felt life swelling great against locked stones.

When her infant child dies, Ann becomes increasingly reclusive and bound to the cycles of the land around her:

> And after that
> She scarcely lived within the cabin's walls,
> But with the cattle moving up the mountain . . .
> Then in the swaying dimness of the forest
> She lay beneath the gnarled mountain laurel
> Or on the cool and calm of fallen oak leaves,
> And heard the rush of wind among the leaves,
> The subtle writhe and shiver of an earth
> Forever tortured by the myriad roots
> Sprawling in darkness downward.

Despite "all the preachers of the country" attempting to restore Ann to her husband, her mind is lost, and she dies embraced by the land she wed. As her body is lowered into the grave, the husband scatters a handful of crushed bones over it—the bones of their dead child.[45]

Religion figures into many of Agee's poems and is treated both reverently and satirically. His early poems tend toward devotion, as do these lines from "A Chorale" that solemnly evoke the Holy Week ceremony known as the Morning Watch, in which Agee had participated as a St. Andrew's student: "Your faith who gave your heart for our safekeeping / Your love who sweated blood while we were sleeping." Here Agee guiltily associated himself with the Disciples, who could not remain awake during Christ's prayer at Gethsemane.[46]

In later poems, however, Agee treated organized religion as a phase of immaturity that he had outgrown and discarded. Perhaps drawing from his experiences singing in choirs at St. John's and St. Andrew's, in "Delinquent" Agee portrayed the mock-devotion that apparently characterized many young choristers' performances:

> Hymning the high gods with oscillations,
> As pliable lips adapt to the air,
> Distracting the flock from divine occupations
> By singing so loudly and looking so fair.
> Limp in their linen that glistens and grates,
> They ogle an octave with unctuous eyes,
> Or lower shy lids as the organ abates,
> Demure as a demon in cherub disguise,
> Till troubled parishioners cannot be sure
> So much naiveté's utterly pure.

Another undated poem reiterates a similar theme: the author's youthful piety has given way to adult rationalism:

> When I was small delight and fear
> Were eminent upon my blood
> Watched I but once into the sun
> Great shadows walked my mind of God.
> . . . .
> But I, and wiser men than I,
> Have since deduced much better sense.
> My brain is very quiet and clear.
> The shadows have departed thence.

In his most ambitious poem, the lengthy and unfinished "John Carter," Agee included a section that could represent his own religious upbringing, with himself disguised as a youth named Leonard:

> Observe the hallmark case of Leonard Dash.
> Sad as a schoolchild, pained in adolescence,
> His frail deistic dreams went all to smash
> With worrying sick about the Actual Presence;
> First Mumsy, then Our Lady was his mash;
> Myrrh was his mouthwash, frankincense his *essence:*
> And he bothered more than any sane youth ought to
> Whether 'twas nice to wear lace on his cotta.
> . . . .
> It flurried Leonard frightfully at times.
> At nights, he thought of one thing and another,
> Of sweet-fleshed maidens bred in palmier climes,

Also of Jesus, Huberts, and his mother.
So finally, when he'd hoarded enough dimes,
He snuk to Boston. . . .

Boston, of course, is not far from Cambridge, where Agee attended Harvard University. Agee included other autobiographical details in his notes for the poem: that John Carter is brought up in "completely faithless Episcopalianism" and endures "an entirely conventional baptism (done because a sore aunt insists it's the polite thing to do)." Perhaps the "sore aunt" was Jessie Tyler, the family's most devout Episcopalian. Whereas Agee grew up at St. John's in Knoxville, with Dr. Walter Whitaker as rector, the poem's title character is raised in "St. Wilfred's" under the leadership of "Paul Inchbald Whitaker, M.A., D.D." At the christening, "Dr. Whitaker let his lip slide up from three highly polished front teeth and said he was delighted to welcome the little fellow." Agee might have inserted his adult self—"uncle Rufus," possibly a nod to Joel Chandler Harris' Uncle Remus—into the poem, in a few lines that reveal his post-religious hedonism: "And then you may agree / With wise old uncle Rufus, when he says / Our race is near its wisest and its best / Wholly in love and prostrate and undressed."[47]

Through the biting sarcasm of "Fellow-Traveler," Agee showed what became of "Leonard Dash" and blamed "Mumsy" for oversaturating his childhood with the religion that turned him away from God:

[I]f only Mumsy had kept mum about the sunnier side of God,
Perhaps I wouldn't have left Him on the seamier side of the sod.

Mumsy you were so genteel
That you made your son a heel.
Sonnybunch must now reclaim
From the sewerpipe of his shame
Any little coin he can
To reassure him he's a man[.][48]

A bedtime verse that Agee recited as a child becomes an object of parody in "John Lamar," an unfinished poem. The four saints—Matthew, Mark, Luke and John—to whom he previously prayed are now four revolutionaries: "Four angels round my bed / Armed sentinels at my head, / Darwin, Einstein, Freud and Marx, / Guard the bed that I lie on."[49]

<hr />

In November 1935, a month after his second TVA article was published, Agee and Via drove south and spent Thanksgiving at St. Andrew's with the Flyes and then vacationed in Anna Maria, Florida. Agee composed many pieces during the stay, including dozens of poems and a now-famous prose work. Recent trips through Knoxville had stirred up memories of his former life there, of his last carefree summer twenty years ago, before his father died. In a journal entry likely from early 1936, Agee noted his progress on a "foot-loose in Knoxville idea," on which he had written "12–15,000 words." This was probably not the same work that he finished in under 2,000 words and published as "Knoxville: Summer of 1915"—which began as an exercise in "improvisation" and was completed, with little revision, in under two hours:

> I was sketching around, vaguely, on a possible autobiographical novel . . . and was so much involved and interested in early childhood memories. I was greatly interested in improvisatory writing, as against carefully composed, multiple-draft writing: i.e., with a kind of parallel to improvisation in jazz, to a certain kind of "genuine" lyrics which I thought should be purely improvised. This text turned up more out of both states of mind, than anything else: specifically, remembrance of the way water from garden hoses looked and sounded at twilight. This brought nostalgia for much that I remembered very accurately; all I had to do was write it; so the writing was easier than most I have managed. It took possibly an hour and a half; on revision, I stayed about 98 per cent faithful to my rule, for these "improvised" experiments, against any revision whatever. There is little if anything consciously invented in it, it is strictly autobiographical.[50]

He spent those ninety minutes well. Unlike his Harvard composition-book sketch about an anonymous family enjoying a last summer evening together before the daughter moves away, in "Knoxville: Summer of 1915" Agee wrote as himself, describing a specific memory of a particular time and place: "We are talking now of summer evenings in Knoxville, Tennessee, in the time that I lived there so successfully disguised to myself as a child." He described Highland Avenue, the houses and trees and the way the neighbors interact. He described the sounds of the locusts, the spray of garden hoses, and the streetcar grinding over its tracks. He described familiar evening rituals: mothers washing dishes after the meal while fathers water their lawns and children play, and the last moments of dusk when his own family gathers on quilts in the backyard: "We all lie there, my mother, my father, my uncle, my aunt, and I too am lying there." He arranged these bits of memory not as a diary entry but as a musical work of art. After its 1938 publication and its later use as a text for a Samuel Barber composition, many regarded it as Agee's signature work—one that has introduced countless readers to his native town.[51]

Leaving "the west coast of Florida" in April, Agee and Via spent "a week in New Orleans" before driving again through his former home state and staying "a last month with some old friend of mine at the school I used to go to in Tennessee." During Agee's time at St. Andrew's, his "old friend" Father Flye introduced him to then-student David McDowell. Agee reacquainted himself with the campus, touring the old buildings and "hiking through the woods" with David. Of course, he could not have foreseen that two decades later McDowell would edit and advocate Agee's works. The two trekked to Piney Point—an area west of campus, not far from Shake-Rag Hollow—which Agee considered "his favorite part of the world," McDowell said. Agee also "wanted to retrace his steps to the Sand Cut, an abandoned sand quarry." When Via and he left St. Andrew's later in May, "after seven months leave" from *Fortune,* Agee took away fresh memories of the school that he would later depict in fiction. Of the month in Sewanee, Agee thanked Flye for his hospitality, stating, "No time or visit ever, anywhere, has been so good and meant so much to me."[52]

Back in New York, *Fortune* assigned Agee an article that would send him to the South again and bring him uncomfortably close to the poverty of farm life. His subjects were the cotton tenant farmers of Alabama, who lived in conditions as primitive as anything his mountaineer ancestors knew. Partnering with photographer Walker Evans, he would document in detail the farmers' experiences and expose the corrupt system that bound their lives in servitude. When Agee boarded the train "early one evening" on June 20, 1936, he had never been more enthusiastic about writing. "This train was going South," he later wrote of the trip. "I was born in the south. I spent my first fifteen years about equally divided between a Tennessee city and Tennessee mountains, and since then I had lived north and had seen the south very little, not at all until two years before. In a limited, entirely unstudied way I knew a good deal about the south in terms of some of its parts, and I a great deal more than loved this country." This was not just an assignment; it was a personal journey, a physical return to the region Agee had written about many times, "projecting all I could from the mountain stuff I knew." He imagined, "What lay ahead of me was in a sense familiar to me, for my childhood had been spent in it and half my ancestry was of the very depths of it." But as he thought of the poor farmers he would be documenting, he could not help but question his own southern credentials:

My father was of mountain people who were tenant farmers. My mother was Michigan born, raised in the south; she was of middle-class, somewhat cultivated, small capitalists. My father died when I was six and though I spent some lucky years in a mountain school most of my life had been middle-class. I have always more resented this fact than not, and have to a degree felt cheated and irreparably crippled of half or more than half of what I am. . . .

   Also, though I knew the south, the Tennessee-mountain-city-valley aspects of it, I knew little or nothing about the cotton country, beyond a rough idea of the look of it and an even sketchier idea of just what the situation was there, beyond what I got out of Tobacco Road, some passages in Faulkner, and a few meetings of the Committee for the Defense of Southern Workers.[53]

As he passed through East Tennessee, "entering Bristol in full dawn" and "stopping in Knoxville," he was welcomed by familiar sensations: "The southern air of the train & passengers. The summer heat." He got off the train in Chattanooga at "about four" that afternoon, noting "the strong June light broken on the buildings, the people at many speeds." Agee, wanting to stay the night before continuing toward Alabama, took a cab to a hotel. "The taxi driver, who said he was the youngest in the city, took me a short cut across the bumping railroad tracks to the Read House, medium priced, the second best hotel in town." The hotel that Agee described had been rebuilt ten years earlier. "The Read House was twelve stories of rather new brick," he wrote. "Outside it looked like a tinted postcard. Inside it looked like a color photograph. Big walnut service desk. Bus-terminal type floor, of polished peanut brittle. Machine made persian rugs, dark reds and purples. Potted palms. Posters of movies. Indirect lighting behind green and cream colored lalique glass. Smooth elevators, like sitting on the cushions in a pneumatic chair." From his "fifth floor" window, he observed the city's "shadows darkening and lengthening but still a lot of daylight." This was the city where at fourteen Agee had spent the better part of a day watching movies, forgetting about family issues and delaying the start of his final semester at St. Andrew's. As he now sat in his hotel looking out over Chattanooga, surely thoughts of those years returned to him: "All the signs. The gliding tops of autos, trucks, and busses, the asphalt, blue in shadow, pale grey-gold in the slicing sunlight; the orchestration of motors; the sharp hiss of air brakes. Noise, and smoke. The smell of a hotel room and the smell of a city I knew in my childhood."[54]

The next day he rented a car from the Matthews Company on Market Street, and after his "first clumsiness with the car," Agee "began to learn its ways" as he departed the city. He later described the drive southward in a characteristically vast sentence:

> I picked up the numbers quickly and got out into the edges of town, gradually gathering speed as the side streets diminished in frequency and importance and obscurity and as the buildings shrank more & more to sun-blinded sheds & shops scattered along sweeps of vacant lots full of rank steaming weeds, dead cars & old tires and bedsprings, and as the street streamed though metamorphosis more and more into road, until at length it became sumptuous, still nearly new, gleaming white, oil-streaked, four lane concrete highway, and lifted itself in a long, slow, steady curve, through surroundings now which were more filling-station and dogstand than edge of city, up the lower shoulder of Lookout Mountain, while behind me the spread and relaxation of the beautiful low-built city I felt affection for, shrank into a unit and shrank in my mirror and I was swinging round the green flank of Lookout Mountain, one of the most hackneyed postcard views in all the South, and the sharp-edged pure white curving road swam strongly up and beneath me in the tremendous silent sunshine, and I was happy.[55]

Having passed through his native state, Agee spent the next two months in Alabama boarding with tenant families while observing and chronicling their lives in detail. Ever since he was a boy—when he took off his shoes and offered them to a mill worker's child in Knoxville—Agee felt compassion for the poor. Father Flye characterized his former pupil as "very tender-hearted, touched to quick sympathy and pity at the sight or thought of suffering, human or other, and incapable of willingly causing it." Agee was deeply affected by what he experienced in Alabama. But he would not publish his account that summer, as expected. In September, after returning to New York, he wrote to Father Flye: "The trip was very hard, and certainly one of the best things I've ever had happen to me. Writing what we found is a different matter. Impossible in any form and length *Fortune* can use; and I am now so stultified trying to do that, that I'm afraid I've lost my ability to make it right in my own way." Over the next three years he reshaped and rewrote his rejected manuscript into something more personal and monumental than any straight piece of journalism.[56]

ⵉⵉⵉⵉⵉⵉⵉⵉⵉⵉⵉⵉⵉ

Tennessee continued to poetically inspire Agee, as in his charming "Lines Suggested by a Tennessee Song." The poem retells the Nativity story in Appalachian dialect and setting: the manger is "a cold black barn," the awe-struck shepherds are slaves laboring on the mountainside, and one of the gifts presented to the child King is "ginseng root from Siler's Bald"—a scenic area on the Appalachian Trail, near Clingman's Dome. The poet could not resist a hillbilly stereotype, as Mary's betrothed was Joseph, "a cousin . . . from down the cove." Agee's verses display the fun he had with the mountain language he knew. Harvard classmate Robert Fitzgerald recalled Agee's humorous recitations of classic poems, such as one by Shelley, "in the accent and pitch of rural Tennessee."[57]

Another poem, "In Memory of My Father (Campbell County, Tenn.)," specifically associates Appalachian details with the area near Jacksboro, where "Mile on mile in mountain folded valley fallen valley lies," and where as a boy on his grandparents' farm, Agee spent nights beneath a "smokesweet quilt":

> Bluely, bluely, styles from stone chimneys crippling smoke of
> hickory larch and cedar wood of ash, of the white oak. The quell
> night blues above.   The quell night blues : branchwaters,
> the black woods, begin to talk.   The blue night blacks above:
> Lamps: bloom in their glasses and the stars: splinter and glister
> glass.   Warmth: slops from the pigsty. In the barn pale hay,
> tusseled in teeth, darkness, a blunt hoof. . . .   throes of a common dream
> : throes in the leaves, and quiet : sweet tended field now meditate your
> children : child, in your smokesweet quilt , joy in your dreams: and
> father, mother : whose rude hands rest you mutual of the flesh : rest in
> your kind flesh well.

> And thou most tender earth:

> Lift through this love thy creatures on the light.

The work, depicting the simple beauty of his father's Tennessee mountain upbringing, could stand as a companion piece to his "Knoxville: Summer of 1915," which with similar, detailed musicality composes the sounds of a cityscape.[58]

Although most of Agee's film writing came later, in 1937 he published a surrealistic script, "Notes for a Moving Picture: The House," set in "a middle-sized provincial industrial city (one hundred thousand to two hundred thousand population; say Knoxville or Chattanooga, Tenn.)." He seemed to be clearly describing Knoxville, with its "small factories, jumbled on a bluff" and "few buildings . . . more than five to seven floors tall . . . of irregular height and period and style of architecture." Along "the main street of this city" can be seen "theaters, restaurants, jewelers, etc.," but "the street is completely deserted. It should be possible to see a quarter to half a mile down it and it should end in air or the dropping of a hill."[59]

After a bizarre and dreamlike parade that includes "a gigantic bright black hearse . . . followed by . . . fifty identical black limousines," the scene shifts to a residential street, focusing on "a large slate-roofed Victorian house" that is "set somewhat back in small grounds." Agee undoubtedly modeled this fictional dwelling on the West Clinch Avenue home of his grandmother and grandfather Tyler. The camera pans over "the grounds, garden, yard . . . the flat, sad, prosperous breadth of housed landscape visible." There is a "sundial at one side" of the yard, which is composed of "short dried grass, [and] dry twiggy earth," and "the sharp leaves of a century plant in the center of a small dry formal garden." Behind the house, a "narrow graveled service path" leads "down past the extinct carriage-house and through the iron gate and into the bare paved alley."[60]

Crossing "the wood floor of the porch whose boards are thickly painted gray," Agee's camera enters through "the gray screen door" into "the dark hallway" and floats past "coarse white lace curtains glazed in sunlight." Agee recalled the scent of the "spuming potted fern" that sat baking behind a hot bay window. The camera lens explores the house as Agee did in his adolescence, taking in "the dark, seedy, fancy furniture, horsehair, bright white antimacassars, brass talons clenching glass globes and sustaining furniture; detail of the heavy and dark, carved mahoganies of table legs; and of carved beds." It examines "the fireplace closed with black-painted gag of fancily cast iron, the mantel uplifting several tiers of small shelves which sustain, on doilies, vases, and figurines of shepherdesses and of fisher-girls," and other knickknacks that Agee used to name as a child, to the amusement of his family. Almost as if cataloging his grandparents' possessions, Agee specified a "similar shot of a glass-faced cabinet containing eggshell, never-used china, a tray of dry butterflies, geological specimens; sets of Victorian books and miscellaneous popular novels of the early twentieth century in cases behind glass . . . glancing detail of china, bare chairs, woodcarving, statuettes, lace, pictures such as an engraving of 'The Lions of Persepolis,' various Victorian patterns of wallpaper, details of ornate picture frames, and many sizes and shapes of mirrors which extend and darken the house."[61]

Then in one swift motion, the camera cranes up through the mansion's ceiling and "comes straight through the shell of beams and roofslate." After appraising all that his grandparents owned and acknowledging a nearby "factory chimney" like the one at his grandfather's marble cutting plant, Agee then destroyed the house in a swirling tempest of imaginary rainstorm and fragmented memory. Under the weight of water, the plaster ceiling collapses onto the piano where Agee once sat for music lessons, crushing it "in a great triple chord." The "fern" whose stench he most associated with the home "spurts upward enormous" and becomes "a shabby fountain." In the morning, as the flood waters recede, "very poor children" roam the street in front of the ruined house, "wading in the deep gutter, clothes rolled high," as young Agee probably did following the rains on Highland Avenue. In "Knoxville: Summer of 1915," the writer had celebrated "the security and simple beauties of childhood." But in this unconventional screenplay he obliterated those things, showing "that not even such a comfortably provincial and culturally remote city would be spared from the corruption of times to come."[62]

In 1937, the same year "The House" appeared in *New Letters in America,* Agee traveled through Knoxville with his mistress, Alma Mailman, on their way to New Orleans. Years later Agee fictionalized this road trip as part of a film scenario, *Bigger Than We Are,* basing the characters John and Celia on himself and Alma. Considering that the story's personae and events closely resembled those from Agee's life, the episode in Knoxville may be factual. If so, Agee drove Alma past "his grandparents' home" on West Clinch but was disappointed to discover that the house had been all but destroyed—not from his imagined deluge but from neglect: "To his shock and sadness, this solid middleclass home has become an unpainted rooming-house." His old home on Highland Avenue had also declined, "gone way downhill from not very high." Perhaps he was indeed short on cash and stopped at "a Bank and [found] the man he knows; a Teller; an old friend of his mother and uncle; a nice and sensitive guy." Agee did know Clifford Glenn, a family acquaintance and teller at the 1913 Hamilton National Bank building, which still stands at 531 South Gay Street. But it is difficult to believe that Agee borrowed thirty dollars from Glenn while telling "an elaborate lie about a couple of guys, friends of his, who have broken down outside town," as John does in *Bigger Than We Are.* The narrative references another section of Gay Street that Agee remembered from childhood, the 300 block's east side, where Sterchi's was located. Around 1930 the nearby Briscoe Building was completely remodeled as the Terminal Building, an Art Deco structure that housed the Union bus lines. That "particularly romantic block" had become "a mixture of 18th century turned slum, with warehouse and bus-terminal," Agee wrote, though the oldest buildings on the block were a century newer than he thought.[63]

Agee's hometown had lost its luster, and the trip with Alma left him disillusioned about their future together. That September he published a poem, "Sunday: Outskirts of Knoxville, Tennessee." Set "in the earliest and chary spring," the poem might have originated with his afternoon drive through the wasted city with Alma beside him. The poem depicts two lovers, "Unharnessed in the friendly sunday air / By the red brambles, on the river bluffs," parked off the main highway beneath "the dogwood flowers." Despite the romantic locale, the writer visualized "How this must end, that now please love were ended," the inevitable dissolution of passion into the "kind contempt" of familiarity and old age.[64]

"Summer Evening," another poem possibly inspired by his most recent Knoxville trip, grew out of a journal entry Agee composed using "automatic writing." Different from the occult practice of the same name in which his grandfather Tyler had dabbled, this sort of automatic writing developed out of the surrealistic desire to exploit the subconscious mind. Agee composed a block of text "quickly, without any preconceived subject," and without stopping to edit or think about what he had just written. After finishing the stream-of-consciousness exercise, Agee then connected his disjointed images and phrases into three solid verses. Published in January 1938, the poem evokes the "locusts" and "dappled shadowed porchswing" of the Highland Avenue childhood he wrote about earlier in "Knoxville: Summer of 1915" and would publish later in the summer of 1938. Although musicians often gathered there to perform, Market Square lacked a bandstand at the time. If at all inspired by Knoxville, Agee's lines "Bandstands every tuesday evening / Bring us to the drawling square" might refer to the regular concerts held at Chilhowee Park during summer months. Agee's memories and images of the Appalachian city, even if composed unconsciously, combine in a poem that is tender and nostalgic.[65]

Other poems reflect the humorous and, in some cases, absurd aspects of the South. That February, his satirical poem, "Dixie Doodle," appeared in *Partisan Review*. As with the "Southern Gentleman" in his first report on the Tennessee Valley Authority, here Agee again lampooned the "old school" conservatives. The "Nashville Agrarians" were a group of traditionalist writers (including future Pulitzer winner Robert Penn Warren) that had coalesced at Vanderbilt University in the 1920s. A decade later Agee caricatured in verse some Agrarians who were publicly opposing "the Tee Vee Aye" agenda: "When the world swings back to sense / (But the world is so damned dense) / An indisputably aryan / Jeffersonian Agrarian / Will be settn awn the Ole Rail Fence, // Swaying lightly with a hot cawn bun, / Quoting Horace and the late Jawn Donne[.]"[66]

Sometime within a few years of that poem's publication, Agee submitted a short story, "In the Middle South," to the same magazine, which rejected it as too descriptive for its minimal action. The setting is "a farm," where "from home to the red road declines a rubbage of densed weedy earth, dry trees, blue, cedars in limestone: white hens in the sunny grass like a washing blown from the line." Agee might have visualized a location similar to the barren farms he saw in Alabama, an area he called "the middle south." However, elsewhere Agee referred to Knoxville as a "mid-Southern industrial city," and here he could have just as well imagined the sort of East Tennessee farm off a main highway where his father's family lived in Jacksboro. The story concerns a farmer and his adult son who attempt to trick a younger stranger into taking "a ruined, and old, car" off their hands for "free, if he can get it off the place." However, "the young man has somehow managed: to get its engine going right here in their very yard: before he even gets it on the road," making himself seem "smarter than they are, to have got it started so easily," using "their own gas" and "their own springwater." This infuriates the son, who feels "angry and cheated," and in a rising tide of vengeance pulls "from khaki pocket a long fat knife" and begins "whittling" chunks out of the young man's dog. The ending is somewhat incomprehensible, but the young man reacts unexpectedly, again thwarting the son's malicious intent.[67]

The violence and graphic descriptions of "In the Middle South" are reminiscent of three prose fragments Agee wrote, around the late 1930s, depicting someone or something being run over on a Knoxville street. Written in sequence, the pieces grow progressively more grotesque. The first, previously unpublished, describes a collision between a horse and a streetcar:

> The horse was pulling the grocery wagon along: thin walls; thin wide iron-bound wheels which made a kind of frail grind and rattle over the grits and irregularities of the pavement. On a rock slanted in towards the rail his left foreleg skidded at just the wrong instant, and the hoof was clamped between the iron rail and the iron wheel of the street car. The car pulled to a stop. The horse recoiling, everything pulled at once: the slender white bone stump of the leg pulled out of its hoof like a bare foot out of a shoe; the horse screamed. People came running from all over the place. The conductor and the boy who drove the wagon quarreled a minute, then the conductor and a lot of the passengers got back in the street car and it moved slowly ahead, banging its bell and shouldering the congestion out of the way.

The piece contains little exaggeration and reads like a report of an actual occurrence. In an obscure, possibly autobiographical reference in *A Death in the Family,* Agee wrote that his uncle Hugh saw "a horse which had fallen in the street." Perhaps it was a memory related to this short piece.[68]

A second fragment, written on the same piece of paper, is related by theme—the victim is a cat instead of a horse—but stylistically different. The narrator sees a cat in the middle of the street that, despite being half flattened, protests noisily. Here Agee writes in the first person, but his exaggerated language stretches the believability of the incident. The piece has been published under the title "Run Over": "I was rounding the corner in to asylum avenue, ambling home in the middle of the afternoon, and there at the curb was a crowd and there in the middle of the crowd was a big thin black cat with wild red blood all over its face and its teeth like long thorns and its tongue curled like that of a heraldic lion. Right across the middle it was as flat as an ironed britches leg. . . . This cat was not lying still nor keeping still: it was as lively as if it were on a gridiron and it was yelling and gasping satanically, the yells sounding like something through a horn whose reed is split." Agee wrote that none of the bystanders "ventured to interfere with these wonderful processes of nature," and added in parenthesis, "Things like these are happening somewhere on the earth every second." While some readers may take the name "Asylum Avenue" as a metaphor, the street, of course, actually existed in Knoxville when Agee lived there.[69]

The third fragment depicts a human victim of a car accident and the grotesque sound of the man's breathing through a bloody gash in his face. The scholar who first titled and published the previous fragment as "Run Over" also published this one, titling it "Give Him Air." However, what he published as "Give Him Air" was only half of what Agee wrote: the editor overlooked the fact that the fragment was continued from a previous page of Agee's handwritten prose. This first half of the fragment, never before published, identifies the location of that accident as West Clinch Avenue— "eleven fifteen" was his grandparents' address on that street:

I was in the living room of eleven fifteen, a warm midafternoon in midsummer, lying on the sofa and reading. It was relatively cool and shadowed and the street sounds went back and forth quietly and distinctly on a far edge of my consciousness. Suddenly is not a sudden enough word for it: there is not any word. I heard it happen I suppose two to five seconds before the rest of my apparatus caught up with it and said, something has hit something a hell of a blow; a car has hit a car. You try and imagine two trip-hammers of solid iron, each about five feet broad, hitting with full force: then say instead that those hammers aren't solid metal, which would give one huge but dull-sounding, kind of totally stunning, blow, but are complicated cages of some flimsy and tinny, some tougher, metal: add in some glass, too: All this hitting at solid trip hammer force makes a more complex, reverberant and terrible noise; and that terrific blow was followed immediately by squealings of metal which a murdered hog would be just faintly capable of imitating, and by the [illegible] bangings of a car hurdling over itself and with each of its sides in turn smacking the street. The car that was doing the squealing was still doing it as I got to the window: low behind on one side, dragging to a stop like a big wild animal whose hind parts are dragged [drugged?] and paralyzed. People were spraying out of houses as far as I could see and them running for it gave the definite impression of bellies to the earth. I moved fast myself, and by the time I got there the crowd was thick and the people had been dragged out of the cars.

The previously published fragment continues on the next manuscript page, excerpted here:

I suppose I may have seen everything in detail, but I don't remember everything, and there's no use inventing it. All I remember is the long blueblack gash made in the asphalt by the dragged axle, which led forty feet right into the hind legs of the mob, and, after I had fought my way through the mob, the man they were looking at. I don't doubt other people were hurt; but I don't recall even seeing them: they couldn't have been hurt as this man was. He was propped up against the ivy on our wall. The right inner forearm and the palm of the right hand were laid open like an anatomical illustration. . . . His whole [missing noun] was snatched off as neatly as a wig off a head, and somebody was wiping the blood and glass away, mainly to give him a chance to breathe, but also apparently in some idiotic hope that he might be able to see; and care to if he could.

Even if the new fragment had not been discovered, the Clinch Avenue location could be inferred from Agee's description of "the ivy on our wall" down along the sidewalk in front of the house, a detail that appears in other writings and in photographs of the 1100 block. If this was based on a real occurrence, it conceivably happened during one of Agee's breaks from St. Andrew's, and close enough to the Tyler home that the wreckage could be seen from a front window. His comment at the end of the piece—"the newspapers said he never regained consciousness, and died on the way to the hospital"—suggests the event was real, and could be verified by a search of local newspapers.[70]

One news story from the period bears a remarkable resemblance to Agee's story fragment, even though the incident happened in winter rather than midsummer. Around 2:20 on the afternoon of January 14, 1924, "Circle Park street car" number twenty-nine passed the Tyler house heading east on Clinch toward Third (now Eleventh) Street, while Matt Moore, a thirty-year-old painter, traveled west in his "Essex touring" car toward the same intersection. One witness saw Moore swerve to miss another automobile;

others said he appeared to drive "blindly" into the intersection. As his car "collided head-on" with the streetcar, Moore "was thrown [through] the windshield." The impact "was heard for blocks in West Knoxville" and undoubtedly drew curious residents to the scene. Bystanders noted the severity of Moore's injuries: "Blood was streaming from a great gash in [his] throat and he was badly cut elsewhere about the head." The paper stated that Moore "was injured probably fatally" and that an hour after the accident he lay "unconscious at the hospital."[71]

Moore died of a skull fracture and brain contusion, according to his death certificate. The serious lacerations to Moore's head and neck, his unconscious state, and the location and loudness of the collision are compatible with the scene Agee described. The news story seems to be further evidence that Agee frequently based his writings on factual incidents. Incidentally, Moore's front seat passenger, Buck Karnes, who "escaped with scratches," had been awarded the Medal of Honor for his actions during the Great War a little over five years earlier. Since 1933 the span crossing the Tennessee River at Alcoa Highway has been named the Buck Karnes Bridge.[72]

The horse, cat, and man fragments—all depicting victims of vehicle accidents—were composed at the same time. Were these all exaggerated descriptions of incidents Agee observed, as "Give Him Air" apparently was? Or were some possibly based on Agee's dreams—subconscious variations of his father's automobile wreck? As pointed out by scholars, the fragments resemble another violent episode: Agee's nightmare of carrying his father's body through the streets of Knoxville—a dream he wrote about later, probably in the mid-1940s.[73]

1940s

Agee reached a milestone in fall 1941 when his cotton tenant book, which he titled *Let Us Now Praise Famous Men,* was finally published. He had tinkered with and expanded the text that *Fortune* rejected five years earlier. Although the book was largely ignored during its initial printing, it would later be regarded as a masterpiece of journalism. Robert Fitzgerald called it "the centerpiece" of Agee's "life and writing." Remembering the summer he spent in Alabama, Agee could not help but compare the experience to his own past, to the people and places he knew intimately: "My father, my grandfather, my poor damned tragic, not unusually tragic, bitched family." A sharecropper's springhouse reminded him of the one on his grandfather Agee's property near Jacksboro: "I stand . . . in a springhouse, of plain boards, straddling a capacious spring, a place such as that which was at my grandfather's farm, with the odor of shut darkness, cold, wet wood, [and] the delighting smell of butter." Of the tenant house occupied by a family he named the Gudgers, Agee wrote, "I remember such square-log double houses in mountain parts of Tennessee." Agee used pseudonyms for most of the real people in the book; and when identifying a couple of landlords, he likely borrowed the name Margraves from his great-grandmother (the surname is not common in Alabama's 1930 census records). A slow drive through a heat-oppressed neighborhood brought to mind the sweltering summer afternoons he spent lying on his grandfather Tyler's shaded, "gray-painted" porch as an "eleven-year-old, male, half-shaped child." In scholar Victor Kramer's assessment, the book "is as much about Agee the reporter as it is about the farmers with whom he lived."[74]

Among Agee's "Suggested" materials near the end of the book, he listed "*Stark Love*, a motion picture, by Karl Brown"—the 1927 film shot in the Appalachians and starring Helen Monday, his possible former classmate from Knoxville. Agee once cited *Stark Love* as a fine example of how greater realism is possible in films than in writing or theater.[75]

The year after the book was published, Agee began reviewing films for *Time* and the *Nation*. Occasionally, he saw movies that sparked comparisons to his Tennessee boyhood. In early 1943 he reviewed the film *Tennessee Johnson* in which Van Heflin played the seventeenth president, Andrew Johnson. The film received a gala opening at Knoxville's Tennessee Theatre on February 17, 1943, with advertisements billing it as "the first showing in the State of Tennessee and the entire Southeast." President Johnson's granddaughter and great-granddaughter attended the screening as well as the preceding banquet at the nearby Andrew Johnson Hotel. Viewing the film in New York, Agee mostly enjoyed Heflin's performance but criticized the film as inauthentic. This draft of the review specifically references "East Tennessee," unlike the version the *Nation* published in January 1943:

> Since I am even more ignorant of the history of my country than most Americans of my age, I can't join the quarrel over *Tennessee Johnson* on any question of basic facts. And since I got in late, I can't say much about the way East Tennesseans were handled, though I know more about East Tennessee. I saw enough to be sure of this: that the dialects ranged all the way from Seaboard women's college Dramat to the Old Homestead, and that there was not an East Tennessean face in the crowd; that little boys should not be presented in new straw hats neatly scissored into imitation ruggedness; and that Van Heflin now and then, by looking like Richard Barthelmess in the first production of *Tol'able David*, was at least more convincing

than anyone else in the crowd. I see no possible excuse for this careless mixture of worn-out stiff-traditional rural types, regarding it as a libel on the Common Man whom it is supposed to flatter, and a neglect of one of the most elementary require-ments, and opportunities, of films. And I doubt whether Shakespeare himself could have gotten away with the lightning transition in which, within three minutes, people who had been on the verge of lynching Van Heflin are ready to elect him Sheriff. . . . It takes longer than that for an East Tennessean to scratch himself.

He immediately saw through Hollywood's mostly shallow representations of his native South. Disney's *Make Mine Music* offended Agee with its "infi-nitely insulting animation of a hill-billy ballad"—a segment that, incidentally, Disney excised from its U.S. DVD release. He justified his indignation in his April 1946 review: "I have hill-billy blood myself."[76]

Even though he traveled through the state less and less frequently, "Agee never lost touch with Tennessee, and he visited Knoxville and the nearby hill country when he could," wrote one journalist. Aside from Father Flye, Agee had other contacts there. By 1940 his mother and stepfather had moved back to St. Andrew's from Maine. Agee, separated from Alma by that time, stopped in Knoxville in spring 1943 on a train ride with Mia Fritsch from Florida to New York. Agee had hoped to show her his hometown, but his throat was uncomfortably sore at the time, and they spent only an hour walking through downtown until the next connecting train came through.[77]

In most of his professional writing, Agee had worked against southern stereotypes by expressing truthfully his own firsthand knowledge of the region. And while he strove for specificity over cliché, he was not always proud of the South. Sometime around 1943, he wrote a piece that would not be published until after his death. "America! Look at Your Shame!" is based on an incident that occurred as Agee rode a New York City bus and heard some white southern military men belittle the black passengers aboard. Agee was reminded of his southern roots and the sort of violence he saw there: "I specially noticed one quite strong young sailor, just across from me. . . . It was the sort of face which only turns up, so far as I know, in the South. . . . I knew the voice just as well, and the special, rather crazy kind of bravery; they made me feel at once as isolated and as matchlessly at home as if I were back in the South again. . . . It is a very special speech, as unattractive to most Northerners as it is dear to natives . . . its special broadenings, lifts, twangs and elisions, even if you didn't know the idiom by heart, which I do, were as charming and miraculous as if, in the same New York bus, a couple of Parsees had saluted each other." But when "the young sailors and soldiers begin to vocalize about the niggers on the bus," Agee imagined confronting them but knew he was no match physically. "Physical cowardice" was one of the ways Agee believed he most differed from his "brave" father. Instead, he planned how he might rationally convince them that their hate-filled speech was wrong: "Look here. What are you fighting this war about. I know how you feel, I know you're from the South, I'm from the South myself, I know (I may be, but the way I say it makes it a lie.). Things are different there, and all this you see here goes against every way you believe is right. But you've got to get used to it." In the end, he remained silent, lacking courage and the belief that speaking to his fellow southerners would do any good.[78]

Agee sympathized with the oppressed and persecuted, and this concern seeped into his subconscious. He detailed an apparent dream in which he was sixteen years old, sitting in the "living-room of a pretty well-to-do substantial, respectable house, say forty years old, in a middle-sized mid-Southern industrial city." Although Agee did not initially specify that city, he later identified it as Knoxville. The house was undoubtedly modeled on the Tyler home, as Agee described the same bay window baking in the summer sun as he had in *Let Us Now Praise Famous Men*. "There were four broad plate-glass windows in the bay: the sun at its hottest and whitest stacked in directly through all four, piling in its heat and its silent light as if it were no more than a mile away: which the thick panes intensified and calmed in transit." In the shelf of the bay window sat a few pots, and "in each pot was an enormous flamboyant and untended fern of the commonest sort: its leaves spilling and spiring all over like a messy fountain whose head is clogged crooked"—recalling the untamed fern in Agee's "Notes for a Moving Picture." The house was "hot with an indoor noontime heat; full of odors." Two characters confront the teenaged, first-person narrator, named Jimmy. "The major was forty-five, grizzling, with a red, meaty, heavily muscled and powerfully composed smooth shaven face: a North-educated Southerner with the pale, [curbedly?] violent blue eyes of a Southerner.... He was Army, he was War, he was ROTC commander at my high school." At the time Agee attended Knoxville High, Major Harry Walter Stephenson led the ROTC. The "violent blue eyes" of the major in the story, titled "Allegiance Dream," recall Agee's description from *Famous Men* of the Civil War prison guards at Andersonville—whose "almost weeping yearning of terror toward brutal-ity, in the eyes, the speech ... is peculiar to the men of the south"—and the "blue-white, reckless, brutal eyes" of the southern soldier in "America! Look at Your Shame!" The other character is "the woman, the lady of the house, prominent Daughter of the Revolution, censor of movies.... She was in uni-form. The formal afternoon uniform of an active and influential woman. Tall sharp heels that could gouge out your soul. Transparent stockings underlaced with burst blood vessels on lavender white shaven flesh." The couple stares menacingly at the narrator, somehow knowing that he has friends around the world who are struggling under, and revolting against, fascist regimes: "They knew; and they were waiting in that silence that made a vacuum of all the earth in its hot noon." Although "Allegiance Dream" is undated, it seems to be a reaction against World War II and related to one of Agee's foreboding "premonitions" from 1945: "I will be killed after long torture, by one or another kind of enemy, probably Stalinists, a few years from now."[79]

The war years were particularly difficult for Agee. He was depressed and disillusioned by the conflict overseas, and even after Victory in Europe Day remained pessimistic about society's ability to recover from the conflict. To Agee, mankind's future looked grim; the devastating use of atomic weaponry would surely become the government's default response in future conflicts. (Agee wrote, in a lauded article for *Time,* that "the bomb split open the universe." It was revealed, only after the destruction of Hiroshima, that the bomb's uranium had been enriched at Oak Ridge, a government town located twenty miles northwest from Knoxville.) His 1945 poem, "Now on the World and on My Life as Well," was likely written just after the war's end:

> Whether by Nature's will or by my own,
> I, who by chance walked safely past a war,
> Shall not by any chance the world has known
> Be here, and breathing, many autumns more.
> Only, with all who in the past have died,
> I had, till lately, faced my death secure,
> Knowing my hunger only was denied,
> Knowing that all I loved was to endure.
> But this year, dying, struck wild, as it fell,
> Ending itself, me, and the world as well.[80]

In his war-induced sorrow, his work seemed futile and pointless now. He wrote to Father Flye of the beginnings of a project based on his experiences at St. Andrew's: "I've started a short novel about adolescence in the 1920's—a fairly good start. But in ten days I haven't come back to it. And by now it looks too flimsy." Agee temporarily put aside the work that years later would become *The Morning Watch.* "With so little time from work and so very little time left for anything faintly recognizable as civilization, it seems rather too obligatory to work only on the best things possible. But those are even harder to hold to—for anyone of my weak will."[81]

Besides the war affecting his work in 1945, he irrationally feared his next birthday. On November 27 he again wrote to Flye: "So I am now 36. For days I have had premonitions: more solemn than any in years. . . . A very strong sense of death." He feared legitimizing the premonition by putting it to paper but continued to write: "I will die during this year, unexpectedly (parallel to my father's death at just that age)." Mia later reported that the year was a particularly tough one for her husband. "Getting him through thirty-six was really something," she said. Agee did not realize just how unfounded was his fear of age thirty-six: he had forgotten the birth year of his father, who actually turned thirty-eight "a month and a day" before he died. But Agee's "sense of death" would resurface throughout the rest of his life—and become increasingly grounded in fact as his health worsened.[82]

By early 1946 Agee and Mia considered relocating to the country. Agee had written to his mother about the possibility. Responding from St. Andrew's, Laura suggested that Sewanee would be a lovely place for the couple to live if not for the local housing shortage at the time. "This mountain country of Tennessee is exceedingly lovely," she wrote, that it "never loosens hold of those who really have seen it." She recommended that her son look into properties in "Gatlinburg & that very *wonderful* Smoky Mt. country," which would be close enough for him to visit her more often. Of course, Agee was on his third marriage, and the Holy Order at St. Andrew's frowned on such things—so she advised that he visit only when the Fathers were away.[83]

Instead of moving south, the Agees moved north out of the city, to a farmhouse James had purchased in Hillsdale, New York. But in 1947 Agee did bring Mia south once more, "to the Tennessee countryside so dear to him and his ancestors." It was among his last few visits—one that may have included stopping by the home of his cousin Gladys, who later could not remember whether the woman with James was "a wife or lover."[84]

Around the time he turned thirty-eight, Agee began a satire, "Two's a Crowd," about "the sexual behavior of the human male." He included a humorous account of his birth, as if his male gender—whether or not he "stuck out" in front—was the only thing his parents cared about:

> I can see them practically as if I were there. My mother bleeding and bellowing and lunging like a tuna, my father heroically fighting down his thirst, the doctor and the nurse busy as bird dogs but with just one thought seriously in mind. Which would it be? Sticking out? Or a hole? The fate of the world depends on it. . . . And then they see it, about the size of a Chinese bean-sprout. . . . My poor father and mother, relieved at last of eight months' need to pretend that they're

equally happy either way, do their level best to soft-pedal their joy.... As for me, I neither know nor give a damn. All I am good for is to yell my head off. And yet a great thing has been offered to me. Through no doing of my own or theirs, I have given my father and mother the best possible opinion of each other and of themselves and of me; even my grandparents, bless their hearts, preen and glow quite a little more because I happened to stick out in front.

Even in this exaggerated scenario, Agee characterizes his father as "heroic," echoing the "brave father" of his early poetry. Agee repeated this theme throughout his career, in various genres. Around the time he satirized his own parents and birth in "Two's a Crowd," he was also at work on novel—a re-creation of his childhood and the events surrounding his father's death as part of a major autobiographical work.[85]

∞∞∞∞∞∞∞∞∞∞

Agee wrote to Father Flye in March 1948 that he had "been very much pre-occupied for several months with a piece of writing," a project "that has so soaked up my interest that I've felt relatively little else to think or talk about." Whereas he had been injecting fragments about his father into his writing for more than two decades, in this novel he would finally examine in detail the event in 1916 that had forever changed his life. The work, he wrote, was "longer than I had foreseen or thought best for it, about my first 6 years, ending the day of my father's burial."[86]

At the time, Agee was involved in Jungian therapy, a form of psychoanalysis in which interpreting dreams was an important facet. He had dreams of "a recurrent city-scape," and remembered "looking uphill" towards a row of "high gray houses on brow of hill" in a city that could be "Knoxville or Nashville." Each time the dream returned, it left him unsettled: "Always fear and an unknown important mood." His earlier works "Notes for a Moving Picture: The House" and "Allegiance Dream" both begin similarly, overlooking a "middle-sized industrial city" with a sense of foreboding, suggesting that this "city-scape" dream originated a decade or more before Agee began the novel.[87]

While Agee had wanted to write about his father's death ever since high school, some scholars believe that the "genesis" of the novel was a dream he had "sometime in the middle or late 1940s." In it, he sees himself walking downtown in a city he first thinks is Chattanooga but then realizes is "Knoxville, in East Tennessee, in the middle of a day towards the middle of the twentieth century." His dream's setting is the same place journalist John

Gunther had visited in May 1945 and called "the ugliest city . . . in America."
For Agee this Knoxville "wasn't as he remembered it from childhood, nor did
he like its looks as well as his memories of it; nor was it as he remembered it
from the middle thirties; he didn't like its looks even as well as that; it was a
blend of the two, and for every old sight which touched him and made him
happy and lonely, there was something new which he disliked." Up Gay Street
he sees that "a crowd was doing some terrible piece of violence" to a man who
had preached truth on the street corner "for everyone to hear." Agee realizes
"this was indeed John the Baptist." As he lifts the body, removing John from
the mob, he senses the bystanders' eyes on him, full of the "terrifying white-
ness" found only in "the eyes of the men of his part of the country." Despite
fearing the mob's reaction he carries the corpse away to "a certain corner, a
certain vacant lot." Agee has forgotten the precise route, and walks with his
burden apparently down Walnut towards St. John's Episcopal, passing "the
dying exquisite houses of the middle nineteenth century, furnished rooms,
doctors' offices, and . . . the harsh gray stone of the church in which he had
been confirmed." He realizes that he is heading towards the wrong bridge,
that he needs to cross "the other viaduct, not Clinch, Asylum." But the closer
he gets to the vacant lot, the more John's corpse begins to decompose. After
waking, Agee realizes that John represented his father. Agee's notes suggest
the sequence was based on an actual nightmare. He wrote, "Dream: If you
know what this means, or whether it means anything, I wish you would tell
me." Asked later whether or not her husband had such a dream, Mia Agee
responded, "It feels like a dream. I would suspect it is an actual dream Jim
had, but that is only conjecture."[88]

Following the nightmarish sequence of carrying his father's body through
Knoxville, back to the corner where they felt most connected, Agee somehow
felt guilty—"I've betrayed my father"—but did not know how or why. He
felt the dream compelling him to find an answer, to examine his childhood
and his relationship with his father: "He should go back into those years. As
far as he could remember; and everything he could remember; nothing he
had learned or done since; nothing except (so well as he could remember)
what his father had been as he had known himself, and what he had seen
with his own eyes, and supposed with his own mind." He wanted to finally
put to rest the idea that he had been a disappointment to his father. "1928
Story," another autobiographical work from the late 1940s, suggests a similar
motivation for Agee exploring his earlier life. Agee's stand-in, Irving, writes
during "the middle, the last half, of the nineteen forties," a time when he feels
a "universal mistrust" in everything and considers "that he had never really

grown up . . . or even wanted [to]." He thinks that writing about it might "amount to something, or maybe at least it would help clear my mind."[89]

The writer was not employing the dream as some convenient literary device to justify his novel; he was on a very real quest to sort out his life before its untimely end. "Now as awareness of how much of life is lost, and how little is left, becomes even more piercing," Agee wrote, "I feel also, and ever the more urgently, the desire to restore, and to make a little less impermanent, such of my lost life as I can, beginning with the beginning and coming as far forward as need be." He planned the novel as "chiefly a remembrance of my childhood, and a memorial to my father; and I find that I value my childhood and my father as they were, as well and exactly as I can remember and represent them." Sometime after he turned thirty-seven—passing what he believed was his father's age at death—Agee wrote a letter to the dead parent whose spirit had haunted him for the past three decades:

> My dear father:
>   This was never my name for you when we knew each other but it has been my name for you for so long, now, that I would be mistaken to try to use the other.
>   Let me explain what I am trying to do here.
>   I have lived, now, a year longer than you were given to live. I feel very heavy in the sense of life and death, and very heavy in my sense of uncertainty and of failure in my life so far, and in the work I want most to do and have felt, for a long time, that I was best fitted to do. My way of trying to handle these things is, to try to recall and understand my life, as well as I can, and to try to write it down as clearly and well as I can. And the more I have thought of this, and the more I have tried, the clearer it has become to me that you have had a great deal more to do with it than any of us could easily imagine. In trying to write about my first few years alive, I am bound to be writing, mainly, about you.

Agee seemed to be defending his choice to become a writer in the first place, doubting that his father would approve of his vocation or his efforts to express their relationship in writing: "If you were alive, and could read this, I cannot believe that you would like it. But if I were to try to make it a thing that you would like, I would fail in that, too, and then I would not even have been true to myself." Concerned that what he wrote might damage family relationships, Agee had told his sister, Emma, "I would never want to do anything to hurt Mother or Father." Around the same time he wrote to his father, he also drafted a letter to his mother, describing his plans for the novel:

> Dearest mother:
>   I had wanted when I saw you to tell you what I was trying to do, and ask whether you would feel willing to help me.

I am trying to write a short book, a novel, beginning with the first things I can remember, and ending with my father's burial. The whole closing section is to be as clear an account as I can make, of everything I can remember, from the morning I woke up and learned that he had died the night before, through to the end of the afternoon of the funeral.

Since I'm mainly trying to write the book from inside my own experience at that age, I may write of this, as of most else in the book, only exactly what I can remember. But that may not be the right way to do it. In any case I know that my own memories are so extremely fragmentary, though very vivid in certain patches, that I'm not sure they may piece together into a coherent account without conjecture and invention, and I'm not sure that I want to do much of either, anywhere in the book, and particularly not on this subject.

So I've wondered about asking you, and Hugh, for whatever you can remember about it. I'm asking a good many questions, which I enclose, separate from this letter, because I realize you may well prefer to have nothing to do with it. If so, don't even bother to look at them. Throw them away. You may not want to remember so distinctly in such detail. And you may have very grave misgivings about my writing about it. In either case I wouldn't want to ask your help.

He may not have actually sent his mother the letter or even solicited family members to help fill in his own recollections. In a page of notes about his father's death, he wrote, "Although my remembrance of the matters which will be told of in the following pages is fragmentary, I have thought it best to invent nothing; I have not even asked the help of others, who were part of the same experience." But for sections where he was unassisted by memory, Agee "took very simple events from his childhood and then allowed his imagination to play over them." The writer found that "invention" was necessary, and actually "served remembrance." His notes suggest that in re-creating his early childhood he used "memories I can infer from my baby"—first-hand experiences from fathering his own child. When he wrote that "marriage in many ways spooked" his father, he was perhaps projecting his own "lasting terror of marriage." But even with his embellishments, the novel would stick remarkably close to events and details from his life—including his father's prior employment in Panama, the familiar nurse who attended the newborn Emma, the neighborhood boys who bullied him, Uncle Frank the mortician, frequent visits with the Tylers, traveling to Elkmont with Uncle Ted and Aunt Kate, his father's fatal wreck, a strange presence felt by family members the night of his death, a visiting cleric from Chattanooga, the funeral in the Tylers' home, his father's burial at Greenwood Cemetery, and the walk to Fort Sanders with Uncle Hugh.[90]

ooooooooooooooo

As Agee continued work on the novel, another chapter of his life was end-ing. Erskine Wright, his stepfather, was dying of cancer. In late January 1949 Agee expressed his sorrow in a letter to Father Flye but said he was unable to visit: "Mother writes that Father Wright sees nobody any more, except you, with occasional visits from Father Spencer. I'm glad you are seeing him. I think it means a great deal to both of them and will continue to, to my mother. . . . It means it must be that last stretch, there. I hope so; I wish it were over. And I wish I could be there, for whatever small use I might be. I can't, until I'm free of this job for *Life,* which goes incredibly slowly." But in mid-February, after receiving news that Father Wright's condition had worsened, Agee dropped what he was doing and traveled to Sewanee. He stayed about a week on the St. Andrew's campus, close to his mother. "Father Wright was suffering a great deal; he was helpless," recalled Mrs. Medford, a nurse and friend of Laura. "Mrs. Wright was worn out from caring for him, and Father Wright didn't ever want her to leave him. She complained. But Rufus told her not to—though he couldn't know what she'd been through—he told her that Father Wright wasn't responsible, that he was suffering. Rufus never wanted to contrary him." Back in 1925 Agee had reluctantly accepted his mother's remarriage to a man quite unlike his father, and over the next two decades Agee's relationship with Erskine Wright—whom he had considered "narrow, moralistic, and rigid"—was little more than a "long estrangement." But perhaps biographers have made more of this than the facts warrant, for Agee had not only attended the finest private schools on his stepfather's tab, but he gave Wright an honored spot in his "Dedication" poem along with his mother's other living relatives. Now as Agee stood beside his stepfather's bed, the two were reconciled. "They made peace when Jim went down there," said Mia Agee. Mrs. Medford remembered that on the night Wright died, Agee remained helpfully nearby: "Rufus came rushing down and said, 'Mrs. Medford, will you come right quick? We think Father is dying.' I just rushed on up there with him. [Father Wright] just breathed a time or two after I got there. . . . Rufus just fell down on his knees and started saying some prayers." Erskine Wright died on February 18, 1949, and was buried three days later in a small cemetery on St. Andrew's campus.[91]

The *Life* feature story that Agee had set aside was published that Sep-tember. "Comedy's Greatest Era" details the pioneering film work of Mack Sennett, Harold Lloyd, Buster Keaton, Harry Langdon, and Charlie Chaplin. Agee was concurrently working on his autobiographical novel, which con-tains a scene in a small movie theater in Knoxville and reveals his mother's aversion to Chaplin's "vulgar" onscreen conduct. In "Comedy's Greatest," he refers to those like his mother as "'Nice' people, who shunned all movies in the early days" and who "condemned the Sennett comedies as vulgar and naive." But he knew there were "millions of less pretentious people," like himself, who "loved their sincerity and sweetness, their wild-animal innocence and glorious vitality." As he wrote this passage, he surely thought of his own experience at the Majestic Theatre, one of several Knoxville movie houses where locals "flocked to the silents": "The reader who gets back deep enough into that world will probably even remember the theater: the barefaced honky-tonk and the waltzes by Waldteufel, slammed out on a mechanical piano; the searing redolence of peanuts and demirep perfumery, tobacco and feet and sweat; the laughter of unrespectable people having a hell of a fine time, laughter as violent and steady and deafening as standing under a waterfall." The article was among Agee's best-received works, in a decade when he supported himself mainly by writing regular film columns in *Time* and the *Nation*.[92]

Agee dedicated one such column to legendary film director D. W. Griffith. Although he "didn't have the luck to see *The Birth of a Nation* until I was in my early twenties," Agee was greatly influenced by the film—particularly the "battle charge" scene, which he called "a perfect realization of a collective dream of what the Civil War was like, as veterans might remember it fifty years later, or as children, fifty years later, might imagine it. I have had several clear mental images of that war, from almost as early as I can remember . . . [and] when I saw that charge, it was merely the clarification, and corroboration, of one of those visions. . . . It is the perfection that I know of, of the tragic glory that is possible, or used to be possible, in war; or in war as the best in the spirit imagines or remembers it." Elsewhere, he stated that the Civil War was the "last war in which there was much nobility," and "the only war that doesn't just purely make me sick at my stomach." Agee, of course, had grown up just down the street from an old fort, which Federal troops defended from a Confederate attack forty-six years before his birth. He described such soldiers as "dark-bearded, coal-eyed, narrow-featured men of it seems a different race, yet who were our grandparents, whose broken old gentleness still trembles along the flagged streets of late spring, were meeting in glades in a level sleet of lead to take each other's souls out." The war, he wrote to Father Flye, "moves me 'historically' as nothing else has which I can remember. I imagine by the Centennial years, there won't be a one alive who was in it, barring some almost unthinkable freak—before whom, if I could find him, I'd feel like dropping on my knees. God bless them all, of both sides." Moved by nostalgia and "clear mental images of that war,"

Agee had suggested in 1937 writing "histories of the Civil War" using only "imagination of what he knows little or nothing of and has never seen." Sometime after that, he began drafting scenes for a planned film about that war. He was apparently undecided about the story's setting, although in one margin he wrote "Tennessee?" as a possibility.[93]

The film concerns "two soldiers," wounded in battle, whose bodies had been inadvertently "abandoned in the deepest part of a ravine . . . exactly where they had fallen late in the afternoon before." One is Union, one Confederate. One has been wounded "in the head," which "had the color and silence of limestone," and "the other . . . was so hurt near the heart that his ribs protruded like fangs" from his uniform. The next morning, one of the men regains consciousness; despite not knowing his location, the landscape reminds him of "an early morning of his childhood, when he had visited his great-uncle's farm." Then the "taste of fresh blood" in the soldier's mouth triggers another early memory: "When he was twelve, he had once chosen to fight a boy no bigger than himself, but much stronger, braver, and more skilful [sic]. He had suffered without resistance so many of these indignities to which the reserved and unaggressive are liable, that the time at last came when not to fight would have meant deeper humiliation than a healthy spirit can support. And so, dreading pain, and violence, and the shame of his sure defeat, he had nevertheless submitted to his oppressor's dearest wish, and had fought." There were a few times in Agee's childhood when he was hesitant or unwilling to fight, beginning with Alvin Tripp on Highland Avenue and apparently continuing with "boys who beat me up" at St. Andrew's. He drew on these personal memories while depicting a wounded Civil War soldier's internal experiences.[94]

The soldier finds the other lying nearby and carries him through the woods, finally seeking help from a family in "a deep mountain cabin." The log structure has "earth floors" and "peppers & popcorn hanging" from the rafters. Similarly, Agee had imagined his father's childhood cabin with "strings of peppers hanging from a rafter, and strings of corn . . . and marks of the axe in the oak logs of the wall and a place where the clay chinking had worked out and a towsack had been prodded in." He wrote that many of the details of the family's way of life could be based on the "Alabama families" he met; the rest could be based on the "mountains I know" from Tennessee.[95]

Like many of Agee's screenplays, the Civil War film treatment reads more like a novel than a script. The project is, unfortunately, one of many he never got around to finishing. But James Agee was not through with the Civil War. He would revisit the subject for two film projects, one about his favorite president—a man he closely associated with his father. His screenplay for *The Blue Hotel* and narration he wrote for the acclaimed film *The Quiet One*, both completed in the late 1940s, aided his transition into the Hollywood phase of his varied career. But he also had two autobiographical novels in the works.[96]

1950s

It had been almost five years since he began writing about his experiences at St. Andrew's. Two events—witnessing his stepfather's death at the school in February 1949 and participating in a religious "symposium" for *Partisan Review* a year later—gave Agee the stimulus needed to roughly finish the story in the spring of 1950. According to his letter to Flye, Agee "worked a week and finished a first draft, anyhow, of the story about Maundy Thursday. . . . between now and leaving town I hope really to finish the story." Remaining faithful to the facts, Agee wrote to Flye from New York, asking the priest for specific details about times of day at St. Andrew's near Holy Week, when the story takes place. The letter also shows that Agee was still working on his Knoxville-based novel at the time: "I've been wanting by the way to ask your help on a few points, some for the story, some for the book: What time, about, is just daylight, *Standard* Time, at St. Andrew's in early April (say April 1) and around April 12? And (as of Knoxville, there can't be much difference), what time is the beginning of dusk; sunset; full darkness on May 18? And what time is *sunrise* at St. Andrew's, April 1 and 12? And just sunlight, on May 18? Just roughly. Standard time in all cases."[97]

In *The Morning Watch*, published in April 1951, Agee fictionalized his private struggles as a student at St. Andrew's School. While critics gave it mixed reviews, those who had worked and lived at the boys' Episcopal school in Sewanee praised Agee's truthful portrayal. The school of the novella "is unmistakably Saint Andrew's," wrote Father Flye, "and the originals of probably all the characters in that story would be easily recognizable by anyone familiar with that place in the early 1920s." As in the cotton tenant book, Agee modeled his characters on real people but renamed them, as shown in a list from his notes—with actual names on the left and pseudonyms on the right:

Dave Mooney—Hobe Gillum
Raymond Kersey—Jimmy Toole
Bob Stewart—George Fitzgerald
Paul Green—Claude Grey

Deaconess Barbour—Deaconess Spenser
Fr. Whitall—Fr. Whitman
Fr. Flye—Fr. Fish
Fr. Lorey—Fr. Weiler
Fr. Orum—Fr. Ogle
Fr. Campbell—Fr. McPhitridge

Agee's descriptions were so accurate that former classmates and teachers were able to identify the persons despite the aliases. For example, the character Willard Rivenburg was recognized as the real-life Clarence Lautzenheiser, who was about seven years Agee's senior. Of the character Rivenburg, Agee wrote, "Nobody knew for sure just how old Willard was, but he looked as many men can only at thirty or so, and then only if they have been through a war, or years of the hardest kind of work. . . . Richard felt a warm rich comforting kind of pride in him and sense of glory as he watched him, as much, in a far quieter way, as when he watched his almost magical ability in sports." Clarence was indeed noted for his athletic ability and may have inspired Agee's 1937 story idea about "love between a twelve-year-old boy and a man of twenty-two, in the Iliadic air of football in a Tennessee mountain peasant school: reaching its crisis during and after a game which is recounted chiefly in terms of the boy's understanding and love; in other words in terms of an age of pure faith." If there was any truth to the scenario, it was probably little more than infatuation on Agee's part, as he depicts in *Morning Watch* with Richard standing close to Willard and feeling "a sense of honor and privilege in having this surprising chance to be so near to him and to watch him so closely, to really see him."[98]

Twelve-year-old Richard, who had lost his father at six, stands in for Agee at that age, and the book re-creates events from his Knoxville childhood as well. He thinks back to "drinking sodapop in Knoxville," and how "boys slightly more worldly than he would twist the bottle deep into the mouth and cock it up vertically to drink, and taking it down, breathless, would pat their stomachs or rub them in circles and gasp, 'Ahhh, good ole whiskey!'" Richard recalls "the terrible thing his uncle had said" about Christ's redemptive crucifixion: "Well who *asked* him to die for me? *I* didn't. He needn't try and collect on the debt . . . because there's no debt, far's I'm concerned." Agee had indeed heard Hugh Tyler make such a statement. And the school chapel's flowers and burning candles cause Richard to remember his father's funeral and imagine the corpse with "the mortal blue dent in the impatient chin."[99]

Among Agee's completed works, *The Morning Watch* remains somewhat neglected—a "largely ignored short novel." Scholars have paid it relatively little attention compared with *Let Us Now Praise Famous Men,* Agee's poetry, film reviews, his second autobiographical novel, and his screenplays.[100]

Screenwriting occupied Agee for most of his remaining career. In the autumn of 1950, he traveled to Los Angeles to script *The African Queen* for John Huston, a man Agee greatly admired and had profiled for *Life* in "Undirectable Director." Working on the film with Huston was somewhat of a consolation for Agee, who missed the chance to adapt Stephen Crane's Civil War story, *The Red Badge of Courage,* for the director. When Twentieth Century–Fox subsequently hired Agee to write and propose film treatments, he returned to the Civil War idea, perhaps with Crane's story still on his mind. Agee set his scenario, titled *Bloodline,* in "the gentle countryside of Middle Tennessee." Shortly after the war ends, a Confederate captain, John Ransome, returns to his ruined plantation to find all his possessions gone except for his prize horse, Shiloh, which had been hidden from looters by Ransome's "faithful former slave, Isaiah." Ransome consults Judge McClanahan, who advises him that moving west would be wise but that the South needs men like Ransome: "I can't imagine any good future here. Only poverty and bitterness and injustice and sorrow, for longer than I hope to live. But never you forget it, Son—this is your home. This is your country. It's broken, now—turned over to cowards and self-seekers and traitors and upstarts and fanatics. If you come back, you may not be able to do much—for yourself *or* your country. But we need every brave and honorable man—every man who really loves his home—to stay with us. Because that kind of animal is pretty near killed off."

The story follows Ransome as he heads west out of Memphis, crosses the Mississippi River by ferry into Arkansas, struggles to reclaim his lost property and family, and finally returns to Tennessee to rebuild his life. Agee finished revising his twenty-five-page treatment in September 1951 and handed it to the studio. It was the second of Agee's Civil War scenarios to remain undeveloped. His next, though only addressing the war peripherally, was successfully produced.[101]

Between the summer and fall of 1952, Agee scripted a five-part television film about Abraham Lincoln for the *Omnibus* series. *Mr. Lincoln* begins with the president's death, and follows the funeral train past villages and clustered mourners as it tours the country. Agee held Lincoln in high regard. Two of his grandparents—Henry Clay Agee and Emma Tyler—were teenagers during Lincoln's presidency, and his own birth was "scarcely one hundred years after the birth of Abraham Lincoln," James Agee wrote. According to one scholar, the boy running behind the funeral train in the film was intended by Agee to represent himself. But if this is so, Agee did not elaborate the fact in his script, only writing, "A little boy runs excitedly towards the train." Lilacs, placed on Lincoln's coffin in the film, were Agee's favorite flower and would be thrown on his own casket a few years after the program aired.[102]

Much of Agee's respect for Lincoln stemmed from a belief that his father, Jay, also endured a primitive childhood, worked hard to make something of his life, and thereby developed strength of character. Reflecting on her first husband's upbringing, Laura once said, "To me, it was always as if it were something like Lincoln." Agee had Lincoln in mind as he wrote parts of his autobiographical novel. In an unused draft for *A Death in the Family*, he imagined that his father had once fancied himself as the president:

> He told himself, smiling with stern self-disgust: And I'm the one thought I was Abe Lincoln.
>
> He could remember sickening daydreams of winning hopeless trials, and of great simple speeches, some funny and some noble. Sometimes he even had a beard. He could remember saving his country, and how his mother had the best room in the White House and smoked her pipe if she damn well had a mind to. Some of the high falutin society people wouldn't even come there any more but all the real people knew she was the salt of the earth and that was how he picked his Cabinet.

Agee wrote another passage, included in the novel, in which Arthur Savage tells Rufus and Emma what a good man their father had been:

> Some people have a hard, hard time. No money, no good schooling, scarcely enough food. Nothing that you children have, but good people to love them. Your daddy started like that. He didn't have one thing. He had to work till it practicly [*sic*] killed him, for every little thing he ever got.
>
> Well, some of the greatest men start with nothing. Like Abraham Lincoln. . . .
>
> Somehow I never got a chance to know Jay—your father—well as I wish. I don't think he ever could have dreamed how much I thought of him. . . . But I always thought your father was a lot like Lincoln. I don't mean getting ahead in the world. I mean a man. Some people get where they hope to in this world. Most of us don't. But there never was a man up against harder odds than your father. And there was never a man who tried harder, or hoped for more.

In another section of the book, the writer envisioned his family visiting an ancient matriarch, a woman born when "Abraham Lincoln was just two years old."[103]

Agee's *Lincoln* script, partly based on Carl Sandburg's biography, cuts from the funeral train all the way back to a *"cabin small and alone, a light in its one window,"* depicting Lincoln's birth, which Agee probably imagined was not much cruder than his father's in Campbell County. As the story progresses, young Abe educates himself, leaves his parents' home in his early twenties, and moves to New Salem: "It was a good town Abe Lincoln had come to; it was the New America in miniature. There were people from the North, and from the South: poor and rather well-to-do; scholarly; and illiterate; and all of them were looking towards a new kind of life with a new kind of hope. There was something like a real democracy, here: for here, it was almost literally true, that nobody looked down on anybody else. They took a man for what he was: and every element in New Salem took young Lincoln into its kindliness and its esteem." As described in the script, the town resembles the kind of place Jay Agee encountered in Knoxville, whose Market Square a local journalist once called "the most democratic place on earth." James Agee knew that his father read law books in such a town and briefly worked as a postmaster, and highlighted such facts about Lincoln's life: "I'm studyin' some about applyin' for a postmastership," says the young Abe. "And I aim to read law, every spare minute." As Jay Agee had delayed his marriage to Laura for financial reasons, so the fictional Lincoln delayed marrying Ann Rutledge: "Ann: my dearest: we *can't* marry yet a while. . . . I'm a poor man. *Very* poor. And in debt. *Bad.* And the only knack I've got with money, is to get worse in debt." Agee was criticized for straying too far from historical records, particularly regarding Lincoln's relationship to Ann Rutledge. It is possible that Agee had his father in mind as he wrote about Lincoln; the converse was certainly true when he wrote his novel.[104]

Incidentally, *Mr. Lincoln* marked the end of Agee's brief stint as a screen actor—consisting of two 1952 films he scripted in which he played a town drunk. Agee, who had acted at Knoxville High School, appeared as the fictional Jack Kelso opposite Royal Dano's youthful Lincoln. The television miniseries was broadcast around the time *Face to Face*—a two-story anthology featuring Agee's adaptation of Stephen Crane's "The Bride Comes to Yellow Sky"—appeared on the big screen. As Frank Gudger, Agee shared the story's first scene of dialogue with Robert Preston, who later portrayed a fictional version of Agee's father in *All the Way Home.*[105]

Just as Agee's sister Emma had followed him into employment at *Time* magazine, so she also acted in at least one film. In *The Steps of Age,* a 1951 mental health documentary, Emma played an unnamed daughter whose widowed mother suffered from "emotional problems." Laura Wright saw the film and wrote to her son about Emma's performance: "Emma I thought did very well too—her part was very short & interrupted & the interior

photography not too clear—but ... I thought she put it over very well—&
her voice was without any artificiality—I thought it 'got across' very well."
Helen Levitt, with whom James had collaborated on *The Quiet One,* produced the film.[106]

∞∞∞∞∞∞∞∞∞

In mid-February 1954, Father Flye's wife, Grace, died at home on St.
Andrew's campus. Agee traveled there to attend the funeral on February 17,
in his final trip to Tennessee. Following the service, Agee comforted a grieving family friend, Mrs. Medford; as he hugged her outside the chapel, he
said, "I know just how you feel." About ten months later he dreamed of the
funeral, and recounted it in a letter to Father Flye: "I think I will tell you, my
dearest friend; last night I had a dream, during which ... your wife and my
beloved friend, as I arrived at St. Andrew's for her burial, stepped out of her
coffin (without stepping back into life) and came towards me up a crowded
aisle in the Chapel, and we embraced and kissed as we always have, after a
long time apart,—as if it were only a few days since we had seen each other.
She is among the Saints, and I think she always was."[107]

By April 1954 Agee was in California, beginning work on the screenplay
for *The Night of the Hunter,* based on Davis Grubb's novel. His first draft was
about twice as long as necessary; and with shooting to begin that summer,
director Charles Laughton rewrote much of the screenplay, causing one to
wonder how many of Agee's original ideas made the final cut. The shooting
script describes the "small one-street river town" (in "Ohio River Country")
as "a picturesque, mid-19th-century remnant of the old river civilization,
which general Progress has left behind." While Cresap's Landing is depicted
as more village than town, one could find parallels in Knoxville, itself a mere
"river town" before railroads connected it to the rest of the country. Coinci-
dentally, a theater named "Bijou" is seen in the film alongside the main road
(Peacock Alley); it is not named as such in the novel, in Agee's draft, or in
the shooting script.[108]

The script contains other elements that at first seem inspired by Agee's
childhood. A father dies, leaving behind a young son, a younger daughter, and
a widow, who in her piety remarries a (believed-to-be) clergyman—as Agee's
mother married Father Wright. The boy covets a pocket watch displayed in a
shop window—as Agee coveted a cap he had seen in a Knoxville store. When
the mother is no longer physically available, the children take refuge with a
surrogate parent—as Agee spent time with Father Flye at St. Andrew's when

Laura forbade her son's visits. But as familiar as these elements might have seemed to Agee, they were already present in the source novel.

However, there are a few surprises in Agee's first-draft script that directly relate to autobiographical descriptions from his earlier works. After the pair of orphaned children raft to safety downriver and are taken in by the matron, Rachel Cooper, the boy, John, explores the inside of the springhouse on her farm:

> Now we see, with him, closely, as he stoops, the crocks and jars standing up to their throats in spring-water, each neatly covered with damp muslin. In a kind of reverent wonder and delight he removes cloths; we see rich blocks of butter, printed into daisy patterns; eggs, all but luminous and jewel-like in this light; he traces one finger tip through cream so rich he makes a trench in it; he smells the cream and sucks his finger and is sharply startled by the sudden deep twang of a bull-frog. He peers around for him. . . . [The bull-frog] is a huge, arty old guy, all jade and silver and gold, big as a catcher's mitt. He glares into our eyes (John's eyes), profoundly affronted, his throat pulsing with outrage.

The passage almost exactly mirrors one from *Let Us Now Praise Famous Men,* in which Agee recalled sensations of standing "in a springhouse . . . a place such as that which was at my grandfather's farm" in Jacksboro, and seeing the "broad affronted eyes, the face and shoulders and great dim belly of a black and jade and golden bullfrog, big as a catcher's mitt, his silver larynx twitching constantly with scarcely controllable outrage."[109]

Another episode sees John in New Economy, "a deeply old-fashioned town." As "he strolls" its sidewalks, which are "well-filled with small-town and rural saunterers," he approaches a "very old-fashioned" farmer's market:

> At the curb, to one side, we see a mixture of old cars and of horse and mule-drawn vehicles. . . . Within the shaded arching of a canvas-covered wagon (the shape and kind which crossed the prairies), a grave, black-eyed woman sits nursing her baby; she wears a sunbonnet which carries out the flaring curve of the wagon-cover.
>
> Along the other side of the walk are shops; shaded market-shelves; and, farther within, market stalls. A yacketing of caged fowls; rattle and rustle of walking and voices; slaughtered hens and calves slung up by their ankles; fresh vegetables; and for John's special notice, a huge old catfish laid out on ice, with eyes like slick coins and whiskers like Fu Manchu.

To anyone familiar with *A Death in the Family,* these descriptions read as an elaboration of Rufus's walk with his father through Knoxville's Market Square, where "in the tail of one wagon a woman sat, her face narrow beneath her flare of sunbonnet, her dark eyes in its shade, like smudges of soot." Father and son did not enter the market house, which was closed at that late hour, but only saw the "white brick wall" of its exterior. But here in his *Hunter* script, Agee describes the market's interior stalls, similar to what one would have seen in Knoxville. The matron Rachel sells produce outside, with her "gaunt old horse and wagon" parked nearby at "a horse-trough." As the heat of the day increases, she protects her horse's head in a peculiar way: "She dips a sponge in the horse-trough, puts it into an old straw hat, and – now we can see – puts the hat, which has holes for the ears, on the horse's head." But the practice was not unusual when Agee was a child, as he wrote about it in an unpublished fragment about summers in Knoxville: "Some of the horses wore sponges and some wore hats just like people but with holes for their ears."[110]

Agee also based a character on an influential figure from his Tennessee childhood. Near the end of his screenplay a priest, Father Scallon, visits Rachel and the children on Christmas Eve. After Scallon suggests that the children might enjoy attending "Midnight Mass" and seeing "the Crib with all the figures," Rachel politely asks the reason for his visit. Scallon replies, "Because I love children, too, Mrs. Cooper." Appearing in neither the source novel nor the finished film, the priest clearly seems to be Agee's tribute to Father Flye. These scenes from Agee's script show that he had reimagined Grubb's scenario and setting in light of his own past.[111]

Agee never saw the film *The Night of the Hunter*. After completing his draft of the script, he remained in California from May to August with his new mistress, Tamara Comstock, whom he had met at a Hollywood party. The few months Agee spent with her were significant in that she provided him a somewhat structured writing environment. During his final productive period, Agee resumed work on the novel he began in the late forties. The fact that the manuscript survived may be attributed to Comstock, who regularly hid the stack of paper in her freezer, as it was "impenetrable to both fire and to Agee's destructive revisionist obsession." However, she was unable to curb his destructive personal habits, particularly his alcohol consumption. After Agee returned to the east coast, his letters to her became increasingly fixated on his failing health. He continued tinkering with two film scripts, one about the Tanglewood music school and one about Colonial Williamsburg, both of which he never finished.[112]

Five days before his death, Agee wrote what would be his final letter to Father Flye. The letter—which, unsent, was later found sitting on the mantel in Agee's home—contained "a movie idea" that begins in the distant past

as "elephants converge from all over Africa." The noble beasts are warned
by "the voice of God" that they "will be taken to be *looked upon,* to be regarded as strange and as wonderful and . . . as funny." A series of vignettes
follow, portraying the mistreatment of circus elephants in the nineteenth
and twentieth centuries. Agee drew from an odd piece of Tennessee lore for
one of these factual episodes. On September 13, 1916—the same month his
aunt Annabel traveled from Nebraska to visit the family—an elephant was
executed in Erwin, Tennessee, about eighty-five miles northeast of Knoxville.
Agee outlined the bizarre scenario: "In a small Tennessee town—out of what
charming provocations you can imagine—Mary went berserk, and killed
three men. The general populace decided, accordingly, that she should be
hanged. They strung her up to a railroad derrick; she broke it down by sheer
weight. They got a stronger derrick: after two hours, Mary died, hanged by
the neck, while 5,000 oafs looked on." His details were mostly right. "Murderous Mary" killed only one man, her unqualified handler, between shows in
Kingsport, Tennessee, after he jabbed her with an elephant goad. To prevent
further tragedy, circus owner Charles Sparks decided the elephant should be
executed. After electrocution was ruled out, hanging was deemed the most
practical option, but it required a train ride forty miles south to the town
of Erwin, site of the next show and the closest available derrick. The first
chain that raised Mary indeed broke, but only because one of the elephant's
ankles was still chained to a railroad track. The same derrick hoisted her up
a second time, and Mary quickly expired. Her body was buried near the rail
yard.[113]

   After explaining the elephant movie to Flye, Agee confessed, "Almost
nobody I've described it to likes this idea, except me. It has its weaknesses,
but I like it. I hope you do." Even if Agee had lived longer, the idea would
have probably gone nowhere. But the scenario is important because it shows
that throughout his career, and even up to his death, Agee continued to draw
inspiration from his native Tennessee.[114]

∞∞∞∞∞∞∞∞∞∞

When Agee died in New York on May 16, 1955, his Knoxville novel—"a
remembrance of my childhood, and a memorial to my father"—was unfinished. David McDowell, whom Agee had met at St. Andrew's nineteen
years prior, edited the manuscript—cutting some chapters, arranging others
as flashbacks, and inserting "Knoxville: Summer of 1915" as a prologue—and
published the novel as *A Death in the Family* in 1957 to wide acclaim. The

work received the 1958 Pulitzer Prize for fiction. Half a century later, the novel was reedited by Michael Lofaro, incorporating Agee's original "dream sequence" as the prologue and other chapters McDowell had cut, and restoring the novel's chronological structure as Agee intended. The new version, subtitled *A Restoration of the Author's Text,* also restores the characters' actual names—which McDowell altered to protect those persons still living in 1957, consequently blurring many of Agee's autobiographical references.[115]

Whereas Agee had previously disguised Knoxville with pseudonyms like Knoxton and Hydesboro, the city is immediately recognizable in *A Death in the Family.* Agee described his former hometown with such accuracy that readers would later be able to easily identify its landmarks and streets—such as the Asylum Avenue Viaduct, the L&N Station, Market Square, Gay Street, and the "middle-sized gracefully fretted wood houses" of Highland Avenue. Scholars like Victor Kramer have noted the degree to which Agee was inspired by his own past: "Agee's final book, unfinished at his death, is largely based on fact: he consciously sought to reconstruct the setting of his childhood." Kenneth Curry considered Agee's novel a "confession" and therefore believed "an enquiry into the factual accuracy beneath his work is legitimate and germane to a consideration of *A Death in the Family.*" Father Flye believed the novel accurately represented Agee's childhood, "a tiny section—three days or so—of his autobiography." Laura Wright waited several months after her son's book was published before sharing her opinion of it:

> So much of it drew me straight into it—and yet mingled with it a great deal else that is a writer's privilege: to use his medium to mould and to drive thro[ugh] abstract things, which were not in reality, true. It is a marvellous [*sic*] mixture of these elements, and I recognize it as a *great and really universal elegy*—since all of it is the essence of *all* deaths—among mankind....
>
> "We" feel the parts in italics are the most beautiful and true, and are really *Rufus at the very top of his gift*—

Despite some minor errors and liberties taken, most events were represented so accurately that Laura asked her daughter, Emma, "How did he know so well how it was?"[116]

Sometimes Agee produced scenes that were in fact imaginary, "including one of the very best scenes in the book, the visit to Great Grandma—that is absolutely fictional," McDowell said. "The priest who visits the house is fictional. A priest did, but he didn't resemble him at all. This is not just simply exactly everything that happened, but a very, very shrewd artist's reworking of material and changing it to fit a theme and a plot." Kramer called the novel "unusual," because of its mixture of "detailed remembrance of specifics" as well as being "an archetypal depiction of events within any family." It is rich with universal themes while being "specific documentation" at the same time: "It is a book about marital love and loss, about initiation of children into life, and about maturation and loss for adults. It is a book about religious faith and the need for religion. It is a book about the urban and rural conflict so many Americans have experienced in this century. Yet, while it is all of these things, it is Agee's specific documentation of his life when he was four, five, and six years old."[117]

∞∞∞∞∞∞∞∞∞∞∞

The early loss of his father bred in Agee a keen awareness of mortality. Although his religious upbringing reinforced the sense of earthly transience, by the 1940s Agee could not shake the fatalistic belief that he would die young like his father. Much of his fiction expresses the outlook that life will never turn out the way you intend: think of the youth obliged to care for an elderly relative instead of pursuing college, or the once-secure Victorian home destroyed in a torrent of rain, or the schoolboy's religious devotion shattered by rationalism, or the perfect childhood ruined when the father dies. Yet despite Agee's flashes of pessimism, as well as his personal struggles with depression and alcoholism, his writings never succumb to despair: they continue to affirm the value of life, in general, and of his own past, in particular. "In all of Agee's writing, there is an elegiac tone, for his are songs to moments which are passing," writes Kramer. "This nostalgia for the past and respect for the moment are his best achievements." Maybe he saw writing as his only means of preserving his life's "slowly dwindling pool" against the "ebbing tide" of time. Had he lived, Agee would have likely finished his Knoxville novel and begun other sections of the multivolume autobiographical work he had in mind—beginning with "The Ancestors" and how his parents met, and ending with "Mia" and all that had happened since his third marriage. Critic Clive James mourned Agee's death and "the absence of that sequence of novels which might have recollected his life—a sequence for the writing of which he had qualifications rivalling Proust's." But Agee could not delay death's arrival; neither could his father or his ancestors before him.[118]

One might argue that Agee would not have become a writer in the first place had his father not died prematurely. But the sudden loss of a parent so robbed him of stability and meaning that as a teenager Agee sought to make sense of his life. During his last few years as a Tennessee resident, he discovered that through writing he was able to express his grief and confusion while preserving moments that had slipped away. Despite his pain originating there, Agee frequently returned—physically and figuratively—to the South. Certainly he saw the extremes of the region as he traveled through it. Sometimes he experienced darkness and violence there, just as he had occasionally seen those traits surface in his father's anger. But much more frequently Agee found comfort and security and inspiration there: it was his home. As journalist Louise Davis wrote, "Agee never got far away from the simplicity of his Tennessee ancestors . . . never lost the sound of the Tennessee mountain ballads that his father had sung to him as a child." In a passage from *A Death in the Family*, Jay has just finished singing Rufus to sleep; and sitting near his son's bed, he thinks about his own unrecoverable past:

> A great cedar, and the colors of limestone and of clay; the smell of wood smoke and, in the deep orange light of the lamp, the silent logs of the walls, his mother's face, her ridged hand mild on his forehead: *Don't you fret, Jay, don't you fret.* . . .
>
> How far we all come. How far we all come away from ourselves. So far, so much between, you can never go home again. You can go home, it's good to go home, but you never really get all the way home again in your life. And what's it all for? All I tried to be, all I ever wanted and went away for, what's it all for? . . .
>
> And God knows he was lucky, so many ways, and God knows he was thankful. Everything was good and better than he could have hoped for, better than he ever deserved; only, whatever it was and however good it was, it wasn't what you once had been, and had lost, and could never have again, and once in a while, once in a long time, you remembered, and knew how far you were away, and it hit you hard enough, that little while it lasted, to break your heart.

James Rufus Agee traveled home every time he wrote about his father and mother, his sister, his aunts and uncles and grandparents—every time he wrote about the farmers of Appalachia, or the religious school for boys, or a neighborhood of middle-class clapboard houses in a southern industrial city, or trolleys clanging down the streets of Knoxville on summer evenings. He traveled there to find parts of himself that he had lost, and in the process he left a great record of love for a region—and a people—that encompassed Knoxville and the hill country of Tennessee down along the Cumberland Plateau. By writing about those places and people, he made his readers care about them, too.[119]

6

"One Familiar and Well-Beloved"

Legacy, 1955–2015

James Agee died at age forty-five on May 16, 1955, suffering a heart attack in a taxi on the way to a doctor's appointment—almost exactly thirty-nine years after his father died in an automobile. At the time, Agee was "no more than a local curiosity" in his former hometown, where the *News-Sentinel* eulogized him as a "poet, critic, magazine and screen writer," who had "published a book of poetry, *Permit Me Voyage*" and "a novel, *The Morning Watch*." The paper quoted magazine editor T. S. Matthews, who said Agee was "the finest writer *Time* ever had." But scarcely any of Agee's work was still in print. *Let Us Now Praise Famous Men* was a little-remembered, short-run book that had not been reprinted in fourteen years, and *A Death in the Family* was still two years away from publication. When he died, Agee was perhaps best known locally as the writer whose Knoxville memories were set to music by Samuel Barber.[1]

Back in 1949, one week before Agee's fortieth birthday, the Knoxville Symphony Orchestra performed Barber's *Knoxville: Summer of 1915,* a work for soprano and orchestra "with words by James Agee, native Knoxvillian, inspired by his childhood memories of Highland Avenue." Some months earlier, the *News-Sentinel* had commented on the composition's role in boosting Knoxville's reputation: "Chambers of Commerce do not always find it worthwhile to keep up with a city's wandering artists since the memories of many such men (and women) run to vinegar instead of wine. But the present recollection is a happy one and quite appropriate to this season of the year." *Partisan Review* had published Agee's prose piece a decade earlier. The work brought Agee more hometown recognition during his lifetime than any of his other writings.[2]

THE BOOK

When *A Death in the Family* was published in November 1957—just before Agee would have turned forty-eight—fans of Barber's composition were pleased to find "Knoxville: Summer of 1915" included as the novel's prologue, lyrically depicting a boy's carefree evening in a Knoxville suburb. Just days after the novel's release, a review appeared in the *News-Sentinel*. An editor noted that "the book, by a former Knoxvillian, was published during the past week." The bottom portion of the article, signed "L.C.T.," was actually written by Lucy Curtis Templeton, a Chi Omega member at UT with Agee's mother and the newspaper's main book critic. "James Agee's book, A Death in the Family, is autobiographical, a poignant account of the death of his own father, who was killed in an automobile accident," she wrote.

> Every review that I have seen of this book refers to the family as "middle-class." By financial standards this might have been the case, but socially and intellectually, it certainly was not. They were exceptionally sensitive and gifted....
>
> Both Laura Tyler Agee and Hugh Tyler were acquaintances of the present writer; in fact Laura, who lives in Connecticut, is a fraternity sister. James Agee, who was called Rufus in those days, she remembers as a lively dark-haired little boy. An aunt who was a member of the family joined an Anglican sisterhood.[3]

Within a week of that article, Lawson McGhee Library made the book available on its shelf of new releases, and by February listed it among the books "most in demand." But the novel received scant local publicity until May, when it won the Pulitzer Prize for fiction. In another write-up, the *News-Sentinel* stressed Agee's connections to the city, that the author "was the grandson of the late ... Joel C. Tyler ... one of the founders of Ty-Sa-Man Machine Co." That business was still thriving in Knoxville, but Agee's family had sold its shares eight years earlier to Nic Knoph Jr., whose father had replaced Jay Agee as bookkeeper in 1916. "Hugh Tyler ... is an uncle, the twin brother of young Agee's mother," the article continued. "The Tyler family lived in a large frame house on the corner of West Clinch Avenue and Twelfth Street." The article also emphasized the novel's autobiographical nature: "Members of the family play a prominent part in the Agee book," which "recounts the effect of a father's death on members of the family, especially a young son. Agee's own father died when the writer was a boy in Knoxville."[4]

In May 1958 the LaFollette Book Club met in that city "at the home of Mrs. W. L. Sharp" to hear a visiting lecturer, Dr. George Ridenour, discuss *A Death in the Family.* The author's grandparents had lived near LaFollette, and Agee's aunt Mossie Hodges still resided there. The *LaFollette Press* wrote that Agee's celebrated novel "is of special interest to people here because of the author's LaFollette connections." The article explained the book's factual basis but misnamed Agee's father and mislocated his car wreck five miles up the road from where it occurred: "His father was the late James Rufus Agee, Sr., with whose untimely death when the son was very young, the book deals. The father was killed in an automobile accident on May 18, 1916, near the present Claxton School, when returning home from a visit in Campbell County with his father, Prof. Henry C. Agee, who was ill. James Agee, Sr. was a brother of Mrs. Mossie Hodges and the late A. F. Agee of LaFollette, and John Agee of Knoxville." Borrowing Lucy Templeton's phrasing, the columnist noted that Agee came "from a family of exceptionally sensitive and gifted people" and that the Tylers' former home in Knoxville "still stands." The fact that the article appeared in a LaFollette newspaper was significant: it applauded the prize-winning novel at the same time that many people in and around that city were shunning it—and its author.[5]

Agee had expressed some concern about fictionalizing intimate details from his family's past. He told his sister, Emma, that in writing the book he did not "want to do anything to hurt Mother or Father." However, he pulled no punches in depicting his parents' marital troubles and his father's struggles with alcohol. Several of Agee's relatives believed he stretched the truth. After reading the novel, Paula Tyler concluded that Jay and Laura were "more intellectual" than their fictional counterparts. Laura reported that her brother Hugh was "hurt" that his character appeared so divisive and angry; in reality, she said, "there was not this bitterness" within the family on the day of the funeral, as depicted. Father Flye believed Joel and Emma Tyler were faithfully rendered in the book but thought the character Andrew was quite unlike Hugh Tyler. "That isn't exactly a good picture of him. He was a gentler person than that and not so . . . caustic," said Flye, who knew the artist to be "charming." But the Tylers (called the Lynches in the novel) were portrayed in a mostly positive light compared to the harshly characterized Agees (renamed the Follets) of Campbell County.[6]

Gladys Agee, daughter of John Agee, had fond memories of her cousin Rufus visiting her family at 1710 Highland Avenue. But later, when she joined the army in the 1940s, James was in New York writing for "leftist" magazines. By then her opinion of him had changed. "Frankly, I was embarrassed by him," she said. His death brought her little closure, because of the publication two years later of "*the* book" and its "scandalous" portrayal of a particular family member.[7]

Alfred Frank Agee was Henry Agee's middle son, the next oldest after Jay. When Frank died of heart failure in 1940, he was remembered fondly "as one of the most affable of LaFollette citizens." He had been "a member [of] the First Baptist Church," a local Mason, had served as a city councilman from 1907 to 1915, and as postmaster from 1922 to 1933. He had brought on his son, Frank Carden Agee, as partner and future successor in the furniture and mortuary business. For decades, Agee Furniture & Undertaking Co. had operated out of two floors of the Adams and Rogers building, a few doors

Detail of a street scene along Central Avenue in LaFollette, circa 1949. The name "Agee's" can be seen directly under the "Frigidaire Appliances" sign, a few doors to the right of Riggs drug store. The mortuary had operated out of the second floor. By this time, almost a decade after Alfred Frank Agee's death, his son Frank Carden Agee ran the furniture business. Postcard image from the author's collection.

east on Central from the corner of Tennessee Avenue, with the furniture store below and the funeral home above it. The 1917 building still stands at that intersection in the center of town. Jerry Sharp, the late curator of the Campbell County Historical Society museum and library, was about four years old when his mother died; he had a memory of the elder Frank Agee coming to the house to take away his mother's body. Sharp remembered there was an elevator—one of the first in the city—in the rear of Agee's store that carried corpses up to the second-floor mortuary. Frank Agee "held the esteem of everyone" in the community, according to his obituary.[8]

So when *A Death in the Family* was published in 1957, Frank's acquaintances and family members were appalled to read about a mortician, Ralph Follet, described as an embarrassing alcoholic and "the worst tail-chaser in LaFollette." In his notes about the funeral, James Agee had remembered Frank arriving at the Tyler house "heavily drunk." But Laura Wright believed the depiction of her brother-in-law was "overdone" in the novel. "That whole part of it was . . . much exaggerated," Laura said. "That was for effect." Frank's niece and nephew, Gladys and Oliver, found the characterization to be completely unlike the "compassionate, intelligent man" they knew. As an example of his kindness, Dr. Oliver Agee remembered his uncle Frank giving him his "first dog" and his "first fishing rod." However, others have remarked that while family members did not react favorably to Frank's depiction, some felt the portrayal was true. For those readers, "common decency," rather than accuracy, was the real issue.[9]

But the book contained other objectionable elements. Grandpa Follet is characterized as a weak pushover and a burden on his wife and loved ones—"sort of useless without ever meaning to be." Agee based the character on his grandfather Henry Clay Agee but renamed—or misnamed—him John Henry, after Gladys's father. Grandmother Mossie Agee had died of a heart attack on December 21, 1943; but her second husband, Thomas Oaks—whom she married less than a year after Henry died—was still living when the published novel called him "an ignorant hand, who couldn't even read or write," even though census records attest that he could do both. Frank's son Wheeler, renamed Jim-Wilson, was described as weak and clingy, "with his poor little washed-out eyes" and "his readiness to cry." Surely Agee remembered that Wheeler died at eight years old in 1918 of a rare bone infection.[10]

To many surviving Agees in Campbell County, the writer's depiction of Frank was libelous—even with the name altered. By the time the novel was published, Frank's son had successfully continued the business and was known for his "hard work, civic responsibility, and community respect." And "out of regard for him alone," many locals rejected the novel for exposing the family's "dirty laundry." Hard feelings lingered even decades after its original publication. A Maryville resident recalled first reading *A Death in the Family* sometime in the 1970s. Not long afterwards, she met the mayor of LaFollette at an event and mentioned reading the book that was partly set in his town. The mayor replied that none of the city or school libraries carried the book, because it portrayed LaFollette's citizens as drunkards. "There is such a thread of truth through it that it made many people believe it was a distortion of truth, and it left them very angry," Dr. Oliver Agee said of the novel. His older sister, Gladys, for example, did not want the author discussed at all in her home. But over the years, Dr. Agee grew to appreciate his cousin's work. "Some of the description is so great. . . . There's no doubt in my mind he was a literary genius."[11]

THE HOUSE

While *A Death in the Family* was being alternately praised and criticized, little notice was given to the late author's former home. Most locals saw no difference between it and the other crumbling Victorians in the neighborhood. But when the house was first sold in July 1884—three decades before Agee's memorable summer evenings there—it sat on what was then Altavia Street, on the western edge of the posh new West End neighborhood, subdivided from a large land tract once owned by W. B. A. Ramsey. Four years later, the area west of Second Creek would incorporate as West Knoxville, with its own mayor and aldermen; the town's recorder and treasurer, Alvis G. Scott, lived in the future Agee home. A rarely noticed remnant from this brief era still, at this writing, lies in the alley between the 1400 blocks of Highland and Forest avenues, where it was placed more than 125 years ago—an iron manhole cover stamped "WEST KNOXVILLE SEWER."[12]

Streetcar tracks were first laid through the neighborhood during the summer of 1888. After a city ordinance passed that December, Altavia Street was renamed Highland Avenue and the house numbered 702. Knoxville annexed West Knoxville in 1897, and the blocks were renumbered by 1900. The house again had a new address, 1505 Highland, which it would keep for more than sixty years.[13]

Owners often rented out rooms, even decades before the neighborhood became known for housing university students. While John Cox lived in the home with his family from 1895 to 1905, he let rooms to boarders. As mentioned, the widowed Laura Agee leased out a few of the spare rooms to university students and a Marine Corps recruiter before selling the house. But there is evidence that the Agees kept boarders even before Jay died: according to city directories, a bookkeeper named Oscar F. Tynes resided with the family in 1914, and a traveling salesman, Archibald P. Spears, boarded there the following year. The John Jett family bought the house from Laura in autumn 1918, and by January 1920 an additional family plus a boarder were living under the same roof—thirteen people in all. The residence, which originally had eight rooms, was advertised in early 1925 as a "modern nine-room house in good condition" with "two baths, large basement, double garage," selling for $7,500.[14]

During the Great Depression, many owners of larger homes could only pay their mortgages by renting out rooms or whole floors. "Nobody could afford to keep them," remembered Martin Hunt, who grew up in the neighborhood at that time. In 1930 a section of the former Agee home was rented

In these two photographs, two-year-old Joann Segaser holds a doll on the front walkway of 1505 Highland, circa 1940. The man standing on the porch is James Shelton, who owned the home for almost two decades. Courtesy of Mark Hipshire and his mother, Joann Hipshire.

out, described in the newspaper as a "newly furnished bedroom and small apartment" with "furnace heat" and a "garage." Home exteriors began to change shape as interiors were increasingly divided into separate spaces. For the first time, 1505 Highland was listed as three apartments in the 1939 city directory. The earlier addition of a second-story bathroom had left an ugly, shed-like appendage hanging off the west side. When the federal census was taken in 1940, there were ten individuals residing in the house: the owners, elderly siblings James and Lizzie Shelton, lived in one apartment; Ethel Campbell, a thirty-four-year-old saleslady, and her two daughters, shared a second unit with a female lodger and a housekeeper; and a young UT instructor, Charles Segaser, and his wife and daughter lived in a third unit. Segaser, who "was studying in UT's Mechanical Engineering graduate school" at the time, worked out a money-saving deal with the landlords: the Sheltons agreed to lower his rent if he regularly "stoked the furnace" in the house's basement, said Mark Hipshire, Segaser's grandson.[15]

The Sheltons were the home's longest owner-residents. James bought the property in October 1927 but would not live in the house for ten more years. His sister Elizabeth moved in around 1930, then fifty years old, and remained in the house through 1949—almost two decades. By comparison, the Agee family lived there fewer than six years; and over the home's seventy-eight-year history, the average occupant stayed about three. One might imagine that families in Agee's day moved from place to place less often than families do now. However, as UT geography professor Charles Aiken stated, "The frequency of turnover of the inhabitants of the 1500 block of Highland Avenue and the Agee house disputes these notions. . . . Agee alluded to the transient nature of the place when he recalled that 'there were few good friends among the grown people.'"[16]

The early 1960s saw a growth in the number of university students renting neighborhood apartments—a "transient population" of young adults who had neither a past nor a future there. The 1962 directory lists a P. H. Hamlin Jr., living in one of the apartments at 1505 Highland. Future UT philosophy professor Phil Hamlin was then a nineteen-year-old student who had not yet read *A Death in the Family* or even heard of James Agee. He had no idea that the house had literary significance; he just liked having a place that "was so close to campus." Sixty years later, as Hamlin examined a well-known photo of the house, he indicated the window to the right of the front door: "My bedroom was that room on the front." His apartment—which he shared with two other men—occupied the eastern half of the ground floor and consisted of two bedrooms, a rear kitchen, and a shared downstairs bathroom. "I think there was a hallway under the stairs, because we could go out the back—we put the trash in the garbage can out back." He entered his ground-floor apartment to the right off the central hallway, just inside the front door before going up the staircase. "You came in the front door, and right in front of you were the stairs to the second floor," Hamlin said. "The stairwell went up, and there were doors in the hall for maybe three rooms up there." He did not remember many details about his apartment, just that most of its double-hung windows did not work. The house was "clearly on its last legs," and Hamlin was among the last tenants to call 1505 Highland home. "It was years later that I realized I had lived in Agee's house." When he finally read the novel, he thought it was "extraordinary."[17]

A *Knoxville Journal* article, "Knox Author Gains Fame," appeared on the front page in early August 1962. It directed readers to a reprint of a recent *Wall Street Journal* editorial by John Chamberlain, who was optimistic that Agee's literary prominence was on the rise. "When the big names of modern American literature are mentioned, the late James Agee is not ordinarily listed among them. But one, two or ten years from now, this situation may well be altered," Chamberlain said. "For on the strength of having won a Pulitzer Prize for his posthumously published novel, *A Death in the Family,* Agee has become a 'sleeper' candidate for immortality. He always had a critical reputation; now he seems on the threshold of achieving popular recognition." Back in May 1955 the few newspaper eulogies seemed to be the last respects Knoxville would ever pay the obscure late author. But with the novel's Pulitzer in May 1958 and the Broadway premiere of *All the Way Home* in 1960—three days after Agee would have turned fifty-one—and another Pulitzer for that play, the author was getting more hometown press in death than he had in life. *Letters of James Agee to Father Flye,* representing the decades-long correspondence between Agee and his mentor, was published in July 1962 to nationwide acclaim. Agee's name was as well known in Knoxville as it ever had been.[18]

But despite the city's growing "popular recognition" of the author, Agee's former childhood home was no more immortal than his body had been. In late August the *Journal* ran a photo of the decrepit house, the front yard's shaggy trees partly obscuring the clapboard structure. The caption, "TIME RUNNING OUT," stated that James Agee's "boyhood home" would soon be torn down "to make way for an apartment house." Developers Gerson and Mathias Bush now owned the property and planned to build a new apartment complex there, requiring the demolition of 1505 and 1509 Highland and an adjacent home on Forest Avenue.[19]

Unlike today, when citywide petitions to save endangered properties are nothing unusual, historical preservation was not the norm in 1962. In fact, many Knoxvillians at that time would have scratched their heads at efforts to save a house that was not even eighty years old and that was, to some, an eyesore. Chester Kilgore, then a university student, recalled that "apathy was rampant regarding saving our historic structures." Consequently, he said, "so many places were lost, and no one cared much one way or the other back then, unless it directly affected them." Aside from a few newspaper articles announcing the development, there is no record of any public comment about the house's fate. Writer and musician R. B. Morris grew up in the Fort Sanders area in the 1950s and '60s and agrees that the city had no interest in saving Agee's home. "I don't know anyone alive who was much aware of the house before it was torn down," said Morris. "There was just no focus on Agee in those days by anyone local (at least in city government or preservation), and thus the house was razed. Not until Hollywood came here around that time was there much of any note of him being from here at all."[20]

By the time the *Journal*'s photograph of 1505 Highland appeared, Hollywood officials had already spent several days "doing research and photographing" the house, in preproduction for a Talent Associates–Paramount Pictures film based on Agee's novel. They were interested in shooting parts of the film in Agee's old neighborhood—even in "the original Agee home," though associate producer Jack Grossberg said the house was "smaller than we would have liked." The *Journal* stated the producers' intent: "Among the problems to be cleared up is an agreement with a Knoxville developer to postpone razing the childhood house of Agee at 1505 Highland Avenue until after it is used in the film." Chamber of Commerce and studio representatives attempted negotiations with the developers, and as late as August 28 newspapers still raised hopes that the home might be used.

But no compromise was reached. Filmmakers were nowhere near ready to begin shooting, as some of the main roles, like the boy Rufus, had not yet been cast. And the Bush brothers were under pressure "to meet financing deadlines" and could not delay demolition long enough for the production's early October start date. Thus, the Chamber of Commerce announced on August 31 that demolition of the old Agee home would begin the following week.[21]

Word spread about the doomed house. On September 4 photographer Ernst Haas came to shoot images of Agee's Knoxville for *Life* magazine. It is ironic that the magazine's editor and Agee's former boss, Henry Luce, chose

The Agee house as it appeared on September 4, 1962, when Ernst Haas photographed it for *Life* magazine. The rocking chairs on the porch were props used for the photo shoot. Courtesy of Fran Allison Young.

such an honor for Agee, who once felt that *Life*'s manufactured photo essays violated the soul and purpose of photography. Haas snapped photos of the L&N Station, a Cades Cove cabin, a Model T being ferried across a river, and several angles of Agee's house. He photographed its front, including a close-up of a bonneted, elderly woman peering through the screen door. Haas shot the house's west side and its awkward second-floor bathroom addition, framing it between porch posts as he stood next door at 1509 Highland. Inside the Agee home, he shot a ghostly image of a boy silhouetted behind a translucent curtain. From an upstairs window, Haas shot down across the porch shingles and through a tree to catch a pedestrian in mid-stride along the sidewalk. Local news station WBIR sent a movie camera to document the occasion.[22]

Reportedly, a separate film crew was expected in town at the end of August "to make a documentary type film of the [Agee] house and its surroundings."

Two photographs of the former Agee house being dismantled in September 1962. From *Knoxville News-Sentinel,* September 13, 1962, © 2017 Gannett-Community Publishing. All rights reserved. Used by permission and protected by the Copyright Laws of the United States. The printing, copying, redistribution, or retransmission of this Content without express written permission is prohibited.

But if such a film was actually made, it has never come to light. WBIR's film, lasting only thirty-five seconds, contains the only known moving images of the dwelling's exterior.[23]

On September 7 a crew began taking the house apart. One newspaper writer lamented, "It's too bad the movie couldn't have been made last year." The making and premiere of *All the Way Home*—Paramount Pictures' version of *A Death in the Family*, partly shot in Agee's old neighborhood—are detailed in the appendix of this volume. But it is worth noting here that while a substitute house was chosen to represent the Agee house exterior, parts of 1505 Highland, the real home, might have actually made it onscreen.[24]

The home was not torn down quickly. A *News-Sentinel* photographer visited the property about five days after demolition began. His two photos show that the roof and front porch were gone, as well as some siding and bricks, probably from one or more chimneys. But most of the house was still there, and there seemed to be a degree of care in the way it was being dismantled. No wrecking ball was being employed here. In fact, some of the materials were piled as though intended for reuse—like the bricks, stacked four feet high in the front yard.[25]

RELICS

A story has been told many times about some of those bricks being saved and reused by another Knoxville novelist, one whose works would also draw curious devotees to the region. Fans of both writers want to believe the story. In 1937 a newly hired lawyer for TVA moved his family to Knoxville—a couple of years after Agee had toured the organization's headquarters there. One of his six children, four-year-old Charles McCarthy Jr., retained memories of growing up in the city and much later used Knoxville as a backdrop for his own acclaimed fiction, including a Pulitzer-winning novel, *The Road*. In September 1962, Charles Jr. was married and living roughly thirty miles from Knoxville when he learned that the Agee house was being torn down. Perhaps he saw the *News-Sentinel* photo of the partially demolished house, or was informed of the bricks by his friend Jim Long, who lived two blocks north of the site. Several publications have since reported that the man now famous as author Cormac McCarthy salvaged bricks from the Agee house and built a fireplace with them. While quotes from the writer himself on the matter have never surfaced, his brothers, Bill and Dennis McCarthy, and friend Walt Clancy confirmed hearing the story directly from Cormac.[26]

If anyone had a literary interest in those bricks, McCarthy seems the most likely person in Tennessee at the time. Notes he wrote while drafting his Knoxville-based novel, *Suttree*, evince his respect for Agee. Many readers consider that novel's opening to be "an homage" to Agee's "Knoxville: Summer of 1915"; some may even share art critic Richard Woodward's opinion that that *Suttree* has "displaced *A Death in the Family* . . . as Knoxville's novel."[27]

For years scholars pointed to a residence on Light Pink Road in Louisville, Tennessee, as the place where Cormac used the bricks. But McCarthy did not purchase that property until 1969, seven years after the Agee house was torn down, and during that interval lived several places outside Tennessee; moreover, the "stone room and chimneys" he constructed onto the Louisville home were of fieldstone, not brick. The real story, it turns out, is much simpler: Cormac hauled the bricks to Sevier County, where in 1962 he and his first wife occupied a Depression-era "shack" on Waldens Creek Road, about five miles west of Goose Gap Road. As the dwelling lacked a heat source, the approach of autumn weather most likely motivated Cormac's masonry project, which may have included building one fireplace in the center of the cabin and one in the rear. The McCarthys relocated a short time later, leaving behind a mortared shrine whose literary significance was lost on all subsequent tenants. The house was demolished in 2004.[28]

Other items were recovered from 1505 Highland. While scouting locations in Fort Sanders one day before *All the Way Home* started shooting there, local film consultant W. Fleming Reeder met a man on the demolition crew. The worker handed Reeder a coin he had found beneath the steps of the former Agee house—a Liberty Head dime minted in 1912, the year the Agees purchased the property. Of course, it could have been dropped by any of the home's subsequent tenants. But it is possible that it rolled to the spot after falling from Jay Agee's pocket or that young Rufus hid it there for safekeeping after Grandpa Tyler gave it to him. Decades after Reeder was given the dime, he passed it on to *News-Sentinel* columnist Don Williams.[29]

Eugene Moser, owner of a Wall Avenue clothing store, visited the demolition site one day and retrieved an old five-paneled door, just like the one propped against a tree in the newspaper photo. One side of the door had a "dark-brown enameled doorknob and metal lock plate" and was coated with cracked, pinkish paint that had obviously been added after the Agees' time. The other side, its knob "white enameled," was a natural "stained wood" color more characteristic of the house's original trim. Moser's daughter inherited the piece and eventually sold it to William Eugene Thomas.[30]

Moser salvaged another item that was much more distinctive, measuring about five feet wide by three feet high by one foot deep, "with ebonized fin-

Two objects, a door and an overmantel, salvaged from the former Agee home in 1962 by Eugene Moser. Courtesy of the East Tennessee Historical Society, Knoxville.

ish, spindle decoration along top edge, centered beveled mirror below." The piece was called an "overmantel," and "could have been bolted or screwed to the top of a fireplace shelf in a living room or on top of a sideboard in a dining room or parlor." Its style hinted at the type of intricate Victorian detail that would have filled the Agee home. Moser passed the overmantel down to his children. Decades after Moser salvaged these items from the Agee home, they were donated to the East Tennessee Historical Society. Eugene Moser "had a true fascination" with James Agee, and his effort to preserve these relics is evidence that not all Knoxvillians were apathetic about the fate of the Agee house.[31]

Roughly five years after the Highland Avenue house was demolished, another Agee artifact was unearthed on the property of the former Tyler home on West Clinch, which had been torn down without local comment by 1961. "Everybody says you better be glad it has [been razed], it had deteriorated so," Laura Wright told Father Flye. "They'd made it into a rooming house or something of the sort. It was nothing to what it had been." But the cottage, Hugh Tyler's former art studio, still stood on the lot for the rest of the decade. Student Jim Harmon and his wife, Lynne McFarland, leased the "guest house" from 1966 to 1968. McFarland remembered discovering the relic in the main home's basement cavity, which a previous tenant had turned into a "sunken garden":

> The guest house was approximately in the center of the block and surrounded by dense vegetation (kudzu, vines, trees, etc.); it could not be seen from any of the streets. . . . The pathway from Clinch going up the hill to the guest house quickly disappeared in the foliage. Another entrance was an informal pathway from 12th Street and ran along the foundation of the missing residence.
>
> The guest house had a main door that faced Clinch, but most people came and went through the patio that faced 12th Street. The guest house was small, consisting of a living room, a bedroom with paneled wood, a bathroom and a little kitchen off the living room. The couple who lived there before we arrived were good with plants and developed the foundation of the original house into a beautiful sunken rock garden. There were peonies, clematis, roses and surprise lilies that only bore a flower in the late summer from a stalk that springs up unexpectedly. . . .
>
> In that sunken garden we found a silver spoon with the monogram "A." We gave this spoon to our friends, John and Mary Mulvany, who were living in New York. John was a big fan of James Agee and this influenced our giving them the spoon. . . .
>
> It was my understanding that the guest house was not rented again after we left in 1968—there were already plans to remove it.

Of course, the lone initial "A" provides no evidence that the object belonged to Agee, considering the home's long list of occupants. But as John Mulvany remembered it, the silver spoon McFarland gave him was more easily identifiable as an Agee relic, because it was engraved with "the initials JRA." In 1968 Mulvany had the spoon with him in New York City when he met Mia Agee. "I returned the spoon to Agee's widow," Mulvany said. He had been "introduced to her by Manny Farber, the film critic, who had been a close friend of Agee."[32]

PREMIERE

At his death, Agee was remembered nationally as a Hollywood screenwriter and film critic. (Some, like Farber, had criticized Agee's reviews for the "decided variance between the critic's words and what actually went on in the film.") But the foundation of Agee's cinematic vocabulary was laid during his Knoxville childhood as he frequented local movie houses with his father. Fittingly then, Knoxville's first major celebration of James Agee took place in and around a movie theater. The Paramount film based on *A Death in the Family* had been partly shot on location in Knoxville over five weeks in autumn 1962. And the buzz created by that event brought Agee extra local recognition and likely prompted Knoxvillians who would not have done so otherwise to read Agee's novel.[33]

All the Way Home opened in October 1963 at the grand Tennessee Theatre, roughly a year after filming began. While publicized as a "world premiere," the film had actually been screened a month earlier "at the first New York Film Festival at the Lincoln Center for the Performing Arts."[34]

In this page from a 1963 edition of its "Merchandising Manual and Press Book," Paramount Pictures touted Knoxville's successful premiere of *All the Way Home* at the Tennessee Theatre. Wallace W. Baumann Collection, McClung Historical Collection, Knox County Library.

Mayor John Duncan named Thursday, October 17, as "All the Way Home Day." For the occasion, cross streets downtown were given signs directing visitors "All the Way Home" to Gay Street, which was temporarily renamed "Agee Street." Knoxvillians crowded its sidewalks that night to catch glimpses of returning celebrities Robert Preston, Michael Kearney, and David Susskind. Antique vehicles used in the film drove the stars from the Andrew Johnson Hotel to the Tennessee Theatre for the ceremony.[35]

Agee visited several of Gay Street's movie houses during his childhood, but it is doubtful he ever caught a show at the Tennessee. The property had been leased for a theater as early as 1920, but the "Moorish Revival"–style venue did not open until October 1928, well after Agee had left the city for New England. He must have glimpsed its exterior during his handful of visits to Knoxville in the 1930s and '40s. But he never saw or imagined it looking anything like this, with his own name on the marquee, declaring in bold letters his connection to the city: "THE KNOXVILLE STORY / BY KNOXVILLE'S JAMES AGEE." The *News-Sentinel* noted that the theater was "practically covered in signs," all proclaiming that "Knoxville is having a world premiere of a top-notch movie tonight. And they all naturally boast of Knoxville's contributions to the movie: Knoxville author, Knoxville setting, much of it filmed in Knoxville and many Knoxvillians cast as extras."[36]

Robert Preston had worked with Agee on *The Bride Comes to Yellow Sky*, and joined the production of *All the Way Home* with a great respect for the writer. Making the film "was a labor of love for me," Preston told a journalist, months before the premiere. "All of us in the film wanted to be part of it and because of the way it was made I know James Agee is not spinning in his grave."[37]

The film was indeed crafted with love, and pains were taken to remain faithful to the tone and locale of Agee's story. It had a successful run in Knoxville, but because of unforeseen circumstances and poor timing, the film failed to repeat the successes of the novel or play and failed at the box office. Even so, its glamorous premiere in 1963 ushered in a new local respect for James Agee and led to the construction of a building in honor of the writer who attracted Hollywood to the city.

AGEE STUDIO

On the morning of the premiere, a bus carrying studio dignitaries, city officials, and members of the press toured downtown filming locations "and points of interest in the life of the late James Agee." It was the first such Agee-related excursion in a city that decades later would host special walking tours and "Agee Ambles" in honor of the writer.[38]

The buses continued out toward the Smoky Mountains, where the party enjoyed a picnic lunch at Cades Cove. In a short ceremony there, Robert Preston, on behalf of Paramount, presented a token to the city—a plaque engraved with Agee's name:

JAMES AGEE MEMORIAL
MOTION PICTURE STUDIO
PRESENTED
WORLD PREMIERE
"ALL THE WAY HOME"
OCTOBER 17, 1963
JOHN J. DUNCAN, MAYOR[39]

It is unclear who originated the idea, but city leaders were certainly inspired by the revenue increase Paramount brought to town. Back in December, Mayor Duncan had toured a Long Island, New York, sound studio, with Paramount arranging a meeting with filmmakers there. On his return, Duncan moved forward with plans to build a cutting-edge sound-recording facility that would lure other Hollywood productions to the area. The city promoted the idea that Knoxville was "rapidly developing into the southeastern United States' first major motion picture production center." The studio, designed to become a gymnasium between recording gigs, was dedicated two years later during the Knoxville premiere of *The Fool Killer*, a film shot in Louisville, Tennessee, starring Anthony Perkins.[40]

In its first few years, Agee Studio hosted such varied activities as Golden Gloves boxing tournaments, square dances, bridge parties, orchestra concerts, ROTC formals, exercise classes, community plays, vehicle registrations, ballets, live dance bands, and archery classes—but never film production. According to one story, the building's close proximity to railroad traffic made it unsuitable for sound recording. In 1969 the city transferred ownership of the studio to the school system, which agreed to build a recreational facility nearby in exchange. Today, West High School's ROTC uses the James Agee Building as a gym. The now-curious plaque, still designating the space as a movie studio, is embedded in a cinderblock wall just inside the front door. Although the visually uninspiring structure on Tobler Lane did not succeed as originally purposed, it still stands as the first Agee monument in Knoxville.[41]

AGEE LIBRARY

Less than a decade later and 120 miles southwest, another structure was erected to honor the writer. In the half-century since Agee was a student there, St. Andrew's School in Sewanee had seen major changes and was no longer the undeveloped school for poor mountain boys. By the fall of 1972, most of the old campus buildings Agee knew were gone, and the student body was now co-ed. For several weeks that semester, students had been rigorously studying James Agee's writings, "short stories, a novella, a novel, poetry, personal journalism, movie criticism, television and movie scripts."[42]

Unfortunately, students did not actually get to read *The Morning Watch*, the novella set at St. Andrew's, because the books did not arrive in time. "The order for *Morning Watch* got mixed up," a former teacher recalled, "and what came was the pamphlet 'Morning Watch' that Methodists or Presbyterians use for Sunday School." Another teacher remembered "Fr. Martinez telling our St. Andrew's kids the story" in lieu of having the novella available for them to read.[43]

This all culminated in what was dubbed Agee Week, October 9–14, when "all classes were suspended to allow a massive immersion in Agee's work—discussion groups, movies, and panels conducted by the novelists, critics, and scholars," said novelist David Madden, one of the participating guests. Separate panels discussed Agee's poetry, *Let Us Now Praise Famous Men, The Morning Watch, The African Queen,* and *A Death in the Family.* Among the many participating Agee scholars and acquaintances were David McDowell, Robert Fitzgerald, Father Flye, and Dwight Macdonald. Family members like Mia Agee and son John, and the author's aunt Annabel Agee and cousin Dr. Oliver Agee also attended the festivities. Madden noted the absence of any scholars from UT Knoxville.[44]

A few Agee films were shown that week, including *All the Way Home, The African Queen,* and *The Bride Comes to Yellow Sky.* In that film, Agee "had a cameo role" as the town drunk, and the students "all cheered when he appeared" onscreen.[45]

On October 14, a solemn prayer service was held at the school chapel, similar to the kind in which Agee must have served as an acolyte "in the innocence of faith." Walter Chambers, the school's director of development, believed that Agee "could have identified, in his own way, with the service of Morning Prayer on the day of the dedication, for I felt that he would have known the words by memory, that he had pondered them in his heart many times in his search for truth." After a recessional hymn, the congregation flowed out of the chapel and up the hill, following a group of young acolytes—one swinging a censer, one carrying a boat of incense, one holding the cross, two holding torches—and priests and faculty along the path to the new Simmonds Building. The James Agee Memorial Library and its Memorial Room were dedicated with prayers and blessings in a ceremony that, to Madden, felt "short" and "hollow compared with, though indispensable to, the informal ceremonies" leading up to it. Despite the prayer service representing the school atmosphere Agee would have recognized, Chambers felt "that Jim would not have been entirely pleased with what he would have called pomp and circumstance, considering it as being pretentious. I was not even sure he would have come." Agee may well have been embarrassed being the subject of a ceremony as overblown as the one he observed there on St. Charles Day forty-eight years earlier. Had attendees possessed a lock of Agee's hair—or even a whisker plucked from the writer's unshaven face and encapsulated in amber—they surely would have venerated it as a holy relic.[46]

Initially, the library contained "8,000 volumes, including an Agee Special Collection of the alumnus' published work and some of his manuscripts, letters and photographs. Also an uncut version of a four-hour TV documentary on Abraham Lincoln." But decades later, faculty members reported that some

Ceremonial procession into the Simmonds Building on St. Andrew's campus during the dedication of the James Agee Library in October 1972. Photo Album of Dedication of Agee Library, University of Tennessee Library, Knoxville. Courtesy of St. Andrew's-Sewanee.

items from the collection had been pilfered over the years, and to preserve them the school donated many of the remaining materials to University of Tennessee, Knoxville, around 2008. As a result, St. Andrew's Agee Library is not the center for researchers it once was. The building, as with the Agee Studio in Knoxville, is mostly unremarkable, and patrons could easily miss the plaque attached to the entrance's cinderblock wall:

THE JAMES AGEE LIBRARY

DEDICATED TO

THE MEMORY OF

JAMES RUFUS AGEE

STUDENT AND WRITER

1909–1955[47]

The school's 1914 chapel that Agee described in *The Morning Watch* was restored in 2016. A small cemetery up the hill is where Agee's mother, Laura Wright, was buried next to Erskine Wright following her death on August 12, 1966. Father Flye's former residence is a short walk from there, moved from another part of campus in 2006 to make way for a new performing arts center.[48]

But another campus landmark with arguably as much historical and literary value has been largely ignored—the small cottage near the school's front entrance where Agee briefly lived. He stayed at the cottage with his mother and sister during their summer vacations at St. Andrew's in 1918 and 1919. When Laura enrolled her son as a student, she continued to live there with Emma while she made him live in a dormitory, but he ran back to the cottage often for motherly comfort.

The house is the last of Agee's Tennessee homes still standing—a literary landmark that deserves to be saved. One hopes that if St. Andrew's-Sewanee ever intends another use for the site, the school's board of directors will choose to move the Agee cottage—as they did with Father Flye's house— rather than destroy it.[49]

1979 DOCUMENTARY

Roughly a decade after *All the Way Home* premiered in Knoxville, a Johnson City native started a project that would bring another film crew to Agee's former neighborhood. And unlike the former film, Hollywood's Academy would not ignore this one.

In 1974 Ross Spears was attending the California Institute for the Arts as a graduate film student when he chose Agee as the subject of his master's thesis. This was a few years before Genevieve Moreau published the first Agee biography, and Spears felt that too little information was available about a writer whose work was becoming increasingly popular.[50]

Spears came to Knoxville in August 1975 to shoot scenes representative of Agee's childhood. Re-creating the family's summer evening gatherings on the lawn, crewmembers and actors assembled at the same Forest Avenue home that Paramount had used thirteen years earlier as the exterior of the Follet residence in *All the Way Home*. For the interior funeral scene, Spears chose a room in the almost seven-thousand-square-foot home at 3106 Kingston Pike, known as the Dulin or Crescent Bluff. At least two scenes were planned that did not appear in the final film—one on the porch of the Kingston Pike home, and a funeral procession near Laurel Avenue and Twelfth Street. The same month, the crew traveled to Sewanee and filmed authentic re-creations of the Morning Watch tradition on St. Andrew's campus and of boys swimming at the Sand Cut nearby.[51]

Over the next few years, Spears collected interviews from some of Agee's closest surviving friends and acquaintances, including Father Flye, John Huston, Robert Fitzgerald, and Agee's former wives. Months before his presidency began, Jimmy Carter spoke on camera of his admiration for Agee and the book *Let Us Now Praise Famous Men*.

Although Spears's documentary, *Agee: A Sovereign Prince of the English Language,* had already been screened at Vanderbilt University back in June, its official "world premiere" was held at Knoxville's Bijou Theatre on October 5, 1979. That evening, Alan Cheuse—not yet known as the author and National Public Radio book critic—observed that the Bijou's "newly renovated" auditorium was "crowded with celebrants . . . loyal local fans of the writer, undergraduates, elder churchmen, the mayor and his wife, teachers from the English Department of the University of Tennessee, critics from New York and Nashville, actors, filmmakers, the director and crew from Knoxville, Los Angeles, and points east." Yet despite Cheuse's impression, James Agee was still "virtually unrecognized and unknown in his own hometown," one local journalist noted.[52]

Besides bringing national attention to his "favorite writer," Spears hoped his film would be appreciated in Knoxville "for many years to come and will be a continual source of community pride." Its premiere turned out to be the only major Agee-related event held in the city during the 1970s. *Agee* was nominated for an Academy Award as Best Feature Documentary in early 1981.[53]

HARD KNOXVILLE REVIEW

Two films about Agee had been partially shot in Knoxville and first screened in that city sixteen years apart. "As it happens, I was at both premieres," said R. B. Morris, a poet and singer-songwriter who had first heard about James Agee as a boy in 1962 when a Paramount film crew showed up in his neighborhood. "I think I was in the fourth grade when *All the Way Home* premiered here. My dad worked at the L&N Station downtown and used to come home from work with reports to us of the filming of the movie.... So there was an early interest in Agee for us." Seeing Ross Spears's film only increased Morris's fascination with Agee. "The fact that I knew well the Fort Sanders houses in both those films and the L&N railyards all pulled me in and inspired me.... It was all part of an ongoing and continually growing interest in Agee and his work." As Morris grew and became involved in the local art and literary scene, "hanging around with older artists and writers," he learned even more about Agee—whose "name was sometimes mentioned with a sort of reverence, and part of that was the fact that he was unheralded in his hometown."[54]

In spring 1982 Morris and another local artist, Eric Sublett, published the second issue of their "little art and literary tabloid," *Hard Knoxville Review.* They dedicated this one to James Agee: "In an attempt to glimpse into a sovereign prince, from what I've gathered of those who knew him and those who researched him much further than I, and from my own observations of his work." Generous excerpts from Agee's works—including *A Death in the Family, Let Us Now Praise Famous Men,* and his book of poetry, *Permit Me Voyage*—filled most of the magazine's twelve pages. "It came out right as the World's Fair got started," Morris said. "We tried to have it sold in the Fine Arts Pavilion, but they apparently weren't interested in promoting local artists. Someone at the pavilion told me later that a bundle of copies sat in the back room for about a month and was still in the bundle when it was thrown away."[55]

Perhaps a handful of fairgoers saw Agee's face glaring back at them from the magazine's newsprint cover that spring. But otherwise, Agee received little attention during the expo, which had markedly altered the city Agee knew. Not only had the old Ty-Sa-Man building and other nearby factories been cleared from the fair site in the Second Creek valley, but several Fort Sanders homes were razed—including one along Forest Avenue that Agee and his father walked past on trips to the movies, and which had stood in for the Agee home in the 1963 film *All the Way Home* and the 1979 documentary

Agee. Affectionately called "The Stateroom" by locals, it had been demolished the fall before publication of "The Agee Issue," which printed Eric Sublett's early-morning photograph of the house.[56]

In late November 1982 an Oak Ridge citizen wrote a letter to the *News-Sentinel* editor suggesting a use for the site of the fair that had closed a month earlier: "Many of us are familiar with tourist attractions of various cities—Underground Atlanta, the Gaslight District of St. Louis, Old Sacramento and Colonial Williamsburg, to name a few. I think Knoxville has a golden opportunity to have such a tourist attraction based on the Knoxville of 1915—the Knoxville of James Agee in his book 'A Death in the Family.'" Such a fanciful idea might have found support in *Hard Knoxville Review*, whose editors had begun envisioning some sort of Agee memorial in Fort Sanders.[57]

Citywide Agee events were sporadic during the eighties, as during the previous decade, but recognition of the writer seemed to be increasing. In 1980 UT's English department sponsored a screening of Ross Spears's documentary on May 2 "to set the tone" for the fifth annual Fort Sanders Street Fair happening the next day along Seventeenth Street between Highland and Laurel. To raise funds for restoring the Custom House on Clinch Avenue, East Tennessee Historical Society held a "preview gala" there on April 14, 1981, featuring "Images of Agee," an exhibit of the photographs Ernst Haas made in 1962 of Agee's house and other related sites; cast members from Cumberland County Playhouse's production of *All the Way Home* performed songs during the event. Eleanor Steber came to UT in February 1982 to perform *Knoxville: Summer of 1915*, the Barber piece she debuted in 1948, and was given "an honorary citizenship award in recognition of all the singer has done to promote Knoxville through this piece of music." (If only Agee had been so honored for writing the text.) In spring 1986, *Knoxville Journal* columnist Vic Weals spotlighted Agee in a few articles that served a dual purpose: they marked seventy years since the car accident that killed Jay Agee while also celebrating Knoxville's literary heritage as part of the statewide Homecoming '86 campaign. Also that spring, *All the Way Home,* Tad Mosel's stage adaptation of Agee's novel, was staged in Knoxville, and the Knox County Public Library screened Spears's documentary. When magazine publisher and Tennessee native Chris Whittle revealed in October 1986 his plans to build a new Whittle Communications campus downtown between the Bijou Theatre and St. John's Episcopal Church, he promised that the media headquarters would feature "James Agee–style writing garrets"—though exactly what connected the dormers to the writer was unclear. And on November 20, 1987, in a ceremony at the Bijou, James Agee was

inducted into the newly established East Tennessee Hall of Fame, along
with five other honorees—Roy Acuff, Clarence Brown, Mary Costa, Grace
Moore, and Patricia Neal. Dr. Oliver Agee and daughter Annabel Agee accepted the award on their cousin's behalf.[58]

Though scattered, Knoxville's appreciation for Agee was significantly more
than the writer received in Nashville, where his great-grandfather had served
in the General Assembly. However, there was one legislative attempt to honor
Agee there, early in the decade. In 1980 the Tennessee Performing Arts Center
opened on Deaderick Street in downtown Nashville, with each of its three
auditoriums carrying the name of a U.S. president from Tennessee: Jackson,
Polk, and Johnson. A state representative from Sparta, I. V. Hillis, believed
the auditorium names should instead reflect the arts and introduced a bill
that would honor three notable artists, each associated with a different section of the state: blues musician W. C. Handy in West Tennessee, composer
Charles Faulkner Bryan in Middle Tennessee, and writer James Agee in East
Tennessee. By early 1981 the measure had received weeks of comment and
debate in the local media. It passed through the House, but was finally out-
voted by the Senate that April, and since then the auditoriums have retained
their original names. Even though the initiative failed, to date it represents
the only major effort to honor James Agee in the western half of the state.[59]

1989 AGEE CONFERENCE

In Knoxville, near the end of a decade largely devoid of major Agee celebra-
tions, author Wilma Dykeman convinced UT's College of Liberal Arts to
host a conference in 1989 to commemorate the fiftieth anniversary of Agee's
Let Us Now Praise Famous Men. Although Agee would have turned eighty
that year, the event's timing was somewhat awkward, as some newspapers
stated incorrectly that the book had been published fifty years prior when it
had actually been forty-eight years. The university's own *Library Development
Review* stated that the date of "composition" was being celebrated when the
book was actually composed over a few years.[60]

In reality, the conference—dubbed "The Agee Legacy: Let Us Now Praise
Famous Men"—marked a half-century since Agee completed the book's
manuscript. Planned events from March 27 to April 1 included an exhibit
of Walker Evans's 1936 Alabama photographs, lectures by visiting scholars,
screenings of the Spears documentary and *All the Way Home*, a walking tour
of Fort Sanders, and readings from Agee's book.[61]

As the conference opened, Dykeman stated: "Agee's vitality and the variety of his writing continue to astonish and challenge us. This week we shall renew acquaintance with the times in which he lived and worked; we shall rediscover a few of the many voices by which he sought to awaken us to the riches and paradoxes and terror of being human. His legacy is in his novels and poems and short stories, journalism and films and film criticism and social commentary. Our main focus will be on that unique achievement, *Let Us Now Praise Famous Men*. At the age of fifty, it remains both timely and timeless."[62]

On March 29, the university hosted a live television broadcast during which David Madden, Ross Spears, Paul Ashdown, and Dykeman discussed the author's life and work. Schools could pay to view the program and ask the panel questions by phone.[63]

The conference was notable for being the first such Agee event in Knoxville, and one that left a remnant on the landscape. On the last day of the conference, a Tennessee Historical Commission marker was dedicated to Agee at the corner of Cumberland and Fifteenth Street. It still stands today; and though difficult to read from a vehicle, the sign contains, for some Knoxvillians and university students who pass the corner daily, the only information they've ever read about Agee:

1E 101

JAMES RUFUS AGEE

Born in Knoxville November 27, 1909, Agee was well-known and respected in the fields of journalism, poetry, fiction, non-fiction, and film. He won a Pulitzer Prize posthumously in 1957 for *A Death in the Family*, a novel based on his youth in the Fort Sanders neighborhood at 1505 Highland Avenue and the trauma of his father's death. He died May 16, 1955.

Planted four blocks south from where he lived, this was the closest anyone had come to establishing a memorial in Agee's former neighborhood. Now visitors to the city at least had a sign letting them know they were in the right area. It would be another fifteen years or so before any kind of physical space was established to welcome Agee pilgrims to Fort Sanders.[64]

PILGRIMS

After the removal of Agee's home, nothing remained on the stripped lot in October 1962 except for "two Trees of Heaven"—a tree variety also known

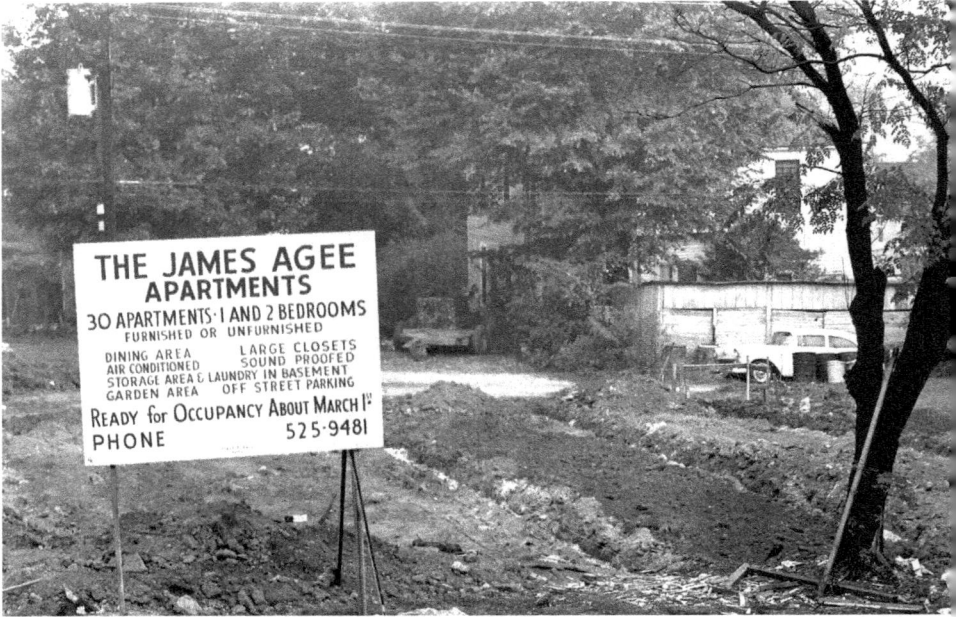

Part of the vacant Highland Avenue lot in October 1962, awaiting construction of the James Agee Apartments. Photo by and courtesy of Alan Shayne.

as Chinese sumac—and "a sign announcing: The James Agee Apartments." Property developers meant the name as a tribute, but the scores of Agee enthusiasts who later traveled to the site felt it more like a slap in the face. Agee's journalistic masterwork *Let Us Now Praise Famous Men* had inspired Danny Lyon's dive into immersive street photography. But in summer 1967, when Lyon arrived in Knoxville to see Agee's birthplace, he was five years too late. Lyon expressed his disappointment in a diary entry: "I was looking for Agee's home, but to my horror found it demolished. . . . It has been replaced by the 'James Agee apartments.' Antique brick and black iron lamps, red doors. Below Agee's name are the words, 'Town and Country Construction.' In a few years such abominable structures will replace all the houses in this Knoxville neighborhood. The Agee apartments seem like some kind of perverse tombstone for this great man."[65]

Agee's Harvard classmate Robert Saudek traveled to Knoxville in October 1971, walked to the street where his friend had grown up, and noted the spot where a couple of old homes—including Agee's—had been torn down nine years earlier:

> In their place has been erected the James Agee Apartments, three middle-brow stories of acne-colored brick, with outside galleries that stretch back from the street like cell-blocks. A tiny pool, coffin-shaped, skinny and dry, sits beneath the cellblocks. . . .
>
> The alley that runs behind the houses of the 1500 block, and was Rufus' alley, gave access to all the backyards, which are still wide and deep but turned to weeds. The trees are out of hand and choking with nondescript vines. The back fences along the alley have been replaced, but their heavy old iron bolts remain. The neighbors still hang their wash out back from clotheslines strung between T-poles. A few small barns, windowless, paintless, and exhausted, have been padlocked for years.
>
> The backyard of 1505 is no longer rough, wet grass. It is concrete clear out to the alley, and beyond it is a tenants' parking lot for the James Agee Apartments. . . .
>
> There was no evidence of curiosity about the black-and-white sign out front, JAMES AGEE APARTMENTS. TOWN AND COUNTRY CONSTRUCTION CO. AGENTS. PHONE 572-2083. Two English department professors at the university had no notion where it was that Agee had lived and written of, although they were sitting three blocks away from that sign. It seemed odd.

Lyon compared the apartment complex to a grave marker; Saudek thought it looked more prisonlike than anything Agee would have recognized. The intended tribute to the author was in name only—with no architectural effort to reflect the character of the homes it replaced or the neighborhood it inhabited.[66]

In late August 1975, just weeks after Ross Spears's documentary film shoot, author David Madden wrote in a letter to the *News-Sentinel* that the loss of Agee's house was "a great disgrace." He noted bitterly that while "Thomas Wolfe's house" had been "fully preserved in Asheville as a national site," pilgrims "who come to Knoxville to visit [Agee's] house find an apartment complex instead."[67]

Paul Ashdown, UT journalism professor emeritus, remembered his first trek to the Agee site: "When I moved to Knoxville in 1977 the first thing I did was to go to Highland Avenue to find James Agee's boyhood home. What I found instead was a cinderblock carbuncle called the James Agee Apartments. So much for Knoxville's sense of history, I thought."[68]

Reflecting on the loss of Agee's house, Jack Neely wrote in April 1986: "It's traditional in most of the world to canonize poets and artists and establish shrines in their memory—often a house they once lived in, renovated and straightened up a little, with regularly scheduled tours where reverent tourists can gaze across a gold velvet rope at the very desk where the Genius composed *this* masterpiece which, of course, won *that* prize." Asheville had its shrine for Wolfe. Oxford, Mississippi, had one for Faulkner. Knoxville had none for Agee. "The Highland Avenue house where he grew up was torn down in 1962," Neely continued. "But the apartment complex which the demolition made way for was named for James Agee. If that's not irony, it's sarcasm."[69]

Even though the city lacked a physical Agee shrine, at least a few Pulitzer-winning writers visited Knoxville looking for traces of the local boy that had inspired them. *Lonesome Dove* author Larry McMurtry wrote in 1999 of his earlier pilgrimages to the city: "Knoxville was James Agee's hometown. I once had an intense Agee phase and had several times drifted around Knoxville, looking for the neighborhood described in his early lyrical prose idyll 'Knoxville: Summer 1915.'" William Kennedy, author of *Ironweed*, came to town in the fall of 1992 and immediately asked, "Can we see James Agee's old neighborhood?" He spent part of the evening walking Highland Avenue while reading lines from Agee's novel. And years later, around 2001, Jack Neely was on Eleventh Street, leading a walking tour of Agee sites, when he spotted author Dale Maharidge, who with Michael Williamson won a Pulitzer in 1990 for *And Their Children After Them*, a book reexamining the families that Agee and Evans had documented fifty years earlier in *Famous Men*.[70]

William Kennedy had left town just before two Agee-related works were exhibited. "Knoxville Summer Evening," a poster by artist Barry Spann, was released locally in November 1992. Above an excerpt from Agee's "Knoxville: Summer of 1915," Spann's illustration depicted trees and pitched roofs of the Fort Sanders neighborhood glowing with the soft, hazy light of sundown. That same month, R. B. Morris, who earlier in life had seen two Agee films open in Knoxville, premiered his own—a screen version of his one-man play *The Man Who Lives Here is Loony*, directed by friend Eric Sublett. Though shot in "six nights during summer 1987 in the attic of the Candy Factory," post-production "was a slow process," taking three years to finish. With the premiere, held at the Bijou Theatre, Morris hoped to change the local perception of Agee: "The image that you have of James Agee in Knoxville that I grew up with, you might have thought he was some retired professor. . . . You always heard him called 'Pulitzer Prize-winning novelist.' He was slightly unreal in that way." Instead, Morris hoped to portray him as "an Everyman . . . a modern man, a modern writer. A man trying to deal with the beginning of the atomic age."[71]

R. B. Morris as "The Man" in his one-act play, *The Man Who Lives Here Is Loony.* Photo by Ric Brooks. Courtesy of Ric Brooks and R. B. Morris.

A few years later, Morris's enthusiasm for Agee influenced a visiting Nashville musician. While in town to produce the V-Roys' next album, Steve Earle met Morris and a group of "hyper-literate hillbillies" whose conversations "began and ended with James Agee." Earle had heard of the author, "mainly in connection with *Let Us Now Praise Famous Men,* which I had never read," but knew little about him. Based on recommendations from Morris and others, Earle picked up a copy of *A Death in the Family.* "I read this book for the first time in Knoxville, where it was possible to actually retrace Agee's (or Rufus's) steps in my spare time," Earle said. "I followed the route that I imagined the city streetcar would have followed out Clinch Avenue and then walked over to Fifteenth and Highland, wondering if the ghost of Hugh James Agee (or Jay Follet) had come that way on his back way home to say a last farewell to the believers." Earle said he now considers Agee "the greatest writer the state has ever produced."[72]

The BBC journeyed to Knoxville in 1995 to commemorate the eightieth anniversary of Agee's "Summer of 1915." Producer Alan Hall and technician Marvin Ware traversed the city on foot, audio equipment in tow, and captured the sounds of a typical sweltering August for an audio documentary that would accompany a performance of Barber's piece by the London Symphony. They recorded cicadas, lawn sprinklers, traffic, a freight train, voices of Knoxvillians, and quotes from Agee's prose and Barber's musical accompaniment—and mixed them into a swirling representation of the city Agee left in his youth.[73]

Of all the interviews Hall conducted during his visit, one stuck out more than the rest. Treading the sidewalks of Fort Sanders, Hall and Ware found "quite by chance a man and his son (the ages of young Agee and his father in 1915), sitting on their porch and happy to share the story of how the man's grandparents had rented the Agee house," said Hall. The man was Mark Hipshire, whose mother and grandparents, the Segasers, lived at 1505 Highland around 1940. His voice opens the program: "Here I am siting on the porch, bringing up Junior, watching the world go by." Hall bookended the thirty-two-minute documentary with Hipshire, whose rumination concludes the piece: "The neighborhood changes and it stays the same, I think."[74]

The documentary was widely praised—in 1997 it won the *Prix Italia* based on its "strong poetic sense of place"—but had not been intended for broadcast in the United States and therefore was not locally influential. According to Paul Ashdown, "not many in town even knew about it." Still, the program proved that outsiders appreciated Knoxville's literary heritage even if the town at large did not. Knoxville historian Jack Neely, whose voice is also heard in the documentary, once lived in the Fort Sanders area. He knew as well as anyone that Agee devotees scouring the city for traces of the writer's past were disappointed to find that Agee's house on Highland Avenue and his grandparents' on Clinch were not saved. The city was not maintaining its literary heritage, Neely suggested in 2001: "If not for James Agee, millions of people around the world might never have heard of us. Every now and then, they come here looking for him. But for all this time, Agee has never had a place here." Paul Ashdown, interviewed in 1983, lamented, "It's too bad that there isn't something of him that survives here. At least in Asheville, Thomas Wolfe's house has been preserved." Ashdown later credited Neely for raising awareness among Knoxvillians of the rich heritage that was being ignored: "Jack's role was to say, hey, we've got a history here, and outsiders know more about it than we do. It's like the city had an inferiority complex, or couldn't separate itself from the fortunes of UT sports."[75]

Such well-known outsiders as Michael Stipe and Garrison Keillor had Agee in mind when they performed in Knoxville. In the middle of R.E.M.'s concert at Thompson-Boling Arena on November 8, 1995, front man Stipe paused the show to read "Knoxville: Summer of 1915." Confused audience members continued making noise through Stipe's recitation until he declared, bluntly, "I'm reading. Let's start over." The singer also "implied that this was one reason he was looking forward to playing Knoxville, [and] that they should feel proud to live in a city that raised James Agee."[76]

In 1999 Keillor brought his *Prairie Home Companion* show to Knoxville for the first time. Broadcast live from the Civic Auditorium on June 26, Keillor closed the summer evening program by remembering the writer that was forever linked to the city. "James Agee came from Knoxville. He wrote about Knoxville in his book, *A Death in the Family*," Keillor said to the local and national audiences. "He wrote a little paragraph that maybe you've heard before, about his father and his mother spreading quilts in the back yard and lying there with his uncle and his aunt, lying there looking up at the sky, talking." Keillor then read an excerpt from the last section of "Knoxville: Summer of 1915." Although brief, the attention was much more influential locally than the BBC documentary, according to Ashdown.[77]

During his visit, Keillor praised Knoxville as "the most beautiful city. It's a city that looks like cities I've seen in picture books when I was a child, with the hills and the river running through it and the steeples. It could be a German city on the Rhine, it could be a city in Provence. It's a magnificent city." Perhaps it was flattery. But Knoxville had improved itself in the half century since Agee last visited, around the time of John Gunther's stinging remarks about its ugliness. Keillor's words were welcomed as rare positive remarks about the city.[78]

AGEE STREET

Had Keillor strolled through Fort Sanders before leaving town, a particular street name might have caught his eye. Just a few weeks prior, the city council voted to change the name of Fifteenth Street north of Cumberland to James Agee Street. Then-mayor Victor Ashe headed an effort to recognize "a number of distinguished figures," including James Agee and Howard Baker. "As mayor, I felt the city should salute those persons of fame and contribution who the city had not recognized over the years. James Agee was a person who immediately came to mind," Ashe explained later. "There was nothing in place which recognized that he ever lived in our city." Ashe and others "felt it was appropriate to honor him by renaming a street in Agee's old neighborhood." The former mayor downplayed his own role in renaming the street, as it only became a reality after the Metropolitan Planning Commission and city council approved it. And renaming a street "didn't require the mayor," Ashe said. "Any group of citizens could have requested a name change." There is a story, though, that Ashe felt strongly enough about honoring Agee that he assigned *A Death in the Family* to councilmembers, after finding out that none of them had read it. Asked about this, Ashe said it could have happened but that he could not recall ever assigning the novel to anyone. But James Agee "was a wonderful writer, and he stirred a great interest in the American public," he said. "The fact that we're still talking about him sixty years after his death must say something."[79]

Other Knoxvillians believed the city should do more to honor Agee, who still had no real place in the city where pilgrims and devotees could stand pensively and pay their respects. Some wondered why Agee had to share half of the street's name, the half south of Cumberland Avenue, with football coach Phillip Fulmer. Naming the entire street after the writer would have been historically justified: although Agee had no ties to UT football, he briefly lived in a small house at the corner of Fulmer Way (then Seventh Street) and Peyton Manning Pass (then Yale Avenue)—a spot directly across from the current stadium's main gates.[80]

However, an idea had been brewing for more than a decade that would finally give Agee his own space: the creation of a park in his former neighborhood. By forming such an area in the part of Knoxville the writer knew best, the city would take a big step toward celebrating both Agee and the historic neighborhood where he lived.[81]

AGEE TOAST

Meanwhile, a gathering north of town initiated what was surely Knoxville's most bizarre annual celebration—toasting a dead man on the spot where he wrecked his car in 1916. The idea began sometime after *Knoxville Journal* columnist Vic Weals published an article in 1986 identifying the site of Jay Agee's accident as "just to the southeast" of where Clinton Highway bridged Beaver Creek in Powell. Weals also pointed out that the blacksmith's cottage, once near the shop where the corpse was carried after the wreck, still stood off the west side of the highway. Local musician and writer Jack Rentfro also worked at the *Journal* and was intrigued by the article. He set out with Jack Neely, driving to the location Weals described near where Emory Road

Jack Neely stands in front of the blacksmith's cottage off Clinton Highway, 1986. The structure was torn down about fifteen years later. Photo by Jack Rentfro. Courtesy of Jack Rentfro and Jack Neely.

intersects Clinton Highway. They found the blacksmith cottage off the side
of the highway, engulfed in kudzu.[82]

But it was not until "some years later" that Rentfro "noticed that there was
a bar on the site" very close to where the accident probably occurred. Neely
and Rentfro "determined that we were obliged to observe the tragic event that
may have launched a literary career." And the NASCAR-themed bar, Checker
Flag, was somehow a fitting landmark, considering that Jay Agee was likely
speeding down Clinton Pike when he lost control of his Model T.[83]

They cannot recall the exact year they inaugurated the event, but it was
sometime around 1999 or 2000. "I do remember the first one was the iffiest,"
Rentfro said, "since we had no idea how we'd be received by the regulars." He
was surprised, though, when "the NASCAR worshipping crowd"—perhaps
fascinated by talk of the "car wreck"—"ended up being thoroughly charmed
by the weirdness." The first meetings were modest: just a handful of attendees
drinking, reading from "dog-eared copies" of Agee's novel, "contemplating
fate," jogging across the four-lane highway to the blacksmith's house, and
maybe "playing didgeridoos to passing Clinton Highway traffic," Neely recalled. Despite a deliberate lack of publicity, event turnout increased annually.
"People just heard about it, and came. As years passed, our band of pilgrims
grew bigger and bigger, sometimes including multiple UT professors, two
of Agee's own cousins, and several musicians who performed by the dart
board. . . . Music included mournful fiddle airs, guitar folk, hymns, drums,
and once a proper string band." The more people came, Neely said, the more
"attendees came to expect a program of some sort. We offered dramatic readings from Agee and related writers." Someone always read aloud the original
newspaper article from the day after the accident.[84]

Another anticipated element, and the most ceremonial, was the Cotter
Pin of Destiny. According to Agee's novel, Jay lost control of his car after a
cotter pin worked itself loose from the steering gear. During an impromptu
investigation in the Checker Flag's rear parking lot, Neely, Rentfro and
others "poked around in the gravel" until they spotted a small metal object.
Even though it looked "more like a porch-swing hook" than a cotter pin,
Neely noted, "the fact that it was in the shape of a question mark added
much to its mystery." Agee Toast tradition dictated that the relic be given
to a different guest at each gathering, and the holder "charged with keeping
it in a safe and worthy place and bringing it back to the Checker Flag the
following May 18." The ritual was always carried out in good humor.

The Checker Flag closed in 2011. Even though the bar soon reopened
under a different name, Neely took it as a sign that the event had run its

course: "As the group grew to include people I didn't even know, I worried that we were challenging fate, driving out to this place on the highway that lacked bus service to drink beer in honor of a man killed in a car wreck on this site.... Some wags christened our annual pilgrimage the Crash Bash. It gave me the heebie-jeebies."[85]

It is unlikely there will be another event to replace the Agee Toast, honoring the man whose fatality inspired *A Death in the Family*. There have been suggestions to rename the current Beaver Creek span as the Jay Agee Memorial Bridge, or at least place a marker near the site to acknowledge its tie to literature.[86]

AGEE AMBLES

Around the time of the first Agee Toast, Jack Neely and fellow Knoxville journalist Scott McNutt organized a different literary gathering to honor Agee—a "marathon" event, sometimes lasting eight hours or more, covering parts of downtown and Fort Sanders that the writer would have recognized. But unlike previous Agee-themed walking tours, the so-called "Agee Amble" was primarily a "pub crawl," with stops at some of downtown's best watering holes.

Neely—who held similar events, "Suttree Staggers," in honor of Cormac McCarthy—led several of these rambling Agee tours between about 1999 and 2007, drawing groups of thirty-five or more, and variously including local participants like Michael Haynes, Jesse Mayshark, Charlie Thomas, Mike Dotson, and Paul Ashdown. While the program changed each time, each Amble featured some rehearsed bits, recitations of Agee's works in unique spaces around town, and occasional multimedia presentations. Actors Greg Congleton and Jayne Morgan performed scenes from *The African Queen* at the corner of Gay and West Church Avenue, while standing on the gunwales of David Phelps' sculpture, "The Oarsman." A reading at Krutch Park from *Let Us Now Praise Famous Men* was accompanied by choreographed movements by members of Circle Modern Dance, led by Mark Lamb. Novelist Brian Griffin coordinated a reading of Agee's letters to Father Flye inside St. John's Episcopal on Walnut Avenue, where Agee had served as a choirboy. The Bistro, next door to Bijou Theatre, "was the single best place for readings," according to Neely; Agee's hilariously incisive film reviews were read "round robin"–style there "over a catfish-and-beer brunch." And the Preservation Pub on Market Square "hosted a long and enthusiastic round of Agee-penned toasts"; for the 2002 Amble, Sundance award-winning filmmaker Paul Harrill arranged a screening at the pub of *In the Street,* the rarely seen "Harlem documentary" that Agee helped photograph.

Always toward the end of the evening, the group replicated the journey Agee made with his father, walking home from the Gay Street movie theater. Flashlights illuminated book pages as "Knoxville: Summer of 1915" was read at the site of Agee's home. And in 2002, the event concluded with a final reading by R. B. Morris, standing at the site of a major Agee memorial that was still two and a half years from being dedicated.[87]

AGEE PARK

Morris and Eric Sublett had contemplated an Agee destination in Fort Sanders ever since they published their "Agee Issue" of *Hard Knoxville Review* in 1982. "We talked to a local property owner in Fort Sanders about donating his property on Twelfth Street for some kind of memorial park to Agee," Morris recalled, but the owner declined. The two artists continued searching for a suitable neighborhood lot for the park, to be "a greenspace in the middle of Fort Sanders" where visitors could "read, picnic and find refuge" while being reminded of Agee's legacy.[88]

It took almost two decades to find one. In the late 1990s the Historic Fort Sanders Neighborhood Association (HFSNA) publically opposed the Metropolitan Planning Commission's efforts to rezone the neighborhood to allow high-density residences. In particular, preservationists feared that the neighborhood's core—"bordered by White Avenue, Grand Avenue, Eleventh Street and Nineteenth Street"—would "lose its listing with the National Register of Historic Places" if many representative properties were destroyed. Architect Randall De Ford, a member of HFSNA, "reached out to the City to be proactive in guiding the future of the neighborhood." De Ford recalled that Mayor Ashe subsequently organized the Fort Sanders Forum, a group of "nearly two dozen people with a variety of . . . interests in Fort Sanders." In eighteen months of proposals, the forum reached two important objectives: "historic zoning and the park." During this time, De Ford formed alliances with Ellen Adcock, Knoxville director of the Department of Administration, and Phil Scheurer, UT vice president of operations.[89]

In an August 1999 meeting, "Scheurer made UT's offer to turn the parking lot beside my house into a park for Fort Sanders, if Wes Goddard and I were willing to have that next to us," De Ford said. The northwest corner lot at Laurel and Agee Street was previously occupied by the large Luttrell mansion, which became a frat house in later life and was finally destroyed by fire in 1971. Since then, the university had used it for student parking. Knowing that Morris had long advocated for an Agee memorial in Fort Sanders, De Ford "told Scheurer and Ellen Adcock that [the park] should honor Agee." The team agreed and created the Agee Park Steering Committee, promptly recruiting Morris, who thought "the little parking lot on James Agee Street would make a good pocket park memorial to Agee, just about a block from his original home on Highland Ave."[90]

Getting the proposal off the ground was "quite a process," according to Morris, and involved multiple negotiations between HFSNA, UT, and the City of Knoxville. The James Agee Steering Committee, chaired by attorney Charles Thomas, partnered with HFSNA and the East Tennessee Foundation. Many supporters joined the effort throughout its progress, including Jack Neely, Wilma Dykeman, Jon Coddington, and Paul Ashdown.[91]

Once UT and the City of Knoxville agreed that the city would lease and maintain the UT-owned property long term—an unexpected cooperation between the two parties—the project was officially announced in April 2001. The *News-Sentinel* praised the collaborative effort to recognize "Agee as one of our own" but remarked that the honor was "belated." Funds still had to be raised, designs drawn, and the site readied for landscaping, and it was two more years before ground was broken. During that period, R. B. Morris held several concerts to benefit the park.[92]

As asphalt was removed and sod planted in June 2003, three marble pillars—between fifteen and twenty-five feet tall—were erected a few blocks west to designate Eleventh Street as the entrance to Fort Sanders. The recent reopening of the Clinch Avenue viaduct, which had been closed to vehicles since the World's Fair, increased the flow of traffic through the heart of the neighborhood.[93]

That November, the park's progress was hastened when Rohm & Haas—whose chemical manufacturing facility on Dale Avenue, adjacent to Fort Sanders, was later bought by Dow Chemicals—awarded the project a $30,000 grant as part of its Community Partnership Initiative.

One month later, two sentinels much larger than the marble pillars progressed down Laurel Avenue toward the park. The eighty-ton trees—two sixty-five-year-old magnolias named Victor and Bill—were in danger of being cut down during construction at a nearby lot. When R. B. Morris suggested relocating the trees to the park, several construction companies and tree experts donated time and labor to make it happen. Neighborhood residents were used to seeing trees and lawns being replaced by asphalt; seeing the reverse happen in Fort Sanders was a rare treat.[94]

The park's next phase of development began in early 2005, with the construction of "a stone terrace and steps flanked by two pillars etched with Agee's words," based on designs by De Ford, who considered the effort "just a small part of giving James Agee what he's due." Organizers hoped to officially dedicate the park in April as part of a planned Agee conference.[95]

2005 AGEE CELEBRATION

When asked what he finds most significant about James Agee, Michael Lofaro, UT professor of American studies and American literature, pointed to "the variety of writing in which [Agee] could excel." Lofaro and Lynn Champion, College of Arts and Sciences director of outreach, envisioned a conference broader in scope than the one held sixteen years earlier for the *Let Us Now Praise Famous Men* anniversary. With this new event, they intended to recognize "the breadth of Agee's achievements" and the "reasons why James Agee and Knoxville are an inseparable part of the American cultural scene." The James Agee Celebration, as they named the conference, was even more ambitious than its predecessor, largely because of Agee materials recently donated to UT's Special Collections by the Agee family and the concurrent "community effort to preserve his memory."[96]

Mostly concentrated during James Agee Week, April 13–17, 2005, roughly twenty events were held in a dozen venues spread between the university and the 100 block of South Gay Street. The Clarence Brown Theatre presented Tad Mosel's *All the Way Home*, and R. B. Morris staged his one-man play, *The Man Who Lives Here is Loony*, at the Carousel Theatre. The East Tennessee History Center exhibited 1915-era artifacts including a Model T and one of L&N Station's original "smoldering" stained glass windows, Agee family photographs, and a re-created section of the Agees' Highland Avenue front porch. Libraries and galleries displayed manuscripts of Agee's screenplays and film reviews, and Walker Evans's photographs for *Let Us Now Praise Famous Men*. Multiple auditoriums screened the Ross Spears films *Agee* and *To Render a Life*, the Michel Viotte documentary *Let Us Now Praise Famous Men (Louons maintenant les grands hommes)*, and the Agee-scripted films *Mr. Lincoln*, *The Night of the Hunter*, and *The African Queen*. The R. B. Morris Band performed; UT's School of Music presented a program of Agee-inspired works, "From Barber to Copland." Over a dozen lectures were given on topics including Agee's poetry, his collaborations with Charles Chaplin and Charles Laughton, the controversial "true" opening of his novel *A Death in the Family*, and his daughter Deedee Agee herself sharing memories of her famous father. A walking tour beginning at the L&N Station wound its way through the Fort Sanders neighborhood, past the former site of the Agee home.[97]

Capping the weeklong celebration, more than 150 people gathered at the corner of Laurel Avenue and James Agee Street at 2:30 p.m. on April 17 to witness the dedication of James Agee Park. Park Committee chairman Charles Thomas opened the ceremony, during which Bill Lyons, Phil Scheurer, and Randall De Ford—representing the City of Knoxville, the University of Tennessee, and the Fort Sanders neighborhood—each spoke before the ribbon was cut and the park officially opened. Climbing the steps up from the sidewalk, guests crossed an inset marble slab engraved with a quote from Agee's "Dedication": "To those who in all times have sought truth and who have told it in their art or in their living." Paul Ashdown read from other Agee works, and the R. B. Morris Band performed. Morris, who had nursed the park idea for two decades, said he was "smiling all the time" and "so pleased" that his dream was now a reality. "This was a long time coming, and it's just the beginning," Morris said.[98]

In honor of her father, Deedee Agee brought "two lilacs, his favorite flower, to the dedication of the new James Agee Park, a grace-filled spot I feel sure he would find holy," she wrote. "Standing there, transplanted ancient magnolias overhead, grand and blooming, I come to a new deep-rooted sense of self, unearthed like truth revealed in epiphany: a not yet fully known dimension of who I am." Interviewed while in town, she said of the park and the conference, "Though I knew my father was a 'favorite son' of Knoxville, perhaps it takes an event such as this to demonstrate his deep appeal."[99]

After decades without much tangible evidence of the city's appreciation, many local fans of Agee's work would agree that the writer had been properly honored. Ashdown called the park dedication "a very good example of community organizing. It began very quietly and under the radar, with a few shakers and movers."[100]

Coordinated with the separate park effort, the Agee Celebration was the largest Agee event ever organized in the city up to that time. Conference chair Michael Lofaro acknowledged its role in preserving the author's local legacy. "Before the celebration, people knew him for a certain book or perhaps a movie like *The African Queen*," said Lofaro. "Now that we've created this context of his work and the many ways he was connected to Knoxville, we can claim that sense of pride and entitlement that comes with being the hometown of a major author." Lofaro later edited *Agee Agonistes*, a volume of lectures from the conference.[101]

∞∞∞∞∞∞∞∞∞∞

As Agee Park was being dedicated, plans were in the works for another tribute to the writer—but an unpublicized one—a block away. In January 2005 developer John Craig of Segundo Properties had purchased two Highland Avenue lots, 1502 and 1508, each containing an existing house across the street from where the Agees once lived. Within two months, architect Randall De Ford sketched a floor plan for a new single-family home to be constructed between the existing houses. Mark Hipshire was consulted about the interior layout based on the few memories his mother had of living in 1505 as a toddler. De Ford's sketch, titled "Reflections on Agee," was "a modern plan, based on the historic form." The proposed house would be "a mirror image" of the Agees' home, sitting directly opposite 1505's lot. To preserve the large magnolia tree in the front yard, the new home's footprint was slightly narrowed by orienting the staircase to one side of the house instead of along its center hall. But the front would have practically duplicated the original, even down to the bay window. Besides helping counteract the continued razing of the neighborhood's original Victorian homes, "Reflections on Agee" would have been a fitting homage to the man who made the block famous. However, Craig abandoned the project and sold the property in 2013. Perhaps another inspired Knoxvillian will one day rebuild the home memorialized in *A Death in the Family*.[102]

2007 NOVEL ANNIVERSARY

Fifty years after that novel's publication, its anniversary was remembered in Knoxville with a couple of events sponsored by the Knox County Public Library. Festivities were small compared to the 1989 *Let Us Now Praise Famous Men* commemoration and the Agee Celebration of 2005. On November 17, Jack Neely led an "Agee Amble" that departed from Lawson McGhee Library. And soprano Jami Rogers and the Knoxville Symphony Orchestra performed Samuel Barber's piece *Knoxville: Summer of 1915* at Church Street United Methodist Church on November 26.[103]

More noteworthy was the release in late December of *A Death in the Family: A Restoration of the Author's Text*, edited by Michael Lofaro in an effort to correct the mistakes of editor David McDowell's original 1957 publication. The new version's most controversial change is the absence of "Knoxville: Summer of 1915" as the prologue that, Lofaro and other scholars argue, Agee never intended. Instead, the novel opens with Agee's nightmare of carrying a badly beaten corpse, later determined to be his father's, through the streets of Knoxville. Aside from retaining Agee's original character names—Laura Agee rather than Mary Follet, etc.—another striking difference from the 1957 edition is the number of new chapters included and their strict chronological arrangement, which original editor David McDowell could not successfully incorporate. Lofaro's restoration of the novel is a major achievement and likely the closest thing to Agee's intended work that the world will ever see.[104]

2009 AGEE CENTENNIAL

Only four years after the last Agee conference, Lofaro initiated another major citywide event to commemorate Agee's hundredth birthday. "This is a great time to get the community to celebrate," said Lofaro of the James Agee Centennial Celebration. Almost twenty planned events were spaced over consecutive weekends between October 23 and November 23. Lofaro felt it was "also a good time to recognize how much work needs to be done on Agee's contribution to film, journalism and his writings across the board." While the conference indeed acknowledged Agee's range as a writer, the James Agee Film Festival made up the bulk of the events during a densely packed first weekend.[105]

As Chaplin inspired Agee's early interest in film, the festival appropriately opened with two Chaplin pictures, *Easy Street* and *Monsieur Verdoux*, shown at the East Tennessee History Center. The Square Room on Market Square screened the Agee-scripted films *The Blue Hotel*, *Genghis Khan*, *The Quiet One*, *The African Queen*, and *The Bride Comes to Yellow Sky*. Also shown were *In the Street*, which Agee helped shoot and direct, and a few home movies captured during the making of *All the Way Home*. R. B. Morris presented "James Agee's Last Letter," an excerpt from *The Man Who Lives Here is Loony*. And at the Bijou Theatre, Ross Spears introduced and screened his documentary, *Agee*, followed that afternoon by a restored version of *The Night of the Hunter*. The much lighter second weekend consisted of "An Afternoon in Agee Park," with readings and comments from R. B. Morris and Randall De Ford.

The following weekend, the Knoxville Museum of Art opened an exhibit about Abraham Lincoln's early life, conveniently timed for the separate screening of Agee's *Mr. Lincoln* miniseries. The East Tennessee History

Center exhibited artifacts to re-create an "East Tennessee Streetscape" as Agee would have remembered it. Guest speakers included novelist David Madden, Metropolitan Museum of Art curator Jeff L. Rosenheim, and *New York Times* book critic Dwight Garner. During "One Last Weekend with Jim," R. B. Morris performed a ticketed concert at the Laurel Theater, and lectures by Michael Lofaro and Paul Ashdown concluded the Centennial Celebration. As he did following the 1989 and 2005 Agee events, Lofaro compiled a volume of essays, *Agee at 100*, based on lectures presented during the conference.[106]

At this writing, Lofaro had no current plans for another Agee conference, and said that while more could be done to honor the writer, what Knoxville has accomplished in the past couple of decades is "certainly on par with other literary figures."[107]

SUMMER OF 2015

Beyond the stone pillars carved with the initials "J A," a few long tables were laden with Styrofoam bowls, plastic spoons, sweating tubs of vanilla ice cream, and sweet toppings in squeeze bottles. Standing beneath a wooden pagoda that offered little shade from the sun, a jazz trio led by Nancy Brennan Strange swung old-fashioned standards like "Swing Low, Sweet Chariot," "Go Tell Aunt Rhoda," and "A Bicycle Built for Two." People of all ages sang and hummed along with varying degrees of familiarity, while reclining on blankets and captain's chairs. A few people were dressed in old styles, but-toned-up, bow-tied, straw-hatted; most wore jeans, shorts, sandals—clothes of modern comfort. It was an unusual sort of gathering, with some talking among acquaintances but mostly people eating ice cream and waiting, antici-pating the event. Trees edged the lot and partly shaded the guests seated on the oval lawn. From parking lot to park, it was a place where people on this summer evening imagined what the neighborhood was like a century ago, back when residents took streetcars or walked to see vaudevilles or movies on Gay Street, or sat talking with family on their front porches.

Once again, Knoxville was celebrating James Agee's "Knoxville: Summer of 1915"—words that first brought the writer local recognition when Samuel Barber set them to music, and words that put the city on the map for count-less readers and listeners around the world. The event, cosponsored by the Knox County Library and the City of Knoxville, marked the centennial of that perfect summer moment from Agee's youth that he expressed so well.

After Jack Neely set the piece's historical context, contrasting the "gritty" reality of 1915 Knoxville to Agee's "idyllic" memories of Highland Avenue,

The "Summer of 1915" centennial gathering in James Agee Park, June 2015.
Photo by the author.

R. B. Morris gently and steadily read those familiar words that the assembly longed to hear: "We are talking now of summer evenings in Knoxville, Tennessee, in the time that I lived there so successfully disguised to myself as a child." Certain words became cues for a keyboardist's subtle accompaniment, emphasizing the work's musicality. At one point, a breeze picked up almost like a crescendo and filled the trees above, and Agee's words seemed even more awake.[108]

People gathered on this evening, June 21, from five to seven, during the time the Agee family would have eaten supper and retired to the back yard. But the sun still cast hard shadows and had not yet diffused to a sky "shining softly and with a tarnish." Absent were the fireflies and cicadas—or locusts, as Agee wrote—that usually appeared with "the unnatural light" of evening. The Agees had fewer afternoon daylight hours in 1915, with the city still in Central Time Zone and without Daylight Savings. Around "half past" six, when Laura cleared the dinner table and Jay watered the lawn, the summer sky over Knoxville was as dark as it is now at 8:30 p.m.[109]

But the time difference did not weaken the immediacy of Agee's words, which imparted an unmistakable grace in the heart of this dense neighborhood. A couple of large brick mansions, built for the Ross and Helm families, still stood to the east and west of the park and represented the once-upperclass Laurel Avenue that Agee crossed while walking to his grandparents' Clinch Avenue home. Directly across the street from the park, on the corner, was a smaller frame house more like the "gracefully fretted wood houses" of Highland. When Agee was born, his relatives Patty Fisk and Jessie Tyler lived in that house, and Laura likely visited them there with the infant Rufus. It was a small connection that few if any locals knew about. But sitting just one block from Agee's former home, pilgrims somehow felt that part of his life had been imprinted on the landscape.[110]

CONCLUSION

Knoxville—and, by extension, Tennessee—had come a long way in honoring this native son. Half a century ago, it allowed his house to be torn down. And aside from being prodded by Hollywood's arrival in 1962—resulting in a film premiere and a short-lived recording studio—the city was slow to recognize Agee's achievements and local connection in any tangible way. That fact was apparent to outsiders who visited the city searching for traces of the writer. It was true regionally as well as on St. Andrew's campus near Sewanee, where the Agee Library dedication of 1972 was apparently the institution's only major celebration of the famous alumnus.

"For a long time Agee was . . . a lost son of Knoxville rather than a favorite son," said R. B. Morris. But Knoxville's citizens and "local artists" saw a "need to bring him forth in the big picture." They were largely responsible for cementing Agee's legacy, fueled by "a growing love and appreciation for his work as well as a growing indignation for how the city had ignored him." Paul Ashdown agreed that "the early interest was essentially local people who were proud of their city and its heritage, and James Agee." The combined, decades-long effort to honor Agee involved individuals with "a literary sensibility" from various disciplines and vocations—students, professors, administrators, local journalists and writers, musicians and artists. "Eventually we coalesced into an effective group that began to force a recognition of him," Morris added, "which manifested in conferences and memorials, plays and publications. And one could say that this was also happening on a national level as well, as Agee's star continued to rise."[111]

As Knoxville embraced Agee, it was also embracing its own important heritage. There was a time when the city believed modernization and urban renewal were its only weapons against the bad national press it had received since the 1920s. Then in the mid-seventies, when the Bijou Theatre was threatened with demolition, a grassroots preservation movement began. By drawing attention to the building's historical value, the now-prominent advocacy group Knox Heritage helped save the structure. Four decades later, one can easily see evidence of preservationists' success all over downtown Knoxville; in fact, the movement has expanded outward in all directions because there are now few historic properties left downtown that have not been revitalized. Is it a stretch to suggest that Agee had something to do with this? That his words somehow inspired a change in how the city viewed itself?[112]

Several weeks after the ice cream social in James Agee Park, *Time* published an article in which writers Pia de Jong and Landon Jones contemplated the relevance of "Knoxville: Summer of 1915." Despite Agee's prose being "nostalgic and sentimental" at times, the writers called it "the most ecstatic piece of writing ever composed about an American summer." More than ever, readers in an increasingly fragmented world connect to the work's "nagging sense of lost community," its "vision of small-town America that we often scoff at as a cliché . . . yet we continue to return to it," wrote de Jong and Jones. They concluded, "We still have something to learn from those summer evenings in Knoxville."[113]

The city certainly appears to have learned something about itself from Agee. That the Agee movement roughly paralleled and even preceded the revival of downtown Knoxville suggests that, by honoring the writer, the city began to acknowledge its own unique identity. Once that happened, protecting its historical and cultural properties naturally followed.

ooooooooooooooo

What about Morris's statement that Agee's reputation has also grown "on a national level"? One might be tempted to think that Knoxville's increasing respect for the writer is nothing more than hometown hubris and provincial pride, that widespread interest in the writer has actually been waning for some time. After all, Google's Ngram Viewer, which graphs how frequently a term or name has appeared in books over a specified time, indicates that the surname "Agee" peaked in popularity in 1980 ("James Agee" peaked in 1975). But Ngram's results are limited to publications in the Google Books database through 2008; it certainly does not contain every printed instance of Agee's name, nor does it consider references in other media. A time-consuming but more accurate method involves listing chronologically the primary and secondary sources, works by and about Agee, published and reissued since his death. By reordering works cited in the most recent (2007) bibliography and adding works published through 2015, one finds that the number of Agee-related books released during each posthumous decade (1955–65, 1966–75, 1976–85, 1986–95, 1996–2005, 2006–15) has remained fairly constant; only one decade saw fewer than fifteen titles published (twelve during 1986–95). In the last ten years, media outlets paid particular attention to the 2013 publication of *Cotton Tenants: Three Families* (the original, rejected manuscript that Agee reworked into *Let Us Now Praise Famous Men*) and the 2007 release of *A Death in the Family: A Restoration of the Author's Text* (the first of twelve planned volumes of *The Works of James Agee*—five of which are now available—being published by the University of Tennessee Press).[114]

Beyond its success as a novel, *A Death in the Family* has been dramatized for stage and screen several times since 1960: Mosel's play *All the Way Home* (with off-Broadway revivals in 1979 and 2006), its 1963 film adaptation by Philip Reisman Jr. (see the appendix for a full account of the production), a 1971 television treatment by Mosel for Hallmark Hall of Fame, NBC's live broadcast of the play in 1981, and a new adaptation of the novel by Robert Lenski for Masterpiece Theatre in 2002.[115]

Mixing drama and music, William Mayer adapted Agee's novel as an opera, *A Death in the Family*, which he premiered in 1983. And while creating their 1954 opera, *The Tender Land*, Aaron Copland and Horace Everett were greatly influenced by the text and images of *Let Us Now Praise Famous Men*.[116]

As Agee often wrote within the forms and sensibilities of music, it is not surprising that his texts have continued to inspire composers for almost eighty years. John Alden Carpenter based his 1936 song "Morning Fair" on Agee's "Sonnet XX." The obvious example is Samuel Barber's often-cited *Knoxville: Summer of 1915*, which still ranks among the most rented works from music publisher G. Schirmer. However, the sixteen-minute piece for soprano and orchestra is not necessarily the most popular setting of an Agee text. In 1938 Barber composed "Sure on this Shining Night," a song for voice and piano (also arranged for choir) based on Agee's poem, "Descriptions of Elysium." If recordings released during the past three decades are any indication, "Sure on this Shining Night" has been performed more than any other Agee lyric; it was also set to choral music by Z. Randall Stroope in 1996 and again by Morten Lauridsen in 2005. "A Lullaby," another of Agee's revisited poems, was set to music at least eight times between 1956 and 2002, by composers Starling Cumberworth, Paul Nelson, Philip G. Klein, Thomas

Pasatieri, Rick Sowash, Dan Welcher, Ricky Ian Gordon, and Paul Moravec. In all, more than twenty musical works have been based on Agee texts and as recently as 2015, with Frederic Sharaf's "A Chorale."[117]

Agee has also been the subject of several documentaries, with particular emphasis on his book about Alabama cotton farmers. One of the first, an hour-long radio program from 1961, was recorded at WBAI studios in New York and rebroadcast in 1968. Director Ross Spears released *Agee* in 1979 and, with Silvia Kersusan, *To Render a Life* in 1992, billed as the first feature film to be based on *Famous Men*.[118]

Four European documentaries—Carol Bell's *Let Us Now Praise Famous Men, Revisited* (a British production that aired on *American Experience* in 1988), producer Alan Hall's aforementioned audio piece for BBC in 1995, French filmmaker Michel Viotte's *Louons maintenant les grands hommes* in 2004, and a second audio documentary Hall recorded in Knoxville in 2007—confirm Agee's international reputation. A couple of Knoxvillians traveling abroad observed this European interest firsthand. Walking past a Parisian bookstore in 1980, Jack Neely spotted Agee's face in the window—a poster advertising a new volume of the writer's works. And in conversations R. B. Morris heard while visiting Paris and London, Agee was generally regarded with "a certain reverence or stature."[119]

This widespread recognition shows that Knoxville is not anomalous in praising the famous writer. In light of the attention Agee has received outside the city, Knoxville acknowledged him quite late: as Morris said, the story of James Rufus Agee's local legacy is one of "belated" fame. In writing, in film, in music, around the world, and at home in Tennessee, Agee remains relevant.[120]

Appendix
"From Low in the Dark"
Film, 1962–1963

James Agee's legacy in East Tennessee took root slowly and was cultivated over decades by individuals who cared deeply about his work. But his reputation might have taken even longer to establish there had Hollywood not invited a flood of media attention to the area between the autumns of 1962 and 1963. The making and premiere of the film *All the Way Home* in Knoxville brought the author and his work into the local consciousness, initially, more so than the novel's earlier publication and Pulitzer reception did. Despite falling into obscurity within a few decades of its release—unlike Agee's novel and its Broadway adaptation—the film is worth considering here in detail as a significant part of the writer's lasting appeal in the region.

∞∞∞∞∞∞∞∞∞∞

Not surprisingly, some of those closest to Agee had balked at the idea of *A Death in the Family* being adapted for the stage or screen. In February 1958 Laura Agee Wright wrote to a friend that the novel was "being much talked of for a *play*—& also for movies." She clearly opposed the dramatization of her family's story, as indicated by her statement "O I hope *not*" and her underscoring *not* three times. It is not known whether she saw the play or film before she died in 1966.[1]

About a month after her letter, Father Flye sent one to David McDowell, the novel's editor, writing, "If the idea of making a play or a movie from that book of Jim's is considered I myself would be cautious and rigidly inflexible. ... What anything connected with or influenced at all by Hollywood would do in making a screen version of *A Death in the Family* would shock and infuriate me to think of." Just as Agee was often highly critical of products manufactured by the big studios, so Flye doubted that any film version of the novel produced for "the American screen" could be "as quiet and exquisitely shaded as . . . the writing." It would only succeed if "done as Jim would have done it, with tenderness and delicacy of perception and taste—as for example *The Quiet One* was done, or the film on Lincoln. . . . A stage or screen version ought no less to have that quality or else not be produced."[2]

After seeing the Broadway debut of Tad Mosel's adaptation, *All the Way Home,* Flye remarked that "it was better than I had expected." The play won its own Pulitzer in 1961. A film version, now inevitable, seemed destined for success.[3]

During his visit to Knoxville in October 1962, Father Flye met cast members from *All the Way Home,* including Michael Kearney, cast as Rufus Follet. Photo by Alan Shayne. Courtesy of Alan Shayne and Michael Kearney.

Screenwriter Philip Reisman Jr. was hired to adapt Mosel's play. Both scripts took the novel's italicized flashback sequences—Jay Follet singing Rufus to sleep, Mary Follet expecting a baby, neighborhood boys teasing Rufus, the family visiting Great-Grandma—and incorporated them seamlessly into the main storyline. Both end with Mary telling Rufus about the baby, hoping it will be a little sister. And much of Reisman's dialogue is more Mosel than Agee. But whereas the play's sparsely dressed stage left much to the audience's imagination, the film script specified actual Knoxville-area places—including "Majestic Theater," "the viaduct," "Forest Avenue," "Highland and Laurel Streets," "L&N Depot," "Gay Street," and "Harbison's haberdashery"—details that begged for an authentic screen treatment. A few of those sites had changed little in the half century since the events occurred.[4]

Reportedly, Reisman had interviewed Father Flye while scripting the film. The priest softened to the movie idea enough that in mid-October 1962 he traveled from New York to Knoxville, where a Hollywood crew was in the process of bringing Agee's story to the big screen. Flye saw filmmakers handling his friend's story with care and finally said after his visit, "I believe that the movie is going to be as nearly as possible in keeping with the spirit of Jim's book."[5]

SCOUTING

The process had begun late that June when a talent scout arrived in town to interview boy actors for the role of six-year-old Rufus Follet. A local newspaper softly announced that David Susskind was producing a film version of Agee's *A Death in the Family*, but it was another two weeks before Knoxvillians heard that it might be shot locally. Although the search for Rufus extended across the state, the studio was—at least initially—"looking for a boy with an East Tennessee accent. People in the South talk differently," said scout Fay Lee, "and we want a boy from this locale since it is a story about this locale."[6]

In late August, Knoxville papers publicized the imminent arrival of crewmembers from Paramount Pictures and its partial subsidiary, Susskind's Talent Associates. It was not the first time Paramount had been to town. Back in the mid-twenties, a studio official visited Knoxville to cast two leading roles for Karl Brown's Appalachian drama *Stark Love*. But the film itself was made roughly fifty miles away on the North Carolina side of the Smokies.[7]

All the Way Home would be the first film shot in Knoxville, in the very neighborhood where James Agee once lived. Whatever he would have thought about his novel being adapted as a film, at least Agee would have applauded the decision to shoot the story in its actual setting. He criticized the 1945 film *A Tree Grows in Brooklyn* because its intricately designed studio facsimile of the Brooklyn streetscape was "as dead as an inch-by-inch description or a perfectly naturalistic painting, compared with accepting instead the still scarcely imagined difficulties and the enormous advantages of submerging your actors in the real thing, full of its irreducible present tense and its unpredictable proliferations of energy and beauty." Two years later, he wrote, "One of the best things that is happening in Hollywood is the tendency to move out of the place—to base fictional pictures on fact, and, more importantly, to shoot them not in painted studio sets but in actual places."[8]

Although "painted studio sets" were used for some interior scenes, almost half of the film would indeed be shot in and around Knoxville. When producers arrived to scout locations, they realized that some of the landmarks Agee

This house, 1412 Forest Avenue, was used for exterior shots of the Follet residence in *All the Way Home*. Father Flye made this photograph while visiting Knoxville in October 1962. The house later appeared in the 1979 documentary *Agee*. SC.MSS.148-1911, James Harold Flye Papers, Vanderbilt University.

described were already gone, such as "old Market Square." After the market house was torn down in early 1960, the city erected concrete awnings—critics called them "toadstools"—that modernized the space and masked the square's Victorian character.[9]

One important landmark that remained was the actual Agee house at 1505 Highland, which art director Richard Sylbert discovered after "scouring a 1915 telephone directory." Producers hoped to use the home as the film's "main setting." Unfortunately, it was already slated for demolition beginning on September 7, one month before filming was to start. Arriving too late, the film crew would lose its most authentic set piece. Equally lamentable was that the house at 1115 West Clinch—where Agee's grandparents had lived for almost three decades, where Agee himself was born in 1909, and where his father's funeral service was held in 1916—had been razed about two years earlier. Father Flye, during his Knoxville visit, may not have realized the house was already gone when he asked to be driven past "the first homesite of the Agees."[10]

Instead, a house at 1412 Forest Avenue, owned by Helene Cooler, was chosen as the Follet (Agee) home out of 150 other candidates. Only the exterior would be shown in the film; the house's interior, like many in the neighborhood, had been converted into apartments. Two larger houses, the Roy Carr residence at 1203 Laurel and the T. C. Wilburn home at 1511 Laurel, would stand in for the Lynch (Tyler) home exteriors and interiors, respectively.[11]

During the first week of September, representatives from the Chamber of Commerce and Paramount Pictures began canvassing Forest, Highland, and Laurel avenues, asking homeowners to sign release forms granting filmmakers permission to photograph their houses for the film. Associate producer Jack Grossberg also secured permissions for shooting downtown. Although not all the locations were used, those selected included L&N Station, Western Avenue Viaduct, and the Bijou Theatre. Gay Street was too busy and polluted with signs of 1960 to be used extensively, so Jackson Avenue was chosen as a substitute, along with West Vine Avenue and the 200 blocks of Commerce and State. But two stores along the main thoroughfare were actually considered, including "the exterior of Hall's Gay Street clothing store," at 318–320 South Gay, "and the interior of Miller's," at the corner of Gay and Union. A cemetery and ferry were among the outlying locations needed.[12]

Fleming Reeder, head of Reeder Productions in Knoxville, produced films "for Industry, Television and Education" from his Ogden Avenue studio. He assisted the Hollywood crew in finding appropriate local settings for *All the Way Home*. Notes penciled throughout his copy of the script indicate he was at least partly responsible for locating a covered bridge, arranging shoots at the cemetery and Cades Cove, and checking for accuracy the script's references to 1915 Knoxville.[13]

Paramount enlisted help from another local studio, Sam Orleans Film Productions, located downtown at 211 West Cumberland, a block east of Gay Street. For years, Orleans had worked as TVA's "official 'cinematographer'" before starting his own company in the 1940s. He "was generally regarded as Knoxville's first resident filmmaker." His company produced a driver-safety film, "The Sixth Wheel," in 1962. Orleans was reportedly "right in the middle of the production" of *All the Way Home* and, subsequently, *The Fool Killer.* But he never got to see the latter film's local premiere, as he died in 1964 when his plane crashed into a Cocke County hillside—the worst air disaster in East Tennessee history.[14]

All the Way Home was scheduled to begin filming on October 8, with stars Jean Simmons and Robert Preston portraying fictional versions of Agee's parents.

CASTING

Robert Preston, enjoying accolades from the summer 1962 release of *The Music Man,* was cast as the father, Jay Follet. He had met James Agee a decade earlier on a film set. "I knew Agee a little bit before he died," said Preston. "He played the role of a drunk and I was the sheriff in '[The] Bride Comes to Yellow Sky.'" Agee had previously reviewed a few Preston films for *Time* magazine. Of *The Macomber Affair,* in which Preston played the title role, Agee wrote in 1947: "None of the three principal players could possibly be improved on."[15]

Agee had much more to say about Jean Simmons, who would portray the mother, Mary Follet. He devoted almost a third of his 1948 *Time* review of Laurence Olivier's *Hamlet* to the young actress: "Jean Simmons, who plays Ophelia ... gives the film a vernal freshness and a clear humanity which play like orchard breezes through all of Shakespeare's best writing, but which are rarely projected by veteran Shakespearean actors.... Young Miss Simmons has an unspoiled talent for speaking with an open voice ... from the heart rather than the roof of the mouth. She has an oblique, individual beauty and a trained dancer's continuous grace." Perhaps confessing his own theatergoing habits, Agee wrote that Simmons "jerks genuine tears during scenes which ordinarily cause Shakespeare's greatest admirers to sneak out for a drink." His appraisal of Simmons continued: "Compared with most of the members of the cast, she is obviously just a talented beginner. But she is the only person in the picture who gives every one of her lines the bloom of poetry and the immediacy of ordinary life."[16]

As much as he respected Simmons and, apparently, Preston, one wonders whether Agee would have endorsed their being cast as his parents. But the actors believed in Agee's story strongly enough that they "went along with any arrangement" to get the film made, agreeing to take "a percentage of the profits," or roughly "one-third of their normal pay." (In one writer's assessment of Paramount's film, "The profits, however, were negligible, although *All the Way Home* was worth making, if, for no other reason, to bring James Agee's poignant novel to the screen.")[17]

Also enhancing the cast was Aline MacMahon, as Rufus's great-aunt Hannah. She was one of the few standouts in Agee's 1944 review of *Dragon Seed*, which he called "an almost unimaginably bad movie." He wrote that MacMahon and Walter Huston, who were made up to appear Asian, "obviously realized that it was much more important to convey the emotions of human beings than the charade mannerisms of Little Theater Chinese." MacMahon was one of four actors in *All the Way Home* who originated their roles on Broadway. The other three were Thomas Chalmers as Grandfather Lynch, Georgia Simmons (no relation to Jean) as Grandmother Follet, and Lylah Tiffany as "Great-Grandma."[18]

John Cullum had some things in common with Agee. Both were born in Knoxville and attended Knoxville High School (and both would later be inducted into the East Tennessee Hall of Fame). As a UT student, Cullum "starred in about fifty Carousel Theater plays," and later stated, "I got my most important [acting] experience there in Knoxville and I feel that it was good training. I am proud to have come from there." He debuted in New York three years after graduating, but subsequently returned to Tennessee to play Governor John Sevier in *Chucky Jack*, an outdoor drama staged in Gatlinburg. His big break on Broadway came in 1960 when he understudied for Richard Burton in *Camelot*. Before Paramount cast him as Uncle Andrew, Cullum had appeared with Robert Preston in *We Take the Town*, "an off-Broadway show" directed by Alex Segal. Cullum could relate well to the Agee tragedy, having lost his mother in a Knoxville car accident in 1956; *All the Way Home* began shooting two days before the sixth anniversary of her death.[19]

Pat Hingle was cast as Jay Follet's brother Ralph. A few years earlier, he had been promised the lead role in the film *Elmer Gantry*, opposite Jean Simmons and directed by her husband Richard Brooks. But then in

February 1959, Hingle fell three stories down an elevator shaft, fractured his skull and multiple other bones, and lost his left pinky. After Burt Lancaster stepped into the *Gantry* role, Hingle narrated *Wild River*, a 1960 film starring Montgomery Clift and shot in East Tennessee's Bradley County. The brief voiceover was one of the only parts he could manage during his yearlong recovery. In 1971 Hingle would reprise his role as Ralph Follet for a television adaptation of Mosel's play.[20]

Wanting an "ordinary-looking kid" to play Rufus, director Segal tested approximately "600 boys from sixteen states." Bruce Keelen of Knoxville was a finalist for the part, but "producers thought he was a bit too large." And although the studio had originally wanted a boy with an authentic twang, Keelen was finally "undone by his Southern accent," Susskind said. Instead, the role was awarded to Michael Kearney of Verona, New Jersey. "He was an adorable child," recalled Alan Shayne, who cast the film along with Michael Shurtleff. "We picked him out of the hundreds of boys I saw because of his just being a little boy, not a professional actor, but a real kid." Kearney, whose only prior film experience was a ten-second bit part opposite Dick Clark in *The Young Doctors*, later recalled auditioning for *All the Way Home:* "We heard about this film they were casting for in New York. They needed a young boy to play the son of Jean Simmons and Robert Preston in the film. The first audition is usually short and sweet: you go in, they say hello, they look at you and make sure you look like your picture—some kids don't—and they give you the once-over and make sure you can speak to them without being too shy. Then they say thank you and let you go. And off I went. There was an order to auditioning: it was an audition, then a first callback, a second, a third. I went back a number of times. But eventually we got the word that I was chosen for the role of Rufus."[21]

The Kearneys were naturally "ecstatic" about the news, and Michael was eager to finally have "a real part." Of his sizeable role, Michael said, "The script has 197 pages. I'm on most of 'em." Family arrangements had to be made quickly since he would be away from home for three or four months: "My grandparents moved in with us. They were going to help Dad take care of the kids at home while Mom and I went to Knoxville." Since the filming schedule required Michael to miss a large chunk of his school year, "the studio hired a young woman down [in Knoxville] named Carol Kress to be my tutor," he said later. Kress taught at Christenberry Junior High School.[22]

The cast assembled in New York on September 24 for the first rehearsal, held "at the Central Plaza jazz emporium on Second Avenue." Segal, a veteran television director, expected the actors to "learn the whole script at once, just as if they were to present a stage play or live-TV drama." He "marked the entire floor" of the rehearsal space with the physical boundaries of certain scenes, blocking the actors' "movements and actions prior to the start of camera work." Kearney had trouble reading the script himself because of his young age. To help him learn his lines, his cousin John Spencer—an actor later known for TV's *The West Wing*—read the script aloud to him. Michael took to memorization so well that he often recited his part, and sometimes the other actors' lines as well, after a single hearing.[23]

When Michael turned seven on October 1, the crew broke from rehearsal and threw him a party. "They got me a cake, and they brought me presents. It was really nice; they treated us so well," he recalled.[24]

ooooooooooooooo

Casting directors Shurtleff and Shayne arrived in Knoxville the next day to officially announce Kearney as the film's Rufus Follet. Shayne would help hire local extras for the film but was largely responsible for helping fit Kearney into the leading role. "My reason for being on location was that Alex Segal . . . insisted I be brought to coach Michael, who was not only very young, but not an actor," said Shayne. "I don't think Michael wanted to be in the picture at all, and I spent most of my time cajoling him and teaching him as much as I could."[25]

Shurtleff was also looking to cast a few locals to stand in for Preston, Simmons, and Kearney, saving the stars from having to be on the set for extended periods while cameras and lights were being set up and focused. Although the stand-ins would not appear on camera, each one was chosen specifically to match the size and complexion of a particular actor. The local paper issued a call for Knoxvillians matching the following descriptions: "Miss Simmons will portray the part of Rufus' mother and her standin should be between the ages of thirty and forty, stand five feet, four and a half inches tall, weigh 120 pounds, have brown hair and be fairly dark complexioned. Preston's standin must also be thirty to forty, six feet, one, weigh 180 pounds, have brown hair and ruddy complexion. The standin for Rufus should be forty-four to forty-five inches tall, be seven years old, blond and fair." Once shooting began, the stand-ins quickly discovered how unglamorous the job was. John Sines, a former UT basketball coach, quit after two days of standing in for Preston, remarking, "Any ape could do that job," and that he "just couldn't afford to stay there for $75 a week." Jean Simmons's stand-in, Betty Henry, faced with missing the UT–Georgia Tech football game one Saturday, resigned her position. And the twelve-hour shifts proved too much for Kearney's stand-in, Michael Dennard. Andrew Hines, Barbara Julian, and Jerry Davis replaced Sines, Henry, and Dennard, respectively.[26]

Locals "with acting experience" were sought for about six small speaking parts, each paying $100 a day. Nonspeaking extras, paid $15 a day, were also needed. A newspaper announcement emphasized the need for "middleaged" extras, rather than the "young attractive girls" who made up the bulk of applicants but which "just aren't needed in the film." By the second week of October, more than one hundred locals had been hired as extras.[27]

Shurtleff and Shayne visited Fort Sanders Elementary School one day, looking to cast a group of boys as Rufus's neighborhood "playmates." Other schools were scouted as well. Back in March the Jernigan boys of 1502 Highland had both appeared in the Carousel Theatre's production of the Tad Mosel play (Victor, eleven, probably had an easy time acting the part of a bully opposite his ten-year-old brother Rusty, who played Rufus). They were cast along with Steve Davis. Tommy Webster, also of Highland Avenue, was later added to the group, and Johnny Giffin portrayed a newspaper boy. Suddenly, these boys were celebrities among their classmates. Tom Southern "was in the fifth or sixth grade" at the time and "was envious of my neighbors and playmates Tommy Webster and Victor and Rusty Jernigan, who got small roles as bullies," Southern said. "They got out of school, and even got to go to New York City for interior filming. They wouldn't tell me how much they got paid, but left the impression it was a small fortune."[28]

PROPS

While the film's human elements were being secured, producers also requested Knoxvillians' help in finding furniture, garments, and other pieces manufactured between the turn of the century and 1920. In less than two weeks, items such as "a 1911 vacuum cleaner, a 1901 piano, a 1906 typewriter, a 1900 sewing machine and a 1915 vase" were loaned, donated, or sold to the production. One of the finds was publicized as "the piano from the old Agee home," though it almost certainly had belonged to a later tenant.[29]

The film required some larger vintage props, including a horse-drawn hearse, a pair of steam locomotives, and a fleet of old vehicles. Bill Dawn, president of the Antique Car Association and owner of a 1915 Mercer, had located a couple dozen autos to be used in the film. Among the recruits was Alvin "Bud" Campbell of South Knoxville and his Ford Model T touring car, the same type driven by Agee's father. Charles and Kenneth Coulter, two brothers from Maryville, each owned Fords used during filming. Vintage car owners living in Knoxville were hired at $35 a day; those living beyond the city limits were paid $50 a day. Bud Campbell said later, "I found out real soon that [$35] wasn't enough. But they did pay me for some days when my car just sat there."[30]

Robert Preston was one of the few members of the cast and crew who knew how to operate a Model T. But despite his familiarity with the car, his clunky costume shoes made it difficult to navigate the brake, low gear, and reverse floor pedals. So he performed his driving scenes without shoes. The old cars were first employed on the afternoon the stars came to Knoxville.[31]

ARRIVAL

After rehearsing in New York for "three or four weeks," the actors—and any crewmembers who had not already left days earlier—boarded the flight to Knoxville on October 7. Michael Kearney had "never flown or even been up close to a plane before" and was initially "terrified" of its loud propellers. The airplane arrived on time, 12:20 p.m., at McGhee-Tyson Airport. Behind a red carpet, unrolled courtesy of the Chamber of Commerce, stood a throng of cheering Knoxvillians. As Kearney remembered, "They threw us a big reception. People were everywhere. The mayor was there, and reporters and cameras . . . and everybody was so excited to see us. It was just a thrill; I had never seen anything like this." Mayor John Duncan welcomed the honored guests and in a ceremonial gesture handed them keys to the city. Robert Preston and a few other stars stopped long enough to sign autographs, while others, like Jean Simmons and John Cullum, slid past the crowd. As she ducked into a waiting car, Simmons politely waved off reporters, saying, "I have a terrible cold, and since we start shooting tomorrow . . ." A row of antique automobiles, many of which would be used during filming, drove guests to the Andrew Johnson Hotel on South Gay Street, where the stars met local fans, signed more autographs, and that evening were treated to a reception dinner hosted by Hamilton National Bank.[32]

FOREST AVENUE

Filming began as scheduled the next morning, October 8. But the first shot was pushed back from eight to nine o'clock as crewmembers cleaned up leaves that the previous day's passing storm had blown all over Forest Avenue. It was the first of the production's many delays.[33] Most of the day's action took

Equipment fills the street in front of 1412 Forest Avenue during the second day of filming. The antique Mercer is parked at left. Crewmembers visible at right include Richard Sylbert (dark jacket and sunglasses), Alex Segal (back to camera), and Jack Grossberg (far right). Photo by and courtesy of Alan Shayne.

place in front of 1412 Forest. Although the house was chosen for its similarity to the Agee home (being roughly a mirror image of the house at 1505 Highland), it was actually much more elaborate, with Italianate details like wide arches between porch posts, a rounded transom, and a second-story porthole window. Years later Michael Kearney remembered it as "that beautiful old white house that had a nice big yard around it and an alley in the back."[34]

Local reporters were on hand to document the start of filming. They watched as almost fifty technicians positioned expensive equipment around the lot, including a "large $125,000 shooting camera . . . two large spotlights . . . steel or aluminum reflectors . . . an enormous Polaroid screen." Michael Hertzberg had been hired as second assistant director and, being about twenty-five at the time, was the youngest crewmember on the set. He did not expect to be promoted so soon. "On the first day of shooting, the director—who was a little off—fired the first assistant director and hired me," said Hertzberg. Immediately after that happened, "Jean Simmons came over to me and said, 'We're all rooting for you.'" He was touched by the gesture: "She was lovely. British actors are as professional as you could get."[35]

Although Segal had rehearsed *All the Way Home* as if it were a play, once filming began he followed protocol by shooting scenes out of sequence to minimize camera setups, with each day's scenes chosen based on location, weather, time of day, health of actors, and any number of other factors. Out of the script's 350 shots, Segal chose to start with those numbered 272–74, in which a milkman and paperboy—played by Howard Grayson and Johnny Giffin—deliver their wares along Forest Avenue. The milkman's horse had more movie experience than many of the local human extras, having previously appeared in *Wild River*.[36]

The main stars were not needed until that afternoon. Preston showed up around two o'clock dangling two earpiece wires connected to his transistor radio, hoping to hear the Giants defeat the Yankees in the World Series. Simmons and Kearney arrived a little later.[37]

Alan Shayne interviewed a group of locals to play neighbors in the Forest Avenue scenes. Several of them appeared fleetingly in "atmosphere" scenes labeled in the script as "Montage" and "Early Evening 'Knoxville: Summer 1915" (shots 119–28), which evoked the novel's prologue. Two boys chased each other in a front yard, three girls strolled along a sidewalk, and a few male extras watered Forest Avenue lawns.[38]

Hundreds of curious onlookers gathered on the sidelines, quietly watching as cameras rolled. One group observed repeated takes of "someone [tossing] a bucket of water out of the window of a house." This may have been the shot (126) in which Mary pulls the kitchen window closed just before Jay showers it with the garden hose. The same evening, Segal captured a scene (shot 134) of the Follets sitting on a quilt in their backyard, singing.[39]

On the second day of shooting on Forest Avenue, producers made an unusual prop request: a supply of live butterflies. Director Segal wanted to photograph Rufus through a window of the home as the boy watched "a butterfly light on a flower." Butterflies, however, were scarce that time of year, and in desperation Segal and art director Richard Sylbert announced that they would pay one dollar for each butterfly brought to the set. "I remember they requested butterflies for a scene," said Kathy Richards, "and my friends and I caught lots of butterflies to take where they were filming." But public response was underwhelming, as the *Boston Herald* reported: "The first day seven were brought in, and the second day seventeen. Then on the third day, an eight-year-old boy showed up with a cardboard box.

'I've got 250 butterflies in here,' he said, 'but they're all dead, so I'll just take fifty cents for each.' He was given $1.00 and told gently that dead butterflies were of no use and that he should take them home and give them a suitable burial." It is not known whether that unscripted flower scene was even shot, as it does not appear in the final film. But a flying butterfly did appear in a scene with the 1915 Mercer after Rufus apparently picks one off the car's grille (shots 73–75).[40]

A couple of times between October 29 and November 1, filmmakers set up behind the Forest Avenue house to shoot encounters between Rufus and the bullies. "The alley was where the kids would chase me and call me names," Kearney recalled. "But they were good kids; they were all local kids." In one of those scenes (shot 63), the boys chase Rufus from Fifteenth (now James Agee) Street into the alley, where he then runs through the backyard of the house to the rear porch. Bystanders congregated in the area to watch the filming, as they did during all local shoots. One man remembered "standing on a street . . . viewing through a vacant lot to the back porch of a house where a scene was being shot."[41]

No one would have recognized the forty-eight-year-old woman and her teenaged son mingling among the crowd of observers. Agee's widow, Mia, and son John arrived near the start of production and stayed in town for about a week but apparently were not interviewed during their trip.[42]

CATERING

Tom Southern's family lived at 1409 Highland, "across the back alley" from the Forest Avenue set. "I saw some of the scenes being filmed, but was in school most of the time," he said. While none of the Southerns appeared on camera, they allowed their property to be used during lunch breaks. "The caterers set up their tables in our back yard," Tom recalled, "and Mother got autographs for me. Robert Preston, Jean Simmons, Pat Hingle, and some lady"—Georgia Simmons—"who added after her signature that she acted with Roy Rogers."[43]

Cast and crew were treated to down-home cooking by Helma's Restaurant of Asheville Highway, which catered the production "round-the-clock" throughout the shoot. Filmmakers arriving on the set each morning had donuts and coffee waiting for them. One of Helma's "location lunches" consisted of "fried chicken, potatoes, lima beans, and pie." On some night shifts, the caterers served "hot soup as late as midnight."[44]

Owner Helma Gilreath was known for her warm personality as well as her food, but she had never fed a film crew before: "Nobody here had ever catered to an entire movie company for two meals a day for three months, no matter where they went. . . . I was so scared the night before the first meal, I thought, 'Can I really do this?'" But the filmmakers greatly enjoyed the meals she prepared. Ronnie Claire Edwards, who played Aunt Sally more than a decade before being cast as Corabeth Godsey on *The Waltons*, remembered, "The food served by the locals was delicious."[45]

Gilreath became friends with Preston on the set. "He would eat anything," she said later, "and lots of it. And he was always so appreciative. The last night [of the film shoot] we served until the wee hours of the morning, and before we left, Mr. Preston came out in the crowd to say good-bye (gave her a big kiss). Not many stars would be so thoughtful." A few years later, she went to see him perform on Broadway in *I Do, I Do*, and they reunited backstage after the show.[46]

CADES COVE

After the first two days of filming in Fort Sanders, the crew moved to Cades Cove. Between October 10 and 14, they shot scenes there of the Follet family visiting an old relative in the country. Michael Kearney remembered "the big Mercer that we all took out to Cades Cove, out to Grandma's house. . . . We did part of that shot on a trailer behind a camera truck, and we did part of it actually driving down the road." A "Girl Scout troop" happened to be "on a field trip" somewhere along Cades Cove Loop Road when they encountered the filmmakers. At least one girl "got Jean Simmons's autograph."[47]

Despite the remote setting, producers were equipped to send and receive calls from California and New York, as the *News-Sentinel* reported: "A car sitting out in the middle of a Cove pasture had a special phone in it."[48]

The crew moved to a location between Nature Trail and Hyatt Lane for the "Great-Grandma" scene (shots 107–15), filmed in front of the George Caughron barn, which blew down during a storm on Christmas Eve 2009. Lylah Tiffany had been cast as Great-Grandma in the Broadway play after she wandered into the New York theater, "snapping the fingers on one purple-veined hand to attract the director's attention." She presented her credentials: "Unicycle rider in vaudeville, carnival and circus acts; concert pianist—I won a scholarship to Chicago Conservatory of Music; fortune teller, voice teacher, manicurist, song writer and playwright, shoe polish salesman, street musician (panhandler), beauty parlor operator ... You name it." Asked whether she could play a woman of 103, Tiffany set her dentures "on the director's desk, letting her cheeks cave in" and said, "What's that ya'll say, sonny?" When the screen version was being cast, Tiffany said, "They didn't say anything about a great-great-grandmother bit. They just asked 'Who's going to play the Lylah Tiffany role?'"[49]

Tiffany proudly recalled crewmembers getting "choked up" during the filming of her scene at Cades Cove. She had been heavily made up for the part, as Kearney recalled later. "Great-Grandma was an experience. I hadn't met her prior to shooting," he said. "I had to walk up to her and say hello. She must have been in makeup all morning being transformed, because she was actually, I believe, in her sixties. But Dick Smith, our makeup artist who was very good at what he did, turned her into a much older woman."

Robert Preston, Jean Simmons, and Michael Kearney pose in front of a Model T while on location in Cades Cove, October 1962. Photo by Alan Shayne. Courtesy of Alan Shayne and Michael Kearney.

Kearney said that his somewhat fearful reaction in that scene was genuine: "She was scary-looking!"[50]

Many in the cast and crew ranked Cades Cove as the high point of the production. A few of the actors "pulled off their shoes and went wading in one of the mountain streams that pour into the cove to join Anthony Creek." Michael Kearney enjoyed seeing animals like the "young calf" used in an unscripted shot and the "small bear" that wandered into the area. "Isn't that the most beautiful place? Like something out of a fairy tale," remarked Lylah Tiffany. Ronnie Claire Edwards said her "memories are mostly of Cades Cove, the feeling that we were being watched," and recalled "Aline MacMahon telling me she, not Jane Darwell, should have played Ma Joad, in *Grapes of Wrath*." MacMahon had no scenes to shoot in Cades Cove but traveled there anyway with fellow cast members.[51]

"What was lovely for me as a kid from the city," said Hertzberg, "was to go out into the Smoky Mountains, which were staggeringly beautiful to a kid who hadn't seen a tree until he was nineteen. I loved it there." Jean Simmons said she would "love to have a log cabin back in those hills." And before leaving Knoxville, associate producer Jack Grossberg stated, "None of us will ever forget the wonderful weekend in Cades Cove."[52]

Preston, Simmons, and director Segal liked the area so much that instead of returning to Knoxville the first night as planned, they stayed with crew-members at Townsend's Valley View Lodge, which at this writing operates as the remodeled Tremont Lodge & Resort on Lamar Alexander Parkway.[53]

But not everyone was ecstatic about filming in the Smokies. The location was particularly taxing on the antique automobiles. After shooting all day in Cades Cove, the cars had to be driven out of the park at night. One Model T owner complained about having to travel that far in the dark, considering the car's underpowered headlights. Vintage car owners thought the filmmakers were often oblivious to the challenges of operating the old machines.[54]

On his last day in the mountains, October 14, Preston met up with his old Air Corps friend and UT's assistant dean of admissions, Grady Adkisson, who had organized a boar hunt "near Walland," several miles north of Townsend. When Preston's first shot missed its target, his companions followed an "old-time custom" and "cut off his shirttail." On his third try, Preston shot a "180-pound Russian boar."[55]

Perhaps Preston thought the experience would help him "fit in to the lo-cale," which he believed was an important part the actor's job: "I'm beginning to feel East Tennessee. You know there's not much of an accent to it—the talk. It's just a feeling of the country, a way of expressing things. I even like the food, like I had always been used to it."[56]

Pat Hingle, as well, thought the film had benefitted so much from the location shoot, which enabled the actors to "soak up some of the flavor and culture of Knoxville," he said. "We could have set up scenery and shot this movie somewhere else, but the people and atmosphere of this city add a unique something to this movie."[57]

By the time the cast and crew returned to Knoxville, the production had reportedly fallen "two or three days behind." Paramount admitted that the planned shooting schedule was "too tight."[58]

BIJOU

All the Way Home opens with Jay and Rufus watching a Charlie Chaplin movie (shots 2–5). The scene was filmed on October 17 inside the Bijou Theatre at 803 South Gay Street. That morning, East High School students David and Bonnie Compton, siblings, and Carol James waited for the school bus at the corner of Gay and Cumberland, near the theater. Alan Shayne, who was downtown looking for extras, approached the three teenagers and asked David if he would like to be in the film. Carol later wrote, "It suddenly popped into my head to ask [Shayne] if he needed us. I asked him in a joking

Preston and Kearney as audience members, Bijou Theatre, October 17, 1962.
Photo by Alan Shayne. Courtesy of Alan Shayne and Michael Kearney.

manner if he would like to have 'two beautiful actresses,' and when he said, 'Yes,' I almost fainted." The students were told to visit Sam Orleans Film Productions, where they would be given contracts and costumes. Carol and the other extras each received $10 for the day's work, appearing as extras in the Bijou scene. "We were part of an audience supposedly watching an old Charlie Chaplin movie. Scenes were shot over and over again from eight o'clock that morning until seven that evening." During her experience, Carol "met the hairdressers, makeup men, camera men, directors, and an assortment of Yankee-speaking people." The extras were given an hour lunch break but had to remain costumed. Walking along Gay Street, Carol "felt rather silly in a blue dress trimmed in white; black stockings; high-topped shoes, which were very uncomfortable; a straw bonnet; and a velvet waist band. Bonnie was wearing a pink linen dress with black bows, high-top shoes, long stockings, and a bow in her hair about a foot long."[59]

The theater had opened in 1909, the year Agee was born, but did not begin regularly screening films until June 1915. While Agee saw movies often during his childhood, his attending the Bijou can only be assumed. Author David Madden, for his novel *Bijou*, imagined a scene in which a "tall, dark man in a rumpled suit" visited the theater in August 1946 "and asked the manager could he walk around, that he used to come here with his father, and that yesterday while he was writing a movie review for *Time* magazine he had been seized by a terrible nostalgia for the Bijou and had impulsively gotten a plane and come down from New York City." Even though Madden discarded the scene, the scenario is plausible, since Agee visited the city at least twice during the forties. The Majestic, which Agee certainly visited, was slightly closer to his home but only a third the size of the Bijou.[60]

As scenes were being filmed for *All the Way Home*, the Bijou was in decline. Three years later, the theater began screening pornography, advertising itself ironically as the Bijou Art Theatre while it fell from cultural relevance, and closed in 1969. In 1975, when Madden heard that the Bijou was in danger of being demolished, he wrote to the *News-Sentinel*, urging the city to save the structure and not repeat the mistake it made a decade earlier by letting go of Agee's childhood home.[61]

LAUREL AVENUE

The exterior of Roy Carr's residence at 1203 Laurel was the Lynch home in the film. It first appears as the Follets drive by in the Mercer, with Uncle Ralph standing on the seat and shouting that the car belongs to him (shots 91–95).

Filmed on October 18, the scene required multiple "trial runs" to time the dialogue to the speed of the car, driven by Preston. Segal was heard to shout, "Too fast, too fast!," until the speed was adjusted. In the film, as the camera pans with the car's southward drive down Twelfth Street toward Laurel, a smaller white house is visible on the corner; Laura Agee once owned that house, which sat at 1116 Laurel Avenue, directly behind her parents' house at 1115 West Clinch.[62]

The funeral procession (shots 295, 320) was filmed along Laurel in front of 1203 around October 20–22. The horse-drawn hearse that had been hired from Cleveland, Tennessee, for the scene was thought to date from "the early 1800s." Hazel Lee Goff, a good friend of Agee's mother, witnessed the filming and reported that "the hearse that took Jay [Agee] to the cemetery was much, much larger and beautifully decorated."[63] In the first tracking shot (295), hearse owner L. J. Murphy is seen up on the seat, wearing a top hat. Holding the reins next to him is Jason Banks, enjoying a break from his normal job as bellhop and waiter at the Andrew Johnson Hotel.

ᴓᴓᴓᴓᴓᴓᴓᴓᴓᴓ

The Lynch home interiors were filmed at 1511 Laurel, a house owned by Mrs. T. C. Wilburn. Built in 1910 for businessman George Helm, the large residence featured "rich mahogany, period furniture, and starred glass windows" inside. Such details are visible in the interior's first appearance in the film, as Andrew Lynch descends the home's grand staircase to answer the telephone call containing Mary's tragic news (shots 210, 212–13).[64]

Flowers, folding chairs, and a casket were set up downstairs in the east room for the funeral service (shots 297–313), filmed around October 26–28. During part of that sequence, Preston was expected to lie motionless in the coffin as the scene played around him. He related the experience to filming *Beau Geste* over twenty years earlier with Gary Cooper. "Remember the scene when he was killed? I carried him in (from the hillside), laid him on a cot, spoke a few words to him, kissed him, then covered him with a flag and got up to blow taps on the trumpet—after first setting fire to his bed," said Preston. "Coop was so sound asleep the prop men had to drag him out of there to put the dummy in for the last shots of the funeral pyre. Most relaxed man I ever saw." Reisman's script specified shots (300, 302) of Jay Follet's body from Rufus's point-of-view—"the outline of his father's forehead and the tip of his nose" and "the waxy image of a man the child once knew." However, in the scene's final edit, Preston's face is visible for about two seconds in a medium shot as Ralph and Grandma Follet seat themselves for the funeral service.[65]

The coffin fascinated young Michael. "I'd never seen a casket before. It was something new to me, kind of an experience for a kid. I remember walking up to it, and kind of looking into it. It was empty. I was just curious," Kearney said. "I was insulated from death. I hadn't lost any close relatives."[66]

A number of locals appeared in that scene. Connie Mayes was one; he "walked up to the widow and said, 'Sorry, Mary.'" Johnny Redwine, known in local music circles, played "Rock of Ages" on a pump organ during the funeral. Michael Kearney said that at the time he thought the man seemed old, "like a fossil. But he showed me how to play the organ."[67]

OTHER INTERIORS

Multiple coffins—about twenty—were required for the scene depicting Ralph Follet's mortuary (shots 142–43, 145, 147). Caskets were set up in the Alcoholics Anonymous building at 208 Market Street, directly across from the old Lawson McGhee Library (the now-extinct address is traversed by West Summit Hill Drive). Originally a two-story dwelling, the space had housed Weaver Funeral Home for decades before the business relocated around 1958. In the scene Ralph (Hingle) calls Jay to relay news of their ailing father. During the conversation, his mother (Georgia Simmons) sits patiently nearby watching him descend into self-pity. Various coffins surround his desk, and the gothic stained window behind him and arched openings at the side of the room truly reflect the building's history as a funeral home. Two other Knoxville interiors, the department store and the saloon, have not been positively identified.[68]

Filmmakers needed a department store for the scene where Aunt Hannah buys Rufus a hat (shots 186–87, 191–95). While Miller's on South Gay Street had been announced during preproduction as a possible interior, that store encompassed about half the block and was split into three large segments, each the width of three normal storefronts. The store shown in the film appears much narrower, and could have been filmed instead behind the main Miller's store at the smaller Miller's Annex, located at 4–6 Market Square (occupied by Café 4 at this writing). The fact that a Miller's executive participated in the film's premiere ceremony suggests the company was somehow involved in the production.[69]

A Knoxville bar or restaurant interior likely portrayed the saloon where Jay stops for a drink on the way home with Rufus (shots 14–19). The curved bar looks similar to the lunch counter once located inside the L&N Station, as confirmed by a former employee. That location would have been convenient, since the station's exterior and rail yard were used in several other scenes.[70]

Kearney said later that he believed these two scenes "were shot in town somewhere." For one thing, studios recycled actors, even for bit parts; yet the faces in these scenes were unfamiliar to Kearney: "They're people I've never seen anywhere else." Also, those locations did not feel like studio sets to him: "I remember being careful where I walked," when shooting the funeral scene inside 1511 Laurel, "because I didn't want to trip over cords" that snaked across the floor. The cables led to "generator trucks outside" that powered the "monster lights" needed to illuminate the sets back then. He recalled the same type of cables on the floor of the saloon. And whereas studio sets often consisted of only "half the room" to allow for camera movement, Kearney said that the locations in question—particularly the bar scene—felt "hot and confining" and "close." He also doubted producers would have built such complicated sets if a Knoxville location already "had the basic look" and could be "dressed up from there."[71]

L&N RAIL YARD

The crew moved to the L&N rail yard at the arrival of the film's "highest paid extras." Paramount spent $200 a day to rent the "two steam locomotives and tenders," including their own "fireman and engineers," from the East Tennessee & Western North Carolina (ET&WNC) Railroad. The biggest expense, $1,600, was transporting the trains from their home in Johnson City to Knoxville and back. Since diesel power had become the norm, the route lacked water and coal refilling stations that steam engines needed. And the engines themselves lacked "automatic safety equipment" and therefore had to be "hauled."[72]

At least two days, October 30 and 31, were spent filming at the rail yard and included a scene of Michael playing near the tracks (shots 47–50). "We worked at the old train station," said Kearney. "I do remember putting the pennies on the track."[73]

Both locomotives had been built around 1904 for Southern Railroad. Several years after appearing in the film, they were sold back to Southern and their original numbers reinstated. ET&WNC 207 became Southern 630 and was eventually restored by Tennessee Valley Railroad in Chattanooga, where it continues to operate as of 2016. ET&WNC 208, the most prominent

Michael Kearney at the
L&N rail yard, crouching
beside ET&WNC 208.
Photo by Alan Shayne.
Courtesy of Alan Shayne
and Michael Kearney.

locomotive in the film, became Southern 722. It was later dismantled for a planned restoration for the Great Smoky Mountains Railroad—a project that fell through for lack of funds. In 2016 its boiler still sat rusting at the company shop yard in Dillsboro, North Carolina.[74]

PRESSURE

After several complex scenes, remote Smoky Mountain locations, funeral processions, and steam trains, *All the Way Home* was almost two weeks behind schedule—even though David Susskind claimed the production was "as on schedule as any of the films I have ever shot."[75]

Some of the delays were unavoidable. The weather had turned increasingly cold and wet. Jean Simmons, who had arrived with a cold in early October, was still suffering sinus issues. She was treated at Fort Sanders Presbyterian on October 31 after a "nasal attack" left her congested and unable to speak clearly. Her scenes the following day were rescheduled. "It was the fall, and it got cold, and it was not pleasant to be filming outside," said Hertzberg. Actors who stayed bundled up between shots had to strip off their coats before cameras rolled and act as if it were the middle of summer. To prevent breath vapor trails on camera during morning and night filming, actors were directed to eat ice cubes before each take. But some of their exhalations were later visible despite the precaution.[76]

The avoidance of post-dubbing dialogue was apparently a major priority on location, as many retakes were blamed on "modern sounds invading the sound tracks." As one reporter wrote, "The blast of a diesel engine's horn, the whoosh of a jet plane, the harmonious sounds of automobile horns and the chug-chug of a bulldozer are just not compatible with scenes of the early 1900s." Noise from jets traveling to and from McGhee-Tyson Airport, roughly twelve miles southwest of downtown, was "the No. 1 problem," according to the film's publicist.[77]

There were other technical issues. "The pace is really determined by how long it takes to light scenes. You needed a million lights," said Hertzberg. While Boris Kaufman "was as good as you could get," the veteran cinematographer "was not known to be a speedy guy." And then there were the mistakes and blunders that plague any motion picture set. Squire D. Neal Adams, a local man hired as an audience member for the Bijou Theatre scene, witnessed much time wasted due to absentmindedness: "After hours of striving for perfection in a particular scene, it was finally shot. Then the film was dropped, and we had to start over again. Finally, they got what they were after again, only to discover after shooting the scene the second time there was no film in the camera."[78]

With an operating cost of roughly $20,000 per day, producers were naturally concerned about going over budget. They had expected to leave town by October 26, telling reporters that "anything not filmed will just have to be cut out of the movie or shot in New York." But the last day of the month found them still in the city with many key night shots needed—about ten days of work. The cast and crew worked long hours, often six days a week.[79]

But pressure was evident even off the set. October was a particularly heavy month, and the intensity peaked around the third week. Robert Preston felt it in his penthouse suite at the Andrew Johnson Hotel the day a visiting reporter noticed the actor "reluctantly turning off the television and newscasts about Cuba to talk about lighter things." The whole country felt it.[80]

Michael Hertzberg recalled that the world news occupied everyone's mind and left a "patina" on everything filmmakers were doing in Tennessee. "This overlay of the Cuban Missile Crisis while trying to make a film in the South in the early sixties—we weren't used to that," he said. "We were working like any person would work, with the strain of our normal jobs, while thinking about death. We were just making a dopey movie, but people were talking about not waking up the next day."[81]

Just as young Rufus Agee had heard snippets of family conversation about a Great War being fought overseas, Michael Kearney, too young to understand the Cuban situation, still sensed that something was wrong: "I don't remember the actual events, but I remember the tension of the time and everyone being concerned. It was kind of a dangerous time, and people were scared."[82]

OFF TIME

Still, the cast and crew found ways to relax during their off hours. Richard Sylbert went fishing for trout "every chance he got." Jean Simmons took her daughter fishing one "chilly, gray" Sunday afternoon; Alan Shayne rode with them in a limousine to "a fishing park outside of town" and sat with Jean "beside a pond" as six-year-old Tracy "caught one fish after another." On October 25 Jean attended a hockey match at the Civic Coliseum with Alex Segal and Michael Hertzberg, watching the Knoxville Knights beat the Greensboro Generals in the season opener. A reporter covering the game noted that Simmons "clapped vigorously" for the home team and was "among the Knights' most robust cheerers." Preston was spotted at Chilhowee Park's Jacobs Building one Friday night, watching a wrestling match. Ric Tillery worked there at the time and remembered Preston as a "very nice man."[83]

One evening, the Hollywood folk dined at Deane Hill Country Club. Carole Gentry Goff was there and got Preston's autograph. "I was so impressed to meet 'really famous people,'" she recalled. On October 28 members of the cast treated the crew to a party at C'est Bon Country and Athletic Club on Alcoa Highway. That night's celebration was apparently rough on the adult cast, as only the kids were called before cameras the following morning of what was dubbed "Children's Day."[84]

Michael Kearney was in play mode most of the time, even on the set. "For me, this was little boy heaven—we had antique cars, we had trains, we had horses. I was climbing on the cars. I don't know what the owners of these cars thought, but if that were my car and a seven-year-old kid was climbing on it, I don't know how I would have felt," he said later. "But everybody was just having a ball." The Andrew Johnson Hotel became Kearney's playground after each day's filming. He described it as "a very nice hotel with very long hallways that I ran laps around day and night. It had no backyard, so I needed a place to play. They knocked on our door a few times about keeping people awake." Guests might have heard strange howling on Halloween night, when, as Kearney's mother recalled, "Michael dressed up as a cub werewolf and charmed hotel guests, the cast and me out of more than $2 and lots of candy." With face paint, fake hair, and fangs applied by Dick Smith, one of Hollywood's top makeup artists, Kearney was surely the best-looking Wolf Man in Knoxville that Halloween.[85]

NIGHT SHOTS

One week before leaving Knoxville, the production switched to "night shift" and tackled all the nighttime scenes that had been held off until the end. On November 4 the crew set up near the Western Avenue Viaduct, the same bridge Jay and Rufus Agee had crossed half a century earlier on their walk home from the movies. The shot (22) is one of the most striking and authentic of the whole film. As Preston and Kearney re-created the event, large floodlights behind the bridge silhouetted their figures as they passed between the L&N Hotel and the L&N Station. About "$25,000 worth of lights" illuminated the set.[86]

Also shot that week were what Kearney remembered as "the Charlie Chaplin scenes at the beginning of the film when we were running down the street." As Preston waddles along the sidewalk, mimicking Chaplin, he appears to be walking with Kearney along a quiet and unfamiliar section of downtown (shot 11). But the two were actually filmed outside the L&N Station's upper entrance. The uniformed man checking crates beside them was probably an actual station worker, as a few were hired as extras. A former L&N employee was there during the night shoot and recalled that "Helma's catered a delicious meal one day . . . on the bottom level." Old City Hall is faintly visible in the background, and parking had to be temporarily prohibited out front. Radio communication between the location shooting and the busy intersection at Western and Henley helped hold back traffic long enough to get the shots.[87]

Traffic control was also necessary on November 5, the night the "vacant lot" scene was filmed (shots 24–25). Since the actual lot that Agee visited with his father was no longer vacant by 1962—at the time it housed a wholesale electrical supply business—filmmakers found another lot a block or so away, at 222 Tenth Street. The lot overlooking the L&N rail yard was dressed with "a stirrup-like tree stump" and a "telephone pole." Across Tenth Street

Robert Preston and Michael Kearney shoot a night scene at
the vacant lot on Tenth Street, November 1962. Photo by Alan
Shayne. Courtesy of Alan Shayne and Michael Kearney.

from the lot, four houses were "rented and vacated" by filmmakers and their
windows lit for night shots. A reporter wrote of the night shoot that the
"old houses . . . appeared to be hosting a gala ball . . . because they were so
brightly lighted." David Susskind explained the need for the extra lighting:
"In order for the houses to appear to be normally lighted, the windows have
to be literally flooded with light."[88]

A thirteen-year-old boy watching from the sidelines that night later recalled those intense lights. "It was 11:30 at night when they filmed the scene. The movie lights were so bright, yet in the film it looked so dark, I was amazed. I'll never forget that night with my dad." Evan McKinley and his father made a special trip to Knoxville so they could watch the filming. "My dad drove me down from Morristown to the film location one night. He and I stood nearby while Robert Preston and the young boy sat on top of the bank looking down at the old L&N Station while an antique steam locomotive came into the station," said McKinley.[89]

Another young bystander whose parent brought her to watch later could not remember exactly where it occurred. "My mother took us to where a scene was being filmed," said Suzanne Province Kear. "Not sure, but I believe it was around Fort Sanders. It was a nighttime scene, and lots of locals congregated in the area. We really couldn't see much, but were just excited about a movie being filmed there."[90]

While there might be seventy-five to one hundred people watching daytime scenes from behind the rope, dropping temperatures typically meant fewer bystanders at night. A few nights that week, low temperatures were at or below freezing. People on the set congregated near "three big coffee urns," and Michael Kearney wore a coat, gloves, and hat between takes.[91]

On November 6, shooting resumed at 1412 Forest Avenue for the back porch "farewell scene" between Preston and Simmons, who had still not fully recovered from her sinus cold. Alex Segal wanted to backlight the actors with a Model T's headlamps before the car had been cranked. The car's owner, Bud Campbell, explained to Segal that the car lacked a battery and had to be running in order for the lights to work. Segal insisted on sending Campbell to connect a separate battery to power the headlights. But Preston objected, saying, "Any fool knows a 1915 Model T's lights won't burn without the engine running." At that, Segal told Campbell to "kill the lights."[92]

∞∞∞∞∞∞∞∞∞∞∞

Only one shot of a downtown storefront made it into the film, but the location has not been identified. While walking with his father along a sidewalk, Rufus stops at the sight of a seminude statuette in the window of Dallinger's, a fictional drug store (shot 9). The whole display window could have been a studio creation—a façade built into a downtown doorway or recessed area. A reverse angle (shot 10) showing Rufus's reaction to the statue also reveals a brick-paved street behind him. Presumably, the scene was filmed somewhere on or adjacent to Gay Street, perhaps near the 200 blocks of South Gay and State streets between Vine and Commerce, or on Jackson Avenue—all areas where the city had permitted Paramount to shoot. Other exterior shots of downtown would never be seen.

DELETED SCENES

In a scripted scene of dialogue (shots 7–8) immediately following the Chaplin film, Rufus complains to his father that the movie stills displayed outside the theater showed things that were not in the film they had just seen: "There wasn't any funny car in the show, Papa. And there wasn't any man with a mushtash like that." Ironically, this short scene is one of several that were filmed—as newspaper reports, publicity stills, and home movies verify—but ultimately deleted from the final cut of *All the Way Home*.

The script contains a few separate episodes (shots 62, 179–84, 261) of older neighborhood boys bullying Rufus. In the first such scene, the boys tease Rufus about his name, singing, "Uh-Rufus, Uh, Rastus, Uh-Johnson, Uh-Brown." However, the finished film only shows the aftermath of that encounter as Rufus runs from the boys through the alley and onto his back porch. After weeks of work, and even a trip to New York in early January for interior shots, the boys "later had a hard time picking themselves out in the background," as practically all their scenes had been cut from the film.[93]

Many local actors who spent long hours standing around in period costumes were similarly disappointed that they had labored in vain. Nelle Sams, marketing secretary at the *News-Sentinel,* was one of several extras used in shots at the L&N rail yard. Sams expected to glimpse herself in the background pulling a suitcase out of an old automobile and straightening the hat and tie of her movie children. For another setup, she was positioned near a "railroad timetable" with a "group of gossiping women." None of her shots were used. Antique car owner Charlie Coulter, upset by his missing footage, said, "After all the hard work we did to have the cars on hand, they didn't use a third of the scenes they filmed. We were disappointed by that."[94]

Knoxville Journal photographer "Brownie" Colquitt was recruited to play the blacksmith in scenes "shot at the blacksmith shop of Roy W. Oglesby on Union School Road, near Hammer Road, in the eastern part of Knox County." He was supposed to appear in cutaway shots with Mary Follet as his character tells her about the accident (shots 198–206). But filmmakers chose to discard the blacksmith footage and only show Mary's reaction to the tragic news. Colquitt's son, Ron, remembered being with his father on the set. "My dad was a blacksmith in this movie but his part got cut." Although his father never appeared onscreen, "he still worked on set doing a lot of jobs," Ron said. "He would take me down to watch them do scenes. Michael Kearney, myself, and one other kid would play during the times where he was needed to shoot." Ron was about a year younger than Kearney. "I remember playing with Rufus on the set, but the people looking over him would not let him play too rough. . . . I couldn't understand that at all."[95]

Around the second or third week of October, when the funeral procession was shot on Laurel Avenue, a cemetery scene (shot 324) featuring the same horse-drawn hearse and antique autos was filmed at New Gray Cemetery in northwest Knoxville. Presumably, New Gray was chosen for its hilled scenery as well as its proximity to the Fort Sanders neighborhood, less than three miles away; Greenwood Cemetery on Tazewell Pike, the actual site of Jay Agee's burial, was more than twice that distance. Photographs by Alan Shayne reveal that a scene of dialogue (shot 326) between Rufus and Walter Starr (played by John Henry Faulk) was also filmed at New Gray, as was a shot of a young girl in a light-colored hat and a dark, striped dress tied with a black bow. When Jean Simmons's young daughter, Tracy, visited her in town, newspapers reported that the girl was promptly given a small part in the film as an extra. "She was visiting me with my mother and thought it would be great fun to dress up in the period clothes we wear in 'All the Way Home' and play games with Mommie," Simmons said. "She looked adorable and Alex Segal the director decided to put her in the picture." None of the cemetery footage made it into the final film.[96]

Before the crew removed the twenty or so coffins from inside the Alcoholics Anonymous building (which depicted Ralph's mortuary in an earlier scene), Segal wanted to get shots of Jean Simmons "picking out a casket," an unscripted sequence. Rains had hit the city that day, November 8, and the entrance area was still wet. As the scene was being prepared, key grip Walter Engels fell while walking on the slick floor, dropping "a sound camera . . . through the front porch." Engels "suffered a severe hip injury" and was driven to the hospital at Fort Sanders. Reportedly, an AA representative called David Susskind at 3:00 a.m. to report damage to the porch and a section of wood flooring, which the crew had scuffed up by dragging a coffin across it. Susskind eventually paid the organization $300 to cover repairs.[97]

The next night, November 9, the dark cloud followed the crew out to East Knoxville, where they set up to film Jay Follet's final onscreen moments. The script required a shot of Robert Preston driving along a rural road (shots 171–72), which Hertzberg said was shot in the area near a ferry. But

Hertzberg did not recall any attempt to depict the crash itself: "My guess is that the ferry was the last scene in the sequence, right before the call" about the accident is made to Mary Follet.[98]

Filmmakers planned an elaborate depiction (shots 173–75) of Jay's Model T being ferried across the river. The scene as Agee described it was re-created on the French Broad River using the old Huffaker ferry, with "ferrymaster Joe Wrinkle" in a small part. On the same property sat the 1830 Huffaker home, which was one of the oldest frame houses left in Knox County until a controversial decision allowed its destruction in 2012. The ferry scene was one of the last on location, two days before the crew's November 11 departure to New York, but also the most difficult—and it did not end well.[99]

As assistant director Michael Hertzberg remembered, "We had to release water upstream to make the water higher." The effort required TVA's cooperation in spilling about forty million gallons from Douglas Dam. But the contrary weather added rain, fog, and wind to an already chilly November night. "We were all wearing winter parkas," said Hertzberg. The crew actually completed a shot of Robert Preston driving the Model T onto the ferry and it floating out onto the water. But Alex Segal wanted an additional shot from Jay's perspective as the car reached the opposite bank. So the ferry was pulled back to shore, and a camera loaded onto it. However, with the wind and added weight, the ferry's front end began dipping into the water. Said a production assistant, "Pumps did no good. About six technicians and everybody on board rushed to save the car. Somebody thoughtfully pulled the plugs to electricity outlets on shore or we'd have all been charged up—maybe electrocuted." The night shoot almost destroyed Campbell's car, along with a film camera. "It really looked like a scene from Dante's Inferno," said Hertzberg, who considers that night "the low point of the shoot" and remembered "Alex Segal punching the production manager, thinking it was his fault." But the night's only casualty was the ferry itself, which sank to the river bottom and was afterwards dubbed the "SS Huffaker." More than fifty years later, one Knoxvillian living near that area reported, "You can still see part of the ferry sticking out of the river when the water is down. Right in front of my house."[100]

The cable ferry—which Hertzberg said "looked like a flat barge with an outhouse on it"—had operated for at least a century and, according to the News-Sentinel, was past due for repairs after "a long history of dumping its passengers and also breaking loose from its cable, taking its cargo for a merry ride downstream." Surprisingly, Paramount announced a return to the Huffaker ferry site in late November to reshoot the scene using stand-ins.

Whether or not that actually happened is unknown, and no trace of the scene appears in the film.[101]

Following the ferry fiasco, the exhausted team returned to Gay Street. But instead of racing back to the Andrew Johnson Hotel, crewmembers remarkably voted to end the day on a constructive note and shoot a needed scene of dialogue (shots 7–8) down the street at the Bijou. "We shot outside of the movie theater the night the ferry sank," Hertzberg recalled. The Bijou's marquee had been made up to read "Gay Theatre." Although Agee likely visited a theater of that name, once located on the street's 400 block, it was a curious choice considering the script specified the name "Majestic," based on Agee's memory. That night's rain had left the sidewalks wet, and technicians found an alternate way to light the area without risk of electrocution. "We shot under the overhang there outside the theater," said Hertzberg. "It was dangerous shooting in the rain with arc lights, so I think they decided on a way to put up lights that wouldn't be dangerous getting wet."[102]

LAST SHOT IN KNOXVILLE

Returning to the vacant lot on Tenth Street on Sunday morning, November 11, Jean Simmons and Michael Kearney were perhaps the last of the out-of-town actors still in Knoxville. Robert Preston had left the day before, and Pat Hingle and Aline MacMahon had flown out on Friday. John Cullum had left almost two weeks earlier. Whether by chance or design, Alex Segal had saved the script's final scene for the last day in Knoxville.[103]

That morning's scene (shots 345-50) was a heavy one. Following an emotional breakdown, Rufus flees his house and runs down the street to the vacant lot, the place he most associates with his father. Mary finds her son there, and they exchange more than three full pages of dialogue. Simmons had battled congestion throughout the Knoxville shoot, and her visible breath vapors indicate how chilly the morning air was. As edited, the scene contains a few of the film's longest takes. In the last shot, mother and son walk up the hill toward Tenth Street as a Model T drives past.

Alex Segal, Boris Kaufman, Jean Simmons, and Michael Kearney departed Knoxville that evening. A small crew stayed for a day or two, long enough to return props and assure that everything was left in order.[104]

∞∞∞∞∞∞∞∞∞∞

Although shooting on location "was very overwhelming" for young Kearney, Knoxville's warm welcome put him at ease, he said later. "The local people

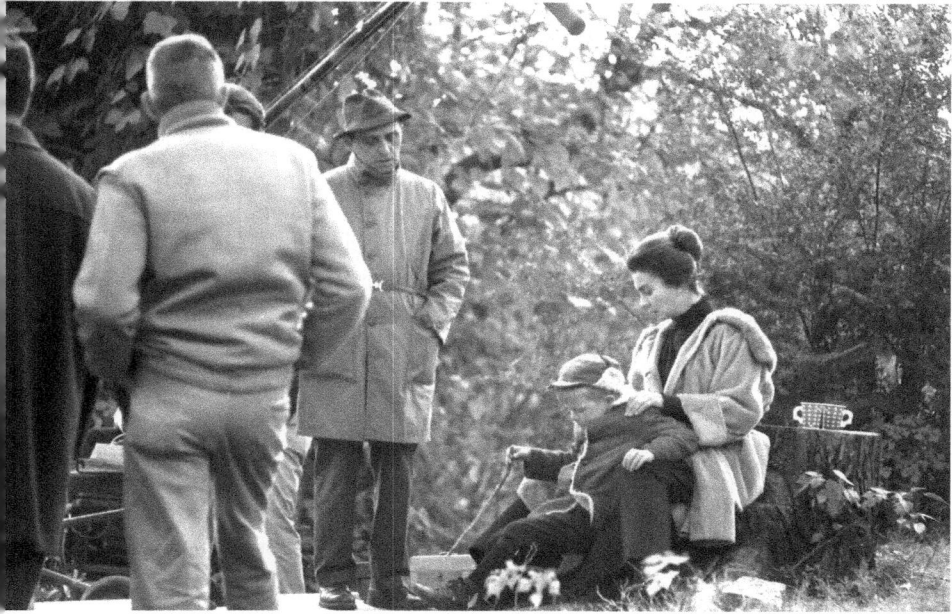

Alex Segal, Michael Kearney, and Jean Simmons at the vacant lot during
filming of the final location sequence, November 11, 1962. Photo by Alan Shayne.
Courtesy of Alan Shayne and Michael Kearney.

were very, very nice to us and went out of their way to make the whole experience great while I was there."[105]

Jack Grossberg said before leaving, "We will take away many fond memories of this city and its people . . . and we hope, as you do, the premiere of *All
the Way Home* can be held here." The City Council had recently requested
that Paramount debut the film in Knoxville. When the event was held there,
almost a year later, Susskind stood on the Tennessee Theatre stage and remarked: "I wouldn't say this unless I really felt it. . . . I've gone on many
locations for other pictures. I don't recall a happier time anywhere than in
Knoxville."[106]

Hertzberg had similar things to say about Knoxville's hospitality: "The
people were lovely and open, and they embraced us. And then of course a lot
of the young girls came down to watch the movie being made, which didn't
hurt." He also felt privileged to have worked with such a "creative team" of
technicians, including Richard Sylbert, Boris Kaufman, Dick Smith, and
Jack Grossberg, "one of my mentors." The director, he said, "was incredibly

talented, but peculiar." In addition to the uncontrollable factors—weather, excess noise, and illness—that filmmakers had to deal with, Hertzberg remembered many delays stemming from Alex Segal's "erratic" behavior on set: "Before we left New York and were rehearsing actors, he came up with the idea that he wanted to get the kids from Tennessee. Somebody told him that he couldn't use non-actors, that it would slow production. He insisted."[107]

Segal found an adaptable actor in Kearney but did not deal well with the inexperienced boys from Knoxville. "The kid that played Rufus was a professional. It was the other kids that were non-professionals; and if they flubbed a line, Segal would kick them in the ass with his boot. There were a lot of fights because of that," Hertzberg said. "If an electrician up on a ladder saw him kick a child, the crewmember would jump on his back. . . . It's the kind of behavior that in those days some very strict or peculiar directors got away with. But not with New York crews." Hertzberg reported that "the same craziness" continued after the move to the New York studio: "That's why it took so long. It was a battle to the end." However, Hertzberg said that Segal's outbursts were never directed at him personally, and admitted that "Alex was really good with actors, coming from the golden age of television."[108]

Kearney vaguely recalled a few "outbursts" on the set but said Segal "was very patient with me. Some directors were a little wacky, as many artists are." To be in show business, Kearney said, "you have to be a little nuts. Some of the most talented people are just out of their minds."[109]

NEW YORK STUDIO

At the end of location work, Jack Grossberg estimated that 40 percent of the film had been shot in Knoxville. But if all the locations identified above were indeed filmed in the vicinity, then the Knoxville scenes make up closer to half of the finished film.[110]

The remaining shots were completed in New York at "DuMont Studios on Sixth Avenue," said Hertzberg, "which was a television studio." Inside the "small" soundstage, a crew built the various rooms of the Follet house, including the central staircase, whose steps went up and turned a corner but then stopped, Kearney recalled: "The bedrooms were in another area," built on the same level as the other sets, "and they were raised, because they had the four steps up into the upstairs hallway" to create the illusion of being on the second floor. But despite the rooms being arranged in sections to facilitate camera movement, there is reason to believe that the house set was designed with particular attention to detail.[111]

As James Agee's old house was being dismantled, several newspapers stated that its furnishings, paneling, doors, and windows were shipped to New York and rebuilt into the Follet interior set. One even claimed that "the stairs [Agee] climbed as a little boy, the very doors he slammed and the fireplace where he sat to warm himself" all appeared in the film. But members of the crew have not been able to confirm these reports. As Albert Brenner, an assistant art director, said, "We used photos of the house as a reference, but no furnishings that I recall." Michael Hertzberg said he "might have heard the stories if they were true" and is "inclined to doubt them" since "it would be expensive and unnecessary to filming."[112]

However, there is evidence that the filmmakers faithfully duplicated the Agee house and, perhaps, actually used parts of it. Producer Jack Grossberg, interviewed a week and a half after demolition began on the house, said, "Even though the real Agee home would have been more difficult to work with—it was smaller than we would have liked—I still think we would have gone with it if we could have." A week earlier, another paper reported that David Susskind paid the property owners $400 for the Agee home, "delaying its demolition by five weeks" so he could salvage what he needed from the structure. As mentioned, newspaper articles throughout September 1962 reveal that the Agee house was taken apart fairly slowly.[113]

Newspapers reported that the Agee porch had been temporarily "grafted" to the rear of the Forest Avenue house. A rear porch was needed there because, like many homes in the neighborhood, the home at 1412 Forest had been split into apartments and the rear porch enclosed. It was used for two exterior scenes: one in which Rufus runs to the porch through the alley to escape the bullies (shot 63), and another in which Jay says goodbye to Mary before he leaves the house for the last time (shot 158). The back porch appears only briefly from afar before the scene cuts to a closer studio shot. A still frame shows the porch looking a bit shabby, as though it was indeed pulled off the front of another house. And the posts are very similar to those seen in photographs of the Agee house taken shortly before its demolition.[114]

While filmmakers mostly succeeded in maintaining continuity between studio sets in New York and the Knoxville exteriors, one scene's revealing error provides more evidence that the Follet interior was a reconstruction of 1505 Highland. As Mary walks out onto the front porch of 1412 Forest with Hannah (shot 59), for a few seconds one can glimpse, through the screen door, the home's actual staircase, which runs up the left side of its central hallway. This is significant, since interior scenes had already shown a right-side staircase in the hall. As the fronts of 1412 Forest and 1505 Highland (both gable-front-and-wing designs) were rough mirror images of each other, one would expect their interior layouts to mirror each other as well. Instead, designers intentionally matched 1505's layout when they created the set. And they would have had a special reason to do this if indeed they reassembled paneling and other pieces from the actual Agee home—pieces that would not have fit together in a mirrored layout. Despite necessary modifications (for example, an arched, rather than rectangular, front transom window to match 1412's), the set's design suggests that producers went to great lengths to faithfully depict Agee's story.

When asked about the house, Michael Kearney said, "I remember they built an exact duplicate in New York. I was amazed, as a kid, to walk into the studio and there it was, front porch and everything. It was incredible. For me it was like going back in time."[115]

∞∞∞∞∞∞∞∞∞

If Knoxville location scenes make up almost half of the film, scenes on the Follet interior set make up the other half. Alan Shayne remembered that Jean Simmons needed his help preparing for one particular scene—not for its emotional content, but for a simple procedure she had to complete while speaking her lines: "She had a scene (later cut from the picture) in which she had to make a bed for her husband, who she thought was still alive." The scene appears as shots 216–18 in the script, just after Mary Follet receives the fateful phone call. "Having been a movie star since she was sixteen, Jean had never made a bed in her life, so I taught her how to make one, hospital corners and all," Shayne said.[116]

The actress's "last scene after four months of shooting" was described as a "rather tearful" one between young Michael and her. Kearney recalled Alex Segal preparing him for those emotional scenes. "There was so much grief later in the film, and at that point I had not experienced anything like that in my life as a seven-year-old kid. But he was trying to think of things that would make me sad," Kearney said. "He would say to me, 'Michael, do you have a dog?' 'Yeah, we have a dog.' 'What if your dog died?' You know, something like that, trying to associate things that would make me sad. He helped me a lot with that." But when tears failed to flow, Segal turned to other methods. "I remember them having this little plastic tube with something like Vicks VapoRub in there, and they'd blow it into our eyes to make them tear up, you know. It's probably not allowed any more," Kearney said. "It would probably be considered cruel today. But I remember Jean Simmons was using it, and I was using it. Then they also had glycerin drops they'd put on our faces to have the tears run down."[117]

Kearney called Simmons and Preston "sweethearts" because of their kindness to him during the production: "It must have been difficult for them to work with a seven-year-old at the time, because I was just being a kid, you know. But they were great people. Robert Preston really made me feel like he was my dad, not only on the set, but also off the set. He was a really warm, caring person, and spent time with me and talked to me even after the camera stopped."[118]

PREMIERE

The premiere of *All the Way Home*—and the first regional Agee celebration—came during Knoxville's frantic effort to modernize itself. Fifteen years after John Gunther infamously snubbed it as America's "ugliest city," Knoxville was still a target for bad press, as in January 1961, when Philip Hamburger wrote in the *New Yorker*, "There is very little to be said for downtown Knoxville. Even third-generation and fourth-generation Knoxvillians, a prideful people, tend to shudder when walking through downtown." Attempting to revamp its image, Knoxville held a successful first Dogwood Arts Festival that April. And over the next year, city government pushed forward a series of redevelopment initiatives: a new Civic Auditorium was opened; Fountain City was annexed; liquor was legalized; the old market house was demolished and the square remodeled as Market Mall; Neyland Stadium, UT Hospital, and McGhee-Tyson Airport were expanded; and construction started on a new swath of streets called the Downtown Loop. A week after Paramount wrapped location shooting in Knoxville, Mayor John Duncan "spoke before a jury at the National Conference on Government in Washington," citing these "progressive movements" as examples of why Knoxville should be designated an "All-America City." Knoxville and ten other cities received the distinction late the following March, out of seventy cities that applied that year.[119]

At the same time, many Knoxvillians saw irony in the title "All-America" being bestowed on a city where most downtown businesses still barred admittance to minorities. Although protests and sit-ins in 1960 had opened to blacks several lunch counters and even the University of Tennessee, entertainment venues remained segregated into 1963. That spring, as the Tennessee Theatre was being considered for the premiere of *All the Way Home*, students mostly from Knoxville College picketed outside the Bijou and the Tennessee. Police arrested more than fifty students, but the demonstrations led those theaters to desegregate by summer. By the time *All the Way Home* screened in Knoxville, whites and blacks could view the film together and be reminded, as Jay Follet advises his son Rufus, "not to use a certain word in referring to people of another race."[120]

On September 12, 1963, officials—including Knoxville mayor John Duncan, Paramount executive Bernard Serlin, Tennessee Theatre manager W. J. Coury, Chamber representative Bob Rule, and Civic Auditorium's Fred McCallum—announced that the film would indeed debut at the Tennessee that fall. Ten years earlier, the venue had hosted the gala opening of *So This is Love*—based on the life of opera star and East Tennessee native Grace Moore—with stars Kathryn Grayson and Merv Griffin in attendance. Now Knoxville anticipated another moment of recognition, another brush with fame. When tickets went on sale the Monday before the premiere, all two thousand available seats sold out in just a few hours.[121]

Downtown hummed with activity on the eve of the event, October 16. While city workers temporarily replaced downtown's "Gay St." signs with new ones reading "Agee St.," crews at the Tennessee were busy hanging curtains and large posters, and even recarpeting the auditorium's aisles. Everything had to be perfect, as NBC was recording the event for its national TV and radio shows *Today* and *Monitor*.[122]

At 6:30 that evening, celebrities arrived at McGhee-Tyson Airport. Recreating the scene from a year earlier, a crowd of fans and press cheered as the stars stepped off the plane but were probably surprised that Preston and Kearney were the only two actors who returned to Knoxville. Jean Simmons remained in England. Aline MacMahon was expected in Hollywood the next day and sent an apology that she would miss the premiere. David Susskind would arrive the next day in time for the premiere. Preston's wife Catherine accompanied him. Kearney arrived with his mother, Irene, his cousin John Spencer, and his manager Betty Geffen.[123]

Fresh Hawaiian leis were placed around the necks of Kearney and Preston, who picked up the boy and said, "Mike, you feel like you've gained forty pounds since the last time I lifted you." Asked about his young co-star's stardom, Preston said, "This hasn't gotten to Mike yet. He was unspoiled when we got him and it was over so fast he was unspoiled when we finished." Back at the Andrew Johnson Hotel, Preston and his wife roomed on the ninth floor, while Kearney and his mother and cousin stayed on the twelfth. Joking with Preston, Michael asked, "If we're such big stars, why aren't we on the seventeenth floor?"[124]

After next morning's breakfast, a caravan of buses took the party of dignitaries on a tour of filming locations, ending in Cades Cove, where a picnic lunch was served. During a short ceremony there, Robert Preston, on Paramount's behalf, presented Mayor Duncan with a cornerstone plaque engraved with the words "JAMES AGEE MEMORIAL MOTION PICTURE STUDIO," the proposed sound-recording facility that the city hoped would attract other Hollywood productions.[125]

That evening, after cocktails and dinner at the hotel, Preston, Kearney, and Susskind—who had arrived that afternoon—were driven in antique cars down the temporarily renamed "Agee Street." A high school band led the procession to the Tennessee Theatre, where UT band members sounded

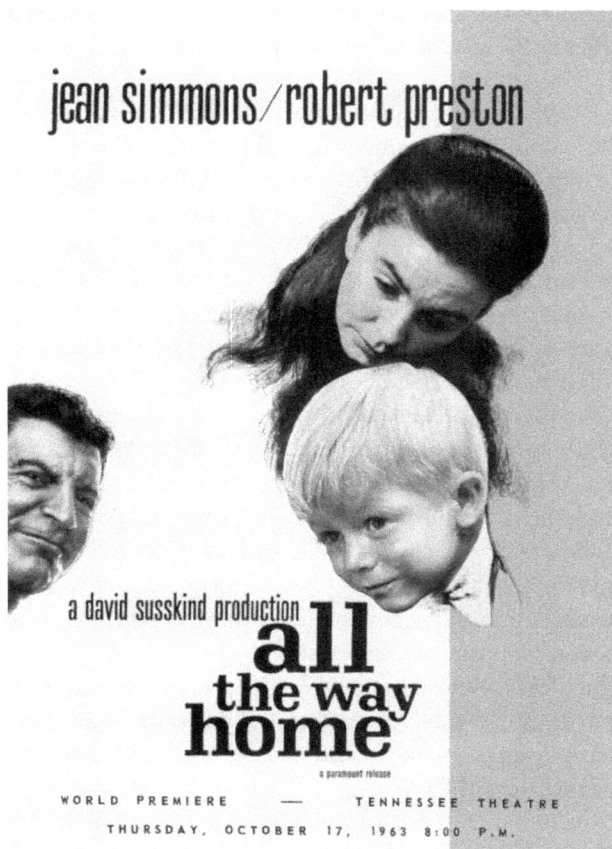

jean simmons / robert preston

a david susskind production
**all
the way
home**

a paramount release

WORLD PREMIERE   —   TENNESSEE THEATRE

THURSDAY, OCTOBER 17, 1963 8:00 P.M.

Program cover from the premiere of *All the Way Home*,
October 17, 1963. Wallace W. Baumann Collection, McClung
Historical Collection, Knox County Library.

the motorcade's arrival. The crowds applauded as each of the stars exited their vehicles. A Morristown teenager who had watched part of the filming a year earlier was there with his family that night. "My whole family went down to watch the parade of stars in the antique cars drive up Gay Street," said Evan McKinley. "We were standing right outside the theater, and I'll never forget Mr. Preston looking down at me, waving, and saying, 'Hi, son!'" Another teen remembered getting his "picture in the paper standing outside the Tennessee Theatre waiting for the stars to arrive in old cars. It was a fun night for a boy of fifteen, and one I will always remember," said Steve Eldridge.[126]

Sometime that night, amidst the mob of star-struck Knoxvillians, one girl was heard shouting, "I've got it, I've got it!" She had picked up the butt of Robert Preston's cigarette off the floor and, grasping it, said, "I'll keep it forever."[127]

At 8:00, Miller's department store executive Byrl Logan opened the ceremony by welcoming UT president Andy Holt to the Tennessee stage. Holt emceed the event, giving some background of the filming before turning over the microphone to the honored guests. David Susskind said he had never been happier on location. Robert Preston said, "This is like coming home . . . and since I never had a home, I'll settle for Knoxville being mine." Apparently, Kearney was overwhelmed by the attention: "I froze. I didn't know what to say." Although the paper reported him crying that night, he did not recall it later. "I remember Robert Preston picked me up behind the podium in the theater, because obviously I wasn't tall enough to reach the mike. And he was whispering things for me to say, and I couldn't hear him," Kearney said. "And I would say, 'What'd you say?' and that got a laugh."[128]

At the end of the ceremony, Susskind, Preston, and young Michael were declared "honorary citizens of Knoxville and honorary colonels in the state." Without missing a beat, Preston replied, "This makes me a double colonel and that means I outrank the governor." Andy Holt retorted, "Now that you are citizens, you can start paying taxes."[129]

Before the film was shown, Preston's wife was introduced from her chair. A local reporter noted that Kearney's mother, Irene, "took her bow from the stage where for a moment she did the Twist with Mr. Preston." Kearney said she was thrilled: "The way they treated my mother, she just had a blast. We were so overwhelmed. We were just small town people from New Jersey thrown in the middle of it. . . . I'd never been through anything like that before." Reflecting on that night more than fifty years later, Kearney considered it an example of the way things were done in "old Hollywood."[130]

For Andy Holt, the premiere even surpassed the pomp and circumstance of the All-America event six months prior. "I've never seen anything like this," he said. After the screening, the festivities continued late into the night, with a Cherokee Country Club reception.[131]

By early November, "nearly 30,000" people had viewed the film at the Tennessee Theatre, making it "the best-attended movie we have shown so far this year," said manager Coury. The film had a successful run in Knoxville theaters and was still playing on one local screen into the first week of January 1965, months after it had closed in most cities.[132]

∞∞∞∞∞∞∞∞∞∞

Reviews were mixed. Critics writing for *New York Times* and *Los Angeles Times* thought that, despite some good performances, the screen translation left out the poetry of Agee's novel, turning a remarkable story into a rather unexceptional film. On the other hand, *Variety* called it "a fine work" that was both "sensitive" and "skillfully filmed." David Susskind apparently considered *All the Way Home* "a monumental flop." Poor timing seemed to be the film's biggest fault. For one, it was overshadowed that year by the earlier release of another black and white movie based on the childhood of a Pulitzer Prize–winning southern writer. At the 1963 Academy Awards, *To Kill a Mockingbird* won three Oscars out of its eight nominations. Comparisons were hard to avoid, as both films took "the perspective of a child's world, touched and transformed by a childhood tragedy." *Mockingbird* contained a direct link to *All the Way Home:* young John Megna played Dill after originating the role of Rufus Follet on Broadway. Knoxvillians may have also noted that both films featured a Carousel Theatre alumnus—John Cullum and *Mockingbird*'s Collin Wilcox had acted together at least once on the UT stage. But as a film *Mockingbird* lacked one kind of authenticity: its fictional town of Maycomb was created on a Hollywood back lot, nowhere near Harper Lee's hometown of Monroeville, Alabama.[133]

And just as the threat of the Cuban Missile Crisis cast gloom over the film's production in Knoxville, so another major news event clouded the nationwide release of *All the Way Home.* President John F. Kennedy had been invited to Knoxville for the October 1963 premiere. Although he of course declined, as did several other political dignitaries, Kennedy reportedly was interested in the film's "cultural aspects." He may never have had a chance to see it. The tragedy that befell him, thirty-six days after the premiere, also doomed the film's theatrical run from the start, as Jean Simmons remembered: "We opened the weekend after President Kennedy was killed. And nobody had the heart to see James Agee's little story about the death of a father figure. It wouldn't have made much money anyway. Today they'd do it for PBS or something."[134]

TELEVISION

Simmons was right: television has been the chosen medium for all subsequent screen adaptations of Agee's novel—including the most recent one for PBS. In 1971 Hallmark Hall of Fame presented the play, reworked by Mosel and starring Joanne Woodward and Richard Kiley as the parents. Filmed at CFTO Studio in Toronto, Hallmark's sets were slightly more elaborate than those of the stage play, most noticeably in the dimensional interior of the Follet house; but the characters were still obviously stuck in a studio. Besides the fact that it reunited David Susskind, Alan Shayne, and Pat Hingle from the 1963 film, the production contained another notable connection. "I knew Jim Agee," said Woodward. "He was one of my heroes when I started out in television." In one of her earliest screen roles, Woodward had played Ann Rutledge in Agee's *Mr. Lincoln* miniseries. "All of us in that play worshipped Jim."[135]

Almost exactly ten years later, in December 1981, "NBC Live Theater" aired Tad Mosel's play in real time from the University of Southern California's Bing Theater, with William Hurt and Sally Field as Jay and Mary Follet. The script had been abridged to fit a two-hour TV slot, but it was otherwise unaltered. During the broadcast, viewers at home saw things they would have observed at a live play: theatergoers entering the building, the curtain rising on the opening scene, the actors moving and speaking from the stage and taking their bows at the end. The program contained fine performances but was a televised play rather than a true screen adaptation.[136]

In 2002 *Masterpiece Theatre* presented a new version of the novel for PBS, scripted by Robert W. Lenski. Auditions for boys aged seven to twelve were held at Knoxville's Bijou Theatre in June 2000, and some locals assumed that producers had chosen to film Agee's story in town. ALT Films, based in Los Angeles, had indeed considered Knoxville, as well as Topeka, Kansas, as possible filming locations. After ruling out the Sunflower State, the production company's cofounder, Marian Rees, felt that Knoxville's downtown lacked the period look of 1915, and that sufficient crew and production services were not available nearby. "But we wanted to come to Tennessee because that's where Agee was," Rees said. "We wanted Tennessee to feel a part of this film. *A Death in the Family* is so widely renowned as a piece of literature, that we were very careful about where we wanted to film it." Rejecting Knoxville, ALT Films instead began shooting in the Nashville area that August. The city's Shelby Park provided the quiet spot where Jay and Rufus Follet sit on the way home from the movies. And its historic Richland and Belmont districts represented the Fort Sanders neighborhood of Agee's youth (Lynch home exteriors were shot at 3712 Richland Avenue; Follet home exteriors at 2807 Oakland Avenue). The Glenn Memorial Women's Club in Springfield, about twenty-five miles north of Nashville, served as the interior of the Joel Lynch home. In Franklin, about seventeen miles south of Nashville, Main Street stood in for Knoxville's Gay Street, the town's old railroad depot for Joel's grain and feed business, and the Toussaint L'Ouverture Cemetery for the final resting place of Jay Follet. In Nolensville, roughly twelve miles east of Franklin, an abandoned farmhouse (burned by firefighters shortly after filming) portrayed the farm of Jay's parents. And in Carthage, about fifty miles east of Nashville, an old truss bridge over the Caney Fork River was used in one of the film's rural driving scenes.[137]

Although the film—which starred Annabeth Gish as Mary, John Slattery as Jay, and James Cromwell as Joel—highlighted some of Middle Tennessee's most picturesque neighborhoods, viewers familiar with the Knoxville locations Agee described had a difficult time suspending disbelief. One Knoxville critic thought downtown Franklin particularly miscast. "Franklin doesn't look anything like Knoxville at any time in this city's history," said Jack Neely. "Franklin was a small, clean, agrarian community. Its historic downtown buildings are all two or three stories tall." Consequently, wide views of the city were avoided, and in all downtown shots the camera never strayed from sidewalks and storefronts. Neely noted by contrast that Knoxville's "Gay Street, especially north of Church, is a well-preserved commercial district of the late 19th and early 20th century architecture," including many buildings with five or more stories. Residential exteriors also disappointed. Audiences expecting "gracefully fretted wood houses," like the type found in Agee's old neighborhood and other parts of Knoxville, saw mostly brick foursquares and bungalows, built ten to twenty years later. Despite the film being produced in Agee's home state, this lack of authenticity overshadowed the film's best moments. As Neely quipped, "I don't understand why *Masterpiece Theatre*, having come this far, didn't come all the way home, so to speak."[138]

RUFUS RETURNS

In the years following the 1963 Knoxville premiere, Michael Kearney occasionally ran into his *All the Way Home* costars. "Georgia Simmons played my grandmother in the film. I worked with her in a couple other things over the years," he said. They both appeared in *The Thanksgiving Visitor*, with Kearney portraying a young Truman Capote. Once Kearney and his mother saw Robert Preston backstage after a Broadway performance in *Ben Franklin in Paris*. When Kearney saw Preston's head, shaved bald for the leading role, he wondered, "Wow, what happened?" And years later, walking along a New York sidewalk, Kearney spotted Lylah Tiffany, the woman whose old-age makeup had once frightened him. When he approached her and told her his name, she did not know who he was until he said, "I'm Rufus."[139]

Kearney returned to Knoxville a couple of times since the premiere. "My wife and I used to do a lot of road trips, just jump in the car and go places. We were on our way down to New Orleans one year and went through Knoxville," he said. They wanted to track down some of the places used in

Michael Kearney returned to Knoxville in September 2015 when *All the Way Home* was screened at the East Tennessee History Center. Here he stands beside a 1916 Model T that was used in the film and owned by Charlie Coulter during the production. The vehicle later belonged to Maryville resident Randy Moats, who died in 2017. Photo by the author. Courtesy of Michael Kearney.

the film, but it had been a couple of decades. "We actually went to the local library and looked up some of the old newspapers. It took me awhile to remember exactly when I was there." After finding some useful articles from 1962, Kearney and his wife drove out to some of the locations. "We found the house we used, which at that time was a frat house. It was an interesting place to revisit," he said. "But we took a ride to Cades Cove and actually found the barn and the area where we did the scenes with Great-Grandma. It was a lot of fun and really brought back some good memories."[140]

As Knoxville celebrated the centennial of James Agee's "Summer of 1915," the Knox County Library screened *All the Way Home* at the East Tennessee History Center early that September. Kearney attended the event with his sister, Eileen, and shared his memories of the production before an appreciative audience. That weekend, he enjoyed seeing the city again and recognizing places he had seen fifty-three years earlier: Gay Street, the Tennessee Theatre, Market Square, the Fort Sanders neighborhood. He toured the house at 1511 Laurel, where he had filmed the funeral scene and first encountered an actual coffin. The grand residence sits immediately west of James Agee Park.

A handful of other film locations remain in Knoxville, including the L&N Station at the corner of Western and Henley. After passenger service ended in 1968, the building stood empty for many years before being occupied by a series of restaurants. In the late 1970s the rail yard was removed in preparation for the 1982 World's Fair. The station building now serves Knoxville as the L&N STEM Academy.

Thanks to preservation efforts in the mid-1970s, the Bijou Theatre was spared its planned demolition and is again a popular live entertainment venue, which since vaudeville days has presented some of the biggest names in show business: the Marx Brothers, John Barrymore, Tallulah Bankhead, and Montgomery Clift, among scores of others. The theater's front section— the former Lamar House, built in 1816 and used as a hotel for more than 150 years—is downtown's oldest commercial building.[141]

Although it did not appear in the film, the Andrew Johnson Hotel housed the production company during the Knoxville shoot and added the stars' names to a long list of notable guests—including Hank Williams Sr., Duke Ellington, Sergei Rachmaninoff, and Amelia Earhart—who had lodged at the hotel since its December 1929 opening. It remained Knoxville's tallest building throughout its half century in business. In 1980, just months after hotel operations ceased, the building was added to the National Register of Historic Places. It was used for various purposes before becoming the headquarters of Knox County Schools. In 2017 the county announced plans to redevelop the building as a commercial property.[142]

Other Knoxville film sites have changed significantly since 1962, with houses, bridges, and streets entirely gone. The house at 1412 Forest Avenue stood in for the Agee home once more—in *Agee*, a 1979 documentary film by Ross Spears—before being torn down in late 1981. As with the original Agee home, apartments now occupy the site. But a few of the street's existing homes are shown in the film, including 1316 Forest (in the lawn-watering scene) and those immediately opposite where 1412 sat. The alley between Forest and Highland also appears onscreen, along with the north side of an old clapboard garage that still stands behind the house at 1415 Highland.[143]

The large corner mansion at 1203 Laurel, used for the Lynch home exterior, was demolished after being "heavily damaged by fire" in 1978. But the adjacent home, still standing at 1213 Laurel, is briefly visible in a tracking shot along the street.[144]

Western Avenue Viaduct was completely replaced with a new, wider version in 1992 as part of the reconfigured freeway onramp. The original viaduct's identification plaques were saved and donated to the East Tennessee Historical Society.

Although Tenth Street no longer exists, the vacant lot was located roughly where today's World's Fair Park Drive intersects Eleventh Street.

∞∞∞∞∞∞∞∞

All the Way Home and its gala premiere established James Agee's local and regional importance in a way that the book on its own could not. In order for Knoxville, the modernized yet still reluctant literary capital of Tennessee, to realize how much its native son was worth, it had to be star-struck, convinced by the alluring presence of Robert Preston and Jean Simmons. And as Hollywood dressed it up in period clothes and flooded it with bright lights, Knoxville looked backwards half a century at its former self—and began to fully appreciate Agee's story.

Now more than half a century after its release, the 1963 film can again be viewed widely. For decades after its theatrical run, it could only be seen in bootleg videos and occasional television airings. Paramount never released the film commercially on VHS or DVD, but since 2012 has made it available as a streaming video through websites like YouTube and Amazon. To date, it remains the most visually authentic screen adaptation of James Agee's novel.

List of Abbreviations

ADITF	*A Death in the Family*
ADITF-R	*A Death in the Family: A Restoration of the Author's Text*
ATWH	*All the Way Home*, shooting script
ETHC	East Tennessee History Center
FWSJ	*Film Writing and Selected Journalism*
JAR	*James Agee Rediscovered*
KG	*Kalamazoo Gazette*
KHS	Knoxville High School
KJ	*Knoxville Journal*
KJT	*Knoxville Journal and Tribune*
KM	*Knoxville Mercury*
KN	*Knoxville News*
KNS	*Knoxville News-Sentinel*
KS	*Knoxville Sentinel*
Letters	*Letters of James Agee to Father Flye*
LP	*LaFollette Press*
LUNPFM	*Let Us Now Praise Famous Men*
MHC	McClung Historical Collection, Knox County Public Library
MP	*Metro Pulse*
MTFCA	Model T Ford Club of America website (http://www.mtfca.com/)
PEM	*Phillips Exeter Monthly*
Poems	*Collected Poems of James Agee*
Prose	*Collected Short Prose of James Agee*
SLD	*Selected Literary Documents*
TMW	*The Morning Watch*

TN   University of Tennessee, Knoxville,
            Special Collections Library
TX   University of Texas, Austin, Harry Ransom
            Humanities Research Center
VU   Vanderbilt University, Jean and Alexander Heard Library,
            Special Collections

Note: Except for newspaper articles and a few other sources, shortened citations have been used throughout the notes; see bibliography for full information. Multiple citations within a note generally follow the order of the text material to which they pertain. Parenthetical references to the main text are sometimes used to aid source identification.

Notes

Preface

1. Hugh Tyler to Helen [Bliss?], Oct. 20, 1948, Hugh Tyler Collection, MHC. For Laura Wright letters, see TN, James Agee and James Agee Trust Collection, circa 1920–2003, MS.2730, box 2 (folder 18), box 3 (folder 2), and box 8 (folder 2). First citations of a collection, except those from MHC, will appear in this format: [library abbreviation (see list above)], [collection], [collection number, if used], [box] [folder], [page(s), if available]. "Hereafter" abbreviations will be noted where applicable.

2. For an example of childhood names, Father Flye interviewed Laura around December 1962 or later, and throughout their conversation Rufus was the only name she used for her son. Similarly, Edwina Dakin Williams, mother of author Tennessee Williams, published a memoir, *Remember Me to Tom,* in which she primarily referred to her son as Tom rather than use his professional name.

3. Agee, *Letters,* 17–133, 170–71.

4. For an example of Agee's first-person recollections, see the detailed notes he wrote concerning the day of his father's funeral, quoted at length in chapter 3 of this volume. *A Death in the Family* notes and fragments, TX, James Agee Collection, 1928–1969, box 5, folder 1, 1–3

5. Agee, movie review, *the Nation,* November 9, 1946, reprinted in *FWSJ,* 265.

Introduction

1. Neely, "Excavating Knoxville Literature," 185, 188–92, 194–96, 199–200, 203.

2. Ibid., 184; Adamson, "The Communications Media," 273; Patton, "Transportation Development," 178–81, 185–86.

3. The first train into Knoxville arrived on June 22, 1855 (Rothrock, *French-Broad Holston Country,* 106). Other sources report "first" arrivals at different times, certainly because two separate railroad lines were inaugurated within three years of each other. The East Tennessee & Georgia Railroad tracks were completed in Knoxville in 1855, and tracks of the East Tennessee & Virginia were completed from Bristol to Knoxville in 1858 (Rule, *Standard History of Knoxville, Tennessee,* 277, 282). A 1922 newspaper article describes the arrival of 1858, "three years before the North and South decided to fight" ("When the First Railroad Train Came to Knoxville," *KN,* Aug. 17, 1922). Sources dating the first train arrival to July 4, 1853, and the building that year of the city's first railroad repair shop, are difficult to reconcile with other information ("Came to Knoxville in Stage Coach; Saw First Railroad Train Arrive," *KN,* Feb. 27, 1925, 12;

"Building of the First Railroad Repair Shops in Knoxville," *KJ*, Aug. 4, 1895). Adding to the confusion is Elisa Buffat's claim to have witnessed "the first train that arrived in Knoxville . . . on the fourth of July 1854" ("Memoirs and Diary of Elisa Buffat [Nee] Bolli," in "Buffat–Bolli Reminiscences," Knox County Library, 21).

4. See MacArthur, "Knoxville's History," 29–45.

5. Wheeler, "James Agee's Knoxville," 50–51; Jack Neely, "A Fair to Remember: Knoxville's National Conservation Exposition of 1913," *MP*, Nov. 11, 2009.

6. Wheeler, "James Agee's Knoxville," 51; Jack Neely, "How the Gritty Knoxville of 1915 Compares to James Agee's Idyllic Memoir," *KM*, June 24, 2015. Neely quotes James Herman Robinson's memoir, *Road Without Turning*.

7. Agee, *ADITF-R*, 54–55, 66–67, 97; Ashdown, "From Almost as Early as I Can Remember," 108; Wheeler, "James Agee's Knoxville," 58; Jack Neely, "The Other World War," *MP*, May 27, 2004; Neely, "1919," in *Knoxville's Secret History*, 107. For more on the race riot, see discussion in ch. 4 of this volume.

8. "Perspective of Knoxville's History During Year Closing," *KS*, Dec. 25, 1913, 12; Allen, ch. 1, *Knoxville, Tennessee*, n.p; Neely, "How the Gritty Knoxville Compares."

9. James Agee, "TVA: Work in the Valley," *Fortune*, May 1935, rpt. in *Complete Journalism*, ed. Ashdown, 199. Two years later, Agee wrote in detail about smoke and how its particles affect industrial cities; see Agee, "Smoke," *Fortune*, June 1937, rpt. in *Complete Journalism*, 286–92.

10. Jack Neely, "Gay Street Cinema: The Sequel," *MP*, April 15, 2004; "Bijou Theater in New Role," *KJT*, June 16, 1915, 8; "Team History (1896–Present)," *Smokiesbaseball .com*, http://www.milb.com/.

11. Miller McDonald, "History of Jacksborough," *Campbell County TNGenWeb*, http://www.tngenweb.org/.

12. Greg Miller, "LaFollette, Tennessee: A City of Dreams," *City of LaFollette*, http://www.lafollettetn.gov/.

13. In June 1906 Frank Agee partnered with two local men to start the Roach Creek Coal & Timber Company ("Southern Coal and Coke Notes," *Black Diamond* 36 [June 30, 1906]: 37). John Henry Agee, whose senior thesis at the University of Tennessee was titled "The Iron Ores of Tennessee," received a mining engineering degree in 1911. The editors of that year's UT yearbook introduced John Agee, the graduate and ROTC member, in this playfully hyperbolic paragraph: "Who would have thought that the coal and iron lands of LaFollette would have sent us this graceful figure, this military hero, this bright and shining torch of knowledge. Of a truth the wag of old, who said that no good thing could come out of Nazareth, did lie most egregiously, and likewise is the modern egotist most grievously mistaken when he prophesies that off the sides of the Cumberlands there cometh no son of Apollo. Never did Venus feel for Adonis half the love which he daily awakens in the fluttering bosoms of Knoxville maidens" (*The Volunteer 1911*, UT yearbook, n.p.).

14. See "Eagle Bluff Section," *Cumberland Trail Conference*, http://cumberlandtrail .org/maps-and-guides/trail-segments/cumberland-mountain/eagle-bluff-section/.

15. See Summerlin, *Longstreet Highroad Guide*, 19.

16. According to biographer Laurence Bergreen, Agee and Alma Mailman "swung through Nashville" on the way to Louisville while on a road trip in 1937 (*James Agee: A Life*, 200). One of Agee's only written references to Nashville is found in a journal entry from around that time. Describing a magazine photograph of a Kentucky highway crime scene, he wrote, "If you drove from Nashville to Louisville on a grayly sunlit day you would see just this in about half your mileage" ([J 4.4: Journal Entry: "Two magazines"], in *JAR*, 85). He mentioned the Shiloh battlefield in southwest Tennessee in his 1933 article about the Tennessee Valley Authority, and specified Memphis as a location in *Bloodline*, a film treatment he wrote in 1951 (see ch. 5 of this volume).

Chapter 1

1. Mark 15:21; 2 Samuel 23:11.

2. James Agee, Autobiographical writing ["I was born"], n.d., TN MS.2730, 4.1 (hereafter TN 4.1); "Huguenot History," *Huguenot Society of America*, http:// huguenotsocietyofamerica.org; P. M. Agee, *Record of the Agee Family*, 6–8, 276, 290–92.

3. James Agee, "Now as Awareness," in *Prose*, 127; Agee, *ADITF-R*, 54–55; Davis, "Agee Story—Part Two," 15.

4. Agee, "Now as Awareness," *Prose*, 126; Agee, [N 25: Fragment: "O my ancestral land"], *JAR*, 326–27 (see notes on 326 for descriptions of Wat Tyler, etc.).

5. Brigham, *Tyler Genealogy*, 217, 414.

6. *Records of the Church of Christ in Granville, Ohio*, book 2, book privately held by First Presbyterian Church of Granville; online database, *Granville Historical Society*, https://www.granvillehistory.org/; Bushnell, *History of Granville*, 322.

7. *Records of the Church of Christ in Granville;* Bushnell, *History of Granville*, 322; Brigham, *Tyler Genealogy*, 414; *Records of the Church of Christ in Granville.*

8. "House of Representatives," *Ohio Statesman*, Jan. 24, 1843, 3; "List of Acts," *Ohio Statesman*, Mar. 13, 1843, 2–3.

9. French, *Historical and Statistical Gazetteer*, 232-40; 1850 U.S. Census, Clinton County, N.Y., population schedule, Ausable, p. 202 (stamped), dwelling 139, family 141, Potter (digital image, *Ancestry.com*); Brigham, *Tyler Genealogy*, 414, 416; Franklin County, Tenn., Death certificate no. 31695 (1929), Jessie Potter Tyler (digital image, *Ancestry.com*). There is disagreement between these last two sources about Jessie's birth year (1855 or 1856) and birthplace (Au Sable Forks or Black Brook, located roughly four miles from each other). For Joel Tyler's birth, see Brigham, *Tyler Genealogy*, 217, 414.

10. 1870 U.S. Census, Will County, Ill., population schedule, Wilmington, p. 20, dwelling 166, family 171, Tyler (digital image, *Ancestry.com*); Durant, *History of Kalamazoo County*, 259.

11. 1870 U.S. Census, population data. The *Michigan State Gazetteer and Business Directory*, 532, stated that Kalamazoo was "the largest incorporated village in the United States" that year. For other details, see Chas. Shober & Co, *Kalamazoo, Michigan,* Map (Madison, WI: J. J. Stoner, 1874), Ruger Map Collection, no. 90, Library of Congress Geography and Map Division, http://hdl.loc.gov; Kalamazoo village directory, 1873, http://kalamazoo

genealogy.org/; "Honorary Members," *KG*, Aug. 10, 1876, 4; "Village Trustees," *KG*, Jan. 6, 1880, 4; National Register of Historic Places Inventory—Nomination Form, Stuart Area Historic District, Kalamazoo, Kalamazoo County, Mich. (National Register no. 83000874).

12. "Joel C. Tyler," *KG*, Mar. 2, 1926, 2; "Personal," *KG*, Sept. 20, 1876, 4; Stephanie Grauman Wolf, "Centennial Exhibition (1876)," *Encyclopedia of Greater Philadelphia*, http://www.philadelphiaencyclopedia.org; *Historical Catalogue . . . Kalamazoo College*, 82.

13. Mike Connell, "Thomas Edison Fell Out of Love with Port Huron," *Port Huron Times Herald*, Nov. 6, 2011; Connell, "Thomas Edison Grew Up in Grand Home," *Port Huron Times Herald*, Nov. 13, 2011; "Member of Pioneer Pt. Huron Family Expires in Maine," *Port Huron Times Herald*, Nov. 7, 1931.

14. "Member of Pioneer Pt. Huron Family Expires"; Connell, "Thomas Edison Grew Up." The Farrand-Edison house (sometimes called the Jenkins house after its original owner) burned in 1870, leaving only the cellar intact. Between 1976 and 1994, archaeologists unearthed Edison artifacts there before a condominium development (Edison Shores) ended the excavations. However, Port Huron protected the footprint of the house; the cellar is buried in a gap between two of the condos. See Connell, "Thomas Edison Grew Up"; "The Search for Thomas Edison's Boyhood Home," http://www.idigit.tv/edison/; "Thomas Edison's Boyhood Home," *Geography at St. Clair Community College*, http://www.sc4geography.net/. This last source includes the only known image of the house, sketched from memory by Emma Tyler's sister, Caroline Farrand Balentine (or Ballentine).

15. *History of St. Clair County, Michigan*, 570, 536–37 (for stepmother and literary guild); Connell, "Thomas Edison Fell Out"; John W. Leonard, "Tyler, Emma Farrand," *Woman's Who's Who of America*, 829; Marcaccio, "Ladies' Library Association of Port Huron, Michigan," 10. Amy Marcaccio—whose work contains rich details about Helen Wheaton Farrand and her life in Port Huron—notes that a group of local teachers formed the Faculty Literary Association (FLA) in 1874 as a spin-off of the Ladies' Library Association, which at that point "was afflicted with internal strife." Emma Farrand was appointed as FLA's vice-president (12–13).

16. *Brown's City Directory of Port Huron*, 14, 47; "Member of Pioneer Pt. Huron Family Expires"; "Tyler, Emma Farrand"; *History of St. Clair County*, 570.

17. Laura Wright, interview with Father Flye (hereafter Wright, interview).

18. For 1882 see *Historical Catalogue . . . Kalamazoo College*, 82; Kalamazoo village directory, 1883, http://kalamazoogenealogy.org; Paula Tyler, interview with Ross Spears (hereafter Tyler, interview).

19. "Personal," *KG*, Sept. 2, 1883, 4; "Michigan Births, 1867–1902," Return of Births, entry for Laura W. Tyler, item 1 p 204 rn 261, May 22, 1884, Kalamazoo, Mich. (database with images, *FamilySearch.org*), https://familysearch.org.

20. *KG*, Feb. 9, 1886, 3; Kalamazoo city directory, 1887; Agee, *ADITF-R*, manuscript variant, 462; "An Unexpected Summons," *KG*, May 7, 1886, 4; "The Late Rufus Tyler," *KG*, May 9, 1886, 3; *KG*, Mar. 31, 1885, 3.

21. Kalamazoo city directory, 1887; Spears and Cassidy, *Agee: His Life Remembered*, 14; Moreau, *Restless Journey*, 25; Wright, interview.

22. Paulin, *Lost Elkmont*, 19; Wright, interview.

23. Sevier County, Tenn., Deed Book S: 164-66, Theodore & Lydia Gardner to R. & J. C. Tyler & Co., July 7, 1888; Deed Book S: 492-95, Valerus & Maria Bruce to R. & J. C. Tyler & Co., June 18, 1889, Register of Deeds Office, Sevierville; Wright, interview; Moreau, *Restless Journey*, 25.

24. Wright, interview; Sevier County, Tenn., Deed Book Z: 535-38, Joel & Emma Tyler, Jessie Tyler & Martha Fiske to Ethel Calkins, W. R. Swaggerty & L. M. Eubanks, Apr. 3, 1899, Register of Deeds Office, Sevierville; Paulin, *Lost Elkmont*, 19.

25. Wright, interview.

26. "Dissolution of Partnership," *KJT*, Jan. 5, 1892, 3; Wright, interview; Howell, "Prominent Knoxvillians," 599; "Historic Downtown Knoxville Walking Tour" brochure, *Knox Heritage*, 2012.

27. "Personal," *KG*, Nov. 7, 1891, 5; 1880 and 1890 U.S. Censuses; Knoxville city directory, 1893; "A Splendid Suburb," *KJT*, Feb. 15, 1889, 4; "Wants Them to Pave," *KJT*, Feb. 13, 1893, 5.

28. "Dissolution of Partnership," *KJT*, Knoxville city directory, 1893.

29. For Paula's birth information see U.S. Social Security death index, *Ancestry.com*. This shows Paula's date of birth as August 27, 1893, but does not give her middle name. The Connecticut Death Index, 1949–2012, on the same website gives her middle initial but lists her birthday as August 24, 1893. Paula Farrand Tyler appears (only her year of birth is listed) in Willis, *History of the Willis Family*, 188. For Paula's quote see Tyler, interview.

30. Knoxville city directory, 1894; Hugh Tyler to Helen [Bliss?], Oct. 20, 1948, South Kent, Conn., Tyler Collection, MHC, 2; Lydia Edison, letter to author, Nov. 17, 2015, Elk, Calif.

31. Tyler, interview.

32. "Sudden Death of Dr. I. W. Fisk," *KG*, Dec. 11, 1891, 1. This article described Sarah Tyler as "seriously ill" at the time. For Martha, see "Pioneer Resident Dies in Knoxville," *KG*, Dec. 10, 1909, 8.

33. Knoxville city directory, 1894; Agee, *ADITF-R*, 88.

34. "A Home in Ashes," *KJT*, Jan. 14, 1895, 4; Lydia Edison, letter; Eric Van Valkenburgh, interview with author, Nov. 7, 2015 (coins); "Jottings," *KG*, Jan. 18, 1895, 9.

35. Knoxville city directories, 1895–97; Record of Deaths, Knoxville, Tenn., Apr. 1895 (*Ancestry.com*); "Mrs. Sarah P. Tyler's Death," *KS*, Apr. 15, 1895, 1; Tyler, interview; Agee, *ADITF*, 119.

36. Seymour, "Outline History," in *History . . . St. John's Episcopal*, 18; Mayo, "James Agee: His Literary Life and Work," 17; Helen H. Turner, "St. John's Branch of the Girls' Friendly Society," in *History . . . St. John's Episcopal*, 189; Dr. Samuel Ringgold, "Sermon," in *History . . . St. John's Episcopal*, 100; Flora Nell Seymour, "Woman's Organizations of St. John's Church," in *History . . . St. John's Episcopal*, 176; St. John's Episcopal Church, Register B, 225; Curry, "Knoxville of James Agee's *ADITF*," 14.

37. Charles Seymour, "Memorials in St. John's Church to the Glory of God," in *History . . . St. John's Episcopal*, 130; *The Volunteer 1902*, UT yearbook, 124.

38. Tyler, interview.

39. Lacey and Yarbro, "Early Unitarian and Universalist Churches," *Tennessee Valley Unitarian Universalist Church*, http://tvuuc.org (pdf), 1; Spears and Cassidy, *Agee: His Life Remembered*, 14.

40. Tyler, interview.

41. Leonard, "Tyler, Emma Farrand"; Bergreen, *James Agee: A Life*, 5 ("wayward"), 6; "The Bethesda Home," *KG*, Nov. 8, 1890, 1; Rule, *Standard History of Knoxville*, 545–46. For syphilis, see Bergreen, 6, which credits an interview with W. M. Frohock for the information.

42. Lacey and Yarbro, "Early Unitarian and Universalist Churches," 2; Rule, *Standard History of Knoxville*, 464.

43. Knoxville city directory, 1897; Sanborn map, Knoxville, 1903, sheet 7; "History of Mayors," *City of Knoxville*, http://www.knoxvilletn.gov; Lucy Curtis Templeton, "Books—Old and New," *KNS*, Aug. 21, 1927; Knoxville city directories, 1897, 1927. By the time the 1897 directory listed the Tylers at 703 West Cumberland, Burnett had published at least two works—an early novel, *Vagabondia*, and a memoir, *The One I Knew the Best of All*—that were partly inspired by her time in Knoxville. See also Jack Neely, "Frances Hodgson Burnett, the Knoxville Years," *KM*, Nov. 18, 2015. For Hugh's memories see Hugh Tyler to James Agee, 3.

44. Knoxville city directory, 1898; Sanborn map, Knoxville, 1903, sheet 1; Hugh Tyler to James Agee, 3.

45. Knox County, Tenn., Deed Book 155: 23, Caroline Hamilton to Joel Tyler, May 3, 1898, Knox County Archives; Aiken, *James Agee's* ADITF (brochure); Knoxville city directories, 1898–1926; Wright, interview; Tyler, interview.

46. Hugh Tyler to Helen Bliss, 3–4.

47. Knox County, Tenn., Deed Book 241:37, Martha Fiske to Jessie Tyler, Aug. 24, 1900, Knox County Archives; Knoxville city directory, 1900; "Michigan Deaths, 1867-1897," Gracie P. Fisk, Feb. 11, 1879, Kalamazoo (database with images, *FamilySearch.org*); "Michigan Deaths, 1867-1897," Arthur P. Fiske, Nov. 26, 1889, Kalamazoo (database with images, *FamilySearch.org*); "Sudden Death of Dr. I. W. Fisk," *KG*, Dec. 11, 1891, 1; Agee, *ADITF-R*, manuscript variant, 511; Tyler, interview.

48. *The Volunteer 1902*, UT yearbook, 124 (Episcopal Club), 60, 140 (Laura's activities); "Nicholson Art League Annual Exhibition," *KS*, Apr. 15, 1902, 5; "Looking Backward," *KNS*, Apr. 16, 1927, 4; Howell, "Prominent Knoxvillians," 621–22.

49. *University of Tennessee Record for 1898*, Mar. 1898, 78; Purcell, *University of Tennessee*; "About Chi Omega," *Chi Omega (Pi Chapter)*, http://www.utkchiomega.com; *Eleusis of Chi Omega* 4 (Feb. 1902): 49; *Eleusis of Chi Omega* 4 (June 1902): 146.

50. Davis, "James Agee and Father Flye," 8; Concannon, "Poetry and Fiction of James Agee," 3; Davis, "Agee Story—Part Two," 15.

51. Davis, "Agee Story—Part Two," 15; Mayo, "James Agee: His Literary Life," 16; Doty, *Tell Me Who I Am*, 2; Spears and Cassidy, *Agee: His Life Remembered*, 14; Agee, Autobiographical writing, TN 4.1.

52. P. M. Agee, *Record of the Agee Family*, 290; Louis N. Agee, *Agee Register*, 575. Concerning the elder James Agee's birthplace, *Ancestry.com* records conflict. One

source ("Family Data Collection—Births") lists his birth in Campbell, Tennessee, on July 9, 1788; but Campbell County was not formed until the early 1800s, as pointed out to me by Bill Claiborne. I am inclined to trust the marriage record between James Agee and Elizabeth Tudor ("U.S. and International Marriage Records, 1560–1900"), which lists his birthplace as Virginia.

53. Chaniott, *Family Reunion,* 4; 1870 U.S. Census, Campbell County, Tenn., population schedule, Jacksboro, p. 7 (stamped), dwelling 95, family 87, Comer (digital image, *Ancestry.com*); U.S. Census, Campbell County, Tenn., population schedule, Fincastle, p. 429 (stamped), dwelling 395, family 388, Comer (digital image, *Ancestry.com*); 1850 U.S. Census, Campbell County, Tenn., population schedule, 17th subdivision, p. 301 (stamped), dwelling 331, family 331, Comer (digital image, *Ancestry .com*); 1860 U.S. Census, Campbell County, Tenn., population schedule, Fincastle, p. 55, dwelling 364, family 357, Agee (digital image, *Ancestry.com*); "Henry Clay and Abraham Lincoln" and "The Statesman," *Henry Clay Estate,* http://henryclay.org; *Goodspeed's History of Tennessee,* 1125–26.

54. "An Eventful Life Brought to a Close, by the Death of Dr. J. H. Agee," *KJT,* Oct. 9, 1899.

55. "Campbell County Courthouse," *History of Campbell County, Tennessee,* http:// www.tngenweb.org; Larry H. Whiteaker, "Civil War," *Tennessee Encyclopedia of History and Culture,* https://tennesseeencyclopedia.net; McDonald, *Campbell County Tennessee USA,* 31; "U.S., Civil War Soldier Records and Profiles, 1861–1865," *Ancestry.com;* "143rd Indiana Infantry in the American Civil War," *Civil War Index,* http://www.civilwarindex .com; *Goodspeed's History of Tennessee,* 1126. For postwar conditions see McDonald, 31–32.

56. "Eventful Life Brought to a Close"; *Goodspeed's History of Tennessee,* 1126.

57. James Harris Agee, speech, in *Journal of the House of Representatives of the State of Tennessee: Adjourned Session of the 36th General Assembly* (Nashville, 1870–71), 724–25.

58. McDonald, *Campbell County Tennessee USA,* 108; Carson Brewer, "Town's History Rises Through Waters of TVA," *KNS,* May 15, 1983, H2.

59. 1880 U.S. Census, Campbell County, Tenn., population schedule, 1st Civil District, p. 362 (stamped), dwelling 24, family 26, Agee (digital image, *Ancestry.com*); "Campbell County Courthouse," *History of Campbell County, Tennessee; State Board of Health Bulletin* 1–2 (1885–87): 1, 17, 46; *State Board of Health Bulletin* 3–4 (1887–89): 5, 216; *State Board of Health Bulletin* 5-6 (1889–90): 186; *Goodspeed's History of Tennessee,* 1125–26; Hamer, "A. Frank Agee," 564; "A. F. Agee, Former Postmaster," *LP,* July 30, 1940.

60. "Eventful Life Brought to a Close"; Campbell County, Tenn., Deed Book 67: 163, Winston Baird to A. J. Agee & A. F. Agee, Sept. 15, 1921, Register of Deeds Office, Jacksboro.

61. Hamer, "A. Frank Agee"; *Tennessee State Gazetteer 1876,* 115; "In Honor of Those Who Served," *LP,* supplement, Nov. 10, 2010, 19.

62. Public member family trees, *Ancestry.com;* "Dog Finds Dead Man," *Muskogee* [Ohio] *Daily Phoenix,* Dec. 18, 1904, 5; "Received Sad News," *Salt Lake Herald,* Dec. 29, 1904, 7; "Sent Up for Life," *Salt Lake Telegram,* May 2, 1905.

63. 1860 U.S. Census, Anderson County, Tenn., population schedule, p. 49 (stamped), dwelling 702, family 702, Lamar (digital image, *Ancestry.com*); 1870 U.S. Census, Anderson County, Tenn., population schedule, 3rd District, p. 14, dwelling 95, family 95, Serelda D. M. Lamar (digital image, *Ancestry.com*); 1880 U.S. Census, Campbell County, Tenn., population schedule, 1st District, p. 361 (stamped), dwelling 1, family 1, Agee (digital image, *Ancestry.com*); Borchers, *Thomas Lamar, the Immigrant*, 2, 238, 241; Roane, Tenn. Marriage license (1843), Lamar-Margraves (digital image, *Ancestry.com*); Wright, interview; Campbell County, Tenn. Marriage license (1877), Agee-Lamar (digital image, *Ancestry.com*); P. M. Agee, *Record of the Agee Family*, 292; Vic Weals, "Annabel Agee," *KJ*, Apr. 30, 1986, C1–2.

64. 1900 U.S. Census, Campbell County, Tenn., population schedule, LaFollette, p. 240 (stamped), dwelling 155, family 159, Henry C. and Mossie Agee (digital image, *Ancestry.com*); *State Board of Health Bulletin* 1 (1885): 1.

65. Wright, interview; Tyler, interview. "We were in Knoxville, and they lived way out," said Paula Tyler, indicating a significant distance between the Tylers' home and the Agees' in Jacksboro. She said that Moss visited the Tylers on at least one occasion and remembered "seeing this country equipage drive up to our house, and Mrs. Agee was sitting in it—not a car but a horse[-drawn carriage]." Paula did not elaborate on the memory, and it is unclear whether Moss had hired the carriage in Knoxville after arriving by train or had traveled by horse and buggy all the way from Campbell County. The latter seems improbable but may have been an unannounced visit that Moss could not afford to make by rail.

66. 1880 U.S. Census; P. M. Agee, *Record of the Agee Family*, 292; Brewer, "Town's History Rises"; 1900 U.S. Census; "A. F. Agee, Former Postmaster."

67. Weals, "Annabel Agee."

68. Wright, interview; Concannon, "Poetry and Fiction," 2; Bergreen, *James Agee: A Life*, 5; 1900 U.S. Census; Mayo, "James Agee," 2; 1910 U.S. Census, Campbell County, Tenn., population schedule, 3rd District, p. 140 (stamped), dwelling 383, family 385, Henry C. Agee (digital image, *Ancestry.com*); Spears and Cassidy, *Agee: His Life Remembered*, 18 (Paula Tyler quote).

69. Agee, Journals, c. 1930s, n.d., TN MS.2730, 8.15 (hereafter TN 8.15); Wright, interview.

70. *Official Register of the United States, 1901*, 2:345; "Civil Service Examination," *KJT*, Apr. 19, 1896; "Postal Examination," *KJT*, Dec. 6, 1896; Leupp, *How to Prepare for a Civil Service Examination*, 281; "Two Local Postoffice Jobs," *KS*, June 26, 1901, 4. Jay might have been appointed in Campbell County, as indicated by the 1905 edition of *Official Register of the United States* (2:696); however, this may be an error, as the publication's 1903 edition states that he was appointed in Knoxville (2:751).

71. "Two Local Postoffice Jobs," *KS*; Agee, Journals, TN 8.15.

72. Wheeler, *Knoxville, Tennessee*, 22, 25; Jack Neely, "The New Knoxvillians," *MP*, June 28, 2007; Neely, *Market Square*, 95 ("dirt farmers," "diversity"), 93 (market house); Agee, *ADITF* drafts, TN MS.2730, 4.13, [1] (hereafter *ADITF* drafts, TN [page]). James Agee wrote of his father's "homesickness" after moving to Knoxville

and his imagining that "he cd have been a big shot if he'd stayed home" in Jacksboro. "Contemptuous of himself for reflecting on it, for wishing he had? A terrific drive towards *something*, & terrific loyalty towards what he comes from. Deep melancholy. Violence. Booze."

73. "Society Gossip," *KS,* June 26, 1901, 5; Knoxville city directory, 1901.

74. "Nicholson Art League Annual Exhibition," *KS,* Apr. 15, 1902, 5.

75. "New Dancing Club to Give German," *KS,* Mar. 3, 1902; "New Dancing Class Has Been Organized," *KS,* Mar. 19, 1902, 5.

76. Agee, *ADITF* drafts, TN [1]; Davis, "Agee Story—Part 2," qtd. in Kramer, *James Agee,* 18; Spears and Cassidy, *Agee: His Life Remembered,* 18 (Paula Tyler quote).

77. *The Volunteer 1903,* UT yearbook; *Eleusis of Chi Omega* 4 (Oct. 1902): 242; *Eleusis of Chi Omega* 5, (Feb. 1903): 92–93; *Eleusis of Chi Omega* 5 (June 1903): 167.

78. *The Volunteer 1904, 1905,* UT yearbooks; *Eleusis of Chi Omega* 6 (Feb. 1904): 59; Chase, *Michigan University Book,* 316. When Mary Emma Farrand graduated in 1877, she was among the first classes of female graduates from the university, but not the first, as is sometimes claimed (in Moreau, *Restless Journey,* 25, for example). A female graduate appears as early as 1874.

79. "Harvey Logan: Wildest of the Wild Bunch," *HistoryNet,* http://www.history net.com; "Kid Curry Found Guilty," *Omaha World-Herald,* Nov. 22, 1902, 1; *Official Register of the United States, 1905,* 2:696; Knoxville city directories, 1902–05; Sanborn map, 1903.

80. Tyler, interview; Spears and Cassidy, *Agee: His Life Remembered,* 18; Wright, interview.

81. Spears and Cassidy, *Agee: His Life Remembered,* 14, 18.

82. "James Agee Will Go to Panama," *KS,* Nov. 27, 1905, 2; Campbell County, Tenn., Deed Book 46: 230, Willie B. Johnston to James Agee, Oct. 31, 1905, Register of Deeds Office, Jacksboro.

83. "James Agee Will Go to Panama."

84. "Panama Canal Zone Employment Records and Sailing Lists—Service Record Cards, 1904-1920," *FamilySearch.org;* "James Agee Will Go to Panama." Jay's "Service Record Card" states that at the time of appointment he lived at "423 Clinch St." But that address does not exist in the city directories or Sanborn maps of the period. Perhaps he still lived in the Vendome, 417 West Clinch, as he did when the 1905 directory was issued earlier that year, or perhaps he lived in the Young Building, 425 West Clinch.

85. "The Workers," *American Experience: Panama Canal,* http://www.pbs.org/wgbh /americanexperience/; "Yellow Fever and Malaria in the Canal," *American Experience: Panama Canal,* http://www.pbs.org/wgbh/americanexperience/; "The Workers."

86. "Panama Canal Zone Employment Records"; *Minutes of Meetings of the Isthmian Canal Commission,* 61 (job start and promotion, salary); Robert J. Karrer, Jr., and David Plowman, "Post of Corozal," *Isthmian Collectors Club Journal 2009* 9, no. 1 (2010): 11; Isthmian Canal Commission, *Annual Report,* 154.

87. "When the Canal Diggers Hear from Home," *Boston Herald,* Aug. 2, 1908, 37.

88. *Investigation of Panama Canal Matters,* 1:898, 936–37, 956.

89. "A Marriage in Panama," *KJT,* June 10, 1906, 9; St. John's Episcopal Church, Register C, 60, 151, 200.

90. "Passenger Ships and Images," *Ancestry.com;* "Agee–Tyler," *KJT,* June 24, 1906, 10.

91. Robert Ellis, "Looking for an Ancestor in the Panama Canal Zone," *National Archives,* https://www.archives.gov; "Church Work on the Isthmus," *Canal Record* 1, no. 14 (1908): 107.

92. "Agee–Tyler." Despite Corozal being specified as the place of marriage, no evidence has been found of an Episcopal church in that small town. The ceremony probably took place at Cristobal, as the newspaper announced initially, at Christ Church Protestant Episcopal. Another Episcopal congregation, St. Paul's, met in the city of Panama, closer to Corozal (Haskins, *Canal Zone Pilot,* 454–55).

93. "Panama Canal Zone Employment Records"; Theodore Roosevelt, "Message to Congress After Returning from the Canal Zone," Dec. 17, 1906, *American Experience: Panama Canal,* http://www.pbs.org/wgbh/americanexperience/; Agee, *ADITF* drafts, TN [1]; "The Workers," *American Experience.*

94. "Passenger Lists of Vessels Arriving at New Orleans, Louisiana, 1903–1945," *Ancestry.com;* Jack Neely, "The Secret Exhibition," *MP,* Feb. 1, 2007.

95. "Panama Canal Zone Employment Records"; Roosevelt, "Message to Congress."

96. Roosevelt, "Message to Congress."

97. "When President Theodore Roosevelt visited Panama Canal in 1906" and "Inspecting Culebra Cut," Prints and Photographs Online Catalog, Library of Congress, http://www.loc.gov/pictures/. For examples of such later opportunities, Jay might have been at Chilhowee Park in 1910 the day Roosevelt appeared before a "fanatical" crowd during the Appalachian Exposition (Jack Neely, "The Strenuous One," *MP,* Oct. 31, 1996). If not there, perhaps Jay was among the Knoxvillians who packed a Gay Street auditorium on September 30, 1912 ("History as Made by Events," *KS,* Dec. 31, 1912, 9) to hear the president's campaign promises of fair labor laws for women and children—issues that excited Jay's mother-in-law and other progressives but apparently not the country's voters at large. Roosevelt was not reelected. And worse, he was injured by a would-be assassin's bullet less than two weeks after leaving Knoxville (Neely, "Strenuous One").

98. Haskins, *Canal Zone Pilot,* 508–10; Roosevelt, "Message to Congress."

99. Neely, *Market Square,* 100–3; "Summary of Principal Local Happenings," *KS,* Dec. 29, 1914, 10.

100. *Eleusis of Chi Omega* 9 (Feb. 1907): 67; *Eleusis of Chi Omega* 9 (May 1907): 177; "New York, Passenger Lists, 1820–1957," *Ancestry.com;* "Panama Canal Zone Employment Records."

101. "Health Report for April," *Canal Record* 1, no. 37 (1908): 293; "Typhoid Fever and Malaria," *Canal Record* 1, no. 3 (1907): 3; Brodhead et al., *The Panama Canal,* 43; Wright, interview; Brodhead et al., *The Panama Canal,* 43; James Agee, "Quinine to You," *Fortune,* Feb. 1934, rpt. in *Complete Journalism,* 101; "Health Report for December," *Canal Zone* 1, no. 20 (1908): 157; Wright, interview.

102. "New York, Passenger Lists"; "Ready for Trouble," *Richmond* [Va.] *Times Dispatch,* June 26, 1908, 9; "Panama Quiet for a While," *Grand Forks* [N.D.] *Daily Herald,* July 12, 1908, 1; "Panama Canal Zone Employment Records"; "New York, Passenger Lists."

103. "Personal Mention," *KJT,* Oct. 29, 1908, 9; "Personal Mention," *KJT,* Nov. 10, 1908, 6; "Panama Canal Zone Employment Records."

104. Wright, interview; "Malaria Symptoms," *WebMD.com*; Spears and Cassidy, *Agee: His Life Remembered,* 18 (Paula Tyler quote).

105. Wright, interview.

106. Agee, "Now as Awareness," *Prose,* 127.

Chapter 2

1. Knoxville city directory, 1909; Knox County, Tenn., Birth certificate, roll M-11, p. 246 (1909), James Rufus Agee (Tennessee State Library & Archives, Nashville). The chapter's first photograph shows a post office worker who resembles a mustached Jay Agee; cf. collage of three Agee family photographs in Haas, "James Agee," photo essay, *Life,* Nov. 1, 1963, 58.

2. "False Alarm Sent as Hallowe'en Prank," *KS,* Nov. 1, 1909, 12; "Milk Bottles Disappear on All-Hallows' Eve," *KS,* Nov. 1, 1909, 11; "Crushing Defeat is Handed Volunteers," *KS,* Nov. 1, 1909, 12; "A Concise Record of Local Events During 1909," *KJT,* Jan. 1, 1910, 4; "Hurrah! Hurrah; Volunteers Scored," *KS,* Nov. 26, 1909, 10; "Tennessee River is Lowest in Years," *KS,* Nov. 4, 1909, 8.

3. "School Book Fund to Be Established," *KS,* Nov. 1, 1909, 12; ad for Majestic, *KS,* Nov. 1, 1909, 6; "Cornerstone-Laying at City High School Building," *KS,* Nov. 10, 1909, 1; Agee, *ADITF-R,* 96; "Exposition Plans Will Be Discussed," *KS,* Nov. 16, 1909, 5; "Views of the Proposed Grounds and Buildings of the Great Appalachian Exposition at Chilhowee Park," *KS,* Nov. 27, 1909, 18; "Work Begins on the Asylum Ave. Viaduct," *KS,* Nov. 23, 1909, 2.

4. James Rufus Agee birth certificate; Laura Wright to James Agee, Nov. 27, 1954, TN MS.2730, 3.2; Davis, "Agee Story—Part Two," 15.

5. Knoxville city directory, 1909; "Dr. Delpeuch [*sic*], Retired Knox Physician, Dies," *KJ,* Aug. 8, 1942, 2; "Knox Philatelist, Albert Delpuech, Dies," *KNS,* Sept. 24, 1968; Agee, *ADITF-R,* 348.

6. Knoxville city directory, 1910; James Agee birth certificate; Hugh Tyler to William Kells Furlong, Jan. 7, 1971.

7. St. John's Episcopal Church Register C, 76; Mayo, 12; Jack Neely, "Excavating Knoxville Literature," 197.

8. 1910 U.S. Census, Campbell County, Tenn., population schedule, 3rd District, p. 140 (stamped), dwelling 383, family 385, Agee (digital image, *Ancestry.com*). In December 1913, Jay deeded about fifty-five acres to his father. See Campbell County, Tenn., Deed Book 55: 534, James and Laura T. Agee to Henry C. Agee, Dec. 3, 1913, Register of Deeds Office, Jacksboro.

9. Knoxville city directory, 1910; Wright, interview.

10. Wright, interview; "Looking Back," *KNS*, Apr. 13, 1936, 8.

11. "Our History," *Corbin, Kentucky*, http://www.corbin-ky.gov; Wright, interview; "Teething vs. Illness," *WebMD.com;* "Teething signs and symptoms," *BabyCenter.com*; "Gastroesophageal Reflux Disease (GERD) in Infants or Children," *WebMD.com;* Agee, Typed letter regarding induction examination, c. 1942 (hereafter Agee, Typed letter).

12. Spears and Cassidy, *Agee: His Life Remembered*, 15 (Laura quote and postcard image); cf. collage of three Agee family photographs, including another studio portrait of Rufus the toddler in a similar outfit (Haas, "James Agee," photo essay, *Life*, Nov. 1, 1963, 58).

13. Agee, *ADITF* drafts, TN [6]. Agee's note of the "train, & tunnel," which appears among other childhood memories, is similar to a statement he wrote in a personal journal for *Let Us Now Praise Famous Men*. Recalling his 1936 train trip south from New York toward Alabama, he was struck by a memory of "the tunnel image of the train" (Agee, [J 1.2: *LUNPFM* Draft and Notes: "This was first one trip, not like any other"], *JAR*, 9). See also Dallas Bogan, "1883 Train Trip from Knoxville to Jellico Described in old Knoxville Daily Tribune," *LP*, rpt., *History of Campbell County, Tennessee*, http://www.tngenweb.org.

14. Bergreen, *James Agee: A Life*, 7.

15. Jay Agee "helped his brothers through college" (Spears and Cassidy, *Agee: His Life Remembered*, 18, Paula Tyler quote), and this likely included Frank's training as a mortician. See also Hamer, "A. Frank Agee"; Curry, "Knoxville of James Agee's *ADITF*," 10; *The Volunteer 1911*, UT yearbook.

16. Knoxville city directory, 1904; Wright, interview; "Savage & Tyler," *American Journal of Commerce* (1903): 32; Sanborn map, Knoxville, 1917, vol. 1, sheet 8; Agee, *ADITF* drafts, TN [6]; Agee, *ADITF-R*, 42.

17. Wright, interview; Knoxville city directory, 1912; Sanborn map, Knoxville, 1917, vol. 1, sheet 96; Agee, "Notes, 1909–16," *ADITF* notes and fragments, TX James Agee Collection 5.1 (hereafter "Notes, 1909–16," TX); Darren Dunlap, "Grant to Help UT Preserve Its History," *KNS*, Dec. 10, 2007, 1; M. J. Slaby, "Preserving UT History," *KNS*, Dec. 25, 2015, 4A; Sanborn maps, Knoxville, 1950, vol. 2, sheet 202.

18. Agee, *ADITF*, 94; Agee, *ADITF* drafts, TN [3].

19. Knox County, Tenn. Birth certificate (1912), Emma Farrand Agee (*Ancestry.com*); Agee, *ADITF-R*, 78–79 (spelling "Margroves" in book could be a transcription error); Bart Pittman, "Knoxville's First Lady Recalls Brilliance of Prize-Winning Author," *KJ*, Sept. 17, 1962, 2 (bassinet).

20. 1910 U.S. Census, Knox County, Tenn., population schedule, Knoxville, p. 97 (stamped), dwelling 44, Victoria Logan (digital image, *Ancestry.com*); 1920 U.S. Census, Knox County, Tenn., population schedule, Knoxville, p. 37 (stamped on reverse side), dwelling 121, family 150, Victoria Logan (digital image, *Ancestry.com*); Arthur G. Seymour Jr. to Kenneth Curry, Feb. 1, 1970, TN MS.2052, 1.1; Agee, "Notes, 1909–16," TX ("spectacles"); Agee, *ADITF* drafts, TN [3] ("Sweetcharryut"); Tyler, interview; Henry Evans, "Miss Goff, Teacher of Nurses, to Retire," *KNS*, Mar. 12, 1961, B4; "Pioneer Knox Nurse, Hazel Lee Goff, Dies," *KNS*, Dec. 9, 1969, 5; Agee, *ADITF* drafts, TN [6, 3].

21. St. John's Episcopal Church, Register C, 84; "Year Book of St. John's Parish, Knoxville," [Sept.] 1912; "Plan of Pews and List of Pew Assignments on June 27, 1913," St. John's Episcopal.

22. Knox County, Tenn., Deed Book 310: 204, R. T. & Belle Wardrep to James and Laura Agee, Nov. 27, 1912, Knox County Archives; Knoxville city directory, 1913; Agee, *ADITF* holograph notes signed, c. 1948, 17 pp., TX James Agee Collection 5.1, [2] (hereafter *ADITF* holograph, TX [page]).

23. Aiken, "Transformation of James Agee's Knoxville," 151; Hess, *Knoxville Campaign,* 281 (anniversary), 275 (memorial); Agee, "David Wark Griffith," *FWSJ,* 361; "Local History as Made in Last Six Months of 1914," *KS,* Dec. 31, 1914, 7; Agee, *ADITF,* 310, 308; Jack Neely, "Rampart Streets," *MP,* Nov. 27, 2003.

24. Aiken, "Transformation," 153–54; Agee, *ADITF,* 3; Agee, *ADITF* drafts, TN [3].

25. Agee, *ADITF,* 3; Knoxville city directory, 1913.

26. Agee, *ADITF,* 3.

27. Knoxville city directory, 1913; Neely, "The Saga of the *Annabell King,*" in *Secret History II,* 26–28; Jack Neely, "A Visit with Dr. Agee," *MP,* Nov. 26, 1998; Knoxville city directory, 1909; "Social Events of the Past Week," *KJT,* June 23, 1912, 8-B ("Miss Agee"); Agee, "Notes, 1909–16," TX 5.1 ("John, Annabel"); Agee, *ADITF,* 6 ("rocking"); "King–Agee," *KS,* Dec. 25, 1914, 6; *KS,* Nov. 27, 1914 (King birthday announcement); *Knoxville Geographic Information System,* www.kgis.org.

28. Knoxville city directory, 1915; "King–Agee"; Agee, *ADITF,* 185.

29. Knox County, Tenn., Deed Book B4: 126, W. H. & Lillie Simmonds to V. C. Trimble, July 22, 1884, Knox County Archives; Aiken, "Transformation," 153.

30. Agee, *ADITF,* 143 ("Morris"), 256 ("ash tray"); Agee, *ADITF-R,* 85 ("back stairs"). An example of a similar, existing house stands at 1522 Highland, which was built at roughly the same time as 1505 and has the same gable-front and wing design. Although lacking the bay window, the front of 1522 is almost a perfect mirror image of the Agee home. While 1522 has a smaller downstairs footprint than 1505, it does share similar interior features, such as the main staircase along the central hallway—opposite the front gable side—as well as a narrow servant staircase down to the kitchen in the rear of the house. For parlor, see Agee, *ADITF,* 191. Agee used the labels "living room" and "sitting room" interchangeably to identify the area where the family usually congregated, the room containing the Morris chair his father favored. However, he never mentioned a parlor, which a family at that time would have reserved as a separate room for formal appointments. Based on a typical Victorian plan—with living and dining rooms and kitchen on one side of the central hallway—the parlor, downstairs bedroom, and bathroom must have been on the other side of the house. For floor coverings, see Agee, *ADITF,* 34, 228, and for "screen doors" see Agee, *ADITF* drafts, TN [3].

31. Agee, *ADITF* holograph, TX [3] ("smoke rings"); Agee, *ADITF* drafts, TN [3] ("rolled," tobacco brands, "blowing"); Agee, *ADITF* holograph, TX [16 ("silk flags"), 4 ("He has little flags")]; "Tobacco Silks," *Kovels,* https://www.kovels.com.

32. Agee, *ADITF* holograph, TX [14 ("the days"), 6 ("high chair," "housework")]; Agee, *ADITF* drafts, TN [3] ("around kitchen," "knee and hip").

33. *ADITF* drafts, TN [3] ("sewing"); Agee, *ADITF* holograph, TX [16] ("softening," "lasts," "cutting").

34. Agee, *ADITF* drafts, TN [3]; Agee, *ADITF,* 89 (Laura singing), 83 (Jay singing), 90 ("Swing Low"); Agee, *ADITF* drafts, TN [3] ("Stand Up"); Agee, "Notes, 1909-16," TX ("hymn-singing"); Halliwell, *Popular Rhymes and Nursery Tales,* 210-11; Tyler, interview. The prayer is traditional and appears in many variations. Rufus later parodied the prayer in a piece of writing; see ch. 5.

35. Agee, "Notes, 1909-16," TX; Agee, *ADITF* holograph, TX [15] ("out to a party"); "Looking Back," *KNS,* Jan. 10, 1938, 6 ("thimble tea"); Agee, *ADITF* drafts, TN [6] ("rose-colored"); Campbell County, Tenn., Marriage license (1914), Hodges-Agee (digital image, *Ancestry.com*); "Agee–King"; Pittman, "Knoxville's First Lady," 2.

36. Agee, *ADITF* holograph, TX [14].

37. Ibid., [15, 14 ("Halloween")]; Agee, *ADITF* drafts, TN [3] ("celluloid"); Agee, "A Birthday," *Prose,* rpt. in *ADITF-R,* 464.

38. Agee, *ADITF* drafts, TN [1]; "Snowfall Made It Look Like Real Christmas," *KS,* Dec. 25, 1915, 14; Agee, *ADITF* drafts, TN [1 ("snow outside," 3 ("Happy Hooligans")].

39. Agee, *ADITF* holograph, TX [14]; Agee, *ADITF* drafts, TN [3] ("being bundled up").

40. Agee, *ADITF* holograph, TX [16 ("poplar"), 7 ("early spring," "wild flowers")]; Agee, *ADITF* drafts, TN [3] ("gutters," "dams").

41. Agee, *ADITF* holograph, TX [14].

42. Agee, *ADITF* drafts, TN [3]; Agee, *ADITF,* 90 ("lying out").

43. Martin Southern, "An Interesting Family," *KNS,* Nov. 27, 1949, 36.

44. Aiken, "Transformation," 155; Neely, "Visit with Dr. Agee"; Tyler, interview; Southern, "An Interesting Family."

45. Agee, *TMW,* 149; Agee, *ADITF* drafts, TN [3].

46. Knoxville city directory, 1915; Agee, *ADITF,* 6.

47. Southern, "Interesting Family"; Agee, *ADITF-R,* 88.

48. For delayed park opening, compare May 1913 Chilhowee ads in *KJT* to those from 1912, 1914, and 1915. For precursors see Ash, *Meet Me at the Fair!,* 15, 24; Neely, "A Fair to Remember," *MP,* Nov. 11, 2009. For daily attractions see Chilhowee Park ad, *KJT,* July 2, 1914, 15. For "firecrackers" see Agee, *ADITF* holograph, TX [16].

49. Agee, *ADITF* holograph, TX [4, 3]; Neely, "Fair to Remember"; "Higher Ground," *Knoxville Museum of Art,* http://www.knoxart.org; Goodman, *First Exposition of Conservation,* 281.

50. "Car Lines of the Knoxville Ry. & Lt. Co.," Knoxville city directory, 1915.

51. Sanborn map, Knoxville, 1917, vol. 1, sheet 106; Agee, *ADITF* holograph, TX [4] ("rolly," "narrow," "dwarf"); Agee, *ADITF-R,* 88 (coaster visible from Magnolia), 91–92 (Rufus on carousel), 96 (concessions); Agee, *ADITF* drafts, TN [3] ("narrow," "dwarf"); "Big Crowd Out at Chilhowee," *KJT,* July 5, 1914, 7.

52. "Big Crowd"; Chilhowee Park ad, *KJT,* June 27, 1915, 11; Agee, *ADITF* drafts, TN [1].

53. Goodman, *First Exposition of Conservation,* 118; "Big Crowd."

54. Agee, "Notes, 1909–16," TX (circus); photos taken during the Appalachian Exposition, 1910, Hist. Photo Copy Project, photo numbers 2011-012-052 through 2011-012-061, MHC; Neely, "A Fair to Remember," *MP,* Nov. 11, 2009; Agee, *ADITF* drafts, TN [3]. Agee's tiny pencil script is notoriously difficult to read; while "fire coming out of pistols" seems the most likely reading, Agee's phrase could also be read as "pre coming out of pistols."

55. Agee, *ADITF* holograph, TX [4 ("outdoor movie"), 15 ("first movie")]; Allen, "Chilhowee Park," *The Play's the Thing,* n.p.; Chilhowee Park ad see *KJT,* May 17, 1914, 5B.

56. Neely, "Fair to Remember"; "Knox Heritage 2014 'Fragile 15' List of Endangered Historic Places," *Knox Heritage,* http://knoxheritage.org.

57. Agee, *ADITF* holograph, TX [11 ("he takes me," "catch a worm"), 3 ("early Saturday," "not catastrophic")].

58. Agee, *ADITF* holograph, TX [15].

59. *KJT,* July 5, 1909, cited in Weals, *Last Train to Elkmont,* 29 ("rest and recreation," Little River Railroad); Paulin, *Lost Elkmont,* 19 (Townsend); Weals, *Last Train to Elkmont,* 27 (Elkmont Special); "Special 4th of July Rates on Knoxville & Augusta and Little River Railroads," ad, *KJT,* June 27, 1915 (in-between stops).

60. The camping group left Knoxville on the evening of October 2 ("Camping Party," *KJT,* Oct. 2, 1914, 9). Lucy Templeton recalled seeing "Laura Tyler, her little daughter, and her son" when the hiking group got to Elkmont ("A Season of Importance," *KNS,* Oct. 19, 1958). Della Yoe, another member of that group, remembered the date of the excursion as October 1914 and recounted the trip in a series of reprinted articles. One particular date, October 4, stuck in her memory because on that day—a few days after departing from Elkmont—the group members had climbed trees and were joyfully swinging from the branches when one woman interrupted: "Girls . . . do you remember that this is the day set apart by the President for prayer for World Peace?" ("Siler's Bald 32 Years Ago," *KNS,* Nov. 6, 1949; "Pierce's ImproveMENT," *KNS,* Nov. 13, 1949; "Clingmans Dome," *KNS,* Nov. 20, 1949). Laura Thornburgh published *The Great Smoky Mountains* (New York: Thomas Y. Crowell, 1937) under the name Laura Thornborough; the University of Tennessee Press later reprinted the book.

61. Agee, *ADITF-R,* 100; public member family trees, *Ancestry.com;* Agee, *ADITF,* 221 ("jump off"); Wright, interview.

62. Paulin, *Lost Elkmont,* 55; National Register of Historic Places Continuation Sheet, Elkmont Historic District, Great Smoky Mountains National Park, Sevier County, Tennessee (National Register no. 94000166), *National Register of Historic Places NPGallery Database,* https://npgallery.nps.gov; map, "Elkmont Tennessee in the early 1920s," rpt. in Paulin, *Lost Elkmont,* 63; National Park Service, app. B: "Cultural and Historic Landscape Assessment for the Elkmont Historic District," *Draft Environmental Impact Statement and General Management Plan Amendment* (Jan. 2006), 17, available online at https://parkplanning.nps.gov; Agee, *ADITF* holograph, TX [16] ("snakes," "fraying water," "peeing"); Agee, *ADITF* drafts, TN [3] ("fast stream").

63. For a detailed study of the Elkmont Historical District and its preservation, see *Draft Environmental Impact Statement* cited in previous note. For a more recent update, see Steve Ahillen, "Elkmont Cabin Preservation Underway," *KNS*, Jan. 27, 2017.

64. Agee, *ADITF-R*, 114; "1915," MTFCA.

65. Dan Sanders, "Jay Follet's Model T," *DanSanders*, http://dansanders.us (this article, originally created as a website resource for *Masterpiece Theatre*, is no longer available); Agee, "Detroit Dynast," *Time*, Apr. 21, 1947, rpt. in Agee, *Complete Journalism*, 343; Agee, "Death of Henry Ford" drafts, *Complete Journalism*, 574. As Paul Ashdown, the editor of *Complete Journalism*, explains in the first footnote (345) to "Detroit Dynast," as well as in the volume's "General Textual Method" section (xxxiv), it is impossible to determine exactly how much Agee contributed to the print versions of his assigned magazine articles, as they often appear heavily edited compared to his drafts.

66. Shannon, *Compilation of the Tennessee Statutes*, 2:2154; Agee, *ADITF-R*, 116–17, 119.

67. Agee, "Boys Will Be Brutes," in *SLD*, 137; Agee, *ADITF-R*, 125.

68. Agee, *ADITF* holograph, TX [2]: "Arthur Savage teaches him to drive the Ford?" See also Jack Neely, "Destiny," *MP*, June 8, 2000; Sanders, "Jay Follet's Model T."

69. Shannon, *Compilation of the Tennessee Statutes*, 2:2153; Tom Kanon, e-mail to author, Dec. 3, 2014.

70. Agee, "American Roadside," in *James Agee: Selected Journalism*, 44.

71. "Directors of Dixie Highway," *KJ*, July 3, 1915, 7; John T. Moutoux, "150-Year-Old Town," *KNS*, Apr. 30, 1933; Brewer, "Town's History." See also ch. 3 discussion of routes between Knoxville and Jacksboro.

72. Agee, "Notes, 1909-16," TX; Tyler, interview; Agee, *ADITF* holograph, TX [15]; Agee, [N 2: Fragment: "Orchard"], *JAR*, 294.

73. Agee, "Notes, 1909-16," TX; Agee, "In Memory of My Father," *Poems*, 60.

74. Agee, *ADITF*, 209–10; Agee, *ADITF* holograph, TX [15] ("looking"); Agee, "Notes, 1909-16," TX ("hunting"); Wright, interview; "Additional Agee Data," *Ansearchin' News: Tennessee Genealogical Magazine*, vol. 37, no. 3 (Fall 1990): 128; public member family trees, *Ancestry.com*.

75. Doty, *Tell Me Who I Am*, 89; Agee, *ADITF* holograph, TX [15, 3 ("Sunday dinner"), 16 ("hens," "ice cream")].

76. Della Yoe, "Some Old West Knoxville Residents," *KNS*, Dec. 26, 1948, B10; Curry, "Knoxville of James Agee's *ADITF*," 2 (cf. Sanborn maps, Knoxville, 1890 sheet 18, 1903 sheet 6, and 1917 sheet 7); Agee, *ADITF-R*, 67–68; Sanborn map, Knoxville, 1917, vol. 1, sheet 7; Martin Southern, "An Interesting Family," *KNS*, Nov. 27, 1949, 36; Southern, "One Hundred and Second Issue."

77. Davis, "Agee Story—Part One," 15 (Hugh quotes); "Personal Mention," *KJT*, Oct. 4, 1908, 9 (winter before); Tyler to Furlong, Jan. 7, 1971 (apprenticeships); Knoxville city directories, 1914-26. See also ch. 4 discussion of Hugh.

78. 1915 State Census, New York County, population schedule, N.Y., p. 41, line 34, Paula Tyler (digital image, *Ancestry.com*); ad, "Paula F. Tyler, Pianist," *KJT*, June 24, 1916, 9. See also ch. 4 discussion of Paula.

79. Knoxville city directory, 1909; "Pioneer Resident Dies in Knoxville," *KG*, Dec. 10, 1909, 8; Knox County, Tenn., Deed Book 246: 429, Jessie Tyler to A. T. Dosser, Feb. 28, 1910, Knox County Archives; "Year Book of St. John's Parish," 1913; Knoxville city directories, 1913–14.

80. Agee, *ADITF-R*, 43–44; Agee, *ADITF* holograph, TX [16] ("tasting"); Agee, *ADITF-R*, 44 ("tall and dark"); Agee, *ADITF* drafts, TN [3] ("tearing"); Robert Fitzgerald, "A Memoir," in Madden and Folks, *Remembering James Agee*, 2nd ed., 74. See also ch. 4 discussion of piano lessons.

81. Tyler, interview; Agee, *ADITF-R*, 46.

82. Agee, *ADITF-R*, 43–46.

83. Waterloo, *Tale of the Time of the Cave Men;* Simon Harmon Vedder, illustration in Waterloo, following p. 210; Harris, *Nights with Uncle Remus;* Agee, *ADITF* drafts, TN [3].

84. "Agee Prose Poem Wins High Praise," *KJ*, Apr. 16, 1948 (Annabel quote); Mayo, "James Agee," 13–14 (Margaret quote).

85. Agee, "James Agee By Himself," in *SLD*, 196 ("Mama"); Neely, "Visit with Dr. Agee" (Oliver quote); Pittman, "Knoxville's First Lady," 2 (Margaret quote).

86. Pittman, "Knoxville's First Lady," 2.

87. Agee, *ADITF* holograph, TX [16]; "Dew Poison," *Dictionary of American Regional English*, http://dare.wisc.edu; Agee, "James Agee by Himself."

88. Davis, "Agee Story—Part Two," 15 (Laura quote); Pat Fields, "Knoxvillian Nostalgically Recalls Visit with Agee in NY," *KJ*, Nov. 2, 1962, 8 (Hazel quote); Davis, "Agee Story—Part Two," 15 (Hugh and Laura quotes); Moreau, *Restless Journey of James Agee*, 36 ("settlement"); Wright, interview.

89. Spears and Cassidy, *Agee: His Life Remembered*, 18.

90. Davis, "Agee Story—Part Two," 15 (Laura quote); Agee, *ADITF*, 198 ("never deceived"); Mayo, "James Agee," 284n89 ("easily identify").

91. Tom Southern, e-mail to author, May 23, 2014 ("running nose"); Southern, "One Hundred and Second Issue" ("mop," "wagon," "red book," "reluctance"); Southern, "An Interesting Family," *KNS*, Nov. 27, 1949, 36 ("Chooten," "pudgy," "shy"); *Boy Mechanic*.

92. Pittman, "Knoxville's First Lady," 2; Knoxville city directories, 1914–15; "Plan of Pews and List of Pew Assignments," St. John's Episcopal; 1910 U.S. Census, Knox County, Tenn., population schedule, Knoxville, p. 83 (stamped), dwelling 243, family 252, Tripp (digital image, *Ancestry.com*); Agee, *ADITF-R*, manuscript variants, 481.

93. Agee, *ADITF* holograph, TX [1]; Agee, *ADITF*, 234.

94. Aiken, *James Agee's* ADITF; Agee, *ADITF*, 243 ("cinders cracking"); Agee, *ADITF* holograph, TX [6] ("Mexican spy"); Agee, *ADITF* drafts, TN [3] ("Pershing," "soldiers"); Agee, "Notes, 1909-16," TX ("crapping").

95. Mayo, "James Agee," 15.

96. Agee, *ADITF*, 194; Homer Clonts, "Van Gilder School," *KNS*, Feb. 7, 1960.

97. Agee, *ADITF* holograph, TX [1]; school records, Knox County Archives; Davis, "Agee Story—Part Two," 15 (Laura quote).

98. "Local History as Made in Last Six Months of 1914," *KS*, Dec. 31, 1914, 7; Agee, *ADITF* drafts, TN [3] ("kindergartlen," "tooby"); Wright, interview.

99. *The Voice 1925,* KHS yearbook; Wright, interview; Tripp to Mayo, Apr. 13, 1968 (baseball); Agee, Typed letter, TN (coordination); "Parent-Teachers Associations in Schools of City," *KS,* Dec. 16, 1914, 11; Agee, *ADITF,* 14.

100. Agee, *ADITF* drafts, TN [3]; 1910 U.S. Census, Knox County, Tenn., population schedule, Knoxville, p. 113 (stamped), dwelling 148, family 153, Johnston (digital image, *Ancestry.com*).

101. School records, Knox County Archives.

102. Agee, "James Agee by Himself," in *SLD,* 195; Agee, *ADITF* drafts, TN [1].

103. Clonts, "Van Gilder School"; Neely, "Lives of the Fort," *MP,* Jan. 24, 2002; Clonts, "Van Gilder School."

104. Mayo, "James Agee," 14–15 (Ann Taylor quote); Agee, *ADITF,* 202 ("began to anticipate"); Agee, *ADITF* drafts, TN [6] ("sometimes with Tripps"); Agee, *ADITF-R,* manuscript variants, 481 ("Everyone knew").

105. Wright, interview; Lucy Templeton, "Some Comment on This and That," *KNS,* Oct. 28, 1962, 48.

106. Agee, *ADITF-R,* manuscript variants, 482.

107. Agee, Typed letter, TN ("small child," "jokes"); Agee, *ADITF* holograph, TX [9].

108. Wright, interview; Agee, *ADITF* holograph, TX [13 ("taken along"), 9 ("complains," "unaware"), 12 ("Mother cuts," "appalled")].

109. Agee, Typed letter, TN; Agee, *ADITF* holograph, TX [12 ("Next time I get," "Whipping again," football), 10 ("Mother tries," "He tries"), 1 ("Hit me")].

110. Agee, *ADITF* holograph, TX [1 ("main rival"), 2 ("competition")]; Agee, *ADITF* drafts, TN [6] ("Mrs. T," "front porch talk").

111. Agee, *ADITF* holograph, TX [12]. Elsewhere, Agee wrote that from "early childhood on I quarreled almost steadily with my sister, 2½ years younger" (Agee, [J 5.6: Journal Entry: "Losses"], *JAR,* 136).

112. Pittman, "Knoxville's First Lady," 2 (Margaret quote); Agee, *ADITF* holograph, TX [10 ("to favor," "gives it up," "jestings"), 9 ("over defends"), 1 ("quite unaware"), 11 ("more than anything"), 1 ("hurt or jealous," "mistrustful"), 10 ("Emma is 'his,'")]; Wright to James Agee, Feb. 27, 1946, TN MS.2730, 2.18. See ch. 4 for discussion of Emma's psychological struggles.

113. Agee, *ADITF* holograph, TX [12].

114. Ibid., [12 ("begins to drink"), 2 ("drinking & moroseness," "blaming me," "Mother")]; Agee, *ADITF,* 92 ("full of great energy," "overheard," "whiskey").

115. Agee, *ADITF* holograph, TX [1 ("Enter her plan"), 11 ("wanted to send"), 12 ("doesn't like")].

116. Ibid., [3, 12].

117. Gay Theatre ad, *KJT,* Dec. 20, 1915, 6.

118. Doty, *Tell Me Who I Am,* 117–18; Agee, [J 4.11: Journal Entry: "Just as When I was Adolescent at Home"], *JAR,* 100–101.

119. Agee, *ADITF,* 17.

120. Knoxville city directory, 1916; Agee to Frances Wickes, qtd. in Davis, *Making of James Agee,* 209–10. Despite Agee's memory of seeing the Chaplin imitator onscreen

during movie outings with his father, Billy West did not begin making the tramp films until 1916, and it is unclear whether any were released before Jay Agee died. See Will Sloan, "The Only and Original," *Partisan,* July 22, 2015, http://www.partisanmagazine .com; "Billy West (I)," *Internet Movie Database,* http://www.imdb.com.

121. Jack Neely, "Gay Street Cinema: The Sequel," *MP,* Apr. 15, 2004; Sanborn map, Knoxville, 1917, vol. 1, sheet 19; Majestic ads, *KJT,* June 6, 1915, 9B, June 13, 1915, 9B, June 20, 1915, 14.

122. Knoxville city directory, 1910. The Majestic first appeared in that year's directory, but had advertised in *KS* at least since the previous November. For other details, see Knoxville city directories, 1914–16; Neely, "Boldest of All the Sounds of Night," 68; Neely, "Hot—and How!," in *Secret History II,* 129.

123. Majestic ads in *KJ* confirm most of the films shown were two-reel shorts or serials. See also Agee, *ADITF,* 11; "Short Film with Eggs in His Pants," forum, 2012, *Charlie Chaplin Club,* http://www.charliechaplinclub.com; Agee, "Comedy's Greatest Era," in *FWSJ,* 18.

124. Agee, *ADITF,* 14; Neely, "Terror on the Wire," in *Knoxville's Secret History,* 42; Agee, *FWSJ,* 265.

125. Allen, *History of Theaters,* 30.

126. Knoxville city directories, 1916–31; Sanborn map, Knoxville, 1950, vol. 1, sheet 19; John F. Weaver, Jr., "The 300 Block of Gay Street, West Side (The Gaps of Gay Street Part 5)," *Knoxville Lost and Found,* http://www.knoxvillelostandfound.blogspot.com; Lois Reagan Thomas, "Credit Union in New Office," *KNS,* Dec. 18, 1989, C6.

127. Agee, *ADITF,* 14 ("store windows," "absorbed faces," "George's"); Allen, *Knoxville, Tennessee,* ch. 1, "Nov., 1915"; Neely, "Christmas in 1915," *KM,* Dec. 16, 2015 ("cosmopolitan," quoting a Dec. 1915 newspaper article); Agee, "Notes, 1909–16," TX ("sign-letters," "walking in dusk"); Agee, *ADITF* drafts, TN [3] ("lighted signs," "Cardui," "Kresses & Woolworths," "Sterchi's"); "Who We Are," *JC Penney Building,* http://www.jcpenneybuilding.com/.

128. "Biographical/Historical Note," Finding Aid for the Morris Bart Firm Records MS.0599, Special Collections Online, TN; Agee, "Notes, 1909–16," TX ("stuffed bear," list of magazines); "Morris Bart, Once Called 'Merchant Prince,' Dies," *KNS,* Mar. 4, 1943, 19; Bert Vincent, "Strolling," *KNS,* Dec. 27, 1961, 17; "I. Beiler, Newsstand Owner, Dies," *KJ,* Jan. 12, 1946; Charles V. Patton, "Educators, Businessmen Met for Long Talks at Newsstand," *KJ,* Apr. 21, 1946 ("high class," "reading matter"); Agee, *ADITF* drafts, TN [3] ("He's a Jew").

129. Agee, *ADITF* drafts, TN [3]; Neely, *Market Square,* 108 (Walker); Agee, *ADITF,* 15; Allen, *Knoxville, Tennessee,* ch. 1, "Aug., 1915" ("Produce Row"); Manning and Jamieson, *Historic Knoxville,* 41 (market house demolished); Neely, *Market Square,* 11, 190; Jack Neely, "A Short Version of the Market Square Farmers' Market's Long History," *KM,* July 16, 2015.

130. Agee, *ADITF,* 73; Agee, "Agee's Memories of His Father's Accident," *ADITF-R,* app. 4, 570; Curry, "Knoxville of James Agee's *ADITF,*" 8; Neely, *Market Square,* 117; Edington's ad, *KJ,* May 17, 1914, 12.

131. Agee, *ADITF,* 15 ("market bar"), 41 ("get a shot"); Neely, *Market Square,* 116; Sanborn map, Knoxville, 1917, vol. 1, sheet 19; Charles Mayo, conversation with author, Jackson, Tenn., Oct. 16, 2015 ("knowing Jay"); Curry, "Knoxville of James Agee's *ADITF,*" 13n8.

132. Neely, *Market Square,* 117; Allen, *Knoxville, Tennessee,* ch. 6, "Saloon"; Knoxville city directory, 1916.

133. *Historic Downtown Knoxville Walking Tour,* site 60; Manning and Jamieson, *Historic Knoxville,* 49; Agee, *ADITF,* 16; Knoxville city directory, 1916; Sanborn map, Knoxville, 1917, sheet 17.

134. *Historic Downtown Knoxville Walking Tour,* site 59; Agee, *ADITF,* 75 ("couplings," "switch engine"), 218 ("smelled like chewing tobacco"), 16 ("stained," "smoldered") 20–21 ("restive," "crumpling"); Aiken, "Transformation," 158-59 (railroad's decline).

135. Agee, *ADITF,* 16–17; "Asylum (Western) Avenue Viaduct," Historic American Engineering Record (HAER) No. TN-29; Jack Neely, "Knoxville's Search for Asylum," *MP,* July 6, 1992, rpt. in Neely, *Knoxville's Secret History,* 92-93.

136. Agee, *ADITF,* 17; Allen, *Knoxville, Tennessee,* ch. 6, "Lights of North Knoxville."

137. Project map, Asylum (Western) Ave Viaduct, HAER No. TN-29, 7.

138. Agee to Frances Wickes, qtd. in Davis, *Making of James Agee,* 209–10.

139. Ibid.

140. Agee, *ADITF,* 19.

Chapter 3

1. Campbell County, Tenn. Marriage license (1877), Agee-Lamar (digital image, *Ancestry.com*).

2. Knoxville city directories, 1912-15; Fields, "Knoxvillian Nostalgically Recalls Visit," *KJ,* Nov. 2, 1962, 8.

3. Agee, *ADITF,* 22-26; "From Bedside of His Father," *KJT,* May 20, 1916, 5 (stroke, Mossie); Agee, "Agee's Memory of His Father's Accident," 569; Doty, *Tell Me Who I Am,* 95 (Annabel quote).

4. Agee, "Agee's Memory of His Father's Accident," 569; "Directors of Dixie Highway Return," *KJT,* July 3, 1915, 7. At that time, driving from Knoxville to the Campbell County line, just northeast of Fincastle, took about 3.25 hours.

5. Although this two-hour difference was discussed as a possibility in Neely's "A Farewell Homage" (*MP,* May 11, 2011), I confirmed it by checking various years of the May 18 edition of the *Sentinel,* beginning with 1916, when sunrise came at 4:28 a.m. Aside from a temporary move to Daylight Savings Time during World War I, Knoxville remained on Central Standard Time until War Time was federally enacted between February 1942 and late September 1945 ("City Business, Industries Plan to Observe New Time," *KNS,* Feb. 4, 1942, 1; "Transportation Pause to Mark Time Change," *KNS,* Sept. 26, 1945, 11). After much controversy, Knoxville entered Eastern Standard Time in April 1946, with the rest of East Tennessee following in September 1947 ("Some Confusion Expected as Time

Changes Sunday," *KNS*, Apr. 21, 1946, 7; "ICC Places Area in Eastern Time Zone," *KNS*, Aug. 29, 1947, 1). These wartime and post-wartime changes had moved Knoxville time forward one hour. The final adjustment came in 1967 with the Federal Uniform Time Act that initiated Tennessee's permanent switch to DST every April ("Anti-DST Bill Fails in Senate," *KNS*, Mar. 28, 1967, 1) and pushed Knoxville's sunrise to 6:28 a.m. that May 18 and every year through 2011 ("Sun and Moon Data for One Day" from the U.S. Naval Observatory website records that May 18 sunrises since 2012 have occurred at 6:27 a.m.).

6. Agee, *ADITF*, 144, 41; Sanborn map, Knoxville, 1917, sheet 32.

7. John T. Moutoux, "150-Year-Old Town to Be Wiped Off Map," *KNS*, Apr. 30, 1933; McDonald, *Campbell County*, 1:10, 109; USGS topo maps of Briceville, 1896, and Maynardville, 1900; Agee, *ADITF*, 45 ("deep country"); Carson Brewer, "Town's History Rises Through Waters," *KNS*, May 15, 1983, H2 (Oliver Agee quote); "Norris Lake Waters Invade Streets of Ancient Loyston," *Clinton Courier*, Mar. 26, 1936, 1.

8. Patton, "Transportation Development," 185–88; Hoskins, "Two main roads ran north and south through Anderson," in *Anderson County*, 79. The 1916 Knoxville city directory describes Clinton Pike as a "continuation of Clinton rd, from Asylum Av w[est] to county line" (710), Asylum Avenue as extending "from 400 Walnut w[est] ... to Clinton pk" (675), and Ball Camp Pike as beginning at "Clinton pk n[ea]r New Gray Cemetery" and continuing "w[est] to Co line" (679). See also Allen, "Ball Camp Pike," ch. 6 of *Knoxville, Tennessee; Agee, ADITF*, 104.

9. Manning and Jamieson, *Historic Knoxville*, 5 (parallel ridges); Vic Weals, "Blacksmith's Family Recalls Life at the Time," *KJ*, May 21, 1986, C1–2 (wood-plank); Knox County court minutes, Jan. 9, 1889, microfilm roll #C.243, vol. J, 453, Knox County Archives (Bell's Bridge built); *We're Having a Meeting at Bell's Campground*, 15 (Fort Menifee description); "D. A. R. Unveils Bell Bridge Marker," *KJ*, June 18, 1928 (built in 1788). At least part of Fort Menifee (or Menifee Station) was still standing in 1931 ("Knoxville's 'Forgotten' Landmarks," *KNS*, Apr. 5, 1931, C1). For distance to Clinton, see "Highway Building," *Anderson County News*, Mar. 10, 1928.

10. *Goodspeed's History of East Tennessee*, 1125 (James Harris Agee); Hill, *Clinton*, 86 (Union Academy); Hoskins, *Anderson County*, 79 (Burnside), 81 (first auto); *Anderson County News*, Apr. 22, 1916.

11. Hoskins, *Anderson County*, 336.

12. "River Bridges Completed," *Anderson County News*, May 6, 1916, 1; "Bridge Opened," *Anderson County News*, May 13, 1916.

13. "Highway Building," *Anderson County News*, Mar. 10, 1928; Carver, "A History of Bridge Building in Tennessee," in *Tennessee's Survey Report*, 76.

14. Agee, *ADITF*, 57; "From Bedside of His Father."

15. Agee, "Agee's Memories of His Father's Accident," 571; Shannon, *Compilation of Tennessee Statutes*, 2:2153 (twenty m.p.h.); Tom Collins, *Legendary Model T Ford*, 78 (speedometers); Roger Karlsson, "re: Questions about 1915 Model T & Accident," forum, Aug. 2015, MTFCA.

16. Karlsson and Royce, "re: Questions about 1915 Model T & Accident," forum, MTFCA; Vic Weals, "Old Cars," *KJ*, June 11, 1986, C2 ("two jars").

17. Agee, "Agee's Memories of His Father's Accident," 571.

18. Knoxville newspapers reported the accident occurred around 8:00 p.m. For other details, see "Found Dead on Clinton Pike," *KJT,* May 19, 1916 ("unusually good"); 1920 U.S. Census, Knox County, Tenn., population schedule, 16th Civil District, p. 260 (stamped on reverse side), dwellings 90–93, families 90–93, Whittenberger, Harvey Bell, Fowler, Samuel M Bell (digital image, *Ancestry.com*). The census page shows most homes north of Bell's Bridge were farms. For loud bridge crossing, see Weals, "Blacksmith's Family Recalls Life," C2.

19. Vic Weals, "Remembering the Wreck," *KJ,* Apr. 23, 1986, C2 (east side); "From Bedside of His Father" ("over road"); Sanders, "Jay Follet's Model T" (bolt, tip-overs); "Found Dead on Clinton Pike"; "Automobile Accident Fatal for James Agee," *KS,* May 19, 1916 (position of body and car); Bill Harper, Steve Jelf, Keith Townsend, and Roger Karlsson, "re: Questions about 1915 Model T & Accident," forum, MTFCA.

20. Mary Dew Moody (great-granddaughter of Will Dew) to author, May 30, 2015. Mary remembered her grandfather, Joe Dew, telling her about the cottage. Her aunt, Martha Dew Childress, was another source of family information. For other details, see Weals, "Blacksmith's Family Recalls Life," C1; 1910 U.S. Census, Knox County, Tenn., population schedule, Civil District 7, p. 26 (stamped), dwelling 203, family 204, Dew; 1920 U.S. Census, Knox County, Tenn., population schedule, 16th Civil District, p. 261 (stamped), dwelling 96, family 96, Dew; 1910 U.S. Census, Knox County, Tenn., population schedule, Civil District 7, p. 26 (stamped), dwelling 201, family 202, Roop. Digital images of the preceding census pages were all accessed via *Ancestry.com.*

21. 1920 U.S. census, Knox County, Tenn., population schedule, 16th Civil District, p. 261 (stamped), dwelling 97, family 97, McConnell. In a conversation with author, June 9, 2016, and subsequent e-mail (Aug. 18, 2016) Diana Wolfram of Powell, Tennessee, remembered that her grandfather Charles went by the nickname Chock and remained in the same house near Beaver Creek until his death in 1955. Dr. Oliver Agee was making a house call to the area in 1951 and stopped to ask directions from an old man sitting along the side of the road. Upon learning the doctor's name, the man replied, "Agee? I heard that name thirty-five years ago. A man was killed in a car accident right near here. I was one of the first ones who found him." According to Dr. Agee, the hairs on his own neck stood up when he heard this (Paul Ashdown, e-mail to author, based on notes from his conversation with Dr. Agee on Mar. 29, 1989). While it is impossible to conclusively identify the old man of Dr. Agee's story, Chock McConnell is a likely candidate. Wolfram was "pretty certain my grandpa was unable to work [by 1951], and it would not have been unusual for him to be sitting around somewhere."

22. "Automobile Accident Fatal"; "Found Dead on Clinton Pike." The latter article states that Tinsley was heading towards Clinton but also reports that he was driving with other men in an automobile. While this may be true, it is more apparent that the *Sentinel's* report came directly from Tinsley's testimony. For other details, see Motorcycle Store ad, *KJ,* May 28, 1916; "Tinsley Sets New Track Record," *Motorcycle Illustrated,* Sept. 23, 1915; *Men of Affairs in Knoxville,* 60–61; Sam Tinsley, phone interview with author, July 30, 2014.

23. "Found Dead on Clinton Pike."

24. Royce, "re: Questions about 1915 Model T & Accident," forum, Aug. 2015, *MTFCA;* Agee, *ADITF,* 147 (carried to blacksmith shop); "Automobile Accident Fatal" (Tinsley telephoned); Keith Gumbinger and Roger Karlsson, "re: Questions about 1915 Model T & Accident," forum, *MTFCA* (storage); Pat Fields, "Knoxvillian Nostalgically Recalls Visit with Agee in NY," *KJ,* Nov. 2, 1962, 8. Fields interviewed Hazel Lee Goff, who said a Ty-Sa-Man employee relayed news of the accident to Laura.

25. 1910 U.S. Census, Knox County, Tenn., population schedule, Civil District 7, p. 26 (stamped), dwelling 200, family 201, Samuel M. Bell (digital image, *Ancestry.com*); Weals, "Remembering the Wreck" ("handsome man"); Sabra Brown (great-niece of Beulah Bell), phone conversation with author, Apr. 21, 2014 (considered improper).

26. Agee, "Agee's Memories of His Father's Accident"; Fields, "Knoxvillian Nostalgically Recalls" (Hazel Goff quote); Agee, *ADITF,* 108. In the original publication of *ADITF,* Arthur Savage was renamed Walter Starr and Hugh, Andrew Lynch.

27. "Found Dead on Clinton Pike" (Delpuech, Cochrane); "Automobile Accident Fatal" ("met death"); Jack Neely, "Destiny," *MP,* June 8, 2000.

28. "Automobile Accident Fatal" ("rather rough"); Sue Watson, e-mail to author, Oct. 17, 2017 (flooded creek reaching porch); Weals, "Blacksmith's family," C1 (grain mill); Agee, *ADITF* holograph, TX [7] ("roads not good"); U.S. Department of Agriculture, *Climatological Data for the United States,* vol. 3, pt. 1, 21, and vol. 3, pt. 2, 29, 37; "Early Wishbone: How Dangerous?" forum, Aug. 6, 2010, *MTFCA;* Bob Coiro, "re: Questions about 1915 Model T & Accident," forum, *MTFCA* ("dance").

29. "Found Dead on Clinton Pike" ("small stone"); Gunnell, *Standard Catalog of Ford,* 11. For an example of steering ratio, Randy Moats demonstrated this for me on November 12, 2016, as I sat behind the wheel of his 1916 Model T. See also "Early Wishbone: How Dangerous?" forum, *MTFCA.*

30. "Automobile Accident Fatal"; "Found Dead on Clinton Pike"; Coiro, "re: Questions about 1915 Model T."

31. Agee, *ADITF,* 147; "What's Wrong with This Picture? (Part II, the Importance of Cotter Pins)," forum, July 2013, *MTFCA;* "Found Dead on Clinton Pike."

32. Bart Pittman, "Knoxville's First Lady Recalls," *KJ,* Sept. 17, 1962, 2 (Brown quote).

33. Doty, *Tell Me Who I Am,* 98; Bergreen, *James Agee: A Life,* 14–15; Agee, *ADITF,* 168; Fields, "Knoxvillian Nostalgically Recalls," 8 (Goff, qtd. in Doty, 96–97).

34. Fields, "Knoxvillian Nostalgically Recalls," 8 (Goff, qtd. in Doty, *Tell Me Who I Am,* 96–97).

35. As reported in *KS* and the *KJT,* the accident occurred "thirteen miles west of the city." However, approximating the 1916 route from downtown Knoxville to the crash site using Google Maps shows a distance of just under ten miles. Historian Jack Neely gives a couple of explanations: (1) the relative straightness of modern roads accounts for a 10–30 percent decrease in distance, and (2) the thirteen-mile figure might have been a guess based on a "1916 odometer" reading. Neely, e-mail to author, May 20, 2016. For other details, see Agee, *ADITF,* 108, 146 (Arthur and Hugh), 135, 165 (Roberts); Knoxville city directory, 1916.

36. Neely, "Destiny," *MP*, June 8, 2000; 1910 U.S. Census, Knox County, Tenn., population schedule, Civil District 7, p. 16 (stamped on reverse side), dwelling 21, family 21, Reagan (digital image, *Ancestry.com*). John Reagan purchased the property in 1902 (Knox County Deed Book 176: 38) and sold it in 1918 (Knox County Deed Book 303: 123). See also Laffitte Howard, "Man of Many Jobs," *KNS*, July 1, 1979, 27.

37. Neely, "Destiny" ("much more aggressive"); Howard, "Man of Many Jobs" ("wouldn't take a bride"); Neely, "Destiny ("Young man"). Howard, in "Man of Many Jobs," records Knoph's reply as "I log with mules." For Nick's positions with company, see Knoxville city directories, 1916–24. For Nick later owning company see Neely, "Destiny."

38. Agee, *ADITF*, 169–73; Doty, *Tell Me Who I Am*, 112 (Flye quote).

39. Joel Tyler, letters to Richard Hodgson, 746–48. See also "Sudden Death of Dr. I. W. Fisk," *KG*, Dec. 18, 1891, 10.

40. Charles Mayo, conversation with author, Oct. 16, 2015, Jackson, Tenn (ghost of Mildred).

41. "Found Dead on Clinton Pike."

42. Agee, *ADITF*, 225 (new cap), 245 (boys retelling newspaper details); Agee, *ADITF* holograph, TX [9, 11] (father's approval); Southern, "One Hundred and Second Issue"; Donn Southern, e-mail to author, May 23, 2014.

43. Tripp to Mayo, Apr. 13, 1968.

44. Vic Weals, "Annabel Agee Recalled," *KJ*, Apr. 30, 1986, C1–2; Doty, *Tell Me Who I Am*, 97 ("such a shock"); Weals, "Annabel Agee Recalled" ("I'll never forget").

45. Knoxville city directory, 1916; "Automobile Accident Fatal for James Agee," *KS*, May 19, 1916.

46. Agee, *ADITF*, 147-48; "Found Dead on Clinton Pike"; Agee, "Agee's Memories of His Father's Accident," 571 ("just on the north side"); Weals, "Remembering the Wreck"; Jack Neely, "Shades," *MP*, May 30, 2002; Matthew Everett, "Agee Assembly," *MP*, May 21, 2008. Due to the certainty with which Weals located the accident "just to the southeast" of the bridge, it is assumed that Beulah Bell, who remembered the night of the wreck, was his information source. Opposite conclusions could be drawn depending on the reasoning. Jack Rentfro, in a message to the author, May 20, 2016, wrote that he assumed Jay Agee crashed on the north side, since it is more likely he would have lost control coming down the hill. But in that case, the Bell family's home would have been the closest place to take Jay's body, rather than the blacksmith shop across the bridge. For description of crash site, see Agee, "Agee's Memories of His Father's Accident," 571; Agee, *ADITF*, 148. One of Agee's journal entries, c. 1937, contains another "wide ditch" reference. While viewing a 1936 magazine photograph of a highway crime scene, in which the victim was found in a car off the side of the road, Agee wrote that "mortal smashups always seem peculiarly appropriate to straightaways. This kind of wide shallow ditch I am fond of. . . . A strong feeling here of the walk up the road from the cars, & of the feet & bodies going sensitive and stepping a little light as they press what they judge to have been close to the exact spot" (Agee, [J 4.4: Journal Entry: "Two magazines"], *JAR*, 85). For "I cannot even remember," see Agee, "Agee's Memories of His Father's Accident," 571.

47. Sam Tinsley, phone interview; Weals, "Remembering the Wreck"; "Tinsley, Tire Firm President, Dies," *KNS,* Mar. 22, 1946, 1; Agee, *ADITF,* 144 ("just as fine"); Tinsley, phone interview.

48. Long, *Notes toward a History,* 5; Chattanooga city directory, 1916. For examples of Robertson in Knoxville, on March 20, 1911, he "conducted the noonday Lenten services" at the church ("1911 Brought Prosperity to Knoxville," *KS,* Dec. 30, 1911, 10). When he preached again at St. John's on the morning of September 22, 1914, Rufus was likely in the congregation ("Local History as Made in Last Six Months of 1914," *KS,* Dec. 31, 1914). For other details, see *Journal of the Eighty-Fourth Annual Convention of the Church in the Diocese of Tennessee* (1916): 9; "James Agee," *KS,* May 20, 1916.

49. Agee, *ADITF* notes and fragments, 6 pp., TX James Agee Collection, 5.1, [1] (hereafter *ADITF* fragments TX [page]).

50. Ibid.

51. Ibid., 1–2.

52. Ibid., 3. For discussion of the novel's portrayal of Frank Agee, see ch. 6 of this volume.

53. Agee, *ADITF-R,* 343.

54. Agee, *ADITF* fragments, TX [2]; Fields, "Knoxvillian Nostalgically Recalls," 8 (Goff quote); Bob Cunningham, "Brightly Colored Coffins and Modish Garments Lessen Horrors of Modern Funeral Rites," *KNS,* Apr. 3, 1927 (Hall quote); Carson Brewer, "This is Your Community," *KNS,* May 6, 1970, 37.

55. Agee, *ADITF* fragments, TX [2]; Discography of American Historical Recordings, adp.library.ucsb.edu.

56. Agee, *ADITF* fragments, TX [2].

57. *KJ,* May 22, 1957, clipping about Savage Gardens, MHC; Agee, *ADITF-R,* 208 ("large lenses"), 325 ("suits as brown"); "Greenville, S. C., Writer Describes Beauties of Savage Rock Garden," *KJ,* Aug. 2, 1932; *Knox Heritage Fountain City Homes Trolley Tour* booklet, 2008, *KnoxHeritage.org.*

58. U.S. Department of Agriculture, *Climatological Data,* 1916, vol. 3, part 2: 38.

59. "Flowers Strewn Over Greenwood," *KNS,* May 18, 1916.

60. "Deaths and Funerals," *KJ,* May 21, 1916; Agee, *ADITF,* 271 (Whitaker); Agee, *ADITF* fragments, TX [1] ("obscurely resented"); Long, *Notes toward a History,* 17, 23, 27–28, 31; Agee, *ADITF,* 307 (fictional priest); Mayo, "James Agee," 286n89 (Hugh Tyler quote); Doty, *Tell Me Who I Am,* 103 (Flye quote).

61. St. John's Episcopal Church, Register C, 256.

62. Neely and Jay, *Marble City,* 10.

63. Agee, *ADITF* fragments, TX [3].

64. Sanborn map, Knoxville, 1917, sheet 93; Hess, *Knoxville Campaign,* 276.

65. Laura Wright, letter to Emma Hunt, *ADITF-R,* app. 7, 578.

66. Weals, "Annabel Agee Recalled" (also in Bergreen, *James Agee: A Life,* 19).

67. Chuck Hamilton, "A Brief History of Christ Church," 3, *Christ Church Chattanooga,* http://christchurch.dioet.org.

68. Doty, *Tell Me Who I Am,* 97 (Annabel Agee quote). John Agee was apparently too busy to travel, because Knoxville papers only mention the arrival in town of "Mrs. John H. Agee . . . and little daughter, Gladys" ("Personal Mention," *KJT,* Sept. 5 and 10, 1916); Mayo, "James Agee," 13–14 ("Rufus would go on rides"); Agee, Autobiographical writing, TN 4.1.

69. Campbell County, Tenn., Marriage record (1917), Oaks-Agee (digital image, *Ancestry.com*); Agee, *ADITF,* 60; 1930 U.S. Census, Campbell County, Tenn., population schedule, 3rd Civil District, p. 246 (stamped on reverse side), dwelling 434, family 475, Oaks (digital image, *Ancestry.com*); Agee to (Aunt) Mossie Hodges, April 1951, qtd. in Spears and Cassidy, *Agee: His Life Remembered,* 155.

70. Martin Southern remembered the Lones tragedy but mistakenly thought it happened "less than a year" after Jay's; see Southern, "One Hundred and Second Issue." For other details, see 1910 U.S. Census, Knox County, Tenn., population schedule, Knoxville, p. 107 (stamped on reverse side), dwelling 58, family 102, Lones (digital image, *Ancestry.com*); "Dr. C. E. Lones is Likely to Live," *KS,* June 4, 1917, 10; "Dr. C. E. Lones Dies of Auto Wreck Injuries," *KS,* June 12, 1917, 16.

Chapter 4

1. Agee, *ADITF* drafts, TN [3]; Agee, *ADITF,* 262 ("killed"); "For the Sufferers," *Life,* Nov. 12, 1914; Jack Neely, "Sudden Move: UT Overrides NC-1 Conservation Zoning," *KM,* June 10, 2015, 13; Neely, "One Last Eulogy for Some UT Landmarks," *KM,* July 15, 2015.

2. Richard N. Owen Sr., *Recollections and Reassurances* (Nashville: Self-published, 1982), 19, Richard N. Owen Collection, AR.768, Southern Baptist Historical Library and Archives, Nashville (partly qtd. in Ashdown "Prophet of Highland Avenue," 63).

3. Knoxville city directory, 1917. Richard Owen, in a telephone interview with Paul Ashdown on January 23, 1988, "recalled that a Marine recruiting officer was also residing in the Agee home" (Ashdown, "Prophet of Highland Avenue," 63). No directory was printed in 1918, but the 1919 directory shows that a Marine recruiter, L. E. Johnson, indeed boarded in the house. See also Jack Neely, "The Other World War," *MP,* May 27, 2004.

4. "World War I Draft Registration Cards," *National Archives,* https://www .archives.gov; "Draft registration cards," *FamilySearch.org.*

5. Eric Van Valkenburgh (Hugh's great-nephew), phone conversation with author, Nov. 7, 2015 (tour of duty, "They put him down," congressman); "Hugh Tyler," *AskArt .com* ("superior officer," "horrific tales"); Carol R. Byerly, "The U.S. Military and the Influenza Pandemic of 1918–1919," *National Center for Biotechnology Information,* http://www.ncbi.nlm.nih.gov; Lydia Edison, letter to author.

6. "Great Liberty Parade, Knoxville, TN, April 1918," MHC Digital Collection photographs, SPC 2009.007.Hahn014-025; *Knox County in the World War,* 427.

7. Neely, "The Other World War."

8. Ibid.; Knoxville city directory, 1915; Knox County, Tennessee, "World War I Draft Registration Cards, 1917–18," Roll 1877374, Draft board 2 (*Ancestry.com*); "U.S., Lists of Men Ordered to Report to Local Board for Military Duty, 1917–18," (*Ancestry.com*); *Knox County in the World War,* 70; Neely, "The Other World War."

9. Agee, Typed letter, TN; "Bedwetting," *WebMD.com;* Agee, *Letters,* 173 ("total anesthesia").

10. Laura Wright to James Agee, Feb. 27, 1946, TN MS.2730, 2.18. Hugh Tyler wrote to his friend Rebecca in 1973 after hearing of Emma's recent mental ailments: "Oh how sad . . . that the once gay and responsive Emma should come to this!" But his descriptions suggest that Emma, then sixty-one, suffered from dementia at the time rather than some psychological deficiency. He hoped his letter "might jog her memory a bit," but wrote, "from what you tell me I doubt it." Hugh asked Rebecca for "the full address of Little Creek Sanitarium." (Hugh Tyler to Rebecca [I failed to note the last name], July 9, 1973, South Kent, Conn., TX 14.3). Since a nursing home by that name has existed in Knoxville since 1940, Hugh's request raises the possibility that Emma was at that facility in 1973 (see *Little Creek Sanitarium,* http://www.little creeksanitarium.com/).

11. Tyler, interview; Long, *Notes toward a History,* app. 5, 13–14.

12. Mayo, "James Agee," 17; Doty, *Tell Me Who I Am,* 4–5; Davis, "James Agee and Father Flye," 8 (Flye quote); Clonts, "Van Gilder"; Rufus Agee school records, Knox County Archives.

13. Maryann Knowles, e-mail to author, Mar. 23, 2015; "History," *Mountain Goat Trail Alliance,* www.mountaingoattrail.org/history/.

14. Moreau, *Restless Journey,* 44; James Harold Flye, Notes for a paper by Father Flye, c. 1970-71, Flye Papers, VU MSS.148, 9.12, [yellow page, A1] (hereafter Flye, Notes for a paper, VU [page]). "Notes for a paper" is an early draft of Flye's "An Article of Faith," in Madden, *Remembering James Agee,* 14–22. See also see Oliver Hodge, interview, part one ("backhouse"); Sanborn map, Sewanee, 1930, sheet 1; Spears and Cassidy, *Agee: His Life Remembered,* 22.

15. I think, but am not certain, that information about the campus having only one telephone at that time came from Flye, Notes for a paper, VU. See also Knox County, Tenn. Death certificate no. 235 (1918), Wheeler Agee (*Ancestry.com*).

16. Knox County, Tenn., Deed Book 303: 303, Laura Agee to J. D. Jett, Sept. 23, 1918, Knox County Archives.

17. Concannon, "Poetry and Fiction," 4; Agee, *ADITF-R,* 200 (Uncle Hugh's copy); Jones, *Grammar of Ornament.*

18. "Higher Ground: Grand Ambitions," *Knoxville Museum of Art,* http:// www.knoxart.org; Jack Neely, "Art in the Afternoon," *MP,* Aug. 6, 2008 ("noted impressionist"); Knoxville city directories, 1910–25; Agee, *ADITF-R,* 341 ("Nell Wylie"); Howell, "Prominent Knoxvillians," 622; Moffatt, "Painting, Sculpture, and Photography," 431; Leeming, *Amazing Grace,* 14 (Tyler and Delaney); Neely, "The Life of Knoxville Artist Beauford Delaney (1901–1979)," *KM,* Feb. 18, 2016.

19. "California, Passenger and Crew Lists, 1882-1959," *Ancestry.com;* "Hugh Tyler," biography and artist bulletins, *AskArt.com.* Rufus practiced drawing while he was married to Alma Mailman (Concannon, "Poetry and Fiction," 4; Agee, *Letters,* 115).

20. Concannon, "Poetry and Fiction," 4; Davis, "Agee Story—Part One," 15 (Laura quote); Neely, "'The Boldest of All the Sounds of Night,'" 68–71; "Bertha Walburn Clark: A Cultural Pioneer (1925–46)," *Knoxville Symphony Orchestra,* https://www .knoxvillesymphony.com.

21. 1920 U.S. Census, New York, N.Y., population schedule, Manhattan borough, p. 224 (stamped on reverse), dwelling 14, family 60, Tyler (digital image, *Ancestry.com*); "Brief History of Diller-Quaile," Kirsten Morgan, e-mail to author; Knoxville city directory, 1924; "New Sounds at an Old Music School," *New York Times,* Feb. 3, 1974 (Rockefellers and Kennedys); Patricia Miller to Mr. MacArthur, ca. 1980, Hugh Tyler Collection, MHC; Spears and Cassidy, *Agee: His Life Remembered,* 18 (Paula quote).

22. "Tennessee Suffrage Leaders," *Tennessee4Me.org,* Tennessee State Museum, http://www.tn4me.org; Anastatia Sims, "Woman Suffrage Movement," *Tennessee Encyclopedia of History and Culture,* https://tennesseeencyclopedia.net; Emma Tyler, "In the Interest of Votes for Women," *KJ,* 1919 newspaper clipping, Lizzie Crozier French Scrapbook, MHC, 24b.

23. Sims, "Woman Suffrage Movement"; Tyler, "In the Interest of Votes for Women."

24. East Tennessee Foundation Suffrage Coalition, *Tennessee Woman Suffrage Memorial,* http://www.tnwomansmemorial.org; Alan Sims, "Local Group Pushes for Memorial Statue to Febb and Harry Burn," *Inside of Knoxville,* Oct. 19, 2017, http:// www.insideofknoxville.com; Davis, *Making of James Agee,* 209 ("felt contempt"); Wilma Dykeman, "Agee Legacy Celebration is Long Overdue Reminder of Knoxville Heritage," *KNS,* Mar. 19, 1989, F3. Dykeman paraphrased a statement Agee had written to her husband, James Stokely.

25. James Harold Flye, Untitled, for a St. Andrew's calendar, 1975, VU MSS.148, 9.13 (hereafter Flye, Untitled, for calendar, VU); Seymour, "Outline History," in *History of One Hundred Years,* 18, 84; *Historic Downtown Knoxville Walking Tour.*

26. Whaley, "Reminiscences," in Seymour, *History of One Hundred Years,* 105; Jack Bryan, "Dr. Walter C. Whitaker, After 22 Years in Knoxville, is More Man than Minister," *KS,* Sept. 15, 1929.

27. Whaley, "Reminiscences," 104–7; Dorothy Whitaker Allen, "A Glimpse," in Seymour, *History of One Hundred Years,* 111.

28. Whaley, "Reminiscences," 107–8; Agee, *ADITF,* 271; Dorothy Allen, "A Glimpse."

29. St. John's Episcopal Church, Register C, 163; Wright, interview.

30. St. John's, Register C, 163; Laura Wright, letter to Emma Hunt, *ADITF-R,* app.7, 578; Neely, "Boldest of All the Sounds," 69 (youth choir); Flye, Untitled, for a calendar, VU.

31. Seymour, "Memorials in St. John's," in *History of One Hundred Years,* 130–31.

32. Knox County, Tenn., Deed Book 362: 169, Joel & Emma Tyler to Laura Agee, Mar. 15, 1919, Knox County Archives; map of 10th Ward, Knoxville, 1926, Knox County Archives; Agee, *ADITF* drafts, TN [1] ("Mother"); Wright, interview ("right behind").

33. Tyler, interview.

34. Davis, "James Agee and Father Flye," 8-9; Flye, Untitled, for a calendar, VU.

35. Flye, Notes for a paper, VU.

36. Flye, "Reflections on Saint Andrew's School—1921," *Holy Cross Magazine*, 1945, 31–32, St. Andrew's–Sewanee Library, folder "Father Flye's articles."

37. Flye, "Introduction," in Agee, *Letters*, 12 (qtd. in Mayo, "James Agee," 20).

38. St. Andrew's grade cards, academic years 1923 and 1924, TN MS.2730, 8.14; Neely, "1919," in *Knoxville's Secret History*, 107; Lakin, "'A Dark Night,'" 34–35; *KJT*, Sept. 18, 1919, qtd. in Lakin, 1.

39. Agee, Autobiographical writing, TN 4.1.

40. Flye, Notes for a paper, VU [white page "A1," 5].

41. Doty, *Tell Me Who I Am*, 5; Gatlin, "Personal and Religious Realism," 50; Spears and Cassidy, *Agee: His Life Remembered*, 22 (Hodge quote).

42. Agee, film review, *Nation*, Apr. 27, 1946, rpt. in *FWSJ*, 232; Flye, Untitled, for a calendar, VU.

43. St. Andrew's grade cards, academic years 1923 and 1924, TN MS.2730, 8.14; Spears and Cassidy, *Agee: His Life Remembered*, 22; Hodge, interview, part one.

44. Spears and Cassidy, *Agee: His Life Remembered*, 22 (Hodge quote).

45. Agee, Typed letter, TN; Mayo, "James Agee," 19 ("mixer," "always reading," quoting Mr. & Mrs. Clyde Medford); Doty, *Tell Me Who I Am*, 6; Spears and Cassidy, *Agee: His Life Remembered*, 22 ("loner," quoting Hodge). Agee, in *TMW*, 99, wrote that Socrates was "one of Richard's nicknames." Oliver Hodge remembered the name, perhaps mistakenly, as "Sophocles" (Spears and Cassidy, *Agee: His Life Remembered*, 22).

46. Robert E. Campbell, "Map of St. Andrew's Campus," Feb. 1940, "Histories: B. Campbell" folder, St. Andrew's-Sewanee Library; "Engineering Report, Properties of St. Andrew's School" (Liverpool & London & Globe Insurance Co., July 1948), 16, St. Andrew's-Sewanee Library; Brown, "The Cottage that Rufus Watched," 18, https://issuu.com. Tom and Burki Gladstone, current occupants at this writing, invited the author to tour the cottage in February 2016.

47. Flye, Notes for a paper, VU [white page "A1," 10]; Doty, *Tell Me Who I Am*, 7 (limited visits, "isolated by death"); Agee, Typed letter, TN ("homesickness"); Agee, *TMW*, 64–65.

48. Sanborn map, Sewanee, 1930, sheet 1; Agee, *TMW*, 33 ("downhill"), 24 ("long room"); postcard image of St. Joseph's, St. Andrew's-Sewanee Library.

49. Agee, Typed letter, TN; Agee, *TMW*, 24.

50. Agee, Typed letter, TN; Hodge, interview, part two. In the same interview, Hodge said, "I was a hillbilly, a mountain type, and I didn't have any high regard for little boys who ran to the teacher. . . . He was, frankly, known among us as a sissy. And he'd run to Father Flye at the drop of anything. . . . But he was no doubt a bright fellow, and some of this was just pure envy [and] jealousy." See also Agee, *TMW*, 63–64 ("friendliness"); Doty, *Tell Me Who I Am*, 7 (painted portraits); "Rough Map," St. Andrew's School Library; "Other Faculty Residence," location 29 on campus map, *St. Andrew's-Sewanee*, http://www.sasweb.org.

51. Flye, Notes for a paper, VU [white page "A1," 4].

52. Flye, Notes for a paper, VU; Agee, *TMW,* 33 ("schoolyard"); Davis, "James Agee and Father Flye," 9; Flye, Notes for a paper, VU [white page "A1," 1] ("not a prodigy").

53. Agee, Typed letter, TN; Flye, Untitled, for a calendar, VU ("not especially prominent"); Agee, Typed letter, TN ("split between"); Mayo, "James Agee," 20–21 (grades); Flye, Notes for a paper, VU [white page, n.p.] ("History"); Agee, history exam, St. Andrew's, May 18, 1923, VU 10.16.

54. Flye, Notes for a paper, VU [white page "A1," 6].

55. Hodge, interview, part two.

56. "Interview with Fr. Flye," *Crest,* 1; Agee, *TMW,* 131–32; Spears and Cassidy, *Agee: His Life Remembered,* 25 (Hodge quote).

57. "Interview with Fr. Flye."

58. Agee, Typed letter, TN ("religiosity"); Flye, Notes for a paper, VU [white page "A1," 8-9]; Agee, *LUNPFM,* 84; Flye, Introduction, in Agee, *Letters,* 11.

59. "St. Andrew's Chapel," *St. Andrew's–Sewanee,* http:www.sasweb.org (1914 structure); "Engineering Report," 11 (chapel measurements, organ); "Ringing the Chocolate Bells," under "Our Traditions," *St. Andrew's–Sewanee,* http://www.sasweb .org; Agee, *TMW,* 121 ("sandstone steps"), 71 ("life-size"), 75 ("font"), 93–94 (organ), 105 ("spangling"), 36 (vestry).

60. "Engineering Report," 11; Agee, *TMW,* 49.

61. Flye, Notes for a paper, VU [white page "A1," 9]; Agee, *TMW,* 29 ("crown"); Agee, *TMW* notes, TX, qtd. in Doty, *Tell Me Who I Am,* 75; "The Morning Watch," under "Our Traditions," *St. Andrew's–Sewanee,* http://www.sasweb.org.

62. Agee, *TMW,* 70 ("deep country"), 45 ("sanctuary lamps"), 94 ("spaced badges," "Madonna"), 35 and 46 ("brimmed"); Rowland, *Holy Week and Easter.*

63. Doty, *Tell Me Who I Am,* 3 (Hugh Tyler quote, citing Mayo, "James Agee," 21), 13–14 (Medford quote), 13 ("lively").

64. Hodge, interview, part two. Hodge was Spears's primary interview subject, but another man's voice is occasionally heard sharing memories along with Hodge. The other man is never officially identified, although at one point Hodge calls him George.

65. Agee, *Letters,* 70, 72.

66. Doty, *Tell Me Who I Am,* 14; Laura Agee, "Man is a Flower of the Field," qtd. in Mayo, "James Agee," 23.

67. Agee, Typed letter, TN; Flye, Notes for a paper, VU.

68. Agee, *TMW,* 61, 65–66.

69. Agee, *LUNPFM,* 124 ("early puberty," "cavernous," "unsentineled," "room to vacant room"), 345 ("shaded boards"), 204 ("stench of ferns"), 124–25 ("trying to read"); Agee, *ADITF,* 90 ("lying out").

70. Hodge, interview, part two; McCoy, *Holy Cross,* 149 (Liston Orum); "Ancient Rites," *New York Times,* Mar. 16, 1924.

71. "Personals," *KNS,* Nov. 27, 1923, 5 ("much improved"); Knox County, Tenn., Deed Book WD 361: 277, Laura T. Agee to George Caldwell, June 9, 1922, Knox County Archives. For "late February" see Flye, "An Article of Faith," in Madden and

Folks, eds., *Remembering James Agee*, 6; Doty, *Tell Me Who I Am*, 14; and Bergreen, *James Agee: A Life*, 30. See also student records, St. Andrew's–Sewanee.

72. "Services Monday for Rev. Wright," *Chattanooga Times*, Feb. 19, 1949; "Rough Map."

73. Agee, [J 2.4: *LUNPFM* Draft: "Can a train trip be had in one sentence"], *JAR*, 39.

74. "West of the Water Tower," *AFI Catalog Silent Film Database*, http://www.afi.com; Agee, [J 2.4: *LUNPFM* Draft: "Can a train trip be had in one sentence"], *JAR*, 39–40.

75. "Personal," *KNS*, Apr. 28, 1924, 5.

76. Jack Neely, "Knoxton High," *MP,* May 7–14, 1998.

77. Kelley, "Education," 246.

78. Agee, "Knoxton High," in *SLD*, 31; John Shearer, "Historic Knoxville High: Did You Know?" *KNS*, May 29, 2010.

79. School records, Knox County Archives; *The Voice, 1925,* KHS yearbook, 199 (date); Agee, "Knoxton High," 35 ("School had begun"); Kelley, "Education," 249; Agee, Typed letter, TN ("Year"); *The Voice, 1925,* KHS yearbook, 23 (Alvin), 48 (Arthur).

80. Agee, "Knoxton High," 31–32.

81. Mayo, "James Agee," 20–21; "Turn to the Right Tonight," *Blue and White Weekly,* KHS, Apr. 24, 1925, 1, *Knoxville Heritage,* http://knoxvilleheritage.com; "Turn to the Right!," *Internet Broadway Database,* http://m.ibdb.com; "Turn to the Right (1922)," *Internet Movie Database,* http://www.imdb.com; Smith, *Turn to the Right,* 4, 11.

82. Smith, *Turn to the Right,* 86.

83. "Turn to the Right Tonight"; Agee, "Knoxton High," 31, 33–34.

84. Agee, "Knoxton High," 30 ("Elmans"-Evans), 30 and 35 ("Sherwood"-Shepherd); 33 ("Hendricks"-Hendrickson), 35 ("Neibert"-Neubert). Miss Neubert is not listed in the 1924 yearbook; "Group Standing" columns showing class averages in various issues of the *Blue and White Weekly* (Dec. 12, 1924; Apr. 3 and 24, 1925, etc.) reveal that she taught juniors. See also Hunt, *Alpha & Omega of the Trojan Dynasty,* 21; "New School Head," *Blue and White Weekly,* May 8, 1925, 1; *The Voice, 1925,* KHS yearbook; Rufus Agee student records, Knox County Archives.

85. Agee, "Knoxton High," 35; "Helen Monday 'Finished' Actress, Says N. Y. Critic," *KNS*, Mar. 3, 1927, 11; "Helen Monday, Back Home, Tells of New Found Movie Chums," *KNS*, Jan. 4, 1927. Paul Wing, *Stark Love*'s assistant director, found Helen at the Economy Drug Store, likely the one at the corner of North Gay and Depot Street, and offered her the role. Helen later said, "Why he ever selected me is more than I can understand . . . for I must have looked like anything but a mountaineer girl. I had my hat pulled over one eye and was trying to look as flapperish as I could." For suggestions that Rufus and Helen knew each other, see Jack Neely, "Glamorous Pajamas and Bonbons," *MP,* Nov. 13, 2013; Doug Mason, "Rare Screening Set," *KNS*, Nov. 11, 2007. Helen's KHS attendance and transfer are confirmed by school records, Knox County Archives. Further confusing the issue, Knoxville papers name only Knoxville High as the school Helen attended; see "Oh, Look What the Press Agents Did to Knoxville's Helen Monday," *KN*, Sept. 25, 1926; "Helen Monday, Back Home"; "Helen Monday's Dubious About Continuing Her Movie Career," *KNS*, Mar. 20, 1927.

86. Agee, "Knoxton High," 35.

87. "Solo Dancer at Les Amis Dance," *KN*, May 26, 1922, 6; "Society," *KN*, Oct. 24, 1922, 7; "600 Attend at Shrine Fete," *KN*, July 30, 1925, 10; "'Safety Last' Will Be Shown to Kids," *KN*, May 24, 1923, 1; "Tables and Chairs," *KN*, May 29, 1925, 14.

88. Emory Place Historic District, Knox County, Tennessee (National Register no. 94001259), *National Register of Historic Places NPGallery Database*, https://npgallery.nps.gov; Tyler Whetstone, "Renovated Knoxville High Will Be 'Anchor' for Community," *KNS*, Aug. 4, 2017.

89. Robert Booker, "How School Became Part of TSD Campus," *KNS*, Aug. 30, 2016; Hugh Tyler, letter to Rebecca, July 9, 1973, TX 14.3.

90. Agee, Autobiographical writing, TN 4.1; Larson, *Summer for the Gods*, 186 (Whitaker); Wheeler, *Knoxville, Tennessee*, 54–55 (Neal and Morgan); Neely, "Bigotry, Militant and Sincere," in *Knoxville's Secret History*, 145–47; Banker, *Appalachians All*, 157–58 (Krutch); Neely, *Market Square*, 112 (Bryan); Lois Reagan Thomas, "The Making of a National Park," *KNS*, Dec. 10, 2000, G6; "Darrow and Scopes Seeing the Smokies," *KN*, Aug. 4, 1925, 1. Future playwright Tennessee Williams was vacationing at Elkmont with his mother and siblings at the time Darrow visited the resort (Williams, *Remember Me to Tom*, 44). See also "Hundreds Here to Pay Tribute," *KN*, July 29, 1925, 1.

91. Mayo, "James Agee," 25–26; Knoxville city directory, 1922; property data, *Knoxville Geographic Information System*, http://www.kgis.org; Agee, Autobiographical writing, TN 4.1.

92. Agee, Typed letter, TN ("profound"); Agee, *Letters*, 51–52 ("bitterness"); Agee, "Infested," *KN*, Aug. 22, 1923, 4. Jack Neely, in "Some June Notes," *KM*, June 1, 2016, points out that the letter was, for all we know, Agee's first published work.

93. Agee, "Further Ideas Briefly Noted," typescript, TN MS.2730, 5.7 ("invalid"); Agee, Typed letter, TN ("lasting terror"); Moreau, *Restless Journey*, 56 (winter).

94. Knoxville city directory, 1925; Polk County, Fla. Marriage license no. 25355 (1925), Wright-Agee (Polk County Clerk, Lakeland); Agee, Typed letter, TN.

95. "Forty Girls Scouts Off to New Townsend Camp," *KN*, June 10, 1925, 3; Bergreen, *James Agee: A Life*, 31 ("early"); "New York, Passenger Lists, 1820–1957," Port of New York, Aug. 29, 1925 (*Ancestry.com*); "Joel C. Tyler Dies," *KJ*, Mar. 2, 1926, 5 (Charleston).

96. "Joel C. Taylor [*sic*] Dies in East," *KN*, Mar. 1, 1926, 1; "New York, New York, Death Index, 1862–1948," entry for Joel Tyler, Manhattan, N.Y., Feb. 28, 1926, citing Death Certificate no. 6203 (*FamilySearch.org*); "Joel C. Tyler," *KG*, Mar. 14, 1926, 15; "Mountain Home Cemetery," *Kalamazoo County, Michigan, Cemeteries*, http://www.rootsweb.ancestry.com (pdf).

97. Moreau, *Restless Journey*, 61; Emma F. Tyler, Will book vol. 11, p. 387, Knox County Archives; Agee, *Letters*, 21 (winter in New York); Personal column, *KNS*, July 11, 1927, 7; "Personal," *KNS*, Nov. 5, 1929, 8 (moved to Knoxville); "Personal," *KNS*, Dec. 18, 1929, 11 (spend Christmas); Manning and Jamieson, *Historic Knoxville*, 56, 71 (decorations); "Mrs. Emma Tyler," *KJ*, Nov. 10, 1931, 9; "Member of Pioneer Pt. Huron Family Expires in Maine," *Port Huron Times Herald*, Nov. 7, 1931.

98. Wright, interview (Jessie qtd. by Laura); Long, *Notes toward a History of Christ Church*, app. 5, 14.

99. Agee, Autobiographical writing, TN 4.1.

100. Davis, "Agee Story—Part Two," 15 (Laura quotes); Agee to (Aunt) Mossie Hodges, April 1951, qtd. in Spears and Cassidy, *Agee: His Life Remembered,* 155.

101. Fitzgerald, "A Memoir," in Agee, *Prose,* 5.

Chapter 5

1. Southern, "One Hundred and Second Issue"; Spears and Cassidy, *Agee: His Life Remembered,* 29 (Flye quote).

2. Agee, "Accomplishments," Guggenheim application, 1932, TN MS.2730, 4.3.

3. Agee, *Peter and Wendy* review," *Blue and White Weekly,* KHS, May 8, 1925, 4, *Knoxville Heritage,* http://knoxvilleheritage.com.

4. Agee, "Bell Tower of Amiens," *PEM,* Dec. 1925, qtd. in Bergreen, *James Agee: A Life,* 32–33. For fleeting moments, see "Now as Awareness," *Prose,* 125. In what appears to be his justification for an autobiographical novel, Agee wrote, "I feel also, and ever the more urgently, the desire to restore, and to make a little less impermanent, such of my lost life as I can, beginning with the beginning and coming as far forward as need be."

5. Mayo, "James Agee," 3; Doty, *Tell Me Who I Am,* 17 (McDowell quote); Bergreen, *James Agee: A Life,* 31.

6. Gatlin, "Personal and Religious Realism," 44 (Coles quote); Davis, *Making of James Agee,* 209 ("If he had lived"); Flye to James Agee, Nov. 23, 1938, typescript, VU MSS148, 9.1; Tom Emblen, "Agee's Writing Inspired by Knoxville Childhood," *Atlanta Journal Constitution,* May 18, 1986 (Kramer quote).

7. Davis, *Making of James Agee,* 209 ("veneration"); Jack Neely, "A Visit with Dr. Agee," *MP,* Nov. 26, 1998 ("identified").

8. Agee, *Letters,* 18; Mayo, "James Agee," 34; Concannon, "Poetry and Fiction," 45; Agee, "Ebb Tide," *PEM,* Nov. 1925, rpt. in *SLD,* 86.

9. Mayo, "James Agee," 29–30; Agee, "Minerva Farmer," *PEM,* Nov. 1925, 39–41. See ch. 1 for photo of Laura Tyler as a UT student, with hair similarly "puffed and knotted." For other details, see Agee, *ADITF,* 89 ("gray eyes"); Edith Snyder Evans, "Miss Staub Has Seen Teaching Methods Change," *KNS,* July 26, 1934; Agee, "Minerva," 41 ("red-haired").

10. Agee, "Catched," *PEM,* rpt. in *SLD,* 54, 63; Agee, *ADITF,* 58.

11. Mayo, "James Agee," 31; Tennessee death certificates filed in Campbell County, 1935–1940 ("Tennessee, Death Records, 1908–58," *Ancestry.com*); Agee, "The Circle," *PEM,* Apr. 1926, rpt. in *SLD,* 24 ("warped"), 18 and 20 (fictionalized LaFollette), 18 ("LaFollette's pride," "largest dwelling"); Glen Oaks mansion historic marker, LaFollette Beautification & Enhancement Board.

12. Mayo, "James Agee," 35; Agee, "Widow," *PEM,* May 1926, rpt. in *SLD,* 84-85; Lydia Edison to the author, Nov. 17, 2015, Elk, Calif. ("husband's body")

13. "Revival On at Central Baptist," *KN,* Oct. 16, 1922; "Union Revival," *KN,* Oct. 19, 1922; "Revival Services at Lincoln Park," *KN,* Nov. 2, 1922; "To Hold Revival at Washington Pike," *KN,* Nov. 22, 1922; "Revival Services at Hayes Chapel," *KN,*

Dec. 11, 1922; "Centenary Revival Continues This Week," *KN,* Dec. 18, 1922; "Man's Man, Former Football Player, to Hold Mission Here," *KNS,* Oct. 23, 1925, 16; Agee, "Revival," *PEM,* May 1926, rpt. in *SLD,* 27; Knoxville city directory 1926; "Moody Revival Ends Tomorrow," *KN,* Dec. 20, 1924, 1; "Sheriff to Hold 'Devastation Day,'" *KN,* May 13, 1925, 7; Robert Fitzgerald, "A Memoir," in Madden and Folks, *Remembering James Agee,* 2nd ed., 62.

    14. Mayo, "James Agee," 43; Jack Neely, "Knoxton High," *MP,* May 7–14, 1998; Agee, *Letters,* 120, qtd. in Paul Ashdown, "James with the Ironically Titled 'LUNPFM,'" in Lofaro, LUNPFM *at 75,* 324; Bergreen, *James Agee: A Life,* 41; Moreau, *Restless Journey,* 66.

    15. Agee, "Jenkinsville I," *PEM,* Dec. 1926, rpt. in *SLD,* 37 ("White Way," "carelessly"), 38 ("General Supply," "Dixie Highway"); Jack Neely, "Beyond John Gunther," *MP,* Mar. 29, 2012. Neely quoted Jennie Bly, alias Audrey Allison, from her book, *Adventures of a Book Agent.* For ad slogan, see A. J. Carroll ad, *KN,* Dec. 13, 1922, 2. However, the slogan "If the best is good enough" was apparently not Carroll's property, for a few other Knoxville companies—including Cherokee Motor, Pace Motor, and Knoxville Outfitting—were marketing with the phrase at the same time.

    16. Agee, "Jenkinsville I," 37 ("hundred yards"), 38 (courthouse, depot, post office); Neely, "Knoxton High"; Agee, "Jenkinsville II," *SLD,* 40–41 ("Seigbert").

    17. Agee, "Jenkinsville II," 40.

    18. Fabre, "Bibliography of the Works of James Agee," 146–48, 163–66; Agee, "Largest Class in History of School Grads," *PEM,* Nov. 1926, 48–52; "319 Seniors Compose Largest Graduating Class," *Blue and White Weekly,* KHS, May 8, 1925, 1.

    19. Agee, "Largest Class," 48, 50. See also ads and article "Year Has Been Success for the Musical Clubs" in *Blue and White Weekly,* KHS, May 8, 1925, 1, 6.

    20. Agee, "Largest Class," 50 (class poem), 51 (class song); *The Voice, 1925,* KHS yearbook, 16 ("Class Poem,"), 17 ("Class Song 1925").

    21. Agee, "From the Life and Letters of an Exeter Man," c. 1926–27, TN MS.2730, 5.5; see pp. 25 ("May Belle"), 8 ("Caesar"), 7 ("sick headache"), 6 ("advisor"), 13 ("Helene"). For another reference to "May Belle," see Agee, "Largest Class," 4; and, similarly, for "Caesar," see Agee, "James Agee by Himself," 1942, *SLD,* 195. For Clarence Brown, see Neely, "National Blue Velvet," in *Knoxville's Secret History,* 25.

    22. Agee, ["When on the Monday after Christmas, Ned Greene finally got home . . ."], untitled draft, n.d., n.p., TN MS.2730, 5.5.

    23. Agee, "Any Seventh Son," *PEM,* June 1927, rpt. in *SLD,* 70, 72–73.

    24. Agee, "Bound for the Promised Land," *PEM,* Jan. 1928, rpt. in *SLD,* 42–45; Knoxville city directory, 1925.

    25. Agee, "A Sentimental Journey," *PEM,* Mar. 1928, rpt. in *SLD,* 46–51.

    26. Agee, *Letters,* 37.

    27. Agee, "A Walk Before Mass," *Harvard Advocate,* Christmas 1929, rpt. in *SLD,* 122–25; Agee, *ADITF-R,* 86–87.

    28. Mayo, "James Agee," 75; Agee, "Boys Will Be Brutes," *Harvard Advocate,* Apr. 1930, rpt. in *SLD,* 137–43; List of Pew Assignments, St. John's Episcopal, 1913.

29. Agee, "Death in the Desert," *Harvard Advocate,* Oct. 1930, rpt. in *Prose,* 61–75; Doty, *Tell Me Who I Am,* 24 ("harvesting"). For Tennessee references, see Agee, "Death in the Desert," *Prose,* 66, 68–69. For similar snake encounter, see Agee, *TMW,* 140–44.

30. Agee, untitled story idea 1, from blue book "Story ideas," TN MS.2730, 4.16.

31. Agee, untitled story idea, from blue book (third in folder), TN MS.2730, 4.16.

32. Agee, untitled story idea 2, from blue book "Story ideas," TN MS.2730, 4.16.

33. Agee, "A Short Story," TN MS.2730, 4.16, [1–4]. This title might simply refer to the name of the assignment; the story opens with this line: "There was a straggle of wagons among the trees surrounding Harrison's Chapel."

34. Agee, *Letters,* 46.

35. "The 1930s," *Tennessee Valley Authority,* https://www.tva.gov; Trevor Stokes, "Defrauded? Headquarters in Tennessee, Not Muscle Shoals," *Florence* [Ala.] *Times Daily,* May 19, 2008; Agee, "Tennessee Valley Authority," *Fortune,* Oct. 1933, rpt. in *FWSJ,* 641 ("106 offices"), 631 ("system begins"); Bergreen, *James Agee: A Life,* 136.

36. Agee, "Tennessee Valley Authority," 631.

37. Ibid.

38. Ibid., 632, 634–35.

39. "News Bits," *KNS,* Jan. 31, 1935, 4; Agee, "T.V.A.: Work in the Valley," *Fortune,* May 1935, rpt. in *James Agee: Selected Journalism,* 65; "Opening Night at TVA Central," *Tennessee Valley Authority,* http://www.tva.com; Patel, *New Deal,* 99; "The Father of Public Power," *TVA Heritage,* https://www.tva.com.

40. Agee, "T.V.A.: Work in the Valley," 64; Jack Neely, "Destiny," *MP,* June 8, 2000.

41. Agee, "T.V.A.: Work in the Valley," 64 ("hundreds of the coffins"), 82 (descriptions of Norris). Paul Ashdown discusses the Agee family connection in his introduction to *Selected Journalism,* xxvii–xxviii.

42. Agee, "Theme with Variations," *Poems,* 53–55.

43. Agee, "Dedication," *Poems,* 8–9.

44. See Agee, *Poems,* for the following: "Sonnet IV," 38; "Sonnet V," 38; "Sonnet XI," 42; "Sonnet XIV," 43; "Sonnet XV," 44. See also Mayo, "James Agee," 103 ("brave father" comparison), 101–3 ("in his strength" comparison). Laura Agee's "Man is a Flower of the Field," from which the "joy and weariness" phrase is quoted, appears in Mayo, 23.

45. Mayo, "James Agee," 39–40 (one Exeter poem), 38 (cycles of land); Agee, *Letters,* 40 ("more or less"); Agee, "Ann Garner," *Poems,* 21 ("Now the blue"), 23 ("And after that"), 24 ("all the preachers").

46. Agee, "A Chorale," *Poems,* 28.

47. See Agee, *Poems,* for the following: "Delinquent," 136; "When I Was Small Delight and Fear," 138–39; "John Carter," 85–86 ("Leonard Dash"), 97 ("completely faithless," "uncle Rufus"), 114, 117 ("sore aunt," Whitaker). For "Dr. Whitaker let his lip," see Agee, *JAR,* 191.

48. Agee, "I. Fellow-Traveler," *Poems,* 145.

49. Tyler, interview (Tyler recalled the original prayer, and Spears connected it to the later poem); Agee, [N 6: Notes for Story and Poem: "John Lamar"], *JAR,* 298.

50. Agee, *JAR*, 319; Doty, *Tell Me Who I Am*, 38; Bergreen, *James Agee: A Life*, 154. As Bergreen interprets it, Agee "compressed the unwieldy mass of recollections into about two thousand shimmering words, less than a fifth of the original length." For "I was sketching," see Agee, program notes from Boston Symphony Orchestra's premiere of Barber's *Knoxville: Summer of 1915*, April 9, 1948, qtd. in Heyman, *Samuel Barber*, 279–80.

51. Agee, "Knoxville: Summer of 1915," *Partisan Review*, Aug.–Sept. 1938, rpt. in *ADITF*, 3–7.

52. Agee, [J 1.4: *LUNPFM* Draft: "We got back from the south late in May"], *JAR*, 11 ("west coast," "seven months"); Doty, *Tell Me Who I Am*, 73 ("hiking," Doty's phrase; "his favorite part," McDowell quote), 74 ("retrace," McDowell quote); Agee, *Letters*, 91.

53. Agee, [J 2.4: *LUNPFM* Draft: "Can a train trip be had in one sentence"], *JAR*, 38 ("early one evening"); Agee, *Letters*, 91–92 (date); Agee, [J 1.1: *LUNPFM* Draft: "It is hard to know whether or not to skip the train"], *JAR*, 4 ("This train," "What lay ahead"), 12–13 ("I was born," "projecting," "My father").

54. Agee, [J 1.2: *LUNPFM* Draft and Notes: "This was first one trip, not like any other"], *JAR*, 9 ("entering Bristol"); Agee, [J 2.4: *LUNPFM* Draft: "Can a train trip be had in one sentence"], *JAR*, 38–40 ("about four," taxi, "Read House"); *Read House Historic Inn and Suites*, http://www.thereadhousehotel.com.

55. R. Ben Sanders to Agee, Aug. 10, 1936, TN MS.2730, 2.1; Agee, [J 2.20: *LUNPFM* Draft: "All the light from the sun was vertical all over the world"], *JAR*, 57–58.

56. Moreau, *Restless Journey*, 36–37; Doty, *Tell Me Who I Am*, 6 (Flye quote); Agee, *Letters*, 94.

57. Agee, "Lines Suggested by a Tennessee Song," *Poems*, 74–75, 71; Fitzgerald, "A Memoir," in Madden and Folks, *Remembering James Agee*, 2nd ed., 63.

58. Agee, "In Memory of My Father (Campbell County, Tenn.)," rpt. in Davis, *Making of James Agee*, app. 1, 253–54. Barson, *Way of Seeing*, 64, compares the two pieces.

59. Agee, "Notes for a Moving Picture: The House," rpt. in *Prose*, 151–52.

60. Ibid., 155-56; Kramer, *James Agee*, 64; Agee, "Notes for a Moving Picture," 159, 163–65. See also Tyler Album 039, Hugh Tyler Collection, MHC, https://www.cmdc .knoxlib.org/cdm/; the photograph shows Paula Tyler standing near a century plant in the family's yard, with part of Hugh's art studio visible behind her.

61. Agee, "Notes for a Moving Picture," 157–58, 162, 165–66.

62. Ibid., 166–67, 169, 171–72; Jack Neely, "Agee the Screenwriter," *City Times*, Aug. 1984, 53–54.

63. Agee, "Bigger Than We Are" (title page: "A Love Story, for Film Documents by James Agee"), typescript, TN MS.2730, 4.22, [22] ("Bigger Than We Are" was Agee's working title). Bergreen, *James Agee: A Life*, 198, accepted the episode as fact. For Clifford Glenn, see Louise McCleary to Kenneth Curry, Oct. 14, 1969, Dr. Kenneth Curry Collection, TN MS.2052, 1.1. See also "322 S. Gay St. – The Terminal Building – The Gaps of Gay Street Part 1," *Knoxville Lost and Found*, http:// knoxvillelostandfound.blogspot.com.

64. Agee, "Sunday: Outskirts of Knoxville, Tennessee," *Poems*, 65–66.

65. Agee, [P 7: Automatic Writing: "small turns"], *JAR*, 202; Davis, "Drinking at Wells," 91, 93–94; Agee, "Summer Evening," *Poems*, 154–55; Neely, "A Musical Crucible," *Market Square*, 54–65. A bandstand-like pavilion would not be built on the square until 1984 (Manning and Jamieson, *Historic Knoxville*, 41). For Chilhowee Park, see Neely, "The Boldest of All the Sounds of Night," 70.

66. Davis, *Making of James Agee*, 33; Mackethan, "I'll Take My Stand" (Agrarian philosophy); Creese, *TVA's Public Planning: The Vision, the Reality*, 113-18 (Agrarians and TVA); Agee, "Dixie Doodle," 8.

67. Agee, "In the Middle South," typescript, TN MS.2730, 2.6, [1–2]; Agee, *LUNPFM*, xiii ("middle south"); Agee, "Allegiance Dream," TN MS.2730, 4.5, [1] ("mid-Southern"); Agee, "In the Middle South," [1–3, 5–6].

68. Agee, untitled fragment ["The horse was pulling the grocery wagon along"], TN MS.2730, 5.5, [3]; Agee, *ADITF*, 135.

69. Agee, untitled fragment ["I was rounding the corner into asylum avenue"], TN MS.2730, 5.5, [3], previously published as "Run Over," *Prose*, 121. For other interpretations see Neely, "Knoxville's Search for Asylum."

70. Agee, untitled fragment ["I was in the living room of eleven fifteen"], TN MS.2730, 5.5, [3–4]; second half published as "Give Him Air," *Prose*, 122–23. For "ivy" see Agee, *ADITF-R*, 67; Hugh Tyler to Helen [Bliss?], 4; "Tyler House Steps," photograph, Tyler Album 053, Hugh Tyler Collection, MHC; "Accident Scene," photograph, NA-3478 A3, Thompson Photograph Collection, MHC, http://www .cmdc.knoxlib.org/cdm/.

71. "Matt Moore Hurt in Crash on W. Clinch," *KN*, Jan. 14, 1924.

72. Tennessee State Library and Archives, Nashville, Tenn., *Tennessee Death Records, 1908–59*, Roll #: 169 (*Ancestry.com*); "Karnes Appreciates His Belated Honor," *KNS*, Mar. 29, 1933, 1.

73. Kramer, *Agee and Actuality*, 114; Lofaro, ed., *ADITF-R*, manuscript variants, 426.

74. Doty, *Tell Me Who I Am*, 66; Fitzgerald, "A Memoir," in Madden and Folks, *Remembering James Agee*, 2nd ed., 39: Agee qtd. in Mayo, "James Agee," 130–31 ("My father,"); Agee, *LUPNFM*, 357 ("springhouse"), 185 ("square-log"), 345 ("gray-painted"); Kramer qtd. in Doty, 39. See also Kramer, "Agee's Use of Regional Material," 74.

75. Agee, *LUNPFM*, 409; Spears and Cassidy, *Agee: His Life Remembered*, 34. When *Stark Love* was released, other viewers familiar with the Smoky Mountains criticized the film as inaccurate; see John T. Moutoux, "Even 'Stark Love' not a True Story of Smokies and Their People, Says One who Knows Them Both," *KNS*, Mar. 11, 1927.

76. *Tennessee Johnson* ad, *KNS*, Feb. 14, 1943; "Service Men Give Military Atmosphere to Ball Here," *KNS*, Feb. 18, 1943, 8; Agee, *Tennessee Johnson* movie review draft, TN MS.2730, 4.26; Agee, movie review, *Nation*, Apr. 27, 1946, rpt. in *FWSJ*, 232.

77. Louise Davis, "Agee Story—Part Two," 15; 1940 U.S. Census, Franklin County, Tenn., population schedule, St. Andrew's, dwelling 141, The Rev. Erskine and Laura Wright (digital image, *Ancestry.com*); Bergreen, *James Agee: A Life*, 278 (stopped in Knoxville).

78. Agee, "America! Look at Your Shame!" *JAR*, 168–71.

79. Agee, "Allegiance Dream," n. d., TN MS.2730, 4.5; *The Voice, 1925,* KHS yearbook, 80 (Stephenson); Agee, *LUNPFM,* 355 ("brutality, in the eyes"); Agee, "America! Look at Your Shame!" *JAR,* 168 ("brutal eyes"); Agee, "Allegiance Dream," TN MS.2730, 4.5 ("the woman, the lady of the house"); Agee, *Letters,* 154 ("premonition").

80. Agee, "Victory: The Peace," *Time,* Aug. 20, 1945, rpt. in *Complete Journalism,* 317; Michael A. Lofaro and Hugh Davis, "The Life and Times of James Agee," in *JAR,* xxvii; Agee, "Now on the World and on My Life as Well," *Poems,* 68.

81. Agee, *Letters,* 152; Bergreen, *James Agee: A Life,* 298–99.

82. Agee, *Letters,* 154; Mia qtd. in Doty, *Tell Me Who I Am,* 68; Agee, *ADITF,* 159 ("month and a day"); Agee qtd. in Doty, 69 ("sense of death").

83. Some sources claim Jim and Mia had been married since "late August" 1944 ("A James Agee Chronology," in Lofaro, *Agee Agonistes,* xxiii; Bergreen, *James Agee: A Life,* 282). However, the couple's daughter Deedee said that "there's some question about whether my parents were ever legally married. . . . They both wanted their being together to be a matter of ongoing choice unsullied by the corrupting hand of the state" (Deedee Agee, "Growing Up with the Jimiagees," 287). If Jim and Mia truly never exchanged vows in a state-recognized ceremony, perhaps they considered themselves wed by common law. Whatever the case, references in this chapter to their relationship (Agee as Mia's husband, Agee's third marriage, etc.) will stand until more information becomes available. On the mountain country, see Laura Wright to James Agee, Feb. 19, 1946, and Feb. 27, 1946, TN MS.2730, 2.18. On February 19, Laura wrote: "*Personally,* we would be glad to have you near enough that we might go to see you, and have you come to see us too, *and Mia with you* . . . but as to the matter of having you come visit us here—it would not be the same as if this was *our house* and we on our own place . . . *This* place so wholly belongs to the Order, & is so entirely under the O. K. of B[isho]p C[ampbell] and, as you know, he is *very stiff* about these things . . . as the Order is a definite leader in taking a stand about the Church's teaching on marriage, etc. etc. . . . This is one reason, if you came to live in Tenn. it would seem better if you were not so near that there would seem to be conscious avoidance of having you come to us[.]"

84. Bergreen, *James Agee: A Life,* 319–20; Davis, "Agee Story—Part One," 15 ("Tennessee"); Don Williams, "James Agee Legacy Focus of Conference," *KNS,* Mar. 19, 1989, 4 ("wife or lover," Williams's phrase).

85. Agee, "Two's a Crowd," drafts, n.d., TN MS.2730, 5.2.

86. Agee, *Letters,* 170–71.

87. For Jungian therapy, see Doty, *Tell Me Who I Am,* 115. In *ADITF-R,* 366, editor Lofaro notes "Agee's ongoing interest in Freudian and Jungian psychoanalysis." For "recurrent city-scape" see Agee, *ADITF* drafts, TN [1].

88. Gatlin, "Personal and Religious," 32 (see also Kramer, *James Agee,* 147); Agee, *ADITF-R,* 10–11; Margaret Ragsdale, "John Gunther, on Visit Here, Finds TVA 'Most Indispensable Thing' Seen in U.S.," *KNS,* May 3, 1945, 18; Gunther, *Inside U.S.A.,* qtd. in Neely, "Requiem for John Gunther," in *Knoxville's Secret History,* 53; Agee, *ADITF-R,* 9 ("wasn't as he remembered"), 4–6, 8, 11–12 ("a crowd"); Doty, *Tell Me Who I Am,* 115 (quoting Agee and Mia).

89. Agee, *ADITF-R*, 12–13 (partly qtd. in Doty, *Tell Me Who I Am*, 87–88); Agee, "1928 Story," *SLD*, 242–43.

90. Agee, "Now as Awareness," *Prose*, 125 (partly qtd. in Mayo, "James Agee," 290, and Doty, *Tell Me Who I Am*, 87). See Agee, *ADITF-R*, for the following: app. 5, 573–74 ("My dear father"); app. 6, 575–76 ("Dearest mother"); app 4: Agee's Memory of His Father's Accident and the Day Before, 568 ("Although my remembrance," "invention"). See also Doty, *Tell Me Who I Am*, 92 (Agee to Emma); Kramer, "Urban and Rural," 109 ("simple events"); Agee, "Notes, 1909–16," TX ("memories"); Agee, *ADITF* drafts, TN [1] ("Marriage"); Agee, Typed letter, TN ("lasting terror").

91. Agee, *Letters*, 176; Doty, *Tell Me Who I Am*, 70; Mayo, "James Agee," 230 (Mrs. Medford quote); Doty, 14 ("narrow," quoting Alma Neuman), 70 ("estrangement," Doty's phrase), 70-71 (quoting Mia and Mrs. Medford); "Services Monday for Rev. Wright," *Chattanooga Times*, Feb. 19, 1949. A month later, Laura wrote to her son: "I have of late been seeing the very beautiful and spiritual significance of his last hours—It was an awful agony—but also, *as a priest*, with his palms up . . . & also joined, he was offering *himself* I am perfectly certain. He was extremely *aware*" (Wright to Agee, Mar. 17, 1949, TN MS.2730, 3.1).

92. Agee, "Comedy's Greatest Era," *Life*, Sept. 3, 1949, rpt. in *FWSJ*, 14.

93. Agee, "David Wark Griffith," *Nation*, Sept. 4, 1948, rpt. in *FWSJ*, 361; Agee, *LUNPFM*, 354 ("last war"); Agee, *Letters*, 183 ("only war"), qtd. in Ashdown, "From Almost as Early," 107; Agee, *LUNPFM*, 355 ("dark-bearded"); Agee, *Letters*, 183 ("moves me"). For "histories of the Civil War," see Agee, "Plans for Work: October 1937," *Prose*, 144; Kramer, *James Agee*, 116. For "Tennessee?" see Agee, Untitled Civil War story, TN MS.2730, 4.11, [loose tan pages, 2] (hereafter Agee, Untitled Civil War story, TN 4.11, [page]).

94. Agee, Untitled Civil War story, TN 4.11, [tan paper with white paper clip, 3, 20]; Agee, *JAR*, 39 ("boys who beat").

95. Agee, Untitled Civil War Story, TN 4.11, [loose tan pages, 2]; Agee, *ADITF-R*, 29 ("strings of peppers"); Agee, Untitled Civil War story, TN 4.11, [loose tan pages, 3] ("Alabama families").

96. Lofaro, "A James Agee Chronology," *ADITF-R*, xxxi.

97. Doty, *Tell Me Who I Am*, 71; Agee, *Letters*, 181, qtd. in Doty, 72.

98. Doty, *Tell Me Who I Am*, 121 (April 1951), 72–73 (Flye's quote), 76–77 (character list); Agee, *TMW*, 39, 41 ("Nobody knew"); Doty, 77 (Clarence); Agee, "Plans for Work: October 1937," *Prose*, 136 ("love"). Agee later detailed the scenario in "Further Ideas Briefly Noted," typescript, TN MS.2730, 5.7. For "sense of honor," see Agee, *TMW*, 41, partially qtd. in Doty, 77.

99. Agee, *TMW*, 54 ("drinking sodapop"), 112–13, ("terrible thing"). See also Mayo, "James Agee," 238n83. For funeral, see Doty, *Tell Me Who I Am*, 79; Agee, *TMW*, 48.

100. Crank, "Body as Sacrifice," 217, 231n1.

101. Doty, *Tell Me Who I Am*, 118; Agee, "Undirectable Director," *Life*, Sept. 18, 1950, rpt. in *FWSJ*, 368–82; Bergreen, *James Agee: A Life*, 357; Ashdown, "From Almost as Early," 114–15 (synopsis); Agee, *Bloodline* revised treatment, TN MS.2730, 8.9, [5]. For

story locations see Agee, *Bloodline* revised treatment; Ashdown, "From Almost as Early," 114–15. For September 1951 see Bergreen, 357; Lofaro, "A James Agee Chronology," xxiii. According to Bergreen, the treatment ran to sixty pages, but the revised treatment—a copy of which is held at UT Knoxville—is only twenty-five pages.

102. Agee's *Lincoln* drafts, dated between July and October 1952, TN MS.2730, 4.28 (hereafter Agee, *Lincoln*, TN 4.28, [page]); Agee, "James Agee by Himself," *SLD*, 196 ("scarcely one hundred years"); Bergreen, *James Agee: A Life*, 370 (boy running). See also David Madden's imaginative piece "Seeing Agee in Lincoln: A Short Story" in *Agee at 100*, 269; Agee, *Lincoln* ep. 1, "The End and the Beginning," TN 4.28, [15] ("little boy runs"); Bergreen, 407 (lilacs).

103. Wright, interview; Agee, *ADITF-R*, 446 ("He told himself," from a variant manuscript), 327–28 ("Some people"), 131 ("just two years old").

104. Agee, *Abraham Lincoln—The Early Years*, 385 ("cabin"); Agee, *Lincoln* ep. 4, "New Salem," TN 4.28, [7–8]; Neely, *Market Square*, 96 ("most democratic"); Agee, *Lincoln* ep. 4, "New Salem," TN 4.28, [33] ("studyin' some"); Agee, *Lincoln* ep. 5, "Ann Rutledge," TN 4.28, [15] ("Ann: my dearest").

105. "Face to Face (1952)," *Internet Movie Database*, www.imdb.com/title/tt0044601/.

106. Della Yoe, "Some Old West Knoxville Residents," *KNS*, Dec. 26, 1948, B10. Yoe wrote that "Emma Agee (Mrs. Don Ling of New York City) . . . has worked on The New Yorker and News Week and is now with Time Magazine." See also Ellis, "American Documentary in the 1950s," 265 ("emotional problems"); Laura Wright to Agee, Jan. 31, 1951, TN MS.2730, 3.2.

107. Franklin County, Tennessee, Death certificate no. 54-02639 (1954), Grace Elenor Flye (digital image, *Ancestry.com*); Doty, *Tell Me Who I Am*, 126 (Agee qtd. by Medford); Agee, *Letters*, 220–21 ("I think"; qtd. in Doty, 126).

108. Couchman, *Night of the Hunter*, 79, 75, 81; Agee (attributed), *The Night of the Hunter*, rpt. in *FWSJ*, 545.

109. Agee, *Night of the Hunter*, 1st draft, TN MS.2730, 6.14, [228]; Agee, *LUNPFM*, 357.

110. Agee, *Night of the Hunter*, 1st draft, TN MS.2730, 6.14, [229–30, (market), 232 (horses)]. See also Agee, *ADITF* holograph, TX [14], for horses, and ch. 2 of this volume for Knoxville summers.

111. Agee, *Night of the Hunter*, 1st draft, rpt. in *The African Queen and The Night of the Hunter: First and Final Screenplays*, 684-85; see Couchman's textual commentary (736) on this scene.

112. Lofaro, "A James Agee Chronology," xxiv; Bergreen, *James Agee: A Life*, 390; Gempp, "Drowned in the Present," 255, 268–76. In his letters to Comstock dated between November 8, 1954, and March 25, 1955, Agee became increasingly focused on his illness and declining stamina.

113. Agee, *Letters*, 230–31; Hilda Padgett, "The Hanging of Mary the Elephant," *Unicoi County History*, Erwin, 1996, *RootsWeb TNGenWeb Project*, http://www.roots web.ancestry.com.

114. Agee, *Letters*, 231–32.

115. Agee, "Now as Awareness," *Prose*, 125; Lofaro, "Idyll or Terror?," 235–49.

116. Kramer, *James Agee*, 142; Curry, "Knoxville of James Agee's *ADITF*," 3; Gatlin, "Personal and Religious," 34 (Flye quote); Laura Wright to Emma Hunt, postmarked Feb. 3, 1958, *ADITF-R*, app. 7, 577; Lydia Edison to author, Nov. 17, 2015 (Laura quote).

117. Spears and Cassidy, *Agee: His Life Remembered*, 173 (McDowell quote); Kramer, *Agee and Actuality*, 16.

118. Kramer, *James Agee*, 158; Agee, "Ebb Tide," *SLD*, 86; Agee, *ADITF-R*, app. 8, 579 (outline of multivolume work); David Denby, "A Famous Man," *New Yorker*, Jan. 9, 2006, 84 (James quote).

119. Davis, "Agee Story—Part One," 11; Agee, *ADITF*, 87.

Chapter 6

1. Doty, *Tell Me Who I Am*, 128. Of course, Jay Agee had died on May 18, 1916. But Moreau, *Restless Journey*, 260, erroneously states that James and his father both died on May 16, a mistake that some chronologies—like those published in *Letters*, 233, and *FWSJ*, 707—make as well. See also Tom Eblen, "Agee's Writing Inspired by Knoxville Childhood," *Atlanta Journal Constitution*, May 18, 1986, A50 ("local curiosity," quoting Paul Ashdown); "Knoxville-Born Writer, Poet and Critic, James Agee, Dies," *KNS*, May 18, 1955. The obituary mistakenly states that Agee scripted the film *The Red Badge of Courage*.

2. "City Orchestra to Play Tone Poem," *KJ*, Nov. 20, 1949; Gunby Rule, "Poet Rewards Knoxville for 'Happy Childhood,'" *KNS*, June 19, 1949, 33.

3. "Father's Death is Topic for Agee Novel," *KNS*, Nov. 17, 1957, 10.

4. "At the Library," *KNS*, Nov. 24, 1957, D2; Carson Brewer, "Knoxvillians Learning More Through Books," *KNS*, Feb. 2, 1958, B8; "Knox Author's Book Wins Pulitzer Prize," *KNS*, May 6, 1958, 13; Nic Knoph Jr. to Paula Tyler, and Laura Wright (copy to James Agee), May 12, 1950, TN MS.2730, 2.14.

5. "LaFollette Book Club Hears Dr. Ridenour Give Review of Book, 'ADITF,'" *LP*, May 29, 1958.

6. Doty, *Tell Me Who I Am*, 92 (Paula quote); Laura Wright to Emma Hunt, Feb. 1958, *ADITF-R*, app. 7, 577–78; Doty, 94 (Flye quote).

7. Don Williams, "Let Us Now Praise Famous Men," *KNS*, Mar. 19, 1989, 4.

8. "A. F. Agee, Former Postmaster, Died at Home Sunday," *LP*, July 30, 1940, rpt. in Lemasters, ed., *Campbell County, Tennessee, Obituaries;* Hamer, "A. Frank Agee," 564. Before the Adams and Rogers building was erected in 1917, Frank's business, originally called Agee & Carden, was located on Tennessee Avenue; see *Cumberland Telephone & Telegraph Directory* (LaFollette, Tenn.), compiled by Greg Miller, Campbell County Historical Society. Jerry Sharp shared his memory of Frank in a conversation with the author, July 2013, LaFollette, Tenn.

9. Agee, *ADITF*, 66; Agee, *ADITF* fragments, TX [2]; Wright, interview; Williams, "Let Us Now"; Annabel Agee, conversation with author, July 10, 2014; Bill Claiborne, phone conversation with author, Nov. 20, 2013; Claiborne, e-mail to author, Nov. 12, 2015.

10. Agee, *ADITF,* 28 ("sort of useless"), 60 (Thomas Oaks), 65 ("washed-out"); Campbell County, Tenn. Death certificate no. 25082 (1943), Mossie Oaks *(Family-Search.org);* 1910 U.S. Census, Anderson County, Tenn., population schedule, p. 14 (stamped), dwelling 41, family 41, Oaks (digital image, *Ancestry.com*).

11. Bill Claiborne, e-mail to author, Nov. 14, 2015. After Frank Carden Agee took over, the company's furniture and undertaking businesses split apart because he "had problems with the [embalming] chemicals." The furniture store continued as Agee & Walters, and the mortuary as Walters Funeral Home. Elizabeth Smiddy, "Sallie Harmon married to Unk Hatmaker," *RootsWeb* thread, Mar. 22, 2008, http://archiver .rootsweb.ancestry.com. Other details are from Nancy Olsen, conversation with author, Sept. 4, 2015 (Maryville resident); Vic Weals, "Annabel Agee recalled," *KJ,* Apr. 30, 1986 ("thread of truth," quoting Oliver Agee); Annabel Agee, conversation with author, Knoxville, July 10, 2014 (Gladys did not want Agee discussed in home); Williams, "Let Us Now" ("literary genius," quoting Oliver).

12. Knox County, Tenn., Deed Book O3: 364, W. B. A. Ramsey (deceased) to W. H. & Lillie Simmonds, Mar. 9, 1876; Deed Book B4: 126, W. H. & Lillie Simmonds to V. C. Trimble, July 22, 1884, Knox County Archives; Rule, *Standard History of Knoxville,* 144; Knoxville city directory, 1888. Perry Held, who at this writing lives on the south side of Highland's 1500 block, alerted me to the existence of the old manhole cover, although he believed it was located in the alley between his home and Laurel Avenue.

13. "New Street Car Line," *KJT,* July 3, 1888; "The Names Changed," *KJT,* Dec. 9, 1888; Gray and Adams, "Government," in Deaderick, *Heart of the Valley,* 104.

14. Knoxville city directories, 1895–1905, 1914–15; Knox County, Tenn., Deed Book 303: 303, Laura Agee to J. D. Jett, Sept. 23, 1918, Knox County Archives; 1920 U.S. Census, Knox County, Tenn., population schedule, Knoxville, p. 35 (stamped), dwelling 168, family 190, Jett (digital image, *Ancestry.com*); classified ads, *KJT,* Aug. 12, 1891, 7, and *KN,* Feb. 12, 1925, 11. See also Tyler Album 058, Hugh Tyler Collection, MHC, https://www.cmdc.knoxlib.org/cdm/; this unlabeled photograph is reputed to be the earliest image of the Agee home. While the street suggests Highland Avenue, close inspection shows significant discrepancies between this unidentified house and the Agee home, including the roof shape, position and size of the chimney, position of the front walkway, shape of porch posts, and a side gable absent in the Agee house (Randall De Ford, e-mail to author, Feb. 4, 2014).

15. Aiken, "Transformation of James Agee's Knoxville," 157; Jack Neely, "Lives of the Fort," *MP,* Jan. 24, 2002 (Hunt quote); classified ad, *KN,* Jan. 17, 1930, 21; 1940 U.S. Census, Knox County, Tenn., population schedule, Knoxville, dwelling 134, Segaser (digital image, *Ancestry.com*); Mark Hipshire, e-mail to author, Feb. 18, 2014.

16. Knox County, Tenn., Deed Book 455: 396, Sam Tunnell to James Shelton, Oct. 1, 1927, Knox County Archives; Knoxville city directories; Aiken, "Transformation," 162.

17. Aiken, "Transformation," 163–64; Phil Hamlin, conversation with author, Knoxville, July 1, 2013.

18. "Knox Author Gains Fame," *KJ,* Aug. 8, 1962, 1; John Chamberlain, "Agee Candidate for Literary Immortality," *Wall Street Journal,* rpt. in *KJ,* Aug. 8, 1962, 4.

19. "Time Running Out," *KJ,* Aug. 24, 1962, 18; "Apartments to be Named for Agee," *KNS,* Sept. 9, 1962.

20. Chester Kilgore to author, Apr. 10, 2016; R. B. Morris, e-mail to author, June 13, 2014.

21. Raymond Flowers, "October Target Date for Filming of Movie," *KJ,* Aug. 23, 1962, 1; Howard Thompson, "Tennessee Testament: Agee's Family Portrait Filmed on the Spot," *New York Times,* Oct. 21, 1962, 135; "Agee Movie May Show During Festival," *KNS,* Sept. 18, 1962, 13; "'Death in the Family' to Be Filmed Here," *KNS,* Aug. 28, 1962, 5; "Demolition of Agee Home Starts," *KNS,* Sept. 7, 1962, 9; "Outside Movie Shots to be Filmed Here," *KJ,* Sept. 1, 1962.

22. "Outside Movie Shots to be Filmed Here"; Bergreen, *James Agee: A Life,* 222; "James Agee" photo essay, *Life,* Nov. 1, 1963, 57–59. One of the images, the elderly woman behind a screen door, was not printed but can still be found among Haas's photos at Getty Images. *KNS* published an image of Haas photographing seven-year-old Chris Maxwell as the boy sat on the porch of the Agee house. The caption reveals that Maxwell was then being considered for the role of Rufus in *All the Way Home* ("Life Subject," *KNS,* Sept. 7, 1962, 9). For WBIR footage see "Ageeana" DVD, Tennessee Archive of Moving Image and Sound (TAMIS), Knox County Library. The short compilation also includes Hugh Tyler's circa 1930 home movies of a trip to Elkmont, behind-the-scenes shots of *All the Way Home,* and other WBIR clips of the actors' arrival and 1963 movie premiere.

23. "'Death in the Family' to Be Filmed Here."

24. "Demolition of Agee Home Starts"; "Agee Movie May Show During Festival," *KNS,* Sept. 18, 1962.

25. "Knoxville—Summer of 1962," photo and caption, *KNS,* Sept. 13, 1962, 9.

26. Davis, "Death in Knoxville," 151; Wes Morgan, "The Route and Roots of *The Road,*" http://web.utk.edu/~wmorgan/; Arnold and Luce, introduction, *Perspectives on Cormac McCarthy,* 4; "Cormac McCarthy: On the Trail of a Legend," *KNS,* Dec. 16, 2007; Cant, *Cormac McCarthy and the Myth of American Exceptionalism,* 20; Davis, "Death in Knoxville," 153; Culverhouse, *Tennessee Literary Luminaries,* 54; Dianne Luce, conversation with Bill McCarthy, Nov. 12-13, 1992, SAMLA conference, Knoxville; Wes Morgan, conversation with Dennis McCarthy, Dec. 5, 2014, Knoxville; Morgan, conversation with Walt Clancy, Oct. 12, 2017, Knoxville.

27. Crews, *Books Are Made Out of Books,* 51-52; Richard B. Woodward, "Cormac McCarthy's Venomous Fiction," *New York Times,* Apr. 19, 1992.

28. Wes Morgan, e-mail to author, Oct. 16, 2017 (citing Blount County, Tenn., deed to McCarthy, Sept. 24, 1969); "Biography," *Cormac McCarthy Society,* http://www.cormacmccarthy.com (residence history); Morgan, conversation with Clancy; Don Williams, "Annie DeLisle," *KNS,* June 10, 1990, E2, qtd. in Arnold and Luce, introduction, 4 ("stone room"); Dennis McCarthy asked Cormac about the bricks and relayed his response to Wes Morgan, who paraphrased the information: "Cormac said that the bricks went into the house on Walden[s] Creek when he lived there in the early '60s. He further said that he made several fireplaces in [the] Light Pink Road

house but that they were made of stone" (Morgan, e-mail to the author, Dec. 5, 2017). See also Dianne Luce and Wes Morgan, e-mails to author, Oct. 11, 2017 (Waldens Creek, Sevier County); Lee (Holleman) McCarthy obituary, *Bakersfield Californian*, Mar. 29, 2009 ("shack," lacked heat), cited in Culverhouse, *Tennessee Literary Luminaries*, 52; Morgan, e-mails to author, Oct. 11, 2017 (chimneys), Dec. 7, 2017 (Depression-era, location, demolished in 2004). I am indebted to McCarthy scholars Wes Morgan and Dianne Luce for their generous help investigating this story.

29. Don Williams, "'Long Journey Home' Involved Lot of Entertaining Details," *KNS*, Nov. 6, 1998, A23.

30. "2009.76.1 Gift of William Eugene Thomas," description of item in East Tennessee Historical Society collection, Michele MacDonald, e-mail to author, Jan. 7, 2014.

31. "2010.11.1 Gift of the Eugene Moser family and son William 'Bill' E. Moser," description of item in East Tennessee Historical Society collection, MacDonald, e-mail to author, Jan. 7, 2014; Jordan, "Bloodline," 110.

32. The 1961 Knoxville city directory, published in October 1960, reported that 1115 West Clinch had been "torn down." The cottage behind it, previously addressed as 1115½, was leased out until being demolished around 1969 (listed as "torn down" in 1970 directory). For Laura's quote, see Wright, interview; McFarland quote from Carroll Bible e-mail to the author, Nov. 29, 2016. Bible remembered the cottage, circa 1968, and his own connection to the tenants: "The path way up to the house was seriously overgrown so it was like entering another dimension. In the midst of the jungle was a small cabin. Living there were a couple—he a student of literature from the cloth of the Beats who eventually split for the coast to write under the name Lone Hawk. His wife was in Philosophy, and we had a mutual friend in Philosophy who had gone to college with me." Mulvany quote from John Mulvany, e-mail to Carroll Bible, Nov. 29, 2016.

33. Farber, "Nearer My Agee to Thee." For Paramount's film see the appendix to this volume.

34. "Agee Film to Premiere in Knoxville," *Jersey Journal,* Sept. 16, 1963, 3.

35. "'Day' Proclaimed for Knox Film Premiere," *KNS,* Oct. 14, 1963, D3; Harry Haun, "Knox Pays Tribute to Agee Movie," *Nashville Tennessean,* Oct. 18, 1963, 42; "Stars 'Fall' on Knoxville for Day," *KNS,* Oct. 17, 1963, 2.

36. "Discover," *Tennessee Theatre,* http://www.tennesseetheatre.com; "'Day' Proclaimed for Knox Film Premiere"; Haun, "Knox Pays Tribute to Agee Movie"; "Stars 'Fall' on Knoxville for Day."

37. John Donovan, "Preston Gains Prestige," *Norfolk Virginian-Pilot,* Jan. 13, 1963, F4 (Preston quote).

38. Dwayne Summar, "Gay to Glitter with Stars, Searchlights," *KNS,* Oct. 13, 1963, 62.

39. "For the Future?" photo caption, *KNS,* Oct. 17, 1963, 2.

40. "Mayor to Learn about Filming," *KNS,* Dec. 2, 1962, 23; Rod Gibson, "Knoxville Had Its Stars for 'All the Way Home,'" *Kingsport Times-News,* Oct. 20, 1963, 8B; "Memorial to Agee," *Boston Herald,* Oct. 27, 1963; Francis Raffetto, "Red Carpet Rolled Out at Knoxville Premiere," *Dallas Morning News,* Apr. 30, 1965.

41. For examples of other uses see *KNS* editions from 1966 (Feb. 6, Apr. 15, Apr. 25, May 15), 1967 (Feb. 3, Feb. 8, Aug. 13), 1968 (Mar. 5, May 30, July 7), and Jan. 12, 1969. Of the building's intended use as a studio, one reporter stated, "The idea never worked" ("All City Employees May Get Salary Hike This Year," *KNS,* Feb. 16, 1969, A7). Information on the close proximity came from Sabra Brown, conversation with author, Apr. 21, 2014. See also "Studio Swap Go-Ahead Given," *KNS,* Feb. 19, 1969, 8; "Construction Starts," *KNS,* Nov. 5, 1969; "Board OK's Funding Football Stadiums," *KNS,* Mar. 11, 1969, 8.

42. "Our History," *St. Andrew's-Sewanee,* http://www.sasweb.org; David Madden, "On the Mountain with Agee," in Madden, *Remembering James Agee,* 3.

43. Sarah Carlos, e-mail to Sherri Bergman, May 6, 2016; Claire Reishman, e-mail to Sherri Bergman, May 6, 2016.

44. Madden, "On the Mountain with Agee," 3 (quote), 1 (absence of UT scholars); "Photo Album of Dedication of Agee Library," TN. The two editions of *Remembering James Agee* contain presentations from the Agee Week conference.

45. Reishman, e-mail to Bergman, May 6, 2016.

46. Agee, *LUNPFM,* 84 ("innocence"); foreword, "Photo Album of Dedication of Agee Library" (Chambers quotes); Madden, "On the Mountain," 9.

47. "James Agee Memorial is Library," *KNS,* Sept. 17, 1972; Susan Core, conversation with author, spring 2015; Julie Jones, e-mail to author, Dec. 9, 2015; Jennifer Benedetto Beals, "A Year in Special Collections," *Library Development Review 2008–09* (UT Libraries), 10.

48. "Rites Wednesday for James Agee's Mother," *KNS,* Aug. 29, 1966, 18; "Other Faculty Residences," location 29 on campus map, *St. Andrew's-Sewanee,* http://www.sasweb.org. The former Agee cottage is shown as location 29 on the map but is not identified as such.

49. Brown, "Cottage that Rufus Watched."

50. Clara Hieronymus, "Spears' Film about Agee Not 'Gloss,'" *Nashville Tennessean,* June 5, 1979, 11.

51. Karen Bossick, "Parts of Agee Story Filmed Here," *KNS,* Aug. 10, 1975, A4; "Kingston Pike & Lyons View Pike Trolley Tour," *Knox Heritage,* 2007, http://www .knoxheritage.org/; Bossick, "Parts of Agee Story"; "St. Andrews Setting of James Agee Film," *Nashville Tennessean,* Aug. 3, 1975.

52. John Branston, "Young Filmmaker's 5-Year Effort is Documentary on James Agee," *KNS,* June 29, 1979, G8; Jim Balloch, "'Agee' Documentary Greeted Well at World Premiere," *KNS,* Oct. 6, 1979, 12; Cheuse, "Return of James Agee," 159–60; Robert Jones, "Film 'Agee' Brings the Writer Back to Knoxville," *KJ,* Oct. 5, 1979.

53. Branston, "Young Filmmaker's 5-Year Effort"; Carson Brewer, "The James Agee Project," *KNS,* Feb. 12, 1976; Clara Hieronymus, "Johnson City Filmmaker Nominated," *Nashville Tennessean,* Feb. 19, 1981, 44.

54. R.B. Morris, e-mail to author, Apr. 23, 2016.

55. Ibid.; R. B. Morris, ed., "The Agee Issue," *Hard Knoxville Review,* Spring 1982; Wayne Bledsoe, "Hard Knoxville Review," *KNS,* Aug. 22, 1984.

56. Aiken, "Transformation," 159–60; Morris, ed., "The Agee Issue," 10–11.

57. "Thoughts on Future Use of Fair Site," *KNS*, Nov. 28, 1982.

58. "Fort Sanders Street Fair to be May 3," *KNS*, Apr. 27, 1980, G4. Unlike similar events held before and after it, the 1980 Fort Sanders Street Fair appears to have been planned with Agee in mind. The neighborhood event was first initiated in spring 1976 with a series of fifteen street fairs "from May to September," including one specifically celebrating "James Agee's Fort Sanders." But no evidence has been found that the Agee-themed fair was actually held ("First of 15 Fort Sanders Fairs is Next Week," *KNS*, Apr. 24, 1976, 5). See also "Historical Center Preview Gala Set Apr. 14 in Knox," *KNS*, Apr. 5, 1981, G1; "Eleanor Steber at UT Sunday," *KNS*, Feb. 19, 1982; ch. 3 of this volume for information on Weals articles; Tom Eblen, "Author's Hometown Now Giving a Nod to Its Literary Son," *Orlando Sentinel*, May 31, 1986; Jane Gibbs DuBose, "Downtown Plans Cost $70 Million," *KNS*, Oct. 2, 1986, A16, qtd. in Ashdown, "Prophet from Highland Avenue," 71 ("garrets"); Sherri Gardner-Howell, "Six Will Be Inducted into Hall of Fame," *KNS*, Nov. 15, 1987.

59. John Egerton, "Honor the Artists at Arts Center," *Nashville Tennessean*, Sept. 14, 1980, 19; Larry Daughtrey, "Bill Would Change Names of Arts Center Auditoriums," *Tennessean*, Jan. 21, 1981, 15; Daughtrey, "Efforts to Rename Arts Auditoriums Hit $75,000 Snag," *Tennessean*, Feb. 4, 1981, 11; "Bid to Rename TPAC Auditoriums Ends," *Nashville Tennessean*, Apr. 30, 1981, 11.

60. "James Agee Now Honored in Home State," *Nashville Tennessean*, Feb. 26, 1989, 62; James B. Lloyd, "The Return of a Knoxville Native Son," *Library Development Review 1988–89* (UT Libraries), 3. According to Bergreen, Agee finished the book after "three years of unremitting labor" (*James Agee: A Life*, 236).

61. Conference brochure, UT, 1989, Agee biographical file, MHC; Williams, "'Let Us Now,'" 3. Also during April, Lawson McGhee Library displayed "unpublished childhood photographs of Agee and some shots of downtown Knoxville in 1915," in an exhibit titled "Remembering James Agee—Knoxville, 1915" ("'Reach, Escape and Dream—Read' Selected as Slogan for Library Week," *KNS*, Apr. 11, 1989, A4).

62. Wilma Dykeman, "Introduction: The Agee Legacy," in Lofaro, *James Agee: Reconsiderations*, 1–2. Dykeman's essay is one of several in the volume that originated as lectures presented during the 1989 conference.

63. Paul Ashdown to author, Aug. 2016. The conference was recorded to videotape, a copy of which is housed in the David Madden Collection, TN MS.2994.

64. Williams, "'Let Us Now Praise Famous Men.'"

65. Thompson, "Tennessee Testament"; "Apartments to be Named for Agee," *KNS*, Sept. 9, 1962; Jack Neely, "Photographer Danny Lyon's Images of a Lost Time and Place," *MP*, July 21, 2010 (including Lyon quote); Amy McRary, "KMA Opens Two Exhibits," *KNS*, Aug. 10, 2014.

66. Robert Saudek, "J. R. Agee '32: A Snapshot Album," in Madden and Folks, *Remembering James Agee*, 2nd ed., 19–21.

67. Jerry David Madden, letter to the editor, *KNS*, Aug. 31, 1975, 31.

68. Paul Ashdown, foreword to Neely, *Knoxville's Secret History*, 4.

69. Jack Neely, "James Agee: A Familiar Face on the Thoroughfares of France," *KNS*, Apr. 30, 1986, W2.

70. McMurtry, *Roads*, 174; Don Williams, "Neptune was One of Many Celebs Paying Visit," *KNS*, Mar. 8, 2002, B5 (quoting Kennedy); Jack Neely, e-mail to author, Dec. 9, 2016.

71. "Barry Spann's Art, James Agee's Words Combined in Poster," *KNS*, Nov. 22, 1992; Betsy Pickle, "Local Writer Strips Away the Agee Aura in Film," *KNS*, Nov. 8, 1992 (including Morris quotes "retired professor," "Everyman").

72. Steve Earle, "Introduction," in Agee, *ADITF*, centennial ed. (Penguin, 2009).

73. Jack Neely, "Knoxville: Summer of 1995," *MP*, August 1995.

74. "Behind the Scenes with Alan Hall," *Third Coast International Audio Festival*, http://www.thirdcoastfestival.org. At this writing, Hall's full audio documentary was available on this website, http://www.thirdcoastfestival.org; "Knoxville: Summer of 1995," produced by Alan Hall.

75. Jack Neely, "A Fort Divided," *MP*, c. August 1998 ("sense of place"); Paul Ashdown, e-mail to author, Apr. 21, 2016 ("not many in town," "Jack's role"); Jack Neely, "Agee Park," *MP*, Apr. 12, 2001; Michaele Orlowski, "Little of Agee Survives in Knoxville," [UT] *Daily Beacon*, May 6, 1983, 6 (Ashdown quote).

76. "1995 Concert Chronology," *R.E.M. Timeline*, https://www.remtimeline.com; Wayne Bledsoe, "R.E.M. Continuing to Define Essence of Alternative Rock," *KNS*, Nov. 9, 1995, B2 (Stipe quote); Neely, "A Live Birth," in *Secret History II*, 155 ("implied").

77. *A Prairie Home Companion*, June 26, 1999, http://www.prairiehome.publicradio .org; Ashdown, e-mail to author, Apr. 21, 2016.

78. Neely, "Beyond John Gunther," *MP*, Mar. 29, 2012 (Keillor quote).

79. "Briefs," *KNS*, June 2, 1999, A4; Victor Ashe, phone interview, Apr. 25, 2016; Ashe, e-mail to author, Apr. 21, 2016 ("city should salute"); Jack Neely, conversation with author, Apr. 20, 2016 (book assignment).

80. Jack Neely, "Bad Signs," *MP*, June 1999; John Mayer, "City Officials Ignore Call to Honor Literary Heritage," *Knoxville Voice*, Nov. 30, 2008.

81. Neely, "Agee Park."

82. Weals, "Remembering the Wreck" ("southeast"); Weals, "Blacksmith's family," *KJ*, May 21, 1986, C1; Jack Neely, "Blacksmith's House," *MP*, May 18, 2000.

83. Jack Neely, "A Farewell Homage to the Checker Flag," *MP*, May 11, 2011.

84. Matthew Everett, "Agee Assembly," *MP*, May 21, 2008; Jack Rentfro to author, May 9, 2016; Neely, "Farewell Homage" ("dog-eared").

85. Neely, "Farewell Homage."

86. Chris Hammond, e-mail to author, May 16, 2016.

87. Neely, e-mails to author, June 24, 2011, Dec. 9, 2016; "Agee Amble II," *MP*, Sept. 19, 2002.

88. Morris, e-mail to author, Apr. 23, 2016; Scott Barker, "Park to Honor Agee," *KNS*, Apr. 10, 2001 ("greenspace").

89. Ed Marcum, "Fort Sanders Residents Studying Ways to Protect Historic Status," *KNS*, Apr. 1, 1998; Randall De Ford, e-mail to author, May 9, 2016.

90. De Ford, e-mail to author, May 9, 2016 ("Scheurer" quotes); Lola Alapo, "James Agee Park Transforming," *KNS*, Nov. 22, 2004; Morris, e-mail to author, Apr. 23, 2016 ("little parking lot").

91. Morris, e-mail to author, Apr. 23, 2016; Alapo, "James Agee Park Transforming"; Barker, "Park to Honor Agee"; Marti Davis, "Pointing to Fort Sanders," *KNS*, June 4, 2003.

92. Don Williams, "City Finally Paying Measure of Respect," *KNS,* Apr. 20, 2001, A21; Randy Kenner, "Agee Park Gets Its Finishing Touches," *KNS,* Apr. 16, 2005, B1.

93. Davis, "Pointing to Fort Sanders."

94. Rachel Kovac, "Mammoth Move," *KNS,* Dec. 20, 2003.

95. Alapo, "James Agee Park Transforming."

96. Lofaro, e-mail to author, May 2, 2016; brochure, James Agee Celebration, UT, 2005 ("breadth"); "Coming Together to Celebrate Noted Knoxville Author," *UTK Library Record 2004–05* (Jan. 2005); Karen Ann Collins, "Agee Remembered, Agee Anew," *Tennessee Alumnus,* Fall 2005, 33 ("community effort").

97. "James Agee Celebration," *Staff Stuff,* Mar. 15, 2005 (Office of the Vice President for Administration and Finance, UT); Fred Brown, "Three Times the History," *KNS,* Mar. 28, 2005.

98. J. J. Stambaugh, "New Park Dedication is One for the Books," *KNS,* Apr. 18, 2005; brochure, James Agee Celebration, UT; Stambaugh, "New Park Dedication" (Morris quote).

99. Deedee Agee, "Knox Visit Deepens Daughter's Identity," *KNS,* June 7, 2005; Collins, "Agee Remembered," 32 (Deedee quote).

100. Ashdown, e-mail to author, Apr. 21, 2016.

101. Collins, "Agee Remembered" (Lofaro quote).

102. Property data and property sale, *Knoxville Geographic Information System,* http://www.kgis.org; Randall De Ford, e-mails to author, Mar. 6 and 7, 2014. Although Highland Avenue would be the most fitting site for such a reconstruction, a more practical site exists, in 2016, one block directly north from the former Agee lot. The vacant Forest Avenue property appears to be four or five lots wide and would accommodate the reconstructed house plus an adjacent parking lot. As no floor plans or interior photographs exist from the old Agee house, the replica's layout would require some interpretation; but measurements could be taken from similar Victorians in the neighborhood, such as the one at 1522 Highland.

103. "Short Quotes and Book Notes," *KNS,* Nov. 11, 2007.

104. For description, see *University of Tennessee Press,* http://utpress.org.

105. Fred Brown, "Four-Week Celebration Recognizes Agee's Contributions to Literature and Film," *KNS,* Oct. 16, 2009.

106. Brochure, "James Agee Centennial Celebration" (UT, 2009), uploaded to *KNS* website, http://web.knoxnews.com.

107. Lofaro, e-mail to author, Apr. 29, 2016.

108. Jack Neely, "How the Gritty Knoxville of 1915 Compares to James Agee's Idyllic Memoir," *KM,* June 24, 2015; Agee, *ADITF,* 3.

109. Agee, *ADITF,* 4.

110. Ibid., 3.

111. "Interview with RB Morris," *Still: The Journal,* Winter 2014, http://www.still journal.net; Morris, e-mail to author, Apr. 23, 2016 ("growing love," "coalesced"); Ashdown, e-mail to author, Apr. 21, 2016.

112. For bad press see Neely, "Beyond John Gunther."

113. Pia de Jong and Landon Jones, "What We Can Learn from the Summer of 1915," *Time*, Aug. 14, 2015.

114. "Agee" and "James Agee," Google Books Ngram Viewer, https://books.google .com/ngrams/; Davis, "James Agee: A Bibliography of Secondary Sources."

115. Mosel, *All the Way Home; All the Way Home,* dir. Alex Segal, screenplay by Philip Reisman, Jr. (USA: Talent Associates/Paramount, 1963); *All the Way Home,* dir. Fred Coe, teleplay by Tad Mosel (USA: Hallmark Hall of Fame, aired Dec. 1, 1971, on CBS); *All the Way Home,* dir. Delbert Mann, play by Tad Mosel (USA: Gideon Productions, aired Dec. 21, 1981, on NBC); *A Death in the Family,* dir. Gil Cates, screenplay by Robert W. Lenski (USA: Alt Films, aired Mar. 25, 2002, on PBS).

116. William Mayer, *A Death in the Family* (WillMayer Music, 1983); Aaron Copland and Horace Everett, *The Tender Land: Opera in Three Acts* (New York: Boosey & Hawkes, 1956).

117. G. Schirmer rental department, e-mail to author, Apr. 11, 2017; "James Agee," *AllMusic.com,* http://www.allmusic.com; "Author: James Agee," *LiederNet Archive,* http://www.lieder.net.

118. "James Agee: A Documentary, on the Life and Work of the Author" (New York: recorded WBAI, 1961; broadcast KPFK, Nov. 16, 1968); *Agee,* dir. Ross Spears (James Agee Film Project, 1979); *To Render a Life:* Let Us Now Praise Famous Men *and the Documentary Vision,* dir. Ross Spears and Silvia Kersusan (James Agee Film Project, 1992).

119. *Let Us Now Praise Famous Men, Revisited,* dir. Carol Bell (Blue Ridge Mountain Films, aired Nov. 29, 1988, on PBS); "Knoxville: Summer of 1995," prod. Alan Hall (BBC Radio 3, broadcast Oct. 3, 1995); *Louons maintenant les grands hommes,* dir. Michel Viotte (France 5/Neria, 2004); "An American Legend: James Agee," prod. Alan Hall (Falling Tree Productions, UK, broadcast Sept. 16, 2007), https:// soundcloud.com; Jack Neely, "James Agee: A Familiar Face on the Thoroughfares of France," *KNS,* Apr. 30, 1986, W2; "Interview with RB Morris."

120. Morris, e-mail to author, Apr. 23, 2016.

Appendix

1. Laura Wright to Emma Hunt, postmarked Feb. 3, 1958, *ADITF-R,* app. 7, 578.

2. James Flye to David McDowell, Mar. 5, 1958, TN James Agee and David McDowell Papers, MS.1500, 2.23 ("If the idea," "done as Jim"); Flye to McDowell, Dec. 1, 1957, TN MS.1500, 2.22 ("American screen"). The day he wrote this earlier letter to McDowell, Flye had viewed an episode of the CBS show *Camera Three,* in which a panel discussion of Agee and his work was interspersed with dramatized scenes from *ADITF.* The broadcast represented the first (partial) adaptation of the novel, roughly three years before the Broadway play premiered. In his letter, Flye was very critical of the production, writing: "I don't care who *played* in this morning's television broadcast the part of Rufus' mother, whom I can never think of in the book except as Mrs. Agee.

If I didn't know or hadn't known all the members of that family so well . . . perhaps the playing and voices of the little scene at the telephone and in the kitchen would have seemed less far from actuality. This was in a bit too high a key, in action and voice. . . . The mother in the scene on the television this morning was not the mother of the book and of fact. Jim would surely have felt so."

3. Kay Morris, "Movie Stars Send Birthday Greetings to Rev. Flye," *Harriman* [Tenn.] *Record,* Nov. 1, 1962 (Flye quote). One source claimed the play's award was the first time in the prize's history that a work had been "twice honored" ("'All the Way Home' to Premiere in Knox," *KNS,* Oct. 12, 1963, 1). In fact, it had happened once before, a decade earlier, with the book *Tales of the South Pacific* and the Rogers and Hammerstein stage musical based on it (Claudia Weissberg, Columbia University, e-mail to author, Aug. 31, 2016).

4. Philip Reisman, Jr., *ATWH,* shooting script (Paman Productions-Paramount Pictures, revised Sept. 5, 1962), copy, TN MS.3541, 1.1, [1, 9, 13, 33, 117, 119].

5. "Agee was Gifted Author, Priest Says," *KNS,* Oct. 14, 1962, 6; Morris, "Movie Stars Send Birthday Greetings" (Flye quote).

6. "Movie Talent Scout Coming," *KNS,* June 29, 1962, 9; "Paramount May Film Movie in Knoxville," *KNS,* July 11, 1962, 28 (Lee quote).

7. Raymond Flowers, "Movie Definitely to Be Filmed in Knox," *KJ,* Aug. 28, 1962, 1. See also ch. 4 discussions of *Stark Love* and Helen Monday.

8. Agee, review of *A Tree Grows in Brooklyn* (film), *Nation,* Feb. 17, 1945, rpt. in *FWSJ,* 168; Agee, review of *Kiss of Death* (film), *Time,* Sept. 15, 1947, rpt. in *FWSJ,* 430.

9. Producers estimated that 40 percent of the film was shot on location (see Pat Fields, "Film Company Slates Knoxville Departure," *KJ,* Nov. 12, 1962). Actually, all the known location shots plus those likely shot in Knoxville make up about half of the finished film. Ray Flowers, "October Target Date for Filming of Movie," *KJ,* Aug. 23, 1962; Neely, *Market Square,* 153–54, 168.

10. Howard Thompson, "Tennessee Testament," *New York Times,* Oct. 21, 1962, 135; "Decision on Film in Knox Expected," *KNS,* Aug. 23, 1962, 29; "Outside Movie Shots to Be Filmed Here," *KJ,* Sept. 1, 1962, 1, 14; Morris, "Movie Stars Send Birthday Greetings" ("first homesite"). Flye may have been confused about the Tylers' former address. On the drive down West Clinch Avenue, he photographed a house that appears to sit near the corner of Thirteenth Street, one block west of 1115 (VU MSS.148, 50.5, [photo SC.MSS.148-1910]).

11. "House Selected for Agee Film Story," *KNS,* Sept. 2, 1962, B11; Powell Lindsay, "City to Be 'Little Hollywood,'" *KNS,* Sept. 23, 1962, B6.

12. "Canvass Set for Movie," *KJ,* Sept. 4, 1962, 8; "Outside Movie Shots"; Lindsay, "'Little Hollywood.'"

13. *ATWH* script, TN MS.3541, 1.1.

14. "Standin Badly Needed for Movie Star Here," *KJ,* Oct. 6, 1962, 12; Jack Neely, "The Last Flight of the Viscount," *MP,* July 15, 2004 ("cinematographer," air disaster); "The Sixth Wheel (1962)," *Internet Movie Database,* http://www.imdb.com; "These were Victims of Crash," *KNS,* July 10, 1964, 3.

15. John Donovan, "Preston Gains Prestige," *Norfolk Virginian-Pilot*, Jan. 13, 1963, F4 (Preston quote); Agee, review of *Macomber Affair* (film), *Time*, Apr. 7, 1947, rpt. in *FWSJ*, 511.

16. Agee, "Olivier's Hamlet," *Time*, June 28, 1948, rpt. in *FWSJ*, 445, 449.

17. "Preston Gains Prestige" ("went along," quoting Preston); Hedda Hopper, "Jean Simmons Star of 'ATWH,'" *Chicago Daily Tribune*, Aug. 20, 1962 ("percentage"); David Hall, "Knoxville Site of Agee Film," *Nashville Tennessean*, Oct. 28, 1962, 10 ("one-third"); Dick, *Engulfed*, 78.

18. Agee, review of *Dragon Seed* (film), *Nation*, Aug. 5, 1944, rpt. in *FWSJ*, 131–32.

19. "Basic Facts," *About John Cullum*, http://www.aboutjohncullum.com; Raymond Flowers, "Knox Man to Play Agee Movie Role," *KJ*, Sept. 21, 1962, 1 ("Carousel"); Charles McMahon, "John Cullum Stays Busy as an Actor," *KNS*, July 7, 1963, 47 (Cullum quote); Flowers, "Knox Man to Play Agee Movie Role," 1–2 (*Chucky Jack, Camelot*); "Cullum Looks Forward to More Broadway Musicals," *KNS*, Oct. 31, 1962, 32 ("off-Broadway"); "Mrs. Cullum Killed in Wreck," *KNS*, Oct. 10, 1956, 1.

20. Alex Witchel, "A Broadway Elder with the Spirit of '76," *New York Times*, Aug. 10, 1997; "Pat Hingle, Star of 'J. B.,' Hurt in 30-Foot Fall from Elevator," *New York Times*, Feb. 21, 1959; "Wild River (1960)," *Internet Movie Database*, http://www.imdb.com; "All the Way Home (1971)," *Internet Movie Database*, http://www.imdb.com.

21. "Unknown Chosen to Play Key Role in First Film," *Springfield* [Mass.] *Union*, Oct. 29, 1963; Raymond Flowers, "New Jersey Youngster Chosen for Movie Role," *KJ*, Oct. 3, 1962, 1, 3 ("too large"). Susskind qtd. in "Agee's Widow, Son to Visit Knoxville," *KNS*, Oct. 3, 1962, 37 ("undone"); Alan Shayne, e-mail to author, Feb. 14, 2017; "Michael Kearney," *Internet Movie Database*, http://www.imdb.com; Michael Kearney, ETHC, Knoxville, Tenn., Sept. 4, 2015.

22. "Unknown Chosen to Play Key Role"; Kearney, ETHC; Powell Lindsay, "Filming Starts Here on 'ATWH,'" *KNS*, Oct. 8, 1962, 1 (Kress).

23. Lindsay, "'Little Hollywood'" (first rehearsal); "Movie Auditions Due to Starts Here Soon," *KJ*, Sept. 28, 1962, 1 ("Central Plaza"); "'ATWH' Rehearsing in New York," *Jersey Journal*, Oct. 16, 1962, 6 ("whole script"); "Unknown Chosen to Play Key Role" (memorization).

24. Kearney, ETHC.

25. Gene Stephens, "Location Crew Starts Filming of Movie Here," *KJ*, Oct. 9, 1962, 1–2; Shayne, e-mail to author.

26. Stephens, "Location Crew Starts Filming"; "All Three Agee Movie Stand-ins Quit," *KNS*, Oct. 17, 1962, 13.

27. Flowers, "New Jersey Youngster"; "3 Knox Boys Get Parts in Agee Movie," *KNS*, Oct. 7, 1962; "'Extras' Needed for Filming of Novel," *KJ*, Oct. 4, 1962, 13 ("middleaged"); Powell Lindsay, "3 Knoxvillians are Movie Stand-ins," *KNS*, Oct. 9, 1962, 17 (one hundred).

28. Jack Neely, "Lives of the Fort," *MP*, Jan. 24, 2002; "17 in Cast of Play about Knoxville," *KNS*, Mar. 4, 1962, 50; "3 Knox Boys Get Parts" (Jernigan, Davis); "Roll 'Em Boys," photo caption, *KNS*, Oct. 8, 1962, 1 (Giffin); Tom Southern, e-mail to author, May 23, 2014

29. "Props Needed for Agee Movie," *KNS,* Sept. 10, 1962, 11; Lindsay, "'Little Hollywood.'"

30. Lindsay, "'Little Hollywood'"; Vic Weals, "Old Cars: ET Model T Owners Recall the Filming," *KJ,* June 11, 1986, C2 (Campbell quote).

31. Weals, "Old Cars."

32. Kearney, ETHC; Pat Fields, "Film Cast Arrives to Begin Work," *KJ,* Oct. 8, 1962, 1–2; Lindsay, "'Little Hollywood'" (red carpet); Kearney, ETHC; Fields, "Film Cast Arrives," 1-2.

33. Lindsay, "Filming Starts Here on 'ATWH.'"

34. Kearney, ETHC.

35. Stephens, "Location Crew Starts Filming," 1–2; Michael Hertzberg, phone interview, June 2, 2016.

36. Reisman, *ATWH* script, TN MS.3541, 1.1 (subsequent shot numbers from this source will appear parenthetically in the text); Lindsay, "Filming Starts Here."

37. Stephens, "Location Crew Starts Filming," 2.

38. Ibid.

39. Tissi Smith, comment on Facebook group "Knoxville Tennessee History & Memories," Feb. 11, 2015, 12:04 p.m., https://www.facebook.com; Stephens, "Location Crew Starts Filming," 2.

40. "Moviemakers Need Butterflies Desperately," *KJ,* Oct. 9, 1962; Kathy Richards, e-mail to author, Oct. 10, 2017; Elinor Hughes, "Theater Notes," *Boston Herald,* Oct. 22, 1962.

41. "'Children's Day' Today on Movie Set," *KJ,* Oct. 29, 1962, A6; "Miss Simmons Ill; Filming Scene Shifted," *KNS,* Nov. 1, 1962, 32; Kearney, ETHC; Jody Davis to author, Apr. 8, 2016.

42. "Agee's Widow, Son to Visit Knoxville," *KNS,* Oct. 3, 1962, 37.

43. Tom Southern, e-mail to author, May 23, 2014.

44. Lindsay, "Filming Starts Here"; Lindsay, "3 Knoxvillians are Movie Stand-ins."

45. Kaye Franklin Veal, "Knoxvillian Recalls Preston as Friendly Man with Appetite," *KNS,* Mar. 24, 1987, A5; Ronnie Claire Edwards, letter to author, Jan. 3, 2015, Dallas.

46. Barbara Ashton Wash, "'I Do, I Do' Remember, Proves Robert Preston," *KNS,* Nov. 17, 1967, 14; Barbara Aston, "Beloved Helma's Founder Dies," *KNS,* Sept. 10, 1993.

47. Kearney, ETHC; Mary Charles Churchill Nash to author, June 7, 2017.

48. "Cades Cove Captivates Movie Cast," *KNS,* Oct. 11, 1962, 2.

49. Ruth Caughron Davis, "George and Delia Caughron Barn in Cades Cove," *Snapshots of the Cove,* http://www.snapshotsofthecove.com/; Pat Fields, "Lylah Tiffany Gets Role in Movie After Long Career in 'Everything,'" *KJ,* Oct. 13, 1962, 14 (Tiffany quote).

50. Fields, "Lylah Tiffany Gets Role" (Tiffany quote); Kearney, ETHC; Neely, "Michael Kearney, the Child Actor of 'ATWH,' Revisits Knoxville," *KM,* Sept. 2, 2015.

51. "Cades Cove Captivates"; Fields, "Lylah Tiffany Gets Role" (Tiffany quote); Ronnie Claire Edwards, letter to author; Pat Fields, "'Five Star Final' Role Started Acting Trend," *KJ,* Oct. 12, 1962, 7 (MacMahon).

52. Hertzberg, phone interview; Lowky Bowman, "Jean Simmons Back in Films," *Baton Rouge Advocate,* Jan. 20, 1963 (Simmons quote); Pat Fields, "Film Company Slates Knoxville Departure," *KJ,* Nov. 12, 1962 (Grossberg quote).

53. "Cades Cove Captivates Movie Cast."

54. Weals, "Old Cars."

55. "First Boar," photo caption, *KJ,* Oct. 16, 1962, 1; "Preston Bags Boar, but Loses Shirttail," *KNS,* Oct. 16, 1962, 6.

56. Pat Fields, "'Simpatico' Key Word to Preston's Success," *KJ,* Oct. 25, 1962, 22 (Preston quote).

57. David Hall, "Knoxville Site of Agee Film," *Nashville Tennessean,* Oct. 28, 1962, 10 (Hingle quote).

58. "Preston Bags Boar," *KNS,* Oct. 16, 1962, 6.

59. Footage from Chaplin's 1914 Keystone comedy "Gentlemen of Nerve" was inserted later; Carol James, "Students Appear in Movie," *Blue and Gray,* East High School, Knoxville, Nov. 21, 1962.

60. "Bijou Theater in a New Role," *KJT,* June 16, 1915; Madden, "James Agee Never Lived in This House," 45.

61. "History," *Bijou Theatre,* https://knoxbijou.com; Jerry David Madden, letter to the editor, *KNS,* Aug. 31, 1975, 31.

62. "Proud Moment," photo caption, *KJ,* Oct. 19, 1962, 26; Sanborn map, Knoxville, 1950, sheet 7.

63. "Cleveland Hearse to Make Movie Debut," *Chattanooga Times,* Oct. 12, 1962; "Knoxville Funeral 1915," photo caption, *KNS,* Oct. 21, 1962, 19; Pat Fields, "Knoxvillian Nostalgically Recalls Visit with Agee in NY," *KJ,* Nov. 2, 1962 (Goff quote); "Long Wait," photo caption, *KJ,* Oct. 19, 1962, 26.

64. Lindsay, "'Little Hollywood.'"

65. Fields, "'Simpatico' Key Word" (Preston quote).

66. Neely, "Michael Kearney."

67. Doris Eckel Melton, comment on Facebook group "Knoxville Tennessee History & Memories," May 5, 2014, 8:51 p.m., https://www.facebook.com ("walked up"); Chuck Sayne to author, Apr. 3, 2016 (Redwine); Fields, "'Simpatico' Key Word" ("Rock of Ages"); Kearney, ETHC.

68. "AA Gets $300 Award Against David Susskind," unidentified newspaper clipping, VU MSS.148, 10.2; Sanborn map, Knoxville, 1917, sheet 19; "History of Weaver Funeral Home," *Dignity Memorial,* http://www.dignitymemorial.com; Don Scruggs and Sue Watson to author, June 10, 2016.

69. Sanborn map, Knoxville, 1950, sheet 19; Chris Hoosier to author, June 16, 2016 (Miller's Annex); Jean Robinette Anderson to author, May 15, 2017 (Miller's Annex); Summar, "Knoxville 'All the Way' for Gala Premiere," 2.

70. Photo "Crescent News Company Lunch Room," N-1408, Thompson Photograph Collection, MHC; Lib Reid to author, June 17, 2016.

71. Kearney, phone interview, June 17, 2016.

72. "Pair of Horses (Iron) Pull 'ATWH,'" *KNS*, Oct. 30, 1962, 7; Lindsay, "'Little Hollywood.'"

73. Kearney, ETHC.

74. Albert Pope to author, Apr. 8, 2016; "Equipment," *Tennessee Valley Railroad,* http://www.tvrail.com; Allen C. Harper, letter, *Great Smoky Mountains Railroad,* http://www.gsmr.com; "Southern Railway 722," *World Public Library,* http://www.worldlibrary.org.

75. "Movie Producer Lauds Knoxvillians' Response," *KJ,* Oct. 24, 1962, 7 (Susskind quote).

76. "Miss Simmons Ill; Filming Scene Shifted," *KNS,* Nov. 1, 1962, 32; Hertzberg, phone interview; Dwayne Summar, "'ATWH' Goes on Night Shift," *KNS,* Nov. 7, 1962, 6.

77. "Film Scene to Be Shot on Viaduct," *KNS,* Nov. 4, 1962, B7; "Agee Movie on Extended Time," *KNS,* Oct. 29, 1962, 29.

78. Hertzberg, phone interview; "Film People Work, Squire Adams Finds," *KNS,* Oct. 21, 1962, 19 (Adams quote).

79. "Film Scene to Be Shot on Viaduct"; "Agee Movie on Extended Time"; Hertzberg, phone interview.

80. Fields, "'Simpatico' Key Word," photo caption.

81. Hertzberg, phone interview.

82. Kearney, phone interview, June 17, 2016.

83. Tom Siler, "Over the Rainbow . . . Cloud 9," *KNS,* May 19, 1964, 16; Shayne and Sunshine, *Double Life,* Kindle ed., n.p. Shayne wrote that after sitting for a long stretch watching her daughter fish, Jean Simmons "seemed quite depressed and finally snapped at Tracy, 'That's enough. We're going back.' The three of us piled into the limousine that was waiting and headed back to town. . . . I was with one of the most beautiful, glamorous movie stars with everything in the world and obviously it wasn't making her happy." Yet Shayne also wrote that "Jean loved to laugh," and echoed James Agee's sentiment in describing her screen presence as "like a breath of fresh air blowing through the lugubrious atmosphere of the movie." See also Hertzberg, phone interview; Roland Julian, "Home Sweet Home—Knights Win," *KNS,* Oct. 25, 1962, 34 (hockey); Ric Tillery, comment on Facebook group "Knoxville Tennessee History & Memories," May 6, 2014, 11:04 a.m., https://www.facebook.com (wrestling match). Preston seemed to be universally liked in Knoxville. But several years later his name came up in the divorce trial of a local "chest surgeon" who accused his wife of having an affair with Preston in fall 1962 while the actor was in town filming the movie. The woman admitted only that "she had seen Mr. Preston here and in New York." Georgiana Fry, "Waterman Gets Divorce, Wife Given Custody," *KNS,* June 28, 1968, 1.

84. Carole Gentry Goff, e-mail to author, Oct. 11, 2017; "'Children's Day' Today on Movie Set," *KJ,* Oct. 29, 1962, A6.

85. Kearney, ETHC; "Young Star Home," *Newark Evening News,* c. Nov. 13, 1962 (Mrs. Kearney quote); Kearney to author, July 6, 2017.

86. Summar, "'ATWH' Goes on Night Shift," *KNS,* Nov. 7, 1962, 6; "Film Scene to Be Shot on Viaduct," *KNS,* Nov. 4, 1962, B7.

87. Kearney, phone interview, Apr. 25, 2015; Lib Reid to author, Apr. 8, 2016 ("Helma's catered"); "Parking Ban Due During Filming," *KJ*, Nov. 1, 1962, 2; Dwayne Summar, "'ATWH' Goes on Night Shift," *KNS*, Nov. 7, 1962, 6.

88. Sanborn map, Knoxville, 1950, sheet 15. The vacant lot was located at the corner of Tenth Street and Forest Avenue. In 1950 the business address would have been 201–205 Tenth Street. See also Sanborn map, Knoxville, 1950, sheet 16 (vacant lot used in film); Howard Thompson, "Tennessee Testament: Agee's Family Portrait Filmed on the Spot," *New York Times*, Oct. 21, 1962, 135 ("stirrup-like"); Summar, "Night Shift" ("rented and vacated").

89. Don Williams, "Filming of Movie Based on Agee Novel Drew Spectators in 1962," *KNS*, Apr. 12, 2002 (McKinley quote).

90. Suzanne Province Kear to author, Apr. 8, 2016.

91. Hall, "Knoxville Site of Agee Film"; McGhee-Tyson Airport, Knoxville, Nov. 4–11, 1962, *Weather Underground;* Summar, "Night Shift."

92. Summar, "Night Shift"; Weals, "Old Cars" (Preston and Segal quotes).

93. "4 Boys in New York for Movie Filming," *KNS*, Jan. 9, 1963, 25; Neely, "Lives of the Fort" ("hard time").

94. Betsy Morris, "She's 'Extra,' and She Doesn't Mind at All," *KNS*, Nov. 11, 1962, E6; Weals, "Old Cars" (Coulter quote).

95. "The Other Side of the Lens," *L&N Magazine*, Jan. 1963; Ron Colquitt to author, Oct. 9, 2016, and Apr. 8, 2016.

96. The cemetery was identified by headstone names and dates shown in Alan Shayne's photographs (copies of which are collected at Tennessee Archive of Moving Image and Sound (TAMIS), Knox County Public Library). See also "Star's Daughter to Make Debut," *KJ*, Oct. 22, 1962, 1; "Jean Simmons' Daughter in Bow," *Boston Record American*, Oct. 29, 1962, 38.

97. "AA Gets $300 Award Against David Susskind"; "Cameraman Hurt in Fall," *KJ*, Nov. 9, 1962; Dorothy Kilgallen, "The Voice of Broadway," *Greensboro* [N.C.] *Record*, Oct. 24, 1963.

98. Hertzberg, phone interview.

99. "Preston Bags Boar, but Loses Shirttail," *KNS*, Oct. 16, 1962, 6 ("ferrymaster"); Haynes Hickman, "'Fragile 15' House in South Knox Razed by Owner," *KNS*, Oct. 12, 2012; Pat Fields, "Film Company Slates Knoxville Departure," *KJ*, Nov. 12, 1962, A2.

100. Hertzberg, phone interview; Leslie Lieber, "Lloyd's Says the Show Must Go On," *This Week*, June 2, 1963, 8 (forty million); Fields, "Film Company Slates" ("Pumps did no good," details other than Hertzberg); Debbie Reynolds, comment on Facebook group "Knoxville Tennessee History & Memories," Apr. 14, 2014, 2:02 a.m., https:// www.facebook.com ("ferry sticking out").

101. Hertzberg, phone interview; Pete Prince, "Knox Ferry Sinks, Possibly Ending Era," *KNS*, Mar. 24, 1963, 28; "Scene Refilming Here Scheduled," *KNS*, Nov. 20, 1962, 11.

102. Hertzberg, phone interview; "Same Ol' Bijou," photo caption, *KJ*, Nov. 10, 1962, 12.

103. "Filming of Agee Movie Ends Today," *KNS*, Nov. 11, 1962, A8; "Cullum Looks Forward to More Broadway Musicals," *KNS*, Oct. 31, 1962, 32.

104. "Filming of Agee Movie Ends Today."

105. Kearney, phone interview, Apr. 25, 2015.

106. Fields, "Film Company Slates" (Grossberg quote); "Premiere Asked," *KNS*, Nov. 7, 1962, 48; *All the Way Home* segment, "Our Stories: 50 Years of East Tennessee on TV," DVD, WBIR-TV (Knoxville, 2006) (Susskind quote).

107. Hertzberg, phone interview.

108. Ibid.

109. Kearney, phone interview, June 17, 2016.

110. Fields, "Film Company Slates."

111. Hertzberg, phone interview; "Production of Rossen's 'Lilith' Inaugurates New Myerberg Studio," *Boxoffice*, July–Sept. 1963, available at *Internet Archive*, https://archive.org; Kearney, phone interview, June 17, 2016.

112. "Outside Movie Shots to Be Filmed Here"; David Hall, "Knoxville Site of Agee Film," *Nashville Tennessean*, Oct. 28, 1962, 10; "Agee Film to Premiere in Knoxville," *Jersey Journal*, Sept. 16, 1963, 3 ("the stairs"); Albert Brenner, e-mail to author, Dec. 22, 2013; Hertzberg, e-mail to author, Jan. 17, 2014. See also articles listed in the following note, and ch. 6 discussion of Agee house demolition.

113. "Agee Movie May Show During Festival," *KNS*, Sept. 18, 1962 (Grossberg quote); "Movie Give Author's Home a New Lease," *Jersey Journal*, Sept. 13, 1962 ("delaying"); "Demolition of Agee Home Starts," *KNS*, Sept. 7, 1962. Even on this first day of demolition, the report stated, "Woodwork, window frames, porch posts and mantle pieces will be salvaged from the house by the movie producers for reassembling into a set in New York City." The next article, "Apartments to be Named for Agee," *KNS*, Sept. 9, 1962, states that the house "is being torn down." A photo caption, "Knoxville—Summer of 1962," *KNS*, Sept. 13, 1962, shows the home with windows, porch, and door removed, and states, "Demolition of the home of the late novelist James Agee has started. . . . Interior pieces will be reassembled in New York." Another article, "Agee Movie May Show During Festival," *KNS*, Sept. 18, 1962, states that the house "is now being torn down." The next article, Lindsay, "'Little Hollywood,'" states that "Paramount has reconstructed in a New York studio the actual Agee home, which is being torn down."

114. Howard Thompson, "Tennessee Testament: Agee's Family Portrait Filmed on the Spot," *New York Times*, Oct. 21, 1962 ("grafted"); Payne, "Two-Prize Agee Novel," *Dallas Morning News*, Jan. 26, 1964 ("grafted"); Sanborn map, Knoxville, 1917, vol. 1, sheet 94; Sanborn map, Knoxville, 1950, vol. 2, sheet 266. The earlier map shows a rear porch on the southwest corner of 1412 Forest; the porch does not appear in the later map.

115. Kearney, phone interview, Apr. 25, 2015.

116. Shayne and Sunshine, *Double Life*, n.p.

117. Earl Wilson, "It Happened Last Night," *Dallas Morning News*, Jan. 11, 1963 ("last scene"); Kearney, phone interview, Apr. 25, 2015.

118. Kearney, phone interview, Apr. 25, 2015.

119. Neely, "Beyond John Gunther," *MP*, Mar. 29, 2012 (Gunther quote); Leon Daniel, "What If You Gave a World's Fair and Nobody Came?" *UPI Archives*, June 4, 1981, http://www.upi.com (Hamburger quote); Albert J. Rogers, "Knoxville is 'All-

America' City," *KNS*, Mar. 28, 1963, 1, 2 (initiatives); "Mayor Plugs City in U.S. Contest," *KNS*, Nov. 17, 1962, 1, 3 ("spoke before a jury").

120. "1960s," *KNS*, July 29, 2012; "53 Arrested During Theater Picketing," *KNS*, Mar. 24, 1963, 1; Lydia X. McCoy, "Fearless: Knoxville's Civil-Rights Foot Soldiers Share Stories from 50 Years Ago," *KNS*, June 16, 2013; Neely, *Tennessee Theatre*, 105–6, 108 ("a certain word").

121. "'ATWH' to Premiere in Knox," *KNS*, Sept. 12, 1963, 1; Dwayne Summar, "Gay to Glitter with Stars, Searchlights," *KNS*, Oct. 13, 1963, 11.

122. Dwayne Summar, "Knoxville Going 'Strictly Hollywood,'" *KNS*, Oct. 16, 1963, 1; Summar, "Gay to Glitter with Stars," 11.

123. Rod Gibson, "Knoxville Had Its Stars," *Kingsport Times-News*, Oct. 20, 1963; Summar, "'Strictly Hollywood,'" 2; Summar, "Knoxville 'All the Way' for Gala 'Home' Premiere," *KNS*, Oct. 18, 1963, 3.

124. Summar, "'Strictly Hollywood,'" 1; Rod Gibson, "Preston Charms Knoxville," *Kingsport Times-News*, Oct. 20, 1963 (Preston quote); "Stars 'Fall' on Knoxville for Day," *KNS*, Oct. 17, 1963, 1 (Kearney quote).

125. Gibson, "Knoxville Had Its Stars"; "Stars 'Fall' on Knoxville," 1.

126. Gibson, "Knoxville Had Its Stars"; Summar, "Knoxville 'All the Way,'" 1; Williams, "Filming of Movie" (McKinley and Eldridge quotes).

127. "Remember When?" *KNS*, June 27, 1999.

128. Summar, "Knoxville 'All the Way,'" 2; Kearney quotes from Neely, "Michael Kearney" ("I froze"), and Kearney, phone interview, Apr. 25, 2015 ("picked me up").

129. Gibson, "Knoxville Had Its Stars."

130. Summar, "Knoxville 'All the Way,'" 2; Kearney, phone interview, Apr. 25, 2015.

131. Summar, "Knoxville 'All the Way,'" 1 (Holt quote); Summar, "Gay to Glitter."

132. "30,000 See 'All the Way Home' Here," *KNS*, Nov. 3, 1963, 20; "At the Theaters," *KNS*, Jan. 2, 1965, 5. Lakemont Drive-In was apparently the last local venue still showing the film at the time.

133. Bosley Crowther, "'ATWH' is Here: Follows Agee's Novel and Mosel's Play," *New York Times*, Oct. 30, 1963; Philip K. Scheuer, "'ATWH' and 'Silence' Shown," *Los Angeles Times*, Feb. 6, 1964; Summar, "'Strictly Hollywood,'" 2 (*Variety* quotes); Jean Simmons, interviewed by James Bawden in 1988, "I'm a Realist," *Classic Images*, http://www.classicimages.com (Susskind quote); "To Kill a Mockingbird (1962)," *Internet Movie Database*, http://www.imdb.com; Harry Haun, "Knox Pays Tribute to Agee Movie," *Nashville Tennessean*, Oct. 18, 1963, 42 ("child's world"); Molyneaux, *Gregory Peck*, 153 (Megna); Gunby Rule, "The Play," *KNS*, Feb. 26, 1953, 19 (Cullum and Wilcox).

134. "Dignitaries Invited to 'Home' Premiere," *KNS*, Oct. 2, 1963, 5; Jean Simmons, Bawden interview.

135. Lawrence Laurent, "'ATWH' is a Tender TV Drama," *Washington Post*, Nov. 28, 1971, 5; Cecil Smith, "Joanne Woodward: Rachel Rachel on Sesame Street," *Los Angeles Times*, Aug. 1, 1971 (Woodward quotes).

136. Dan Sullivan and Sylvie Drake, "Going 'ATWH' via TV," *Los Angeles Times*, Dec. 23, 1981.

137. *A Death in the Family,* dir. Gil Cates, perf. Annabeth Gish and John Slattery (ALT Films/PBS, 2002); "See an Agee Film," *KNS,* June 9, 2000, 7 (auditions); Don Williams, "Writer James Agee Put Both Heart and Soul into His Work," *KNS,* June 9, 2000, A23 (locals assumed); Melonee McKinney, "Time Traveling," *Nashville Tennessean,* July 11, 2000, 1W, 3W (Knoxville, Rees quote); Rose French, "Franklin 'Best' Setting for Agee Film," *Nashville Tennessean,* Aug. 5, 2000, 1B, 6B (Shelby Park, Richland, Springfield); Mae Ambrose, e-mail to author, May 8, 2017 (Ambrose, secretary of the Richland–West End Neighborhood Association, identified the Lynch home and believed, correctly, that the Follet home was in the Belmont neighborhood); Melonee McKinney, "Franklin Plays 1915 Knoxville," *Nashville Tennessean,* Aug. 4, 2000, 1W (Main Street, depot); Marilee Spanjian, "New Clothing Store is Just an Illusion," *Nashville Tennessean,* July 28, 2000, 1W (cemetery); French, "Franklin 'Best' Setting," 6B (Nolensville and Carthage).

138. Jack Neely, "Masterpiece Theatre Doesn't Make It Quite ATWH," *MP,* Aug. 10, 2000. Homes that compose Nashville's historic Richland-West End neighborhood were built between 1905 and 1925. See "RWENA History," *Richland–West End Neighborhood Association,* http://www.rwena.org.

139. Kearney, phone interview, Apr. 25, 2015; Neely, "Michael Kearney."

140. Kearney, phone interview, Apr. 25, 2015.

141. *Historic Downtown Knoxville Walking Tour* (L&N Station, Bijou).

142. Ibid.; "Opening Dec. 17," *KNS,* Nov. 26, 1929; "Floridian Buys Andrew Johnson Hotel for $1.07 Million," *KNS,* Nov. 28, 1979; "Hotel, Knoxville College Put on Historic Register," *KNS,* July 30, 1980, C10; "Knox Co. Seeking Proposals for the AJ Building," *KNS,* Apr. 18, 2017.

143. Aiken, "Transformation of James Agee's Knoxville," 160.

144. "Fire Heavily Damages Victorian Mansion," *KNS,* Nov. 29, 1978, D1.

Selected Bibliography

Writings by James Agee

Abraham Lincoln—The Early Years. In *The Lively Arts: Four Representative Types,* by Rodney E. Sheratsky and John L. Reilly. New York: Globe Books, 1964.

The African Queen and The Night of the Hunter*: First and Final Screenplays.* Edited by Jeffrey Couchman. Knoxville: University of Tennessee Press, 2017.

Agee: Selected Literary Documents. Edited by Victor A. Kramer. Troy, NY: Whitston Publishing, 1996.

"Agee's Memories of His Father's Accident and the Day Before." N.d. In Agee, *A Death in the Family: A Restoration of the Author's Text,* ed. Lofaro. Appendix 4: 569–72.

"Allegiance Dream." N.d. TN MS.2730, box 4, folder 5.

Autobiographical writing. N.d. TN MS.2730, box 4, folder 1.

Collected Poems of James Agee. Edited by Robert Fitzgerald. Boston: Houghton Mifflin, 1968.

Collected Short Prose of James Agee. Edited by Robert Fitzgerald. Boston: Houghton Mifflin, 1968.

Complete Journalism. Edited by Paul Ashdown. Knoxville: University of Tennessee Press, 2013.

Cotton Tenants: Three Families. Edited by John Summers. Brooklyn: Melville House, 2013.

A Death in the Family. 1957. Reprint, New York: Vintage Books, 1998.

A Death in the Family: A Restoration of the Author's Text. Edited by Michael A. Lofaro. Knoxville: University of Tennessee Press, 2007.

"Dixie Doodle." *Partisan Review* 4 (Feb. 1938): 8. Available at *Partisan Review Online,* Boston University, http://hgar-srv3.bu.edu.

Film Writing and Selected Journalism. New York: Library of America, 2005.

"Infested." *Knoxville News,* August 22, 1923, 4.

James Agee Rediscovered: The Journals of Let Us Now Praise Famous Men *and Other New Manuscripts.* Edited by Michael A. Lofaro and Hugh Davis. Knoxville: University of Tennessee Press. 2005.

James Agee: Selected Journalism. Edited by Paul Ashdown. Knoxville: University of Tennessee Press. 1985.

"Largest Class in History of School Grads." *Phillips Exeter Monthly,* November 1926, 48–52.

Letters of James Agee to Father Flye. New York: George Braziller, 1962.

Let Us Now Praise Famous Men. [With Walker Evans.] 1941. Reprint, New York: Ballantine Books, 1978.

"Minerva Farmer." *Phillips Exeter Monthly.* November 1925, 39–41.

The Morning Watch. 1950. Reprint, New York: Ballantine Books, 1969.

Review of *Peter and Wendy* (book). *Blue and White Weekly,* Knoxville High School, May 8, 1925, 4. Knoxville Heritage website. http://knoxvilleheritage.com.

Interviews

Agee, Annabel. Interview with author. Knoxville, July 10, 2014.

Hamlin, Phil. Interview with author. Knoxville, July 1, 2013.

Hertzberg, Michael. Phone interview with author. June 2, 2016.

Hodge, Oliver. Interview with Ross Spears. Mid-1970s. Digitized audio recording. "Sound Recordings from Our Archives," Agee Films website, http://www.ageefilms.org.

Kearney, Michael. Phone interview with author, April 25, 2015.

———. Phone interview with author, June 17, 2016.

Tinsley, Sam. Phone interview with author. July 30, 2014.

Tyler, Paula. Interview with Ross Spears. Circa 1977. Digitized audio recording. "Sound Recordings from Our Archives," Agee Films website, http://www.ageefilms.org.

Wright, Laura. Mrs. Wright talking to Father Flye. December 1962 and later. Five-inch audio tape. Vanderbilt University, Heard Library, Father James Harold Flye Papers, MSS 148, Box 57: Series 14, Item 22.

Letters

Agee, James. Typed letter regarding induction examination. Circa 1942. TN MS.1998, box 1, folder 12. (Agee writes to a psychiatrist recommended by Lionel Trilling and Mia Fritsch of *Fortune* magazine, telling of his background and relevant psychological details before his induction examination for military service.)

Edison, Lydia. Letter to author. November 17, 2015, Elk, Calif.

Flye, James Harold. Letter to David McDowell. December 1, 1957, from Wichita. TN MS.1500, box 2, folder 22.

———. Letter to David McDowell. March 5, 1958. TN MS.1500, box 2, folder 23.

Tripp, Dr. A. B. Letter to Charles Mayo. April 13, 1968, Memphis. Scanned letter provided by Charles Mayo.

Tyler, Hugh. Letter to James Agee. March 25, 1955, Knoxville. TN MS.2730, box 2, folder 14.

———. Letter to Helen [Bliss?]. October 20, 1948. South Kent, Conn. Hugh Tyler Collection. McClung Historical Collection, Knox County Library.

———. Letter to William Kells Furlong. January 7, 1971. Hugh Tyler Collection. McClung Historical Collection, Knox County Library.

Tyler, Joel. Letters to Richard Hodgson. *Journal of the American Society for Psychical Research* 11 (1917): 746–48.

Wright, Laura. Letters to James Agee. Various. TN MS.2730, box 2, folder 18; box 3, folder 2; box 8, folder 2.

———. Letter to Emma Hunt. Postmarked February 3, 1958. In Agee, *A Death in the Family: A Restoration of the Author's Text,* ed. Lofaro. 577–78.

Library Collections

Knox County Library, McClung Historical Collection
    Hugh Tyler Collection.
    "Buffat-Bolli Reminiscences." 1908, 1916. Bound typed manuscript.
Library of Virginia, Richmond
    Robert Young Clay Papers, 45033.
St. Andrew's–Sewanee School, Sewanee, Tenn., Agee Library
    Folder: "Engineering Report Properties of St. Andrew's School."
    Folder: "Father Flye's articles."
    Folder: "Histories: B. Campbell."
    Folder: "St. Andrew's II."
    Folder: "St. Andrew's History—Misc. Notes."
University of Tennessee, Knoxville, Special Collections Library
    All the Way Home, shooting script by Philip Reisman Jr. Paman Productions–Paramount Pictures, revised September 5, 1962. Copy, MS.3541, 1.1.
    James Agee and James Agee Trust Collection, c. 1920–2003, MS.2730.
    James Agee and David McDowell Papers, 1919–1985, MS.1500.
    James Agee Papers, c. 1936–1955, MS.1998.
    Dr. Kenneth Curry Collection, MS.2052.
    Photographs of Tenn. Cities Collection, MS.0951.
University of Texas, Austin, Harry Ransom Humanities Research Center
    James Agee Collection, 1928–1969, TXRC98-A10.
Vanderbilt University, Jean and Alexander Heard Library, Special Collections
    Father James Harold Flye Papers, 1904–1983, MSS.148.

Newspapers

Anderson County [Tenn.] *News*
Chattanooga Times
Chicago Daily Tribune
Clinton [Tenn.] *Courier*
Dallas Morning News
Jersey Journal [Jersey City, N.J.]
Kalamazoo Gazette

Kingsport [Tenn.] *Times-News*
Knoxville Daily Journal and Tribune
Knoxville Journal
Knoxville Journal and Tribune
Knoxville Mercury
Knoxville News
Knoxville News-Sentinel
Knoxville Sentinel
LaFollette [Tenn.] *Press*
Metro Pulse [Knoxville, Tenn.]
Nashville Tennessean
New York Times
Port Huron Times Herald

Books, Articles, and Theses

Adamson, June. "The Communications Media." In Deaderick, *Heart of the Valley*, 273–336.

Agee, Louis N. *Agee Register: A Genealogical Record of the Descendants of Mathieu Agee, a Huguenot Refugee to Virginia*. Baltimore: Gateway Press, 1982.

Agee, Deedee, "Growing Up with the Jimiagees." In Lofaro, *Agee Agonistes*, 287–96.

Agee, P. M. *A Record of the Agee Family*. Independence, Mo.: N.p., 1937.

Aiken, Charles S. *James Agee's* A Death in the Family: *A Walking Tour of the Neighborhood*. Brochure. Knoxville: University of Tennessee, 2005.

———. "The Transformation of James Agee's Knoxville." *Geographical Review* 3 (April 1983): 150–65.

Allen, Ronald. *A History of Theaters in Knoxville, TN, 1872–1982*. Knoxville: Ronald R. Allen, 2010.

———. *Knoxville, Tennessee: Summer, 1915–Spring, 1916*. Knoxville: Ronald R. Allen, 2008.

Ash, Steven V. *Meet Me at the Fair! A Pictorial History of the Tennessee Valley Agricultural and Industrial Fair*. Knoxville: Tennessee Valley Fair, 1985.

Ashdown, Paul. "From Almost as Early as I Can Remember: James Agee and the Civil War." In Lofaro, *Agee Agonistes*, 105–24.

———. Introduction. *James Agee: Selected Journalism*. Ed. Ashdown. Knoxville: University of Tennessee Press, 1985, xiii–xliv.

———. "Prophet from Highland Avenue: James Agee's Visionary Journalism." In Lofaro, *James Agee: Reconsiderations*, 59–81.

Arnold, Edwin T., and Dianne C. Luce, eds. *Perspectives on Cormac McCarthy*. Jackson: University Press of Mississippi, 1999.

Banker, Mark T. *Appalachians All: East Tennesseans and the Elusive History of an American Region*. Knoxville: University of Tennessee Press, 2011.

Barson, Alfred T. *A Way of Seeing: A Critical Study of James Agee.* Amherst: University of Massachusetts Press, 1972.

Bergreen, Laurence. *James Agee: A Life.* 1984. Reprint, New York: Penguin, 1985.

Borchers, Donnis Mott. *Thomas Lamar, the Immigrant: 300 Years of Descendants.* Omaha, Neb.: Self-published, 1977.

The Boy Mechanic. Vol. 1, *700 Things for Boys to Do.* Chicago: Popular Mechanics, 1913.

Brigham, Willard I. *Tyler Genealogy: The Descendants of Job Tyler, of Andover, Massachusetts, 1916–1700.* Vol. 1. Plainfield, N.J.: C. B. Tyler; Tylerville, Conn.: R. U. Tyler, 1912.

Brodhead, Michael J., Carol R. Byerly, Jon T. Hoffman, and Glenn F. Williams. *The Panama Canal: An Army's Enterprise.* Washington, D.C.: Center of Military History, United States Army, 2009.

Brown, Paul F. "The Cottage that Rufus Watched." *St. Andrew's–Sewanee School Magazine,* Spring 2016, 18–19.

Brown's City Directory of Port Huron. Port Huron, Mich.: C. E. Brown, 1870.

Bushnell, Rev. Henry. *History of Granville, Licking County, Ohio.* Columbus, Ohio: Hann & Adair, 1889.

Cant, John. *Cormac McCarthy and the Myth of American Exceptionalism.* New York: Routledge, 2008.

Carver, Martha. *Tennessee's Survey Report of Historic Bridges.* Nashville: Ambrose, 2008.

Chaniott, Sara Hollingsworth. *Family Reunion, A Campbell County, Tennessee Family History Book.* LaFollette, Tenn.: Board of Directors of Campbell County Historical Society, 2005.

Chase, Theodore R. *The Michigan University Book, 1844–1880.* Detroit: Richmond, Backus, 1880.

Cheuse, Alan. "The Return of James Agee." Ch. 11 in *Listening to the Page: Adventures in Reading and Writing.* New York: Columbia Univ. Press, 2001.

Collins, Tom. *The Legendary Model T Ford.* Iola, Wis.: Krause, 2007.

Concannon, Jeanne M. "The Poetry and Fiction of James Agee: A Critical Analysis." PhD diss., University of Minnesota, 1968.

Couchman, Jeffrey. *The Night of the Hunter: Biography of a Film.* Evanston, Ill.: Northwestern University Press, 2009.

Crank, James A. "The Body as Sacrifice: *The Morning Watch* and Ritual Violence." In Lofaro, *Agee Agonistes,* 217–33.

Creese, Walter L. *TVA's Public Planning: The Vision, the Reality.* Knoxville: University of Tennessee Press, 2003.

Crews, Michael Lynn. *Books Are Made Out of Books: A Guide to Cormac McCarthy's Literary Influences.* Austin: University of Texas Press, 2017.

Culverhouse, Sue. *Tennessee Literary Luminaries: From Cormac McCarthy to Robert Penn Warren.* Charleston, S.C.: History Press, 2013.

Curry, Kenneth. "The Knoxville of James Agee's *A Death in the Family.*" In *Tennessee Studies in Literature,* Vol. 14. Knoxville: University of Tennessee Press, 1969, 1–14.

Davis, David A. "Death in Knoxville." *Southern Literary Journal* 44 (Fall 2011): 151–54.

Davis, Hugh. "James Agee: A Bibliography of Secondary Sources." In Lofaro, *Agee Agonistes,* 299–331.

———. "Drinking at Wells Sunk Beneath Privies: Agee and Surrealism." In Lofaro, *Agee Agonistes,* 85–104.

———. *The Making of James Agee.* Knoxville: University of Tennessee Press, 2008.

Davis, Louise, "The Agee Story—Part One: Two Deaths in the Family." *Nashville Tennessean Magazine,* February 8, 1959, 10–11, 20.

———. "The Agee Story—Part Two: He Tortured the Thing He Loved." *Nashville Tennessean Magazine,* February 15, 1959, 14–5, 21.

———. "James Agee and Father Flye." *Nashville Tennessean Magazine,* June 4, 1972, 8–10.

Deaderick, Lucile, ed. *Heart of the Valley: A History of Knoxville, Tennessee.* Knoxville: East Tennessee Historical Society, 1976.

Dick, Bernard F. *Engulfed: The Death of Paramount Pictures and the Birth of Corporate Hollywood.* Lexington: University Press of Kentucky, 2015.

Doty, Mark A. *Tell Me Who I Am: James Agee's Search for Selfhood.* Baton Rouge: Louisiana State University Press, 1981.

Durant, Samuel W. *History of Kalamazoo County.* Kalamazoo, Mich.: Everets, 1880.

Ellis, Jack C. "American Documentary in the 1950s." Ch. 11 in *Transforming the Screen: 1950–1959,* ed. Peter Lev. Los Angeles: University of California Press, 2003.

Fabre, Genevieve. "A Bibliography of the Works of James Agee." *Bulletin of Bibliography* 24 (May–Aug. 1965): 147–66.

Farber, Manny. "Nearer My Agee to Thee." *Cavalier,* December 1965. Reprinted in *Cinema Comparat/ive Cinema* 2, no. 4 (2014): 39–41. Available online at http://www.ocec.eu.

French, John Homer. *Historical and Statistical Gazetteer of New York State.* New York: Heart of the Lakes, 1860.

Gatlin, Rochelle. "The Personal and Religious Realism of James Agee." Ph.D. diss., University of Pennsylvania, 1978.

Gempp, Brian. "Drowned in the Present: The Correspondence of James Agee and Tamara Comstock." In Lofaro, *Agee Agonistes,* 253–83.

Goodman, W. M. *The First Exposition of Conservation and Its Builders.* Knoxville: Knoxville Lithographing, 1914.

Goodspeed's History of Tennessee: Containing Historical and Biographical Sketches of Thirty East Tennessee Counties. 1887. Reprint, Nashville: Charles and Randy Elder, 1972.

Gray, Aelred J., and Susan F. Adams. "Government." In Deaderick, *Heart of the Valley,* 68–144.

Gunnell, John. *Standard Catalog of Ford.* 4th ed. Iola, Wis.: Krause, 2007.

Haas, Ernst. "James Agee." Photo essay. *Life,* November 1, 1963, 57–67.

Halliwell, James Orchard. *Popular Rhymes and Nursery Tales.* London: John Russell Smith, 1849.

Hamer, Philip M. "A. Frank Agee." In *Tennessee: A History, 1673–1932,* Vol. 4, 564. New York: American Historical Society, 1933.

Harris, Joel Chandler. *Nights with Uncle Remus*. Boston: Houghton Mifflin, 1911.

Haskins, William C., ed. *Canal Zone Pilot, Guide to the Republic of Panama*. Panama: A. Bienkowski, 1908.

Hess, Earl J. *The Knoxville Campaign: Burnside and Longstreet in East Tennessee*. Knoxville: University of Tennessee Press, 2012.

Heyman, Barbara B. *Samuel Barber: The Composer and His Music*. New York: Oxford University Press, 1992.

Hill, Stephanie A. *Clinton*. Charleston, S.C.: Arcadia, 2011.

Historical Catalogue of the Students of Kalamazoo College and of Kalamazoo Theological Seminary, 1851–1902. Kalamazoo, Mich.: Ihling Bros. & Everard, 1903.

Historic Downtown Knoxville Walking Tour. Brochure. Knoxville: Knox Heritage, 2013.

History of St. Clair County, Michigan. Chicago: A. T. Andreas, 1883.

Hoskins, Katherine. *Anderson County: Historical Sketches*. Clinton, Tenn.: K. B. Hoskins, 1987.

Howell, Alice L. "Prominent Tennesseans." In Deaderick, *Heart of the Valley*, 482–624.

Hunt, William D. *The Alpha & Omega of the Trojan Dynasty*. Knoxville: Self-published, 1988.

"Interview with Fr. Flye." *Crest*, February 12, 1969. Copy of article in "St. Andrew's History—Misc. Notes" folder, St. Andrew's-Sewanee Library.

Investigation of Panama Canal Matters: Hearings Before the Committee on Interoceanic Canals. Vol. 1. Washington, D.C.: Government Printing Office, 1906.

Isthmian Canal Commission. *Annual Report of the Isthmian Canal Commission*. Washington, D.C.: Government Printing Office, 1907.

Jones, Owen. *The Grammar of Ornament*. London: Quaritch, 1910.

Jordan, Jessica. "Bloodline." BA thesis, Wesleyan University, 2013.

Kelley, Paul. "Education." In Deaderick, *Heart of the Valley*, 237–72.

Knox County in the World War. Knoxville: Knoxville Lithographing Co., 1919. Available online at Internet Archive, https://archive.org.

Kramer, Victor A. *Agee and Actuality: Artistic Vision in His Work*. Troy, N.Y.: Whitston, 1991.

———. "Agee's Use of Regional Material in *A Death in the Family*." *Appalachian Journal* 1 (Autumn 1972): 72–80.

———. *James Agee*. Boston: G. K. Hall, 1975.

———. "Urban and Rural Balance in James Agee's *A Death in the Family*." In Lofaro, *James Agee: Reconsiderations*, 104–18.

Lacey, Jean, and Karen Yarbro. "Early Unitarian and Universalist Churches." Tennessee Valley Unitarian Universalist Church website. http://tvuuc.org.

Lakin, Matthew. "'A Dark Night': The Knoxville Race Riot of 1919." *Journal of East Tennessee History* 72 (2000): 1–29.

Larson, Edward J. *Summer for the Gods: The Scopes Trial and America's Continuing Debate over Science and Religion*. New York: Basic Books, 2008.

Leeming, David. *Amazing Grace: A Life of Beauford Delaney*. New York: Oxford University Press, 1998.

Lemasters, Paul W., ed. *Campbell County, Tennessee, Obituaries, 1821–1959, Surnames A–H.* LaFollette, Tenn.: Campbell County Historical Society, 2001.

Leonard, John W. "Tyler, Emma Farrand." In *Woman's Who's Who of America: A Biographical Dictionary of Contemporary Women of the United States and Canada, 1914–1915,* 829. New York: American Commonwealth, 1914.

Leupp, Francis E. *How to Prepare for a Civil Service Examination.* New York: Hinds, Noble & Eldredge, 1898–99.

Lofaro, Michael A. "Idyll or Terror? The True Introduction to Agee's *A Death in the Family.*" In Lofaro, *Agee Agonistes,* 235–49.

———, ed. *Agee Agonistes: Essays on the Life, Legend, and Works of James Agee.* Knoxville: University of Tennessee Press, 2007.

———, ed. *James Agee: Reconsiderations.* Tennessee Studies in Literature, Vol. 33. Knoxville: University of Tennessee Press, 1992.

———, ed. Let Us Now Praise Famous Men *at 75: Anniversary Essays.* Knoxville: University of Tennessee Press, 2017.

Long, Grady M. *Notes toward a History of Christ Church Parish 1900–1960.* 1969. Christ Church Chattanooga website, http://christchurch.dioet.org.

MacArthur, William J. "Knoxville's History: An Interpretation." In Deaderick, *Heart of the Valley,* 1–67.

Mackethan, Lucinda H. "I'll Take My Stand: The Relevance of the Agrarian Vision." *Virginia Quarterly Review,* Autumn 1980: http://www.vqronline.org.

Madden, David. "James Agee Never Lived in This House." In *The Last Bizarre Tale: Stories,* 40–54. Knoxville: University of Tennessee Press, 2014

———, ed. *Remembering James Agee.* Baton Rouge: Louisiana State University Press, 1974.

Madden, David, and Jeffrey Folks, eds. *Remembering James Agee.* 2nd ed. Athens: University of Georgia Press, 1997.

Manning, Russ, and Sondra Jamieson. *Historic Knoxville and Knox County: A Walking and Touring Guide.* Norris, Tenn.: Laurel Place, 1990.

Marcaccio, Amy. "The Ladies' Library Association of Port Huron, Michigan: Woman's Struggle for Intellectual Recognition in a Post-Civil War Community." BA thesis, Kalamazoo College, Fall 1980.

Mayo, Charles W. "James Agee: His Literary Life and Work." PhD diss., George Peabody College for Teachers, 1969.

McCoy, Adam Dunbar. *Holy Cross: A Century of Anglican Monasticism.* Wilton, Conn.: Morehouse-Barlow, 1987.

McDonald, Miller. *Campbell County Tennessee USA.* Vol. 1. LaFollette, Tenn.: County Services Syndicate, 1993.

McMurtry, Larry. *Roads.* New York: Simon & Schuster, 2000.

Men of Affairs in Knoxville. Knoxville: Journal and Tribune, 1921

Michigan State Gazetteer and Business Directory. Vol. 3. Detroit: R. L. Polk, 1877.

Minutes of Meetings of the Isthmian Canal Commission, October, 1905, to March, 1907. Washington, D.C.: Government Printing Office, 1908.

Moffatt, Frederick C. "Painting, Sculpture, and Photography." In Deaderick, *Heart of the Valley*, 424–38.

Molyneaux, Gerard. *Gregory Peck: A Bio-Bibliography*. Westport, Conn.: Greenwood, 1995.

Moreau, Genevieve. *The Restless Journey of James Agee*. New York: Morrow, 1977.

Mosel, Tad. *All the Way Home: A Drama in Three Acts*. New York: Samuel French, 1961.

Neely, Jack. "The Boldest of All the Sounds of Night: Music in the Early Life of James Agee." In Lofaro, *Agee Agonistes*, 67–72.

———. "Excavating Knoxville Literature." In *Knoxville Bound*, ed. Judy Loest with Jack Rentfro, 182–204. Knoxville: Metro Pulse Publishing, 2004.

———. *Knoxville's Secret History*. 2nd ed. Knoxville: Scruffy City, 1999.

———. *Market Square*. Knoxville: Market Square District Association, 2009.

———. *Secret History II*. Knoxville: Scruffy City, 1998.

———. *The Tennessee Theatre: A Grand Entertainment Palace*. Knoxville: Historic Tennessee Theatre Foundation, 2015.

Neely, Jack, and Aaron Jay. *The Marble City: A Photographic Tour of Knoxville's Graveyards*. Knoxville: University of Tennessee Press, 1999.

Official Register of the United States, 1901. Vol. 2. Washington, D.C.: Government Printing Office, 1901.

Official Register of the United States, 1903. Vol. 2. Washington, D.C.: Government Printing Office, 1903.

Official Register of the United States, 1905. Vol. 2. Washington, D.C.: Government Printing Office, 1905.

Patel, Kiran Klaus. *The New Deal: A Global History*. Princeton, N.J.: Princeton University Press, 2016.

Patton, Edwin P. "Transportation Development." In Deaderick, *Heart of the Valley*, 178–236.

Paulin, Daniel L. *Lost Elkmont*. Charleston, S.C.: Arcadia, 2015.

Purcell, Aaron D. *University of Tennessee*. Chicago: Arcadia, 2007.

Rothrock, Mary U., ed. *The French Broad–Holston Country: A History of Knox County, Tennessee*. Knoxville: East Tennessee Historical Society, 1946.

Rowland, E. J. *Holy Week and Easter: The Services Explained*. St. Leonards on Sea: Christ Church Publishing, 1956. Available online at *Project Canterbury*, http://anglicanhistory.org.

Rule, William, ed. *Standard History of Knoxville, Tennessee*. Chicago: Lewis, 1900.

Saudek, Robert. "J. R. Agee '32: A Snapshot Album." In Madden, *Remembering James Agee*, 23–34.

Seymour, Charles M. *History of One Hundred Years of St. John's Episcopal Church in Knoxville, Tennessee 1846–1946*. Knoxville: Vestry of St. John's Parish, 1947.

Shannon, Robert T., comp. and ed. *A Compilation of the Tennessee Statutes*. Nashville: Tennessee Law Book Publishing Co., 1917.

Shayne, Alan, and Norman Sunshine. *Double Life: A Love Story from Broadway to Hollywood*. New York: Open Road Media, 2013.

Smith, Winchell. *Turn to the Right.* New York: Samuel French, 1916. Available online at *Forgotten Books,* https://www.forgottenbooks.com.

Southern, Martin. "One Hundred and Second Issue." *Annals,* July 19, 1968. Scanned document provided by the Southern family.

Spears, Ross, and Jude Cassidy, eds. *Agee: His Life Remembered.* New York: Holt, Rinehart and Winston, 1985.

Summerlin, Vernon and Kathy. *Longstreet Highroad Guide to the Tennessee Mountains.* Atlanta: Longstreet Press, 1999.

U.S. Department of Agriculture Weather Bureau. *Climatological Data for the United States by Sections, 1916.* Vol. 3, pts. 1 and 2. Washington, D.C.: Weather Bureau, 1917.

Waterloo, Stanley. *The Tale of the Time of the Cave Men, Being the Story of Ab.* London: Adam and Charles Black, 1904.

Weals, Vic. *Last Train to Elkmont: A Look Back at Life on Little River in the Great Smoky Mountains.* Knoxville: Olden Press.

We're Having a Meeting at Bell's Campground: The History of Bell's Campground and Bell's Campground United Methodist Church. Powell, Tenn.: Bell's Campground United Methodist Church, 1980.

Wheeler, William Bruce. "James Agee's Knoxville." In Lofaro, *Agee Agonistes,* 49–65.

———. *Knoxville, Tennessee: A Mountain City in the New South.* 2nd ed. Knoxville: University of Tennessee Press, 2005.

Williams, Edwina Dakin, as told to Lucy Freeman. *Remember Me to Tom.* New York: Putnam, 1963.

Willis, Charles Ethelbert. *A History of the Willis Family of New England and New Jersey.* Richmond, Va.: Whitmore & Garrett, 1917.

Index